INTRODUCTION TO LANGUAGES AND THE THEORY OF COMPUTATION

John C. Martin
North Dakota State University

McGraw-Hill, Inc.
New York   St. Louis   San Francisco   Auckland   Bogotá
Caracas   Lisbon   London   Madrid   Mexico   Milan
Montreal   New Delhi   Paris   San Juan   Singapore
Sydney   Tokyo   Toronto

To MY PARENTS

This book was set in Times Roman by Publication Services.
The editor was David M. Shapiro.
The cover was designed by John Hite.
Project supervision was done by Publication Services.
R. R. Donnelley & Sons Company was printer and binder.

INTRODUCTION TO LANGUAGES AND THE THEORY OF COMPUTATION

3 4 5 6 7 8 9 0   DOC DOC   9 5 4 3 2

ISBN 0-07-040659-6

Library of Congress Cataloging-in-Publication Data

Martin, John C.
    Introduction to languages and the theory of computation / John C. Martin.
        p.   cm.
    Includes bibliographical references and index.
    ISBN 0-07-040659-6
    1. Sequential machine theory.   2. Computable functions.
I. Title.
QA267.5.S4M29   1991
511.3—dc20   90-42807

ABOUT THE AUTHOR

John C. Martin attended Rice University both as an undergraduate and as a graduate student, receiving a B.A. in Mathematics in 1966 and a Ph.D. in 1971. After leaving graduate school, he taught for two years at the University of Hawaii in Honolulu, and in 1973 he accepted a position at North Dakota State University. Since then he has taught both mathematics and computer science courses at NDSU, where he is currently an associate professor of computer science.

CONTENTS

Preface   xi

Introduction   xiii

Part I   Mathematical Notation and Techniques   1

1   Basic Mathematical Objects   3

1.1   Sets   3
1.2   Functions   7
1.3   Logical Statements   11
1.4   Proofs   16
1.5   Relations   21
1.6   Languages   24
     Exercises   28

2   Mathematical Induction and Recursive Definitions   33

2.1   The Principle of Mathematical Induction   33
2.2   The Strong Principle of Mathematical Induction   40
2.3   Recursive Definitions   44
     Exercises   52

Part II   Regular Languages and Finite Automata   55

3   Regular Expressions and Regular Languages   57

3.1   Definitions: Regular Expressions and the Corresponding Languages   57
3.2   Examples and Applications   60
     Exercises   64

4 Finite Automata   66

4.1	The Memory Required to Recognize a Language	66
4.2	Definitions and Representations	70
4.3	Extending the Notation: The Function δ^*	73
4.4	Distinguishing One String from Another	76
4.5	Unions, Intersections, and Complements of Regular Languages	79
	Exercises	82

5 Nondeterminism   86

5.1	Nondeterministic Finite Automata	86
5.2	Nondeterministic Finite Automata with Λ-Transitions	91
5.3	The Equivalence of FAs, NFAs and NFA-Λs	96
5.4	Algorithms and Examples	100
	Exercises	103

6 Kleene's Theorem   108

6.1	To Each Regular Expression There Corresponds a Finite Automaton	108
6.2	To Each Finite Automaton There Corresponds a Regular Expression	114
	Exercises	119

7 Minimal Finite Automata   121

7.1	A Minimum-State FA for a Regular Language	121
7.2	Minimizing the Number of States in an FA	125
7.3	A More Efficient Algorithm for Marking Pairs	131
7.4	The Uniqueness of the Minimum-State FA	134
	Exercises	137

8 Regular Languages and Nonregular Languages   141

8.1	A Criterion for Regularity	141
8.2	The Pumping Lemma: Another Way to Prove a Language Nonregular	143
8.3	Decision Problems and Decision Algorithms	147
8.4	Regular Languages and Programming Languages; Finite Automata and Computers	151
	Exercises	153

Part III   Context-Free Languages and Pushdown Automata   157

9 Context-Free Languages   159

9.1	Definitions and Introduction	159
9.2	Examples: Natural Languages, Programming Languages, Algebraic Expressions, and Others	161
9.3	Unions, Concatenations, and *'s of CFLs	168
9.4	Regular Languages and Regular Grammars	172
	Exercises	175

10 Derivation Trees and Ambiguity   180

10.1 Definitions and Examples   180
10.2 An Unambiguous CFG for Algebraic Expressions   187
       Exercises   194

11 Simplified Forms and Normal Forms   196

11.1 Eliminating Λ-Productions from a CFG   196
11.2 Eliminating Unit Productions from a CFG   201
11.3 Eliminating Useless Variables from a CFG   204
11.4 Chomsky Normal Form   208
       Exercises   210

12 Pushdown Automata   213

12.1 Introduction by Way of an Example   213
12.2 Definitions   217
12.3 More Examples   220
12.4 Deterministic PDAs   223
12.5 The Two Types of Acceptance Are Equivalent   227
       Exercises   230

13 The Equivalence of CFGs and PDAs   232

13.1 For Any CFG There Is a PDA   232
13.2 For Any PDA There Is a CFG   236
       Exercises   242

14 Parsing   244

14.1 Top-Down Parsing   244
14.2 Recursive Descent   251
14.3 Bottom-Up Parsing   255
       Exercises   260

15 CFLs and Non-CFLs   263

15.1 The Pumping Lemma and Examples   263
15.2 Intersections and Complements   270
15.3 Decision Problems for CFLs   274
       Exercises   276

Part IV Turing Machines, Their Languages, and Computation 277

16 Turing Machines 279

16.1 Models of Computation 279
16.2 Definitions; TMs as Language Acceptors 282
16.3 Combining Turing Machines 288
16.4 Computing a Function with a TM 292
      Exercises 295

17 Variations of Turing Machines 298

17.1 TMs with Doubly-Infinite Tapes 298
17.2 TMs with More Than One Tape 303
17.3 Nondeterministic TMs 305
17.4 Universal Turing Machines 311
      Exercises 315

18 Recursively Enumerable Languages 319

18.1 Recursively Enumerable and Recursive 319
18.2 Enumerating a Language 322
18.3 Not All Languages Are Recursively Enumerable 324
18.4 Examples 329
      Exercises 331

19 More General Grammars 334

19.1 Unrestricted Grammars 334
19.2 Grammars and Turing Machines 338
19.3 Context-Sensitive Grammars 343
19.4 Linear-Bounded Automata and the Chomsky Hierarchy 345
      Exercises 350

20 Unsolvable Decision Problems 353

20.1 The Halting Problem 353
20.2 Other Unsolvable Problems Relating to TMs 356
20.3 Post's Correspondence Problem 359
20.4 Applications to Context-Free Languages 365
      Exercises 368

21 Computability: Primitive Recursive Functions 370

21.1 Computable Functions 370
21.2 Primitive Recursive Functions 373
21.3 More Examples 379
21.4 Primitive Recursive Predicates 382
21.5 Some Bounded Operations 385
      Exercises 391

22 Computability: μ-Recursive Functions 394

22.1 A Computable Total Function That Is Not Primitive Recursive 394
22.2 Unbounded Minimalization and μ-Recursive Functions 395
22.3 Gödel Numbering 397
22.4 All Computable Functions Are μ-Recursive 401
22.5 Nonnumeric Functions 407
       Exercises 411

Part V   Introduction to Computational Complexity 413

23 Tractable and Intractable Problems 415

23.1 Growth Rates of Functions 415
23.2 The Time Complexity of a Turing Machine 420
23.3 Tractable Decision Problems: The Class $\mathscr{P}$ 423
23.4 Nondeterminism and the Class $\mathscr{NP}$ 426
23.5 NP-Completeness 430
       Exercises 433

24 Some NP-Complete Problems 435

24.1 NP-Completeness of the Satisfiability Problem 435
24.2 Other NP-Complete Problems 442
       Exercises 448

References 450

Bibliography 453

Index 456

PREFACE

This book presents an introduction to the theory of computation, designed specifically for the undergraduate student. It emphasizes formal languages, automata, and computability, and it includes a brief discussion of computational complexity and NP-completeness.

Early exposure to the topics covered in this text can have several benefits for students. It introduces them to profound computational questions and to aspects of the subject that will not quickly become obsolete; it helps to provide a perspective on computer science as a discipline, rather than a collection of diverse technologies; and it clearly demonstrates the power of mathematical tools and formal methods as well as their applicability to computing.

The potential benefits of studying these topics are greatest if they come early in the students' careers, after perhaps a year's worth of coursework in computer science. The difficulty is that even though such students may have had calculus or discrete mathematics, it is not to be expected that they have acquired much familiarity with axiomatic approaches or much proficiency at formal reasoning. Obviously, it is important to avoid overwhelming them with mathematical notation. However, it is just as important that the topics be discussed in the language that is appropriate (that of mathematics) and that the students see the precision and clarity mathematical language makes possible. I believe the approach I have adopted makes this book distinctive: to start out comparatively slowly by introducing the needed mathematical tools in the context in which they will be used, and to explain and demystify them with examples and discussion—not to sacrifice mathematical rigor or precision, but to make the mathematics more intelligible. As the students progress through the book and acquire more experience with mathematical formalism, it will not be necessary to supplement the formalism with as much exposition.

The first part (Chapters 1 and 2) contains some mathematical preliminaries. In particular, Chapter 2 is devoted to mathematical induction, recursive definitions, and applications to languages and related topics. These two chapters are more detailed and complete than the mathematical preliminaries sections of most other books in this field and can be treated as an integral part of the book rather than as an isolated reference section. These chapters, and thus the entire book, can be read by a student who has not already had a thorough course in discrete mathematics. With students who have had such a background, Part I may be omitted, although it may be necessary to introduce the notation and terminology in Section 1.6, and it may be desirable to look briefly at a few examples in Chapter 2 having to do with formal languages.

The book contains enough material for a full year course. Preliminary versions have been used at North Dakota State University, in a three-quarter sequence required for computer science majors and recommended for the sophomore year (although many students take it as juniors or seniors). It would be reasonable to use the book as the basis for a one-semester course covering regular and context-free languages and some of the theory of Turing machines. In addition, since Parts IV and V are substantially independent of the first three Parts (except for Chapter 19 and the last section of Chapter 20), it would also be possible to use it in a course on Turing machines, computability, and complexity.

I would like to express my gratitude to all those people who have contributed in any way to this book. I must especially single out D. Bruce Erickson, who was an unfailing resource in times of confusion or indecision. I have also benefited from, and appreciate greatly, the conversations I have had with Davis Cope, Jim Hoffman, Paul Juell, Ken Magel, Lloyd Olson, Mark Pavicic, Warren Shreve, and Vasant Ubhaya. My editor at McGraw-Hill, David Shapiro, has been kind, encouraging, and useful at every step, and Ingrid Reslmaier and everyone else at McGraw-Hill with whom I have had any contact have been uniformly helpful. The following reviewers gave many valuable suggestions during early drafts of the manuscript: Stanley Ahalt, Ohio State University; Edward Ashcroft, Arizona State University; Timothy Margush, University of Akron, Ohio; Michael Quinn, Oregon State University; Klaus Sutner, Stevens Institute of Technology; and Jie Wang, Boston University. Finally, and most importantly, I thank my wife Jan for her patience, her forbearance, and her support during all the phases of this project.

John C. Martin

INTRODUCTION

This book is mostly about the theory of computation. "Computation", what a computer does, can refer to a number of seemingly very different activities: adding and subtracting numbers, sorting lists of names into alphabetical order, formatting a page of text, to name just a few of the most familiar. The variety of these activities makes it difficult to talk about them as a whole, which we must do if we are to discuss the *theory* of computation, without lapsing into vague generalities.

One is tempted to sidestep the question of exactly what computation is by returning to the second sentence above: computation is what a computer does. But then we must ask exactly what a computer is, and at this point we run the risk of getting bogged down in a discussion of hardware and technology. What is the minimum, in terms of memory, speed, etc., below which something should not be called a computer? Exactly what does a state-of-the-art supercomputer have in common with a programmable hand calculator?—or, for that matter, with a state-of-the-art supercomputer of twenty years ago? It's not exactly *actual* computers we are concerned with—they are too diverse, too ill-defined, and too complicated— but computers in the abstract. We are interested in the unifying features of all computers, the features that they have in common, that distinguish them from other pieces of hardware (compact disk players, for example, or hair dryers). Since "computers in the abstract" can best be described in terms of what they do (computation), we are back where we started.

Fortunately, we can use the ideas of an English mathematician named Alan Turing to help us answer both questions: what a computer is, and what it does. Some fifty years ago, well before the invention of the electronic digital computer, Turing attempted to formalize precisely the notion of an *effective procedure,* or *algorithm*—what a human being does, in other words, when he or she sits down with a pencil and paper to solve some problem in a systematic, step-by-step way. His approach was to identify the fundamental, primitive operations involved in the process, and to define an abstract *machine* capable of performing those operations according to clearly specifiable rules. The resulting abstract device, which came to be called a Turing machine, is very simple conceptually (the moves it makes consist essentially of reading symbols on a long tape, one at a time, and replacing them by other symbols), and yet it is extremely powerful. In fact Turing claimed at the time, and all the evidence since then tends to support his claim, that any conceivable algorithmic procedure can be accomplished by a Turing machine with an appropriate set of built-in rules.

It would be very easy to construct a hardware implementation of a Turing machine (or at least a hardware approximation—the "tape" in the abstract version is assumed to have unlimited length), and it is easy to write a program, in practically any high-level programming language, to simulate such a machine. But in a way, this is beside the point. The abstraction underlying Turing machines is so simple that the best way to understand is abstractly. In fact, since a Turing machine is not a particularly *efficient* way of solving complex problems, there is no reason to build one, except just for the fun of it. The significance of the Turing machine is that it is an *abstract model of computation*. To be a little more explicit: once we have the notion of a Turing machine, we may *define* "computation" to be, roughly speaking, that which can be carried out by a Turing machine. This can be made into a precise definition, since the notion of a Turing machine is precisely definable; and it is justified by the theoretical power of these machines, to which we referred above. By studying what Turing machines are or are not capable of, we are able to study computation itself, and what is or is not effectively computable by any procedure whatsoever.

Turing machines are not the only abstract models of computation. A number of other researchers have attempted to capture in a mathematical definition the nature of computation, or of an effective procedure. Now it is not possible to prove that a particular mathematical definition is a correct formulation of an intuitive idea like that of computation; but it is possible to compare one mathematical definition with another. One of the most convincing arguments in support of Turing's claim for the generality of his "computing machine" is that all the independent approaches, including Turing machines, can be demonstrated to be equivalent in their computing power. Although some of the other abstract models resemble modern computers more closely in their details, Turing machines are among the easiest to describe and the most well-known.

We are now in a better position to understand what "the theory of computation" means. To summarize: the theory of computation deals in part with abstract models of computation such as Turing machines, the types of problems that they are able to solve, and the types of problems that they are *not* able to solve. Studying these abstractions allows us to study computers without worrying about the intricacies of a particular architecture, and without worrying about the limitations imposed by a specific set of hardware. We are able to strip away the nonessentials and study the properties that all computers have in common, the power and the potential of computers in general as well as their inherent limitations.

The theory of computation, however, has come to include other topics as well. In Parts II and III of this book we look at several abstract devices less general than Turing machines. Although they can be viewed as rudimentary models of computation, and thus can help to set the stage for Turing machines, they arise naturally in various settings in computer science. Looking briefly at them now will also help us to understand better the "languages" part of the book's title.

In the 1950s, Noam Chomsky introduced a formal device called a *context-free grammar* for modeling certain properties of language. A particular context-free grammar contains a number of *grammar rules,* and specifies a particular language: the language consisting of all the strings that can be generated using the rules. Although Chomsky was interested primarily in "natural" language, it was quickly recognized that context-free grammars were of great value to computer science, since they could be used to describe and to define the syntax of programming languages and other important formal languages. The theory of context-free grammars was applied to compiler design and other areas of computer science.

Within a few years of the introduction of context-free grammars, it was shown that they were equivalent in their language-describing ability to certain abstract machines called *pushdown automata*. "Equivalent" means, on the one hand, that for any context-free grammar, there is a pushdown automaton that can *recognize* the corresponding language—that is, process an arbitrary string and determine whether or not it belongs to the language; and on the other hand, for any pushdown automaton, the language it recognizes can be generated by some context-free grammar.

Around the same time, an even simpler abstract machine, a *finite automaton,* was introduced. Although such devices were originally used by McCulloch and Pitts to model neuron nets, they were also applied to the design of switching circuits, and more recently to the solution of miscellaneous software problems arising in compiler design and text editing. The basic idea underlying a finite automaton, or "finite-state machine", is a very general one: a system that is at each moment in one of a finite number of discrete, easily identifiable states, and that moves among these states in a predictable way depending on inputs to the system. Like pushdown automata, finite automata can be formulated as *language recognizers*. The corresponding languages are very simple, although they too have important applications in computer science. Simple language-generating formalisms can be described that are equivalent to finite automata, in the same way that context-free grammars are equivalent to pushdown automata.

Now a Turing machine, like a modern computer, can process "input" (the symbols on its tape initially) and produce "output" (the symbols remaining on its tape after it has finished its sequence of moves). Both these simpler abstract machines are also models of computation, in the sense that they process input strings and produce output—although in their simplest form, the output they produce will contain only yes-or-no answers. They may therefore be compared to Turing machines, and there is a natural hierarchy in terms of computing power into which they all fit: pushdown automata are more restrictive, and finite automata drastically more so, owing to their severely limited "memory". Studying this hierarchy leads us to study Turing machines' language-recognizing abilities also, and to consider the languages they are capable of describing. As one might hope, there is a way of generating these languages using grammars more general than context-free grammars; as a result, there is a hierarchy of language types corresponding to the various abstract machines.

It may seem unduly restrictive to focus on the problem of recognizing strings in a language. Certainly when we arrive at Turing machines we shall be discussing a wider range of types of computation. But language recognition is not as specialized an activity as it might seem at first. A general solution to any *decision problem* (a problem for which every specific instance can be answered yes or no) can be viewed as a language-recognition algorithm. To take a familiar numerical example, solving the problem: given an integer n, is it prime? amounts to examining input strings (representations of integers) and distinguishing those that represent primes from those that don't—in other words, recognizing the language of strings that represent primes. Furthermore, in the case of a problem requiring an answer more complicated than yes/no, there is often a closely related decision problem whose solution is at least comparable to that of the original. For example, if f is a function, being able to answer the question: given x and y, is $f(x) = y$? is tantamount to being able to compute $f(x)$ for an arbitrary x. Thus it is reasonable to use the problem of language recognition as a unifying theme in our discussion of abstract models of computation.

Up to this point, we have mentioned those aspects of the theory of computation that concern solving problems, or performing computations, *in principle*. We have ignored questions of speed, efficiency, memory capacity, all those issues that can obviously not be ignored in practice, when specific computational problems need to be solved. In the last part of the book. we look briefly at these more practical questions. We develop a way of classifying problems according to their inherent complexity, which allows us to separate the problems that are solvable in principle but hopelessly difficult in practice from those that can feasibly be solved in a realistic amount of time. Again a model of computation such as a Turing machine is useful. Although it is not itself an efficient computer, it can be used as a yardstick: if we use an appropriate scheme for classifying problems, it is possible to draw conclusions about the feasibility of solving a particular problem on a real computer, based on how it compares to other problems when solved on a Turing machine.

The theory of computation, then, has combined a number of elements drawn from quite different areas: mathematics, linguistics, biology, electrical engineering—and, of course, computer science. Remarkably, these disparate elements fit together into a coherent, even elegant, theory. To a great extent, the way they fit together into a theory is what dictates the organization of this book and the order in which the topics are discussed. It is helpful to be able to start with relatively simple models, to develop mathematical notation for them, and to formulate and answer in a simple setting questions that will be harder or impossible to answer later on. However, the reason for studying the individual topics is not so much that they fit into an elegant theory, as that each is an important and useful topic in its own right.

PART

I

MATHEMATICAL NOTATION AND TECHNIQUES

In practically every theoretical textbook, if there is an opening chapter in the form of mathematical preliminaries, it will include somewhere near the beginning a discussion of sets. The reason is that sets are generally accepted as the primitive "undefined" objects of mathematics, the objects in terms of which everything else is defined. In this theoretical computer science textbook, we shall study languages and abstract "machines." A language is nothing more than a set of strings, or words, that are composed of symbols from some other set, the alphabet. The underlying components of an abstract machine are sets, and the way the machine works is described by specifying certain rules that take the form of functions from one set to another. The first two "basic mathematical objects" are therefore sets and functions, and the first two sections of Chapter 1 present notation and terminology we will need in dealing with these objects.

Since our discussions will involve logical reasoning, it is appropriate to spend a little time talking about logical statements and arguments. These might seem even more basic to our enterprise than sets and functions. The reason they don't come first is that it's easier to talk about logic if we use a few tools pertaining to sets. In Section 1.4, we look very briefly at some of the most fundamental types of logical argument used in proofs. The remaining sections of Chapter 1 introduce

1

the idea of a relation on a set (a generalization of a function from a set to itself) and some of the notation that will get us started on our study of languages.

Chapter 2 returns to proof techniques and discusses another type, proof by mathematical induction, that is particularly appropriate in discrete mathematics and will be useful for us in this book. A closely related idea is that of inductive, or recursive, definition. We will see later in the chapter that it will be an effective way of defining languages, and, when used along with mathematical induction, will help us establish properties of languages.

CHAPTER

1

BASIC
MATHEMATICAL
OBJECTS

1.1 SETS

The first question in discussing sets is how to specify one. The two most common ways are to enumerate the elements (either completely or in such a way as to make it clear what the remaining ones are) and to give a property that characterizes the elements of the set. Standard notation for the two approaches is illustrated by these examples.

$$A = \{11, 12, 21, 22\}$$
$$B = \{3, 3.1, 3.14, 3.141, 3.1415, 3.14159, \ldots\}$$
$$C = \{x \mid x \text{ is a positive integer whose decimal representation}$$
$$\text{has two digits, each either 1 or 2}\}$$

The set A has four elements. B is an infinite set, whose elements are the approximations to π obtained by giving some initial number of decimal digits. At least, that's probably the way most people would fill in the "$\ldots$," even if they were not able to produce any other elements of B beyond the six that are shown. C is identical to A, since it has the same elements.

To say that x is an element of the set A, we write $x \in A$. Using this notation, we might write

$$D = \{x \in B \mid x < 3.1415\}$$

to specify the set $\{3, 3.1, 3.14, 3.141\}$. We would read this "the set of elements x in B such that $x < 3.1415$."

If A and B are sets, A is a subset of B if every element of A is an element of B. This is written $A \subseteq B$. Saying that two sets are equal (i.e., have the same elements) is equivalent to saying that each is a subset of the other. Thus, when we want to prove that $A = B$, there will normally be two parts to the proof: proving that $A \subseteq B$ and proving that $B \subseteq A$.

If we have a set A, we may consider another set A', the *complement* of A, consisting of all elements not in A. Of course this makes sense only in the context of some "universal" set U that contains all the elements we might ever consider.

$$A' = \{x \in U \,|\, x \notin A\}$$

where $\notin$ means "is not an element of." If A is the set $\{1, 2\}$, A' might mean the set of all integers not equal to 1 or 2, or the set of all real numbers not equal to 1 or 2, or any number of other possibilities, but the set U that is intended is usually clear from the context.

For any two sets A and B, we can form the *union* of the two, $A \cup B$, and the *intersection* of the two, $A \cap B$.

$$A \cup B = \{x \,|\, x \in A \quad \text{or} \quad x \in B\}$$

$$A \cap B = \{x \,|\, x \in A \quad \text{and} \quad x \in B\}$$

For example,

$$\{1, 2, 3, 4\} \cup \{2, 4, 6, 8\} = \{1, 2, 3, 4, 6, 8\}$$

$$\{1, 2, 3, 4\} \cap \{2, 4, 6, 8\} = \{2, 4\}$$

A and B are *disjoint* if they contain no elements in common. We can write this as $A \cap B = \varnothing$, where $\varnothing$ is the *empty set*—the set with no elements. If A, B, and C are sets, then we may write $A \cup B \cup C$ to mean $\{x \,|\, x$ is an element of at least one of the three sets A, B, and $C\}$. Of course we can also write $(A \cup B) \cup C$ and $A \cup (B \cup C)$, which are defined differently:

$$(A \cup B) \cup C = \{x \,|\, x \in A \cup B \quad \text{or} \quad x \in C\}$$

$$A \cup (B \cup C) = \{x \,|\, x \in A \quad \text{or} \quad x \in B \cup C\}$$

As you can verify, all three of these sets are equal. Similarly, $A \cap B \cap C = (A \cap B) \cap C = A \cap (B \cap C)$. More generally, if $A_1, A_2, \ldots$ are sets, we write

$$\bigcup_{i=1}^{10} A_i$$

to mean the set $\{x \,|\, x \in A_i$ for at least one i with $1 \le i \le 10\}$;

$$\bigcup_{i=1}^{\infty} A_i = \{x \,|\, x \in A_i \text{ for at least one } i \ge 1\}$$

$$\bigcap_{i=1}^{N} A_i = \{x \mid x \in A_i \text{ for every } i \text{ with } 1 \le i \le N\}$$

and so forth. Still more generally, if $P(i)$ is some condition involving i, we might write something like

$$\bigcup_{P(i)} A_i$$

to mean $\{x \mid x \in A_i \text{ for at least one } i \text{ satisfying } P(i)\}$. For example,

$$\bigcup_{i \text{ is prime}} A_i = A_2 \cup A_3 \cup A_5 \cup A_7 \cup \ldots$$

$$= \{x \mid x \in A_i \text{ for at least one prime } i\}$$

The *difference* of two sets A and B is the set

$$A - B = A \cap B' = \{x \mid x \in A \quad \text{and} \quad x \notin B\}$$

With the union, intersection, complementation, and difference operations, one can construct arbitrarily complicated expressions, and it is often necessary to manipulate expressions using a few basic rules. Here is a list of some standard set identities. A, B, and C represent arbitrary sets. As before, $\emptyset$ denotes the empty set, and U stands for the universal set.

The *commutative* laws:

$$A \cup B = B \cup A \tag{1.1}$$
$$A \cap B = B \cap A \tag{1.2}$$

The *associative* laws:

$$A \cup (B \cup C) = (A \cup B) \cup C \tag{1.3}$$
$$A \cap (B \cap C) = (A \cap B) \cap C \tag{1.4}$$

The *distributive* laws:

$$A \cup (B \cap C) = (A \cup B) \cap (A \cup C) \tag{1.5}$$
$$A \cap (B \cup C) = (A \cap B) \cup (A \cap C) \tag{1.6}$$

The *De Morgan* laws:

$$(A \cup B)' = A' \cap B' \tag{1.7}$$
$$(A \cap B)' = A' \cup B' \tag{1.8}$$

Other laws involving complements:

$$(A')' = A \tag{1.9}$$
$$A \cap A' = \emptyset \tag{1.10}$$

$$A \cup A' = U \tag{1.11}$$

Other laws involving the empty set:

$$A \cup \varnothing = A \tag{1.12}$$

$$A \cap \varnothing = \varnothing \tag{1.13}$$

Other laws involving the universal set:

$$A \cup U = U \tag{1.14}$$

$$A \cap U = A \tag{1.15}$$

Rules (1.7) and (1.8), the De Morgan laws, are particularly useful. Let us give a proof of (1.8), to illustrate how identities of this type are proved.

To show $(A \cap B)' \subseteq A' \cup B'$, let $x \in (A \cap B)'$. Then by definition of complement, $x \notin A \cap B$. By definition of intersection, x is not an element of both A and B; therefore, either $x \notin A$ or $x \notin B$. Thus $x \in A'$ or $x \in B'$, so $x \in A' \cup B'$ by definition of union.

To show $A' \cup B' \subseteq (A \cap B)'$, let $x \in A' \cup B'$. Then $x \in A'$ or $x \in B'$. Therefore, either $x \notin A$ or $x \notin B$. Thus x is not an element of both A and B, and so $x \notin A \cap B$. Therefore $x \in (A \cap B)'$.

As an illustration of how some of these rules may be applied, let us simplify the expression $A \cup (B - A)$.

$$A \cup (B - A) = A \cup (B \cap A') \quad \text{(by definition of } -\text{)}$$

$$= (A \cup B) \cap (A \cup A') \quad \text{(by (1.5))}$$

$$= (A \cup B) \cap U \quad \text{(by (1.11))}$$

$$= A \cup B \quad \text{(by (1.15))}$$

For any set A, we may consider the set whose elements are the subsets of A. This set, sometimes referred to as the *power set* of A, is often written 2^A. The reason for this notation is that if A has n elements, then 2^A has 2^n elements (see Exercise 2.10). To illustrate, suppose $A = \{1, 2, 3\}$; then

$$2^A = \{\varnothing, \{1\}, \{2\}, \{3\}, \{1, 2\}, \{2, 3\}, \{1, 3\}, \{1, 2, 3\}\}$$

Notice that $\varnothing$ and A are included: the empty set is a subset of every set, and any set is a subset of itself.

Here is another definition involving sets. Given two sets A and B, we may consider the new set of all "ordered" pairs (a, b), where $a \in A$ and $b \in B$. The set of all these ordered pairs is called the *Cartesian product* of A and B, and is denoted $A \times B$. "Ordered" means simply that the pair (a, b) is different from the pair (b, a). If A has n elements and B has m elements, then $A \times B$ has nm elements. For example,

$$\{a, b\} \times \{0, 1, 2\} = \{(a, 0), (a, 1), (a, 2), (b, 0), (b, 1), (b, 2)\}$$

More generally, the set of all "ordered n-tuples" $(a_1, a_2, \ldots, a_n)$, where $a_i \in A_i$ for each i, is denoted $A_1 \times A_2 \times \cdots \times A_n$.

1.2 FUNCTIONS

Next to sets, the most important types of objects in mathematics are functions. The functions you see most often in algebra and calculus courses involve real numbers and have formulas such as x^2, $\log_2(x)$, and $\sin x$. Each of these expressions specifies a real number that is associated with a real number x; in the second case, it is necessary to say a positive real number x, since $\log_2(x)$ makes sense only if $x > 0$. More generally, a function associates with each element of one set a single element of another set. The first set is the *domain* of the function, the second set the *codomain*. If the name of the function is f, and the domain and codomain of f are A and B, respectively, the element of B that f associates with an element x of A is written $f(x)$. We write

$$f : A \to B$$

to indicate that f is a function with domain A and codomain B. In informal terminology, we say f *assigns* an element of B to each element of A; or f *maps* an element x of A to the element $f(x)$ of B. A slightly more precise way of describing a function eliminates the need for such undefined terms as "assigns," "associates," or "maps"; we shall discuss it a little later. But for most of our purposes, the informal terminology is perfectly adequate.

Sometimes there seems to be a certain arbitrariness about the codomain of a function. For example, consider the function f, whose domain is the set of real numbers, given by the formula $f(x) = x^2$. Let $\mathcal{R}$ be the set of real numbers, and let $\mathcal{R}^+$ be the set of nonnegative real numbers. We might say $f : \mathcal{R} \to \mathcal{R}$, since for every real number x, x^2 is a real number. We might also say $f : \mathcal{R} \to \mathcal{R}^+$, since for every real number x, x^2 is a nonnegative real number. To confuse the matter more, if we were only interested in considering $f(x)$ for nonnegative values of x, we might say $f : \mathcal{R}^+ \to \mathcal{R}$, or $f : \mathcal{R}^+ \to \mathcal{R}^+$. To be precise, these are really four different functions, even though their values for a given x are all described by the same formula. To specify a function, we must say what its domain and codomain are, and we must state the rule that determines the value $f(x)$ that is assigned to each x in the domain. This is a law that is often broken: people speak of "the function $f(x) = x^2$," or "the function $\log_2(x)$." One common convention is to assume that the domain is the largest set for which the formula makes sense—for x^2, $\mathcal{R}$; for $\log_2(x)$, $\{x \in \mathcal{R} \mid x > 0\}$. However, this still leaves the codomain up in the air. In many cases, it may not matter, but in defining a function we shall try to specify both sets.

It is occasionally desirable to discuss a set of functions whose domains, though possibly different, are all subsets of some fixed set A. In this situation, so that we can compare functions in the set even though they have different domains, they are referred to as *partial functions* on A. A partial function on A is a function whose domain is part of A; it is sometimes viewed as a function on A that is *undefined* at certain points of A. In contrast, a *total* function on A is a function that is defined at each point of A. We will have occasion to use partial functions later in this book, but until further notice, "a function with domain A" will always mean a total function on A.

Here are a few examples of functions. Let H be the set of human beings, alive and dead. Let $\mathcal{N} = \{0, 1, 2, \ldots\}$, the set of *natural numbers*.

1. $f_1 : \mathcal{N} \to \mathcal{N}$, defined by the formula $f(x) = x^2$
2. $f_2 : H \to H$, defined by the rule $f(x) =$ the mother of x
3. $f_3 : H \to \mathcal{N}$, defined by the rule $f(x) =$ the number of siblings of x
4. $f_4 : \{1, 2, \ldots, 100\} \to H$, defined by $f(x) =$ the xth-tallest living man in America

We've already noticed that if $f : A \to B$, there may be elements y of B that do not correspond to any x in A—i.e., for which there is no $x \in A$ with $f(x) = y$. The *range* of the function f is the set $\{y \in B|$ there is at least one x in A with $f(x) = y\}$. In our examples, the range of f_1 is the set of all nonnegative integers that are perfect squares. The range of f_2 is the set of all human females with at least one child. Assuming we don't count half-brothers or half-sisters as siblings, the range of f_3 is probably $\{0, 1, \ldots N\}$ for some N less than 50. (*Probably*, because it may be the case that one pair of parents had 41 children but no pair of parents ever had 40.) The range of f_4 is the set of the 100 tallest living men in America.

It is useful to introduce a little more notation at this point. If $f : A \to B$ and A_1 is a subset of B, we write $f(A_1)$ to mean the subset of B consisting of all the elements $f(x)$ for $x \in A_1$. In other words,

$$f(A_1) = \{y \in B|y = f(x) \text{ for at least one } x \in A_1\}$$

In a sense this is misleading notation, for now when we write $f(X)$, X might be either an element of A or a subset of A; generally, however, no confusion will arise. In terms of this notation, if $f : A \to B$, the range of f can be written $f(A)$. It is always true that $f(A) \subseteq B$, but these two sets may not be the same—see below.

If $f : A \to B$, we say f is *one-to-one*, or *injective*, or an *injection*, if the same element y in B cannot be $f(x)$ for more than one x in A. In other words, f is one-to-one if, whenever $f(x_1) = f(x_2)$, then $x_1 = x_2$. To say it yet another way, f is one-to-one if, whenever x_1 and x_2 are elements of A and $x_1 \neq x_2$, $f(x_1) \neq f(x_2)$. If $f : A \to B$, f is *onto*, or *surjective*, or a *surjection*, if every element of B is $f(x)$ for some $x \in A$—or equivalently, if $f(A)$ (the range of f) is equal to B (the codomain of f). If f is both one-to-one and onto, f is *bijective*, or a *bijection*. Of our four examples, only f_1 and f_4 are one-to-one. f_2 is not, since there are two people having the same mother; f_3 is not, since there are two people having the same number of siblings. None of our four functions is onto: in all four cases, we can see that the range of the function is strictly smaller than the codomain.

The terminology "one-to-one," although standard, is potentially confusing. It doesn't mean that one element of A is mapped to (only) one element of B. This property goes without saying—it's part of what it means to say $f : A \rightarrow B$. Nor does it mean that for one $y \in B$, there's one $x \in A$ with $f(x) = y$. There may be no such x if f is not onto. What it does mean is that only one element x of A is mapped to the one element $f(x)$ of B.

To a large extent, whether f is one-to-one or onto depends on how we have specified the domain and codomain. To go back to our first example, it doesn't make sense to ask whether "the function $f(x) = x^2$" is one-to-one or onto, as the following illustrates.

[handwritten: R = real]
[handwritten: $R+$: real > 0 .]

1. $f : \mathcal{R} \rightarrow \mathcal{R}$ defined by $f(x) = x^2$ is neither one-to-one nor onto. *[handwritten: $x_1=-1$, $x_2=1$, $x_1 \neq x_2$ but $f(x_1)=f(x_2)$]*
2. $f : \mathcal{R} \rightarrow \mathcal{R}^+$ defined by $f(x) = x^2$ is onto but not one-to-one. *[handwritten: $x_1=-1, x_2=1$ Ranf $= R+$]*
3. $f : \mathcal{R}^+ \rightarrow \mathcal{R}$ defined by $f(x) = x^2$ is one-to-one but not onto. *[handwritten: $x_1=1, x_2=2$ ∵ R include $R>0$ ($R+$) & $R<0$.]*
4. $f : \mathcal{R}^+ \rightarrow \mathcal{R}^+$ defined by $f(x) = x^2$ is both one-to-one and onto.

If $f : A \rightarrow B$ and $g : B \rightarrow C$, then for $x \in A$, $f(x) \in B$, and since g is defined on B, it is possible to talk about $g(f(x))$. More generally, if $f : A \rightarrow B$, $g : B_1 \rightarrow C$, and the range of f is a subset of B_1 (so that g is defined at every point of the form $f(x)$), then $g(f(x))$ makes sense. The function $h : A \rightarrow C$ defined by $h(x) = g(f(x))$ is called the *composition* of g and f and is written *[handwritten: $f \rightarrow g \rightarrow h$]* $h = g \circ f$. For example, the function h from $\mathcal{R}$ to $\mathcal{R}$ defined by $h(x) = \sin(x^2)$ is the composition of g and f (*i.e.*, $g \circ f$), where $g(x) = \sin x$ and $f(x) = x^2$. The composition of f and g (*i.e.*, $f \circ g$), on the other hand, is given by the formula $(\sin x)^2$. When you're computing $g \circ f(x)$, take the formula for $g(x)$ *[handwritten: $\Rightarrow g(f(x))$]* and replace every occurrence of x by $f(x)$. You can verify that if $f : A \rightarrow B$, $g : B \rightarrow C$, and $h : C \rightarrow D$, then the functions $h \circ (g \circ f)$ and $(h \circ g) \circ f$ from A to D are equal, and either one is computed as follows: For $x \in A$, first take $f(x)$; then apply g to that element of B to obtain $g(f(x))$; then apply h to that element of C to obtain $h(g(f(x)))$.

The preceding paragraph introduces one slightly subtle point. We said $h \circ (g \circ f) = (h \circ g) \circ f$, rather than $h \circ (g \circ f)(x) = (h \circ g) \circ f(x)$. In general, when we say that two functions f and g are equal, we are saying three things: first, that f and g have the same domain; second, that they have the same codomain; and third, that for each x in the domain, $f(x)$ and $g(x)$ are the same. Here again, it is easy to be careless and to regard as "equal" two functions that have the same value at each element in the intersection of the two domains (i.e., at each point where they are both defined). But we shall usually be strict about observing the technicality.

Suppose $f : A \rightarrow B$ and $g : B \rightarrow C$, and assume that f and g are both one-to-one; then $g \circ f$ is also. To say that $g \circ f$ is one-to-one means that whenever $g \circ f(x_1) = g \circ f(x_2)$, $x_1 = x_2$; but if $g(f(x_1)) = g(f(x_2))$, then, since g is one-to-one, $f(x_1) = f(x_2)$, and thus, since f is one-to-one, $x_1 = x_2$. If f and g are both assumed to be onto, on the other hand, then $g \circ f$ is also. For any $z \in C$, there is a $y \in B$ with $g(y) = z$, since g is onto; and for any $y \in B$ there is an $x \in A$ with $f(x) = y$, since f is onto. Therefore, for any $z \in C$ there is an $x \in A$ with $g(f(x)) = g \circ f(x) = z$. Finally, it follows by combining these facts that if f and g are both bijections, then so is $g \circ f$.

If $f : A \to B$ is a bijection (one-to-one and onto), then for any $y \in B$, there is at *least* one $x \in A$ with $f(x) = y$, since f is onto; and for any $y \in B$, there is at *most* one $x \in A$ with $f(x) = y$, since f is one-to-one. Therefore, for any $y \in B$, it makes sense to speak of *the* $x \in A$ for which $f(x) = y$, and we denote this x by $f^{-1}(y)$. We may now speak of the function f^{-1} from B to A. $f^{-1}(y)$ is the element $x \in A$ with $f(x) = y$. Notice that substituting $x = f^{-1}(y)$ in this formula gives us immediately the formula $f(f^{-1}(y)) = y$, or $f \circ f^{-1}(y) = y$. On the other hand, for $x \in A$, $f(f^{-1}(f(x))) = f \circ f^{-1}(f(x)) = f(x)$, and therefore, since f is one-to-one and f has the same value at x as at $f^{-1}(f(x))$, $f^{-1}(f(x)) = x$. These two formulas summarize the "inverse function" f^{-1}:

$$\text{for every } x \in A, \ f^{-1}(f(x)) = x$$

$$\text{for every } y \in B, \ f(f^{-1}(y)) = y$$

Remember that it makes sense to discuss the function f^{-1} only when f is a bijection. You can verify that for any bijection $f : A \to B$, $f^{-1} : B \to A$ is also a bijection.

The relation between f and f^{-1} is symmetric: if the inverse function of f is f^{-1}, then the inverse function of f^{-1} is f. The formula for this is $(f^{-1})^{-1} = f$, and it is easily verified by using the definition of $(f^{-1})^{-1}$: $(f^{-1})^{-1}(x)$ is the element y of B for which $f^{-1}(y) = x$; but $f^{-1}(f(x)) = x$; therefore, since f is one-to-one, $y = (f^{-1})^{-1}(x) = f(x)$.

Recall that at the end of Section 1.1 we defined the Cartesian product $A \times B$ of two sets A and B, or more generally, the Cartesian product $A_1 \times A_2 \times \ldots \times A_n$ of n sets. In this book, one way in which Cartesian products will often be used is to consider a function of more than one variable. When a quantity depends on two or more independent variables, it is appropriate to view it as a function whose domain is (some subset of) a Cartesian product. We might, for example, try to predict a person's risk of contracting a certain disease during the next year on the basis of the person's sex, age, income, and city. If this were possible, we could consider the function

$$DP : S \times A \times I \times C \to [0, 1]$$

Here $S = \{\text{male, female}\}$, $A = I = \mathcal{N}$, $C = \{x | x \text{ is a city in the US}\}$, and $[0,1]$ means the set of all real numbers between 0 and 1. If the probability that a 22-year-old male resident of Hettinger, N.D., earning 11,300 dollars a year will contract the disease during the next year is 0.0003, then we would say that

$$DP(\text{ male, 22, 11300, HettingerND}) = 0.0003$$

The standard arithmetic operations on real numbers can also be interpreted as functions in this way. We might write $+ : \mathcal{R} \times \mathcal{R} \to \mathcal{R}$, except that $+(a, b)$ is normally written $a + b$. Division $(/)$ could be described as a function from $\mathcal{R} \times (\mathcal{R} - \{0\})$ to $\mathcal{R}$, since a/b makes sense for any pair of real numbers (a, b) for which $b \neq 0$.

1.3 LOGICAL STATEMENTS

Whether the abstract objects we are discussing are as basic as sets and functions or as complicated as theoretical models of computation, our discussions will attempt to present the logical properties of these objects: to define as precisely as we can the particular objects we are interested in studying, and to investigate the logical consequences of the definitions. Both the definitions and the subsequent discussion will involve logical *statements* and logical *arguments*, and it is therefore appropriate to spend some time on the rudiments of logic and proofs.

To begin at the beginning: the primitive objects in logic are *statements*. These are assertions that can be given *truth values*—i.e., that are either true or false (and not both). This requires a little qualification. The statement $1 < 2$ is true; the statement $1 > 2$ is false; the truth value of the statement $x < 2$ obviously depends on the value of the variable x. We may if we wish regard all three of these as statements involving some variable x. (x doesn't actually appear in the first two, but it does no harm to say they "involve" x.) x is an element of some universe, which in this case we might take to be the set $\mathcal{R}$ of real numbers. Each of the three statements, then, has a *truth set*: the set of real numbers x for which the statement is true. The essential difference between the three statements is that their truth sets are different: the entire set $\mathcal{R}$, the empty set, and the set $\{x \in \mathcal{R} | x < 2\}$, respectively. In general, then, we shall consider statements "over" some universe U (i.e., statements involving a variable x whose values are elements of U), and each such statement has a truth set that is a subset of U. If p is a statement over U, and if we denote the variable by x, we often write $p = p(x)$ to emphasize the fact that the statement depends on x. We shall let $T(p) = T(p(x))$ denote the truth set of p:

$$T(p(x)) = \{x \in U | p(x) \text{ is true}\}$$

Sometimes we want to consider statements with more than one variable, such as "x is the brother of y," or "$x < y$ and $y < z$." The variables may belong to different universes: in the statement "x is an element of A," we might choose x to be a variable over $\mathcal{R}$ and A to be one over $2^{\mathcal{R}}$. It is worth pointing out that limiting ourselves to one variable in our discussion does not really prohibit statements like these. In order to consider the statement $x \in A$, for example, we could take as our single universe the set $\mathcal{R} \times 2^{\mathcal{R}}$. We may define functions $\pi_1 : \mathcal{R} \times 2^{\mathcal{R}} \to \mathcal{R}$ and $\pi_2 : \mathcal{R} \times 2^{\mathcal{R}} \to 2^{\mathcal{R}}$ by the formulas $\pi_1(x, A) = x$ and $\pi_2(x, A) = A$, and we can now view the statement as involving the single variable (x, A), since it can be rewritten $\pi_1(x, A) \in \pi_2(x, A)$. In particular, it still makes sense to talk about the truth set of the statement, which is now a subset of $\mathcal{R} \times 2^{\mathcal{R}}$. Fortunately, we won't need to be this formal or this technical very often, but it explains why we are able to speak of logical statements as having one variable.

If $p(x)$ and $q(x)$ are statements over U, we say $p(x)$ *logically implies* $q(x)$, or simply $p(x)$ implies $q(x)$, if $T(p(x)) \subseteq T(q(x))$—in other words, if $q(x)$ is true whenever $p(x)$ is true. The notation $p \Rightarrow q$ will mean that p implies q. Statements p and q are *logically equivalent* (written $p \Leftrightarrow q$) if each implies the other. This is the same as saying that their truth sets are equal. To take an example, let p_1, p_2, and p_3 be defined as follows:

$$p_1 : x < 2$$

$$p_2 : x^2 < 4$$

$$p_3 : 2x < 4$$

If we assume that the universe is still $\mathcal{R}$, then the truth set of p_1 is $\{x \in \mathcal{R} | x < 2\}$, that of p_2 is $\{x \in \mathcal{R} | -2 < x < 2\}$, and that of p_3 is the same as that of p_1. Thus p_1 and p_3 are equivalent, while p_2 implies both p_1 and p_3 but is not equivalent to either. Logically speaking, knowing the truth set of a statement tells you all you need to know about the statement. Two equivalent statements, such as $x < 2$ and $2x < 4$, may sound different, but they say essentially the same thing.

Just as we can combine sets to form new sets, using the operations of union, intersection, and complementation, we can combine statements to form new statements, using the logical operations OR, AND, and NOT, which are usually denoted by the symbols $\vee$, $\wedge$, and $\neg$, respectively. Since the logical content of a statement is embodied in its truth set, we may *define* the statement $p \wedge q$ by saying what its truth set is—and it is exactly what you would expect. We define $p \wedge q$ to be true precisely when p and q are both true:

$$T(p \wedge q) = T(p) \cap T(q)$$

Similarly,

$$T(p \vee q) = T(p) \cup T(q)$$

$$T(\neg p) = T(p)'$$

Once we have made these definitions, we may easily come up with rules of logical equivalence, based on the set identities in Section 1.1. For example, consider the two statements

$$r : \neg(p \wedge q)$$

$$s : (\neg p) \vee (\neg q)$$

We have $T(r) = T(p \wedge q)' = (T(p) \cap T(q))'$, and $T(s) = T(\neg p) \cup T(\neg q) = T(p)' \cup T(q)'$. Since these two sets are equal, according to (1.8) in Section 1.1, we conclude that r and s are equivalent. In exactly the same way, you can translate each of the identities in Section 1.1 into the corresponding equivalence.

Another important logical operation is the *conditional* operation, denoted $\rightarrow$. We read the statement $p \rightarrow q$ as "if p, then q." What should its truth set be? Consider a man lying in bed, not yet quite awake, saying to himself, "If today is Monday, I'm late for work." Obviously the statement should be considered true if in fact it is Monday and he is late for work. Obviously it should be false if it is Monday and he is not late for work. The less obvious question is, if today is Sunday, is his statement true or false? Normally we do not say that he is making a false statement just because he is too sleepy to know that it's Sunday—irrespective of whether he is actually late for work or not. If today is not Monday, we give him the benefit of the doubt and say that his statement is correct. Another way to look at this is that the man is willing to commit himself as to his being late for work only if the first condition (that today is Monday) is true. If today is not Monday he doesn't want to express an opinion, and thus it is not appropriate to accuse him of lying in this case. At any rate, the conditional statement $p \rightarrow q$ is defined to be true except when it's obviously false: it's true unless p is true and q is not. In other words,

$$T(p \rightarrow q) = (T(p) \cap T(q)')'$$

$$= T(p)' \cup T(q)$$

It follows from this formula that

$$(p \rightarrow q) \Leftrightarrow (\neg p \lor q)$$

Notice that the conditional statement $p \rightarrow q$ is different from $p \Rightarrow q$. $p \rightarrow q$ is a statement on the same level as p, over the same universe; it may be true or false, and its truth set is a subset of the universe. $p \Rightarrow q$ is not a logical statement in the same sense, or over the same universe—it is a "meta-statement," a statement about statements.

Conditional statements come in many guises, even apart from the fact that there are seemingly different statements such as $\neg p \lor q$ (and we shall see others soon) that are equivalent to $p \rightarrow q$. There are a number of ways besides "if p, then q" to express in words the statement $p \rightarrow q$, and they appear frequently enough, in this book and elsewhere, that you should be able to recognize them. One of the most common is "p only if q." The statement "He went only if he had the car" means the same as "If he went, he had the car." A few other ways of saying $p \rightarrow q$ are indicated below.

> if p then q
>
> p only if q
>
> not p unless q
>
> q follows from p
>
> p is sufficient for q
>
> q is necessary for p
>
> q is a consequence of p

The *biconditional* statement $p \leftrightarrow q$ is a shortened form of $(p \rightarrow q) \land (q \rightarrow p)$. Using two different ways of expressing the conditional, we might read this "p only if q, and p if q," but it is usually shortened to "p *if and only if* q." The statement $q \rightarrow p$ is called the *converse* of $p \rightarrow q$. For this reason, you sometimes see statements like "If p, then q, and conversely," which is another way of expressing the biconditional statement $p \leftrightarrow q$.

We saw earlier that by definition, $p \rightarrow q$ is true unless p is true and q is not. Thus, saying that $p \rightarrow q$ is *always* true, or that $p \rightarrow q$ is equivalent to the statement TRUE, or that it has truth set U, is the same as saying that it's not possible for p to be true and q not to be true. But this is the same as saying that whenever p is true, q must be true—in other words, $p \Rightarrow q$. This is the relationship between $p \to q$ and $p \Rightarrow q$: the second expresses the fact that the first is always true. Similarly, saying that the biconditional statement $p \leftrightarrow q$ is always true is the same as saying that p and q are logically equivalent. When you encounter a *proof* in a theoretical book such as this one, it will typically be a proof that some statement q follows from some set of assumptions p, or that two statements p and q are equivalent. The proof may begin "We shall prove that if p, then q," or "We shall prove that p if and only if q"; and it may contain statements such as "r follows from s," or "if r then s, and conversely." In most cases, what is actually being expressed is a logical relationship between statements. A slightly more accurate version of the first statement, for example, might be "We shall prove that 'if p then q' is always true," or "We shall prove that p logically implies q." We shall say more about proofs in the next section.

We must talk a little more precisely about variables in statements. Consider the three statements

$$(x - 1)^2 < 4$$

$$\text{for every } x, (x - 1)^2 < 4$$

$$\text{there exists } x \text{ so that } (x - 1)^2 < 4$$

All of them involve a variable called x, but there is an obvious difference between the use of x in the first statement and the use of x in the other two. In the first, the variable x is a *free* variable. Any specific value in the universe might be substituted for x; for some values, the resulting statement might be true, and for others it might be false. The statement depends on x: $(x - 1)^2 < 4$ is different from $(y - 1)^2 < 4$, since x and y may refer to different elements of the universe. In the second statement, however, it makes no sense to substitute a value for x: "For every 5, $(5 - 1)^2 < 4$" is nonsense, and so is "For every 2, $(2 - 1)^2 < 4$." The statement is not about a number; it is about the universe of numbers, and it is either true or false, period. Whether it is true or false depends on the universe. For $\mathcal{R}$, it is obviously false. The phrase "for every" is called a *quantifier*, and we say that the variable x is *bound* to that quantifier; it is a *bound* variable, not free. The other basic quantifier is "there exists," and the x in the third statement is also bound to the quantifier. In the statement "For every x, $x + y > x$," x is a bound variable and y is free. Going back to the beginning of this section, when we speak of a statement $p(x)$, and refer to its truth set, we are assuming x is a *free* variable.

In the statement "For every x, $(x - 1)^2 < 4$," the phrase "for every x" has a certain *scope*—namely, the statement $(x - 1)^2 < 4$—and outside that statement x means something different, if it means anything at all. If you have studied a language like Pascal, you may be reminded of the scope of a variable in a procedure, and in fact the situations are very similar. If a Pascal procedure contains a declaration of an identifier A, then the scope of that declaration is limited to the procedure and any other procedures within it. To refer to A outside the procedure is either an error or a reference to some other identifier declared outside the procedure.

One must exercise a certain amount of care in using sentences with more than one quantifier: "For every x, there exists x so that $(x - x)^2 < 4$" is illegal, because for a specific occurrence of x in "$(x - x)^2 < 4$," it is impossible to tell which quantifier x is bound to. The statement "for every x, there exists y so that $(x - y)^2 < 4$" is perfectly valid. The quantifiers "for every" and "there exists" are often denoted $\forall$ and $\exists$, respectively, and parentheses are used to indicate clearly the scope of each. Our last sentence would be written

$$\forall x (\exists y ((x - y)^2 < 4))$$

You can perhaps appreciate better the importance of the scope of quantifiers by comparing this statement with another that is superficially similar:

$$\exists y (\forall x ((x - y)^2 < 4))$$

If we interpret both these as statements about the set of real numbers, then in the first statement the entire clause $\exists y ((x - y)^2 < 4)$ is within the scope of "$\forall x$." This means intuitively that we can interpret "$\exists y$" as "There exists a number y, which may depend on x." The first statement is clearly true, since y could be chosen to be x, for example. The second, however, is false, since it asserts that there is a single number y that satisfies the inequality no matter what x is. That this is false can be seen by considering $x = y + 2$.

To most people, a sentence written in English looks less intimidating than a formula sprinkled with $\forall$'s, $\exists$'s, $\wedge$'s, and so on. That is why most textbooks write statements out in words, and that is why we will not be using the $\forall$ and $\exists$ notation very much after we leave this chapter. However, in order to work with a logical statement, particularly one involving quantifiers, it is essential that you be able to dissect the statement and isolate its basic logical constituents. Often, writing it out in a formula can be helpful here, because it forces you to identify the logical components of the statement and the relationships between them. In particular, it forces you to specify the scope of each quantifier. We give two examples and refer you to the exercises for several others.

Example 1.1. Let the universe be $\mathcal{N}$. Consider the statement "p is prime," involving the free variable p. Let us write this as a formula, using logical operators and quantifiers, standard relational operators on integers ($>$, $=$, etc.), and the multiplication operator $*$. "p is prime" means that $p > 1$ and the only divisors of p are 1 and p. In other words, $p > 1$ and for any integer k, if k divides p, k must be 1 or p. "k divides p" can be written

$$\exists m (p = k * m)$$

and so the complete statement "p is prime" can be written

$$(p > 1) \wedge \forall k (\exists m (p = k * m) \rightarrow (k = 1 \vee k = p))$$

Example 1.2. Suppose we try to express in a formula the statement "Every nonempty set of natural numbers has a smallest element." We consider two types of variables: those over $\mathcal{N}$, which we write in lower-case, and those over $2^{\mathcal{N}}$, for which we use upper-case.

Our first reformulation is: "For every A, if there are any elements in A, then there is an element x in A so that $x \leq$ every element of A." The last part can be restated "For every y, if $y \in A$ then $x \leq y$." The entire statement then takes the form

$$\forall A(\exists z(z \in A) \rightarrow \exists x(x \in A \wedge \forall y(y \in A \rightarrow x \leq y)))$$

Since most of the statements that we prove in this book involve quantifiers in some form, there is one more issue pertaining to them that it will be helpful to discuss: how to negate a quantified statement. Saying "It is not true that for every x, $p(x)$" is equivalent to saying "There exists x so that not $p(x)$"; similarly, "There does not exist x so that $p(x)$" is equivalent to "For every x, not $p(x)$." These basic rules are straightforward but must be applied carefully in the case of a statement with several quantifiers. Consider the statement "For every x, there exists y so that for every z, $p(x, y, z)$." The discussion will be easier if we revert temporarily to the symbolic form of the quantifiers: remember that $\exists$ means "there exists" and $\forall$ means "for every." Let s be the statement

$$\forall x(\exists y(\forall z(p(x, y, z))))$$

To negate s, we proceed one step at a time

$$\begin{aligned}
\neg s &= \neg(\forall x(\exists y(\forall z(p(x, y, z))))) \\
&= \exists x(\neg(\exists y(\forall z(p(x, y, z))))) \\
&= \exists x(\forall y(\neg(\forall z(p(x, y, z))))) \\
&= \exists x(\forall y(\exists z(\neg p(x, y, z))))
\end{aligned}$$

In words, not s means "There exists x so that for every y, there exists z so that not $p(x, y, z)$."

1.4   PROOFS

People think of proofs as belonging to mathematics; students beginning a course in theoretical computer science are sometimes surprised—let's face it, sometimes dismayed—to find that a good part of the book is in the "theorem-proof" format. Perhaps the first question to be considered in this section should be why proofs are appropriate or necessary in this book. A superficial answer is that a proof convinces the students that the result is true, but this answer leaves something to be desired. A student reading a geography book is happy to accept without proof the statement that Ulan Bator is the capital of Mongolia; no doubt most students would be prepared to believe an author's assertion that a language is regular if and only if it can be recognized by a finite automaton (see Chapter 6). This aspect of proofs should certainly not be unduly minimized; in developing or in learning a theory, a proof is useful in eliminating doubt as to the truth of a statement. But there are other reasons for proofs as well, and in a course like this they are probably even more important. A theory is not simply a collection of facts. To understand a theory, you must understand how one fact is connected to another, and how two concepts that may be defined in very different ways turn out to be closely related. A good proof certainly convinces the reader that a result is true, but it also helps him to understand *why* it is true; it allows him to put the result in perspective and to relate it to the rest of the theory. A bad (but correct) proof, on the other hand, still leaves no doubt as to the correctness of the result being proved, but doesn't give the reader any more insight than he had before into the result or its significance.

In a typical step in a proof, we derive some statement from certain assumptions or hypotheses, from statements we have already derived, and from certain other generally accepted facts, using general principles of logical reasoning. How strict we are as to what constitutes a "generally accepted fact" and what constitutes an acceptable "general principle of logical reasoning" will determine how formal, or how detailed, our proof will be. If we are being exceptionally careful, then on the one hand we will declare at the outset what *axioms* we are adopting and allow no other "generally accepted facts"; and on the other hand, we will enumerate all the specific rules of logical inference that are to be allowed, and we will justify each step in the argument by a reference to one of these rules. At the opposite extreme, one might say "It is obvious that this statement follows," trusting that the reader can fill in the gaps. Whether one should aim more toward the first approach or toward the second depends largely on who the reader is likely to be. Outside a course in mathematical logic, it is hardly ever feasible to provide *every* detail of a proof, as in the first approach; to do so would make the proof too long and laborious to be very helpful. But of course, as mathematics teachers know very well, what is obvious to one person is not obvious to another, and if there is any doubt, it is generally desirable to give some sort of reason for each step in the proof.

There is nothing magical about a proof. Proofs are essentially nothing more than convincing logical arguments. Students tend to be intimidated by proofs, perhaps because it is sometimes difficult to decide when something is a proof, and perhaps because they have seen too many that make heavy use of "it is obvious." One learns to understand proofs, and ultimately to construct them, by studying many examples and by having one's own efforts criticized. In this section, we shall look briefly at a few of the most fundamental forms of proof, and in the next chapter we will study in more detail a more specialized proof technique, which is nevertheless applicable in a variety of settings and will be indispensable in the rest of the book.

Usually what we are trying to prove involves a statement of the form $p \rightarrow q$. A *direct* proof is to *assume* that the statement p is true, and to show using this assumption that q is true. Our first example illustrates this approach.

Example 1.3. *To prove*: For any integers a and b, if a and b are odd, then ab is odd.

Proof. We must start by saying precisely what it means for an integer to be odd. Let us take this as our definition: An integer n is odd if there exists an integer x so that $n = 2x + 1$. Let us now take any a and b and assume that both are odd. Then there is an integer x so that $a = 2x + 1$, and there is an integer y so that $b = 2y + 1$. We wish to show that there is an integer z so that $ab = 2z + 1$. Let us therefore calculate ab.

$$ab = (2x + 1)(2y + 1)$$

$$= 4xy + 2x + 2y + 1$$

$$= 2(2xy + x + y) + 1$$

Thus we may take z to be $2xy + x + y$.

This is an example of a *constructive* proof. We are trying to prove a statement of the form "There exists z so that . . . ." We prove it by constructing z — saying exactly what it is.

Two other comments about this proof are in order. The first has to do with the quantifier "there exists" in the definition of odd. We said "There is an integer x so that $a = 2x + 1$," and subsequently we wrote the equation $ab = (2x + 1)(2y + 1) = \ldots$. Strictly speaking, this is slightly careless. In the first statement, x is a bound variable, bound to the quantifier "there is." In the equation, which of course is outside the scope of the quantifier, we continue to use x as if it means some specific element, contrary to the rule formulated in Section 1.3. This sort of carelessness with "there exists" is not uncommon, and often relatively harmless. In this situation it seems clear what we have in mind: the fact that we say "There exists x" in one case and "There exists y" in the other is a tip-off that we intend to use these specific numbers later. But it would have been more precise, perhaps, to say

there exists x so that $a = 2x + 1$; choose such an x, and call it x_1. There exists x so that $b = 2x + 1$; choose such an x, and call it x_2. Then $ab = (2x_1 + 1)(2x_2 + 1) = \ldots$

If you feel that this is being too fussy, consider a more serious violation of the rule. Suppose we have an argument that begins "For every x, $p(x)$ is true; therefore, x is. . . ." In this case there is no clue as to what the x is that we're talking about in the second statement. The only thing that's different here is that it's the "for every" quantifier instead of "there exists," but our failure to observe the scope of the quantifier has resulted in nonsense.

Secondly, since our proof actually involved the quantified statement "For any integers a and b, . . . ," it is appropriate to point out something that would *not* be a proof: to give an example of a and b for which the statement is true. If we say "Let $a = 45$ and $b = 11$; then $a = 2(22) + 1$ and $b = 2(5) + 1$; therefore $ab = (2(22) + 1)(2(5) + 1) = \ldots = 2(247) + 1$," we have proved nothing except that $45(11)$ is odd. Finding a value of x so that the statement $p(x)$ is true proves the statement "There exists x so that $p(x)$." It does not prove the statement "For every x, $p(x)$." Finding a value of x so that the statement $p(x)$ is false *disproves* the statement "For every x, $p(x)$" (or, if you prefer, proves the statement "It is not the case that for every x, $p(x)$"); this is a "proof by counterexample." Of course, proving that "For every x, $p(x)$" is false is not the same as proving "For every x, not $p(x)$." Again, one cannot prove a statement of the form "For every x, . . ." by giving an example.

The alternative to a direct proof is an *indirect* proof, and the simplest form of indirect proof uses the fact that $p \to q$ is equivalent to $\neg q \to \neg p$. The second conditional statement is called the *contrapositive* of the first. You are familiar with this equivalence in everyday speech: "If I drive, I don't drink" is equivalent to "If I drink, I don't drive," or "If it's not true that I don't drink, then I don't drive." A general argument uses some of the equivalences obtained from the set identities in Section 1.1, plus the fact mentioned in Section 1.3, that $p \to q$ is equivalent to $\neg p \lor q$.

$$p \to q \Leftrightarrow \neg p \lor q$$
$$\Leftrightarrow q \lor \neg p$$
$$\Leftrightarrow \neg(\neg q) \lor \neg p$$
$$\Leftrightarrow \neg q \to \neg p$$

The last equivalence uses the same rule as the first, except with $\neg q$ and $\neg p$ instead of p and q, respectively. A "proof by contrapositive" that $p \to q$ is true assumes that $\neg q$ is true and proves that $\neg p$ is true.

Example 1.4. *To prove*: For any positive integers i, j, and n, if $ij = n$, then either $i \leq \sqrt{n}$ or $j \leq \sqrt{n}$.

Proof. The statement we wish to prove is of the general form "For every x, if $p(x)$ then $q(x)$." For each x, the statement "If $p(x)$ then $q(x)$" is equivalent to "If not $q(x)$ then not $p(x)$," and therefore (by a "general principle of logical reasoning"!) the statement we wish to prove is equivalent to this: For any positive integers i, j, and n, if it's not the case that $i \leq \sqrt{n}$ or $j \leq \sqrt{n}$, then $ij \neq n$.

If it's not true that $i \leq \sqrt{n}$ or $j \leq \sqrt{n}$, then $i > \sqrt{n}$ and $j > \sqrt{n}$. We use the fact that if a and b are numbers with $a > b$, and $c > 0$, then $ac > bc$. Applying this to the inequality $i > \sqrt{n}$, with $c = j$, we obtain $ij > \sqrt{n}\,j$. Since $n > 0$, we know that $\sqrt{n} > 0$, and we may apply the same fact again to the inequality $j > \sqrt{n}$, this time letting $c = \sqrt{n}$, to obtain $j\sqrt{n} > \sqrt{n}\sqrt{n} = n$. We now have $ij > j\sqrt{n} > n$, and it follows that $ij \neq n$.

The second paragraph in this proof illustrates the claim made earlier that a complete proof with no details left out is usually not feasible. Most people would agree that the statement being proved here is relatively simple, and our proof probably includes more detail than would normally be found; still, we have left out a lot. To mention just a few of the details that were ignored:

1. $\neg(p \lor q)$ is equivalent to $\neg p \land \neg q$; therefore, if it's not true that $i \leq \sqrt{n}$ or $j \leq \sqrt{n}$, then $i \not\leq \sqrt{n}$ and $j \not\leq \sqrt{n}$.
2. For any two real numbers a and b, exactly one of the conditions $a < b$, $a > b$, and $a = b$ holds; therefore, if $i \not\leq \sqrt{n}$, then $i > \sqrt{n}$; similarly for j.
3. For any two real numbers a and b, $ab = ba$; therefore, $\sqrt{n}\,j = j\sqrt{n}$.
4. For any real numbers a, b, and c, if $a > b$ and $b > c$, then $a > c$; therefore, if $ij > j\sqrt{n} > n$, then $ij > n$.

Even if we include all these details, we still have not made completely explicit all the rules of inference we have used to arrive at the final conclusion, and we have used a number of facts about real numbers that could themselves be proved from more fundamental axioms. Again, the moral is simply that a proof needs to contain enough detail to be convincing, but exactly how much that means is often a subjective judgment.

A variation of proof by contrapositive is *proof by contradiction*. In its most general form, proving by contradiction that some statement is true involves showing that if it is not true some contradiction results. A contradiction is simply a false statement, one equivalent to the statement FALSE. Formally, if it can be shown that $\neg q$ implies FALSE, then ($\neg$ FALSE) implies q; ($\neg$ FALSE) is the same as TRUE, and saying that TRUE implies q is the same as saying that q is true. If we wish to show by contradiction that $p \to q$ is true, we assume $p \to q$ is false. Since $p \to q$ is equivalent to $\neg p \vee q$, this means we assume $\neg(\neg p \vee q)$, or $p \wedge \neg q$, is true. From this we try to derive some statement that contradicts a statement we know to be true—possibly p, or possibly some other statement.

Example 1.5. *To prove*: For any sets A, B, and C, if $A \cap B = \varnothing$ and $C \subseteq B$, then $A \cap C = \varnothing$.

Proof. Suppose this is not the case. Then using the comments in Section 1.3 about the negation of quantified statements, we may say that there exist sets, which we may call A, B, and C, for which the conditional statement is false. Since $p \to q$ is false precisely when p is true and q is false, we know that $A \cap B = \varnothing$ and $C \subseteq B$, but $A \cap C \neq \varnothing$. Therefore, there exists x so that $x \in A \cap C$. If we choose such an element x, then $x \in A$ and $x \in C$. Since $C \subseteq B$ and $x \in C$, then $x \in B$. Therefore $x \in A$ and $x \in B$, so $x \in A \cap B$. This contradicts the assumption that $A \cap B = \varnothing$, and the proof is complete.

There is not always a clear line between a proof by contrapositive and one by contradiction. Any proof by contrapositive that $p \to q$ is true can easily be transformed into a proof by contradiction: instead of assuming that $\neg q$ is true and deriving $\neg p$, assume that p and $\neg q$ are true and derive $\neg p$; then the contradiction is that p and $\neg p$ are both true. In Example 1.3, it was slightly easier to argue by contradiction, since we wanted to use the assumption that $C \subseteq B$. A proof by contrapositive would assume that $A \cap C \neq \varnothing$ and would try to show that

$$\neg((A \cap B = \varnothing) \wedge (C \subseteq B))$$

This would be more complicated, if only because the desired statement is more complicated.

We conclude our brief discussion of proofs with two more examples, which illustrate a *vacuously* true statement and a proof by *cases*.

Example 1.6. *To prove*: The empty set is a subset of every set.

Proof. Let us first restate the proposition this way: For every set A, and for every x, if $x \in \varnothing$, then $x \in A$. The conditional statement is $p \to q$, where p is always false. (By definition of $\varnothing$, it is impossible that $x \in \varnothing$.) We say that the statement is *vacuously* true, and the proposition follows.

Example 1.7. *To prove*: For any sets A and B, if $A \neq B$, then $(A \cap B') \cup (A' \cap B) \neq \varnothing$.

Proof. $A = B$ is equivalent to $(A \subseteq B) \wedge (B \subseteq A)$, and thus $A \neq B$ is equivalent to $(A \nsubseteq B) \vee (B \nsubseteq A)$. The statement we wish to prove is therefore of the form

$$(p_1 \vee p_2) \rightarrow q$$

Typically one proves this by proving both $p_1 \rightarrow q$ and $p_2 \rightarrow q$. To say it another way, we need to show that in either of the two cases $A \nsubseteq B$ and $B \nsubseteq A$, the conclusion is true. In the first case, since it's not true that every element of A is an element of B, there exists an element of A that is not an element of B; choose such an element x. Then $x \in A$ and $x \in B'$, and thus $x \in A \cap B'$. Therefore, $x \in (A \cap B') \cup (A' \cap B)$, and this set is not empty. The second case is handled exactly the same way.

Reading and understanding proofs is difficult. Not surprisingly, constructing them yourself is even more difficult, and you don't learn how by reading a brief discussion like this one. The purpose of the discussion has been to introduce you to some of the logical techniques most commonly used in proofs, which you will encounter over and over, in some form or other, as you progress through the book. Whenever possible, the proofs will be constructive; and often the actual construction is important for its own sake, in addition to proving the result. One thing to keep in mind: although a proof should do more than just convince, it fails if it does not convince. Cultivate a critical attitude. When you read a proof, ask yourself, "Am I convinced by this step?" When you try to write a proof, read over what you have written and ask, "If I didn't believe the result already, would this proof convince me?"

1.5   RELATIONS

In calculus, when you draw the graph of a function $f : \mathcal{R} \rightarrow \mathcal{R}$, you are marking certain pairs (x, y) in $\mathcal{R} \times \mathcal{R}$, those for which $y = f(x)$. One might identify the function with its graph and say that the function *is* this set of pairs. Defining a function this way makes it unnecessary to say that a function is a "rule," or a "way of assigning," or some other such mathematically imprecise phrase. In general, we might define a function $f : A \rightarrow B$ to be a subset f of $A \times B$ so that for each $a \in A$, there is exactly one element $b \in B$ for which $(a, b) \in f$. The value of b corresponding to a (the value of b for which $(a, b) \in f$) is what we usually write $f(a)$.

A function from A to B is a restricted type of correspondence between elements of the set A and elements of the set B—restricted in that to an $a \in A$ there must correspond one and only one $b \in B$. A bijection from A to B is even more restricted: in the ordered-pair definition, for any a there must be one and only one pair (a, b), and for any b there must be one and only one pair (a, b). If we relax both these restrictions, we might say that an element of A could correspond to several elements of B, or possibly to none, and an element of B could correspond to several elements of A, or possibly to none. Such a correspondence would no longer necessarily be a function, either from A to B or from B to A, but it would still make sense to describe it by specifying a subset of $A \times B$. For an element $a \in A$, a would correspond to, or be "related" to, an element $b \in B$ if the pair (a, b) was in the subset. The mathematical name given to such a subset of $A \times B$ is a *relation* from A to B. We will be primarily interested in the case when $A = B$; in that case, we call it a *relation on A*.

You are familiar with many examples of relations on sets, even if you have not seen them described this way before. If A is the set $\mathcal{N}$ of natural numbers, consider the relation of equality. Normally we write $a = b$; if we were thinking of $=$ as a subset of $\mathcal{N} \times \mathcal{N}$, we could just as easily write $(a, b) \in =$. Of course, the first way is more familiar, and for that reason, if R is an arbitrary relation on A we often write aRb instead of $(a, b) \in R$. In words, we would say a is *related* to b in both cases—or, if there were some doubt as to which relation was meant, related to b via R. The subset $=$ of $\mathcal{N} \times \mathcal{N}$ is the set $\{(0, 0), (1, 1), \ldots\}$, containing all pairs (i, i). The relation on $\mathcal{N}$ specified by the subset

$$\{(0, 1),$$
$$(0, 2), (1, 2),$$
$$(0, 3), (1, 3), (2, 3),$$
$$\ldots\}$$

is the relation $<$. Other simple relations on $\mathcal{N}$ include $\leq$, $>$, $\geq$, $\neq$. A relation on $\mathcal{N}$ of a slightly different type is the "congruence mod n" relation. If n is a fixed positive integer, we say a is congruent to b mod n (in symbols, $a \equiv_n b$) if $a - b$ is a multiple of n. To illustrate, let $n = 3$. As a subset of $\mathcal{N} \times \mathcal{N}$, $\equiv_3$ contains $(0,0)$, $(1,1)$, $(1,4)$, $(4,1)$, $(7,10)$, $(3,6)$, $(8,14)$, $(76,4)$, and every other pair (a, b) with $a - b$ divisible by 3.

There are a number of special types of relations on a set, but the type we will be particularly interested in is called an *equivalence relation*, and it is characterized by three properties called *reflexivity, symmetry*, and *transitivity*. In general, let R be a relation on a set A. As we noted earlier, we shall write aRb, instead of $(a, b) \in R$, to indicate that an element a is related via R to an element b.

1. R is *reflexive* if for every $a \in A$, aRa. (In other words, R is reflexive if every element is related to itself.)
2. R is *symmetric* if for every a and b in A, if aRb, then bRa. Two elements may or may not be related, but if the relation is symmetric one cannot be related to a second without the second being related to the first.
3. R is *transitive* if for any a, b and c in A, if aRb and bRc, then aRc.
4. R is an *equivalence relation* on A if R is reflexive, symmetric, and transitive.

Of the examples given above, the two relations $=$ and $\equiv_n$ on $\mathcal{N}$ are the only two that are equivalence relations. You can check easily that the relation of equality is reflexive, symmetric, and transitive; let us show that $\equiv_n$ also has these properties, for any fixed positive integer n.

First, $\equiv_n$ is reflexive: for any $a \in N$, $a \equiv_n a$, since $a - a$ is a multiple of n (it is $0 * n$). Second, the relation is symmetric: if $a \equiv_n b$, then $a - b$ is a multiple of n, say kn; but then $b - a = (-k)n$, so $b \equiv_n a$. Finally, it is transitive: if $a \equiv_n b$ and $b \equiv_n c$, then $a - b = kn$ and $b - c = mn$, for some integers k and m; but then $a - c = (a - b) + (b - c) = kn + mn = (k + m)n$. Since $a - c$ is a multiple of n, $a \equiv_n c$.

The relation $<$ on $\mathcal{N}$ is neither reflexive nor symmetric. It is not always the case that $a < a$—in fact, it is never the case; and if $a < b$, it is not true that $b < a$. The relation $\leq$ is reflexive but not symmetric. Both of these relations are transitive. The relation $\neq$ is symmetric but neither reflexive nor transitive.

Let us consider a very simple type of equivalence relation on a set A, which turns out to be a useful example because in fact, as we shall see, any equivalence relation can be viewed as being of this type. Suppose that we have a *partition* of A: a collection of subsets, any two of which are disjoint, which together contain all the elements of A. We may think of the elements of A as being distributed into a number of bins, each bin corresponding to a subset in the partition. Every element is in some bin, and no element is in more than one. Now let us define the relation E on A as follows: aEb means a is in the same bin as b. It is obvious that E is an equivalence relation: any element of A is in the same bin as itself; if a is in the same bin as b, then b is in the same bin as a; and if a and b are in the same bin, and b and c are in the same bin, then a and c are in the same bin. The elements in the bin containing a are precisely the elements (including a) that are related to a via E.

Now suppose R is any equivalence relation on a set A. If a is any element of A, we denote by $[a]_R$ (or simply $[a]$) the *equivalence class containing a*—i.e.,

$$[a]_R = \{x \in A \,|\, xRa\}$$

Notice that the "equivalence class containing a" really does contain a, since aRa (because R is reflexive). Notice also that since A is symmetric, saying that $x \in [a]$ is really the same as saying that $a \in [x]$, or aRx. The reason is that if $x \in [a]$, then xRa; but then by symmetry aRx, so that $a \in [x]$.

Now the point is that these equivalence classes form a partition of A, so we can think of them as bins. Certainly every element is in some equivalence class, since, as we have seen, $a \in [a]$. The other condition we need, in order to conclude that the sets $[a]$ form a partition of A is that any two equivalence classes $[a]$ and $[b]$ are either disjoint or identical. Let us show that if $[a]$ and $[b]$ are not disjoint, then $[a] \subseteq [b]$; the same argument will show that $[b] \subseteq [a]$, and thus $[a] = [b]$.

If $[a] \cap [b] \neq \varnothing$, then some x is an element of both $[a]$ and $[b]$. As we have already observed, since $x \in [a]$, aRx. Let y be any element of $[a]$. Then

yRa (by definition of $[a]$)

aRx

xRb (by definition of $[b]$)

Since R is transitive, it follows that yRb. We may conclude that $[a] \subseteq [b]$.

We have shown that the equivalence classes of R form a partition of A. Furthermore, two elements a and b are related, or "equivalent," if and only if they are in the same equivalence class; this is true since on the one hand $a \in [a]$, and on the other hand b is equivalent to a if and only if $b \in [a]$. The conclusion is that abstractly, the arbitrary equivalence relation R is no different from the relation E described above, where the bins are the equivalence classes.

To be a little more explicit, here are eight ways of saying the same thing:

$$aRb$$

a and b are in the same equivalence class

$$a \in [b]_R$$

$$b \in [a]_R$$

$$[a]_R = [b]_R$$

$$[a]_R \subseteq [b]_R$$

$$[b]_R \subseteq [a]_R$$

$$[a]_R \cap [b]_R \neq \emptyset$$

Let us identify the distinct equivalence classes in our congruence-mod-n example. For any $a \in \mathcal{N}$, the integers related to a are all those differing from a by a multiple of n.

$$[0] = \{0, n, 2n, 3n, \ldots\}$$

$$[1] = \{1, n + 1, 2n + 1, \ldots\}$$

$$[2] = \{2, n + 2, 2n + 2, \ldots\}$$

$$\cdots$$

$$[n - 1] = \{n - 1, 2n - 1, 3n - 1, \ldots\}$$

Clearly, these n equivalence classes are distinct, since no two of the integers $0, 1, \ldots, n - 1$ differ by a multiple of n. They also account for all the elements of $\mathcal{N}$. Therefore, since any equivalence class is either disjoint from all of these or equal to one of these, these are all the distinct equivalence classes.

1.6   LANGUAGES

When we speak of languages, we must begin by specifying an *alphabet*, which contains all the legal symbols that can be used to form words in the language. An alphabet is a finite set of symbols. Often in this book, it will be sufficient to consider an alphabet with only two symbols, usually called either a and b or 0 and 1, although their names are arbitrary. Occasionally, we will even use a one-symbol alphabet. Although alphabets like $\{a, b\}$ might not seem at first to allow very interesting languages, they are not really too restrictive for our purposes. In the first place, many phenomena that we will be discussing can occur even in these simple settings, where examples are easier to describe; and in the second place, as you are aware, words constructed from multi-symbol alphabets can be encoded using only two symbols. In the memory of a computer, everything is ultimately expressible in terms of "binary" digits.

If Σ is an alphabet, a *string* over Σ is simply some number of elements of Σ (possibly none) placed in order. We could be more mathematical here, and say that a string of length k is a function f from $\{1, 2, \ldots, k\}$ to Σ, so that the ith symbol in the string is $f(i)$, but normally we can get by with the informal definition. If we take our alphabet to be $\{a, b\}$, some strings over this alphabet are a, baa, aba, and $aabba$. A very important string, which is a string over Σ no matter what Σ is, is the *null* string (the string with no symbols), denoted by Λ. (To avoid confusion, we will never consider an alphabet that has a symbol called Λ.) If x is a string over an alphabet Σ, the *length* of x is the number of symbols in the string, and we will denote this by $|x|$. Thus $|aba| = 3$, $|a| = 1$, and $|\Lambda| = 0$. Notice that when we write a, we might be referring either to the symbol in the alphabet or to the string of length 1. Is there a difference? There would be, at least a technical one, if we were using some definition of string such as the one above involving functions; in general, however, it will not be necessary to distinguish between them. So strings of length 1 over Σ are the same as elements of Σ.

If we take some alphabet Σ, the set of *all* strings over Σ will be denoted by Σ^*. To illustrate for $\Sigma = \{a, b\}$:

$$\{a, b\}^* = \{\Lambda, a, b, aa, ab, ba, bb, aaa, aab, aba, abb, baa, \ldots\}$$

A *language* over Σ will be a set of strings over Σ—i.e., a subset of Σ^*. Here are some examples of languages over $\{a, b\}$. In the fourth example, we introduce a piece of notation that will often be helpful: $N_a(x)$ and $N_b(x)$ denote the number of a's and the number of b's, respectively, in the string x.

$\{\Lambda, a, aa, aab\}$

$\{x \in \{a, b\}^* \mid |x| \leq 8\}$

$\{x \in \{a, b\}^* \mid |x| \text{ is odd}\}$

$\{x \in \{a, b\}^* \mid N_a(x) \geq N_b(x)\}$

$\{x \in \{a, b\}^* \mid |x| \geq 2 \text{ and the first and last symbols of } x \text{ are both } b\}$

When we compare a "language," as we have defined it, to specific well-known languages, we may prevent some confusion by considering what the basic strings are that make up these other (written) languages. Although we would inevitably run into problems in trying to "define" a natural language like English precisely, it is clear that English is not simply a set of words; it would make more sense to think of it as a set of legal sentences. If we adopt this approach, then of course the alphabet contains not only 26 letters, but a blank symbol and punctuation symbols as well. How can we interpret a programming language like Pascal as a set of strings? The most reasonable way is to say that the strings are complete Pascal programs. Thus in general, even though we may speak of "words" in a language, it should be kept in mind that single words (i.e., strings) may incorporate rules of syntax or grammar that were used in their construction.

Since languages are merely sets of strings, new languages can be constructed using any of the set operations discussed earlier in this chapter. The union of two languages over an alphabet Σ is also a language over Σ, as is the complement of Σ. In the second case, the universal set is taken to be the language Σ^* of all strings over Σ; thus, $L' = \Sigma^* - L$. Notice that any two languages can be considered to be over a common alphabet: if $L_1 \subseteq \Sigma_1^*$ and $L_2 \subseteq \Sigma_2^*$, then L_1 and L_2 are both subsets of $(\Sigma_1 \cup \Sigma_2)^*$. Of course this creates the potential for confusion: if L_1 is viewed as a subset of Σ_1^*, then L_1' should be $\Sigma_1^* - L_1$, but if it is viewed as a language over $\Sigma_1 \cup \Sigma_2$, L_1' should be $(\Sigma_1 \cup \Sigma_2)^* - L_1$. Normally it will be clear which alphabet is the appropriate one to use.

In addition to the standard set operations, there is an operation on strings that allows us to construct new strings as well as new languages. This is the *concatenation* operation. If x and y are elements of Σ^*, the concatenation of x and y is the string xy formed by writing the symbols of x and the symbols of y consecutively. If $x = abb$ and $y = ba$, $xy = abbba$. You may check that just as in unions and intersections of sets and in composition of functions, the associative law holds: $(xy)z = x(yz)$. Thus we may concatenate several strings without worrying about the order in which the concatenations occur. We say that a string x is a *substring* of another string y if there are strings z and w, either or both of which may be null, so that $y = zxw$. The string *car* is a substring of each of the strings *descartes*, *vicar*, *carthage*, and *car*, but not of the string *charity*.

At this point some new notation and definitions are in order. First we introduce notation that will be helpful for combining individual symbols of the alphabet. If Σ is an alphabet, and $a \in \Sigma$, we write a^k to denote the string $aa \ldots a$ having k consecutive a's: $a^0 = \Lambda$, $a^1 = a$, $a^2 = aa$, and so on. Next, for $k \geq 0$,

$$\Sigma^k = \{x \in \Sigma^* \mid |x| = k\}$$

Now we may extend our notation so as to be able to talk about concatenating strings and languages, rather than individual symbols and alphabets. If $x \in \Sigma^*$ and $k \geq 0$, $x^k = xx \ldots x$ (i.e., k copies of x concatenated). Again $x^0 = \Lambda$. If $L_1, L_2 \subseteq \Sigma^*$,

$$L_1 L_2 = \{xy \mid x \in L_1 \text{ and } y \in L_2\}$$

For example,

$$\{in, out\}\{come, law, door\} = \{income, inlaw, indoor,$$
$$outcome, outlaw, outdoor\}$$

Notice the similarity to the Cartesian product of two sets. But see Exercise 1.35. If $L \subseteq \Sigma^*$ and $k \geq 0$,

$$L^k = \overbrace{LL \ldots L}^{k}$$

(i.e., the set of all strings that can be obtained by concatenating k elements of L). $L^0 = \{\Lambda\}$. If $L \subseteq \Sigma^*$,

$$L^* = \bigcup_{i=0}^{\infty} L^k$$

Just as Σ^* means all the strings that can be obtained by concatenating any number of symbols from Σ, L^* consists of all strings that can be obtained by concatenating any number of strings from L. Notice that Λ is always an element of L^*, no matter what L is. Finally, we denote by L^+ the set of all strings obtainable by concatenating *one* or more elements of L:

$$L^+ = \bigcup_{i=1}^{\infty} L^k$$

You can check that $L^+ = L^*L = LL^*$. L^* and L^+ may in fact be equal—see Exercise 1.31.

We have looked at several ways of describing languages. In most cases, the languages we wish to describe are infinite (i.e., have an infinite number of strings). However, we are obviously interested in specifying, or describing, these languages in ways that are finite. It is possible to distinguish two basic approaches, which can be illustrated by examples.

$$L_1 = \{ab, \ aba, \ bb, \ bab, \ abba\}^* \cup \{b\}\{bb\}^*$$
$$L_2 = \{x \in \{a, b\}^* | N_a(x) \geq N_b(x)\}$$

In the first case, the definition consists of a description of how an arbitrary string in the language can be *constructed*: it can be obtained either by concatenating an arbitrary number of strings, each of which is either ab, aba, bb, bab, or $abba$, or by concatenating the string b with an arbitrary number of copies of bb. In the second case, the definition specifies a property that characterizes the strings in the language. In other words, it tells how to *recognize* a string in the language: count the number of a's and the number of b's, and compare the two. There is not always a hard and fast line separating these two approaches. A definition like

$$L_3 = \{byb | y \in \{a, b\}^*\}$$

which is another way of writing the last language in our original group of examples, could be interpreted as a method of generating strings in L_3 (start with an arbitrary string and add b to each end) or as a method of recognizing elements of L_3 (examine the symbols on each end, assuming that the length is at least 2). Even a definition like that of L_1, which clearly belongs in the first category, might immediately suggest a way of determining whether some arbitrary string belongs to L_1; and there might be obvious ways of generating all strings in L_2, though the definition is clearly of the second type. As we progress in this book we shall be studying, on the one hand, more and more general ways of *generating* languages, beginning with methods similar to that in the definition of L_1; and on the other hand, corresponding methods of greater and greater sophistication for *recognizing* strings in these languages. The second approach will consist of specifying an *abstract machine* whose operation embodies the method of recognizing the language: a precise description of the machine will be a way of specifying precisely which strings are in the language. These abstract machines will be fairly primitive initially, since it turns out that languages such as L_1 can be recognized relatively easily. A language like L_2 will require a more powerful type of abstract machine to recognize it, as well as a more general method of generating it; and before we are through we shall study machines equivalent in power to the most sophisticated computer.

EXERCISES

1.1. Describe the set $\{0, -1, 2, -3, 4, -5, \ldots\}$ in a way that does not involve "...."

1.2. Describe the set $\{1/2, 1/4, 3/4, 1/8, 3/8, 5/8, 7/8, 1/16, 3/16, 5/16, 7/16, \ldots\}$ in a way that does not involve "...."

1.3. In each case, find a simpler expression representing the same set. (Assume that A and B are sets.)
(*a*) $A - (A - B)$
(*b*) $A - (A \cap B)$
(*c*) $(A \cup B) - A$
(*d*) $(A - B) \cup (B - A) \cup (A \cap B)$
(*e*) $(A' \cap B')'$
(*f*) $(A' \cup B')'$

1.4. In each case, find an expression for the indicated set that involves A, B, C, and the three operations $\cup$, $\cap$, and $'$.
(*a*) $\{x \mid x \in A$ or $x \in B$ but not both$\}$
(*b*) $\{x \mid x$ is an element of exactly one of the three sets A, B, and $C\}$
(*c*) $\{x \mid x$ is an element of exactly two of the three sets A, B, and $C\}$
(*d*) $\{x \mid x \in A$ or $x \in B$ or $x \in C$ but not all three$\}$

1.5. For each integer n, denote by C_n the set of all real numbers less than n, and for each positive integer n let D_n be the set of all real numbers less than $1/n$. Express each of the following sets in a simpler form that does not involve unions or intersections. (For example, the answer to (*a*) is C_{10}.)
(*a*) $\cup_{n=1}^{10} C_n$
(*b*) $\cup_{n=1}^{10} D_n$
(*c*) $\cap_{n=1}^{10} C_n$
(*d*) $\cap_{n=1}^{10} D_n$
(*e*) $\cup_{n=1}^{\infty} C_n$
(*f*) $\cup_{n=1}^{\infty} D_n$
(*g*) $\cap_{n=1}^{\infty} C_n$
(*h*) $\cap_{n=1}^{\infty} D_n$
(*i*) $\cup_{n=-\infty}^{\infty} C_n$
(*j*) $\cap_{n=-\infty}^{\infty} C_n$

1.6. In this problem, as usual, $\mathcal{R}$ denotes the set of real numbers, $\mathcal{R}^+$ the set of non-negative real numbers, $\mathcal{N}$ the set of natural numbers (nonnegative integers), and $2^{\mathcal{R}}$ the set of subsets of $\mathcal{R}$. $[0, 1]$ denotes the set $\{x \in \mathcal{R} \mid 0 \le x \le 1\}$. In each case, say whether the indicated function is one-to-one and whether it is onto. Give reasons. If it is not onto, find its range.

(a) $f_a : \mathcal{R}^+ \to \mathcal{R}^+$ defined by $f_a(x) = x + a$ (where a is some fixed element of $\mathcal{R}^+$)

(b) $d : \mathcal{R}^+ \to \mathcal{R}^+$ defined by $d(x) = 2x$

(c) $t : \mathcal{N} \to \mathcal{N}$ defined by $t(x) = 2x$

(d) $g : \mathcal{R}^+ \to \mathcal{N}$ defined by $g(x) = [x]$ (the largest integer $\leq x$)

(e) $i : 2^{\mathcal{R}} \to 2^{\mathcal{R}}$ defined by $i(A) = A \cap [0, 1]$

(f) $u : 2^{\mathcal{R}} \to 2^{\mathcal{R}}$ defined by $u(A) = A \cup [0, 1]$

1.7. Suppose A and B are sets and $f : A \to B$. Let S and T be subsets of A.

(a) Is the set $f(S \cup T)$ a subset of $f(S) \cup f(T)$? If so, give a proof; if not, give a counterexample (i.e., specify sets A, B, S, and T and a function f).

(b) Is the set $f(S) \cup f(T)$ a subset of $f(S \cup T)$? Give either a proof or a counterexample.

(c) Repeat part (a) with intersection instead of union.

(d) Repeat part (b) with intersection instead of union.

(e) In each of the first four parts where your answer is no, what extra assumption on the function f would make the answer yes? Give reasons for your answer.

1.8. Suppose A and B are sets, $f : A \to B$, and $g : B \to A$. If $f(g(y)) = y$ for every $y \in B$, then f is _____ and g is _____. Give reasons for your answers.

1.9. Let $A = \{2, 3, 4, 6, 7, 12, 18\}$ and $B = \{7, 8, 9, 10\}$.

(a) Define $f : A \to B$ as follows: $f(2) = 7$; $f(3) = 9$; $f(4) = 8$; $f(6) = f(7) = 10$; $f(12) = 9$; $f(18) = 7$. Find a function $g : B \to A$ so that for every $y \in B$, $f(g(y)) = y$. Is there more than one such g?

(b) Define $g : B \to A$ as follows: $g(7) = 6$; $g(8) = 7$; $g(9) = 2$; $g(10) = 18$. Find a function $f : A \to B$ so that for every $y \in B$, $f(g(y)) = y$. Is there more than one such f?

1.10. Let f_a, d, t, g, i, and u be the functions defined in Exercise 1.6. In each case, find a formula for the indicated function.

(a) $g \circ d$

(b) $t \circ g$

(c) $t \circ t$

(d) $d \circ f_a$

(e) $f_a \circ d$

(f) $g \circ f_a$

(g) $u \circ i$

(h) $i \circ u$

1.11. In each case, show that f is a bijection and find a formula for f^{-1}.

(a) $f : \mathcal{R} \to \mathcal{R}$ defined by $f(x) = x$

(b) $f : \mathcal{R}^+ \to \{x \in \mathcal{R}^+ | 0 < x \leq 1\}$ defined by $f(x) = 1/(1 + x)$

(c) $f : \mathcal{R} \times \mathcal{R} \to \mathcal{R} \times \mathcal{R}$ defined by $f(x, y) = (x + y, x - y)$

1.12. Denote by p, q, and r the statements $a = 1$, $b = 0$, and $c = 3$, respectively. Write each of the following statements symbolically, using p, q, r, $\wedge$, $\vee$, $\neg$, and $\to$.

(a) Either $a = 1$ or $b \neq 0$

(b) $b = 0$ but neither $a = 1$ nor $c = 3$

(c) It is not the case that both $a \neq 1$ and $b = 0$

(d) If $a \neq 1$, then $c = 3$, but otherwise $c \neq 3$

(e) $b = 0$ only if either $a = 1$ or $c = 3$

(f) If it's not the case that either $a = 1$ or $b = 0$, then only if $c = 3$ is $a \neq 1$

1.13. Which of these statements are true?

(a) If $1 + 1 = 2$, then $2 + 2 = 4$

(b) $1 + 1 = 3$ only if $2 + 2 = 6$

(c) ($1 = 2$ and $1 = 3$) if and only if $1 = 3$

(d) If $1 + 1 = 3$, then $1 + 2 = 3$

(e) If $1 = 2$, then $2 = 3$ and $2 = 4$

(f) Unless $2 + 2 = 4$, $1 + 1 \neq 2$

(g) Only if $3 - 1 = 2$ is $1 - 2 = 0$

1.14. The most common way of analyzing a compound statement involving simple statements p and q is to construct a *truth table* that shows the truth value for each combination of truth values of p and q. Below are truth tables for the statements $p \wedge q$, $p \vee q$, $\neg p$, and $p \rightarrow q$ (which may in fact be taken as the definitions of these statements).

p	q	$p \wedge q$	$p \vee q$	$\neg p$	$p \rightarrow q$
T	T	T	T	F	T
T	F	F	T	F	F
F	T	F	T	T	T
F	F	F	F	T	T

Truth tables for more complicated statements can be built by finding the truth tables for the component parts from which the statements are constructed. For example, to find the truth table for

$$p \wedge ((\neg q) \rightarrow (\neg p)),$$

we would find truth tables for $\neg q$ and $\neg p$, then combine them using the basic truth table for a conditional to obtain the table for $\neg q \rightarrow \neg p$, and use the truth table for $\wedge$ to get the final result shown.

p	q	$\neg q$	$\neg p$	$\neg q \rightarrow \neg p$	$p \wedge (\neg q \rightarrow \neg p)$
T	T	F	F	T	T
T	F	T	F	F	F
F	T	F	T	T	F
F	F	T	T	T	F

From the truth table it is now obvious that the statement is equivalent to $p \wedge q$.

Construct truth tables for these statements, and use the results to find all logical implications and logical equivalences among them (which statements imply which others, and which are equivalent to which others).

(a) $q \rightarrow p$

(b) $p \leftrightarrow q$

(c) $(p \rightarrow q) \wedge (p \rightarrow \neg q)$

(d) $p \vee (p \rightarrow q)$

(e) $p \wedge (p \rightarrow q)$

(f) $(p \rightarrow q) \wedge (\neg p \rightarrow q)$

(g) $p \leftrightarrow (p \leftrightarrow q)$

(h) $q \wedge (p \rightarrow q)$

1.15. Show that the statements $p \vee q \vee r \vee s$ and $(\neg p \wedge \neg q \wedge \neg r) \rightarrow s$ are equivalent.

1.16. In each case, say whether the statement is true or false, if the universe specified by the quantifiers is the one indicated. Here $(0, 1)$ means the set $\{x \in \mathcal{R} | 0 < x < 1\}$, and $[0, 1]$ means $\{x \in \mathcal{R} | 0 \leq x \leq 1\}$.

(a) $\forall x (\exists y (x > y))$, where $U = (0, 1)$

(b) $\forall x (\exists y (x > y))$, where $U = [0, 1]$

(c) $\exists y (\forall x (x > y))$, where $U = (0, 1)$

(d) $\exists y (\forall x (x > y))$, where $U = [0, 1]$

(e) $\forall x (\exists y (x \geq y))$, where $U = (0, 1)$

(f) $\forall x (\exists y (x \geq y))$, where $U = [0, 1]$

(g) $\exists y (\forall x (x \geq y))$, where $U = (0, 1)$

(h) $\exists y (\forall x (x \geq y))$, where $U = [0, 1]$

1.17. Let R be a relation on a set S. Write a formula involving quantifiers that expresses the fact that R is not transitive.

1.18. Referring to Example 1.1, write symbolic statements using quantifiers to say each of these things:

(a) Every integer greater than 1 has at least one prime factor.

(b) There is exactly one prime that is divisible by 2.

1.19. In each case, a relation on the set $\{1, 2, 3\}$ is given. Of the three properties, reflexivity, symmetry, and transitivity, determine which ones the relation has. Give reasons.

(a) $R = \{(1, 3), (3, 1), (2, 2)\}$

(b) $R = \{(1, 1), (2, 2), (3, 3), (1, 2)\}$

(c) $R = \varnothing$

1.20. In general, a relation on a set can be reflexive or not reflexive, symmetric or not symmetric, and transitive or not transitive—eight possible combinations in all. The relations in Exercise 1.19 illustrate three of the eight. Construct relations on $\{1, 2, 3\}$ that illustrate the other five.

1.21. Consider the following "proof" that any relation R on a set A that is both symmetric and transitive must also be reflexive:

> Let a be any element of A. Choose some $b \in A$ so that aRb. Then since R is symmetric, bRa. Now since R is transitive, and since aRb and bRa, it follows that aRa. Therefore R is reflexive.

Your answer to Exercise 1.20 shows that this proof is not correct. What is the flaw? At what point did it go wrong?

1.22. Three relations are given on the set of all nonempty subsets of $\mathcal{N}$. In each case, say whether the relation is reflexive, whether it is symmetric, and whether it is transitive.

(a) R is defined by: ARB if and only if $A \subseteq B$.

(b) R is defined by: ARB if and only if $A \cap B \neq \varnothing$.

(c) R is defined by: ARB if and only if $1 \in A \cap B$.

1.23. How would your answer to Exercise 1.22 change if in each case R were the indicated relation on the set of *all* subsets of N?

1.24. In each case, a set A is specified, and a relation R is defined on it. Show that R is an equivalence relation.

(a) $A = 2^S$, for some set S. An element X of A is related via R to an element Y if there is a bijection from X to Y.

(b) A is an arbitrary set, and it is assumed that for some other set B, $f : A \to B$ is a function. For $x, y \in A$, xRy if $f(x) = f(y)$.

(c) Suppose U is the set $\{1, 2, \ldots, 10\}$. A is the set of all statements over the universe U—i.e., statements involving at most one free variable, which can have as its value an element of U. (Included in A are the statements FALSE and TRUE.) For two elements r and s of A, rRs if $r \Leftrightarrow s$.

1.25. In Exercise 1.24a, if S has exactly ten elements, how many equivalence classes are there for the relation R? Describe them. What are the elements of the equivalence class containing $\{a, b\}$ (assuming a and b are two elements of S)?

1.26. In Exercise 1.24b, if A and B are both the set of real numbers, and f is the function defined by $f(x) = x^2$, describe the equivalence classes.

1.27. In Exercise 1.24c, how many equivalence classes are there? List some elements in the equivalence class containing the statement $(x = 3) \lor (x = 7)$. List some elements in the equivalence class containing the statement TRUE, and some in the equivalence class containing FALSE.

1.28. Let A be any set, and let R be any equivalence relation on A. Find a set B and a function $f : A \to B$ so that for any $x, y \in A$, xRy if and only if $f(x) = f(y)$.

1.29. Again refer to Exercise 1.24a. Assuming that S is finite, find a function $f : 2^S \to \mathcal{N}$ so that for any $x, y \in 2^S$, xRy if and only if $f(x) = f(y)$.

1.30. Let n be a positive integer. Find a function $f : \mathcal{N} \to \mathcal{N}$ so that for any $x, y \in \mathcal{N}$, $x \equiv_n y$ if and only if $f(x) = f(y)$.

1.31. Let L be a language. It is clear from the definitions that $L^+ \subseteq L^*$. Under what circumstances are they equal?

1.32. (a) Find an example of languages L_1 and L_2 over $\{a, b\}$ for which $(L_1 \cup L_2)^* \neq L_1^* \cup L_2^*$.

(b) Find an example of languages L_1 and L_2 over $\{a, b\}$ for which $L_1 \not\subseteq L_2$, $L_2 \not\subseteq L_1$, and $(L_1 \cup L_2)^* = L_1^* \cup L_2^*$.

1.33. Show that if A and B are languages over Σ and $A \subseteq B$, then $A^* \subseteq B^*$.

1.34. Show that for any language L, $L^* = (L^*)^* = (L^+)^* = (L^*)^+$.

1.35. For a finite set S, denote by $|S|$ the number of elements of S. Is it always true that for finite languages A and B, $|AB| = |A||B|$? (For example, if A has 3 elements and B has 4, does the concatenation AB always have 12?) Either prove it or find a counterexample.

1.36. List some elements of $\{a, ab\}^*$. Can you describe a simple way to recognize elements of this language?

1.37. (a) Consider the language L of all strings of a's and b's that do not end with b and do not contain the substring bb. Find a finite language S so that $L = S^*$.

(b) Show that there is no language S so that the language of all strings of a's and b's that do not contain the substring bb is equal to S^*.

CHAPTER
2

MATHEMATICAL INDUCTION AND RECURSIVE DEFINITIONS

2.1 THE PRINCIPLE OF MATHEMATICAL INDUCTION

The theory of languages and computation is full of statements over the universe of natural numbers, statements involving a variable N. Of course, such statements are not unique to this subject; they are widespread in other areas of computer science and mathematics. Here are two examples from early in this book. Don't worry if you don't understand exactly what they say.

1. A language with N elements is regular.
2. If L is a language corresponding to a regular expression with N operations, then L is recognized by a finite automaton.

There are many other statements that do not involve an integer explicitly but can be reformulated so that they do.

3. For any two strings x and y, the reverse of the string xy is equal to the reverse of y followed by the reverse of x.

One way to introduce N into this statement would be to make the assertion for strings y of length N. The result might be

3. For any string y of length N, and any string x, the reverse of the string xy is equal to the reverse of y followed by the reverse of x.

Why would one want to write it this way? It may seem as though the N unnecessarily clutters up what was originally a simple statement about strings. In fact, as we shall soon see, it suggests an approach that we might take to proving the statement.

When we have such a statement, we will typically want to show that it is true for all values of N greater than or equal to some starting value. (In each of the three statements above, the starting value happens to be 0.) This section describes a useful method for doing this. The statement in our first illustration is a simple numerical formula.

Example 2.1. Consider the statement

$$2^0 + 2^1 + 2^2 + \cdots + 2^N = 2^{N+1} - 1$$

Let us try to prove this statement for every integer $N \geq 0$. There are no obvious algebraic things to do to the left-hand side, no doubt partly because the number of terms being added depends on N. Since no better approach occurs to us, we try writing the formula out for the first few values of N, to see if we can detect any sort of pattern.

$$
\begin{array}{lll}
N = 0: & 2^0 = 2^1 - 1 & \text{(i.e., } 1 = 2 - 1) \\
N = 1: & 2^0 + 2^1 = 2^2 - 1 & \\
N = 2: & 2^0 + 2^1 + 2^2 = 2^3 - 1 & \\
N = 3: & 2^0 + 2^1 + 2^2 + 2^3 = 2^4 - 1 & \\
N = 4: & 2^0 + 2^1 + 2^2 + 2^3 + 2^4 = 2^5 - 1 &
\end{array}
$$

If we're actually doing the arithmetic to check the formulas, we will certainly notice before long that to check the formula at a certain stage, say $N = 4$, we don't need to add all the numbers on the left side $(2^0 + 2^1 + 2^2 + 2^3 + 2^4)$—we just need to take the left side of the previous formula $(2^0 + 2^1 + 2^2 + 2^3)$, which we've already calculated, and add 2^4. Now when we calculated $(2^0 + 2^1 + 2^2 + 2^3)$, we obtained $2^4 - 1$. So our answer for the left side for $N = 4$ is

$$(2^4 - 1) + 2^4 = 2 * 2^4 - 1 = 2^{4+1} - 1$$

Sure enough, the formula is correct when $N = 4$. At this point, we probably realize that the same thing will happen at each step! Let's back up and see if we can make this into a convincing proof.

Example 2.1.   Proof Number 1. To show:

$$2^0 + 2^1 + \cdots + 2^N = 2^{N+1} - 1 \quad \text{for every } N \geq 0$$

$N = 0:$
$$2^0 = 2^{0+1} - 1$$

$N = 1:$
$$2^0 + 2^1 = (2^1 - 1) + 2^1 \qquad \text{(by using the result for } N = 0)$$
$$= 2 * 2^1 - 1 = 2^2 - 1 = 2^{1+1} - 1$$

$N = 2:$
$$2^0 + 2^1 + 2^2 = (2^2 - 1) + 2^2 \qquad \text{(by using the result for } N = 1)$$
$$= 2 * 2^2 - 1 = 2^{2+1} - 1$$

$N = 3:$ $2^0 + 2^1 + 2^2 + 2^3 = (2^3 - 1) + 2^3$ (by using the result for $N = 2$)

$$= 2 * 2^3 - 1 = 2^{3+1} - 1$$

. . .

Continue this process. The formula is true for every $N \geq 0$.

Is this convincing? It would probably convince most people, but if we look at it critically, we see the ending is weak. We used "Continue this process" to call attention to the fact that the cases we checked exhibit a common pattern and that this pattern is repeated at each step. But we didn't actually say *what* the pattern is, and so in a sense "Continue this process" is supposed to convey the most important idea in the proof! Surely we can do better than that. Let's try to describe more explicitly what makes this work: not just for $N = 0$, or $N = 1$, or $N = 2$, but for an *arbitrary* value of N, which we'll call $N = K$. To be specific, let's describe what we do to check the formula when $N = K + 1$, assuming that we've already checked it when $N = K$.

$$2^0 + 2^1 + \cdots + 2^K + 2^{K+1} = (2^0 + 2^1 + \cdots + 2^K) + 2^{K+1}$$

$$= (2^{K+1} - 1) + 2^{K+1} \text{ (using the result when } N = K)$$

$$= 2 * 2^{K+1} - 1$$

$$= 2^{(K+1)+1} - 1$$

We've just verified that for any $K \geq 0$, the truth of the formula for $N = K + 1$ follows from the truth of the formula for $N = K$. To say it differently: if we know the formula holds when $N = K$, we may conclude that it holds when $N = K + 1$. Our proof will surely be clearer if we include this general step.

Example 2.1.   Proof Number 2. To show:

$$2^0 + 2^1 + 2^2 + \cdots + 2^N = 2^{N+1} - 1 \text{ for every } N \geq 0$$

$N = 0:$ $2^0 = 2^{0+1} - 1$

$N = 1:$ $2^0 + 2^1 = (2^1 - 1) + 2^1$ (by using the result for $N = 0$)

$$= 2 * 2^1 - 1 = 2^2 - 1 = 2^{1+1} - 1$$

$N = 2:$ $2^0 + 2^1 + 2^2 = (2^2 - 1) + 2^2$ (by using the result for $N = 1$)

$$= 2 * 2^2 - 1 = 2^{2+1} - 1$$

$N = 3:$ $2^0 + 2^1 + 2^2 + 2^3 = (2^3 - 1) + 2^3$ (by using the result for $N = 2$)

$$= 2 * 2^3 - 1 = 2^{3+1} - 1$$

. . .

In general, for $N = K + 1$,

$$2^0 + 2^1 + \cdots + 2^{K+1} = (2^0 + 2^1 + \cdots + 2^K) + 2^{K+1}$$

$$= (2^{K+1} - 1) + 2^{K+1} \text{ (using the result for } N = K)$$

$$= 2 * 2^{K+1} - 1$$

$$= 2^{(K+1)+1} - 1$$

Therefore, the formula holds for every $N \geq 0$.

This is certainly better. But since we will be using this type of argument a great deal, let's consider whether we can polish it a little, and exhibit its true nature more clearly. We might say, somewhat paradoxically, that our second version is both more than is required and less than a completely convincing proof. It's *more* than is required because we've checked the formula for four specific values of N. This was helpful initially, when we were looking for the pattern, but it's not really necessary now. We could leave out the case $N = 3$, the case $N = 2$, even the case $N = 1$. All of these cases are taken care of by our general argument for $N = K + 1$. The three cases correspond to the values 2, 1, and 0, respectively, of K. Of course, we *can't* leave out the case $N = 0$, because that's what starts the whole thing off. As soon as we know the formula holds for $N = 0$, our general argument tells us it holds for $N = 1$; as soon as we know it for $N = 1$, our general argument tells us it holds for $N = 2$; and so forth.

This second version is *less* than a completely convincing proof simply because to the extent that the cases $N = 1$, $N = 2$, and $N = 3$ are presumed to be necessary for the proof, the two elements of the proof that *are* crucial are obscured. What are they? The first element is checking the formula in the case that starts us off: $N = 0$. The second is the general argument that once we know the formula for some arbitrary value of N ($N = K$), we may conclude it for the next value of N ($N = K + 1$). These two facts together are what allow us to say that the formula holds for all $N \geq 0$. Obviously, neither by itself would be enough: the case $N = 0$ might happen to hold by some fluke—or, for that matter, the formula might hold for the first 7,000 values of N, by an even more misleading fluke—and on the other hand, it wouldn't help to know that the truth of the formula for any value of N implied the truth for the next value, if we could never show that the formula was true for some value in the first place.

There are so many statements that can be proved by exactly this method that it is useful to formulate a general principle, called the *principle of mathematical induction*, to apply whenever we encounter such a statement, and to introduce terminology that will emphasize the two essential ingredients of the proof. In order to state the principle as concisely as possible, we give the name $P(N)$ to the statement involving N that we are trying to prove.

PRINCIPLE OF MATHEMATICAL INDUCTION. Suppose $P(N)$ is a statement involving an integer N, and we wish to prove that $P(N)$ is true for all values of N beginning with some starting value N_0. To do this, it is sufficient to show these two things:

1. $P(N_0)$ is true.
2. For any integer $K \geq N_0$, if $P(K)$ is true, then $P(K + 1)$ is true.

Thus, anytime we have a statement involving some integer N and we announce that we intend to prove the statement using the principle of mathematical induction, or more commonly, "by induction," this will always* mean that we have two things to show: first, that the statement is true for whatever value of N we're starting with (in our introductory example, $N = 0$); second, that its truth for some value $N = K$ implies its truth for $N = K + 1$. These two parts of an induction proof are referred to as the *basis* step and the *induction*, or *inductive*, step. The induction step consists of proving that the statement $P(K + 1)$ is true, *assuming* that $P(K)$ is true. The assumption that $P(K)$ is true is called the *inductive hypothesis*.

Now we are ready to return to our example for the third and final version of the proof.

Example 2.1.   Proof Number 3 (by induction). Let $P(N)$ be the statement:

$$2^0 + 2^1 + \cdots + 2^N = 2^{N+1} - 1$$

We shall show that $P(N)$ is true for all $N \geq 0$.

Basis step: To show that $P(0)$ is true. $P(0)$ is the statement $2^0 = 2^1 - 1$, and this is certainly true.

Induction hypothesis: $K \geq 0$ and $P(K)$: i.e.,

$$2^0 + 2^1 + \cdots + 2^K = 2^{K+1} - 1$$

Statement to be shown in induction step: $P(K + 1)$: i.e.,

$$2^0 + 2^1 + \cdots + 2^{K+1} = 2^{(K+1)+1} - 1$$

Proof of induction step:

$$\begin{aligned}
2^0 + 2^1 + \cdots + 2^{K+1} &= (2^0 + 2^1 + \cdots + 2^K) + 2^{K+1} \\
&= (2^{K+1} - 1) + 2^{K+1} \quad \text{(using the inductive hypothesis)} \\
&= 2 * 2^{K+1} - 1 \\
&= 2^{(K+1)+1} - 1
\end{aligned}$$

Whether or not you follow this format exactly, you should get into the habit of always

- Writing out precisely the statement that is to be shown in the basis step;
- Writing out precisely the induction hypothesis;
- Writing out precisely the statement that is to be shown in the inductive step;
- Pointing out exactly where in the inductive step you use the inductive hypothesis.

These steps may seem laborious at first, but you will find that they help immeasurably in working your way through the proof. Often, once you have done the first three of these four steps, you will find that the actual details of completing the proof are entirely straightforward. Another way to say this is that once it's clear in your mind exactly what it is you're trying to do, actually doing it usually isn't

---

* Unless, that is, we are using the slightly different Strong Principle of Mathematical Induction (see Section 2.2).

so difficult. The reason the four steps are useful is that they help you to clarify for yourself exactly what you're trying to do. In this book, although we may not label the steps of an induction proof quite so formally after the first few chapters, they will always be clearly identifiable.

Before we leave our example altogether, let us contrast Proof Number 1 to Proof Number 3, and say once again why, even though Number 3 involves unfamiliar notation and terminology, it is still preferable.

Most importantly, it calls attention to the two crucial elements of the argument, those that we've labeled the basis step and the induction step. Those two elements were present, remember, in Proof Number 1; they were just obscured. In the second place, formulating a "principle" as we have, and being able to refer to it by name at the beginning of a proof, are useful in themselves. If there are 100 situations in this book in which we use the principle of mathematical induction (don't worry, there probably aren't), we're much more likely to understand them if we identify explicitly the common principle that is operating in all of them, than we are if we treat them as 100 isolated statements whose proofs are intuitively plausible but unrelated. This is one of the reasons for mathematical definitions and terminology in the first place: they take a little getting used to, but they allow us to classify things, and to abstract the common element among seemingly different things. When you read, as one often does in computer science books or papers, "It can be shown by induction that . . . ," you already know a good bit about the proof—in fact, you have a framework for the proof. If the details are not supplied, you can add them.

Not every statement involving integers is appropriate for mathematical induction. Consider the statement

$$(2^N + 1)(2^N - 1) = 2^{2N} - 1$$

which we may view as a statement about integers $N \geq 0$, though it's also true for other numbers N. It would be silly to prove this using the principle of mathematical induction. It's not that we couldn't; it's just that when we came to the induction step, the reason we would give for the desired conclusion would very likely not require the inductive hypothesis. In this case, the conclusion for $K + 1$ could be obtained, just like the conclusion for N in the first place, by expanding the left side of the formula and using laws of exponents. The proof would not be a "real" induction proof, and it would be misleading to classify it as one.

The question arises, then: when is mathematical induction desirable? (Or, if you prefer, when is it necessary?) A general rule of thumb is that whenever a proof contains " . . . ," or "Repeat this process for each N," or "Continuing in this manner, one can see," or any other such phrase, the proof could be made more precise by using mathematical induction. To say that none of these phrases should ever be used in a proof is unreasonable. " . . . " can be useful, and in a simple enough situation it may require little or no explanation. When you are writing a proof and you find yourself using one of these phrases, the important thing is to be aware of the mathematical induction argument that could be substituted, so that you can decide whether it would make the proof clearer. When you encounter one of these phrases while reading a proof, you should realize that it is very likely a substitute for an induction argument. In that case, if the argument doesn't seem obvious to you, you might find that supplying the details of the induction helps you to understand the proof better. In the early stages of this book, we shall err on the side of caution. In the later chapters, don't be too surprised if you see "Continuing in this manner," or even just " . . . ," used from time to time.

The second example illustrates the fact that it's not only numerical formulas to which induction can be applied.

Example 2.2. Let L be a language in Σ^*, for some alphabet Σ. Consider the statement

$$\text{If } L^2 \subseteq L, \text{ then } L^+ \subseteq L$$

Here we have the situation mentioned in the opening paragraph of this section. The statement does not explicitly involve an integer N, and therefore as it stands is not appropriate for the application of the principle of mathematical induction. However, we may easily recast the statement to correct this, if we recall from Chapter 1 that

$$L^+ = \bigcup_{N=1}^{\infty} L^N$$

This suggests that we choose as $P(N)$ the statement $L^N \subseteq L$. Obviously the statement is true for $N = 1$, but let's specifically start our induction proof with $N = 2$, just to illustrate the fact that the starting value in an induction proof needn't be 0 or 1. In order to prove this by induction, we could try a few cases, as we did in Example 2.1, to help us guess the idea behind the inductive step. But it may not be necessary. The key to any induction proof is to figure out how to use the inductive hypothesis in order to prove the induction step; let's go directly to that problem. In our final proof, we will include the basis step as well. The inductive hypothesis will be

$$K \geq 2 \text{ and } L^K \subseteq L$$

(Note: one point in this problem that may cause confusion at first is that we have another "hypothesis" floating around: the assumption that $L^2 \subseteq L$. This is the assumption that makes the statement true in the first place. Obviously, if we didn't know something about L in addition to its being a language in Σ^*, we could not expect to say that $L^N \subseteq L$ for any $N \geq 1$—a language with only one string in it illustrates this. This assumption has nothing to do with the inductive hypothesis; it's available to us free, in both the basis step and the induction step.) In the induction step we wish to show

$$L^{K+1} \subseteq L$$

The question we must ask, then, is: how can we say something about L^{K+1} if we know something about L^K? That is, how can we use the inductive hypothesis? What we need is something that allows us to express L^{K+1} in terms of L^K. But once we have said that, the solution presents itself:

$$L^{K+1} = L^K L$$

(Or $L^{K+1} = LL^K$; either will work.) If we are assuming that $L^K \subseteq L$, then it follows that $L^K L \subseteq LL = L^2$. But then we're done, because we also know that $L^2 \subseteq L$. Now that we've figured out the crucial step, we can afford to be a little more concise in our official proof.

Example 2.2.   Proof by induction. Let $L \subseteq \Sigma^*$, and assume $L^2 \subseteq L$. Let $P(N)$ be the statement:

$$L^N \subseteq L$$

We shall prove $P(N)$ for every $N \geq 2$.

Basis step: To show that $P(2)$ is true. $P(2)$ is the statement $L^2 \subseteq L$, and this is true because of our assumption. (It *is* our assumption.)

Induction hypothesis: $K \geq 2$, and $P(K)$: i.e., $L^K \subseteq L$.

Statement to be shown in induction step: $P(K + 1)$: i.e., $L^{K+1} \subseteq L$.

Proof of induction step: $L^{K+1} = L^K L \subseteq LL$, since $L^K \subseteq L$ (this is the induction hypothesis); but $LL = L^2 \subseteq L$, because of our original assumption.

2.2   THE STRONG PRINCIPLE OF MATHEMATICAL INDUCTION

There are situations where induction is clearly the appropriate technique to prove a statement, and yet the version we have formulated of the induction principle isn't quite sufficient. Again, it's easiest to illustrate by an example.

Example 2.3. This statement is also phrased in terms of languages, although it could be restated in a purely arithmetic form:

If Σ is an alphabet, and $a \in \Sigma$, $\{a^N | N \geq 12\} \subseteq \{aaa, aaaaaaa\}^*$

To simplify notation, let $L = \{aaa, aaaaaaa\}$. In order to recast the statement as one of the form "For every integer $N \geq N_0$, ...," we let $P(N)$ be this statement:

$$P(N) : a^N \in L^*$$

Then our statement is simply that $P(N)$ is true for every $N \geq 12$. If we try a straightforward induction proof, the basis step presents no difficulty.

$$a^{12} = (aaa)^4 \in L^*$$

The problem comes in the induction step. If we assume that $a^K \in L^*$, there's no obvious way to use that to show that $a^{K+1} \in L^*$, since a^{K+1} cannot be formed by concatenating a^K with either a^3 or a^7. What we need seems to be that either a^{K-2} or a^{K-6} is an element of L^*, so that we could concatenate either a^3 or a^7 to get a^{K+1}—and therefore, since we could get a^{K+1} by concatenating two elements of L^*, a^{K+1} would be in L^*. However, we can construct an intuitive argument almost the same way we did in Example 2.1, except that we need a few more cases before the pattern becomes clear.

$N = 12:$ $a^{12} = (a^3)^4 \in L^*$

$N = 13:$ $a^{13} = a^7(a^3)^2 \in L^*$

$N = 14:$ $a^{14} = (a^7)^2 \in L^*$

$N = 15:$ $a^{15} = a^{12}a^3 \in L^*$ (since, by the case $N = 12$, $a^{12} \in L^*$)

$N = 16:$ $a^{16} = a^{13}a^3 \in L^*$ (since, by the case $N = 13$, $a^{13} \in L^*$)

$N = 17:$ $a^{17} = a^{14}a^3 \in L^*$ (since, by the case $N = 14$, $a^{14} \in L^*$)

. . .

This is as plausible intuitively as Proof Number 1 of Example 2.1, but our principle of mathematical induction doesn't quite take care of it. So we formulate a second principle, called the strong principle of mathematical induction (sometimes referred to as course-of-values induction). The only difference is that we're allowed to use a slightly stronger inductive hypothesis: in order to prove $P(K + 1)$ in the induction step, we make the assumption not only that $P(K)$ is true, but that all the statements $P(N_0)$, $P(N_0 + 1)$, $\ldots$, $P(K)$ are true. The intuitive content is thus almost the same; in both cases, the induction principle captures the idea of proving the statements $P(N)$ in sequence, and for each N after the first one using statements we've already proved to prove the current statement.

STRONG PRINCIPLE OF MATHEMATICAL INDUCTION. Suppose $P(N)$ is a statement involving an integer N, and we wish to prove that $P(N)$ is true for all values of N beginning with some starting value N_0. To do this, it is sufficient to show these two things:

1. $P(N_0)$ is true.
2. For any integer $K \geq N_0$, if the statement $P(N)$ is true for every N satisfying $N_0 \leq N \leq K$, then $P(K + 1)$ is true.

We now use this to prove the statement in Example 2.3.

Example 2.3. **Proof by induction.** Let $L = \{aaa, aaaaaaa\}$. Let $P(N)$ be the statement: $a^N \in L^*$. We shall prove $P(N)$ for every $N \geq 12$.
    Basis step: To prove $P(12)$: i.e., $a^{12} \in L^*$. $a^{12} = (a^3)^4$, and since $a^3 \in L$, it follows that $a^{12} \in L^*$.
    Inductive hypothesis: $K \geq 12$, and $P(N)$ is true for all N with $12 \leq N \leq K$ (i.e., for all N with $12 \leq N \leq K$, $a^N \in L^*$).
    Statement to be shown in induction step: $P(K + 1)$: i.e., $a^{K+1} \in L^*$.
    Proof of induction step:

case 1: $K = 12$. $a^{K+1} = a^{13} = a^7(a^3)^2 \in L^*$.
case 2: $K = 13$. $a^{K+1} = a^{14} = (a^7)^2 \in L^*$.
case 3: $K \geq 14$. Then $K - 2 \geq 12$. Since the inductive hypothesis is that $P(N)$ is true for every N with $12 \leq N \leq K$, we may conclude that $a^{K-2} \in L^*$. Therefore, $a^{K+1} = a^{K-2}a^3 \in L^*$, since both a^{K-2} and $a^3 \in L^*$.

You should make sure you understand why we needed to consider three cases in the inductive step. We wanted to apply the inductive hypothesis to a^{K-2}. The problem is that the inductive hypothesis applies only to integers $N \geq N_0$ (i.e., $N \geq 12$), and $K - 2 \geq 12$ only for $K \geq 14$. So we have to take care of the cases $K = 12$ and $K = 13$ separately—just as we had to handle them separately in our preliminary intuitive proof. It's important to remember that the proof of the inductive step must work for *any* $K \geq N_0$, and sometimes this requires considering special cases. An extreme example of the absurdity that might result if we ignore this requirement is the following statement.

Example 2.4. Let $P(N)$ be the statement: If S is any set of N husbands, all the elements of S have the same wife. To show $P(N)$ for every $N \geq 1$. (You might guess that there's nothing special about "husbands" and "wife" in this statement. We could just as easily substitute "triangles" and "area," or "horses" and "color," etc.)

Basis step: $P(1)$ is the statement: For any set S of 1 husband, all the elements of S have the same wife. This is clearly true.

Induction hypothesis: $K \geq 1$, and for any set S of K husbands, all the elements of S have the same wife.

Statement to be proved in induction step: For any set S of $K + 1$ husbands, all the elements of S have the same wife.

Proof of induction step: Let S be any set $\{H_1, H_2, \ldots, H_{K-1}, H_K, H_{K+1}\}$ of husbands. Let $T = \{H_1, H_2, \ldots, H_K\}$ and $R = \{H_1, \ldots, H_{K-1}, H_{K+1}\}$. T is just S except with the element H_{K+1} deleted, and R is just S except with the element H_K deleted. Then both T and R are sets of K husbands; thus, by the inductive hypothesis, all the husbands in T have the same wife, and all the husbands in R have the same wife. This wife is the wife of H_{K-1}, who is an element of both T and R. But every element of S is in either T or R. If an element of S is in T, he has the same wife as H_{K-1}, and if an element of S is in R, he has the same wife as H_{K-1}; therefore, every husband in S has the same wife as H_{K-1}, and in particular, all the elements of S have the same wife.

Obviously, the statement being "proved" here is false. But don't let that prejudice you: if you prefer, for "husbands" and "wife" substitute "xxx's" and "yyy" (this would produce a statement that, if it meant anything, might be true), and see if the *proof* is valid. If it is, of course, we have a problem, having by a seemingly legitimate method proved a false statement.

The basis step is unobjectionable. The argument in the induction step seems valid until you try it for some specific values of K, when you realize (at the point where H_{K-1} is assumed to have a wife) that the K in the inductive hypothesis is tacitly assumed to be at least 2 in the proof. It's a correct induction proof except that the induction step fails for just one value; and therefore it's completely incorrect.

Let's look at one more illustration of the strong principle of mathematical induction.

Example 2.5. First recall that a *prime* is a positive integer, 2 or bigger, that has no positive integer divisors except itself and 1. Let $P(N)$ be the statement: N either is prime or can be factored as a product of primes. We show $P(N)$ for every $N \geq 2$.

Basis step: $P(2)$ is the statement: 2 either is prime or can be factored as a product of primes. This is true: 2 is prime.

Inductive hypothesis: $K \geq 2$, and for every integer N with $2 \leq N \leq K$, N either is prime or can be factored as a product of primes.

Statement to be proved in induction step: $K + 1$ either is prime or can be factored as a product of primes.

Proof of induction step: If $K + 1$ is prime, the statement is true. If not, then by definition of prime, $K + 1 = R * S$, where R and S are positive integers and neither R nor S is equal to 1 or $K + 1$. But then R and S must both be greater than 1 and less than $K + 1$. Therefore, by the inductive hypothesis, both R and S are either prime or factorable as a product of primes. In any case, since $K + 1 = R * S$, it follows that $K + 1$ is factorable as a product of primes, and the statement is true.

We have two slightly different principles of mathematical induction. When is one appropriate, and when is the other? The usual answer is that the first one is appropriate unless it's not adequate (that is, unless in proving the statement for $N = K + 1$ you need to assume the truth of the statement, not only for $N = K$ but for smaller values of N as well), and then the second must be used. Our last inductive proof in this section illustrates the fact that if you want to be on the safe side, you can always use the strong principle of induction, whether it's necessary or not.

Example 2.6. Consider the following fragment of a Pascal program: Assume that all variables are of type Integer.

Read(X,N);

Y := 1;

For I := 1 To N Do

    Y := Y * X;

Writeln(Y)

You can figure out what this does even if you haven't programmed in Pascal. The variables X and N are assigned values from the input. The variable Y is given the initial value 1, and a loop is repeated N times; each time, the value of Y is replaced by its old value multiplied by X. The final value of Y is printed out. We would like to make a statement about the value ultimately printed out by this program fragment, in terms of the values input to X and N. We do this in a slightly roundabout way, as follows. For any integer L, let $P(L)$ be the statement: If the input value for X is x, then after the loop has been iterated L times, the resulting value of Y is x^L. If we can show that $P(L)$ is true for any $L \geq 0$, then it will follow that the value printed out is x^n, where n is the value input to N.

    Basis step: $P(0)$ is the statement: If the input value for X is x, then the value of Y that results from 0 iterations of the loop is x^0. This is true, since if the statement in the loop has not been executed, the initial value of Y, which is 1, has been left unchanged.

    Inductive hypothesis: $K \geq 0$, and for any L with $0 \leq L \leq K$, if the input value for X is x, then after L iterations of the loop the value of Y is x^L.

    Statement to be proved in inductive step: If the input value for X is x, then after $K + 1$ iterations of the loop the value of Y is x^{K+1}.

    Proof of inductive step: It is clear from looking at the statement in the loop that the value of Y after $K + 1$ iterations is x times the value of Y after K iterations. Since $0 \leq K \leq K$, it follows from the inductive hypothesis that the value after K iterations is x^K. Therefore, the value after $K + 1$ iterations is $x * x^K = x^{K+1}$.

Although the program fragment here is certainly very simple, this example should suggest that the principle of mathematical induction can be a useful technique for verifying the correctness of programs.

One other comment about this last proof. There were several integers floating around in the example, if we include program variables: X, x, N, I, Y, n. We chose to formulate our statement in terms of none of them, but a new integer we called L. This often happens. In such a case, it's not enough to decide that we're going to prove something by induction—we must decide exactly which integer to use for the induction. In this example, we might say that we proved the result *by induction on the number of iterations of the loop,* or *by induction on L.*

You may occasionally encounter the principle of mathematical induction in a disguised form that might be called the "minimal counterexample principle." We close this section by returning to Example 2.2, and giving an alternative proof to illustrate this principle.

Example 2.2.   Alternative Proof. Recall that in this example, L is a language in Σ^* and L^2 is assumed to be a subset of L. $P(N)$ is the statement: $L^N \subseteq L$. We wish to prove $P(N)$ for every $N \geq 2$.

Just as in a typical induction proof, we start by verifying that the statement holds for the starting value of N—in this case, it's obvious. Now, if it's *not* true that $P(N)$ is true for all $N \geq 2$, then there must be a minimal value of N greater than or equal to 2 for which $P(N)$ fails, say $N = K$. Since we have verified that $P(2)$ is true, $K > 2$. Therefore $K - 1 \geq 2$, and since $K - 1$ is less than the minimal value K, $P(K - 1)$ must be true. So we have:

$$L^{K-1} \subseteq L \text{ and } L^K \nsubseteq L$$

But $L^K = LL^{K-1}$, and therefore $L^K \subseteq LL \subseteq L$. We have derived a contradiction, and we may conclude that our original assumption was false. Therefore, $P(N)$ is true for all $N \geq 2$.

You can probably see the close resemblance between this proof and our previous proof by induction. Most people prefer the induction proof, because it's a direct proof and not a proof by contradiction, but both are equally valid. The principle on which the second proof depends is sometimes called the *Well-Ordering Principle for the Natural Numbers*: Any nonempty set of positive integers has a smallest element. This is certainly intuitively plausible, as much so as the principle of mathematical induction, and in fact the two principles can be shown to be equivalent. The most well-known axiomatization of the natural numbers, the *Peano* axioms, includes an axiom that embodies the principle of mathematical induction. In spite of their intuitive plausibility, neither the induction principle nor the well-ordering principle follows from other standard properties of the integers.

2.3   RECURSIVE DEFINITIONS

Most people who have completed a course in Pascal (or any other programming language that supports recursion) would recognize this:

```
Function Factorial(N: Integer): Integer;
Begin
    If N = 0 then
        Factorial := 1
    Else
        Factorial := N * Factorial(N−1)
End;
```

as the function that computes $N!$, the factorial of a nonnegative integer N, recursively. If you studied this in a Pascal course, you were probably told that it was not an efficient way to compute $N!$, because of the overhead involved with recursive calls. Here we are concerned not with efficiency, but with the fact that this recursive algorithm could equally well be taken as the definition of $N!$:

$$N! = \begin{cases} 1 & \text{if } N = 0 \\ N * (N - 1)! & \text{otherwise} \end{cases}$$

This is a simple example of a recursive, or *inductive*, definition. There is an obvious analogy to the principle of mathematical induction: the "basis" part of the definition defines the function for some starting value ($N = 0$), and the "inductive" part defines the function for an arbitrary value (corresponding to $K + 1$ in the induction step of a proof), assuming that its value for $N - 1 (= K)$ has already been defined. Clearly this does indeed define a function whose domain is the set of all nonnegative integers. But if you feel that "clearly" is a little too strong, you are encouraged to construct a proof using mathematical induction that this definition specifies the value of $N!$ for every $N \geq 0$.

The factorial function is a numerical function, but the technique of recursive definition applies also to other types of functions, as well as to sets—in particular, languages. In order to define a language, we specify certain strings that are in the language to start with, and we give a general method for constructing new elements, starting with strings we already know are elements.

Example 2.7. Let L be a language over an alphabet Σ. We have defined L^* in Section 1.6 to be the language

$$L^* = \bigcup_{k=0}^{\infty} L^k$$

where L^k is the set of all strings formed by concatenating k elements of L, and $L^0 = \{\Lambda\}$. The languages L^k can be defined recursively as follows:

$$L^0 = \{\Lambda\}$$

$$\text{For } k \geq 0, \ L^{k+1} = L^k L$$

Thus for any k, any $x \in L^k$, and any $y \in L$, $xy \in L^{k+1} \subseteq L^*$. This suggests a more direct way of defining L^* recursively:

1. $\Lambda \in L^*$.
2. For any $x \in L^*$ and any $y \in L$, $xy \in L^*$.
3. No string is in L^* unless it can be obtained by using rules 1 and 2.

To illustrate, let $L = \{a, ab\}$. We start out with Λ. One application of rule 2 adds the strings $\Lambda a = a$ and $\Lambda ab = ab$—i.e., the strings in $L^1 = L$. A second application gives us Λa, Λab, aa, aab, aba, and $abab$, so that we have the elements of $L^0 \cup L^1 \cup L^2$. Any concatenation of k elements of L can be produced from the definition by using k applications of rule 2.

An even simpler illustration is to let $L = \Sigma$. Then a string of length k in Σ^*, which is a concatenation of k elements of Σ, can be produced by k applications of rule 2.

It is interesting to compare the nonrecursive description of L^k, "the set of all strings formed by concatenating k elements of L," with the recursive definition above. The non-recursive definition seems reasonably clear, and it doesn't require much ingenuity to determine which strings are included in L^k. Still, when you actually construct these strings, you don't concatenate k strings at once, you concatenate two strings. The recursive definition is both more consistent with the fact that concatenation is a *binary* operation, and more explicit about exactly how the concatenation is done: a $(k + 1)$-fold concatenation is obtained by concatenating an element of L^k and an element of L. It has a dynamic, or algorithmic, quality that the other lacks. If we were determined to avoid inductive definition, we could say something like

$$L^k = \overbrace{(\ldots((LL)L)\ldots)L}^{k \text{ factors}}$$

or give an equivalent definition in words. Either way, we leave ourselves open to the same objection as in our initial attempt to prove the statement in Example 2.1. Rather than using "$\ldots$" to suggest the general step, the inductive definition comes right out and says it.

Example 2.8. We wish to define the reverse of a string, which we think of as a function from Σ^* to Σ^*. Example 2.7 tells us that any string in Σ^* other than Λ is of the form xa, for some $x \in \Sigma^*$ and some $a \in \Sigma$; therefore, if the recursive part of our definition tells us what the reverse of xa is, assuming we already know what the reverse of x is, then it will effectively define the value of the function at every element of Σ^*.

We define the reverse $REV(x)$ of an element x of Σ^* as follows:

1. $REV(\Lambda) = \Lambda$.
2. For any $x \in \Sigma^*$ and any $a \in \Sigma$, $REV(xa) = aREV(x)$.

Let's apply the definition to the string 100. First we notice that the reverse of a string of length 1 is obtained from the definition by writing the string as the concatenation of Λ and itself.

$$
\begin{aligned}
REV(100) &= REV((10)0) \\
&= 0REV(10) \quad \text{(to get this we let } x = 10 \text{ and } a = 0 \text{ in rule 1)} \\
&= 00REV(1) \quad \text{(here we chose } x = 1) \\
&= 00REV(\Lambda 1) \\
&= 001REV(\Lambda) \quad \text{(here we chose } x = \Lambda) \\
&= 001\Lambda \quad \text{(here we used rule 1)} \\
&= 001
\end{aligned}
$$

Example 2.9. Let Σ be an alphabet. The language *PAL* of palindromes over Σ (defined nonrecursively as the set of strings that are equal to their reverse) can be defined as follows:

1. $\Lambda \in PAL$.
2. For any $a \in \Sigma$, $a \in PAL$.
3. For any $x \in PAL$ and any $a \in \Sigma$, $axa \in PAL$.
4. No string is in *PAL* unless it can be obtained by using rules 1, 2, and 3.

You can see that the palindromes that can be constructed by using rules 1 and 3 are those of even length, and those obtained from rules 2 and 3 are the ones of odd length.

In Example 2.7, we commented on the algorithmic, or constructive, nature of the recursive definition of L^k. In the case of a language like *PAL*, this aspect of the recursive definition can be useful both from the standpoint of generating elements of the language and from the standpoint of recognizing elements of the language. The definition says, on the one hand, that we can construct palindromes by starting with either Λ or a single symbol, and continuing to concatenate a symbol onto both ends of the current string; on the other hand, it says that if we wish to test a string to see if it's a palindrome, we may first compare the leftmost and rightmost symbols, and if they're equal, reduce the problem to testing the substring obtained by deleting them.

Example 2.10. Let Σ be the alphabet $\{i, (,), +, -\}$. Below is a recursive definition of the language AE of fully parenthesized algebraic expressions involving the binary operators $+$ and $-$ and the identifier i. ("Fully parenthesized" means exactly one pair of parentheses for every operator.)

1. $i \in AE$.
2. For any elements x and y of AE, the strings $(x + y)$ and $(x - y)$ are both elements of AE.
3. No string is in AE unless it can be obtained by using rules 1 and 2.

Some of the strings we obtain from this definition are i, $(i + i)$, $(i - i)$, $((i + i) - i)$, and $((i - (i - i)) + i)$.

In Examples 2.7, 2.9, and 2.10, let us consider briefly the last statement in the definition. In each case, we're defining a set. The previous statements describe elements in the set. The last statement finishes the definition by specifying which elements are *not* in the set: everything not described explicitly by the previous statements. If we ended the definition before the last statement, one would probably still assume that the previous statements can produce all the elements of the set; but one thing that has no place in a definition is ambiguity, and the last statement is intended to remove it.

One might still question, however, whether this last statement is sufficient to specify precisely what is and what is not in the set. Sometimes people are even a little more explicit. In Example 2.10, we might say "No string is in AE unless it can be obtained by *a finite number of applications of* rules 1 and 2." This is certainly what we intended the original definition to mean. Here the precaution hardly seems necessary, as long as it is understood that "string" means something of finite length, but in a recursive definition like the following, it is perhaps more appropriate. Suppose we define a set $\mathscr{F}$ of subsets of the natural numbers like this:

1. For any natural number n, $\{n\} \in \mathscr{F}$.
2. For any $A \in \mathscr{F}$ and any natural number n, $A \cup \{n\} \in \mathscr{F}$.
3. Nothing is in $\mathscr{F}$ unless it can be obtained by using rules 1 and 2.

One could ask whether an infinite set can be an element of $\mathscr{F}$. On the one hand, it seems as though the answer should be no, since the only way rule 2 could produce an infinite set would be for the set A to be infinite already. On the other hand, the only way to use the definition to show that an infinite set B is *not* in $\mathscr{F}$ is to show that none of the infinite sets $B - \{n\}$ is in $\mathscr{F}$. In this case, specifying that rules 1 and 2 are to be used a finite number of times in obtaining elements of $\mathscr{F}$ might make the definition more precise. We will not always be this explicit in our recursive definitions, and it is common not to be. But remember that we think of a recursive definition as a *constructive*, or *algorithmic* definition. It should always be understood that the things being defined are those that can be obtained by using the statements in the definition a finite number of times.

This discussion brings us back to the relationship between proofs by induction and inductive definitions. Because of the obvious similarity between the two techniques, it is not surprising that mathematical induction is usually the appropriate method for proving statements about objects defined inductively. As our next example illustrates, the number of applications of the definition required to obtain the object is often the natural choice for the integer on which to base the inductive proof. And, as we shall also discover, doing it this way may allow us to simplify the proof somewhat.

Example 2.11. Consider the language L^*, where $L = \{a, ab\}$. For convenience, we restate the recursive definition of L^* in this particular case:

1. $\Lambda \in L^*$.
2. For any $x \in L^*$, both xa and xab are elements of L^*.
3. No strings are in L^* unless they are obtained by using rules 1 and 2.

Let us prove the following statement using mathematical induction:

> For any $x \in L^*$, x does not begin with b and does not contain the substring bb.

Since any $x \in L^*$ can be obtained by using rule 1 together with N applications of rule 2 (for some $N \geq 0$), we may formulate our statement in terms of this N:

> If $x \in L^*$ is obtained from Λ by N applications of rule 2 (i.e., if x is the concatenation of N elements of L), then x does not begin with b and does not contain the substring bb.

Now in all our proofs by mathematical induction up to this point, we have been careful to state explicitly the basis step, the induction hypothesis, and the statement to be proved in the induction step, all in terms of N. Let us consider whether there is a more natural procedure in this case. If we wrote out the statement above for $N = 0$, it would reduce to this:

> Λ does not begin with b and does not contain the substring bb.

In other words, the basis step in the induction proof is simply to show that the desired conclusion holds for the string defined in the basis step of the recursive definition.

The inductive step is to show that from the assumption that the conclusion holds for strings x obtained by K applications of rule 2, it follows that it holds for strings obtained by $K + 1$ applications—i.e., for strings of the form xa and xab. Suppose we ignore K altogether and prove what seems like a simpler statement: whenever the conclusion holds for some string x, it also holds for the strings xa and xab. You can easily see that this is sufficient to complete the inductive step. (Suppose y is obtained in $K + 1$ applications of rule 2, and we know that any x obtained in K applications satisfies the desired property. Then for some such x, $y = xa$ or $y = xab$. But if we have proved that for any x satisfying the property, xa and xab do also, the desired conclusion then follows for y.) It is reasonable, then, to proceed as follows.

Inductive hypothesis: For some string x, x does not begin with b or contain the substring bb.

Statement to be proved in inductive step: xa and xab do not begin with b and do not contain bb.

Proof of inductive step: If $x = \Lambda$, xa and xab obviously begin with a, not b; otherwise, xa and xab cannot begin with b since x doesn't. It is clear that since x does not contain bb, xa and xab cannot either.

It should be emphasized that although this proof looks a little different from our previous proofs by induction, we are not really using a different principle of mathematical induction in this example. There is an underlying natural number N involved, and as we saw above, we could formulate all our steps in terms of N. It's just that since the N we have chosen is the one naturally associated with the recursive definition, our inductive proof ends up following the definition also, so closely that it is not necessary, or even helpful, to mention N explicitly.

We shall see several other proofs by induction, both in this chapter and later on, where this idea is helpful.

The relationship between inductive definitions and proofs using mathematical induction is so close that in inductive proofs we often use inductive definitions without even being aware of it. We have only to return to our examples to illustrate this. In Example 2.1, we proved that

$$2^0 + 2^1 + \cdots + 2^N = 2^{N+1} - 1$$

and if we examine the proof carefully we find that in effect we used inductive definitions of both the sum on the left side and the exponential on the right. When we say

$$(2^0 + \cdots + 2^N) = (2^0 + \cdots + 2^{N-1}) + 2^N$$

we're using something like the following definition of $S_N = 2^0 + \cdots + 2^N$:

$$S_N = \begin{cases} 1 & \text{if } N = 0 \\ S_{N-1} + 2^N & \text{if } N \geq 1 \end{cases}$$

and the law of exponents that allows us to say that $2 * 2^{K+1} = 2^{(K+1)+1}$ is for all practical purposes an inductive definition of 2^N:

$$2^N = \begin{cases} 1 & \text{if } N = 0 \\ 2 * 2^{N-1} & \text{if } N \geq 1 \end{cases}$$

Although it is common, when dealing with something as simple as $2^0 + \cdots + 2^N$, to avoid mentioning the inductive definition explicitly, you should be aware that it is often helpful to keep it in mind. You're invited to see if you can spot the inductive definitions that are implicitly involved in Examples 2.2 and 2.3.

We shall close this section with two more examples of inductive proofs based on inductive definitions. The first is a useful fact about the reverse of a string, defined in Example 2.8, and the second uses that fact to establish that the nonrecursive definition of the language *PAL* given in Example 2.9 is indeed equivalent to the recursive definition.

Example 2.12.   Proof by induction of a property of *REV*. Recall that in Example 2.8, we defined the reverse function recursively as follows:

$$REV(\Lambda) = \Lambda; \qquad \text{for any } x \in \Sigma^* \text{ and } y \in \Sigma, REV(xa) = aREV(x).$$

In this example, we wish to show that for any two strings x and y, $REV(xy) = REV(y)REV(x)$. In order to use the principle of mathematical induction, we need an integer N on which to base the induction. The two obvious choices for N in this case are probably $|x|$ and $|y|$; in fact, the way we've chosen to define REV makes $|y|$ a slightly more appropriate choice (see Exercise 2.17). Thus, let $P(N)$ be the statement:

$$\text{If } x, y \in \Sigma^* \text{ and } |y| = N, \; REV(xy) = REV(y)REV(x)$$

We show $P(N)$ is true for all $N \geq 0$.

   Basis step: $P(0)$ is the statement: if $x, y \in \Sigma^*$ and $|y| = 0$, then $REV(xy) = REV(y)REV(x)$. But if $|y| = 0$, $y = \Lambda$.

$$
\begin{aligned}
REV(xy) &= REV(x\Lambda) \\
&= REV(x) \quad \text{(since } x\Lambda = x) \\
&= \Lambda REV(x) \\
&= REV(\Lambda)REV(x) \quad \text{(using the definition of } REV) \\
&= REV(y)REV(x)
\end{aligned}
$$

   Inductive hypothesis: $K \geq 0$, and if $x, y \in \Sigma^*$ and $|y| = K$, $REV(xy) = REV(y)REV(x)$.

   Statement to be shown in inductive step: if $x, y \in \Sigma^*$ and $|y| = K + 1$, $REV(xy) = REV(y)REV(x)$.

   Proof of inductive step: Since $|y| = K + 1$, we may write $y = za$, where $|z| = K$ and $a \in \Sigma$. Then

$$
\begin{aligned}
REV(xy) &= REV(x(za)) \\
&= REV((xz)a) \\
&= aREV(xz) \quad \text{(using the definition of } REV) \\
&= a(REV(z)REV(x)) \quad \text{(by the inductive hypothesis)} \\
&= (aREV(z))REV(x) \\
&= REV(y)REV(x) \quad \text{(using the definition of } REV)
\end{aligned}
$$

Example 2.13.   Proof by induction that both definitions of *PAL* are equivalent. We now have an inductive definition of the reverse of a string (Example 2.8), as well as an inductive definition of the language *PAL* that doesn't mention the reverse function explicitly (Example 2.9). We may consider the language $PAL1 = \{x \in \Sigma^* | REV(x) = x\}$, and we would be surprised if they turned out not to be the same. Let us show that they are indeed equal.

Part I: We show that $PAL \subseteq PAL1$. For convenience, we restate the definition of *PAL* from Example 2.9.

1. $\Lambda \in PAL$.

2. For any $a \in \Sigma$, $a \in PAL$.
3. For any $x \in PAL$ and any $a \in \Sigma$, $axa \in PAL$.
4. No string is in PAL unless it can be obtained by using rules 1, 2, and 3.

Just as in Example 2.11, it is appropriate to base the induction on the number of applications of rule 3 required to produce the element of PAL—and to simplify the proof accordingly, so that it follows the steps in the definition. Notice that the basis step now requires two cases, since elements of PAL obtained by zero applications of rule 3 include both Λ and elements of Σ.

Basis step: We show that $\Lambda \in PAL1$ and for every $a \in \Sigma$, $a \in PAL1$. The first statement follows from the first part of the definition of REV: $REV(\Lambda) = \Lambda$, and thus $\Lambda \in PAL1$. In the second case we have

$$
\begin{aligned}
REV(a) &= REV(\Lambda a) \\
&= aREV(\Lambda) \quad \text{(by definition of } REV\text{)} \\
&= a\Lambda \quad \text{(by definition of } REV\text{)} \\
&= a
\end{aligned}
$$

Inductive hypothesis: For some $x \in PAL$, $x \in PAL1$; i.e., $REV(x) = x$.
Statement to be shown in inductive step: For any $a \in \Sigma$, $axa \in PAL1$.
Proof of inductive step:

$$
\begin{aligned}
REV(axa) &= REV((ax)a) \\
&= aREV(ax) \quad \text{(by definition of } REV\text{)} \\
&= a(REV(x)REV(a)) \quad \text{(by Example 2.12)} \\
&= (aREV(x))REV(a) \\
&= (aREV(x))a \quad \text{(since } REV\,(a) = a\text{, as shown above)} \\
&= axa \quad \text{(by the inductive hypothesis)}
\end{aligned}
$$

Therefore $axa \in PAL1$.

Part II: We show that $PAL1 \subseteq PAL$. Let $P(N)$ be the statement: If $x \in PAL1$ and $|x| = N$, then $x \in PAL$. We must show $P(N)$ is true for every $N \geq 0$.
Basis step: Since $\Lambda \in PAL$ by the definition of PAL, $P(0)$ is true.
Inductive hypothesis: $K \geq 0$, and if $x \in PAL1$ and $|x| \leq K$, then $x \in PAL$.
Statement to be shown in inductive step: If $x \in PAL1$ and $|x| = K + 1$, $x \in PAL$.
Proof of inductive step: If $|x|$ is 1, $x \in PAL$ by definition of PAL; so we might as well assume that $|x| \geq 2$. Therefore $x = ayb$, for some a and $b \in \Sigma$ and some string y. Since $x \in PAL1$, $REV(x) = x$. But $REV(x) = REV(ayb) = bREV(ay)$, by the definition of REV. The only way ayb can equal $bREV(ay)$ is for a to equal b. Thus $x = aya$. Now we have

$$
\begin{aligned}
REV(x) &= aREV(ay) \\
&= aREV(y)REV(a) \quad \text{(using Example 2.12)} \\
&= aREV(y)a \quad \text{(as shown above, } REV(a) = a\text{)}
\end{aligned}
$$

and $x = aya$. Therefore, since $REV(x) = x$, it follows that $REV(y) = y$. This means that $y \in PAL1$; but then since $|y| \leq K$, the inductive hypothesis implies that $y \in PAL$. Finally, using the definition of PAL, we conclude that $aya = x \in PAL$.

EXERCISES

In any problem where there is a statement, with no other explanation, the statement is one that it is appropriate to prove using mathematical induction, and you are to supply the proof.

2.1. For every $N \geq 1$, $1 + 2 + 3 + \cdots + N = N * (N + 1)/2$.

2.2. For every $N \geq 1$, $1^2 + 2^2 + \cdots + N^2 = N * (N + 1) * (2N + 1)/6$.

2.3. For every $N \geq 1$, $1/(1 * 2) + 1/(2 * 3) + \cdots + 1/(N * (N + 1)) = N/(N + 1)$.

2.4. If r is a real number not equal to 1, then for every $N \geq 0$, $r^0 + r^1 + \cdots + r^N = (1 - r^{N+1})/(1 - r)$.

2.5. For every $N \geq 4$, $N! > 2^N$.

2.6. If x is a real number greater than -1, then for every $N \geq 0$, $(1 + x)^N \geq 1 + Nx$.

2.7. For every $N \geq 0$, N is either even or odd. (By definition, an integer N is even if there is an integer I so that $N = 2 * I$; N is odd if there is an integer I so that $N = 2 * I + 1$.)

2.8. For every $N \geq 108$, there are integers I_N and J_N, both ≥ 0, so that $N = 7 * I_N + 19 * J_N$.

2.9. $1 + 1/2 + 1/3 + \cdots$ is infinite; that is, for every $N \geq 0$, there is an integer $K_N \geq 1$ so that $1 + 1/2 + \cdots + 1/K_N > N$.

       Hint: the sum $1/(K + 1) + 1/(K + 2) + \cdots + 1/(2 * K)$ is at least how big?

2.10. For every $N \geq 0$, the number of subsets of a set with N elements is 2^N.

2.11. For every $N \geq 0$, $N * (N^2 + 5)$ is divisible by 6.

2.12. The numbers a_N, for $N \geq 0$, are defined recursively as follows:

$$a_0 = -2; \quad a_1 = -2; \quad \text{for } N \geq 2, a_N = 5 * a_{N-1} - 6 * a_{N-2}$$

Show that for every $N \geq 0$, $a_N = 2 * 3^N - 4 * 2^N$.

2.13. The Fibonacci numbers F_N ($N \geq 0$) are defined as follows:

$$F_0 = 0; \quad F_1 = 1; \quad \text{for } N \geq 2, F_N = F_{N-1} + F_{N-2}$$

Show that for every $N \geq 0$, $F_N = C * (A^N - B^N)$, where

$$C = \frac{1}{\sqrt{5}}, \quad A = \frac{1 + \sqrt{5}}{2}, \quad \text{and} \quad B = \frac{1 - \sqrt{5}}{2}$$

2.14. The total time $T(N)$ required to execute a particular recursive sorting algorithm on an array of N elements is one second if $N = 1$; otherwise it's no more than $C * N + 2T(N/2)$ (for some constant C independent of N). Show that if N is a power of 2, say $N = 2^K$, then

$$T(N) \leq N * (CK + 1) = N * (C * \log_2 N + 1)$$

This is a relatively simple example of the "run-time analysis" of recursive algorithms.

The next three problems refer to the function REV defined in Example 2.8. The property established in Example 2.12 may be helpful.

2.15. For any string x, $REV(REV(x)) = x$.

2.16. For any string x and any $N \geq 0$, $REV(x^N) = (REV(x))^N$.

2.17. (a) In Example 2.12, the formula $REV(xy) = REV(y)REV(x)$ was proved by induction on $|y|$. Can you give a proof using induction on $|x|$ instead?

(b) Suppose that instead of the definition in Example 2.8, the following is substituted:

$$REV(\Lambda) = \Lambda; \qquad \text{for any } x \in \Sigma^* \quad \text{and} \quad a \in \Sigma, REV(ax) = REV(x)a.$$

Show that the statement in Example 2.12 is still true: For any strings x and y, $REV(xy) = REV(y)REV(x)$.

2.18. No string in the language AE (Example 2.10) contains the substring)(.

2.19. Any prefix of a string in AE (Example 2.10) contains at least as many ('s as)'s.

2.20. In each part below, a recursive definition is given of a particular language in $\{a, b\}^*$. Give a simple nonrecursive definition in each case. Assume that each definition includes an implicit last statement: "Nothing is in L unless it can be obtained by the previous statements."

(a) $a \in L$; if $x \in L$, then xa and xb are elements of L

(b) $a \in L$; if $x \in L$, then bx and xb are elements of L

(c) $a \in L$; if $x \in L$, then ax and xb are elements of L

(d) $a \in L$; if $x \in L$, then xb, xa, and bx are elements of L

(e) $a \in L$; if $x \in L$, then xb, ax, and bx are elements of L

(f) $a \in L$; if $x \in L$, then $xb \in L$; if $x \in L$ and x doesn't end with a, then $xa \in L$

(g) $\Lambda \in L$; $b \in L$; $bb \in L$; if $x \in L$, then xa, xab, and $xabb$ are elements of L

2.21. Give recursive definitions for each of the following sets.

(a) The set S of numbers divisible by 7

(b) The set T of strings in $\{0, 1\}^*$ containing the substring 00

(c) The set U of strings in $\{0, 1\}^*$ not containing the substring 001

(d) The set V of strings of the form $0^N 1^N$ $(N \geq 0)$

2.22. (a) Give a recursive definition of $|x|$, the length of an element x of Σ^*.

(b) Use your definition to show:

(i) For any strings x and y, $|xy| = |x| + |y|$

(ii) For any string x and any $N \geq 0$, $|x^N| = N * |x|$

(iii) For any string x, $|REV(x)| = |x|$ (see Example 2.8)

2.23. $\{0, 10\}^+ = \{x \in \{0, 1\}^* | x$ ends with 0 and 11 is not a substring of $x\}$.

2.24. For each $N \geq 0$, define strings A_N and B_N as follows:

$$A_0 = 0; \quad B_0 = 1; \quad \text{for } N > 0, \ A_N = A_{N-1}B_{N-1}; \ B_N = B_{N-1}A_{N-1}$$

(a) For every $N \geq 0$, the strings A_N and B_N, which are of the same length, differ in every symbol.

(b) For every $N \geq 0$, A_{2N} and B_{2N} are palindromes—i.e., $REV(A_{2N}) = A_{2N}$ and $REV(B_{2N}) = B_{2N}$.

(c) For every $N \geq 0$, A_N contains neither the substring 000 nor the substring 111.

2.25. The "pigeonhole principle" says that if $N + 1$ objects are distributed among N pigeonholes, there must be at least one pigeonhole that ends up with more than one object. A slightly less trivial-sounding formulation says that if $f : A \rightarrow B$, and the sets A and B have $N + 1$ and N elements, respectively, then f is not one-to-one. (Do you see that these are really the same statement?) Prove the second version of the statement.

2.26. Suppose S and T are both finite sets of strings, and we have a function $e : S \to T$. e can be thought of as an encoding of the elements of S, using the elements of T as code words. If we have this situation, we can encode S^* by letting the code string for $x_1 x_2 \ldots x_N$ be $e^*(x_1 \ldots x_N) = e(x_1)e(x_2)\ldots e(x_N)$. The encoding of S has the *prefix property* if, for any $x_1, x_2 \in S$, the code word $e(x_1)$ is not a prefix of $e(x_2)$. In particular, then, the function e is one-to-one. Show that if the encoding e has the prefix property, then every element of T^* can be decoded in at most one way—i.e., the encoding e^* is one-to-one.

2.27. Consider this recursive definition of a language $L \subseteq \{a, b\}^*$:

> $a \in L$; if $x \in L$, xx and bax are elements of L; nothing is in L unless it can be obtained by (a finite number of applications of) the first two statements.

In this exercise we are concerned not so much with what language these specific conditions produce as with alternative ways of defining the same thing. The definition specifies a fixed string that the language must contain and gives two operations under which the language is *closed*: concatenating a string with itself, and concatenating ba onto the beginning of a string. (Saying that a set is closed under an operation means that if the operation is applied to elements of the set, the result will be an element of the set.) There are certainly other languages in $\{a, b\}^*$ that contain the string a and are closed under these two operations: $\{a, b\}^*$ itself is one such language; the set of all strings containing at least one a is another.

(a) Show that L is the smallest such language—i.e., if L_1 is any such language, then $L \subseteq L_1$. (L is said to be the closure of the set $\{a\}$ with respect to these two specified operations.)

(b) Show that L is the intersection of all such languages.

PART
II

REGULAR EXPRESSIONS AND FINITE AUTOMATA

As we saw in Chapter 1, there are at least two approaches to the problem of describing in some finite way a language that is likely to be infinite. One is to describe a method of *generating* the language: either generating the strings in the language by using string operations to combine individual symbols and simpler strings, or using set operations to generate the language itself from simpler languages. Another approach is to specify a mechanism for *recognizing* strings in the language. In a sense, of course, this is what we do any time we give a criterion for membership in the language; but in the present context "recognize" is to be interpreted in an algorithmic sense. To recognize a language means to have a method of determining for any string whether or not it is in the language.

In Part II, we investigate a class of simple languages, the *regular* languages. Taking the first approach, we may describe such a language as one that can be generated from the null string and the individual symbols in the alphabet, using a finite number of applications of certain standard operations. A *regular expression* is a notational device for representing the symbols and the operations used in this construction, and so our first characterization of regular languages is that a language is regular if it can be described by a regular expression.

If we try to use the second approach to describe what distinguishes regular languages, we arrive at a different sort of finiteness condition. We consider how much it is necessary to "remember" in order to recognize a language, assuming that in processing a string we restrict ourselves to a single pass through the string, from left to right. This leads to the definition of an abstract recognizing device called a *finite automaton*, whose memory is limited to its being able to distinguish among a fixed finite number of states. Our second characterization is that a language is regular if it can be recognized by a finite automaton. Although seemingly more roundabout, this approach in fact gives us more insight into what it means for a language *not* to be regular. It has the additional advantage that it can be generalized directly, beginning in Part III, so as to handle the other abstract machines and languages in the hierarchy we shall be considering. Along the way, we will discover other characterizations of regular languages, as well as algorithms that allow us to translate one description of a language into another description of a different type. (For example, given a regular expression, we will be able to construct an equivalent finite automaton.)

In investigating regular languages and finite automata, we encounter in a particularly simple setting questions that we will pursue when we look at more complex languages and machines. The difference is that here the questions often have simple answers. In Part II, we develop notation and techniques that will help us later, when we study more sophisticated models of computation. But this part is not only of theoretical interest. Regular languages themselves come up in real life, and there are practical problems—within computer science as well as without—whose solutions can be handled by finite-state devices. As we go along, we shall point some of these out.

CHAPTER 3

REGULAR EXPRESSIONS AND REGULAR LANGUAGES

3.1 DEFINITIONS: REGULAR EXPRESSIONS AND THE CORRESPONDING LANGUAGES

Three basic operations for constructing new languages from existing ones are union, concatenation, and the "closure" operation *. When we start with the simplest possible languages—those containing a single string that is either the null string or of length 1—the languages that we obtain by using a combination of these operations are the *regular* languages. Such languages can therefore be described by an explicit formula involving unions, concatenations, and *s. It is common to simplify the formula slightly, by leaving out the set brackets {, } and replacing $\cup$ by $+$; the result is called a *regular expression*.

If you study these examples, you should get a good idea of the rules for writing regular expressions.

Language	Regular expression representing the language
1. {Λ}	Λ
2. {0}	0
3. {001} (i.e., {0}{0}{1})	001
4. {0, 1} (i.e., {0} $\cup$ {1})	$0 + 1$
5. {0, 10} (i.e., {0} $\cup$ {10})	$0 + 10$
6. {1, Λ}{001}	$(1 + \Lambda)001$
7. {110}*{0, 1}	$(110)(0 + 1)$
8. {0, 10}*({11}* $\cup$ {001, Λ})*	$(0 + 10)^*((11)^* + 001 + \Lambda)^*$
9. {1}*{10}	1^*10
10. {10, 111, 11010}*	$(10 + 111 + 11010)^*$

We interpret a regular expression as representing the "most typical" string in the language to which the expression corresponds. For example, 1^*10 stands for "any string consisting of the substring 10 preceded by arbitrarily many 1's."

If we try to spell out in a little more detail what we meant in the first paragraph by "the languages that we obtain by using a combination of these operations," we might say something like this: languages containing only Λ or a string of length 1, together with those that can be obtained from such languages by a finite sequence of steps, each step consisting of applying one of the three operations to languages that were obtained at an earlier step. For example, in number 9 above we could obtain the language in three steps:

1. apply concatenation to $\{1\}$ and $\{0\}$, yielding $\{10\}$;
2. apply * to $\{1\}$, yielding $\{1\}^*$; and
3. apply concatenation to $\{1\}^*$ and $\{10\}$, yielding $\{1\}^*\{10\}$.

It is exactly this type of definition, involving a sequence of steps in which operations are applied to objects obtained earlier in the sequence, that can be simplified by using recursion. We begin with certain "basic" languages that correspond to regular expressions, and we specify operations that can be applied to any languages in this class to produce new languages in the class. However, we are interested not only in the languages that can be obtained by applying the three language operations, but also in the regular expressions themselves, which can be obtained by applying the three regular expression operations (using + instead of $\cup$). The recursive definition below, therefore, defines two things at once: regular expressions and the corresponding languages.

Definition 3.1. A *regular expression* over the alphabet Σ, and the corresponding language, are defined as follows:

1. $\varnothing$ is a regular expression, corresponding to the empty language $\varnothing$.
2. Λ is a regular expression, corresponding to the language $\{\Lambda\}$.
3. For each symbol $a \in \Sigma$, a is a regular expression corresponding to the language $\{a\}$.
4. For any regular expressions r and s over Σ, corresponding to the languages L_r and L_s, respectively, each of the following is a regular expression over Σ, corresponding to the language indicated.

$$(rs), \text{ corresponding to } L_r L_s$$

$$(r + s), \text{ corresponding to } L_r \cup L_s$$

$$(r^*), \text{ corresponding to } L_r^*$$

5. Only those things that can be produced using parts 1–4 are regular expressions over Σ.

A language over the alphabet Σ is a *regular language* if there is some regular expression over Σ corresponding to it.

A few comments about the definition are in order. First, the regular expression with which we begin the definition is $\varnothing$, corresponding to the empty language. From the earlier examples, you can see why it is helpful to be able to use Λ in building up more complicated regular expressions, and it is even more obvious that the single symbols of the alphabet are crucial regular expressions, but it is not obvious that $\emptyset$ will be helpful in constructing regular expressions. In fact, we seldom use it in larger expressions; we don't expect to see regular expressions of the form

$$(((((0 + 1)^*)\emptyset)((\emptyset + (01))^*))\emptyset)$$

although according to our definition they are legal. (This one, in fact, corresponds to the empty language.) The main reason for including $\emptyset$ is consistency. Theorem 3.2 is one example (there will be others in later chapters) where we want to say that to every something-or-other there corresponds a regular expression, and without $\emptyset$ we would need to make exceptions for trivial special cases.

Second, since regular expressions correspond to languages, and since we have enlarged our set of notation in the case of languages to include expressions like L^2, it seems reasonable to make an unofficial addition to the language of regular expressions: if r is a regular expression, we will sometimes write (r^2) to stand for the regular expression (rr), (r^3) to stand for $((rr)r)$, and so forth; and (r^+) will stand for the regular expression $((r^*)r)$.

Third, if the definition is compared with some of the examples, it will appear that they are not legitimate regular expressions after all. For example, according to the definition, $((00)1)$ is a regular expression corresponding to $\{001\}$, and $(0(01))$ is another, but clearly the definition doesn't allow 001. Unfortunately, we can't just leave out the parentheses in part 4 of the definition; if we did it would follow, for example, that $0 + 1$ corresponds to $\{0, 1\}$, and $0 + 11$ corresponds to $\{0, 1\} \{1\}$. But it would seem equally unfortunate not to allow 011 as a regular expression. We can resolve the difficulty the same way we do in ordinary algebraic notation. The arithmetic expression $a + b * c$ is interpreted as $a + (b * c)$, because we say that $*$ has higher *precedence* than $+$. In this way, we can often dispense with parentheses. In a similar way, $a + b + c$ is interpreted as $(a + b) + c$, because among operations of equal precedence, those to the left are performed first. Of course $(a + b) + c$ and $a + (b + c)$ have the same value if a, b, and c are numbers; but we are speaking of how the expression is defined, and our convention gives us an unambiguous definition.

Let us stipulate at this point that in regular expressions the operation $*$ has highest precedence, concatenation next, and $+$ lowest. Secondly, we specify that operations *associate to the left*—e.g., that $a + b + c$ is to be interpreted as $(a + b) + c$.

Now we may allow as a regular expression anything that, if it were fully parenthesized according to our rules of precedence, would be legitimate according to the definition. For example, $(001)^*$ stands for $(((00)1)^*)$, and $1^*10 + 11^*$ stands for $((((1)^*1)0) + (1(1)^*))$.

However, at this point we may go even a little farther. To return for a moment to arithmetic: when we write $1 + 6 = 5 + 2$, we are making a statement about numbers, not about expressions. If we adopt the same approach here, we may agree to identify two regular expressions if the languages they represent are equal.

This allows us to formulate rules for simplifying regular expressions. Here are five examples.

$$1^*(1 + \Lambda) = 1^*$$

$$1^*1^* = 1^*$$

$$0^* + 1^* = 1^* + 0^*$$

$$(0^*1^*)^* = (0 + 1)^*$$

$$(0 + 1)^*01(0 + 1)^* + 1^*0^* = (0 + 1)^*$$

Rules such as these can be useful. When we follow an algorithm that produces a regular expression, as we shall be doing later, and end up with one that takes two lines to write, it would be nice to know if in fact it could be reduced to ten or twelve symbols. We could have concerned ourselves with this back in Chapter 1; identities such as the ones above are actually statements about languages, disguised as statements about regular expressions. What the last one says is that the language of all strings of 0s and 1s (i.e., the right side) can be expressed as the union of two languages: one consisting of all strings containing the substring 01, the other consisting of all strings in which all the 1s precede all the 0s. Rather than attempt a systematic study of the "algebra" of regular expressions, we give a few examples that illustrate some of the important principles. More examples can be found in the exercises.

3.2. EXAMPLES AND APPLICATIONS

Example 3.1. Let L be the language of all strings of 0s and 1s that have even length. (Since 0 is even, L contains Λ.) Is L regular, and if so, what is a regular expression corresponding to it?

We can answer this by realizing that if a string has even length, it can be thought of as consisting of a number, possibly zero, of strings of length 2 concatenated. And, conversely, any such concatenation has even length. Since we can easily enumerate the strings of length 2, we may write the answer:

$$(00 + 01 + 10 + 11)^*$$

Example 3.2. Let L be the language of all strings of 0s and 1s that have odd length. We can use the previous example: odd length means in particular length at least one, and so we may view L as the language of all strings consisting of a single symbol followed by an even-length string. Since we have a regular expression for even-length strings, and since we can easily find one for strings of length 1, a regular expression for L is

$$(0 + 1)(00 + 01 + 10 + 11)^*$$

You may ask why we couldn't have described the language in this example as the set of strings consisting of an even-length string followed by a single symbol, which would have led to

$$(00 + 01 + 10 + 11)^*(0 + 1)$$

The answer is that we could, and this brings up a point that is worth commenting on. For any regular expression, there are many others that correspond to the same language.

Since a little earlier we mentioned the problem of *simplifying* a regular expression, it might seem as though there is a single regular expression that is the simplest, or one that most concisely expresses the language. This is not necessarily the case, and in fact the regular expression we choose may depend on the aspect of the structure that we wish to emphasize. In this example, the two regular expressions we wrote are equally simple; the first is more appropriate if we want to call attention to the first symbol of the string, the second if we want to emphasize the last symbol of the string. If for some reason we wanted to emphasize the *third* symbol of the string, it might very well be better to use the more complicated regular expression

$$0 + 1 + (00 + 01 + 10 + 11)(0 + 1)(00 + 01 + 10 + 11)^*$$

The first two terms are necessary to take care of the length-1 case.

Example 3.3. Let L be the language of all strings of 0s and 1s containing at least one 1. Here are three regular expressions corresponding to L:

$$0^*1(0 + 1)^*$$

$$(0 + 1)^*1(0 + 1)^*$$

$$(0 + 1)^*10^*$$

The first expresses the fact that a string in L can be decomposed as follows: an arbitrary number of 0's (possibly none), the first 1, and then any arbitrary string. The second, which in some sense is the most general, or the closest to our definition of L, expresses the fact that a string in L has a 1, both preceded and followed by an arbitrary string. The third is similar to the first, but emphasizes the last 1 in strings in L.

Example 3.4. Let L be the set of all strings of length less than or equal to 6. There is no doubt that L is regular: a simple, but unpleasant, regular expression corresponding to it is

$$\Lambda + 0 + 1 + 00 + 01 + 10 + 11 + 000 + \cdots + 111110 + 111111$$

The only question is whether or not we can find a regular expression that we can feasibly write in its entirety, without using "$\cdots$" to abbreviate. There is one for the set of strings of length exactly 6:

$$(0 + 1)(0 + 1)(0 + 1)(0 + 1)(0 + 1)(0 + 1)$$

or, in our extended notation, $(0 + 1)^6$. If we're careful, we can modify this so that it will suffice. We may view a string of length 6 or less as being in fact a concatenation of six things, some or all of which may be Λ. Therefore, if we use the expression above, but allow Λ as a third choice in each of the six factors, we obtain $(0 + 1 + \Lambda)^6$.

Example 3.5. $L = \{x \in \{0, 1\}^* | x$ ends with 1 and does not contain the substring 00$\}$. The defining property of L can be stated in another way that may be easier to work with: an equivalent criterion for membership of a string x in L is that 1 be a substring of x and every 0 appearing in x be followed immediately by 1. If every 0 is followed immediately by 1, then the only 0's occur in substrings of the form 01, and of course all the remaining symbols are 1's. This means that every string in L corresponds to the regular expression $R = (1 + 01)^*$. On the other hand, in any string corresponding to R, each 0 is followed immediately by 1. Thus L is a subset of the language corresponding to R, the subset of all strings in R containing 1. This extra constraint simply means that Λ can't be included, and that L corresponds to the regular expression

$$(1 + 01)^+ = (1 + 01)^*(1 + 01)$$

Example 3.6. For an example from real life, with a flavor that's a little different, let us enlarge the alphabet. Take

$$\Sigma = \{P, M, D, E, 0, 1, 2, 3, 4, 5, 6, 7, 8, 9\}$$

Here P should be thought of as "+", M as "−", D as "."—the letters are used to avoid typographical confusion. (E, though, really means the symbol E.) To make the example simpler to write, let S, which stands for "sign," be the regular expression $\Lambda + P + M$. Let DIG ("digit") be the regular expression $0 + 1 + 2 + 3 + 4 + 5 + 6 + 7 + 8 + 9$. Consider the regular expression

$$S \ DIG^+(D \ DIG^+ + D \ DIG^+E \ S \ DIG^+ + E \ S \ DIG^+)$$

What language does this correspond to? Of course one answer is

$$\{S\}\{0, 1, 2, 3, 4, 5, 6, 7, 8, 9\}^+(\{D\} \cdots)$$

A better way to ask the question is, perhaps, does this language correspond to anything useful? A typical string has this form: first a sign (plus, minus, or possibly neither); one or more digits; then *either* a decimal point and one or more digits, which may or may not be followed by an E, a sign, and one or more digits, *or* just the E, the sign, and one or more digits. (If it serves no other purpose, this example should at least convince you that one regular expression is worth several lines of prose.) The answer, as programmers may have realized, is that this is the specification for a real constant in the Pascal programming language. If it's in exponential format, no decimal point is needed. If there is a decimal point, there must be at least one digit immediately preceding and following it.

The following theorem is hardly more than a restatement of part of Definition 3.1, but we record it for future reference.

Theorem 3.1. The class of regular languages is closed under the operations of union, concatenation, and $*$.

Proof. The theorem says simply that if L_1 and L_2 are regular languages, then so are $L_1 \cup L_2$, L_1L_2, and L_1^*. This is immediate from the definition, since if R_1 and R_2 are regular expressions corresponding to L_1 and L_2, respectively, then $(R_1 + R_2)$, (R_1R_2), and $(R_1)^*$ are regular expressions corresponding to the three languages.

In Chapter 4, we shall return to Theorem 3.1: specifically, to the closure of the class of regular languages under the union operation. There we will be concerned with recognizing languages, and it will be useful to give an alternative proof of the result. The proof will provide an explicit algorithm for recognizing $L_1 \cup L_2$, given that we have ways of recognizing L_1 and L_2; in addition, it will enable us to add two other operations, intersection and complement, to the list of operations under which the class of regular languages is closed.

We finish this section with a result that illustrates how the inductive nature of our definition of regular expressions makes it easy to fashion inductive proofs of statements about regular expressions.

Theorem 3.2. Every finite language is regular.

Proof. "Finite" means having exactly N elements, for some $N \geq 0$, and this suggests (doesn't it?) a proof using mathematical induction.

Statement to be proved: For any $N \geq 0$, any language having exactly N elements corresponds to some regular expression.

Basis step: Consider $N = 0$. A language with 0 strings is $\varnothing$, which according to Definition 3.1 corresponds to the regular expression $\varnothing$.

Induction hypothesis: Suppose K is an arbitrary integer ≥ 0, and assume that any language with exactly K elements corresponds to a regular expression.

Induction step: We wish to show that any language with $K + 1$ elements corresponds to a regular expression. Let L be our language. We may express L as the union of two languages L_1 and L_2, where L_1 has K elements and L_2 has one element. By our inductive hypothesis, L_1 corresponds to some regular expression r_1. If we can find a regular expression r_2 corresponding to L_2, then according to part 4 of Definition 3.1, the regular expression $(r_1 + r_2)$ corresponds to the language $L_1 \cup L_2$, which is L.

We have therefore reduced the problem to showing that a language with one element corresponds to a regular expression. This one element is a string of some unknown length; let's finish the proof by using mathematical induction again, this time on the length of the string.

Statement to be proved: For any $N \geq 0$, any string of length N (or, more precisely, the language whose only element is the string of length N) corresponds to a regular expression.

Basis step: Consider $N = 0$. The language containing the string of length 0 corresponds, according to part 2 of Definition 3.1, to the regular expression Λ.

Induction hypothesis: Suppose K is an arbitrary integer ≥ 0, and assume that every language whose only element is a string of length K corresponds to a regular expression.

Induction step: We wish to show that any language whose only element is a string of length $K + 1$ corresponds to a regular expression. Let x be a string of length $K + 1$. Then x can be expressed as ya, where $|y| = K$ and $|a| = 1$. Now by our inductive hypothesis, the language consisting of y alone corresponds to a regular expression r, and by part 3 of Definition 3.1, the language consisting of the string a corresponds to the regular expression a. Therefore, by part 4 of Definition 3.1, the language $\{y\}\{a\} = \{ya\}$ corresponds to the regular expression (ra).

If you compare this proof with the first few sentences in Example 3.4, you might wonder why we constructed a proof using mathematical induction—in fact using mathematical induction twice—at all. What's wrong with the following proof?

> Let L be a finite language. Then if L has N elements, $L = \{x_1, \ldots, x_N\}$, where each x_i is a string. Any string is of the form $ab \ldots c$, where $a, b, \ldots c \in \Sigma$, and so corresponds to the regular expression $ab \ldots c$. Therefore, if r_i is a regular expression corresponding to the string x_i for each i, then L corresponds to the regular expression $r_1 + r_2 + \cdots + r_N$.

My answer is that this is a perfectly good way to convince yourself of the truth of the theorem, which is after all a simple one. When you read the shorter paragraph, though, you should be aware of the two places where "$\cdots$" showed up: once in the definition of L, and once in the discussion of a single string. Since we are still near the beginning of the book, the inductive proof was given, to illustrate again the close connection between recursive definitions and inductive proofs; after reading it, you should understand that both ellipses were replaced by induction proofs, which used the parts of Definition 3.1 involving + and concatenation, respectively.

EXERCISES

3.1. Find a regular expression corresponding to the language $(\{ab, aab, abaabb\}^* \cup \{abbba\})\{abb\}\{b, baa\}^*$.

3.2. What is the shortest string of a's and b's not in the language corresponding to the regular expression $b^*(abb^*)^*a^*$?

3.3. Consider the two regular expressions

$$R_1 = a^* + b^* \qquad R_2 = ab^* + ba^* + b^*a + (a^*b)^*$$

(a) Find a string corresponding to R_1 but not to R_2.
(b) Find a string corresponding to R_2 but not to R_1.
(c) Find a string corresponding to both R_1 and R_2.
(d) Find a string corresponding to neither R_1 nor R_2.

3.4. Simplify these regular expressions.
(a) $(01 + 10 + 0110 + 1001)^*$
(b) $(0(0 + 1)^*)^+$
(c) $01((01)^*01 + (01)^*) + (01)^*$
(d) $(01 + \Lambda)^*$
(e) $(10 + 01)^*1001(10 + 01)^* + (01)^*(10)^*$
(f) $(10 + 01)^*10(10 + 01)^*01(10 + 01)^* + (10 + 01)^*01(10 + 01)^*10(10 + 01)^*$

3.5. Find a way to generalize each part of Exercise 3.4. For example, a generalization of (a) might be: For any two regular expressions R and S, $(R + S + RS + SR)^* = (R + S)^*$.

3.6. What is true of the language corresponding to a regular expression that does not involve the * operator? Why?

3.7. Find regular expressions corresponding to each of the languages defined recursively below.
(a) $\Lambda \in L$; if $x \in L$, then $aabx$ and xbb are elements of L; nothing is in L unless it can be obtained from these two statements.
(b) $a \in L$; if $x \in L$, then $aabx$, $xaab$, and xbb are elements of L; nothing is in L unless it can be obtained from these two statements.

3.8. Find regular expressions corresponding to each of the languages defined in Exercise 2.20.

3.9. Find a regular expression corresponding to each of the following subsets of $\{0, 1\}^*$.
(a) The language of strings containing exactly two 0s.
(b) The language of strings containing at least two 0s.
(c) The language of strings that do not end with 01.
(d) The language of strings that begin or end with 00 or 11.
(e) The language of strings containing no more than one occurrence of the string 00. (The string 000 should be viewed as containing two occurrences of 00.)
(f) The language of strings in which the number of 0's is even.

(g) The language of strings in which every 0 is followed immediately by 11.

(h) The language of strings that do not contain the substring 110.

(i) The language of strings that contain both the substring 11 and the substring 010.

3.10. Describe as simply as possible the language corresponding to each of the following regular expressions.

(a) $0^*1(0^*10^*1)^*0^*$

(b) $((0+1)^3)^*(\Lambda + 0 + 1)$

(c) $(1+01)^*(0+01)^*$

(d) $(0+1)^*(0^+1^+0^+ + 1^+0^+1^+)(0+1)^*$ (Give an answer of the form: all strings containing both the substring _____ and the substring _____.)

3.11. In Example 3.6, we constructed a regular expression corresponding to real constants in the Pascal programming language. Modify the regular expression so that it removes the restrictions on the number of digits before and after the decimal point.

3.12. Using mathematical induction, show that if L is a regular language, then the language L^N is regular for every $N \geq 0$.

3.13. Suppose R is a regular expression over an alphabet Σ. Show that if for each symbol of R that is an element of Σ another regular expression over Σ is substituted, the result is a regular expression over Σ. Mathematical induction would be appropriate.

3.14. Let C and D be regular expressions over Σ.

(a) Show that the formula $R = C + RD$, involving the variable R, holds if the regular expression CD^* is substituted for R.

(b) Show that if Λ is not in the language corresponding to D, then the only regular expression R for which $R = C + RD$ is CD^* (i.e., any other one must correspond to the same language.)

3.15. The function $REV : \Sigma^* \to \Sigma^*$ is defined in Example 2.8. If L is a language, let $REV(L)$ denote the language $\{REV(x) | x \in L\}$.

(a) If r is the regular expression $(001 + 11010)^*1010$, and L_r is the corresponding language, give a regular expression corresponding to $REV(L_r)$.

(b) Taking this example as a model, give a recursive definition of a function $RREV$ from the set of regular expressions over Σ to itself, so that for any regular expression r, the language corresponding to $RREV(r)$ is the reverse of the language corresponding to r. Using mathematical induction, give a proof that your function $RREV$ has this property.

(c) Show that if L is a regular language, then $REV(L)$ is regular.

CHAPTER

4

FINITE AUTOMATA

4.1 THE MEMORY REQUIRED TO RECOGNIZE A LANGUAGE

One of the reasons for beginning our study of the theory of computation with languages is that this approach suggests a natural way to start out slowly: begin with simple languages and consider the minimal requirements for a machine that is able to process them. (At this stage, "process" means recognize.) In fact, the simple languages we have in mind have already been introduced—the regular languages of the preceding chapter. In this chapter, we re-introduce them: they can be characterized in terms of the "memory" required to recognize them. As we begin to study machines that are simple models for computation, it seems appropriate to talk about memory. Perhaps what is meant by the term is a little vague so far, but let us try to make it more precise by looking more carefully at the problem of recognizing a language. As mentioned previously, when we talk in Part II about recognizing a language, we will restrict ourselves to a single pass from left to right. This restriction is somewhat arbitrary, but it helps us to clarify what information must be "remembered" (information about the initial portion of the string seen so far), and it allows us to classify languages on the basis of how much we need to remember at each step in order to recognize the language.

Before we proceed, however, it may be helpful to standardize our idea of the recognition process a little further. Describing the process in terms of examining a string and then deciding whether the string is in the language suggests that we don't make any decisions until we have reached the end of the string. Instead, it's convenient to view the process in a slightly different way; there's no harm in assuming that any decision we would make for a string x we go ahead and make, as a tentative decision, even if x is only an initial substring of a longer string. In other words, after looking at a symbol we make a decision about the entire substring we have received so far, without worrying about whether we have reached the end. When we do finally reach the end, we will simply take as our final decision the most recent tentative decision, made for the entire string as a result of its being an initial substring of itself.

If at some stage in our processing we remember the entire substring we've received so far, we obviously have all the information we could possibly need in order to make the decision that we need to make at this stage. It seems reasonable to ask, however, whether we need to remember that much.

To get us started, suppose the language L is all of $\{0, 1\}^*$. In this trivial case, there's no need to remember the substring, because the decision will be the same for all substrings. In other words, since there's no need to distinguish between one substring and any other, there's no need to remember that we have one substring rather than another.

Consider a slightly less trivial example.

Example 4.1. Let L be the language of all strings in $\{0, 1\}^*$ that end with the substring 10. Then the decision that is made for any string depends only on its last two symbols. There's no need to distinguish between one string that ends in 10 and any other string that ends in 10. Be careful, however. You might be tempted to lump together all strings that don't end with 10 and remember only the fact that the substring doesn't end with 10, but this is not correct. Suppose you have received the string 01011. If you remember only that it doesn't end with 10, you have no way of distinguishing it from, say, 100—now or in the future. But if the *next* symbol received turns out to be 0, then in the first case you'll have 010110, which is in the language; and in the second case you'll have 1000, which is not. Therefore, you have to be able to remember enough now to distinguish between 01011 and 100, so that you will be able one symbol later to distinguish between 010110 and 1000: not because the decision made about them now is different, but because the decision made after subsequent symbols are received might be different. Nevertheless, L is a very simple language to recognize. Roughly speaking, once you have received at least two symbols, you can remember the last two symbols of the current substring and forget everything else. There are at most four possible cases, and you just have to be able to remember which you've got. In fact, as we shall see in Example 4.4, we can get by with three cases overall.

The next example illustrates the opposite extreme.

Example 4.2. Take L to be the language PAL defined in Example 2.9: the set of strings in $\{0, 1\}^*$ equal to their reverse. For example, 0, 0110110110, and 10101 are palindromes, but 1101 is not. Even though this is a simple language to describe, the problem of recognizing it is much harder, from the standpoint of the memory required. As the previous examples suggest, another way of saying how much we must remember is to say how many distinct substrings must be distinguished. The answer for this language is *all* of them. That is, if we consider any two possible choices, say x and y, for the substrings that we might have received up to the current time, there is at least one choice for the string of subsequent symbols, say z, which would cause us to make one decision in the case of x and the opposite decision in the case of y. More concisely, for any two strings x and y, there is a string z such that one and only one of the two strings xz and yz is in the language. This fact may not be completely obvious, but see Exercise 4.13. The result is that we can't forget anything, because no matter what string x we've received so far, we must distinguish it from every other possible string; we must remember that it is x and not something else.

Example 4.3. Let's consider again the language

$$L = \{x \in \{0, 1\}^* | x \text{ ends in 1 and doesn't contain the substring 00}\}$$

which we introduced in Example 3.5. There we saw that L is a regular language corresponding to the regular expression $(1 + 01)^+$. Now we will be able, as in Example 4.1 above, to describe in an alternative way what it is that makes L a relatively simple language.

Suppose that in the course of trying to recognize L we have currently processed several symbols, say the substring s. The easiest case to dispose of is that in which s already contains 00 as a substring. This means that s is not in L, and no matter what symbols we see subsequently, the resulting string will never be in L. In this case, which we'll call case N, the only thing we need to remember is that 00 has already occurred.

Now consider two other cases, in both of which 00 has not yet occurred: case 0, in which the last symbol of s is 0, and case 1, in which the last symbol is 1. If we are in case 1, s is in L; in this case, if the next symbol is 0 we will have case 0 and if the next symbol is 1 we will still have case 1. In case 0, the symbols 0 and 1 would take us to case N and case 1, respectively. These three cases account for almost all substrings. The only one left out is Λ. This case must be distinguished from the other three: from case N, because for the substring Λ, unlike the substrings of case N, there are subsequent symbols that would cause the string to be in L; from case 0, because the subsequent symbol 0 would cause different decisions in the two cases; and from case 1, because the decision for the current substring is already different.

We have therefore classified all strings in $\{0, 1\}^*$ into four types, in such a way that when we are processing substrings to determine membership in L, we *don't* need to remember what the substring is; we only need to remember which of the four types we have.

We can summarize this example by the schematic diagram in Fig. 4-1.

We may, on the one hand, interpret a diagram such as Fig. 4-1 as a flowchart, or illustration, of the algorithm we use when processing strings. The short arrow to the circle labeled Λ tells us where to begin, when we have examined no symbols yet. The double circle indicates that if we are at that point in the algorithm when we reach the end of the string we are processing, then our answer should be "Yes, the string is in L." Beyond that, the four regions correspond to the four types of substrings described in the example, and the arrows tell us, for each possible

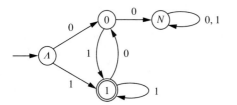

FIGURE 4-1
Recognizing the language in Example 4.3.

symbol that comes next, how much to remember. For example, if at some point we find ourselves in case 0 (that is, the substring we have received so far ends in 0 and doesn't contain 00) and the symbol we receive next is 1, the arrow labeled 1 instructs us to forget everything except the fact that the new substring ends with 1 and doesn't contain 00. In fact, saying it this way is a little misleading. Although it is helpful in understanding the algorithm to think of case 0, for example, as meaning "The substring we have received so far ends in 0 and doesn't contain 00," even that is more than we have to remember. We can forget what the significance of the cases is, as long as we can keep them straight—as long as we can manage to remember that we're in case 0 and not case 1, case Λ, or case N. It can be a purely mechanical procedure, so simple a machine could do it. The short arrow to the circle labeled Λ indicates that we start there in the flowchart, with the null string; the double circle around 1 indicates that the current substring is actually an element of L.

This leads us to the other possible interpretation of the diagram, which is the one we will adopt. We will think of it as representing an *abstract machine* that would work as follows: the machine is at any time in one of four possible *states*, which we have arbitrarily labeled Λ, 0, 1, and N. When it is activated initially, it is in state Λ. The machine receives symbols of the alphabet (0 or 1) as *inputs*, and as a result of being in a certain state and receiving a certain input, it moves to the state specified by the arrow labeled with that input. Finally, certain of the states (in our example, only state 1) are *accepting* states. The machine is in an accepting state if and only if the current substring is an element of L.

It seems reasonable to refer to something of this sort as a "machine," since one could visualize an actual piece of hardware that would work according to these specifications. But we should realize that the machine is distinct from any particular hardware implementation of it. In fact, it might exist only in software form, so that the input symbols are input data to a program, output consists simply of substrings and yes-or-no answers for each one, and representation of states depends on the programming language being used and the programmer's ingenuity. We call it an *abstract* machine because it is a specification, in some minimal sense, of what is to be done, and the machine description carries with it no indication of what sort of physical status things like "state" and "input" have. The abstraction that is at the heart of the machine is the *set* of states and the *function* that specifies, for each combination of state and input symbol, the state the machine goes to next. The property that is crucial, and (as we shall see shortly) that gives the machine its name, is the finiteness of the set of states. To say again why this is significant: if there are N states, then the problem of recognizing the language requires that we—or the machine—remember, not the entire substring that has occurred so far, but simply which of the N states the machine is in as a result. Being able to distinguish between these states (or equivalently, being able to distinguish between strings that lead to these different states) constitutes the only form of memory the machine has; it is not surprising that with such a severely restricted capacity to remember, the machine can recognize only rather simple languages. In fact, as we shall see, the languages that can be recognized in this way are precisely the same as the regular languages, the simplest in the hierarchy of languages we shall be considering. It may not be obvious from the regular-expression approach that there are languages that are not regular; at the point we have now reached, it is perhaps more plausible that there are, and this new approach will allow us to produce many simple examples before long. The language *PAL* in Example 4.2 is a prime candidate—see Theorem 4.3.

4.2   DEFINITIONS AND REPRESENTATIONS

Now that we have isolated the essential aspects of machines of this type, and have a bare-bones description involving sets and functions, we provide this description with the status of a formal mathematical definition. This will give us something to fall back on in subsequent discussion, as well as providing a body of convenient notation to work with.

Definition 4.1. A *finite automaton*, or *finite-state machine* (henceforth abbreviated FA), is a 5-tuple $(Q, \Sigma, q_0, \delta, A)$, where Q is a finite set (whose elements we will think of as *states*), Σ is a finite set (whose elements we will think of as *input symbols*), $q_0 \in Q$ (we will think of the state q_0 as the *initial* state), δ is a function from $Q \times \Sigma$ to Q, (the *transition* function, or *next-state* function), and $A \subseteq Q$ (A is the set of *accepting* states).

A comment may be in order here, even at the cost of interrupting the development. If this is the first time in your life you have ever encountered a definition that begins: "a ____ is a 5-tuple (__,__,__,__,__), where . . .," your reaction may be "Is this really necessary?" or maybe something even more emphatic. Unless you're planning to become a mathematician, you might be reassured by an article entitled "Can We Make Mathematics Intelligible?" by R. P. Boas, which appeared in *The American Mathematical Monthly* a few years ago. Professor Boas says,

> There is a test for identifying some of the future professional mathematicians at an early age. These are students who instantly comprehend a sentence beginning "Let X be an ordered quintuple $(a, T, \pi, \sigma, \mathcal{B})$, where . . ." They are even more promising if they add, "I never really understood it before."

He goes on to emphasize the importance of providing examples to motivate abstract definitions, of which the definition above is certainly one. All right then, is this really necessary? How can a machine be a 5-tuple? The answer is that there are certainly ways we could avoid mentioning 5-tuples in the definition. Stating it as we have allows us to talk about five things at once as though it is one "object" we are talking about. It will allow us to say "Let $M = (Q, \Sigma, q_0, \delta, A)$ be an FA," instead of "Let M be an FA with state set Q, input alphabet Σ, initial state q_0, transition function δ, and set of accepting states A." In other words, like most mathematical notation, it is just a way of being precise and concise at the same time. And of course, like a lot of mathematical notation, it takes a little getting used to.

This is a good place to mention that although diagrams such as Fig. 4-1 are used almost universally to describe simple FAs, they are not the only way. You specify a finite automaton $(Q, \Sigma, q_0, \delta, A)$, first by saying what the three sets

Q, Σ, and A are; then by saying what the initial state q_0 is; and finally, and most importantly, by saying what the function δ is. A diagram is very often an effective way to describe the function, and if the number of states is manageable, it is perhaps the way that conveys most quickly the essential structure. But functions can be described by tables of values, for example, and this would be a perfectly acceptable substitute for a picture. If we took this approach for Example 4.3, we would end up with something like this.

Table of values for the transition function in Example 4.3

		input	
		0	**1**
	Λ	0	1
state	0	N	1
	1	0	1
	N	N	N

Example 4.4   (Continuation of Example 4.1). Let's go back to the language $L = \{0, 1\}^*\{10\}$ of all strings ending in 10. We have already seen that if you have received at least two inputs, you can forget all but the last two. It may not be completely obvious, however, just how many states are required by an FA accepting L. Initially the machine has received no input, and until it gets at least two symbols it must remember the inputs it has received. A straightforward way to proceed is shown in Fig. 4-2, which gives both a *state diagram* for an FA and a *transition table* for the function δ.

The states labeled Λ, 0, and 1 are "temporary" states that the FA uses only until it has received two inputs, and from that point on it cycles back and forth among the

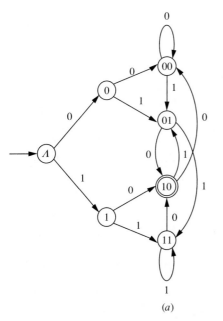

(a)

FIGURE 4-2
A finite automaton recognizing $\{0, 1\}^*\{10\}$: (*a*) Transition diagram; (*b*) Transition table.

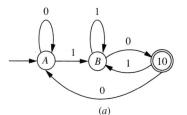

	input	
state	**0**	**1**
Λ	0	1
0	00	01
1	10	11
00	00	01
01	10	11
10	00	01
11	10	11

FIGURE 4-2(*b*)

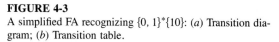

(*a*)

FIGURE 4-3
A simplified FA recognizing $\{0, 1\}^*\{10\}$: (*a*) Transition diagram; (*b*) Transition table.

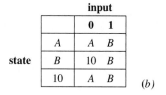

	input	
state	**0**	**1**
A	*A*	*B*
B	10	*B*
10	*A*	*B*

(*b*)

other four, "remembering" the last two symbols it has received. If we look carefully at this diagram, though, we may be able to simplify the FA. Consider the two states 0 and 00. Neither is an accepting state, so starting from either one we will need at least one more symbol to have a string in the language. But the rows in the transition table corresponding to these states are the same; regardless of which we start in, the input 0 will take us to 00 and the input 1 will take us to 01. Since two strings that cause the machine to be in these respective states don't need to be distinguished now (neither state is an accepting state) and can't be distinguished one symbol later (the machine will then be in the same state), we conclude that the two states don't really represent two cases that need to be distinguished at all. We could merge them into one, and call it state *A*. In the same way, all three states 1, 01, and 11 can be merged into one, called *B*. We have therefore reduced the number of states to four. But we can go one step further: notice that since states 0 and 00 are now the same, and since 1 and 01 are now the same, there is no difference between the rows in the table corresponding to Λ and 0. Since neither of these is an accepting state, we could have lumped Λ in with 0 and 00 as well. We now have three states, *A*, *B*, and 10, and it is clear that the number cannot be reduced any more. If we wished, we could describe state *A* as representing "no progress toward 10," meaning that the machine has received either no input or an input string having last symbol 0 but not last two symbols 10. *B* stands for "halfway there," or last symbol 1. As we noted after Example 4.3, though, these intuitive descriptions of the states are not needed to specify the abstract machine completely. The final result is pictured in Fig. 4-3*a*.

One final comment: the analysis that led to the simplification of the FA in this example can be turned into a systematic procedure for finding the FA with the minimum number of states that recognizes the same language as a given FA. This will be discussed in more detail in Chapter 7.

4.3 EXTENDING THE NOTATION: THE FUNCTION δ^*

If $M = (Q, \Sigma, q_0, \delta, A)$, we now have a concise way of writing "the state to which the machine M goes if it is in state q and receives input symbol a." It is $\delta(q, a)$. We would like an equally concise way of writing "the state in which M ends up, if it begins in state q, and receives the string x of several input symbols." Let us write this as $\delta^*(q, x)$. We may think of δ^*, then, as an extension of the transition function δ, which is defined on $Q \times \Sigma$, to the larger set $Q \times \Sigma^*$. We can give a recursive formula for δ^*, using the same principle as in Example 2.8. There we wished to define $REV : \Sigma^* \to \Sigma^*$. We began by saying what $REV(\Lambda)$ is; then, since any string of length greater than 1 can be expressed as xa for some $x \in \Sigma^*$ and some $a \in \Sigma$, we needed only to say how $REV(xa)$ is obtained from $REV(x)$.

Here, if q is any element of Q, we want to say what $\delta^*(q, xa)$ is, in terms of $\delta^*(q, x)$. We want $\delta^*(q, xa)$ to mean the state M ends up in, if it begins in state q and receives first the string x of input symbols, then the one extra symbol a. But the state M gets to from q using the string x is $\delta^*(q, x)$; and from any state p, the state M goes to with one additional input a is $\delta(p, a)$. It follows that the recursive part of our definition should define $\delta^*(q, xa)$ to be $\delta(\delta^*(q, x), a)$. For the basis part of the definition, we must define $\delta^*(q, \Lambda)$. With the null string of inputs, we don't expect M to change state, and so we let $\delta^*(q, \Lambda)$ be q.

Definition 4.2. Let $M = (Q, \Sigma, q_0, \delta, A)$ be an FA. Define the function

$$\delta^* \ : \ Q \times \Sigma^* \to Q$$

recursively as follows.

1. For any $q \in Q$, $\delta^*(q, \Lambda) = q$
2. For any $y \in \Sigma^*$, $a \in \Sigma$, and $q \in Q$, $\delta^*(q, ya) = \delta(\delta^*(q, y), a)$

This definition looks rather formidable, but we can see from an example that using it to calculate $\delta^*(q, x)$ amounts to just what you would expect: processing the symbols of x one at a time, and seeing where the transition function δ takes us at each step. Suppose M contains the transitions shown in Fig. 4-4.

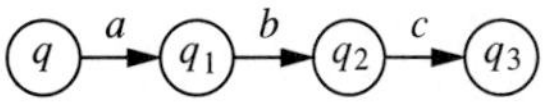

FIGURE 4-4

Let us use the definition to calculate $\delta^*(q, abc)$.

$$\delta^*(q, abc) = \delta(\delta^*(q, ab), c)$$

$$= \delta(\delta(\delta^*(q, a), b), c)$$

$$= \delta(\delta(\delta^*(q, \Lambda a), b), c)$$

$$= \delta(\delta(\delta(\delta^*(q, \Lambda), a), b), c)$$

$$= \delta(\delta(\delta(q, a), b), c)$$

$$= \delta(\delta(q_1, b), c)$$

$$= \delta(q_2, c)$$

$$= q_3$$

Other properties you would expect δ^* to satisfy can be derived from our definition. For example, an obvious generalization of statement 2 of the definition is the formula

$$\delta^*(q, xy) = \delta^*(\delta^*(q, x), y)$$

which should hold for any $q \in Q$ and any two strings x and y. The proof is by mathematical induction, and the details are left to you in Exercise 4.5.

Notice also that in the sample calculation above, since the definition starts out with Λ instead of strings of length 1, we found $\delta^*(q, a)$ by expressing a as $a\Lambda$ and applying part 2 of the definition. Fortunately, it turned out to be simply $\delta(q, a)$; for strings of length 1 (i.e., elements of Σ), δ and δ^* can be used interchangeably.

The function δ^* allows a concise statement of what it means for an FA to accept a string, and therefore facilitates our second characterization of regular languages.

Definition 4.3. Let $M = (Q, \Sigma, q_0, \delta, A)$ be an FA. A string $x \in \Sigma^*$ is *accepted* by M if $\delta^*(q_0, x) \in A$. x is *rejected* by M if it is not accepted. The *language accepted, or recognized, by M* is the language $L(M) = \{x \mid x \text{ is accepted by } M\}$. If L is a language in Σ^*, L is accepted, or recognized, by M if $L = L(M)$.

It is worth calling attention to the last statement in Definition 4.3, because of what it does *not* say. It does not say that L is accepted by M if all the elements of L are accepted by M. If it did, we could use the FA pictured in Fig. 4-5 to recognize any language, no matter how complex. The power of a machine doesn't lie in the number of strings it accepts, but in its ability to discriminate—to accept some and reject others. To accept a language, an FA has to accept all the strings in the language *and* reject all the strings in its complement.

FIGURE 4-5

As we've already suggested, the languages that can be recognized by FAs are exactly the same as the regular languages. It will be easier to demonstrate this in Chapter 6, when we have a little more machinery, and will be able to give other characterizations of these languages as well. In the meantime, we record the result officially as Theorem 4.1.

Theorem 4.1. A language $L \subseteq \Sigma^*$ is regular (i.e., corresponds to a regular expression over Σ) if and only if there is an FA that recognizes L.

Proof. Postponed until Chapter 6.

To recapitulate: in the light of our earlier discussion, we can now say that a language L is regular if and only if it is possible to classify all strings into some finite number N of types, so that once we have processed any substring in the course of recognizing L, it is not necessary to remember the substring, but only which of the N types it is. The N types correspond to the states of an FA that recognizes L. As this suggests, a language like *PAL* (Example 4.2) cannot be regular, since we have already seen that to recognize *PAL* requires that we be able to distinguish between any two elements of an infinite set of strings, and this seems to require an infinite set of states. For a slightly more careful proof, see Theorem 4.3.

Example 4.5. This time we start with a transition diagram, or state diagram (Fig. 4-6), and see what language the corresponding FA recognizes.

We begin by considering the state labeled A. It is both the initial state and an accepting state; thus we know immediately that Λ is in the language. What strings cause the machine to be in state A? Clearly the answer is strings of 0's of even length. If we want a regular expression, $(00)^*$ will work. The other accepting state is B. We can see that to reach B, one must have come from A via 1, possibly after visiting 0. The easiest way to reach B from A is with the string 11—but once the machine is in state B, any subsequent even-length string of 1's returns the machine to B. So the strings that get us from A to B are even-length strings of two or more 1's, corresponding to the regular expression $11(11)^*$—except that they could be preceded by an even-length string of 0's. The regular expression we want is therefore $(00)^*11(11)^*$.

The state labeled D serves the same purpose in this example that state N did in Example 4.3: once the machine reaches D, it stays there forever; a substring causing the machine to reach state D is a substring that permanently disqualifies any string containing it from being in the language.

The labels 0 and 1 are intended to suggest that we are halfway toward the pair of identical symbols that leads to an accepting state. In both cases, if the next symbol is the same as the most recent one, we will return to an accepting state; if not, the machine goes to state D.

What is the language this machine recognizes? We have determined that even-length strings of 0's are the ones that result in state A; even-length strings of 0's followed by even-length strings of two or more 1's are the ones that result in state B; we may therefore describe the language as the set of all strings consisting of an even number of 0's followed by an even number of 1's. The corresponding regular expression is $(00)^* + (00)^*11(11)^*$, or $(00)^*(11)^*$.

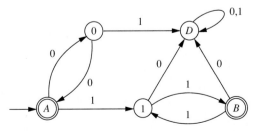

FIGURE 4-6

The method we used in this example to find a regular expression corresponding to the language recognized by the FA probably looked a little haphazard. Don't be concerned. When we show the equivalence between regular languages and languages recognized by FAs, we will describe a systematic procedure to solve this problem.

4.4 DISTINGUISHING ONE STRING FROM ANOTHER

As the next example will indicate, there are situations where it is easy to see in a general way how the machine should work, and yet the number of states required makes it awkward to give either a transition diagram or a table of values for the transition function.

Example 4.6. For an integer $N \geq 1$, let

$$L_N = \{x \in \{0, 1\}^* \mid |x| \geq N \text{ and the } N^{\text{th}} \text{ symbol from the right is } 1\}$$

There is a straightforward way to construct an FA recognizing L_N: create a distinct state for every possible substring of length N or less, just as we did in Example 4.4. For each i, the number of strings of length exactly i is 2^i. If we add these numbers for all the values of i from 0 through N, we obtain $2^{N+1} - 1$ (see Example 2.1), and so this is the total number of states. We illustrate for $N = 3$ in Fig. 4-7.

The eight states representing strings of length 3 are at the right. Not all the transitions from these states are shown, but the rule is simply

$$\delta(abc, d) = bcd$$

The accepting states are the four for which the third-from-last symbol is 1.

So far so good; but suppose N is 20 instead of 3. The principle is still the same, but instead of fifteen states, there are now $2^{21} - 1 = 2,097,151$. There is no confusion about how the machine should work, and we could give explicit formulas, similar to the one above for $N = 3$, for the transition function. Moreover, perhaps we shouldn't be too dismayed at the number of states, since for that matter, any portion of the memory of a computer that can accommodate 21 bits can be in 2^{21} possible states, in the sense that there are that many possible choices for the informational content. Nevertheless, we may still ask whether there isn't some simpler FA that would work, possibly some radically different approach that would cut down the number of required states to a manageable size. The answer is essentially no. Although it is possible to reduce the number somewhat, the absolute minimum is still at least 2^{20}; we can see this by considering the strings among which the machine must distinguish in order to produce the correct answer. (To be continued.)

It has been clear since Examples 4.1 and 4.2 that the difficulty of recognizing a particular language is tied to the number of strings that must be distinguished. The reason for having two distinct states in an FA in the first place is that they serve to distinguish some strings from others. Two strings x and y *need* to be distinguished by the machine if there is some string z so that one of the strings xz and yz should be accepted by the machine and the other shouldn't. We have taken time out from our example to define more formally the notion of two strings

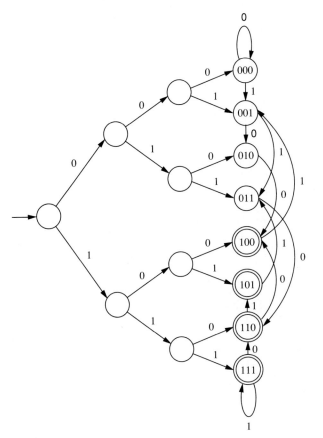

FIGURE 4-7
A finite automaton recognizing L_3.

needing to be distinguished in the course of recognizing the language L, and to establish a relationship between the number of strings that need to be distinguished and the number of states required by any FA recognizing the language.

Definition 4.4. Let L be a language in Σ^*. For any two strings x and y in Σ^*, x and y are *distinguishable with respect to L* if there is a string z, which may depend on x and y, so that one and only one of the strings xz and yz is in L. In this case, the string z is said to distinguish x and y with respect to L. The strings x and y are *indistinguishable* with respect to L if this is not the case—i.e., for every string z, xz and yz have the same status: either both are in L or neither is in L.

We may illustrate this definition by returning to Example 4.3, where we let L be the language of strings of 0's and 1's that end in 10. The two strings 01011 and 100 are distinguishable with respect to L, since concatenating with 0 produces an element of L in the first case and not in the second. The strings 0 and 100 are indistinguishable. $0z \in L$ if and only if z ends in 10, and the same is true for $100z$; therefore $0z \in L$ if and only if $100z \in L$.

Theorem 4.2. If $L \subseteq \Sigma^*$ and for some integer n there are n elements of Σ^*, any two of which are distinguishable with respect to L, then any FA that recognizes L must have at least n states.

(Note that we are not assuming L to be regular. There may be no FA recognizing L; the theorem says only that if there is one, it can have no fewer than n states.)

Proof. Suppose $M = (Q, \Sigma, q_0, \delta, A)$ is an FA recognizing L, and let S be any set of strings, any two of which are distinguishable with respect to L. The idea of the proof is to show that any two strings in S must cause M to end up in different states. In other words, the states $\delta^*(q_0, x)$ corresponding to the elements x of S are all distinct. Since by assumption we may choose S to have n elements, it follows that there must be at least n states.

Let x and y be arbitrary elements of S. Our assumption is that any two elements of S are distinguishable with respect to L. Therefore, there is a string z so that of the two strings xz and yz, only one is in L. Now M recognizes L; this means that the strings w for which $\delta^*(q_0, w) \in A$ are precisely the strings in L.

Thus of the two states $\delta^*(q_0, xz)$ and $\delta^*(q_0, yz)$, only one is in A. In particular,

$$\delta^*(q_0, xz) \neq \delta^*(q_0, yz)$$

According to Exercise 4.5, we therefore have

$$\delta^*(\delta^*(q_0, x), z) \neq \delta^*(\delta^*(q_0, y), z)$$

We're almost finished. Let us denote by p and q the states $\delta^*(q_0, x)$ and $\delta^*(q_0, y)$, respectively. We know that $\delta^*(p, z) \neq \delta^*(q, z)$, and it follows that $p \neq q$. This is what we needed to show.

Example 4.6 (continued). According to Theorem 4.2, if we can produce a set of n elements, any two of which are distinguishable with respect to L_{20}, then any FA accepting L_{20} must have at least n states. We claimed above that the minimum number of states is at least 2^{20}. Let us show this by demonstrating that any two strings of length 20, of which there are 2^{20} in all, are distinguishable with respect to L_{20}.

Let x and y be two distinct strings of length 20. "Distinct" means they differ in the ith symbol, for some i with $1 \leq i \leq 20$. Of course, if $i = 1$, then they differ in the 20th symbol from the right; in this case, they are distinguishable with respect to L_{20}, since one is in L and the other is not. (This means that in Definition 4.4, we are taking $z = \Lambda$.) Otherwise $1 < i$; in this case take z to be any string of length $i - 1$. The two strings xz and yz still differ in the ith position, but now the ith position is exactly 20th from the right. In other words, one of the strings xz and yz is in L but the other isn't. Therefore, x and y are distinguishable with respect to L_{20}.

Examples like this one, together with Theorem 4.2, will help us to appreciate Chapter 5, in which we show that a slight change in the rules by which an FA operates often *can* reduce drastically the number of states.

For now, let's finish this section by proving something that we have suspected for some time, but that Theorem 4.2 now allows us to demonstrate convincingly.

Theorem 4.3. The language *PAL* of all palindromes in $\{0, 1\}^*$ is not regular.

Proof. We've already stated (see Example 4.2 and Exercise 4.13) that any two strings in $\{0, 1\}^*$ are distinguishable with respect to *PAL*. This would certainly do it, because if someone claimed to have an FA with n states recognizing *PAL*, all we'd have to do to prove him wrong, according to Theorem 4.2, is produce $n + 1$ strings, any two of which would then be distinguishable. In fact, to prove the theorem it isn't necessary to show that any two strings are distinguishable. It's sufficient to show that for any n we can find $n + 1$ pairwise distinguishable strings, and we can do this by exhibiting an infinite set of strings, any two of which are distinguishable. For example, consider the strings 1, 11, 111, and so forth: all strings of the form 1^K for $K \geq 1$. To show that any two of these are distinguishable with respect to *PAL*, we just need to show that for any two distinct integers J and K, there's a string z so that only one of the strings $1^J z$ and $1^K z$ is a palindrome. That's easy: take z to be the string 01^J. Then $1^J z = 1^J 01^J$, which is certainly a palindrome, and $1^K z = 1^K 01^J$, which isn't a palindrome since $J \neq K$.

We will return to nonregular languages in Chapter 8. In addition to the technique used here, there are other methods for demonstrating languages nonregular. Definition 4.4 will also come up again; the distinguishability relation (actually, to be precise, the *in*-distinguishability relation) can be used in an elegant description of a "minimum-state" FA recognizing a given language. This will be discussed in Chapter 7.

4.5   UNIONS, INTERSECTIONS, AND COMPLEMENTS OF REGULAR LANGUAGES

We observed in Theorem 3.1 that from the definition of regular expressions and the corresponding languages, it follows that the union, concatenation, and * of regular languages are all regular. (If we have regular expressions corresponding to languages L_1 and L_2, the definition specifies three new regular expressions, corresponding to the three languages $L_1 \cup L_2$, $L_1 L_2$, and L_1^*.) Theorem 4.1 gives an alternative characterization of regular languages, and the question arises: if we have an FA recognizing L_1 and another recognizing L_2, is there a correspondingly simple way to produce FAs that recognize $L_1 \cup L_2$, $L_1 L_2$, and L_1^*?

In Chapter 6 we shall prove Theorem 4.1, that to every FA there corresponds a regular expression, and to every regular expression there corresponds an FA. The proof will be constructive, and so, in a sense, we will be able to answer the question in the preceding paragraph as follows: Given FAs recognizing L_1 and L_2, find corresponding regular expressions R_1 and R_2; then find FAs corresponding to the regular expressions $R_1 + R_2$, $R_1 R_2$, and R_1^*. In fact, the process isn't really as roundabout as this might suggest. The FA corresponding to $R_1 + R_2$, for example, is obtained by first "combining" the two FAs in a straightforward way to form a slightly more general kind of machine (a *nondeterministic* FA, or NFA), and then using another algorithm to eliminate the "nondeterminism" and produce an equivalent ordinary (i.e., "deterministic") FA.

However, there is a more direct approach that we can use right now to produce an FA recognizing the union of the two languages. In addition to being a little less circuitous, this approach also has the advantage that it will allow us to handle the other standard set operations, intersection and complement, in almost the same way. The remaining operations—concatenation and $*$—are not really *set* operations, but operations that depend on the fact that these are sets of *strings*; they will have to wait until Chapter 6.

Suppose we have languages L_1 and L_2 over Σ that are recognized by the respective FAs $M_1 = (P, \Sigma, p_0, \delta_1, A_1)$ and $M_2 = (Q, \Sigma, q_0, \delta_2, A_2)$. We wish to find an FA $M = (R, \Sigma, r_0, \delta, A)$ to recognize $L_1 \cup L_2$. This means intuitively that in processing a string, M needs to keep track of the status of both M_1 and M_2 simultaneously, as they process the string, and to accept whenever one or the other accepts. This may sound complicated, but abstractly it's very simple. The machine M_1 "remembers" that it's in a particular state, and so does M_2. What does M need to remember? Both the state M_1 is in and the state M_2 is in—a pair of states. This suggests that we take as the states of M, pairs (p, q), where $p \in P$ and $q \in Q$. In other words, we take R to be the set $P \times Q$. Initially M_1 is in state p_0 and M_2 is in state q_0, so initially M should be in state (p_0, q_0). If M is in state (p, q) and receives input a, it should go to the state represented by the pair $(\delta_1(p, a), \delta_2(q, a))$, since $\delta_1(p, a)$ and $\delta_2(q, a)$ are the states to which M_1 and M_2, respectively, would go. Finally, since M is to accept a string whenever either M_1 or M_2 does, the accepting states of M should be the pairs (p, q) for which either $p \in A_1$ or $q \in A_2$. That's all there is to it! Moreover, exactly the same construction works for the two languages $L_1 \cap L_2$ and $L_1 - L_2$, except for the definition of accepting states. In the first case (p, q) should be an accepting state if p and q are both accepting states in their respective machines—i.e., if $p \in A_1$ and $q \in A_2$; in the second case, (p, q) should be an accepting state if $p \in A_1$ and $q \notin A_2$. It should be pretty clear that this construction will do the job, but for the sake of completeness we do things a little more carefully in the following proof. We include a fourth language, the complement L'_1 of L_1. Of course, we could obtain this from the third case by noticing that $L'_1 = \Sigma^* - L_1$; and if we look carefully at the FA that would be produced, we can see that it is essentially the same as the one described in the proof. But it's even easier to construct it directly.

Theorem 4.4. If L_1 and L_2 are regular languages in Σ^*, then $L_1 \cup L_2$, $L_1 \cap L_2$, $L_1 - L_2$, and L'_1 are all regular languages.

Proof. We take care of the first three cases first. Suppose L_1 and L_2 are recognized by $M_1 = (P, \Sigma, p_0, \delta_1, A_1)$ and $M_2 = (Q, \Sigma, q_0, \delta_2, A_2)$, respectively. Define $M = (R, \Sigma, r_0, \delta, A)$ recognizing $L_1 \cup L_2$ as follows:

$$R = P \times Q$$

$$r_0 = (p_0, q_0)$$

$$A = \{(p, q) | p \in A_1 \text{ or } q \in A_2\}$$

$$\delta : R \times \Sigma \rightarrow R \text{ is defined by } \delta((p, q), a) = (\delta_1(p, a), \delta_2(q, a))$$

Then a simple mathematical induction argument (Exercise 4.18) shows that for any $x \in \Sigma^*$ and any $(p, q) \in R$,

$$\delta^*((p, q), x) = (\delta_1^*(p, x), \delta_2^*(q, x))$$

Now x is accepted by M if and only if $\delta^*((p_0, q_0), x) \in A$. By the formula above, this is the same as saying

$$(\delta_1^*(p_0, x), \delta_2^*(q_0, x)) \in A$$

By definition of A, this will happen if and only if either $\delta_1^*(p_0, x) \in A_1$ or $\delta_2^*(q_0, x) \in A_2$—in other words, if and only if $x \in L_1 \cup L_2$.

For $L_1 \cap L_2$ and $L_1 - L_2$, the same argument works, except that for $L_1 \cap L_2$ we define $A = \{(p, q) | p \in A_1$ and $q \in A_2\}$ and for $L_1 - L_2$ we define $A = \{(p, q) | p \in A_1$ and $q \notin A_2\}$.

We construct M_1' to recognize L_1' as follows:

$$M_1' = (P, \Sigma, p_0, \delta_1, P - A_1)$$

M_1' accepts a string x if and only if $\delta^*(p_0, x) \in P - A_1$; this is equivalent to saying $\delta^*(p_0, x) \notin A_1$, or in other words, M_1 doesn't accept x. Therefore, M_1' recognizes L_1'.

It often happens that the FA we need is even simpler than the construction would seem to indicate. This is illustrated by the following example.

Example 4.7. Let L_1 and L_2 be the following subsets of $\{0, 1\}^*$:

$$L_1 = \{x | 00 \text{ is not a substring of } x\}$$

$$L_2 = \{x | x \text{ ends with } 01\}$$

L_1 and L_2 are recognized by the FAs pictured in Fig. 4-8a.

If we apply the construction in the theorem to this example, we obtain an FA with nine states. In drawing the transition diagram, we begin with the initial state (A, P). Since $\delta_1(A, 0) = B$ and $\delta_2(P, 0) = Q$, we have $\delta((A, P), 0) = (B, Q)$. Similarly, $\delta((A, P), 1) = (A, P)$. Then we calculate $\delta((B, Q), 0)$ and $\delta((B, Q), 1)$. As soon as a new state is introduced in this process, we calculate the transitions from this state. At some point we obtain the partial diagram in Fig. 4-8b. At each step up to this point (after we drew the transitions from the initial state), there was at least one state to which arrows had been drawn but from which we hadn't drawn arrows. In other words, all six of the states from which arrows are drawn are reachable from the initial state. At this point, however, since we have drawn all the transitions from these states, it is clear that the other three states are not reachable from the initial state—and therefore that they need not be included in the final diagram. This is a general principle that is explored more fully in Exercise 4.16: states in an FA that are unreachable from the initial state may be omitted without affecting the language recognized by the FA.

Suppose now that we wish the FA to recognize the language $L_1 - L_2$. Then we designate (A, P) and (B, Q) as accepting states (i.e., those pairs (X, Y) of the six, for which X is either A or B and Y is not R), and obtain the machine pictured in Fig. 4-8c.

There is a further simplification we can make, though; none of the states (C, P), (C, Q), or (C, R) is an accepting state, and once the machine enters one of these states,

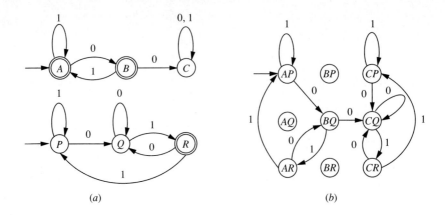

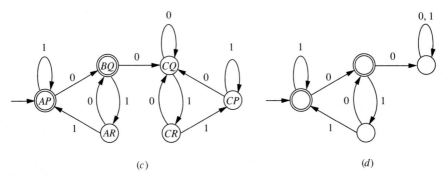

FIGURE 4-8
An FA to recognize $L_1 - L_2$.

it remains in one of them. This implies that we could replace all of them with a single
state, obtaining the FA shown in Fig. 4-8d.

EXERCISES

4.1. For each of the FAs pictured in Fig. 4-9, (*i*) characterize the strings that cause the
FA to be in each state; (*ii*) describe the language recognized by the FA; and (*iii*)
give a regular expression corresponding to the language.

4.2. For each of the languages in Exercise 3.9, draw an FA recognizing the language.

4.3. For each of the following regular expressions, draw an FA recognizing the corresponding language.
(*a*) $(0 + 1)^* 110^*$
(*b*) $(11 + 10)^*$
(*c*) $(1 + 110)^* 0$

4.4. Draw an FA that recognizes the language of all strings of 0's and 1's of
length ≥ 1 that, if they were interpreted as binary representations of integers, would represent integers evenly divisible by 3. Leading 0's are permissible. (Suggestions: How would you test a number for divisibility by 3
in a Pascal program? How much do you need to know (i.e., to "remember") about an integer to determine whether it's divisible by 3? Finally,

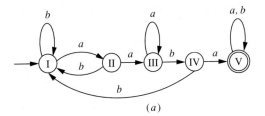

(a)

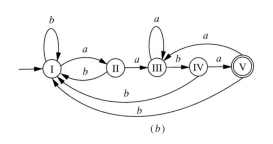

(b)

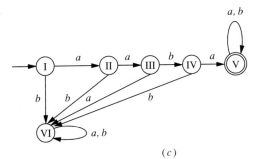

(c)

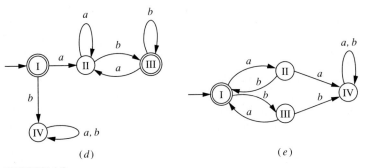

(d)　　　　　　　　　　　(e)

FIGURE 4-9

if a string of 0's and 1's represents the integer N, what integer is represented by the string obtained by concatenating 0 onto the right?)

Problems 4.5, 4.6, and 4.7 all refer to an FA $(Q, \Sigma, q_0, \delta, A)$.

4.5. Using mathematical induction, show that for any x and y in Σ^*, and any $q \in Q$,

$$\delta^*(q, xy) = \delta^*(\delta^*(q, x), y)$$

One choice for $P(N)$ is the statement: If $y \in \Sigma^*$ and $|y| = N$, then for any $x \in \Sigma^*$ and any $q \in Q$,

$$\delta^*(q, xy) = \delta^*(\delta^*(q, x), y)$$

4.6. Show that if for some state q, $\delta(q, a) = q$ for every $a \in \Sigma$, then $\delta^*(q, x) = q$ for every $x \in \Sigma^*$.

4.7. Show that if for some state q and some string x, $\delta^*(q, x) = q$, then for every $N \geq 0$, $\delta^*(q, x^N) = q$.

4.8. For the FA in Exercise 4.1(d), show that there cannot be any other FA with fewer states recognizing the same language.

4.9. Show that there cannot be an FA with three states recognizing the language of all strings of 0's and 1's of length ≥ 2 in which the second symbol from the left is 0.

4.10. Show that there cannot be an FA having fewer than four states recognizing the language of all strings of 0's and 1's in which both the number of 0's and the number of 1's are even.

4.11. Let N be a positive integer, and let $L = \{x \in PAL | |x| = 2N\} = \{yREV(y)| |y| = N\}$. What can you say about the minimum number of states in any FA that recognizes L? Give reasons for your answer.

4.12. Exercise 2.25 introduces the "pigeonhole principle." Explain what this principle has to do with the proof of Theorem 4.2.

4.13. Show the statement in Example 4.2: Any two strings of 0's and 1's are distinguishable with respect to the language *PAL*. (Suggestion: If $|x| = |y|$ and $x \neq y$, it is easy to find a string z distinguishing the two strings. If $|x| < |y|$, write $y = y_1 y_2$, where $|y_1| = |x|$. Then show that a string w can be found with $|w| = |y_2|$ so that $wREV(w) REV(x)$ distinguishes x and y.)

4.14. (a) Show that if L is a regular language and F is a finite language, then $L \cup F$, $L \cap F$, and $L - F$ are regular.

(b) Show that if L is a non-regular language and F is a finite language, then $L \cup F$ and $L - F$ are nonregular.

4.15. Languages such as that in Example 4.1 are regular for what seems like a particularly simple reason: in order to test a string for membership, we need examine only the last few symbols. More precisely, there is an integer N and a set S of strings of length N so that for any string x of length N or greater, x is in the language if and only if the final substring of x of length N is one of the elements of S. (In Example 4.1, we may take N to be 2 and S to be the set $\{10\}$.) Show that any language having this property is regular. Suggestion: first show that the subset of the language consisting of all strings in the language with length $\geq N$ is regular, then use Exercise 4.14.

4.16. Suppose $M = (Q, \Sigma, q_0, \delta, A)$ is an FA. If p and q are elements of Q, we say q is *reachable* from p if there is a string x in Σ^* so that $\delta^*(p, x) = q$.

(a) Let M_1 be the FA obtained from M by deleting any states that are not reachable from q_0 (and of course deleting any transitions to or from such states). Show that M_1 and M recognize the same language.

(b) It would seem as though another reasonable way to simplify the FA without affecting the language it accepts would be to eliminate any states from which no accepting states are reachable. However, we cannot in general talk about "the FA obtained by deleting any states from which no accepting states are reachable." Why not?

4.17. Let $M = (Q, \Sigma, q_0, \delta, A)$ be an FA. Let $M_1 = (Q, \Sigma, q_0, \delta, R)$, where R is the set of states from which some state in A is reachable (see Exercise 4.16). What is the relationship between the language recognized by M_1 and the language recognized by M? Prove your answer.

4.18. This problem refers to the proof of Theorem 4.4. Suppose $M_1 = (P, \Sigma, p_0, \delta_1, A_1)$ and $M_2 = (Q, \Sigma, q_0, \delta_2, A_2)$ are FAs, and M is the FA constructed as in the proof of Theorem 4.4. Using mathematical induction, show that for any $x \in \Sigma^*$ and any $(p, q) \in R$, $\delta^*((p, q), x) = (\delta_1^*(p, x), \delta_2^*(q, x))$.

4.19. Let M_1, M_2, and M_3 be the FAs pictured in Fig. 4-10, recognizing languages L_1, L_2, and L_3, respectively. Draw FAs recognizing these languages.
(a) $L_1 \cup L_2$
(b) $L_1 \cap L_2$
(c) $L_1 - L_2$
(d) $L_1 \cap L_3$
(e) $L_3 - L_2$

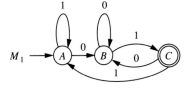

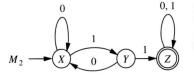

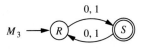

FIGURE 4-10

CHAPTER
5

NONDETERMINISM

5.1 NONDETERMINISTIC FINITE AUTOMATA

In this chapter, we shall consider an abstract machine very similar to an FA, still having finitely many "states" and some sort of "next-state" function, but with the rules relaxed somewhat, and an element of *nondeterminism* introduced. We shall see that the new machines are capable of recognizing exactly the same languages as finite automata, but often they can be constructed more easily, and sometimes they can have dramatically fewer states than equivalent FAs. You will recall that at this point we have stated, but not proved, that a language is regular if and only if it can be recognized by an FA. We deferred the proof because, surprisingly, it is easier to prove even more: that regular expressions, FAs, and the machines we are about to describe are all equivalent, with respect to the languages to which they correspond.

Example 5.1. Let's begin by considering a relatively trivial example of how relaxing the rules might lead to a simplification. Consider the FA corresponding to Example 4.3, pictured in Fig. 5-1a. This recognizes the language of all strings of 0's and 1's ending with 1 and not containing 00. The state labeled N is a "dead" state: once the FA enters that state, it stays there forever. The machine continues to receive and process input, but it could just as well be shut down—the input string on which it is working will never be accepted.

With this in mind, suppose we just leave this state out, ending up with the diagram in Fig. 5-1b. This is no longer a transition diagram for an FA, since it does not include

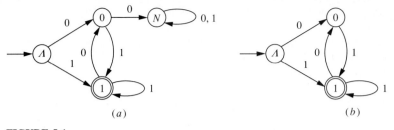

FIGURE 5-1

a transition from state 0 on input 0. But it would be simple enough to relax the rules for FAs slightly in order to accommodate it: just don't require that there be a value of the next-state function for *every* state-input pair. If in processing a string the machine finds itself unable to process the next symbol, it can quit early, and the decision it reaches is that the string is not in the language. The criterion for accepting a string is still the same: that the state reached as a result of processing the string be an accepting state.

Example 5.2. In our second example, we consider a more substantial departure from the rules. Consider the language *L* of all strings of 0's and 1's that have three consecutive occurrences of the same symbol: either 000 or 111. We can easily find a regular expression for this language:

$$(0 + 1)^*(000 + 111)(0 + 1)^*$$

It is also not difficult to construct an FA recognizing *L*. A diagram of such a machine is given in Fig. 5-2*a*. Compare this to the diagram in Fig. 5-2*b*.

     The second diagram fails to be a diagram of an FA, partly for the same reason as in the previous example, but in addition for what seems to be a more serious reason. In state *A*, with input 0, for example, there are two arrows we might follow, and it is therefore unclear what should happen. Because of this ambiguity, it is difficult to interpret the diagram in either of the ways we did previously: as an algorithm for recognizing the language while remembering as little as possible, or as an abstract machine. (For an algorithm or a machine, presumably, the action to be taken at each step should be specifiable in a clear and unambiguous way.)

    On the other hand, there is an obvious sense in which Fig. 5-2*b* seems to reflect the structure of the regular expression accurately. Moreover, once we agree on how to interpret it, it is easier to understand than the FA pictured in Fig. 5-2*a*. For any string in *L*, it is easy to describe a path in the diagram that corresponds to the string and that terminates at the circle labeled *B*: Start at *A* and continue looping back to *A* until the first occurrence

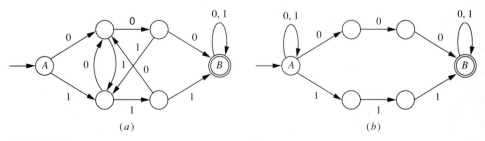

FIGURE 5-2

of either 000 or 111 is encountered; use those three symbols to get to B; then loop back to B once for each remaining symbol. Furthermore, for any string not in L, it is clear that there is no path corresponding to the string that starts at A and ends at B.

We now have a way of making sense of Fig. 5-2b. It is not the same as the way we interpreted a diagram of an FA. The difference is that instead of asking whether *the* path corresponding to a string leads to an accepting state, we are now asking whether *some* path corresponding to the string leads to an accepting state. We might compare this to the problem of trying to decide directly whether a string x (say 0111011000101, for example) corresponds to the regular expression $(0 + 1)^*(000 + 111)(0 + 1)^*$. There are many ways we could attempt to match them, since any initial substring of x matches $(0 + 1)^*$. Some of them do not work—using the substring 011 or 011101100 to match $(0 + 1)^*$, for example—but if there is at least one way we can match them, we conclude that x does indeed correspond to the regular expression.

Let us return to the problem of defining an abstract machine whose structure is pictured by the diagram—possibly relaxing slightly our requirements for a machine in the process, as noted earlier. As in our discussion for FAs, we have in mind a 5-tuple $(Q, \Sigma, q_0, \delta, A)$. Of the five objects, all but the fourth are identical to the corresponding components of an FA. (Fig. 5-2b indicates six states, including an initial state and exactly one accepting state.) The transition function δ is where the crucial difference will come. As we saw in the two previous examples, for a particular combination of a state and an input symbol, there may be no states specified by the diagram, or there may be several. What this suggests is that if we want a transition function δ on $Q \times \Sigma$, its value should be not an element of Q but a *subset* of Q, possibly with no elements, possibly with several. Our interpretation will be that $\delta(q, a)$ represents the set of states that the machine can legally be in, as a result of being previously in state q and processing input symbol a. This means that we are viewing the machine as *nondeterministic*: at some point it may have a choice of moves, and when this happens it selects a move in some unspecified way. As we shall see presently, the nondeterminism is more apparent than real; there is a corresponding ordinary FA that faithfully simulates the actions of the nondeterministic machine. In any case, let us now give a more formal definition.

Definition 5.1. A nondeterministic finite automaton, abbreviated NFA, is a 5-tuple $(Q, \Sigma, q_0, \delta, A)$, where Q and Σ are nonempty finite sets, $q_0 \in Q$, $A \subseteq Q$, and $\delta : Q \times \Sigma \rightarrow 2^Q$. Q is the set of states, Σ is the alphabet, q_0 is the initial state, and A is the set of accepting states. As usual, 2^Q means the set of subsets of Q.

As in the case of FAs, we need notation that will allow us to define the language recognized by an NFA M. In particular, we wish to define $\delta^*(p, x)$, the set of states M can legally be in as a result of starting in state p and processing the symbols in the string x. We begin by recalling Definition 4.2. There we said

$$\delta^*(p, ya) = \delta(\delta^*(p, y), a)$$

We shall also give a recursive definition here, but let us start with what may seem like a more straightforward approach. If $x = a_1 a_2 \ldots a_n$, then what it means to say that M can legally be in state q after processing x is this: There is a sequence of states $p_1, p_2, \ldots, p_n = q$ so that M can get to state p_1 from state p by processing a_1; and for any subsequent i, M can get to state p_i from p_{i-1} by processing a_i. A simpler way to say "M can get to state p_i from p_{i-1} by processing a_i" is just

$$p_i \in \delta(p_{i-1}, a_i)$$

So our initial formulation of δ^* is the following.

Definition 5.2 **(Nonrecursive definition of δ^* for an NFA).** If $x = a_1 a_2 \ldots a_n$ and $p \in Q$,

$\delta^*(p, x) = \{q \in Q \,|\, \text{for some sequence } p_0, p_1, \ldots, p_n \in Q$

with $p_0 = p$ and $p_n = q$, $p_i \in \delta(p_{i-1}, a_i)$ for each i with $1 \le i \le n\}$

This lends itself to a recursive formulation, just as in Section 4.3. If $y = a_1 \ldots a_{n-1}$, so that $x = ya_n$, we would like to describe $\delta^*(p, x)$ in terms of $\delta^*(p, y)$. An element of $\delta^*(p, y)$, according to the definition above, is a state r for which there is a sequence $p = p_0, p_1, \ldots, p_{n-1} = r$ so that for each i with $1 \le i \le n - 1$, $p_i \in \delta(p_{i-1}, a_i)$. We may therefore say that

$$\delta^*(p, ya_n) = \{q \,|\, q \in \delta(r, a_n) \text{ for some } r \in \delta^*(p, y)\}$$

A slightly more concise statement is

$$\delta^*(p, ya_n) = \bigcup_{r \in \delta^*(p,y)} \delta(r, a_n)$$

This is the recursive part of the definition. The basis part is the same as in Section 4.3, except that we need to write a set instead of a state.

Definition 5.2a **(Recursive definition of δ^* for an NFA).** Let $M = (Q, \Sigma, q_0, \delta, A)$ be an NFA. Define $\delta^* : Q \times \Sigma^* \to 2^Q$ recursively, as follows.

1. For any $q \in Q$, $\delta^*(q, \Lambda) = \{q\}$.
2. For any $y \in \Sigma^*$, $a \in \Sigma$, and $q \in Q$,

$$\delta^*(q, ya) = \bigcup_{p \in \delta^*(q,y)} \delta(p, a)$$

In Chapter 4, we showed that certain expected properties of δ^* follow from the definition. For example, $\delta^*(q, xy) = \delta^*(\delta^*(q, x), y)$ and $\delta^*(q, a) = \delta(q, a)$, for any $q \in Q$, any strings x and y in Σ^*, and any $a \in \Sigma$. One can derive the analogous properties here also. We show the second and refer you to Exercise 5.7 for the first, the statement of which must be modified slightly. If $q \in Q$ and $a \in \Sigma$,

$$\delta^*(q, a) = \delta^*(q, \Lambda a) = \bigcup_{p \in \delta^*(q,\Lambda)} \delta(p, a)$$

$$= \bigcup_{p \in \{q\}} \delta(p, a) = \delta(q, a)$$

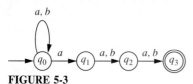

FIGURE 5-3
Transition diagram for Example 5-3.

It is now a simple matter to say, in terms of δ^*, what it means for a string x to be accepted by an NFA $M = (Q, \Sigma, q_0, \delta, A)$. In the case of an FA, this meant that $\delta^*(q_0, x) \in A$. As we have seen, we want "x is accepted by M" to mean that there is a sequence of moves M can make, starting in q_0 and processing the symbols of x, that will lead to an accepting state—in other words, that at least one of the states in which M can end up after processing x is an accepting state.

Definition 5.3. Let $M = (Q, \Sigma, q_0, \delta, A)$ be an NFA. A string $x \in \Sigma^*$ is accepted by M if $\delta^*(q_0, x) \cap A \neq \emptyset$. The language recognized by M is $L(M) = \{x \mid x$ is accepted by $M\}$. If $L \subseteq \Sigma^*$, L is recognized by M if $L = L(M)$.

Perhaps another example will help to clarify just how the function δ^* can be computed.

Example 5.3. Let $M = (Q, \Sigma, q_0, \delta, A)$, where $Q = \{q_0, q_1, q_2, q_3\}$, $\Sigma = \{a, b\}$, $A = \{q_3\}$, and δ is given by the following table.

		input	
		a	b
	q_0	$\{q_0, q_1\}$	$\{q_0\}$
state	q_1	$\{q_2\}$	$\{q_2\}$
	q_2	$\{q_3\}$	$\{q_3\}$
	q_3	$\emptyset$	$\emptyset$

Then M may be represented by the transition diagram in Fig. 5-3.

Let us calculate $\delta^*(q_0, x)$ for a few strings x of increasing length, using Definition 5.2a.

$$\delta^*(q_0, \Lambda) = \{q_0\} \text{ (by definition of } \delta^*)$$

$$\delta^*(q_0, a) = \delta(q_0, a) = \{q_0, q_1\} \text{ (from the table)}$$

$$\delta^*(q_0, b) = \delta(q_0, b) = \{q_0\}$$

$$\delta^*(q_0, aa) = \bigcup_{p \in \delta^*(q_0, a)} \delta(p, a) \text{ (by definition of } \delta^*)$$

$$= \bigcup_{p \in \{q_0, q_1\}} \delta(p, a) \text{ (by the previous calculation)}$$

$$= \delta(q_0, a) \cup \delta(q_1, a)$$

$$= \{q_0, q_1\} \cup \{q_2\}$$

$$= \{q_0, q_1, q_2\}$$

$$\delta^*(q_0, ba) = \bigcup_{p \in \delta^*(q_0, b)} \delta(p, a)$$

$$= \delta(q_0, a)$$

$$= \{q_0, q_1\}$$

$$\delta^*(q_0, aaa) = \bigcup_{p \in \delta^*(q_0, aa)} \delta(p, a)$$

$$= \delta(q_0, a) \cup \delta(q_1, a) \cup \delta(q_2, a)$$

$$= \{q_0, q_1\} \cup \{q_2\} \cup \{q_3\}$$

$$= \{q_0, q_1, q_2, q_3\}$$

$$\delta^*(q_0, baa) = \bigcup_{p \in \delta^*(q_0, ba)} \delta(p, a)$$

$$= \delta(q_0, a) \cup \delta(q_1, a)$$

$$= \{q_0, q_1, q_2\}$$

That's probably enough to get an idea of what is necessary in general. At this point, we see that aaa is accepted by M, and baa is not. In fact, as you can see from studying the diagram in Fig. 5-3, $\delta^*(q_0, x)$ contains q_1 if and only if x ends with a; for any y with $|y| = 2$, the set $\delta^*(q_0, xy)$ contains q_3 if and only if x ends with a; and, therefore, the language recognized by M is

$$\{x \in \{a, b\}^* \mid |x| \geq 3 \text{ and the third symbol from the right is } a\}$$

This example illustrates the fact, pointed out at the beginning of this section, that an NFA recognizing a language may have many fewer states than the simplest FA recognizing the language. This language is essentially the one we called L_3 in Example 4.6. As we saw there, any FA recognizing L_N must have at least 2^N states. Our example shows that for $N = 3$ we may reduce the number of states from 8 to 4 by using an NFA. The improvement for larger N is even more dramatic, since we may in the same way find an NFA with $N + 1$ states recognizing L_N.

5.2 NONDETERMINISTIC FINITE AUTOMATA WITH Λ-TRANSITIONS

It will be helpful to carry one step further our program of generalizing FAs by relaxing the rules. So far, we have allowed for the possibility that a particular combination of state and input symbol may leave the machine either no moves or a choice of moves. A way to generalize this further is to allow a move with no input. We think of such a move as a Λ-transition—a move that needs only the null string as input. As in the case of NFAs, the purpose of such a generalization is to simplify the process of finding an abstract machine recognizing a given language or to provide a simpler description of such a machine. In particular, proofs such as that of Kleene's Theorem in the next chapter, in which we are

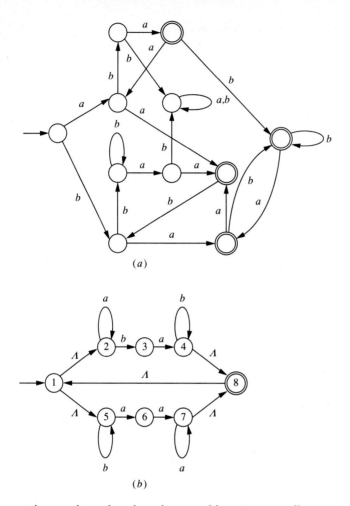

(a)

(b)

FIGURE 5-4

trying to show that there is a machine corresponding to some language, will be simplified considerably. The next example illustrates how this might happen.

Example 5.4. Look at Fig. 5-4a and see if you can describe (using a regular expression or any other way) the language recognized by the FA pictured there. If you have not read Chapter 6, in which we will formulate an algorithm for finding a regular expression equivalent to a given FA, the chances are you will have trouble, even though the FA shown is the simplest possible one (the one with the fewest possible states) recognizing this language.

   Now look at Fig. 5-4b, in which some of the arrows are labeled with Λ. If we assume that what it means for a string to be accepted by this machine is the same as for NFAs— i.e., that the string correspond to at least one path starting in the initial state and ending in an accepting state—it is perfectly obvious what the language is. There are two paths from 1 to 8, corresponding to the regular expressions a^*bab^* and b^*aaa^*; the Λ-transition from 8 back to 1 means that we may continue to iterate one or the other of these paths as often as we wish—in other words, that we may include all strings formed by concatenating one or more strings, each of which corresponds to one of these two regular expressions. Thus, one regular expression that corresponds to the language is $(a^*bab^* + b^*aaa^*)^+$. Although the number of states in Fig. 5-4b is only slightly lower than the number in Fig. 5-4a, the second diagram is much easier to understand.

If you wish, you may try to convince yourself that the machines in Figs. 5-4a and 5-4b correspond to the same language. (See Example 5.7 near the end of this chapter.) In any case, it is straightforward to give a precise definition of the generalization of NFAs illustrated by Fig. 5-4b. The only difference is that the domain of the transition function δ now contains pairs of the form (q, Λ) as well as those of the form (q, a).

Definition 5.4. A nondeterministic finite automaton with Λ-transitions (abbreviated NFA-Λ) is a 5-tuple $(Q, \Sigma, q_0, \delta, A)$, where Q and Σ are nonempty finite sets, $q_0 \in Q, A \subseteq Q$, and

$$\delta : Q \times (\Sigma \cup \{\Lambda\}) \rightarrow 2^Q$$

As before, we need to define an extended function δ^* in order to give a precise definition of acceptance of a string by an NFA-Λ. The idea is the same: we want $\delta^*(q, x)$ to be the set of all states in which the NFA-Λ can legally end up as a result of starting in state q and processing the symbols in x. However, there is now a slight complication, since "processing the symbols in x" allows for the possibility of Λ-transitions interspersed among ordinary transitions. To illustrate: if $x = ab$, and the path in Fig. 5-5 leads from q_0 to an accepting state, then we wish to say that x is accepted, since $a\Lambda\Lambda b\Lambda = x$.

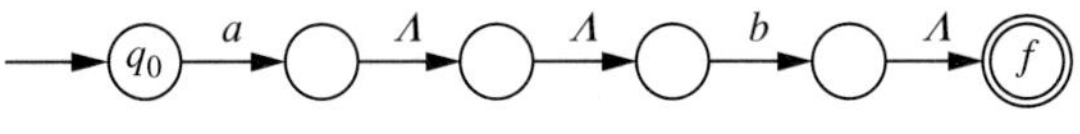

FIGURE 5-5

Just as we did for NFAs, we will begin with a nonrecursive definition that captures in a straightforward way, if not an especially elegant one, the intuitive idea. It is an obvious adaptation of Definition 5.2.

Definition 5.5   (Nonrecursive definition of δ^* for an NFA-Λ). Let $M = (Q, \Sigma, q_0, \delta, A)$ be an NFA-Λ. If $x = a_1 \ldots a_n \in \Sigma^*$ and $p, q \in Q$, we say M moves from state p to state q by a sequence of transitions corresponding to x if there are an integer $m \geq n$, a sequence $b_1, b_2, \ldots, b_m \in \Sigma \cup \{\Lambda\}$ satisfying $b_1 \ldots b_m = x$, and a sequence of states $p = p_0, p_1, \ldots, p_m = q$ so that for each i with $1 \leq i \leq m$, $p_i \in \delta(p_{i-1}, b_i)$.
   For $x \in \Sigma^*$ and $p \in Q$,

$$\delta^*(p, x) = \{q \in Q | \text{there is a sequence of transitions}$$

$$\text{corresponding to } x \text{ by which } M \text{ moves from } p \text{ to } q\}$$

Coming up with a reasonable recursive formulation is a little harder this time. The recursive part of the definition will still involve an extra alphabet symbol, but if we have the set S of states that M may be in before that symbol is processed, we obtain the new set by allowing all possible transitions from elements of S on that symbol, as well as subsequent Λ-transitions. This suggests that we also need to modify the basis part of the recursive definition in Definition 5.2a: $\delta^*(q, \Lambda)$ will be the set containing not only q, but any other states that the NFA-Λ can reach from q by using Λ-transitions. Both these modifications can be described in terms of the Λ-*closure* of a set S of states: the set of all states that can be reached by starting at an element of S and using only Λ-transitions. This is defined recursively.

Definition 5.6. Let $M = (Q, \Sigma, q_0, \delta, A)$ be an NFA-Λ. For a subset S of Q, the Λ-closure of S is the subset $\Lambda(S) \subseteq Q$ defined recursively as follows:

1. Every element of S is an element of $\Lambda(S)$;
2. For any $q \in \Lambda(S)$, every element of $\delta(q, \Lambda)$ is an element of $\Lambda(S)$; and
3. No elements of Q are in $\Lambda(S)$ unless they can be obtained using rules 1 and 2.

To repeat, what is being defined here is simply the set of states that can be reached from elements of S using nothing but Λ-transitions. It should be clear from this verbal description what set that is, but perhaps it is worthwhile to translate the recursive definition into an algorithm for calculating $\Lambda(S)$.

Algorithm to calculate $\Lambda(S)$: Start with $T = S$; at each step, add to T the union of all the sets $\delta(q, \Lambda)$ for $q \in T$; stop when this step doesn't change T; $\Lambda(S)$ is the final value of T.

For example, if we take S to be $\{4\}$ in the NFA-Λ pictured in Fig. 5-4b, we obtain $\{4, 8\}$ after the first step, $\{4, 8, 1\}$ after the second, $\{4, 8, 1, 2, 5\}$ after the third, and the same after the fourth. $\Lambda(\{4\})$ is therefore $\{4, 8, 1, 2, 5\}$.

It should now be easy enough to understand the recursive formulation of the definition of δ^* in an NFA-Λ, given Definition 5.2a and the comments after the nonrecursive definition.

Definition 5.5a   (Recursive definition of δ^* for an NFA-Λ). Let $M = (Q, \Sigma, q_0, \delta, A)$ be an NFA-Λ. The extended transition function $\delta^* : Q \times \Sigma^* \to 2^Q$ is defined as follows:

1. For any $q \in Q$, $\delta^*(q, \Lambda) = \Lambda(\{q\})$,
2. For any $q \in Q$, $y \in \Sigma^*$, and $a \in \Sigma$,

$$\delta^*(q, ya) = \Lambda(\bigcup_{p \in \delta^*(q, y)} \delta(p, a))$$

A string x is accepted by M if $\delta^*(q_0, x) \cap A \neq \varnothing$. The language recognized by M is $L(M) = \{x \in \Sigma^* | x \text{ is accepted by } M\}$.

Example 5.5. Let's continue to use the NFA-Λ pictured in Fig. 5.4b to illustrate how δ^* might be calculated. It is clear from the picture that the string aba should be accepted; let's calculate $\delta^*(q_0, aba) = \delta^*(1, aba)$ and see if the definition gives the same result.
We could start from the top and work down:

$$\delta^*(1, aba) = \Lambda\left(\bigcup_{p\in\delta^*(1,ab)} \delta(p, a)\right)$$

$$= \Lambda\left(\bigcup_{p\in\Lambda(\ldots)} \delta(p, a)\right)$$

$$= \cdots$$

but at this point we begin to suspect it might be easier to start from the bottom (i.e., the left) and work up, calculating $\delta^*(1, \Lambda)$, then $\delta^*(1, a)$, then $\delta^*(1, ab)$, and finally $\delta^*(1, aba)$.

$$\delta^*(1, \Lambda) = \Lambda(\{1\})$$
$$= \{1, 2, 5\}$$

$$\delta^*(1, a) = \Lambda\left(\bigcup_{p\in\delta^*(1,\Lambda)} \delta(p, a)\right)$$
$$= \Lambda(\delta(1, a) \cup \delta(2, a) \cup \delta(5, a))$$
$$= \Lambda(\varnothing \cup \{2\} \cup \{6\})$$
$$= \Lambda(\{2, 6\})$$
$$= \{2, 6\}$$

$$\delta^*(1, ab) = \Lambda\left(\bigcup_{p\in\delta^*(1,a)} \delta(p, b)\right)$$
$$= \Lambda(\delta(2, b) \cup \delta(6, b))$$
$$= \Lambda(\{3\})$$
$$= \{3\}$$

$$\delta^*(1, aba) = \Lambda\left(\bigcup_{p\in\delta^*(1,ab)} \delta(p, a)\right)$$
$$= \Lambda(\delta(3, a))$$
$$= \Lambda(\{4\})$$
$$= \{4, 8, 1, 2, 5\}$$

Since $\delta^*(1, aba) \cap A \neq \varnothing$, aba is indeed accepted.

This is not intended to convince you that going through these calculations is necessary to decide whether a string is accepted, in an example as simple as this one—only that going through the calculations is feasible and yields results that correspond to your intuition. If you were looking at Fig. 5-4b, you would no doubt argue along these lines instead: The string $\Lambda aba\Lambda$ is the same as aba; the picture contains this sequence of transitions, beginning in state 1 and ending in state 8:

$$1 \xrightarrow{\Lambda} 2 \xrightarrow{a} 2 \xrightarrow{b} 3 \xrightarrow{a} 4 \xrightarrow{\Lambda} 8$$

It follows that aba is accepted.

5.3   THE EQUIVALENCE OF FAs, NFAs, AND NFA-Λs

We began our discussion of NFAs by thinking of them as obtained from FAs by relaxing the rules. Strictly speaking, an FA is not quite an NFA, since the transition function is in one case a function from $Q \times \Sigma$ to Q and in the other a function from $Q \times \Sigma$ to 2^Q. However, a function from $Q \times \Sigma$ to Q can in an obvious way be identified with a function from $Q \times \Sigma$ to 2^Q whose values are all sets with one element, so it is natural to think of an FA as a special type of NFA. Of course, in order to say this, we must be sure that the two slightly different definitions of a string being accepted will yield the same answer when applied to any particular string. You should convince yourself that this is the case.

Similarly, an NFA can be thought of as a special type of NFA-Λ, one in which, for each $q \in Q$, $\delta(q, \Lambda) = \varnothing$ (i.e., one in which there are no Λ-transitions). Again, we should be a little careful. If we start with an NFA, we have a definition in terms of δ^* of a string being accepted. When we view the NFA as an NFA-Λ, we have another definition of acceptance. In both cases, x is accepted if $\delta^*(q_0, x) \cap A \neq \varnothing$, but the extended transition function δ^* is defined differently in these two cases. That the two definitions agree for each string x follows from the fact that when we view an NFA as an NFA-Λ, $\Lambda(S) = S$ for every $S \subseteq Q$, so that the two functions δ^* turn out to be the same.

When we introduced these two generalizations of FAs, we did so with the claim that they recognized exactly the same languages as FAs. In other words, allowing nondeterminism doesn't enlarge the class of languages that we are able to recognize. It is clear from the last two paragraphs that any language that is recognized by an FA can be recognized by an NFA, and any language that is recognized by an NFA can be recognized by an NFA-Λ. It is time to complete the loop by showing that any language that is recognized by an NFA-Λ can be recognized by an FA.

Theorem 5.1. Let $L \subseteq \Sigma^*$, and suppose L is recognized by the NFA-Λ $M = (Q, \Sigma, q_0, \delta, A)$. There is an FA $M_2 = (Q_2, \Sigma, q_2, \delta_2, A_2)$ recognizing L.

Proof. The proof has two main parts: first, to find an NFA M_1 (without Λ-transitions) recognizing L; and second, to find an FA that is equivalent to this NFA. Because of their length, the two parts are further subdivided into several steps.

   PART 1. We shall find an NFA $M_1 = (Q_1, \Sigma, q_1, \delta_1, A_1)$ recognizing L.

(a) Definition of M_1 (Eliminating the Λ-transitions).
   We may let $Q_1 = Q$ and $q_1 = q_0$. The problem is simply to define the transition function δ_1 so that, if in the machine M we can get from a state p to a state q using certain symbols together with Λ-transitions, then in M_1 we can get from p to q using only those symbols without the Λ-transitions. If in the machine M the initial state q_0 is not an accepting state but it is possible to get from q_0 to an accepting state using only Λ-transitions, then no matter how we define the transition function in M_1, the null string will still not be accepted, since by definition $\delta_1^*(q_0, \Lambda)$ contains no states except q_0; in this case we will also need to relabel q_0 as an accepting state in M_1.

Essentially, we have the solution already, as a result of defining the function δ^* for the NFA-Λ M. For any $q \in Q$ and $a \in \Sigma$, define

$$\delta_1(q, a) = \delta^*(q, a)$$

Let's pause long enough to make sure we understand the significance of this. According to Definition 5.5a, we have

$$\delta^*(q, a) = \delta^*(q, \Lambda a)$$

$$= \Lambda\left(\bigcup_{p \in \delta^*(q,\Lambda)} \delta(p, a)\right)$$

$$= \Lambda\left(\bigcup_{p \in \Lambda(\{q\})} \delta(p, a)\right)$$

The best way to interpret this is one step at a time. $\bigcup_{p \in \Lambda(\{q\})} \delta(p, a)$ is the set of states that can be reached from q, using the input symbol a but possibly also Λ-transitions beforehand. $\Lambda(\bigcup_{p \in \delta^*(q,\Lambda)} \delta(p, a)\ )$ is the set of states that can be reached from q, using the input symbol a but allowing Λ-transitions both before and after.

What we have accomplished so far is to define δ_1 so that if M can move from p to q using the input a together with Λ-transitions, M_1 can move from p to q using the input a alone.

Finally, as we mentioned before, it may be necessary to make q_0 an accepting state in M_1; let

$$A_1 = \begin{cases} A \cup \{q_0\} & \text{if } \Lambda(\{q_0\}) \cap A \neq \varnothing \text{ in } M \\ A & \text{otherwise} \end{cases}$$

If $x \in \Sigma^*$, $\delta_1^*(q, x)$ is the set of states M_1 can reach, starting from q, using the symbols of x. $\delta(q, x)$ is the set of states M can reach, starting from q, using the symbols of x together with Λ's. In order to complete the proof that M_1 recognizes the same language as M, we need to show that these sets are the same, at least for every x with $|x| \geq 1$. ($\delta_1^*(q, \Lambda)$ and $\delta^*(q, \Lambda)$ may be different, and this is the reason for defining A_1 as we did.) That they are equal is not surprising, since that was really the point of our definition of δ_1; in spite of the the rather involved definitions of δ^* and δ_1^*, the proof is not too bad.

(b) We show that if $|x| \geq 1$ and $q \in Q$, then $\delta_1^*(q, x) = \delta^*(q, x)$.
The proof is by mathematical induction on $|x|$. The basis step is easy: for $|x| = 1$, we showed right after Definition 5.2 that $\delta_1^*(q, x) = \delta_1(q, x)$, and $\delta_1(q, x)$ is defined to be $\delta^*(q, x)$.

In the induction step, the induction hypothesis is that K is an integer at least 1, and that for any $q \in Q$ and $y \in \Sigma^*$ with $|y| = K$, $\delta_1^*(q, y) = \delta^*(q, y)$. We wish to show that if $q \in Q$ and $|x| = K + 1$, then $\delta_1^*(q, x) = \delta^*(q, x)$. But if $|x| = K + 1$, we may write $x = ya$, where $|y| = K$ and $a \in \Sigma$. Then

$$\delta_1^*(q, x) = \delta_1^*(q, ya)$$

$$= \bigcup_{p \in \delta_1^*(q,y)} \delta_1(p, a) \text{ (by Definition 5.2)}$$

$$= \bigcup_{p \in \delta^*(q,y)} \delta_1(p, a) \text{ (by the inductive hypothesis)}$$

$$= \bigcup_{p \in \delta^*(q,y)} \delta^*(p, a) \text{ (by definition of } \delta_1)$$

We are hoping to show that this set is $\delta^*(q, ya)$. What we now notice is that the Λ-closure of this set is precisely the definition of $\delta^*(q, ya)$. But each of the sets $\delta^*(p, a)$ is itself a Λ-closure, by definition of δ^*, and it follows easily that the union is also. (See Exercise 5.6.) In other words, this set is equal to its Λ-closure, and therefore equal to $\delta^*(q, ya)$. This completes the induction.

(c) We show that M_1 recognizes L.

Since M recognizes L, we know that a string x is in L if and only if $\delta^*(q_0, x) \cap A \neq \emptyset$; on the other hand, x is accepted by M_1 if and only if $\delta_1^*(q_0, x) \cap A_1 \neq \emptyset$.

First consider the case when $\Lambda(\{q_0\}) \cap A = \emptyset$ in M. A_1 is defined to be A. If $|x| \geq 1$, we have shown that $\delta^*(q_0, x) = \delta_1^*(q_0, x)$, and so x is in L if and only if x is accepted by M_1. But if $x = \Lambda$, x is not accepted by either M or M_1 in this case; it follows that M_1 recognizes L.

In the other case, when $\Lambda(\{q_0\}) \cap A \neq \emptyset$, then $A_1 = A \cup \{q_0\}$. Λ is accepted by both M and M_1. If $|x| \geq 1$, $\delta^*(q_0, x) = \delta_1^*(q_0, x)$. Either this set contains an element of A (in which case M and M_1 both accept x), or this set contains neither q_0 nor any elements of A (in which case M and M_1 both reject x). It is impossible for the set to contain q_0 and no elements of A: if $q_0 \in \delta^*(q_0, x)$, then since $\delta^*(q_0, x)$ is the Λ-closure of another set (by definition), $\delta^*(q_0, x)$ contains $\Lambda(\{q_0\})$ and thus contains an element of A. It follows that M and M_1 accept exactly the same strings.

PART 2. We show that for any NFA $M_1 = (Q_1, \Sigma, q_1, \delta_1, A_1)$ recognizing L, there is an FA $M_2 = (Q_2, \Sigma, q_2, \delta_2, A_2)$ recognizing L.

(a) Definition of M_2.

Here the feature that we are trying to eliminate is nondeterminism. States in M_2 must be defined so that for each combination of state and input symbol, exactly one state results. We use what looks like a trick but in fact is already partly suggested by the definition of NFA. The transition function δ_1 takes a pair (q, a) to a set of elements of Q_1. Note the singular: we may think of the function as taking (q, a) to *several elements* of Q_1 or to *a set* of elements of Q_1. This suggests that the nondeterminism is only apparent—that it arises from our notion of what a state is. If we say that a state is one of the elements of the original set Q_1, we are forced to interpret the machine as making arbitrary choices. Suppose instead that we call a state a subset of Q_1. Let s be such a subset. For any element p of s in which M_1 begins, there is a set $\delta_1(p, a)$ of (possibly several) elements of Q_1 to which M_1 may go on input a; but for the single subset s of elements of Q_1 in which M_1 starts, there is a single subset of elements of Q_1 in which M_1 may end up: namely, the union of the sets $\delta_1(p, a)$ for all the elements $p \in s$. To each state-input pair, there corresponds one and only one state. Moreover, the machine obtained this way clearly simulates in a natural way the action of the original machine, provided that we define the initial and final states correctly. Thus, we have eliminated the nondeterminism by what we might call the *subset construction*: states in Q_2 are subsets of Q_1.

This discussion should help you to understand the following definition of $M_2 = (Q_2, \Sigma, q_2, \delta_2, A_2)$.

$$Q_2 = \text{the set of subsets of } Q_1$$

$$q_2 = \{q_1\}$$

$$\delta_2(q, a) = \bigcup_{p \in q} \delta_1(p, a) \text{ for } q \in Q_2 \text{ and } a \in \Sigma$$

$$A_2 = \{q \in Q_2 | q \cap A_1 \neq \varnothing\}$$

The last definition is the correct one because what it means for a string to be accepted in M_1 is that, starting in q_1, the set of states (i.e., elements of Q_1) that M_1 might end up in should contain an element of A_1.

(b) We show that M_2 recognizes L.
This will follow from the formula

$$\delta_2^*(q_2, x) = \delta_1^*(q_1, x) \text{ (for every } x)$$

which we now prove using mathematical induction on $|x|$. Since M_2 is an FA, $\delta_2^*(q_2, x)$ is defined in Definition 4.2. δ_1^* is defined in Definition 5.2a above.
If $|x| = 0$,

$$\delta_2^*(q_2, x) = \delta_2^*(q_2, \Lambda)$$

$$= q_2 \text{ (by definition of } \delta_2^*)$$

$$= \{q_1\} \text{ (by definition of } q_2)$$

$$= \delta_1^*(q_1, \Lambda) \text{ (by definition of } \delta_1^*)$$

$$= \delta_1^*(q_1, x)$$

The induction hypothesis is that $K \geq 0$ and that for any y with $|y| = K$, $\delta_2^*(q_2, y) = \delta_1^*(q_1, y)$. We wish to show that if $|x| = K + 1$, then $\delta_2^*(q_2, x) = \delta_1^*(q_1, x)$. For such an x, we write $x = ya$, where $|y| = K$. Then

$$\delta_2^*(q_2, x) = \delta_2^*(q_2, ya)$$

$$= \delta_2(\delta_2^*(q_2, y), a) \text{ (by definition of } \delta_2^*)$$

$$= \delta_2(\delta_1^*(q_1, y), a) \text{ (by the induction hypothesis)}$$

$$= \bigcup_{p \in \delta_1^*(q_1, y)} \delta_1(p, a) \text{ (by definition of } \delta_2)$$

$$= \delta_1^*(q_1, ya) \text{ (by Definition 5.2a)}$$

$$= \delta_1^*(q_1, x)$$

That M_1 and M_2 recognize the same language is now easy to see. A string x is accepted by M_2 if and only if $\delta_2^*(q_2, x) \in A_2$; but using the fact we have just established, as well as the definition of A_2, we see that x is accepted by M_2 if and only if $\delta_1^*(q_1, x) \cap A_1 \neq \varnothing$. In other words, x is accepted by M_2 if and only if x is accepted by M_1.

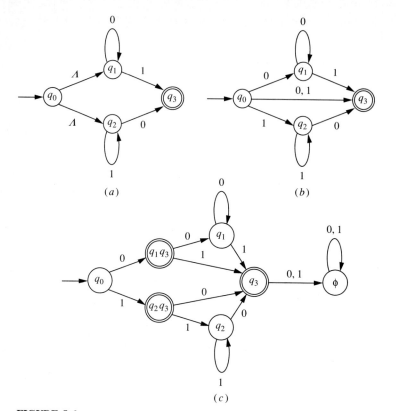

FIGURE 5-6
Obtaining an FA from an NFA-Λ.

5.4 ALGORITHMS AND EXAMPLES

It is important to realize that, at this point, we have not only a theorem but an algorithm. In fact, we have two algorithms: one that allows us to find an NFA equivalent to a given NFA-Λ and one that allows us to find an FA equivalent to a given NFA. Fortunately, although some of the details in the proof were difficult, the algorithms themselves are easy to apply, as the next example demonstrates.

Example 5.6. Let $M = (Q, \Sigma, q_0, \delta, A)$ be the NFA-Λ pictured in Fig. 5-6a. Fig. 5-6b shows an NFA $M_1 = (Q_1, \Sigma, q_0, \delta_1, A_1)$ equivalent to it, and Fig. 5-6c shows the resulting FA $M_2 = (Q_2, \Sigma, \{q_0\}, \delta_2, A_2)$. Let us look at some of the steps involved in obtaining these.

Suppose we wish to find $\delta_1(q_0, 0)$. By definition,

$$\delta_1(q_0, 0) = \delta^*(q_0, 0) = \Lambda\left(\bigcup_{p \in \Lambda(\{q_0\})} \delta(p, 0)\right)$$

In an involved example, we might feel more comfortable carrying out each step literally: calculating $\Lambda(\{q_0\})$, finding $\delta(p, 0)$ for each p in this set, taking the union of the $\delta(p, 0)$s, and calculating the Λ-closure of the result. In an example this simple, we can easily see that from q_0 with input 0, M can move to state q_1 (using a Λ-transition to q_1 first) or to state q_3 (first to q_2 with Λ, then from there to q_3 with 0). There are no Λ-transitions from q_1 or q_3, so $\delta_1(q_0, 0) = \{q_1, q_3\}$. Similarly, $\delta_1(q_0, 1) = \{q_2, q_3\}$. The table shows the remaining values of δ_1.

q	$\delta_1(q, 0)$	$\delta_1(q, 1)$
q_0	$\{q_1, q_3\}$	$\{q_2, q_3\}$
q_1	$\{q_1\}$	$\{q_3\}$
q_2	$\{q_3\}$	$\{q_2\}$
q_3	$\varnothing$	$\varnothing$

Finally, since $\Lambda(\{q_0\})$ does not contain q_3, $A_1 = A = \{q_3\}$. Thus the diagram in Fig. 5-6*b*.

Now we apply the second algorithm, the subset construction, to obtain an FA from this NFA. It is often helpful in this step to start by constructing a table such as the preceding one.

Perhaps the first step should be to say why the FA shown in Fig. 5-6*c* has only seven states and not sixteen, the number of subsets of $\{q_0, q_1, q_2, q_3\}$. We have seen this sort of thing before, in Section 4.5. Rather than start by drawing all sixteen states, we draw a particular state only at the point when it's needed—i.e., only when a sequence of transitions allows M_2 to enter it. In this way, the resulting diagram contains only those states that are reachable from the initial state.

From $\{q_0\}$, the two states that can be reached with one symbol are $\{q_1, q_3\}$ and $\{q_2, q_3\}$. If we now want $\delta_2(\{q_1, q_3\}, 0)$, we have only to consult the table:

$$\delta_2(\{q_1, q_3\}, 0) = \delta_1(q_1, 0) \cup \delta_1(q_3, 0) = \{q_1\} \cup \varnothing = \{q_1\}$$

Since this set has not appeared yet, we add it as a new state. If we continue in this way, we eventually reach a point where for each state q we have drawn so far, $\delta_2(q, 0)$ and $\delta_2(q, 1)$ are both already drawn, at which point we have all the reachable states.

Notice that $\delta_2(\{q_3\}, 0) = \delta_2(\{q_3\}, 1) = \varnothing$. In a diagram like that in Fig. 5-4*b*, this would mean that no arrows originated at state q_3, but now it means that we need the state $\varnothing$ to complete the diagram. Obviously, whenever $\varnothing$ appears as a state in this type of construction, $\delta_2(\varnothing, a) = \varnothing$ for every $a \in \Sigma$.

Example 5.7. For our last, somewhat more ambitious example, we return once more to the NFA-Λ pictured in Fig. 5-4*b*. If the NFA-Λ is $M = (Q, \Sigma, 1, \delta, A)$, then again we may without difficulty construct the table that shows the values of the transition function δ_1 in the NFA M_1. For completeness, we include the values of δ in tabular form, as well as the Λ-closure of each state of M.

You may wish to draw the NFA that we obtain, using the first algorithm. As you can see by examining the last two columns of the table, a picture would require quite a few arrows (36, in fact, two of which would have two labels), and would therefore be of dubious value in displaying the essential behavior of the NFA. Instead, let us go directly to the FA M_2. The second table shows the states of M_2 (more or less in the order of their appearance) and the transitions. The Roman numerals are introduced to make the picture less cumbersome.

The resulting FA is shown in Fig. 5-7. This is not exactly the FA shown in Fig. 5-4*a*. That one has one fewer state; it is easy to see from Fig. 5-7 that states

q	$\delta(q, a)$	$\delta(q, b)$	$\delta(q, \Lambda)$	$\Lambda(\{q\})$	$\delta(q, a)$	$\delta(q, b)$
1	$\varnothing$	$\varnothing$	$\{2, 5\}$	$\{1, 2, 5\}$	$\{2, 6\}$	$\{3, 5\}$
2	$\{2\}$	$\{3\}$	$\varnothing$	$\{2\}$	$\{2\}$	$\{3\}$
3	$\{4\}$	$\varnothing$	$\varnothing$	$\{3\}$	$\{1, 2, 4, 5, 8\}$	$\varnothing$
4	$\varnothing$	$\{4\}$	$\{8\}$	$\{1, 2, 4, 5, 8\}$	$\{2, 6\}$	$\{1, 2, 3, 4, 5, 8\}$
5	$\{6\}$	$\{5\}$	$\varnothing$	$\{5\}$	$\{6\}$	$\{5\}$
6	$\{7\}$	$\varnothing$	$\varnothing$	$\{6\}$	$\{1, 2, 5, 7, 8\}$	$\varnothing$
7	$\{7\}$	$\varnothing$	$\{8\}$	$\{1, 2, 5, 7, 8\}$	$\{1, 2, 5, 6, 7, 8\}$	$\{3, 5\}$
8	$\varnothing$	$\varnothing$	$\{1\}$	$\{1, 2, 5, 8\}$	$\{2, 6\}$	$\{3, 5\}$

	q	$\delta_2(q, a)$		$\delta_2(q, b)$	
I	$\{1\}$	$\{2, 6\}$	(II)	$\{3, 5\}$	(III)
II	$\{2, 6\}$	$\{1, 2, 5, 7, 8\}$	(IV)	$\{3\}$	(V)
III	$\{3, 5\}$	$\{1, 2, 4, 5, 6, 8\}$	(VI)	$\{5\}$	(VII)
IV	$\{1, 2, 5, 7, 8\}$	$\{1, 2, 5, 6, 7, 8\}$	(VIII)	$\{3, 5\}$	(III)
V	$\{3\}$	$\{1, 2, 4, 5, 8\}$	(IX)	$\varnothing$	(X)
VI	$\{1, 2, 4, 5, 6, 8\}$	$\{1, 2, 5, 6, 7, 8\}$	(VIII)	$\{1, 2, 3, 4, 5, 8\}$	(XI)
VII	$\{5\}$	$\{6\}$	(XII)	$\{5\}$	(VII)
VIII	$\{1, 2, 5, 6, 7, 8\}$	$\{1, 2, 5, 6, 7, 8\}$	(VIII)	$\{3, 5\}$	(III)
IX	$\{1, 2, 4, 5, 8\}$	$\{2, 6\}$	(II)	$\{1, 2, 3, 4, 5, 8\}$	(XI)
X	$\varnothing$	$\varnothing$	(X)	$\varnothing$	(X)
XI	$\{1, 2, 3, 4, 5, 8\}$	$\{1, 2, 4, 5, 6, 8\}$	(VI)	$\{1, 2, 3, 4, 5, 8\}$	(XI)
XII	$\{6\}$	$\{1, 2, 5, 7, 8\}$	(IV)	$\varnothing$	(X)

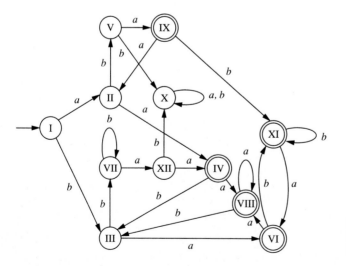

FIGURE 5-7
FA obtained from the NFA-Λ in Figure 5.4b.

IV and VIII could be combined into one. That the FA in Fig. 5-4a is indeed the one with the fewest states, as we claimed in Example 5.4, is not so obvious, but this fact can easily be obtained by the technique described in Chapter 7.

EXERCISES

5.1. In Fig. 5-8 is a transition diagram of an NFA-Λ. For each string indicated below, say whether the NFA-Λ accepts it.

    (*a*) *aba*

    (*b*) *abab*

    (*c*) *aaabbb*

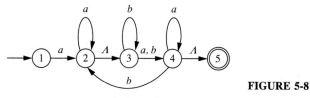

FIGURE 5-8

5.2. Find a regular expression corresponding to the language recognized by the NFA-Λ pictured in Fig. 5-8. You should be able to do it by inspection, without applying any complicated algorithms.

5.3. In each part of Fig. 5-9, two NFA-Λs are illustrated. Decide whether the two accept the same language. If not, find a string that is accepted by one but not by the other.

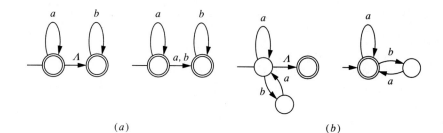

(*a*)   (*b*)

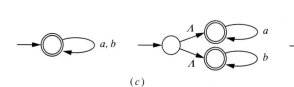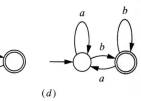

(*c*)   (*d*)

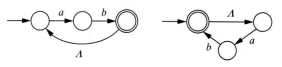

(*e*)

FIGURE 5-9

q	$\delta(q, a)$	$\delta(q, b)$	$\delta(q, \Lambda)$
1	$\varnothing$	$\varnothing$	$\{2\}$
2	$\{3\}$	$\varnothing$	$\{5\}$
3	$\varnothing$	$\{4\}$	$\varnothing$
4	$\{4\}$	$\varnothing$	$\{1\}$
5	$\varnothing$	$\{6, 7\}$	$\varnothing$
6	$\{5\}$	$\varnothing$	$\varnothing$
7	$\varnothing$	$\varnothing$	$\{1\}$

5.4. A transition table is given for an NFA-Λ with the seven states numbered 1–7. Find:

(a) $\Lambda(\{2, 3\})$

(b) $\Lambda(\{1\})$

(c) $\Lambda(\{3, 4\})$

(d) $\delta^*(1, ba)$

(e) $\delta^*(1, ab)$

(f) $\delta^*(1, ababa)$

5.5. Let $M = (Q, \Sigma, q_0, \delta, A)$ be an NFA-Λ. Let $S, T \subseteq Q$.

(a) Show that $\Lambda(S) = \cup_{p \in S} \Lambda(\{p\})$.

(b) Show that $\Lambda(\Lambda(S)) = \Lambda(S)$.

(c) Show that $\Lambda(S \cup T) = \Lambda(S) \cup \Lambda(T)$.

(d) Draw a transition diagram illustrating the fact that $\Lambda(S \cap T)$ and $\Lambda(S) \cap \Lambda(T)$ are not always the same. Which is always a subset of the other?

(e) Draw a transition diagram illustrating the fact that $\Lambda(S')$ and $\Lambda(S)'$ are not always the same. Which is always a subset of the other? Under what circumstances are they equal?

5.6. Let M be as in Exercise 5.5. A set $S \subseteq Q$ is called Λ-*closed* if $\Lambda(S) = S$. Show that the union of two Λ-closed sets is Λ-closed, and that the intersection of two Λ-closed sets is Λ-closed.

5.7. Let $M = (Q, \Sigma, q, \delta, A)$ be an NFA.

(a) Show that for every $x, y \in \Sigma^*$ and every $q \in Q$,

$$\delta^*(q, xy) = \bigcup_{p \in \delta^*(q, x)} \delta^*(p, y)$$

(Refer to Exercise 4.5.)

(b) Show that this formula is still true if M is an NFA-Λ.

(Both parts of this exercise get rather messy, but it is primarily a question of using the definitions of δ^* and $\Lambda(S)$.)

5.8. Conceivably, an NFA-Λ might allow Λ-transitions from some states to themselves. Is it possible that the language recognized by an NFA-Λ might be different if all such transitions were deleted? Why?

5.9. Suppose $M = (Q, \Sigma, q_0, \delta, A)$ is an NFA-Λ recognizing a language L. Let M_1 be the NFA-Λ obtained from M by adding Λ-transitions from each element of A to q_0. What language does M_1 recognize?

5.10. Let $M = (Q, \Sigma, q_0, \delta, A)$ be an NFA-Λ recognizing a language L.

(a) How could you modify M to obtain an NFA-Λ recognizing L in which there are no transitions to the initial state?

(b) How could you modify M to obtain an NFA-Λ recognizing L in which there is only one accepting state and there are no transitions from that state?

5.11. Let $M = (Q, \Sigma, q_0, \delta, A)$ be an NFA-Λ recognizing a language L; assume that there are no transitions to q_0, that A has only one element q_f, and that there are no transitions from q_f (see Exercise 5.10).

(a) Let M_1 be obtained from M by adding Λ-transitions from q_0 to every state that is reachable from q_0 in M. What language does M_1 accept?

(b) Let M_2 be obtained from M by adding Λ-transitions to q_f from every state from which q_f is reachable in M. What language is accepted by M_2?

(c) Let M_3 be obtained from M by adding both the Λ-transitions in (a) and those in (b). What language is accepted by M_3?

(d) Let M_4 be obtained from M by adding Λ-transitions from p to q for every p and q for which q is reachable from p in M. What language is accepted by M_4?

5.12. Suppose M is an NFA-Λ with exactly one accepting state q_f that recognizes the language $L \subseteq \{a, b\}^*$. We wish to modify M so that it recognizes $L\{a\}^*$.

(a) Draw a transition diagram illustrating the fact that adding a single a-transition from q_f to itself does not always accomplish this.

(b) Describe the way you *would* modify M to accomplish this.

5.13. Suppose M is an NFA-Λ recognizing $L \subseteq \Sigma^*$. Describe how you would modify M to obtain an NFA-Λ recognizing $REV(L) = \{REV(x) | x \in L\}$.

5.14. (Refer to Exercise 4.16.) Let $M = (Q, \Sigma, q_0, \delta, A)$ be an FA.

(a) Show that if every state other than q_0 from which no element of A can be reached is deleted, then what remains is an NFA recognizing the same language.

(b) Show that if all states not reachable from q_0 are deleted and all states other than q_0 from which no element of A can be reached are deleted, what remains is an NFA recognizing the same language.

5.15. For each of these regular expressions over $\{a, b\}$, draw an NFA-Λ recognizing the corresponding language.

(a) $(a + b)^* ababb(a + b)^*$

(b) $(a + b)^*(abb + abab)(a + b)^*$

(c) $(a + b)(ab)^*(baa)^*$

(d) $(a + b)^* aab(a + b)^3$

(e) $aba^* + a(ab + ba)^* bb$

5.16. For each of the NFA-Λs shown in Fig. 5-10, find a regular expression corresponding to the language it recognizes.

5.17. In each part of Fig. 5-11 is pictured an NFA-Λ $M = (Q, \Sigma, q_0, \delta, A)$. Follow the algorithm of this chapter to find an equivalent FA. Start by constructing a table that shows $\delta^*(q, a)$ and $\delta^*(q, b)$ for each $q \in Q$. Use this table to draw an NFA equivalent to M. Then apply the subset construction: determine the subsets of Q that will appear as states in the resulting FA, construct a transition table for the FA, and, finally, draw a transition diagram. (In the first three parts, M is already an NFA, so the first two steps are unnecessary.)

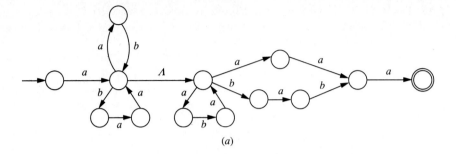

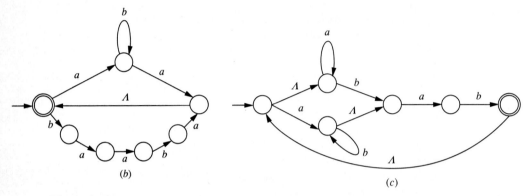

(a)

(b)

(c)

FIGURE 5-10

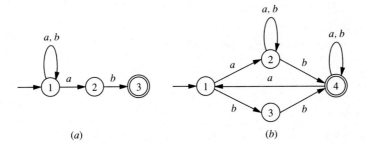

(a)

(b)

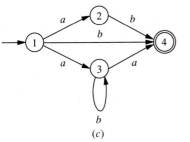

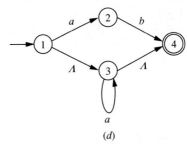

(c)

(d)

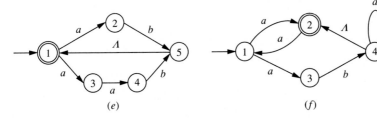

(e)

(f)

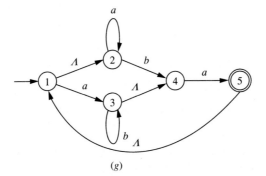

(g)

FIGURE 5-11

CHAPTER
6

KLEENE'S THEOREM

6.1 TO EACH REGULAR EXPRESSION THERE CORRESPONDS A FINITE AUTOMATON

In this chapter we fulfill the promise, made in Chapter 4, to demonstrate the equivalence of two ways of describing regular languages: using regular expressions (the way that gives the languages their name) and using finite automata. We have two statements to prove, and we give each one the status of a theorem.

Theorem 6.1 (**Kleene's Theorem, Part 1**). If R is a regular expression over the alphabet Σ, and L is the language in Σ^* corresponding to R, then there is a finite automaton M recognizing L.

Proof. Relying on the main result of the last chapter, we shall actually show that there is an NFA-Λ recognizing L. The proof is constructive—i.e., it includes an algorithm to produce the NFA-Λ. Combined with the algorithms presented in Theorem 5.1, this will yield an algorithm to take a regular expression and produce an equivalent FA.

For convenience, we restate the definition of a regular expression over Σ and the corresponding language, given originally in Chapter 3.

1. $\varnothing$ is a regular expression, corresponding to the empty language.
2. Λ is a regular expression, corresponding to the language $\{\Lambda\}$.
3. For each $a \in \Sigma$, a is a regular expression, corresponding to the language $\{a\}$.
4. For any regular expressions r and s over Σ, corresponding to the languages L_r and L_s, respectively, each of the following is a regular expression over Σ, corresponding to the language indicated.

(rs), corresponding to $L_r L_s$

$(r + s)$, corresponding to $L_r \cup L_s$

(r^*), corresponding to L_r^*

5. Only those things that can be produced using rules 1–4 are regular expressions over Σ.

The form of the definition is that certain basic regular expressions are specified, and a rule (rule 4) is given that can be applied to regular expressions to produce new regular expressions. As we saw in Chapter 2, if we use mathematical induction to establish the property of regular expressions stated in the theorem and base the induction on the number N of applications of rule 4 needed to produce the regular expression, the format of the proof will follow closely that of the definition, and it will not be necessary to mention N explicitly.

The basis step of the proof is to show that the languages corresponding to the regular expressions specified in rules 1–3 can be recognized by NFA-Λ's. The NFA-Λs that work for $\varnothing$, Λ, and $a \in \Sigma$ are shown in Figs. 6-1a, 6-1b, and 6-1c, respectively.

These are all extremely simple NFA-Λs, and it wouldn't have been much harder to give FAs in these three cases. Although the diagrams alone probably suffice, you are encouraged to describe more formally what the NFA-Λ is in each case and to prove that it recognizes the language indicated.

In the induction step, if we assume that r and s are regular expressions for which the corresponding languages can be recognized by NFA-Λs, we must show that any regular expression obtained from r and s by applying rule 4 also has this property. Again, there are three cases. Schematic diagrams intended to convey the essential idea of the construction in each case are shown in Fig. 6-2.

Case 1. Suppose $R = (rs)$. Let L_r and L_s be the languages corresponding to r and s, and let L correspond to R. Then $L = L_r L_s$. Suppose the NFA-Λs $M_r = (Q_r, \Sigma, q_r, \delta_r, A_r)$ and $M_s = (Q_s, \Sigma, q_s, \delta_s, A_s)$ recognize L_r and L_s, respectively. We may assume (by renaming states if necessary) that $Q_r \cap Q_s = \varnothing$. We wish to construct $M = (Q, \Sigma, q_0, \delta, A)$ to recognize $L_r L_s$. The idea is very simple: let the initial state of M be q_r, let the accepting states be the elements of A_s, and create Λ-transitions from every element of A_r to q_s. Strings in $L_r L_s$ will correspond to paths that begin at q_r, travel to an element of A_r, jump to q_s by a Λ-transition, and finish at an element of A_s. (Refer to Figure 6-2a; in the figure, A_r is represented as having the two elements f_r and f_r', and $A_s = \{f_s, f_s'\}$.) More formally, define M as follows:

$$Q = Q_r \cup Q_s \qquad q_0 = q_r \qquad A = A_s$$

for $q \in Q$ and $a \in \Sigma$,

$$\delta(q, a) = \begin{cases} \delta_r(q, a) & \text{if } q \in Q_r \\ \delta_s(q, a) & \text{if } q \in Q_s \end{cases}$$

for $q \in Q$,

$$\delta(q, \Lambda) = \begin{cases} \delta_r(q, \Lambda) & \text{if } q \in Q_r - A_r \\ \delta_s(q, \Lambda) & \text{if } q \in Q_s \\ \delta_r(q, \Lambda) \cup \{q_s\} & \text{if } q \in A_r \end{cases}$$

On the one hand, if $x \in L_r L_s$, then $x = x_r x_s = x_r \Lambda x_s$, where $x_r \in L_r$ and $x_s \in L_s$. In the terminology of Definition 5.5, M moves from q_0 to some state $q' \in A_r$ by a sequence of transitions corresponding to x_r; M moves from q' to q_s by a Λ-transition,

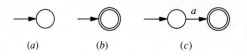

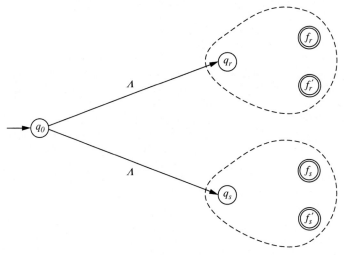

FIGURE 6-1
NFA-Λs for basic regular expressions.

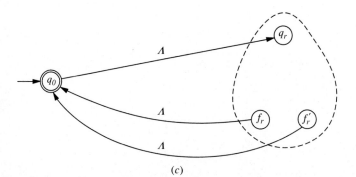

FIGURE 6-2
NFA-Λs for concatenation, union, and *.

according to the third part of the definition of $\delta(q, \Lambda)$; and M moves from q_s to an element of A by a sequence of transitions corresponding to x_s. It follows that M moves from q_0 to an element of A by a sequence of transitions corresponding to x, and thus that x is accepted by M.

On the other hand, if x is accepted by M, there is a sequence of transitions corresponding to x, beginning at q_r and ending at some element of A_s. One of them must therefore be from an element of Q_r to an element of Q_s, and the only choice, according to the definition of δ, is a Λ-transition from an element of A_r to q_s. Since $Q_r \cap Q_s = \emptyset$, all the transitions previous to this in the sequence are between elements of Q_r, and all subsequent ones are between elements of Q_s. It follows that $x = x_r \Lambda x_s = x_r x_s$, where $x_r \in L_r$ and $x_s \in L_s$.

Case 2. Suppose $R = (r + s)$. As before, the corresponding languages L_r and L_s are recognized by NFA-Λ's $M_r = (Q_r, \Sigma, q_r, \delta_r, A_r)$ and $M_s = (Q_s, \Sigma, q_s, \delta_s, A_s)$, where $Q_r \cap Q_s = \emptyset$, and $L = L_r \cup L_s$. This time construct $M = (Q, \Sigma, q_0, \delta, A)$ as follows:

Let q_0 be a new state, not in either Q_r or Q_s

$$Q = Q_r \cup Q_s \cup \{q_0\}$$

$$A = A_r \cup A_s$$

$\delta : Q \times \Sigma \to Q$ is defined as follows:

$$\delta(q_0, \Lambda) = \{q_r, q_s\}$$

$$\delta(q_0, a) = \emptyset \quad \text{for every} \quad a \in \Sigma$$

for $q \in Q_r \cup Q_s$ and $a \in \Sigma \cup \{\Lambda\}$,

$$\delta(q, a) = \begin{cases} \delta_r(q, a) & \text{if } q \in Q_r \\ \delta_s(q, a) & \text{if } q \in Q_s \end{cases}$$

Roughly speaking, M consists of both the NFA-Λs M_r and M_s, with a new initial state and Λ-transitions from it to q_r and q_s; see Fig. 6-2b. If $x \in L_r$, M moves from q_0 to q_r by a Λ-transition and from q_r to an element of A_r (therefore, an element of A) by a sequence of transitions corresponding to x. It follows that $\Lambda x = x$ is accepted by M. A similar argument works if $x \in L_s$. Conversely, if x is accepted by M, there is a sequence of transitions corresponding to x, starting at q_0 and ending either at an element of A_r or at an element of A_s. The first transition in the sequence must be a Λ-transition from q_0 to q_r or q_s, since there are no other transitions from q_0; thereafter, since $Q_r \cap Q_s = \emptyset$, either all are between elements of Q_r or all are between elements of Q_s. x must therefore be an element of $L_r \cup L_s$.

Case 3. Finally, suppose $R = (r^*)$. Let $M_r = (Q_r, \Sigma, q_r, \delta_r, A_r)$ recognize L_r, and let $L = L_r^*$. Define $M = (Q, \Sigma, q_0, \delta, A)$ as follows (see Fig. 6-2c):

Again, let q_0 be a new state, not in Q_r

$$Q = Q_r \cup \{q_0\}$$

$$A = \{q_0\}$$

for $q \in Q$ and $a \in \Sigma$,

$$\delta(q, a) = \begin{cases} \delta_r(q, a) & \text{if } q \in Q_r \\ \varnothing & \text{if } q = q_0 \end{cases}$$

for $q \in Q$,

$$\delta(q, \Lambda) = \begin{cases} \delta_r(q, \Lambda) & \text{if } q \in Q_r - A_r \\ \delta_r(q, \Lambda) \cup \{q_0\} & \text{if } q \in A_r \\ \{q_r\} & \text{if } q = q_0 \end{cases}$$

Suppose $x \in L_r^*$. If $x = \Lambda$, clearly x is accepted by M. Otherwise, for some $m \geq 1$, $x = x_1 x_2 \ldots x_m$, where each $x_i \in L_r$. M moves from q_0 to q_r by a Λ-transition; for each i, M moves from q_r to an element f_i of A_r by a sequence of transitions corresponding to x_i; and, for each i, M moves from f_i back to q_0 by a Λ-transition. It follows that $(\Lambda x_1 \Lambda)(\Lambda x_2 \Lambda) \ldots (\Lambda x_m \Lambda) = x$ is accepted by M. Conversely, if x is accepted by M, there is a sequence of transitions corresponding to x, beginning and ending at q_0. Since the only transition from q_0 is a Λ-transition to q_r, and the only transitions to q_0 are Λ-transitions from elements of A_r, it is clear that x can be decomposed in the form $x = (\Lambda x_1 \Lambda)(\Lambda x_2 \Lambda) \ldots (\Lambda x_m \Lambda)$, where, for each i, there is a sequence of transitions corresponding to x_i from q_r to an element of A_r. Therefore, $x \in L_r^* = L$.

We have shown in each of the three cases that there is an NFA-Λ recognizing L, and so the proof is complete.

It often happens that you look at a regular expression and see immediately how to construct a simple NFA-Λ, or even an FA, that recognizes the corresponding language. As always, though, relying on intuition alone increases the risk of error. Although the constructions described in Theorem 6.1 may seem tedious when every step is included, and they often don't lead directly to the simplest possible answer, they are guaranteed to produce a correct solution in even the most complicated example. The next example illustrates all three of the constructions in the theorem, as well as the fact that one can often make simplifications along the way.

Example 6.1. Let $R = (00 + 1)^*(10)^*$. We first illustrate the literal application of the algorithm, without worrying about possible simplifications. We begin with the primitive (zero-operation) regular expressions that appear in R. These are shown in Fig. 6-3a. The NFA-Λs corresponding to 00 and 10 are now constructed using concatenation and are shown in Fig. 6-3b. Next, form the NFA-Λ corresponding to $(00 + 1)$, as in Fig. 6-3c. Figs. 6-3d and 6-3e illustrate the NFA-Λs corresponding to $(00 + 1)^*$ and $(10)^*$, respectively. Finally, these are combined using concatenation, and the resulting NFA-Λ is shown in Fig. 6-3f.

In fact, it was clear at several points along the way that there were Λ-transitions and states that were not serving any useful purpose. Even without worrying about finding the simplest possible machine recognizing the language, we may simplify the answer considerably. The six parts of Fig. 6-4 parallel those of Fig. 6-3 and incorporate some of these obvious simplifications.

Although straightforward simplifications such as these are harmless enough, in a more complicated example it may not be so obvious which Λ-transitions can be done away with this way. Don't forget that Chapter 5 provides a general algorithm for converting any NFA-Λ into an FA. We have not yet dealt with the problem of how to find the

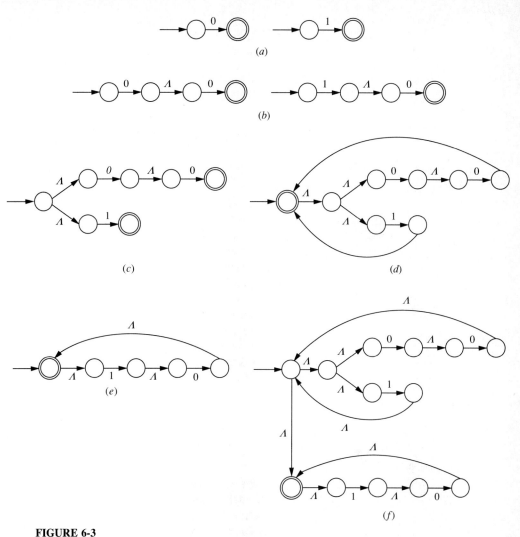

FIGURE 6-3
An NFA-Λ for $(00 + 1)^*(10)^*$.

simplest FA recognizing a regular language, but we shall consider that problem in the next chapter.

You should notice also that although it was not stated in quite this form, Theorem 6.1 contains implicitly algorithms for constructing NFA-Λs to recognize the union, concatenation, and * of languages recognized by given NFA-Λs. For example, in Examples 4.4 and 4.5, we determined that the FAs pictured in Figs. 6-5a and 6-5b recognize the languages corresponding to $(0 + 1)^*10$ and $(00)^*(11)^*$, respectively. We may apply two of the algorithms described in the proof of Theorem 6.1 (making one simplification in the second step) to obtain the NFA-Λ in Fig. 6-5c recognizing the language corresponding to

$$((0 + 1)^*10 + (00)^*(11)^*)^*$$

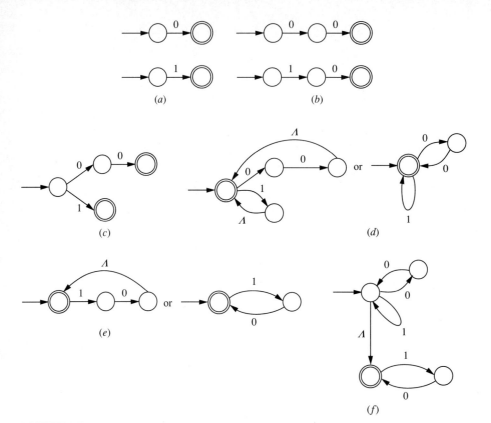

FIGURE 6-4
A simplified NFA-Λ for $(00 + 1)^*(10)^*$.

6.2   TO EACH FINITE AUTOMATON THERE CORRESPONDS A REGULAR EXPRESSION

Theorem 6.2   (Kleene's Theorem, Part 2). If $M = (Q, \Sigma, q_0, \delta, A)$ is an FA recognizing a language L, there is a regular expression over Σ corresponding to L.

Proof. Again, we are looking for an inductive proof. There are several ways one might attempt to proceed. The simplest would seem to be induction on the number of states in the FA. Although a proof based on this idea can be carried out, it entails some complications, and we try a slightly different tack.
 For elements p and q of Q, we let

$$L(p, q) = \{x \in \Sigma^* | \delta^*(p, x) = q\}$$

$L(p, q)$ is the set of strings that allow M to reach state q if it begins in state p. If we could show that each language $L(p, q)$ corresponded to a regular expression, then since the language recognized by M is the union of the languages $L(q_0, q)$ for all the elements q of A, a regular expression for L could be obtained by combining these individual regular

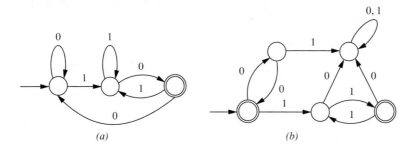

(a)   (b)

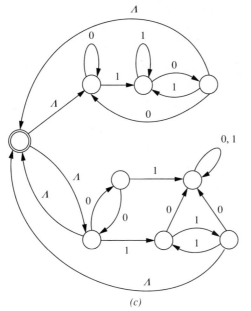

(c)

FIGURE 6-5
An NFA-Λ for $((0 + 1)^*10 + (00)^*(11)^*)^*$.

expressions using $+$. Therefore, we concentrate on finding an inductive proof that each language $L(p, q)$ is regular.

On exactly what integer shall we base the induction? One possibility is to use the number of other states through which there are paths from p to q; but the proof will go more smoothly if we involve this number indirectly, as follows.

First, to make it easier to formulate a statement $P(J)$, we assume that the elements of Q are labeled using the integers 1 through N. Next, we formalize the idea of a path *going through* a state s. If $x \in \Sigma^*$, we say x represents a path from p to q through s if we can write $x = yz$ for some y and z with $|y|, |z| > 0$, $\delta^*(p, y) = s$, and $\delta^*(s, z) = q$. Finally, for $J \geq 0$ we define the set $L(p, q, J)$ as follows:

$$L(p, q, J) = \{x \in \Sigma^* \mid x \text{ corresponds to a path from } p \text{ to } q \text{ that goes through} \\ \text{no state numbered higher than } J\}$$

Notice that $L(p, q, N) = L(p, q)$, since N is the highest-numbered state in the FA. Thus it will be sufficient to show that $L(p, q, N)$ is regular, and we do this by showing that

$L(p, q, J)$ is regular for each J. Now we are ready for the induction. Let $P(J)$ be the statement

$P(J)$: For every p and q with $1 \leq p, q \leq N$, the language $L(p, q, J)$ is regular.

We wish to show that $P(J)$ is true for all J satisfying $0 \leq J \leq N$.

For the basis step, we must show $L(p, q, 0)$ is regular. A path from p to q can go from p to q without going through any state numbered higher than 0 (i.e., without going through *any* state) only if it corresponds to a single symbol, or if $p = q$ and the path corresponds to the string Λ. Thus $L(p, q, 0)$ is a subset of $\Sigma \cup \{\Lambda\}$. Since every finite language is regular, $L(p, q, 0)$ is regular.

The induction hypothesis is that $0 \leq K \leq N - 1$ and that for every p and q with $1 \leq p, q \leq N$, the language $L(p, q, K)$ is regular. We wish to show that for every p and q with $1 \leq p, q \leq N$, $L(p, q, K + 1)$ is regular.

A string x is in $L(p, q, K + 1)$ if it represents a path from p to q that goes through no state numbered higher than $K + 1$. There are two ways this can happen: the path could bypass the state $K + 1$ altogether, in which case x is actually an element of $L(p, q, K)$, or the path could go from p to $K + 1$, possibly looping back to $K + 1$ several times, and then go from $K + 1$ to q, never going through any states numbered higher than $K + 1$. In the second case, $x = x_1 y x_2$, where

$$\delta^*(p, x_1) \quad = \quad K + 1$$

$$\delta^*(K + 1, y) \quad = \quad K + 1$$

$$\delta^*(K + 1, x_2) \quad = \quad q$$

If we include all the looping from $K + 1$ back to itself within the string y, then $x_1 \in L(p, K + 1, K)$ and $x_2 \in L(K + 1, q, K)$; this says simply that before arriving at $K + 1$ the first time, and after leaving $K + 1$ the last time, the path goes through no state numbered higher than K. Furthermore, if $y \neq \Lambda$ (i.e., if the path does loop from $K + 1$ back to $K + 1$ at least once), and each of the separate loops in the path y is represented by a string y_i, so that $y = y_1 y_2 \ldots y_I$, then each y_i is an element of $L(K + 1, K + 1, K)$, and thus $y \in L(K + 1, K + 1, K)^*$. In any case, what we have discovered is that

$$L(p, q, K + 1) = L(p, q, K) \cup L(p, K + 1, K)L(K + 1, K + 1, K)^*L(K + 1, q, K)$$

This may look terrible, but never mind. The important thing is that by the inductive hypothesis, each of the sets on the right side is regular, and the entire expression is obtained by applying the operations of union, concatenation, and * to regular languages. It follows that $L(p, q, K + 1)$ is regular.

Let us recapitulate the steps in the proof, not in the order we mentioned them, but in the order they need to be used.

1. For each pair of states p and q, and each J with $0 \leq J \leq N$, $L(p, q, J)$ is regular. This was proved by induction on J.
2. $L(p, q) = L(p, q, N)$; therefore $L(p, q)$ is regular.
3. $L = \cup_{q \in A} L(q_0, q)$; therefore L is regular.

As usual, we are interested not only in the result itself, but in the algorithm provided by the proof. The theorem tells us that there is a regular expression corresponding to a given FA—the algorithm tells us how to find it. The following example illustrates the steps involved.

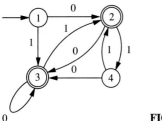

0

FIGURE 6-6

Example 6.2. Let $M = (Q, \Sigma, 1, \delta, A)$ be the FA pictured in Fig. 6-6. Let us construct for each J a table showing the languages $L(p, q, J)$ (to be precise, the corresponding regular expressions) for the various combinations of p and q. $L(p, q, 0) = \{a | \delta(p, a) = q\}$, if $p \neq q$, and $L(p, p, 0) = \{a | \delta(p, a) = p\} \cup \{\Lambda\}$. These values are shown in the first table below.

$L(p, q, 0)$ and $L(p, q, 1)$

		q		
	1	**2**	**3**	**4**
1	Λ	0	1	$\varnothing$
p **2**	$\varnothing$	Λ	0	1
3	$\varnothing$	1	$0 + \Lambda$	$\varnothing$
4	$\varnothing$	1	0	Λ

$L(p, q, 2)$

		q		
	1	**2**	**3**	**4**
1	Λ	0	$1 + 00$	01
p **2**	$\varnothing$	Λ	0	1
3	$\varnothing$	1	$0 + 10 + \Lambda$	11
4	$\varnothing$	1	$0 + 10$	$11 + \Lambda$

$L(p, q, 3)$

		q		
	1	**2**	**3**	**4**
1	Λ	$0 + (1 + 00)(0 + 10)^*1$	$(1 + 00)(0 + 10)^*$	$01 + (1 + 00)(0 + 10)^*11$
p **2**	$\varnothing$	$0(0 + 10)^*1 + \Lambda$	$0(0 + 10)^*$	$1 + 0(0 + 10)^*11$
3	$\varnothing$	$(0 + 10)^*1$	$(0 + 10)^*$	$(0 + 10)^*11$
4	$\varnothing$	$(0 + 10)^*1$	$(0 + 10)^+$	$(0 + 10)^*11 + \Lambda$

Notice that $L(p, 1, 0) = \varnothing$ for every $p \neq 1$; this is obvious from Fig. 6-6, since there are no transitions to state 1. In fact, if $p \neq 1$, $L(p, 1, J)$ will be $\varnothing$ for each J, for the same reason.

We begin to use the recursive formula for $L(p, q, N)$. For example,

$$L(1, 2, 1) = L(1, 2, 0) \cup L(1, 1, 0)L(1, 1, 0)^*L(1, 2, 0)$$
$$= \{0\} \cup \{\Lambda\}\{\Lambda\}^*\{0\}$$
$$= \{0\}$$

Again, we can save ourselves some work. $L(1, 2, 1)$ is the same as $L(1, 2, 0)$. If we think about why, we see that $L(p, q, 1) = L(p, q, 0)$ for every p and q. $L(p, q, 1)$ is the set of strings that represent paths from p to q never going through any state numbered higher than 1. But, as we've already noticed, this really means never going through any state numbered higher than 0; since there are no transitions to state 1, there are no paths through it.

Here are some of the sets $L(p, q, 2)$:

$$L(1, 2, 2) = L(1, 2, 1) \cup L(1, 2, 1)L(2, 2, 1)^*L(2, 1, 1)$$
$$= \{0\} \cup \{0\}\{\Lambda\}^*\varnothing$$
$$= \{0\}$$

$$L(1, 3, 2) = L(1, 3, 1) \cup L(1, 2, 1)L(2, 2, 1)^*L(2, 3, 1)$$
$$= \{1\} \cup \{0\}\{\Lambda\}^*\{0\}$$
$$= \{1, 00\}$$

$$L(1, 4, 2) = L(1, 4, 1) \cup L(1, 2, 1)L(2, 2, 1)^*L(2, 4, 1)$$
$$= \varnothing \cup \{0\}\{\Lambda\}^*\{1\}$$
$$= \{01\}$$

If you're careful, you can fill in some terms easily, just looking at Fig. 6-6. $L(2, 2, 2) = \{\Lambda\}$, since the only nontrivial paths from state 2 to state 2 go through states numbered higher than 2. In fact, except for single transitions, all nontrivial paths from state 2, as well as all those to state 2, go through state 3 or state 4. This means that

$$L(2, 2, 2) = L(2, 2, 0)$$
$$L(2, 3, 2) = L(2, 3, 0)$$
$$L(2, 4, 2) = L(2, 4, 0)$$
$$L(3, 2, 2) = L(3, 2, 0)$$
$$L(4, 2, 2) = L(4, 2, 0)$$

Next,

$$L(3, 3, 2) = L(3, 3, 1) \cup L(3, 2, 1)L(2, 2, 1)^*L(2, 3, 1)$$
$$= \{0, \Lambda\} \cup \{1\} \{\Lambda\}^*\{0\}$$
$$= \{0, 10, \Lambda\}$$

$L(3, 4, 2)$, $L(4, 3, 2)$, and $L(4, 4, 2)$ are calculated similarly. Now we are ready to calculate $L(p, q, 3)$. We do two such calculations and leave the others to you.

$$L(1, 2, 3) = L(1, 2, 2) \cup L(1, 3, 2)L(3, 3, 2)^*L(3, 2, 2)$$
$$= \{0\} \cup \{1, 00\}\{0, 10, \Lambda\}^*\{1\}$$
$$= \{0\} \cup \{1, 00\}\{0, 10\}^*\{1\}$$

$$L(4, 4, 3) = L(4, 4, 2) \cup L(4, 3, 2)L(3, 3, 2)^*L(3, 4, 2)$$
$$= \{11, \Lambda\} \cup \{0, 10\}\{0, 10, \Lambda\}^*\{11\}$$
$$= \{0, 10\}^*\{11\} \cup \{\Lambda\}$$

Notice that some of the expressions of the form $L(p, q, 3)$ have been simplified slightly. The preceding calculation of $L(4, 4, 3)$ is a typical example.

There is no need to calculate the complete table for $L(p, q, 4)$; we need only $L(1, 2, 4)$ and $L(1, 3, 4)$, since 2 and 3 are the only accepting states.

$$L(1, 2, 4) = L(1, 2, 3) \cup L(1, 4, 3)L(4, 4, 3)^*L(4, 2, 3)$$
$$= \{0\} \cup \{1, 00\}\{0, 10\}^*\{1\} \cup (\{01\} \cup \{1, 00\}\{0, 10\}^*\{11\})$$
$$(\{0, 10\}^*\{11\})^*(\{0, 10\}^*\{1\})$$

$$L(1, 3, 4) = L(1, 3, 3) \cup L(1, 4, 3)L(4, 4, 3)^*L(4, 3, 3)$$
$$= \{1, 00\}\{0, 10\}^* \cup (\{01\} \cup \{1, 00\}\{0, 10\}^*\{11\})(\{0, 10\}^*\{11\})^*\{0, 10\}^+$$

(In both cases, when we substituted for $L(4, 4, 3)$ in the expression $L(4, 4, 3)^*$, we omitted the Λ-term.) Finally, if we denote the two regular expressions by $R(1, 2, 4)$ and $R(1, 3, 4)$, the one we want is $R = R(1, 2, 4) + R(1, 3, 4)$. The two are very similar and allow us to simplify the formula for R to obtain

$$R = 0 + (1 + 00)(0 + 10)^*1 + (01 + (1 + 00)(0 + 10)^*11)((0 + 10)^*11)^*((0 + 10)^*1 + (0 + 10)^+)$$

It would no doubt be possible to simplify this further, but we have not discussed any systematic method for doing so. The important thing at this point is to make sure you understand the steps of the algorithm. The exercises give you an opportunity to practice the algorithm at your leisure.

EXERCISES

6.1. In the construction in Case 1 of Theorem 6.1, give an example (i.e., draw a transition diagram) to illustrate the fact that the two sets Q_r and Q_s must be disjoint for the resulting NFA-Λ to recognize the language L_rL_s.

6.2. In Case 2 of Theorem 6.1, give an example to illustrate the fact that Q_r and Q_s must be disjoint for the resulting NFA-Λ to recognize $L_r \cup L_s$.

6.3. In Case 1 of Theorem 6.1, consider this alternative to the construction described, assuming that M_r has only one accepting state: eliminate the Λ-transition from the accepting state of M_r to q_s and merge these two states into one. Either show that this would work in general or give an example to show that it doesn't always work.

6.4. In Case 2 of Theorem 6.1, suppose that instead of a new state q_0 and Λ-transitions from it to q_r and q_s, we make q_r the initial state of the new NFA-Λ and create a Λ-transition from it to q_s. Again, either prove that this always works or give an example to show that it doesn't.

6.5. Finally, in Case 3 of Theorem 6.1, suppose that instead of adding a new state q_0, with Λ-transitions from it to q_r and to it from each accepting state of M_r, we make q_r both the initial state and the accepting state, and create Λ-transitions from each accepting state of M_r to q_r. Prove that this always works or give an example to show that it doesn't.

6.6. In each case below, find an NFA-Λ recognizing the language corresponding to the regular expression, by applying literally the algorithm in the chapter. Do not attempt to simplify the answer.
  (a) $((ab)^*b + ab^*)^*$ (b) $aa(ba)^* + b^*aba^*$ (c) $(ab + (aab)^*)(aa + a)$

6.7. In Figs 6-7a and 6-7b are pictured FAs M_1 and M_2, recognizing languages L_1 and L_2, respectively. Draw NFA-Λs recognizing each of these languages, using the constructions in this chapter.
  (a) L_1L_2 (b) $L_1L_1L_2$ (c) $L_1 \cup L_2$
  (d) L_1^* (e) $L_2^* \cup L_1$ (f) $L_2L_1^*$
  (g) $L_1L_2 \cup (L_2L_1)^*$

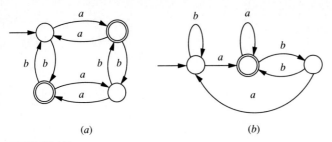

(a) (b)

FIGURE 6-7

6.8. Use the algorithm of Theorem 6.2 to find a regular expression corresponding to each of the FAs shown in Fig. 6-8. In each case, if the FA has n states, construct tables showing $L(p, q, J)$ for each J with $0 \le J \le n - 1$.

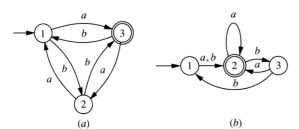

(a) (b)

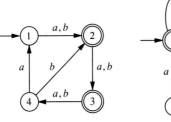 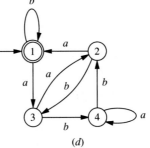

(c) (d)

FIGURE 6-8

MINIMAL
FINITE
AUTOMATA

7.1 A MINIMUM-STATE FA FOR A REGULAR LANGUAGE

We wish to pursue further the question of how many states are required in an FA that is to recognize a given language L. A little terminology will be helpful at this point. If S is a set of strings, any two of which are distinguishable with respect to L, let us call S a *pairwise distinguishable* set, or a PD set. It will be understood in this discussion that "PD" means PD with respect to some fixed language L.

So far, we have a "negative" result, Theorem 4.2: If S is a PD set with n elements, then any FA recognizing L must have at least n states. A corresponding positive result would be that for some PD set containing n elements, there actually is an FA with n states that recognizes L.

If L is regular, there is *some* FA recognizing L with, say, n_1 states. Our negative result then says that no PD set can have more than n_1 elements. In other words, if we want an FA recognizing L to have a state set the same size as some PD set, the PD set needs to be as large as possible. With this in mind, we say that a PD set S is *maximal* if for any string x, there is some element of S that is indistinguishable from x with respect to L—in other words, if adding any elements to S would produce a set that is no longer PD. It may not be obvious that a maximal PD set actually has the maximum number of elements that any other PD set can have, but we shall see before long that it does.

The positive result we might hope for is that if S is any maximal PD set, say with n elements, there is an FA recognizing L with n states. In fact, this is true, but it will be convenient to formulate the result a little differently, in terms of equivalence classes.

Let us define a relation I_L on Σ^*:

For $x, y \in \Sigma^*$, $x I_L y$ means x and y are indistinguishable with respect to L; in other words, for every $z \in \Sigma^*$, either xz and yz are both in L, or xz and yz are both in L'.

Lemma 7.1. I_L is an equivalence relation on Σ^*.

Proof. It is obvious that I_L is reflexive and symmetric, perhaps less obvious that it is transitive. Suppose $x I_L y$ and $y I_L w$. We must show that $x I_L w$. Take any $z \in \Sigma^*$. If $xz \in L$, then $yz \in L$, since $x I_L y$, and therefore $wz \in L$, since $y I_L w$. Similarly, if $xz \notin L$, then $wz \notin L$. Therefore $x I_L w$.

We may now consider the set of equivalence classes with respect to I_L. For the rest of this chapter, "equivalence class" means equivalence class with respect to the relation I_L, for whatever language L we happen to be talking about. The next lemma shows that talking about equivalence classes is really just another way of talking about maximal PD sets of strings.

Lemma 7.2. S is a maximal PD set if and only if S contains exactly one string from each equivalence class.

Proof. Suppose S contains one string from each equivalence class. Then S is PD, since two strings in different equivalence classes are distinguishable. S must be a maximal PD set, since any string in Σ^* belongs to some equivalence class and is therefore indistinguishable from the element of S belonging to that equivalence class.

On the other hand, suppose S is a maximal PD set. Then any two elements of S belong to different equivalence classes, since they are distinguishable; and every equivalence class must be represented in S, because if there were a string x for which S contained no element equivalent to x, then the set obtained from S by adding x would still be PD, and S could not be maximal.

It follows in particular from Lemma 7.2 that if L is regular, all maximal PD sets have the same number of elements, namely, the number of equivalence classes.

We will be able to construct a minimum-state FA recognizing L in terms of these equivalence classes. But it may be easier to understand if we start from what seems like the other end, by supposing that we have an FA $M = (Q, \Sigma, q_0, \delta, A)$ recognizing L and having the minimum number of states. Adapting the notation of Chapter 6, we let

$$L_q = \{x \in \Sigma^* | \delta^*(q_0, x) = q\}$$

for any $q \in Q$.

If x and y are two strings belonging to the same L_q (i.e., if $\delta^*(q_0, x) = \delta^*(q_0, y)$), M does not distinguish between x and y, so, since M recognizes L, x and y must be indistinguishable with respect to L—i.e., $x I_L y$. On the other hand, if $x I_L y$, there is no need for M to distinguish between x and y; on the grounds that a minimum-state FA has only the states that are necessary, we might predict that $\delta^*(q_0, x) = \delta^*(q_0, y)$ and thus that x and y belong to the same L_q. Obviously, more detail is needed for a proof, but let us assume for the moment that this reasoning is correct and see what conclusion we may draw. We have a partition of Σ^* consisting of all the sets L_q, and two strings are in the same L_q if and only if they are equivalent with respect to the relation I_L. It follows that

> the sets L_q determined by a minimum-state FA are simply the equivalence classes of I_L.

This suggests a way to construct the minimum-state FA recognizing L. As long as the equivalence class containing x, which we denote $[x]$, is already one of the sets L_q in a minimum-state FA, why not simply say that $[x]$ *is* the state q? In other words, we obtain the FA we want by taking the set of states to be the set of equivalence classes of I_L. This might have seemed rather abstract and/or unnatural if we had made this definition without any preamble, but we have been led to it naturally by considering the sets L_q. In addition, recall the early part of Chapter 4. There we identified a state with the set of strings satisfying some property, where the property represented all the information we needed to remember at that stage. This is another indication that our definition of state is reasonable; the state we are in at any point is determined by the strings that have gotten us to that point.

Once we have decided that the states in our FA should be the equivalence classes of I_L, it is fairly clear how to complete the definition of the FA. The initial state is the equivalence class corresponding to the string Λ; the transition function is computed by concatenating the input symbol onto any of the strings corresponding to the current state; and the accepting states are simply those equivalence classes containing elements of L.

We are almost ready to formulate a precise definition embodying these intuitive ideas. But there is one detail that we should look at more closely. How are we defining the transition function δ? We said earlier, "by concatenating the input symbol onto any of the strings corresponding to the current state." This means that if we start with an equivalence class q containing a string x, then $\delta(q, a)$ should be the equivalence class containing xa. Symbolically (letting $[x]$ denote the equivalence class containing x), $\delta([x], a) = [xa]$. This seems harmless enough at first; but a potential difficulty arises when we consider two strings x and y. It should be the case that $\delta([x], a) = [xa]$ and $\delta([y], a) = [ya]$, but suppose $[x] = [y]$. (Remember, this is just another way of saying $x I_L y$.) Obviously, unless $[xa] = [ya]$, we have an inconsistency. Another way to describe the difficulty is to say that our definition of $\delta([x], a)$ seems to depend not just on the set $[x]$ and the symbol a, but on the particular element of $[x]$ we have in mind (namely, x). Fortunately, as the next lemma shows, there isn't really a problem at all.

Lemma 7.3. I_L is *right invariant* with respect to concatenation: i.e., if $x I_L y$, then for any $a \in \Sigma$, $xa I_L ya$. Equivalently, if $[x] = [y]$, then for any $a \in \Sigma$, $[xa] = [ya]$.

Proof. Suppose $x I_L y$, and let $a \in \Sigma$. We must show that for any $z \in \Sigma^*$, xaz and yaz are either both in L or both not in L. But for any $z' \in \Sigma^*$, xz' and yz' are either both in L or both not in L. By applying this in the case $z' = az$, we have the desired result.

This lemma removes the only obstacle to defining the minimum-state FA we want.

Theorem 7.1. Let L be a regular language in Σ^*. Define $M_L = (Q_L, \Sigma, q_0, \delta, A)$, where

Q_L is the (finite) set of equivalence classes with respect to I_L

$q_0 = [\Lambda]$

$A_L = \{q \in Q_L | q \cap L \neq \emptyset\}$

$\delta : Q \times \Sigma \longrightarrow Q$ is defined by $\delta([x], a) = [xa]$ (for every $x \in \Sigma^*$ and $a \in \Sigma$)

M_L is an FA recognizing L, and M_L has the fewest states of any FA recognizing L.

Proof. We have already observed that Q_L is finite, and Lemma 7.3 shows that our definition of δ is legitimate. Thus, there is no doubt that M_L is an FA. A formula that will be useful in verifying that M_L recognizes L is the following:

$$\delta^*([x], y) = [xy] \text{ (for any } x, y \in \Sigma^*)$$

This is proved by induction on $|y|$. The basis step is easy, since if $|y| = 0$, then $y = \Lambda$, and $\delta^*([x], \Lambda) = [x] = [x\Lambda]$. The first equality uses Definition 4.2, the definition of δ^*.

For the induction step, let the induction hypothesis be that $K \geq 0$ and that $\delta^*([x], y) = [xy]$ for every $x \in \Sigma^*$ and for every y with $|y| = K$. We wish to show that for any y with $|y| = K + 1$, and any $x \in \Sigma^*$, $\delta^*([x], y) = [xy]$. First we write $y = y_1 a$, where $|y_1| = K$ and $a \in \Sigma$. Then

$$\begin{aligned}
\delta^*([x], y) &= \delta^*([x], y_1 a) \\
&= \delta(\delta^*([x], y_1), a) \text{ (by Definition 4.2)} \\
&= \delta([xy_1], a) \text{ (from the induction hypothesis)} \\
&= [xy_1 a] \text{ (from the definition of } \delta) \\
&= [xy]
\end{aligned}$$

M_L accepts x if and only if $\delta^*([\Lambda], x) \in A$. Using the formula we have just proved, we see that this is true if and only if $[x] \in A$, and because of the definition of A this is true if and only if $[x] \cap L \neq \emptyset$. We would like to show that saying $[x] \cap L \neq \emptyset$ is the same as saying $x \in L$.

Certainly, if $x \in L$, then $[x] \cap L \neq \emptyset$. On the other hand, if $[x] \cap L \neq \emptyset$, there is a string $y \in L$ so that $y \in [x]$, or $y I_L x$. This means that for any z, yz and xz are both in L or both not in L. If we choose $z = \Lambda$, then since $y \in L$, we may conclude that $x \in L$. Therefore, M_L accepts x if and only if $x \in L$.

Finally, as we showed in Lemma 7.2, a set consisting of one string from each element of Q_L is a PD set with respect to L, and thus Theorem 4.2 implies that any FA recognizing L must have at least as many states as M_L.

Example 7.1. Let L be the language $\{x \in \{0, 1\}^* | x \text{ ends with } 10\}$. (This is the language considered in Examples 4.1 and 4.4.) Consider the strings $x_1 = \Lambda$, $x_2 = 1$, and $x_3 = 10$.

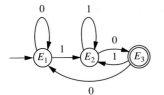

FIGURE 7-1
A minimum-state FA recognizing $\{0, 1\}^*\{10\}$.

On the one hand, the set $\{x_1, x_2, x_3\}$ is PD with respect to L. We can show this easily by finding, for each pair of strings in this set, a string z that distinguishes them relative to L. For example: $x_10 \notin L$ and $x_20 \in L$; $x_1\Lambda \notin L$ and $x_3\Lambda \in L$; $x_20 \in L$ and $x_30 \notin L$.

On the other hand, we can easily show that $\{x_1, x_2, x_3\}$ is a maximal PD set. Let y be any string. If y ends with 10, y is clearly indistinguishable from x_3 with respect to L; if y ends with 1, y is indistinguishable from x_2; and otherwise (if $y = \Lambda$, $y = 0$, or y ends with 00), y is indistinguishable from x_1.

We may conclude that the equivalence classes are the sets

$$E_1 = \{x \,|\, x \text{ does not end with 1 or 10}\}$$

$$E_2 = \{x \,|\, x \text{ ends with 1}\}$$

$$E_3 = \{x \,|\, x \text{ ends with 10}\}$$

We now have the states of our minimum-state FA. To draw the transitions, we observe that

$$E_10 \subseteq E_1 \qquad E_11 \subseteq E_2$$

$$E_20 \subseteq E_3 \qquad E_21 \subseteq E_2$$

$$E_30 \subseteq E_1 \qquad E_31 \subseteq E_2$$

This means that a minimum-state FA recognizing L can be drawn as in Fig. 7-1. Not surprisingly, this is the same FA that we came up with in Example 4.4, except for the names given to the states.

7.2 MINIMIZING THE NUMBER OF STATES IN AN FA

A reasonable question to ask, after Example 7.1, is how one can find a maximal PD set relative to L. In the example, we had an unfair advantage, since we already had an FA recognizing L and it was clear that it had as few states as possible. Theorem 7.1 provides an abstract description of a minimum-state FA recognizing L, but as it stands it may not seem especially useful, since there's no obvious way to find a maximal PD set or even to determine how many elements there are in such a set—and therefore no obvious way to find out what the minimum-state FA looks like. Recall that if we have a regular expression corresponding to

L, Chapters 5 and 6 tell us how to find an FA recognizing L, of which we *can* draw a diagram. Therefore, a more pertinent question might be this: Given an FA recognizing L, is it a minimum-state FA recognizing L, and if not, how can we modify it so as to obtain one? As it turns out, the abstraction described in Theorem 7.1 will help us to answer this.

Suppose $M = (Q, \Sigma, q_0, \delta, A)$ is an FA recognizing L. There is one obvious way in which we might be able to reduce the number of states: eliminate any states that are not reachable from q_0. What remains is still an FA recognizing the same language (see Exercise 4.16). Here is an algorithm to do this.

Let $Q_0 = \{q_0\}$; for $N \geq 1$, let $Q_N = Q_{N-1} \cup \{\delta(q, a) | q \in Q_{N-1}, a \in \Sigma\}$. If K is the smallest N for which $Q_N = Q_{N-1}$, then Q_K is the set of states reachable from q_0.

For the remainder of this discussion, we shall assume that in the finite automaton M we start with, all states are reachable from q_0.

In Section 7.1, we obtained a minimum-state FA "abstractly" by taking the equivalence classes of I_L to be the states. The states, in other words, constitute a partition of Σ^*: every string belongs to one and only one of these sets. If we knew what this partition looked like, we would know what the minimum-state FA looked like. But the not-necessarily-minimal FA that we have determines a partition of Σ^* also: the partition consisting of the sets L_q ($q \in Q$). (L_q contains all the strings that cause M to be in state q.) By considering the relationship between these partitions, we may be able to see how the two FAs are related.

The crucial observation is that if two strings x and y are in the same L_q (i.e., $\delta^*(q_0, x) = \delta^*(q_0, y)$), they are in the same equivalence class, so $x I_L y$. To see this, use the definition of I_L. Take any $z \in \Sigma^*$ and consider xz and yz. Since $\delta^*(q_0, x) = \delta^*(q_0, y)$, we may conclude that

$$\begin{aligned} \delta^*(q_0, xz) &= \delta^*(\delta^*(q_0, x), z) \\ &= \delta^*(\delta^*(q_0, y), z) \\ &= \delta^*(q_0, yz) \end{aligned}$$

Since M recognizes L, this means that $xz \in L$ if and only if $yz \in L$. This is true for any z, and thus $x I_L y$.

What does this tell us about the two partitions? It says that each L_q is a subset of some equivalence class—or, to say it another way, no L_q can intersect more than one equivalence class. Consider an equivalence class $[x]$; since every string in $[x]$ belongs to some L_q, and since every L_q that contains an element of $[x]$ is a subset of $[x]$, it follows that $[x]$ is actually a union of L_q's.

It may be helpful at this point to look again at Example 4.4. Figure 7-2 shows the original FA we drew for this language (a); the minimum-state FA we arrived at (b); the partition of $\{0, 1\}^*$ corresponding to the original FA (c); and the partition of $\{0, 1\}^*$ created by the equivalence classes of I_L (d). The main thing you're supposed to notice here is simply that the partition in Fig. 7-2c is *finer* than that in d: each set in the second partition is the union of sets in the first.

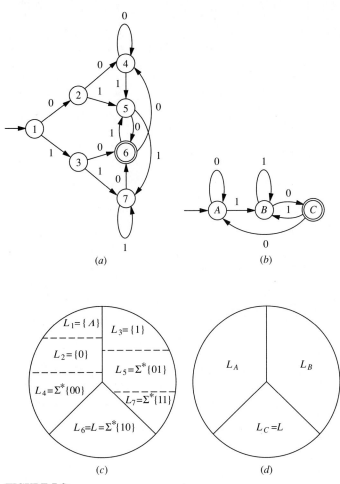

FIGURE 7-2
The L_q partitions of Σ^* for the FAs in Example 4.4.

Saying that several distinct L_q's are subsets of the same equivalence class is the same as saying that a set of several distinct states in M corresponds to one state in our minimum-state FA. On the one hand, this allows us to formulate a

Criterion for M to be a minimum-state FA. If each equivalence class with respect to I_L is identical to a single set L_q, the number of states in M is the minimum possible; if there are distinct states p and q so that L_p and L_q are subsets of the same equivalence class, the number of states in M is not minimal.

On the other hand, it tells us, if M is not minimal, how we need to modify M so as to obtain a minimum-state FA: identify each set of states that correspond to a single state in the minimum-state FA, and "merge" the states in each such set into a single state. It is helpful to describe the problem in terms of *pairs* of states. We have reduced the problem to identifying those pairs (p, q) for which L_p and L_q are subsets of the same equivalence class. Obviously, we can do this if we can solve the opposite problem, whose solution turns out to be more straightforward: identify those pairs (p, q) for which L_p and L_q are subsets of different equivalence classes. Let us introduce temporary notation for this. We shall write

$p \cong q$ if L_p and L_q are subsets of the same equivalence class, $p \not\cong q$ otherwise.

Remember: $p \cong q$ means that p and q are ultimately to be merged into one state in our minimal FA. It will also be helpful to rephrase the condition $p \not\cong q$. If $x \in L_p$ and $y \in L_q$, $p \not\cong q$ means simply that x and y are distinguishable with respect to L. Notice that saying *there exist* $x \in L_p$ and $y \in L_q$ that are distinguishable is equivalent to saying that for *any* $x \in L_p$ and $y \in L_q$, x and y are distinguishable; this is true because each L_p is a subset of a single equivalence class.

We make three observations, which will serve as the basis for an algorithm to find the pairs (p, q) with $p \not\cong q$.

1. If exactly one of the two states p, q is in A, then $p \not\cong q$. The reason is that if $x \in L_p$ and $y \in L_q$, exactly one of the strings x, y is in L, and this obviously implies that x is distinguishable from y.

2. If $\delta^*(r, w) = p$, $\delta^*(s, w) = q$, and $p \not\cong q$, then $r \not\cong s$. In particular, if $\delta(r, a) = p$, $\delta(s, a) = q$, and $p \not\cong q$, then $r \not\cong s$. To see the first statement, suppose $x \in L_r$ and $y \in L_s$; then $xw \in L_p$ and $yw \in L_q$. Since $p \not\cong q$, xw and yw are distinguishable; therefore, so are x and y.

3. If $r \not\cong s$, there is a string $z \in \Sigma^*$ so that exactly one of $\delta^*(r, z)$, $\delta^*(s, z)$ is in A. (If $x \in L_r$ and $y \in L_s$, then x and y are distinguishable with respect to L. Let z be a string so that exactly one of xz, yz is in L; then exactly one of $\delta^*(r, z)$, $\delta^*(s, z)$ is in A.)

These observations suggest some algorithm like the following:

Algorithm 7.1 (For identifying pairs (p,q) with $p \not\cong q$). List all (unordered) pairs of states (p, q) for which $p \neq q$. Make a sequence of passes through the pairs. On the first pass, mark each pair of which exactly one element is in A. On each subsequent pass, mark a pair (r, s) if there is an $a \in \Sigma$ for which $\delta(r, a) = p$, $\delta(s, a) = q$, and the pair (p, q) is already marked. After a pass in which no new pairs are marked, stop. The marked pairs (p, q) are the ones with $p \not\cong q$.

Let us first make sure that the algorithm is correct. By observation 1, any pair (p, q) marked on the first pass satisfies $p \not\cong q$; by observation 2, any pair (p, q) marked on a subsequent pass also satisfies $p \not\cong q$; and by observation 3, any pair (p, q) for which $p \not\cong q$ will be marked within $|z| + 1$ passes, where z is a string for which exactly one of $\delta^*(p, z)$, $\delta^*(q, z)$ is in A. The pass on which a particular pair is marked may depend on the order in which the pairs are processed in each pass.

Before we look at an example, let us make sure we understand how to finish up once we have found all pairs (p, q) with $p \not\cong q$. Consider some state p. If $p \not\cong q$ for every other state q, no other states of M will be merged with p in forming the minimum-state FA M_1. But if there is at least one other state q

with $p \cong q$, which will be true if (p, q) remains unmarked at the termination of Algorithm 7.1, then all such states q will be merged with p to form a single state of M_1. By observation 1 above, either all these states of M are accepting states or none of them is; the resulting state in M_1 will be designated an accepting state in the first case and not in the second. The only remaining question is how to determine the transitions. Suppose $\delta(p, a) = q$ and $\delta(r, a) = s$ in M. If it turns out that $q \cong s$, so that q and s are merged into a single state t, obviously the resulting transitions on the symbol a from both the state in M_1 corresponding to p and the state in M_1 corresponding to r, whether they are the same or not, will go to t. What seems at first like a less obvious question is what to do if $p \cong r$, so that both are merged into some state u. Fortunately, there will not be any question as to where transitions from u go, since by observation 2 it must be true that $q \cong s$ also.

It is now reasonably clear how to obtain a minimum-state FA, starting with an arbitrary FA. For completeness, however, we present the algorithm more formally.

Algorithm 7.2 (Given $M = (Q, \Sigma, q_0, \delta, A)$, to obtain a minimum-state FA $M_1 = (Q_1, \Sigma, q_1, \delta_1, A_1)$ with $L(M_1) = L(M)$). Let us assume that the states in Q are numbered from 1 through N. For each $I \in Q$, $f(I)$ will denote the state in Q_1 corresponding to I.

Initialize Q_1 to be empty. Determine the pairs (I, J) for which $I \cong J$, using Algorithm 7.1. For each I from 1 to N: if $J \not\cong I$ for each J with $1 \le J < I$, add a new state to Q_1, and let this new state be $f(I)$; otherwise, choose any $J < I$ with $J \cong I$, and let $f(I) = f(J)$.

q_1 is defined to be $f(q_0)$.

$A_1 = f(A) = \{f(I) | I \in A\}$

δ_1 is defined as follows: For $p \in Q_1$ and $a \in \Sigma$, $\delta_1(p, a) = f(\delta(I, a))$, where I is any element of Q with $f(I) = p$.

Example 7.2. Let us illustrate the algorithm for the same FA we looked at in Example 4.4, pictured in Fig. 7-2a. First, we apply Algorithm 7.1 to mark pairs of states. Figure 7-3a shows all pairs (I, J) for which $I \ne J$. The pairs marked 1 are those of which exactly one element is in A; they are marked on pass 1. The pairs marked 2 are those marked on the second pass. For example, consider the pair $(2, 5)$. $\delta(2, 0) = 4$ and $\delta(5, 0) = 6$; since the pair $(4, 6)$ was marked on pass 1, $(2, 5)$ is marked.

A third pass doesn't produce any additional marked pairs. For example, $\delta(1, 0) = 2$ and $\delta(2, 0) = 4$, but $(2, 4)$ is not marked. Similarly, $\delta(1, 1) = 3$ and $\delta(2, 1) = 5$, but $(3, 5)$ is not marked. Therefore, if on the third pass the pair $(1, 2)$ is the first pair to be tested, it will not be marked on that pass.

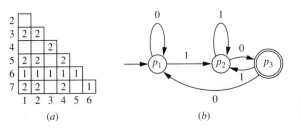

(a) (b)

FIGURE 7-3
Minimalizing the FA in Fig. 7-2a.

When the third pass has been completed, Algorithm 7.1 terminates. The remainder of Algorithm 7.2 consists of making a pass through the seven states, creating as many states in the minimal FA as necessary in the process, and then determining the transitions. Let p_1 be the new state $f(1)$. Since $1 \cong 2$, no state in the new FA is created corresponding to state 2, but $f(2) = p_1$. Since $1 \not\cong 3$ and $2 \not\cong 3$, we create a new state $p_2 = f(3)$; since $1 \cong 4$, $f(4) = p_1$; since $3 \cong 5$, $f(5) = p_2$. $I \not\cong 6$ for each $I < 6$, so there is a third state $p_3 = f(6)$. p_3 will be an accepting state, since 6 is. Finally, $3 \cong 7$, thus $f(7) = p_2$.

To determine $\delta_1(p_1, a)$ (for a either 0 or 1), we choose I (e.g., $I = 1$) with $f(I) = p_1$. Since $\delta(1, 0) = 2$ and $f(2) = p_1$, we have $\delta_1(p_1, 0) = p_1$. Since $\delta(1, 1) = 3$ and $f(3) = p_2$, $\delta_1(p_1, 1) = p_2$. Similarly, we can see that $\delta_1(p_2, 0) = p_3$, $\delta_1(p_2, 1) = p_2$, $\delta_1(p_3, 0) = p_1$, and $\delta_1(p_3, 1) = p_2$.

The resulting FA for this example is shown in Fig. 7-3b. Of course, except for state names, it is the same FA found in Example 7.1, as well as in Example 4.4.

We conclude this section by proving that the FA M_1 produced by Algorithm 7.2 is in general a minimum-state FA recognizing the same language as M.

Theorem 7.2. Let $M = (Q, \Sigma, q_0, \delta, A)$ be an FA. Let $M_1 = (Q_1, \Sigma, q_1, \delta_1, A_1)$ be the FA obtained by applying Algorithm 7.2 to M. Then $L(M_1) = L(M)$, and M_1 has the fewest states of any FA accepting this language.

Proof. The algorithm actually produces the set Q_1 and a function $f : Q \to Q_1$ with $f(q_0) = q_1$. The transition function $\delta_1 : Q_1 \times \Sigma \to Q_1$ obtained from the algorithm satisfies the condition

$$\delta_1(f(q), a) = f(\delta(q, a)) \text{ for every } q \in Q \text{ and } a \in \Sigma$$

by definition. We have already discussed the fact that because of observation 2, defining $\delta_1(f(q), a)$ this way does indeed make sense. It is straightforward to check using mathematical induction on $|x|$ that for every $x \in \Sigma^*$,

$$\delta_1^*(f(q), x) = f(\delta^*(q, x)) \tag{7.1}$$

(see Exercise 7.13).

We can use this formula to show that $L(M) = L(M_1)$. On the one hand, if $x \in L(M)$, then $\delta^*(q_0, x) \in A$. By definition of A_1, $f(\delta^*(q_0, x)) \in A_1$; thus by (7.1), $\delta_1^*(f(q_0), x) = \delta_1^*(q_1, x) \in A_1$. Therefore, $x \in L(M_1)$. On the other hand, if $x \in L(M_1)$, $\delta_1^*(f(q_0), x) \in A_1$, which together with (7.1) implies that $f(\delta^*(q_0, x)) \in A_1$. We would like to show that $\delta^*(q_0, x) \in A$. By definition of A_1, $f(\delta^*(q_0, x)) = f(q)$ for some $q \in A$. If $q \neq \delta^*(q_0, x)$, then these two states yield the same value for f. This means that $q \cong \delta^*(q_0, x)$—i.e., that the pair $(q, \delta^*(q_0, x))$ is not marked by Algorithm 7.1. But observation 1 shows that since one of these two states is an element of A, the other must also be. Therefore, $\delta^*(q_0, x) \in A$, and $x \in L(M)$.

Let $L = L(M) = L(M_1)$. We know that M_1 recognizes L. That it is a minimum-state FA recognizing L is now easy to see. Theorem 7.1 tells us that the minimum number of states in an FA recognizing L is the number of equivalence classes of I_L. But in our construction of M_1, distinct states of M corresponding to the same equivalence class were merged, so that the resulting states correspond precisely to the equivalence classes. Therefore, M_1 must be minimal.

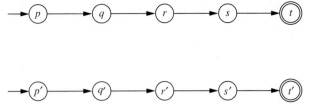

FIGURE 7-4

7.3 A MORE EFFICIENT ALGORITHM FOR MARKING PAIRS

In our example, Algorithm 7.1 required only one pass beyond the first, but in general this is too much to expect, and the potential inefficiency becomes more serious. On each pass, it is necessary to consider every unmarked pair (r, s), and, in the worst case, calculate $\delta(r, a)$ and $\delta(s, a)$ for every symbol in Σ.

If it should happen that each new pass resulted in only one or two more marked pairs, this would indeed be a time-consuming process. The problem is that in a situation like that pictured in Fig. 7-4, if on a particular pass we tested the pairs (p, p'), (q, q'), (r, r'), and (s, s') in that order, it might be that the only one we would mark would be (s, s'), and the time it took us to test (p, p'), (q, q'), and (r, r') would have been wasted.

One change that this suggests is the following (referring again to Fig. 7-4): when we test (p, p') and find that $\delta(p, a) = q$ and $\delta(p', a) = q'$, if the pair (q, q') isn't yet marked, we keep track of this information by inserting (p, p') into a set that contains pairs from which it's possible to get in one step to (q, q'). If and when (q, q') gets marked, at that point, we also mark all the pairs in that set (and, for each such pair that gets marked, we also mark all the pairs in *its* set, and so on). One pass becomes more complicated, but now one pass (beyond the first) is all that's necessary.

At this point, we present the algorithm more carefully. Because of its added complexity, and specifically because of its recursive aspect, it is written in a "pseudo-code" (Pascal-like) format. MARKR is a recursive procedure.

Algorithm 7.1a (For identifying pairs (p, q) with $p \not\equiv q$.)

    BEGIN
        List all (unordered) pairs (p, q) with $p \neq q$;
(1)   FOR each pair (p, q) with $p \neq q$ DO
        IF exactly one of p, q is in A THEN
          Mark (p, q)
        ELSE
          Initialize the set $S(p, q)$ to be empty;
(2)   FOR each pair (p, q) with $p \neq q$ DO
        IF (p, q) is not marked THEN
(3)   FOR each $a \in \Sigma$ DO

```
              BEGIN
                 r := δ(p, a);
                 s := δ(q, a);

              IF  r ≠ s  THEN
                 IF (r, s) is not marked THEN
(4)                 Insert (p, q) into S(r, s)
                 ELSE
(5)                 MARKR(p, q)
              END
        END.
        Procedure MARKR(p, q) is as follows:
        BEGIN
           Mark (p, q);
           FOR each pair (r, s) in S(p, q) DO
              MARKR(r, s)
        END;
```

We shall look at an example illustrating Algorithm 7.1*a*, but first let us verify that it works. We leave it to you to check that any pair (p, q) marked by the algorithm is indeed a pair for which $p \not\equiv q$. The less obvious question is whether the algorithm marks all such pairs. As we noticed in observation 3, if $p \not\equiv q$, there is a string z so that exactly one of $\delta^*(p, z)$, $\delta^*(q, z)$ is in A. If $p \not\equiv q$, we may show, using mathematical induction on the length of the shortest such string, that (p, q) is marked during execution of the algorithm.

If $p \not\equiv q$, let $l(p, q)$ be the length of the shortest string z for which exactly one of $\delta^*(p, z)$, $\delta^*(q, z)$ is in A. The basis step in the induction is to show that if $l(p, q) = 0$, then (p, q) is marked by the algorithm. This is clear, since $\delta^*(p, \Lambda) = p$ and $\delta^*(q, \Lambda) = q$, and thus (p, q) is marked in the first FOR-loop.

Suppose that $K \geq 0$ and for any (r, s) with $l(r, s) = K$, (r, s) is marked. We wish to show that if $l(p, q) = K + 1$, then (p, q) is marked. Choose z so that $|z| = K + 1$ and exactly one of $\delta^*(p, z)$, $\delta^*(q, z)$ is in A. We may write $z = az_1$, where $|z_1| = K$ and $a \in \Sigma$. Let $r = \delta(p, a)$ and $s = \delta(q, a)$. Since exactly one of $\delta^*(r, z_1)$, $\delta^*(s, z_1)$ is in A, and since no string shorter than z_1 can satisfy this property (because $l(p, q) = K + 1$), we have $l(r, s) = K$. By the induction hypothesis, we know that the pair (r, s) is marked. If this happens before the pair (p, q) is processed in the loop (2), then line (5) will be executed for the pair (p, q), which causes it to be marked. Otherwise, when the symbol a is processed in loop (3), the pair (p, q) is inserted into the set $S(r, s)$; in this case, when (r, s) is marked, all the pairs in this set will be marked as a result of executing the procedure MARKR with the pair (r, s).

Example 7.3. We illustrate Algorithm 7.1*a* (and the correspondingly modified version of Algorithm 7.2) on the FA pictured in Fig. 7-5*a*. Figure 7-5*b* shows the pairs (p, q) with $p \not\equiv q$, at a point midway through the algorithm. In the box corresponding to each pair (p, q), the top portion contains the pairs in the set $S(p, q)$; the bottom portion is used

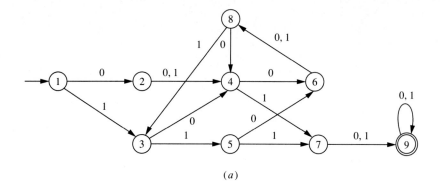

(a)

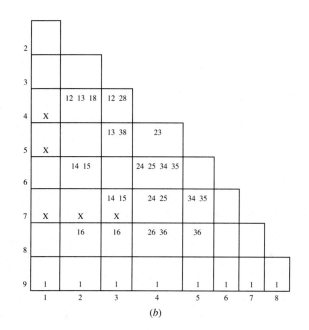

(b)

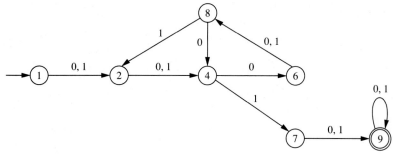

(c)

FIGURE 7-5
Algorithm 7.1a illustrated.

for marking the pair. Pairs marked 1 are those marked in loop (1) of the algorithm. The order in which the remaining pairs are processed is one column at a time, top-to-bottom (i.e., $(1, 2), (1, 3), \ldots, (1, 8), (2, 3), (2, 4), \ldots, (2, 8), (3, 4), \ldots, (7, 8)$). Figure 7-5b illustrates the contents of the table just before testing the pair (4,5).

Let us begin at that point. $\delta(4, 0) = 6 = \delta(5, 0); \delta(4, 1) = 7 = \delta(5, 1)$. Since in this case (4,5) is not inserted into any set $S(p, q)$, we can see that it will never be marked.

Next is (4,6). $\delta(4, 0) = 6$ and $\delta(6, 0) = 8$, so we insert (4,6) into the set $S(6, 8)$. Similarly, (4,6) is inserted into $S(7, 8)$.

$\delta(4, 0) = 6$ and $\delta(7, 0) = 9$. Since (6,9) is marked, we mark (4,7). At this point $S(4, 7) = \{(2, 4), (2, 5)\}$. Calling MARKR with (2,4) causes (2,4) to be marked, as well as the pairs (1,2), (1,3), and (1,8) in the set $S(2, 4)$. Calling MARKR with (2,5) causes only that pair to be marked.

$\delta(4, 0) = 6$ and $\delta(8, 0) = 4$. (6,4) (or (4,6)) is still unmarked, so (4,8) is inserted into $S(4, 6)$.

Let us summarize the next few steps. (5,6) is inserted into $S(6, 8)$ and $S(7, 8)$. (5,7) is marked, which causes (3,4), (3,5), (1,2), (2,8), (1,6), (1,3), and (3,8) to be marked. (5,8) is inserted into $S(4, 6)$; then it is marked, causing (3,6) to be marked. (6,7) is marked. (6,8) is marked, which causes (4,6) and (5,6) to be marked, and the marking of (4,6) results in that of (4,8) and (2,6). Finally, (7,8) is marked.

The result is that the pairs (2,3) and (4,5) remain unmarked. In the rest of Algorithm 7.2, new states in the minimum-state FA are created for each of the states 1, 2, 4, 6, 7, 8, and 9 in the original FA. The result (with these numbers used for the states) is shown in Fig. 7.5c.

7.4 THE UNIQUENESS OF THE MINIMUM-STATE FA

Before we leave the subject of minimum-state FAs we should notice one more thing. We now have a way of starting with an FA M and finding an FA M_1 with the fewest possible states recognizing the same language. If we have two FAs recognizing the same language and apply the minimization algorithm to both, the resulting FAs will have the same number of states. One might ask whether they will *look* the same; in other words, is there only one minimum-state FA recognizing a given language? If we are careful to formulate correctly the notion of two FAs "looking the same," we can see from our earlier discussion that the answer is yes. The effect of applying Algorithm 7.1 to M, which recognizes the language L, is to leave unmarked those pairs of states (p, q), and only those, for which L_p and L_q are both subsets of the same equivalence class. This means that for any equivalence class C, all the states p for which $L_p \subseteq C$ are merged into one, say P, by Algorithm 7.2. The subsets L_P in the resulting FA M_1 are identical to the equivalence classes; in other words, two strings x and y cause M_1 to be in the same state if and only if x is equivalent to (indistinguishable from) y. We expect, therefore, that M_1 will look the same as the minimum-state FA M_L described in Theorem 7.1, whose states are simply these equivalence classes.

To be a little more explicit: we have $M = (Q, \Sigma, q_0, \delta, A)$; the FA $M_L = (Q_L, \Sigma, q_L, \delta_L, A_L)$ described in Theorem 7.1; and the FA $M_1 = (Q_1, \Sigma, q_1, \delta_1, A_1)$ obtained from Algorithm 7.2. From the above, we may define

$$i : Q_L \to Q_1$$

where for any equivalence class $C \in Q_L$, $i(C)$ is the state of M_1 to which the strings in C correspond. This is the same as saying

$$i([x]) = \delta_1^*(q_1, x)$$

for every $x \in \Sigma^*$. i is one-to-one, since two inequivalent strings cannot cause M_1 to be in the same state. Therefore, since Q_L and Q_1 are the same size, i is a bijection. Furthermore, since the initial state q_L of M_L is $[\Lambda]$, we have

$$i(q_L) = i([\Lambda]) = \delta_1^*(q_1, \Lambda) = q_1$$

Recall that in the FA M_L, a state (an equivalence class) is accepting if and only if the equivalence class contains an element of L. If $i([x]) \in A_1$, then $\delta^*(q_1, x) \in A_1$, which means that $x \in L$. Obviously, $[x]$ contains an element of L (namely, x), and so $[x] \in A_L$. On the other hand, if $[x] \in A_L$, some element of $[x]$, say y, belongs to L; but since $y \in [x]$, yI_Lx, thus $x \in L$. Therefore, $\delta_1^*(q_1, x) = i([x]) \in A_1$. We conclude that the function i preserves accepting states: $i([x])$ is an accepting state in M_1 if and only if $[x]$ is an accepting state in M_L.

Let us consider the relationship between i and the two transition functions δ_1 and δ_L. For any $a \in \Sigma$,

$$\begin{aligned}
i(\delta_L([x], a)) &= i([xa]) \text{ (by definition of } \delta_L) \\
&= \delta_1^*(q_1, xa) \text{ (by the formula for } i \text{ above)} \\
&= \delta_1(\delta_1^*(q_1, x), a) \text{ (by the definition of } \delta_1^*) \\
&= \delta_1(i([x]), a)
\end{aligned}$$

We may represent this relationship pictorially as in Fig. 7-6. Starting at $[x]$, you end up at the same place, whether you first follow the arrow across to $\delta_L([x], a) = [xa]$ and then down to $i([xa])$, or whether you first go down to $i([x])$ and across to $\delta_1(i([x]), a)$.

The significance of this is that the transitions in the FA M_L are preserved in the FA M_1: the top part of Fig. 7-6 is identical to the bottom, except that the states are designated $[x]$ and $[xa]$ in one case, $i([x])$ and $i([xa])$ in the other. Since the transition shown is arbitrary, what this tells us is that the transition diagram for M_L is identical to that for M_1, except for this difference in the way states

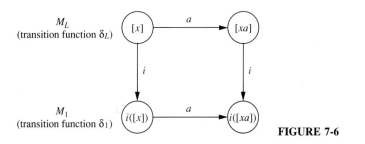

FIGURE 7-6

are labeled. "Identical" is not too strong a word here, since the two pictures have accepting states in exactly the same places, as we have already noticed.

This is the appropriate formulation of two FAs "looking the same." But remember our original question: is there only one minimum-state FA recognizing a given language L? What we have seen so far is that, except for the labels of the states, any minimum-state FA looks the same as M_L; it follows then that any two minimum-state FAs recognizing L look the same.

The notion of two FAs looking the same is formulated more precisely in the following definition.

Definition 7.1. If $M_1 = (Q_1, \Sigma, q_1, \delta_1, A_1)$ and $M_2 = (Q_2, \Sigma, q_2, \delta_2, A_2)$ are FAs with alphabet Σ, and $i : Q_1 \rightarrow Q_2, f$ is an *isomorphism from* M_1 *to* M_2 if i is a bijection from Q_1 to Q_2 satisfying these conditions:

$$i(q_1) = q_2$$

for any $q \in Q_1, i(q) \in A_2$ if and only if $q \in A_1$

for every $q \in Q_1$ and $a \in \Sigma, i(\delta_1(q, a)) = \delta_2(i(q), a)$

M_1 is *isomorphic to* M_2 if there is an isomorphism from M_1 to M_2.

There may be some question at this point as to whether it is quite accurate to say that "M_1 is isomorphic to M_2" really means "M_1 looks the same as M_2." In particular, we would certainly agree that the relation "looks the same as" ought to be symmetric and transitive: if M_1 looks the same as M_2, M_2 looks the same as M_1; and if M_1 looks the same as M_2 and M_2 looks the same as M_3, then M_1 looks the same as M_3. But it is not immediately obvious that the relation "is isomorphic to" has these properties. To remove any doubt, we prove a preliminary lemma.

Lemma 7.4. The relation $\sim$ on the set of FAs over Σ, defined by

$$M_1 \sim M_2 \text{ if } M_1 \text{ is isomorphic to } M_2$$

is an equivalence relation.

Proof. It is easy to see that the relation is reflexive, since for any FA $M = (Q, \Sigma, q_0, \delta, A)$, the identity function from Q to Q, the function i defined by $i(x) = x$, is an isomorphism from M to M.

Let $i : Q_1 \rightarrow Q_2$ and $j : Q_2 \rightarrow Q_3$ be isomorphisms from M_1 to M_2 and from M_2 to M_3, respectively. We must show that there is an isomorphism from M_2 to M_1, which will show that $\sim$ is symmetric, and that there is an isomorphism from M_1 to M_3, which will show that $\sim$ is transitive.

Since i and j are both bijections, $i^{-1} : Q_2 \rightarrow Q_1$ is a bijection and $j \circ i : Q_1 \rightarrow Q_3$ is a bijection. For any $p \in Q_2$ and $a \in \Sigma$,

$$i(i^{-1}(\delta_2(p, a))) = \delta_2(p, a)$$

by definition of the function i^{-1}. But since i is an isomorphism from M_1 to M_2,

$$i(\delta_1(i^{-1}(p), a)) = \delta_2(i(i^{-1}(p)), a) = \delta_2(p, a)$$

Since i is one-to-one and

$$i(i^{-1}(\delta_2(p, a))) = i(\delta_1(i^{-1}(p), a))$$

it follows that

$$i^{-1}(\delta_2(p, a)) = \delta_1(i^{-1}(p), a)$$

This is the formula i^{-1} needs to satisfy in order for it to be an isomorphism from M_2 to M_1. In addition, since for any $q \in Q_1$, q is an accepting state if and only if $i(q)$ is, it is also true that for any $p \in Q_2$, p is an accepting state if and only if $i^{-1}(p)$ is; and finally, since $i(q_1) = q_2$, $i^{-1}(q_2) = q_1$. Therefore, i^{-1} is an isomorphism from M_2 to M_1.

Now we show that $j \circ i$ is an isomorphism from M_1 to M_3.

$$\begin{aligned} j \circ i(\delta_1(q, a)) &= j(i(\delta_1(q, a))) \\ &= j(\delta_2(i(q), a)) \\ &= \delta_3(j(i(q)), a) \\ &= \delta_3(j \circ i(q), a) \end{aligned}$$

The second equality holds because i is an isomorphism, the third because j is. It is easy to check that for any $q \in Q_1$, q is an accepting state if and only if $j \circ i(q)$ is, and clearly $j \circ i(q_1) = q_3$. Therefore M_1 is isomorphic to M_3.

Theorem 7.3. If M_1 and M_2 are both minimum-state FAs recognizing a language $L \subseteq \Sigma^*$, M_1 is isomorphic to M_2.

Proof. This follows easily from our earlier discussion together with Lemma 7.4.

EXERCISES

7.1. For which languages $L \subseteq \{a, b\}^*$ is there only one equivalence class with respect to the relation I_L?

7.2. Let x be a string in $\{a, b\}^*$. How many equivalence classes are there of the relation I_L, where $L = \{x\}$? Describe them.

7.3. Find a language L so that no equivalence class of I_L has more than one element.

7.4. Consider the language $L = \{a^N b^N | N > 0\}$.
   (a) Show that L constitutes a single equivalence class with respect to I_L (i.e., any two elements of L are equivalent, and no element of L is equivalent to an element of L').
   (b) Show that for any $i \geq 0$, the string a^i is distinguishable from every other string with respect to L.
   (c) Show that $a^5 b$ and $a^6 b^2$ are not distinguishable with respect to L.
   (d) What are the distinct equivalence classes of I_L?

7.5. Consider the language $L = \{x \in \{a, b\}^* | N_a(x) = N_b(x)\}$.
   (a) Show that if $N_a(x) - N_b(x) = N_a(y) - N_b(y)$, x and y are not distinguishable with respect to L.

(b) Show that if $N_a(x) - N_b(x) \neq N_a(y) - N_b(y)$, x and y are distinguishable.

(c) What are the distinct equivalence classes of I_L?

7.6. Let L be the language of "balanced" strings of parentheses—i.e., all strings that are the strings of parentheses in legal algebraic expressions. For example, ()() and ((())) are in L, (() and ())() are not. Describe the distinct equivalence classes of I_L.

7.7. Let $M = (Q, \Sigma, q_0, \delta, A)$ be an FA recognizing a language L. As in Section 7.2, if $p, q \in Q$, $p \cong q$ means that the sets L_p and L_q are both subsets of the same equivalence class with respect to I_L. (Assume that $L_p \neq \phi$ for every p.)

(a) Suppose $\delta(p, a) = \delta(q, a)$ for every $a \in \Sigma$. Can we conclude that $p \cong q$? Why?

(b) Show that if $p \cong q$, then for every $x \in \Sigma^*$, $\delta^*(p, x) \in A$ if and only if $\delta^*(q, x) \in A$.

(c) Show that if for every $x \in \Sigma^*$, $\delta^*(p, x) \in A$ if and only if $\delta^*(q, x) \in A$, then $p \cong q$.

7.8. Let M be as in Exercise 7.7. Show that $\cong$ is an equivalence relation on Q, and that the states in Q that are merged in the minimization algorithm are precisely the elements of an equivalence class of $\cong$.

7.9. Let $M = (Q, \Sigma, q_0, \delta, A)$ be an FA.

(a) Suppose $Q_1 \subseteq Q$, $Q_1 \cap A = \emptyset$, and for every $q \in Q_1$ and $a \in \Sigma$, $\delta(q, a) \in Q_1$. Show that for any $p, q \in Q_1$, $p \cong q$.

(b) Suppose $Q_1 \subseteq A$ and for every $q \in Q_1$ and $a \in \Sigma$, $\delta(q, a) \in Q_1$. Show that for any $p, q \in Q_1$, $p \cong q$.

7.10. For each of the FAs pictured in Fig. 7-7, find a minimum-state FA recognizing the same language. (It's possible that the given FA may already be minimal.)

7.11. Find a minimum-state FA recognizing the language corresponding to each of these regular expressions.

(a) $(a^*ba + b^*a)(ab)^*$

(b) $(aba)^*b + (b^*a)^*$

7.12. Find a minimum-state FA recognizing the language recognized by each of the NFA-Λs in Fig. 7-8.

7.13. Suppose $M_1 = (Q_1, \Sigma, q_1, \delta_1, A_1)$ and $M_2 = (Q_2, \Sigma, q_2, \delta_2, A_2)$ are FAs and $f : Q_1 \rightarrow Q_2$ satisfies the condition $f(\delta_1(q, a)) = \delta_2(f(q), a)$ for every $a \in Q_1$ and $a \in \Sigma$. Show that $f(\delta_1^*(q, x)) = \delta_2^*(f(q), x)$ for every $q \in Q_1$ and every $x \in \Sigma^*$.

7.14. Show that two isomorphic FAs recognize the same language.

7.15. (a) How many one-state FAs over the alphabet $\{a, b\}$ are there, no two of which are isomorphic?

(b) How many two-state FAs over the alphabet $\{a, b\}$ are there (in which both states are reachable from the initial state and at least one state is accepting), no two of which are isomorphic?

(c) How many distinct languages are recognized by the FAs in (b)?

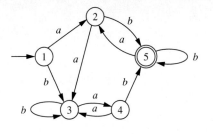

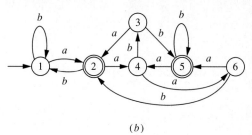

(a)

(b)

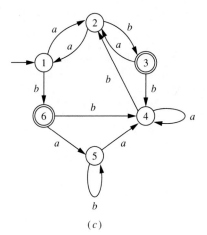

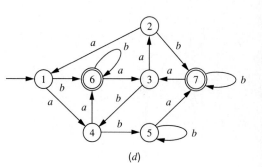

(c)

(d)

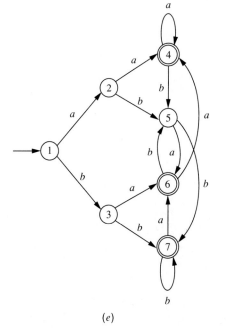

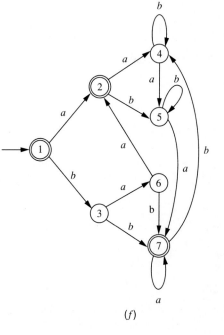

(e)

(f)

FIGURE 7-7

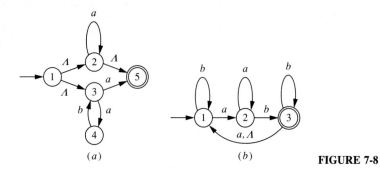

(a)   (b)

FIGURE 7-8

7.16. Show that the FAs described by these two transition tables are isomorphic. The states are 1–6 in the first, I–VI in the second; the initial states are 1 and I, respectively; the accepting states in the first FA are 5 and 6, in the second IV and V.

q	$\delta(q, a)$	$\delta(q, b)$
1	3	5
2	4	2
3	1	6
4	4	3
5	2	4
6	3	4

q	$\delta(q, a)$	$\delta(q, b)$
I	II	V
II	I	IV
III	III	II
IV	II	III
V	VI	III
VI	III	VI

7.17. Describe in general how you might go about determining whether two FAs are isomorphic.

CHAPTER

8

REGULAR LANGUAGES AND NONREGULAR LANGUAGES

8.1 A CRITERION FOR REGULARITY

As a result of Theorem 4.3, we have one example of a language that is not regular: the language of palindromes over the alphabet $\{0,1\}$. However, we may extract from Chapters 4 and 7 a general criterion for a language L to be regular, and this will allow us to identify many other nonregular languages. The criterion involves the relation I_L, that of indistinguishability with respect to L, introduced in Section 7.1.

Theorem 8.1 (Myhill–Nerode). A language L in Σ^* is regular if and only if the set of equivalence classes of the relation I_L is finite. L is nonregular if and only if there is an infinite subset of Σ^*, any two elements of which are distinguishable with respect to L.

Proof. First, notice that the two statements really say the same thing. To say that two strings are distinguishable with respect to L is the same as saying that they are in different equivalence classes of I_L. Thus, on the one hand, if the set of equivalence classes of I_L is finite, then any pairwise distinguishable set of strings has at most as many elements as there are equivalence classes of I_L, and, in particular, there can be no infinite pairwise distinguishable set. On the other hand, if the set of equivalence classes is infinite, then a set consisting of one string from each is an infinite set, any two elements of which are distinguishable with respect to L.

If the set of equivalence classes of I_L is finite, the proof of Theorem 7.1 shows there is an FA with exactly that many states recognizing L. (In the statement of that theorem, we assumed L to be regular; but the proof used only the finiteness condition.) Conversely, Theorem 4.2 says that if there is a pairwise distinguishable set with n elements, any FA recognizing L has at least n states; it follows that if there is an infinite pairwise distinguishable set, there can be no FA recognizing L.

A finite automaton's "memory" resides in its finite set of states. It is capable of remembering only that the current input string corresponds to one state rather than another. Theorem 8.1 is just another way of saying that a language is regular if and only if that type of memory is sufficient to recognize it.

In the proof of Theorem 4.3, we considered the infinite set of strings $S = \{1, 11, 111, \ldots\}$. If we are attempting to recognize the language of palindromes, and the current input string is one of the elements of S, say 1^k, we must be able to remember the number k in some form or other; if what comes afterward is 01^j, for example, we must be able to compare j and k, since the entire string is a palindrome if and only if the two are equal. With a fixed number of states, there is a limit to the size of the k that can be remembered. This is the intuitive reason that the language of palindromes is not regular.

We may now use the same principle to exhibit a number of other nonregular languages.

Example 8.1. Let $L = \{0^n 1^n | n \geq 0\}$. Again, it is intuitively obvious that recognizing L will be too much for any FA, because we must remember how many 0's we've seen so that we will be able to determine whether there are exactly as many 1's. To use Theorem 8.1, we consider the infinite set $S = \{0^n | n \geq 0\}$. Any two elements of S, say 0^i and 0^j, can be distinguished by the string 1^i, since $0^i 1^i \in L$ but $0^j 1^i \notin L$. Therefore, L is not regular.

Example 8.2. Let L be the set of all legal algebraic expressions involving the identifier A, the operator $+$, and left and right parentheses. (We considered a similar language in Example 2.10.) It would be simple enough to give a recursive definition of L, but we save that until the next chapter, since L will be a useful example of a context-free language. To show that L is not regular, we can ignore much of its structure altogether. We will use only the fact that the string $(^i A)^j$ is in L if and only if $i = j$. We may therefore copy Example 8.1 and let $S = \{(^n | n \geq 1\}$. If $1 \leq m < n$, then $(^m A)^m \in L$ and $(^n A)^m \notin L$. This shows that S is an infinite set that is pairwise distinguishable with respect to L.

Example 8.3. For yet another example where the set $S = \{0^n | n \geq 0\}$ can be used to prove a language nonregular, take L to be the language $\{ww | w \in \{0, 1\}^*\}$ of all strings of even length whose first and second halves are identical. Here we must be just a little more imaginative to find a string z that distinguishes 0^n and 0^m when $m \neq n$; but $z = 1^n 0^n 1^n$ will do. $0^n z \in L$, and $0^m z \notin L$.

Exercise 8.1 asks you to get even a little more mileage out of the set $\{0^n | n \geq 0\}$ or some variation of it. We close this section with one more example.

Example 8.4. Let $L = \{a, abb, abbaaa, abbaaabbbb, \ldots\}$. A string in L consists of groups of a's alternated with groups of b's. It begins with a single a, and each group of identical symbols has one more symbol than the previous group. Here we may take the set S to be L itself. Let x and y be distinct elements of L; suppose x ends with the group a^j and y ends with the group a^k, for example. Then $xb^{j+1} \in L$, but $yb^{j+1} \notin L$. Obviously, a similar argument will work in the other three cases.

8.2 THE PUMPING LEMMA: ANOTHER WAY TO PROVE A LANGUAGE NONREGULAR

Our next result also uses the finiteness of the set of states of a finite automaton to derive a property that is common to all regular languages. This will provide another technique for showing languages nonregular, since if a property is shared by all regular languages and certain languages can be shown not to have the property, then these languages cannot be regular.

Suppose M is an FA recognizing a language L. The property we are interested in has to do with paths through M that contain "loops." If a string x is in L and the path corresponding to x contains a loop, in the sense that processing the symbols of x causes M to return at least once to a state it has been in previously, there are many other paths that also correspond to strings in L: paths that visit exactly the same states but take the loop a different number of times. This simple observation will turn out to provide a powerful tool, and it will be worthwhile to formulate it carefully so that the tool will be as useful as possible.

Let $M = (Q, \Sigma, q_0, \delta, A)$, and suppose that Q has N elements. For any $x \in L$ with $|x| \geq N$, if we write $x = a_1 a_2 \ldots a_N y$, the sequence of states

$$q_0$$
$$q_1 = \delta^*(q_0, a_1)$$
$$q_2 = \delta^*(q_0, a_1 a_2)$$
$$\ldots$$
$$q_N = \delta^*(q_0, a_1 a_2 \ldots a_N)$$

must contain some state at least twice. This is where our loop comes from. Suppose $q_i = q_{i+p}$, where $0 \leq i < i + p \leq N$. Then

$$\delta^*(q_0, a_1 \ldots a_i) = q_i$$
$$\delta^*(q_i, a_{i+1} \ldots a_{i+p}) = q_i$$
$$\delta^*(q_i, a_{i+p+1} \ldots a_N y) = q_f \in A$$

To simplify notation, let $u = a_1 \ldots a_i$, $v = a_{i+1} \ldots a_{i+p}$, and $w = a_{i+p+1} \ldots a_N y$. (See the diagram in Fig. 8-1.) Since $\delta^*(q_i, v) = q_i$, then

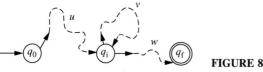

FIGURE 8-1

$\delta^*(q_i, v^m) = q_i$ for every $m \geq 0$ (see Exercise 4.7), and it follows from this that $\delta^*(q_0, uv^mw) = q_f$ for every $m \geq 0$. Since $p > 0$ and $i + p \leq N$, we have proved the following result.

Theorem 8.2. Suppose L is a regular language recognized by some FA with N states. For any $x \in L$ with $|x| \geq N$, x may be written as $x = uvw$, for some u, v, and w satisfying

$$|uv| \leq N$$

$$|v| > 0$$

$$\text{for any } m \geq 0, uv^mw \in L$$

This result is often referred to as the Pumping Lemma, since we may think of it as taking an arbitrary string of sufficient length in L and "pumping up" a portion of it, by introducing additional copies of v, to obtain many more distinct elements of L.

Many theorems are easy to understand and apply but difficult to prove. This one is relatively simple to prove, but applying it correctly requires some care, simply because of the logical complexity of the statement. It may be helpful first to restate it in a way that seems to weaken it slightly but makes it a little clearer what the point is that will be essential for the applications.

Theorem 8.2a   (Pumping Lemma). Suppose L is a regular language. There is an integer N so that for any $x \in L$ with $|x| \geq N$, there are strings u, v, and w so that $x = uvw$ and

$$|uv| \leq N \tag{8.1}$$

$$|v| > 0 \tag{8.2}$$

$$\text{for any } m \geq 0, uv^mw \in L \tag{8.3}$$

This theorem describes a property of regular languages, and, as we observed earlier, we can apply it to show a language nonregular if we can show that the property fails to hold for the language. This is done by assuming that the statement about L is true and deriving a contradiction. The statement is of the form: "There is an N so that for any $x \in L$ with $|x| \geq N$, ..." We assume it is true; we therefore have some integer N, although we don't know what it is. If we can find a specific string x with $|x| \geq N$ so that the statements involving x in the theorem would lead to a contradiction, we're done. (The statement in the theorem says that for *any* x with $|x| \geq N$, ...; therefore, for our specific x, ...; but this leads to a contradiction; therefore, the statement in the theorem leads to a contradiction.) But remember that we don't know what N is. So, in effect, we must show that for *any* N, we can find an $x \in L$ with $|x| \geq N$ so that the statements about x in the theorem lead to a contradiction. We are free to pick x, as long as $|x| \geq N$. Since we don't know what N is, we must specify x in terms of N.

One other very important point: once we have chosen x, we are *not* free to choose the way in which our string x is broken into u, v, and w. Theorem 8.2a says simply that there *is* a way that will cause (8.1)–(8.3) to be true. We are choosing an x that will lead to a contradiction; this means that once we have chosen x, we need to show that *any* choice of u, v, and w satisfying (8.1)–(8.3) produces a contradiction.

Let us illustrate, using as an example one of the languages that we know from Section 8.1 is nonregular.

Example 8.5. Take $L = \{0^n 1^n \mid n \geq 0\}$. Using Theorem 8.2a, we wish to show that L is nonregular. Suppose L is regular, and let N be the integer in Theorem 8.2a. We must show that no matter what N is, we may find x, with $|x| \geq N$, that produces a contradiction. Let $x = 0^N 1^N$. According to Theorem 8.2a, there are strings u, v, and w so that $x = uvw$ and conditions (8.1), (8.2), and (8.3) in the theorem hold. We don't know exactly what u, v, and w are, but (8.1), (8.2), and (8.3) allow us to determine their general form. From (8.1) we can see that $uv = 0^k$ for some k, so from (8.2) we have $v = 0^j$ for some $j > 0$. Then (8.3) says that $uv^m w \in L$ for every $m \geq 0$. But

$$uv^m w = (uv)v^{m-1}w$$
$$= 0^k(0^j)^{m-1}0^{N-k}1^N \qquad (w = 0^{N-k}1^N, \text{ since } uv = 0^k)$$
$$= 0^{N+j(m-1)}1^N$$

and this string is clearly not in L if $m > 1$. This contradiction shows that our original assumption that L was regular cannot be true.

Before we leave this example, it is worth looking a little more closely at our choice of x. We didn't have a lot of choice, since a string in L is determined by its length. But the only assumption about x in the pumping lemma is that $|x| \geq N$. With just a little more effort, we could have obtained a contradiction with $x = 0^M 1^M$ where M is any number $N/2$ or bigger. This assumption would no longer imply that $uv = 0^k$; there would be two other cases to consider. If v contained both 0's and 1's, then $v = 0^i 1^j$, so for any $m > 1$, $uv^m w$ would contain 10, which would make it impossible for it to be in L. If v were 1^j, then we could obtain a contradiction in the same way we did originally.

Again, the point is that in using the pumping lemma to show L nonregular, we are free to choose x any way we wish, as long as $|x| \geq N$, and we try to choose it so that obtaining a contradiction will be as easy as possible. But once we have selected x, we must be careful to show that a contradiction follows inevitably. Unless we can show that every conceivable case leads to a contradiction, we haven't accomplished anything.

Example 8.6. Let

$$L = \{x \in \{0, 1\}^* \mid x \text{ contains equal numbers of 0's and 1's}\}$$

The proof that L is nonregular starts exactly the same way. Assume L is regular, and let N be the integer in Theorem 8.2a. Again, let's try $x = 0^N 1^N$. Exactly the same argument as in Example 8.5 shows that if $x = uvw$ and (8.1), (8.2), and (8.3) of the theorem hold, then $v = 0^j$ for some $j > 0$, and we get the same contradiction as before. $uv^m w$ cannot be in L if $m \neq 1$, since it doesn't have equal numbers of 0's and 1's.

Here we have a better example of the importance of choosing x appropriately. We can see this by looking at a choice of x that would *not* be appropriate. Suppose $x = (01)^N$. This x is certainly in L, and $|x| \geq N$. But look what happens when we try to get a contradiction. If $x = uvw$, we have these possibilities:

1. $v = (01)^j$ for some $j > 0$
2. $v = 1(01)^j$ for some $j \geq 0$

3. $v = (10)^j$ for some $j > 0$

4. $v = (01)^j 0$ for some $j \geq 0$

Unfortunately, none of the conditions (8.1), (8.2), and (8.3) gives us any more information about v, except for some upper bounds on j. In cases 2 and 4 we can obtain a contradiction, since the string v that is being pumped has unequal numbers of 0's and 1's. In the other two cases, however, there is no contradiction, since for this L, obtaining a contradiction means producing a string $uv^m w$ with unequal numbers of 0's and 1's. We cannot be sure that these other cases don't occur, and thus with this choice of x we are simply unable to complete the proof.

Example 8.7. $L = \{0^n x | x \in \{0, 1\}^*$ and $|x| \leq n\}$. Another description of L is that it is the set of all strings of 0's and 1's so that at least the first half consists of 0's. Assume L is regular, and let N be the integer in Theorem 8.2a. What string shall we start with in order to obtain a contradiction? It obviously can't be all 0's, for then no other string obtained by pumping would have anything but 0's. Suppose we try our old standby, $x = 0^N 1^N$. Then if $x = uvw$ and (8.1), (8.2), and (8.3) hold, it follows as before that $v = 0^j$ for some $j > 0$. In this example, pumping is a little misleading: We do not obtain a contradiction by looking at strings with additional copies of v, since they have even more 0's in the front. However, (8.3) says in particular that $uv^0 w = uw \in L$. This gives us our contradiction, since $uw = 0^{N-j} 1^N \notin L$. Therefore, L is not regular.

Often it is possible to get by with a weakened form of the pumping lemma. Here are two versions that ignore many of the conclusions of Theorem 8.2a but are still strong enough to show certain languages nonregular.

Theorem 8.3   (Weak form of pumping lemma). Suppose L is an infinite regular language. There are strings u, v, and w so that $|v| > 0$ and $uv^m w \in L$ for every $m \geq 0$.

Proof. This follows immediately from Theorem 8.2a: no matter how big the integer N in the statement of that theorem is, L contains a string at least that long since L is infinite.

Theorem 8.3 would suffice for Example 8.5, as you are asked to show in Exercise 8.2, but it is not enough to take care of Examples 8.6 or 8.7.

Theorem 8.4   (Even weaker form of pumping lemma). Suppose L is an infinite regular language. There are integers p and q, with $q > 0$, so that for every $m \geq 0$, L contains a string of length $p + mq$. In other words, the set of integers $LENGTHS(L) = \{n | L$ contains a string of length $n\}$ contains the "arithmetic progression" of all integers $p + mq$ (where $m \geq 0$).

Proof. This follows from Theorem 8.3, since we may take $p = |u| + |w|$ and $q = |v|$.

Theorem 8.4 would not be enough to show the language in Example 8.5 nonregular, but we shall use it in our next example.

Example 8.8. Let $L = \{0^n | n$ is prime $\} = \{0^2, 0^3, 0^5, 0^7, 0^{11}, \ldots\}$. According to Theorem 8.4, in order to show that L is nonregular, we just need to show that the set of primes cannot contain an infinite arithmetic progression of the form $\{p + mq | m \geq 0\}$; in other words, for any $p \geq 0$ and $q > 0$, there is an integer m so that $p + mq$ is not prime.

"Not prime" means factorable into factors 2 or bigger. We could choose $m = p$, which would give $p + mq = p + pq = p(1 + q)$, but we're not certain that $p \geq 2$. Instead, let $m = p + 2q + 2$. Then

$$p + mq = p + (p + 2q + 2)q$$

$$= (p + 2q) + (p + 2q)q$$

$$= (p + 2q)(1 + q)$$

and this is not prime.

This example obviously has a different flavor from those preceding, and seems to have more to do with arithmetic, or number theory, than with languages. Yet it illustrates the fact, which will become even more obvious in the later parts of this book, that many questions about computation can be formulated in the context of language theory. What we have found in this example is that there is no finite automaton that can take an arbitrary integer and determine whether it is prime; solving this problem for arbitrarily large integers requires more memory than an FA has.

One might hope at this point that for any nonregular language L, the pumping lemma can be used to prove it is nonregular, using some sufficiently clever choice of a string x. In other words, one might hope that the converse of Theorem 8.2a is true—that if the conclusions of the pumping lemma hold, then L is regular. The next example shows that this is not correct, and therefore that the pumping lemma cannot be adapted to prove languages regular.

Example 8.9. Let

$$L = \{a^i b^j c^j | i \geq 1, j \geq 0\} \cup \{b^j c^k | j, k \geq 0\}$$

Let us show first that the conclusions of Theorem 8.2a hold. Take N to be 1, and suppose $x \in L$ with $|x| \geq N$. There are two cases. If $x = a^i b^j c^j$ where $i \geq 1$, let $u = \Lambda$, $v = a$, $w = a^{i-1} b^j c^j$. Any string of the form $uv^m w$ is still of the form $a^l b^j c^j$ and is therefore an element of L (whether $l = 0$ or not). If $x = b^i c^j$, again let u be Λ and v the first symbol in x. Again, $uv^m w \in L$ for every $m \geq 0$.

However, L is not regular, as you can show using Theorem 8.1. The details are almost identical to those in Example 8.1 and are left as an exercise (Exercise 8.3).

8.3 DECISION PROBLEMS AND DECISION ALGORITHMS

Finite automata are our first step toward a general model of computation. An FA is a very rudimentary computer. It receives input, and it produces output of the form "yes" or "no," in the sense that the input string may or may not cause the FA to end up in an accepting state. The problems it can solve are *decision* problems: problems that can be answered yes or no, like "Given a string x of a's and b's, does x contain more than two occurrences of the string baa?" or "Given a string of 0's and 1's that is the binary representation of a natural number n, is n divisible by 7?" A decision problem like the first one consists of a set of specific *instances*; in this case, an instance is a particular string of a's and b's. An instance of a problem corresponds to asking the general question in one particular case.

The fact that an FA is limited to solving decision problems is not so significant. What makes it a primitive model of computation is that the algorithm it embodies cannot involve remembering more than some fixed amount of information. A decision problem for which every instance can be answered subject to this constraint is inherently fairly simple, and thus probably not very interesting.

In this section, we are interested not so much in decision problems that FAs can solve, as in decision problems having to do with FAs and regular languages themselves. There are a number of questions that arise naturally in connection with FAs, some of which we already have decision algorithms to answer. Here is a list that is not by any means exhaustive.

1. Given an FA M and a string x, does M accept x?
2. Given an FA M, is there a string that it accepts? (Equivalently, is $L(M) = \varnothing$?)
3. Given an FA M, is $L(M)$ finite?
4. Given two FAs M_1 and M_2, are there any strings that are accepted by both?
5. Given two FAs M_1 and M_2, is $L(M_1)$ a subset of $L(M_2)$?
6. Given two FA's M_1 and M_2, do they accept the same language? (In other words, is $L(M_1) = L(M_2)$?)
7. Given two regular expressions R_1 and R_2, do they correspond to the same language?
8. Given an FA M, is it a minimum–state FA accepting the language L(M)?

Problem 1 has an easy solution: give the string x as input to M and see what happens. If it causes M to end up in an accepting state, the answer is yes, otherwise the answer is no. The reason this is acceptable as an algorithm is that M behaves deterministically (i.e., we can predict by examining the specifications of M exactly what steps it will take, and what its conclusion will be on input x), and its processing of x is guaranteed to terminate after exactly $|x|$ moves and produce an answer.

Chapter 7 gives a decision algorithm for problem 8. Apply the minimization algorithm to M and see if the number of states is reduced. Of the remaining problems, some are closely related to others. In fact, if we had an algorithm to solve problem 2, we could obtain algorithms to handle problems 4, 5, 6, and 7. For problem 4, we could first apply the algorithm presented in Section 4.5 to construct an FA M recognizing $L(M_1) \cap L(M_2)$; we could then use the algorithm for problem 2 on this new FA. For any M_1 and M_2, there is a string in $L(M_1) - L(M_2)$ if and only if $L(M_1)$ is not a subset of $L(M_2)$. Therefore, problem 5 could be done the same way, but with $L(M_1) - L(M_2)$ instead of $L(M_1) \cap L(M_2)$. Problem 6 can be reduced to problem 5, since two sets are equal precisely when each is a subset of the other. Finally, problem 7 can be reduced to problem 6, since we have an algorithm from Chapter 6 to find an FA corresponding to a given regular expression.

The two that remain are 2 and 3. With regard to 2, one might ask how an FA could fail to accept any strings. A trivial way, which we could detect by looking at the FA's specifications, would be for it to have no accepting states. But even if there are accepting states, it is possible for them all to be unreachable from the initial state. We may determine this by calculating recursively, as in Chapter 7, the states that are reachable. If $M = (Q, \Sigma, q_0, \delta, A)$, define the sets T_k as follows.

$$T_0 = \{q_0\}$$

$$\text{for } k \geq 1, \; T_k = T_{k-1} \cup \{\delta(q, a) | q \in T_{k-1}, a \in \Sigma\}$$

T_k is the set of states reachable in one step from T_{k-1}—or equivalently, T_k is the set of states reachable from q_0 by strings of length k.

Decision Algorithm for problem 2. **(Given an FA M, is $L(M) = \varnothing$?)** Continue to compute the set T_k until either T_k contains an element of A, or $T_k = T_{k-1}$. In the first case, $L(M) \neq \varnothing$. In the second case, if $T_k \cap A = \varnothing$ for the last k considered, then $L(M) = \varnothing$.

If N is the number of states in M, one of these two cases must occur by the time T_N has been computed. This means that the following algorithm would also work:

Give M input strings in increasing order of length; if no strings of length less than N are accepted, then M does not accept any strings.

Notice, though, that this approach is likely to be much less efficient. For example, if we test 0101100 and later test 01011000, all but the last step of the second test is duplicated effort.

It is interesting that this second version starts out sounding like a completely simple-minded approach. (Does M accept any strings? Well, try some strings and see!) The aspect of the solution that rescues it from hopeless simple-mindedness is that if all strings of length less than N have been tried without success, we know we can quit. Without this proviso, it wouldn't be an algorithm at all—only a shot in the dark.

In the case of Problem 3, the simple-minded approach of trying strings would seem to have no chance at all of success. But again, the trick is to identify a finite range of string lengths so that having tested, if necessary, all the strings in that range, we will know the answer. The pumping lemma in its original version, Theorem 8.2, turns out to be useful here. Again, let N be the number of states in the FA M. In the first place, the pumping lemma tells us that if M accepts even one string of length N or greater, then $L(M)$ is infinite, since for some fixed strings u, v, and w with $|v| > 0$, $L(M)$ contains the infinite set $\{uv^m w | m \geq 0\}$.

On the other hand, if $L(M)$ is infinite, there must be a string x satisfying $N \leq |x| < 2N$ that is accepted. To see this, suppose $L(M)$ is infinite and there is no such x. There must be strings of length $\geq 2N$ that are accepted, since $L(M)$ is infinite. Choose one of minimal length, say z. Apply the pumping lemma to z: z can be written $z = uvw$, where $|uv| \leq N$, $|v| > 0$, and, in particular, $uv^0 w = uw \in L(M)$. But $|uw| \geq 2N - N$, since $|uvw| \geq 2N$ and $|v| \leq N$, and $|uw| < |uvw| = |z|$. Therefore, one of these two cases must occur: either

$N \leq |uw| < 2N$ or $2N \leq |uw| < |z|$. Our original assumption was that there was no x in $L(M)$ with $N \leq |x| < 2N$, and so we are left with the second case. But this contradicts our choice of z as the shortest string of length $\geq 2N$ in $L(M)$. It follows that our original assumption is false.

We have proved that the following algorithm is a solution to Problem 3:

Decision Algorithm for Problem 3 **(Given an FA *M*, is *L(M)* finite?)** Give M input strings in increasing order of length, beginning with length N. If no strings of length less than $2N$ are accepted, then $L(M)$ is finite; otherwise $L(M)$ is infinite.

There are at least two reasons for discussing decision problems such as those above and for trying to find corresponding decision algorithms. One is the obvious reason: solutions to the problem may be useful in specific cases. To take a not entirely frivolous example where problem 6 comes up, picture your poor instructor grading an exam question that asks for an FA recognizing a particular language. He or she knows a solution, presumably; a student turns in a totally different solution. The instructor is honor-bound to expend at least *some* effort trying to decide whether the two solutions are equivalent. (You are free to decide for yourself, however, how likely it is that he or she will implement the entire decision algorithm sketched above.) If the answer to a specific instance of the problem is the primary concern, then whether there is an efficient solution—one that can actually be carried out—is at least as important as whether there is a solution in principle. Someone who needed to solve problem 2 for an FA with 100 states could not afford even to consider the second version of the decision algorithm above and might look for ways to shortcut the first.

Aside from the question of finding efficient algorithms, however, there is another reason to consider these decision problems, a reason that will assume greater significance as we progress farther in the book. It is simply that not all decision problems can be solved; problems can be posed for which it can be proved that no decision algorithm could possibly exist. In fact, we won't have to go far to find examples. Although later on we shall consider decision problems that are not directly related to languages and computation, the first example historically of an "unsolvable" problem, and the first we shall consider, is problem 1 above, stated for a more general model of computation called a Turing machine. Its unsolvability was proved by Turing in the 1930s. That such problems could exist at all, and that there could be examples so basic and simple to state, came as a shock to mathematicians and logicians when it first became known (there were no "computer scientists" at the time, since this discovery predated, though not by very long, the development of the modern computer), and the idea is shocking even today. Completely aside from questions of efficiency, and even aside from physical considerations such as the speed of an electrical impulse, the number of atoms available in the universe from which to construct memory devices, and so on, there are definite theoretical limits on what it is possible for a computer, or a human being, or even a superhuman being who is constrained by the same rules of logic that we are, to compute. We will be investigating these matters in much more detail later. For the moment, it is reassuring to find that most of the obvious questions one can think of to ask about regular languages do have answers, and that we can exhibit algorithms guaranteed, in principle at least, to find them.

8.4 REGULAR LANGUAGES AND PROGRAMMING LANGUAGES; FINITE AUTOMATA AND COMPUTERS

When you hear the word "languages" in the context of computer science, you naturally think first of programming languages: Pascal, C, COBOL, and so forth. In our ascent up the hierarchy of formal languages, we have only reached the first plateau, that of regular languages. We can stop for a moment at this point, however, and ask what the relationship is between regular languages and the programming languages you're familiar with. The answer is almost obvious: programming languages are not regular. We saw in Example 8.2, for example, that a smaller language that is imbedded in most programming languages, that of algebraic expressions involving parentheses, is not regular. If finite automata are not capable of distinguishing between valid algebraic expressions and other strings, it doesn't seem likely that an FA could distinguish between a valid Pascal program and something that's not one. If a string purported to be a Pascal program and was invalid only because it contained an assignment statement whose right side was an invalid expression, how could an FA detect the problem without being able to recognize valid expressions?

More to the point, however, we can give a *proof* that Pascal is not regular, using exactly the same idea as in Example 8.2. All you need to know about Pascal is that the following string:

PROGRAM A; BEGIN BEGIN ... BEGIN END ... END END.

is a valid Pascal program (although it obviously doesn't accomplish anything) if the number of BEGINs is at least 1 and the same as the number of ENDs, and not otherwise. With this in mind, let S be the infinite set containing the strings

PROGRAM A; BEGIN

PROGRAM A; BEGIN BEGIN

PROGRAM A; BEGIN BEGIN BEGIN

...

Then any two strings in S, with m and n BEGINs, respectively, are distinguished relative to Pascal by the string consisting of m ENDs, separated by blanks, followed by a period. Therefore, by Theorem 8.1, Pascal is not regular.

While regular languages are not rich enough in structure to be programming languages, they do occur naturally in the context of programming languages. Example 3.6 provides a regular expression that specifies the proper syntax for a real constant appearing in a Pascal program statement. More generally, the *tokens* of a programming language can typically be described by a regular expression. Tokens include identifiers, literals, operators, reserved words, and punctuation. The first phase in compiling a program written in a high-level language such as Pascal is that of *lexical analysis*: identifying and classifying the tokens into which the individual characters are grouped. There are programs called lexical-analyzer generators; they are given as input a set of regular expressions that specify the structure of tokens, and they produce a software version of an FA that can be incorporated as a token-recognizing module in a compiler.

If regular languages aren't qualified to be programming languages, even less, it would seem, are finite automata equipped to be computers. There are a number of obvious differences, some more significant than others, having to do with memory, output capabilities, programmability, and so on. We have seen several examples of problems that are out of reach for any FA but could be handled easily by any programmer on just about any computer.

This point seems obvious, doesn't it? But if we think a little more carefully, we realize that some qualification is necessary. Take a problem that is impossible for a finite automaton, that of recognizing the language $L = \{0^n 1^n | n \geq 0\}$, for example. We could write a computer program to do this, and we could run it on our desktop computer, which, we suppose, is a modest micro. Exactly how big an element of L our computer could handle depends on the computer itself and on the way we have programmed it; but in any case, there will come a point at which some string x in L is *too* big. In other words, our physical computer, the one on the desk, can't recognize L at all, but only the finite subset of L consisting of all the strings shorter than x. This is a little disconcerting, since in order to recognize any finite language, a finite automaton is sufficient.

We might carry the argument further. For the sake of this discussion, let us pin down what our computer consists of: the central unit, with its chips, power supply, and, let's say, one disk drive, which contains a disk with the operating system and any other software we are using; the video monitor; and the keyboard. All input will be assumed to come from the keyboard, and, for simplicity, the only output device will be the monitor. When the computer is turned on, the operating system is loaded into the computer's memory, and the cursor on the screen is prompting us for the new date, but before we have hit any keys on the keyboard, we could say that the computer is in its initial state. Thereafter, depending on what state the computer is in, and what key we press, the computer enters another state. The current state of the computer is specified by the current information content of each bit of memory, and the complete electrical configuration of the system, including which pixels of the screen are activated. In our simplified version, we can essentially ignore output, since the contents of the monitor screen are specified by the current state. Unrealistic or unhelpful as this may seem, the point is clear: it can be argued that a specific computer does in fact behave like a finite automaton.

Nevertheless, this is not the way computers are viewed, and it is not the way we shall view them in this book, for at least two reasons. The first is that it is obviously not a useful viewpoint, just as it is not useful to view a human being as an assemblage of elementary particles if one wishes to study human behavior. The number of elementary particles is too vast, and the interactions between them too little understood. The number of states in the machine above may be described as finite, but in most ways that's a misleading description, since as far as we are concerned there is no practical difference whatsoever between a number that large and infinity.

Secondly, the point of formulating abstract models such as finite automata is to free ourselves from the need to worry about physical limitations like memory size. Obviously, there are many languages, including some regular ones, that no physical computer will ever be able to recognize; but it still makes sense to distinguish between the logical problems that arise in recognizing some of these, and the problems that arise in recognizing others. Finite automata and computers are different in principle, and what we are studying is what each is capable of in principle, not what a specific, imperfect, physical implementation of a computer can do in practice. As we progress further, we shall introduce abstract models that resemble a computer more closely. There will never be a perfect physical realization of any of them; but studying the conceptual model is still the best way to understand the potential, and the limitations, of their imperfect physical realizations.

EXERCISES

8.1. In each of the following cases, prove that the language L is nonregular by showing that any two elements of the infinite set $\{a^n | n \geq 0\}$ are distinguishable with respect to L.

(a) $L = \{a^n b a^{2n} | n \geq 0\}$

(b) $L = \{a^i b^j c^k | k > i + j\}$

(c) $L = \{x \in \{a, b\}^* | N_a(x) < 2N_b(x)\}$

(d) $L = \{x \in \{a, b\}^* | \text{no initial substring of } x \text{ has more } b\text{'s than } a\text{'s}\}$

8.2. Show that Theorem 8.3 can be used to show that $\{0^n 1^n | n \geq 0\}$ is not regular.

8.3. Using Theorem 8.1 show that the language in Example 8.9 is not regular.

8.4. Using the Pumping Lemma (Theorem 8.2a) show that each of these languages is not regular.

(a) Each of the languages in Exercise 8.1

(b) $L = \{x \in \{a, b\}^* | x \text{ is a palindrome}\}$

(c) $L = \{ww | w \in \{a, b\}^*\}$

(d) The language L of algebraic expressions in Example 8.2.

8.5. Here is a "proof," using the pumping lemma, that the language L of all strings of a's and b's of length 100 is not regular. Since the result being "proved" is false (all finite languages are regular), the proof cannot be correct. What is the flaw in the proof?

> Assume that L is regular. By the pumping lemma, if we choose an element of L, say $w = a^{100}$, there are strings x, y, and z, with $|y| > 0$, so that every string of the form $xy^k z$ (where $k \geq 0$) is in L. Since there are infinitely many different strings of this form, this contradicts the fact that L is finite. Therefore, L is not regular.

8.6. For each statement below, decide whether it is true or false. If it is true, prove it; if not, give a counterexample. All parts refer to languages over $\{a, b\}$.

(a) If $L_1 \subseteq L_2$ and L_1 is not regular, then L_2 is not regular.

(b) If $L_1 \subseteq L_2$ and L_2 is not regular, then L_1 is not regular.

(c) If L_1 and L_2 are nonregular, then $L_1 \cup L_2$ is nonregular.

(d) If L_1 and L_2 are nonregular, then $L_1 \cap L_2$ is nonregular.

(e) If L is not regular, then L' is not regular.

(f) If L_1 is regular and L_2 is nonregular, then $L_1 \cup L_2$ is nonregular.

(g) If L_1 is regular, L_2 is nonregular, and $L_1 \cap L_2$ is regular, then $L_1 \cup L_2$ is nonregular.

(h) If L_1 is regular, L_2 is nonregular, and $L_1 \cap L_2$ is nonregular, then $L_1 \cup L_2$ is nonregular.

(i) If $L_1, L_2, \ldots$ are regular, then $\cup_{n=1}^{\infty} L_n$ is regular.

8.7. Below are a number of languages over $\{a, b\}$. In each case, decide whether the language is regular or not, and prove that your answer is correct.

(a) L is the set of all strings x beginning with a non-null string of the form ww.

(b) L is the set of all strings x having some non-null substring of the form ww.

(c) L is the set of all strings x having some non-null substring of the form www. (This is harder, but with an extra fact, which you are hereby allowed to assume, it is not so bad. The extra fact is that there are arbitrarily long strings of a's and b's that do not contain any non-null substring of the form www. In fact, such strings can be obtained using the construction in Exercise 2.24.)

(d) $L = \{x \in \{a, b\}^* | x$ is not a palindrome$\}$

(e) $L = \{x \in \{a, b\}^* | x$ begins with a palindrome of length $\geq 3\}$

(f) $L = \{x \in \{a, b\}^* | N_a(x)$ is a perfect square$\}$

(g) $L = \{x \in \{a, b\}^* |$ in every initial substring of x, the number of a's and the number of b's differ by no more than 2 $\}$

(h) $L = \{x \in \{a, b\}^* |$ in every substring of x, the number of a's and the number of b's differ by no more than 2 $\}$

(i) $L = \{x \in \{a, b\}^* | N_a(x)$ and $N_b(x)$ are both divisible by 5$\}$

(j) $L = \{x \in \{a, b\}^* |$ there is some integer $k > 1$ so that $N_a(x)$ and $N_b(x)$ are both divisible by $k\}$

8.8. A set S of non-negative integers is an *arithmetic progression* if for some integers n and p, $S = \{n, n + p, n + 2p, \ldots\}$. Let A be a subset of $\{a\}^*$, and let $S = \{|x| \mid x \in A\}$.

(a) Show that if S is an arithmetic progression, A is regular.

(b) Show that if A is regular, S is the union of a finite number of arithmetic progressions.

8.9. This problem involves languages of the form

$$L = \{x \in \{a, b\}^* | N_a(x) = f(N_b(x))\}$$

for some function f from the set of natural numbers to itself. Example 8.6 shows that if f is the function defined by $f(n) = n$, then L is nonregular. If f is any constant function (e.g., $f(n) = 4$), L is regular. One might ask whether it is necessary to restrict f quite so severely in order for L to be regular.

(a) Show that if L is regular, the function f must be bounded—i.e., there must be some integer B so that $f(n) \leq B$ for every n. (Suggestion: suppose not, and apply the pumping lemma to strings of the form $a^{f(n)}b^n$.)

(b) Show that if f is defined by $f(n) = n$ MOD 2, then L is regular.

(c) The function in (b) is *eventually periodic*: there are integers N_0 and P with $P > 0$ so that for any $n \geq N_0$, $f(n) = f(n + P)$. Show that if f is any eventually periodic function, L is regular.

(d) Show that if L is regular, f is eventually periodic. (Suggestion: use the pumping lemma on strings of the form $b^n a^{f(n)}$.)

8.10. Describe decision algorithms to answer each of these questions.
  (a) Given two FAs M_1 and M_2, are there any strings that are accepted by neither?
  (b) Given a regular expression R and an FA M, are the corresponding languages equal?
  (c) Given an NFA-Λ M and a string x, does M accept x?
  (d) Given two NFA-Λs, do they accept the same language?
  (e) Given an NFA-Λ M and a string x, is there more than one sequence of transitions corresponding to x that causes M to accept x?

8.11. According to Theorem 7.3, there is essentially only one minimum-state FA recognizing a given language; any two are isomorphic. Use this to describe another decision algorithm to answer the question "Given two FAs, do they recognize the same language?"

PART

III

CONTEXT-FREE LANGUAGES AND PUSHDOWN AUTOMATA

We saw in Part II that regular languages can be characterized elegantly in a number of ways, but the finite-automaton characterization makes it clear that these languages are fairly specialized. Finite automata are primitive models of computation, and the languages they are capable of recognizing do not exhibit a very rich structure. We are now ready to consider languages that permit more variety and sophistication in their syntax. The first characterization of these languages, involving *context-free grammars*, consists of a simple recursive method of specifying the grammar rules by which strings in the languages can be generated. These rules are reminiscent of the grammar rules in natural languages like English; to a considerable extent, the syntax of natural languages, as well as that of programming languages and other "formal" languages, can be described this way. Although this characterization does not make it immediately obvious that every regular language is of this type, it is not difficult to find a subclass of the context-free grammars, that of *regular* grammars, corresponding precisely to the class of regular languages.

Just as in the simpler case, it is useful to try to describe context-free languages in terms of an abstract recognizing device. Here it is possible to build on the idea of a finite automaton in a straightforward way: we may consider starting with an FA and adding an auxilliary memory. For the resulting machine to be genuinely more powerful than an FA, the added memory must be potentially infinite; but it is sufficient to impose upon this extra memory a very simple organization, that of a *stack*. The resulting machines, *pushdown automata*, are shown in Chapter 13 to be equivalent to context-free grammars in the same way that FAs are equivalent to regular expressions, except that it is necessary here to formulate them as nondeterministic devices—that is, unlike the earlier case, the nondeterminism cannot always be eliminated.

Given a context-free grammar and a string derivable from that grammar, a particular derivation often gives rise to a particular way of interpreting the string. (An analogous situation in English is an interpretation of a sentence based on "diagramming" it—i.e., exhibiting the syntax rules underlying its construction.) This means in particular that some grammars for a language may be more appropriate than others. Normally, it is desirable to work with an *unambiguous* grammar, one in which every string has an essentially unique derivation. In addition, it may be worthwhile to transform the grammar so that certain potentially undesirable features are eliminated or so that all the grammar rules have a similar form. These aspects of context-free grammars are discussed in Chapters 10 and 11. Moreover, in addition to the basic problem of recognizing strings in the language, there is now the problem of *parsing* strings: constructing derivations in a particular grammar for the language. Since there are standard ways of associating nondeterministic pushdown automata with context-free grammars, so that a sequence of moves by which the machine accepts a string corresponds to a derivation of the string in the grammar, the problem of parsing is related to the problem of trying to modify a pushdown automaton to obtain an equivalent one that is deterministic. Some simple approaches to this problem are discussed in Chapter 14.

Finally, although context-free grammars and pushdown automata represent a substantial increase in complexity over regular expressions and finite automata, these languages are still not general enough to include all interesting or useful formal languages. Techniques similar to those in Chapter 8 can be used to exhibit simple languages that are not context-free: these are mentioned in Chapter 15. Just as in the case of regular languages, these techniques can also be used to find algorithms for certain decision problems associated with context-free languages, and a few of these are discussed.

CHAPTER
9

CONTEXT-FREE
LANGUAGES

9.1 DEFINITIONS AND INTRODUCTION

We have encountered a number of languages, including some that we know now to be nonregular, that we can easily define recursively. By selecting one and reformulating the definition just slightly, we are led to the notion of a *grammar*, which is a powerful tool for describing and analyzing languages. A specific type of grammar called a *context-free* grammar can be used to describe the languages that we want to consider in this part.

Example 9.1. In Example 2.9, we gave a recursive definition of the language *PAL* of all palindromes over an alphabet Σ. In the case when $\Sigma = \{a, b\}$, the definition can be restated as follows:

1. $\Lambda, a, b \in PAL$;
2. For any $S \in PAL$, aSa and $bSb \in PAL$; and
3. No string is in *PAL* unless it can be obtained by using rules 1 and 2.

Let us view the symbol S for the moment as a *variable*, representing an arbitrary element of *PAL*, whose value we wish to compute (by a sequence of "recursive calls," if you like). The rules 1 and 2 could be restated informally this way:

1. S could take the value Λ, a, or b; and
2. S could take the value aSa or bSb, where the new S is yet to be computed.

Suppose we think of the symbol $\rightarrow$ as meaning "could take the value"; then we might write, for example,

$$S \rightarrow aSa \rightarrow abSba \rightarrow ab\Lambda ba = abba$$

159

and we would clearly have used rules 1 and 2 to obtain an element of *PAL*. Using the →
notation, the rules could be rewritten

$$S \rightarrow a \mid b \mid \Lambda$$

$$S \rightarrow aSa \mid bSb$$

The vertical bar is to be interpreted as "or." We note for future reference that in an
expression such as "*aSa|bSb*," the two alternatives are *aS a* and *bS b*, not *a* and *b*—in
other words, the concatenation operation takes precedence over |. In the terminology we
are adopting, *S* is a *variable*, *a* and *b* are *terminal symbols*, or simply *terminals*, and
rules 1 and 2 consist of a total of five *grammar rules*, or *productions*. The idea is that
we start with the symbol *S* (or in general, if there are several variables, with the one that
has been designated as the "start" symbol) and use productions to substitute other strings
for variables until eventually we have a string with nothing but terminals; at this point we
have derived a string in the language.

Let us now give the general definition illustrated by this example.

Definition 9.1.   A *context-free grammar* (CFG) is a 4-tuple $G = (V, \Sigma, S, P)$, where:

V and Σ are finite sets with $V \cap \Sigma = \varnothing$: V is the set of *variables*, or *nonterminal*
symbols, and Σ is the alphabet of *terminal symbols*, or *terminals*;
$S \in V$ is the *start* symbol; and
P is a finite set of *productions*, or *grammar rules*, of the form $A \rightarrow \alpha$, where $A \in V$
and $\alpha \in (V \cup \Sigma)^*$.

Suppose we have a CFG $G = (V, \Sigma, S, P)$. We will reserve the symbol
→ for individual productions, but we will write $\alpha \Rightarrow_G \beta$ when the string β
can be obtained from the string α by replacing some variable that appears on the
left side of a production in G by the corresponding right side: in other words, if
$\alpha = \alpha_1 A \alpha_2$, $\beta = \alpha_1 \gamma \alpha_2$, and one of the productions in G is $A \rightarrow \gamma$. In this
case, we shall say α derives β, or β is derived from α, in one step. If there is
no question as to which CFG is being referred to, we usually shorten $\Rightarrow_G$ to $\Rightarrow$.
More generally, we write $\alpha \Rightarrow_G^* \beta$ if α derives β in zero or more steps—i.e.,
either $\alpha = \beta$, or there exist an integer $k \geq 1$ and strings $\alpha_0, \alpha_1, \ldots, \alpha_k$, with
$\alpha_0 = \alpha$ and $\alpha_k = \beta$, so that for each i with $0 \leq i \leq k - 1$, $\alpha_i \Rightarrow_G \alpha_{i+1}$.
Again, we often shorten $\Rightarrow_G^*$ to $\Rightarrow^*$.

Definition 9.2.   Let $G = (V, \Sigma, S, P)$ be a CFG. The language generated by G is

$$L(G) = \{x \in \Sigma^* \mid S \Rightarrow_G^* x\}$$

A language L is a *context-free language* if there is a CFG G so that $L = L(G)$.

In our second example, there is a little more variety in terms of variables.

Example 9.2.   Suppose we want a CFG that generates the language of all *non*-palindromes
over $\{a, b\}$. How might we go about it? A string x that is not a palindrome can be described
this way: as we work our way in from both ends, we may encounter symbols that agree,
for a while, but at some point we will find a symbol on the left that is different from the

corresponding one on the right. This suggests that we might begin with productions of this form:

$$S \rightarrow aSa \mid bSb \mid A$$

A is a second variable that stands for any string of length ≥ 2 whose first and last symbols are different. So far, we know that if our non-palindrome looked like $ab\ldots aa$, for example, it would have a derivation beginning

$$S \Rightarrow aSa \Rightarrow aAa$$

We need productions starting with A. The only requirement is that in a string derivable from A, the first and last letters be different; after that, what we get is arbitrary. Let's try

$$A \rightarrow aBb \mid bBa$$

where B stands for "any string at all." Now it's easy to finish up. "Any string at all" consists of a, followed by anything at all; b, followed by anything at all; or nothing.

$$B \rightarrow aB \mid bB \mid \Lambda$$

Our complete CFG has $V = \{S, A, B\}$ and $\Sigma = \{a, b\}$, and P is the set containing the productions

$$S \rightarrow aSa \mid bSb \mid A$$

$$A \rightarrow aBb \mid bBa$$

$$B \rightarrow aB \mid bB \mid \Lambda$$

The discussion should have made it clear that this CFG is a correct solution. In general, of course, to show that a CFG generates a language, we must show first that every string in the language can be derived from the grammar and second that no other strings can.

The string $ababaa$ has the derivation

$$S \Rightarrow aAa \Rightarrow abBaa \Rightarrow abaBaa \Rightarrow ababBaa \Rightarrow abab\Lambda aa = ababaa$$

9.2 EXAMPLES: NATURAL LANGUAGES, PROGRAMMING LANGUAGES, ALGEBRAIC EXPRESSIONS, AND OTHERS

The word "grammar" in this chapter is not just a coincidence. In fact, the languages to which context-free grammars were originally applied were "natural" languages such as English. These grammars are capable of describing much of the grammar, or syntax, of English, although as we shall see, to expect to arrive at a complete description of a natural language like English using a context-free grammar is probably unrealistic.

Even a basic, unadorned English sentence can take a bewildering variety of forms, but one of the simplest is

⟨subject⟩ ⟨verb phrase⟩ ⟨object⟩

which is illustrated by these familiar examples:

Gentlemen prefer blondes
Coughs and sneezes spread diseases
Faint heart ne'er won fair lady
The early bird catches the worm

To handle sentences of this sort, we could start by writing the production

$$S \ \rightarrow \ \langle \text{subject} \rangle \ \langle \text{verb phrase} \rangle \ \langle \text{object} \rangle$$

where we think of the start variable S as standing for an arbitrary sentence in our language and the three bracketed terms as our additional variables. If our goal is simply to be able to derive our four example sentences, we might attempt to finish up with something like this:

$\langle \text{subject} \rangle \rightarrow \langle \text{noun phrase} \rangle$ and $\langle \text{subject} \rangle \mid \langle \text{noun phrase} \rangle$
$\langle \text{noun phrase} \rangle \rightarrow \langle \text{article phrase} \rangle \langle \text{adjective phrase} \rangle \langle \text{noun} \rangle$
$\langle \text{article phrase} \rangle \rightarrow \langle \text{article} \rangle \mid \Lambda$
$\langle \text{adjective phrase} \rangle \rightarrow \langle \text{adjective} \rangle \mid \Lambda$
$\langle \text{verb phrase} \rangle \rightarrow \langle \text{adverb} \rangle \langle \text{verb} \rangle \mid \langle \text{verb} \rangle$
$\langle \text{object} \rangle \rightarrow \langle \text{noun phrase} \rangle$
$\langle \text{article} \rangle \rightarrow$ the
$\langle \text{adjective} \rangle \rightarrow$ faint $\mid$ fair $\mid$ early
$\langle \text{noun} \rangle \rightarrow$ gentlemen $\mid$ blondes $\mid$ coughs $\mid$ sneezes $\mid$ diseases $\mid$ heart $\mid$ lady $\mid$ bird $\mid$
    worm
$\langle \text{adverb} \rangle \rightarrow$ ne'er
$\langle \text{verb} \rangle \rightarrow$ prefer $\mid$ spread $\mid$ won $\mid$ catches

The productions with $\langle \text{subject} \rangle$ on the left side allow several noun phrases joined by "and." The "Λ-productions" (those with Λ on the right) are supposed to take care of the cases when there is no article or no adjective. A derivation of the third sentence in this grammar is

$S \Rightarrow \langle \text{subject} \rangle \langle \text{verb phrase} \rangle \langle \text{object} \rangle$
 $\Rightarrow \langle \text{noun phrase} \rangle \langle \text{verb phrase} \rangle \langle \text{object} \rangle$
 $\Rightarrow \langle \text{article phrase} \rangle \langle \text{adjective phrase} \rangle \langle \text{noun} \rangle \langle \text{verb phrase} \rangle \langle \text{object} \rangle$
 $\Rightarrow \Lambda \langle \text{adjective phrase} \rangle \langle \text{noun} \rangle \langle \text{verb phrase} \rangle \langle \text{object} \rangle$
 $\Rightarrow \langle \text{adjective} \rangle \langle \text{noun} \rangle \langle \text{verb phrase} \rangle \langle \text{object} \rangle$
 $\Rightarrow$ faint $\langle \text{noun} \rangle \langle \text{verb phrase} \rangle \langle \text{object} \rangle$
 $\Rightarrow$ faint heart $\langle \text{verb phrase} \rangle \langle \text{object} \rangle$
 $\Rightarrow \cdots$
 $\Rightarrow$ faint heart ne'er won fair $\langle \text{noun} \rangle$
 $\Rightarrow$ faint heart ne'er won fair lady

You have probably figured out already that this grammar is inadequate as a description of even a tiny portion of "real" English. In addition to the four relatively reasonable sentences above, it also generates sentences like

> faint bird and the fair sneezes and fair bird and gentlemen and bird ne'er catches early heart

The problem might simply be that we have not been careful enough and that our categories are too broad. We certainly haven't, and they certainly are. There are many different types of nouns; if a sentence has as its subject a noun like "gentlemen," it's unlikely that a noun like "coughs" could be substituted without producing nonsense. At the very least, it would be necessary to distinguish between a singular noun such as "bird" and a plural such as "coughs." But beyond that, you can still sense that the most enormous context-free grammar is going to run into difficulties in trying to capture the subtleties of established usage and idiom. In a natural language like English, one suspects that no matter what grammar is being used, there will be sentences that are "grammatically correct" but somehow not quite right. What *is* right depends a lot on the context. A *context-free* grammar is given that name because if $\alpha A \beta$ appears in a derivation, where A is a variable, it is always legitimate to use any production $A \rightarrow \gamma$ to replace A by γ, independent of the context—i.e., regardless of what α and β look like. In a context-free language, one string that can be obtained by applying the productions is just as good, and makes just as much sense, as any other.

The point is illustrated more explicitly by the grammar with these productions:

$$S \rightarrow \langle noun \rangle \langle verb \rangle \langle object \rangle$$
$$\langle noun \rangle \rightarrow \text{Joe} \mid \text{Jim} \mid \text{Jane}$$
$$\langle verb \rangle \rightarrow \text{reminded}$$
$$\langle object \rangle \rightarrow \langle noun \rangle \mid \langle pronoun \rangle$$
$$\langle pronoun \rangle \rightarrow \text{himself} \mid \text{herself}$$

More than one sentence derivable from this grammar doesn't quite work: "Joe reminded herself" and "Jane reminded himself," for example. These two could be eliminated in a straightforward way, at the cost of complicating the grammar. We could introduce variables $\langle$masculine noun$\rangle$, $\langle$feminine pronoun$\rangle$, and so on, and use productions such as

$$S \rightarrow \langle masculine\ noun \rangle \langle verb \rangle \langle masculine\ pronoun \rangle$$

A more subtle problem is "Joe reminded Joe." Normally, we don't say this, unless we have in mind two different people named Joe, but there's no obvious way to prohibit it without also prohibiting "Joe reminded Jim" or "Jim reminded Joe." (At least, there is no obvious way short of scrapping this grammar and finding another in which we have a different production for every sentence we want to end up with. This trivial option is available here, since the language is finite.) "Joe reminded himself" and "Joe reminded Jim" are perfectly good English

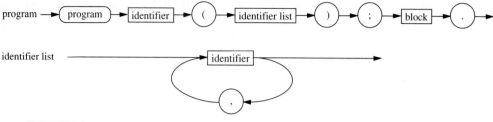

FIGURE 9-1
Syntax diagram from Pascal.

sentences. To distinguish these from "Joe reminded Joe" requires using *context*, and this is forbidden in a context-free grammar.

The next example should help to indicate how context-free grammars might be useful to computer science.

Example 9.3. Most introductory Pascal textbooks have an appendix in the back containing "syntax diagrams." Some also have an appendix with "BNF rules." "BNF" stands for "Backus-Naur Form"; this is a system of notation, introduced in 1959 by Backus, which is equivalent to a context-free grammar. Syntax diagrams are a pictorial way of saying the same thing.

A typical syntax-diagram appendix for Pascal begins with a diagram like that in Fig. 9-1. The corresponding BNF rules might look like this:

$$\langle \text{program} \rangle ::= \text{program} \ \langle \text{identifier} \rangle \ (\langle \text{identifier list} \rangle); \langle \text{block} \rangle.$$

$$\langle \text{identifier list} \rangle ::= \langle \text{identifier} \rangle \ \{ \ , \ \langle \text{identifier} \rangle \ \}$$

If we view these as productions in a CFG, the variables are those things within $\langle \rangle$, just as in our English example. In Fig. 9-1, the variables are within rectangles. The symbol $::=$ is what we write $\rightarrow$. The $\{\}$ notation is the principal difference between BNF and normal CFG notation — and in fact was not part of the original BNF system. $\{...\}$ means zero or more occurrences of whatever is inside the brackets. This is simply a way of saying iteratively what we normally say recursively; we could replace the second BNF rule above by the following:

$$\langle \text{identifier list} \rangle ::= \langle \text{identifier} \rangle \ , \ \langle \text{identifier list} \rangle \ | \ \langle \text{identifier} \rangle$$

Either version says that an identifier list is a sequence of one or more identifiers separated by commas. The diagram also says this, since to traverse the "identifier list" arrow completely you must go through the "identifier" box once, but you can loop back through the box as often as you wish, provided that each time you go through the comma first.

Most of the syntax of Pascal can be described this way. Of course, the grammar gets reasonably complicated. Before you finally understand what the legal definition of a "block" is, you must cope with variables such as $\langle \text{constant definition} \rangle$, $\langle \text{simple type} \rangle$, $\langle \text{unpacked structured type} \rangle$, $\langle \text{record section} \rangle$, $\langle \text{case label} \rangle$, $\langle \text{function heading} \rangle$, $\langle \text{referenced variable} \rangle$, and so forth. Another variable with a large definition is $\langle \text{statement} \rangle$, as you might expect. But for the most part, this context-free grammar describes — in fact, *defines*, since this was the original description given by Wirth, who developed Pascal — what is legal Pascal and what isn't. This doesn't mean, however, that if you are writing a Pascal program and have managed to construct something in which there are no violations of the BNF rules, all your problems are solved. In the first place, of course, these rules embody the *syntax* of Pascal, and there are plenty of opportunities for mistakes in *semantics*—using grammatically correct statements in incorrect ways. In addition, there are subtle aspects of Pascal syntax that are not included in this, or any, CFG; it is possible to write a program that satisfies the BNF rules and still doesn't compile. A more accurate statement is that the syntax of the executable portion of a Pascal program can be described by a CFG. We shall come back to this issue in Chapter 15.

Most of the examples of context-free grammars that we discuss in this book will be relatively small in comparison to the BNF description of Pascal. We are interested not so much in the complexities of a specific language as in the properties of context-free languages in general, and most of these can be illustrated by examples that are more tractable.

Example 9.4. As promised in Example 8.2, we show that the language of legal algebraic expressions is a context-free language: to be specific, algebraic expressions involving a single identifier a, the binary operations $+$, $-$, $*$, and $/$, and left and right parentheses.

A recursive definition of this language uses the observation that if we have two legal expressions, the new strings obtained either by joining the two using one of the four operations or by enclosing one within parentheses are also legal expressions—and that except for the string a, these rules account for all possible expressions. The most straightforward way to obtain a context-free grammar embodying these rules is to use the productions

$$S \rightarrow S + S \mid S - S \mid S * S \mid S/S \mid (S) \mid a$$

If we wanted, for example, to obtain the string

$$a + (a * a)/a - a$$

we could do it with the derivation

$$S \Rightarrow S - S \Rightarrow S + S - S \Rightarrow a + S - S \Rightarrow a + S/S - S$$
$$\Rightarrow a + (S)/S - S \Rightarrow a + (S * S)/S - S \Rightarrow a + (a * S)/S - S$$
$$\Rightarrow a + (a * a)/S - S \Rightarrow a + (a * a)/a - S \Rightarrow a + (a * a)/a - a$$

It is easy to see that there are many other derivations as well. For example,

$$S \Rightarrow S/S \Rightarrow S + S/S \Rightarrow a + S/S \Rightarrow a + (S)/S$$
$$\Rightarrow a + (S * S)/S \Rightarrow a + (a * S)/S \Rightarrow a + (a * a)/S$$
$$\Rightarrow a + (a * a)/S - S \Rightarrow a + (a * a)/a - S \Rightarrow a + (a * a)/a - a$$

We are tempted to say that the first is more natural than the second. The first starts with the production

$$S \rightarrow S - S$$

and signifies that we are interpreting the original expression as the difference of two other expressions. This seems correct, since normally the expression would be evaluated as follows:

1. Evaluate $a * a$; call its value A;
2. Evaluate A/a; call its value B;

3. Evaluate $a + B$; call its value C; and

4. Evaluate $C - a$.

The expression "is" the difference of the subexpression with value C and the subexpression a. The second derivation, on the other hand, interprets the expression as a quotient. There's no doubt that the grammar allows this derivation, but the derivation does not in any sense reflect our view of what the correct structure of the expression is.

One possible conclusion is that the context-free grammar we have given for the language might not be the most appropriate. In the first place, as we shall discuss in the next chapter, it is often desirable to choose a CFG for which there is not this need to choose between two derivations of a string—for which a string can *have* only one derivation (except for trivial differences as to the order in which two variables in a given string are chosen for replacement). If a CFG allows essentially only one derivation of each string, it is called *unambiguous*. We shall discuss this concept in more detail, and give a precise definition, in the next chapter. In the second place, there are standard conventions for interpreting algebraic expressions, having to do with the precedence of operators and with the left-to-right order of evaluation. For example, $*$ has higher precedence than $+$, and thus in the evaluation of $a + b*c$, the multiplication must be performed first. Similarly, $a - b + c$ means $(a - b) + c$, not $a - (b + c)$. The context-free grammar above has nothing in it that suggests these conventions, or that suggests that the two derivations given above are not equally appropriate. This helps explain why it is referred to as *ambiguous*. We shall come back to this example, and when we do we shall find a grammar that addresses both these issues.

Example 9.5. Let's try to come up with a CFG G generating the language

$$L = \{x \in \{a, b\}^* | x \text{ contains unequal numbers of } a\text{s and } b\text{s}\}$$

We start off with the observation that if we could find a CFG G_1 for the language L_1 of strings with more as than bs, we could certainly find another, G_2, for the opposite language L_2 (more bs than as), and we could combine them as follows. Let A be the start symbol of G_1 and B that of G_2, and relabel the other variables if necessary so that no variable appears in both V_1 and V_2; then let G contain the productions

$$S \rightarrow A \mid B$$

(where S, the start symbol of G, appears in neither G_1 nor G_2), as well as all the productions in both G_1 and G_2. The resulting grammar would give us what we want, since any string in the language must have either more as than bs or vice-versa, and must therefore be derivable from either A or B.

We now concentrate on G_1. As we saw in Example 9.1, the problem is essentially how to define L_1 recursively. Certainly $a \in L_1$, and both xa and $ax \in L_1$ for any $x \in L_1$. This suggests productions

$$A \rightarrow a \mid Aa \mid aA$$

It is less obvious how to add bs. However, if we have two elements x and y of L_1, combining them produces at least two more as than bs, and this allows us to add a single b and still obtain an element of L_1. We could add the b at the left, at the right, or between the two. Corresponding productions are

$$A \rightarrow bAA \mid AAb \mid AbA$$

It should be reasonably clear that the productions

$$A \rightarrow a \mid Aa \mid aA \mid bAA \mid AAb \mid AbA$$

produce only strings with the desired property. (You are invited in Exercise 9.10 to prove this using mathematical induction.) We shall supply the proof of the opposite direction: every string with more as than bs is derivable from A using these productions. In fact, we can eliminate either $A \rightarrow Aa$ or $A \rightarrow aA$, and the remaining ones still suffice.

At this point, let us introduce a little notation. For any string z, let

$$DIFF(z) = N_a(z) - N_b(z)$$

$$= \text{(the number of } a\text{s in } z) - \text{(the number of } b\text{s in } z)$$

To prove: If $G_1 = (\{A\}, \{a, b\}, A, P_1)$, where P_1 contains the productions

$$A \rightarrow a \mid aA \mid bAA \mid AAb \mid AbA$$

then for any string x with $DIFF(x) > 0$, $x \in L(G_1)$.

The proof is by induction on $|x|$. For the basis step, we must show that if $|x| = 1$ and $DIFF(x) > 0$, then $x \in L(G_1)$. But this is clear, since in this case $x = a$, and $A \Rightarrow a = x$.

In the induction step, assume that $K \geq 1$ and that for any y with $|y| \leq K$ and $DIFF(y) > 0$, $y \in L(G_1)$. We wish to show that if $|x| = K + 1$ and $DIFF(x) > 0$, then $x \in L(G_1)$. We consider three cases.

Case 1. $x = by$ for some y. Since $DIFF(x) \geq 1$, $DIFF(y) \geq 2$. If we could decompose y in the form $y = y_1 y_2$, where $DIFF(y_1) > 0$ and $DIFF(y_2) > 0$, we could apply our inductive hypothesis to y_1 and y_2, since $|y_1| \leq K$ and $|y_2| \leq K$. In order to find y_1 and y_2, we consider initial substrings of y. The shortest, Λ, has $DIFF$ 0. The longest, y, has $DIFF$ at least 2. Each time an extra symbol is added to an initial substring of y, $DIFF$ changes by 1. Therefore, there is an initial substring y_1 for which $DIFF(y_1) = 1$. Let y_2 be the remaining part of y. Then $x = by = by_1 y_2$, and since $DIFF(y) \geq 2$, we must have $DIFF(y_2) > 0$.

The inductive hypothesis tells us that y_1 and y_2 are both elements of $L(G_1)$—i.e., both are derivable from A. Therefore, since $x = by_1 y_2$, we may derive x from A by starting with the production $A \rightarrow bAA$, then deriving y_1 from the first A and y_2 from the second.

Case 2. $x = yb$ for some y. The proof is virtually the same as in Case 1, except that the derivation begins with

$$A \Rightarrow AAb$$

Case 3. $x = aya$ for some y. We assume that x contains at least one b, since otherwise it is easy to derive x using only the productions $A \rightarrow a$ and $A \rightarrow aA$. Our goal is to show that $x = wbz$ for some strings w and z with $DIFF(w) > 0$ and $DIFF(z) > 0$. It will follow from the induction hypothesis that w and z can both be derived from A, and this will show that x can be derived from A, starting with

$$A \Rightarrow AbA$$

To show that x can be decomposed in this form, suppose that x has n bs, with $n \geq 1$. For each i with $1 \leq i \leq n$, let w_i be the substring of x occurring before the ith b, and z_i the substring following the ith b. In other words,

$$x = w_i b z_i$$

where the b shown is the ith one. We know that $DIFF(w_1) > 0$, since x begins with a. If $DIFF(w_n) > 0$, we may let w be w_n and z be the string (with at least one a) following the last b, and we have the result we want. Otherwise, let m be the smallest value of i for which $DIFF(w_i) \leq 0$. We know, then, that $m \geq 2$. But $DIFF(w_m)$ is no smaller than $DIFF(w_{m-1}) - 1$, since w_m has only one more b than w_{m-1}. Therefore, $DIFF(w_{m-1}) = 1$. Since $x = w_{m-1}bz_{m-1}$, and $DIFF(x) > 0$, we may conclude that $DIFF(z_{m-1}) > 0$, and thus letting $w = w_{m-1}$ and $z = z_{m-1}$ gives us our result. The proof is now complete.

With this preliminary result out of the way, it is easy enough to complete our context-free grammar. $V = \{S, A, B\}$, and P contains the productions

$$S \;\rightarrow\; A \mid B$$

$$A \;\rightarrow\; a \mid aA \mid bAA \mid AAb \mid AbA$$

$$B \;\rightarrow\; b \mid bB \mid aBB \mid BBa \mid BaB$$

9.3   UNIONS, CONCATENATIONS, AND *'s OF CFLs

In the preceding example, we found a CFG for a language L by expressing L as the union of two languages and finding a CFG for each one. The same technique allows us to conclude in general that the union of two CFLs is a CFL. The following theorem expresses this result as well as the corresponding ones involving concatenation and $*$.

Theorem 9.1. If L_1 and L_2 are CFLs, the languages $L_1 \cup L_2$, L_1L_2, and L_1^* are also CFLs.

Proof. The proof is constructive: if we have CFGs generating the languages L_1 and L_2, we shall show how to construct new CFGs generating the three new languages. Suppose

$$G_1 = (V_1, \Sigma, S_1, P_1) \quad \text{and} \quad G_2 = (V_2, \Sigma, S_2, P_2)$$

generate L_1 and L_2, respectively.

(1) **We construct** $G_U = (V_U, \Sigma, S_U, P_U)$ **generating** $L_1 \cup L_2$. We repeat the construction in Example 9.5. First, rename elements of V_2 if necessary so that $V_1 \cap V_2 = \varnothing$; let

$$V_U = V_1 \cup V_2 \cup \{S_U\}$$

where S_U is a new symbol not in V_1 or V_2; then let

$$P_U = P_1 \cup P_2 \cup \{S_U \;\rightarrow\; S_1 \mid S_2\}$$

On the one hand, if $x \in L(G_1)$, then $S_U \Rightarrow^* x$ in the grammar G_U, because we may use the production $S_U \rightarrow S_1$ and continue with the derivation of x in G_1. Similarly for $x \in L(G_2)$. Therefore

$$L(G_1) \cup L(G_2) \subseteq L(G_U)$$

On the other hand, if x is derivable from S_U in G_U, the derivation must begin

$$S_U \Rightarrow S_1 \quad \text{or} \quad S_U \Rightarrow S_2$$

In the first case, all subsequent productions used must be productions in G_1, since no variables in V_2 are involved, and thus $x \in L(G_1)$; in the second case, $x \in L(G_2)$. Therefore,

$$L(G_U) \subseteq L(G_1) \cup L(G_2)$$

(2) We construct $G_C = (V_C, \Sigma, S_C, P_C)$ generating $L_1 L_2$. Again, make sure by relabeling if necessary that $V_1 \cap V_2 = \emptyset$, and let

$$V_C = V_1 \cup V_2 \cup \{S_C\}$$

This time let

$$P_C = P_1 \cup P_2 \cup \{S_C \rightarrow S_1 S_2\}$$

If $x \in L(G_1)L(G_2)$, then $x = x_1 x_2$, where for each i, $x_i \in L(G_i)$. We may derive x in G_C as follows:

$$S_C \Rightarrow S_1 S_2 \Rightarrow^* x_1 S_2 \Rightarrow^* x_1 x_2 = x$$

where the second step is the derivation of x_1 in G_1, the third that of x_2 in G_2. Conversely, if x can be derived from S_C, x can be derived from $S_1 S_2$, and therefore $x = x_1 x_2$, where each x_i can be derived from S_i in G_C. But since $V_1 \cap V_2 = \emptyset$, being derivable from S_i in G_C implies being derivable from S_i in G_i, and thus $x \in L(G_1)L(G_2)$.

(3) We construct $G^* = (V, \Sigma, S, P)$ generating L_1^*. Let

$$V = V_1 \cup \{S\}$$

where $S \notin V_1$. L_1^* contains strings of the form $x = x_1 x_2 \ldots x_k$, where each $x_i \in L_1$. Since x_i can be derived from S_1, in order to derive x from S we need only to be able to get strings of S_1's. This suggests that we include the productions

$$S \rightarrow S_1 S \mid \Lambda$$

in P. Therefore, let

$$P = P_1 \cup \{S \rightarrow S_1 S \mid \Lambda\}$$

The proof that $L_1^* \subseteq L(G^*)$ is straightforward. If $x \in L(G^*)$, it is clear that either $x = \Lambda$ or x can be derived from some string of the form S_1^k in G. In the latter case, since the only productions in G beginning with S_1 are those in G_1,

$$x \in L(G_1)^k \subseteq L(G_1)^*$$

Before we give applications of the theorem, notice that it really was necessary in parts 1 and 2 to make sure that $V_1 \cap V_2 = \emptyset$. Consider the two CFGs having the productions

$$S_1 \rightarrow XA \quad X \rightarrow c \quad A \rightarrow a$$

and

$$S_2 \rightarrow XB \quad X \rightarrow d \quad B \rightarrow b$$

respectively. If we applied the construction in part 1 with the two CFGs as they are, the resulting CFG would allow this derivation:

$$S \Rightarrow S_1 \Rightarrow XA \Rightarrow dA \Rightarrow da$$

but da is not in either of the two CFLs.

Example 9.6. Let $L = \{a^i b^j c^k | j > i + k\}$. It may not be obvious at first that this has anything to do with Theorem 9.1. You might be tempted at first to write L as a concatenation $L_1 L_2 L_3$, where these three languages contain strings of as, strings of bs, and strings of cs, respectively. This approach is doomed to failure: L contains both $a^1 b^3 c^1$ and $a^1 b^4 c^2$, but if we allowed L_1 to contain a^1, L_2 to contain b^3, and L_3 to contain c^2, then $L_1 L_2 L_3$ would also contain $a^1 b^3 c^2$, and this is incorrect. Fortunately, there's a trick: notice that

$$a^i b^{i+k} c^k = a^i b^i \, b^k c^k$$

The only difference between this and a string x in L is that x has at least one extra b in the middle:

$$x = a^i b^i \, b^m \, b^k c^k \quad \text{(for some } m > 0)$$

Thus the correct way to write L as a concatenation is $L = L_1 L_2 L_3$, where

$$L_1 = \{a^i b^i \,|\, i \geq 0\}$$
$$L_2 = \{b^m \,|\, m > 0\}$$
$$L_3 = \{b^k c^k \,|\, k \geq 0\}$$

Part 2 of Theorem 9.1, applied twice, therefore reduces the problem to finding CFGs for these three languages.

A recursive definition for L_1 is the following:

$$\Lambda \in L_1; \quad \text{for any } x \in L_1, \ axb \in L_1; \quad \text{nothing else is in } L_1$$

This suggests that these productions will generate L_1:

$$A \rightarrow aAb \mid \Lambda$$

L_3 is almost identical and can be generated by

$$C \rightarrow bCc \mid \Lambda$$

Finally, L_2 can be generated by the productions

$$B \rightarrow bB \mid b$$

(Note: $B \rightarrow b$, not $B \rightarrow \Lambda$, since we want only strings of one or more b's.)

We just need to concatenate the three start symbols and add a production that allows us to get this string from the new start symbol. The final CFG $G = (V, \Sigma, S, P)$ is shown below.

$$V = \{S, A, B, C\} \quad \Sigma = \{a, b, c\}$$
$$P = \{S \rightarrow ABC$$
$$A \rightarrow aAb \mid \Lambda$$
$$B \rightarrow bB \mid b$$
$$C \rightarrow bCc \mid \Lambda\}$$

A derivation of $ab^4 c^2 = (ab)(b)(b^2 c^2)$, for example, is

$$S \Rightarrow ABC \Rightarrow aAbBC \Rightarrow a\Lambda bBC \Rightarrow abbC$$
$$\Rightarrow abbbCc \Rightarrow abbbbCcc \Rightarrow abbbb\Lambda cc$$

Example 9.7. Our theorem gives us a way of finding CFGs for languages obtained from simpler ones using unions, concatenations, and $*$. This should already remind you of regular languages, which can be obtained from very simple languages using these three operations, so let's look at an example where we find a CFG for a regular language. Let L be the language corresponding to the regular expression

$$(abb + b)^*(ab)^*$$

Rather than starting from scratch with single symbols, we may take some obvious shortcuts. A CFG to generate the language $\{abb\}$ has the single production $A \rightarrow abb$. One for generating $\{b\}$ has the production $B \rightarrow b$. Therefore, we may obtain the language $\{abb\} \cup \{b\}$ by using the productions

$$C \rightarrow A \mid B$$
$$A \rightarrow abb$$
$$B \rightarrow b$$

The next obvious shortcut is to eliminate the variables A and B altogether and to use the productions

$$C \rightarrow abb \mid b$$

Part 3 of Theorem 9.1 tells us that the productions

$$D \rightarrow CD \mid \Lambda$$
$$C \rightarrow abb \mid b$$

will give us all strings in $\{abb, b\}^*$ from the variable D. Next, the same method suggests

$$E \rightarrow FE \mid \Lambda$$
$$F \rightarrow ab$$

as a way of deriving $\{ab\}^*$ from the start symbol E. Finally, we may obtain the concatenation of the two languages by adding the production $S \rightarrow DE$. The final CFG has start symbol S, other variables C, D, E, and F, and productions

$$S \rightarrow DE$$
$$D \rightarrow CD \mid \Lambda$$
$$C \rightarrow abb \mid b$$
$$E \rightarrow FE \mid \Lambda$$
$$F \rightarrow ab$$

It is probably clear from this example that all regular languages are context-free. Rather than giving the straightforward inductive proof that the example suggests, however, we consider in the next section whether it might be possible to identify a particular type of "regular" CFG that is naturally associated with regular languages.

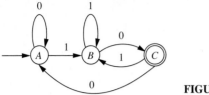

FIGURE 9-2

9.4   REGULAR LANGUAGES AND REGULAR GRAMMARS

At the end of the last section, we saw that Theorem 9.1, together with properties of regular expressions, allowed us to construct a CFG for any regular language. If we now approach regular languages via finite automata, instead of regular expressions, we find that not only can a regular language be generated by a CFG, but it can be generated by a CFG of a particularly simple type. These CFGs provide yet another characterization of regular languages.

Let's begin with the FA in Fig. 9-2, which is the same as that in Fig. 4-4*a*. The accepting state is now also given a letter as a name, for reasons that will shortly be obvious. The language recognized by this FA is $\{0, 1\}^*\{10\}$, the set of all strings ending in 10. Consider such a string, say $x = 110001010$. Suppose we trace the progress of this string through the states of the finite automaton, as follows.

Substring processed so far	State
Λ	A
1	B
11	B
110	C
1100	A
11000	A
110001	B
1100010	C
11000101	B
110001010	C

If we list the lines of this table consecutively, with "$\Rightarrow$" in between, we obtain

$$A \Rightarrow 1B \Rightarrow 11B \Rightarrow 110C \Rightarrow 1100A \Rightarrow 11000A \Rightarrow 110001B \Rightarrow$$
$$1100010C \Rightarrow 11000101B \Rightarrow 110001010C$$

All it takes to convert this into a derivation of 110001010 in a CFG is to declare as productions

$$A \to 1B, \quad B \to 1B, \quad B \to 0C, \quad C \to 0A, \quad A \to 0A, \quad \text{and} \quad C \to 1B$$

—and one more, $C \to \Lambda$, which allows us to get rid of the C at the end. By now you have noticed that our variables are the three states A, B, and C, the start variable is the initial state, and for each state P and each $a \in \Sigma$, if $\delta(P, a) = Q$, we have a production $P \rightarrow aQ$. Finally, for each accepting state F, we have a production $F \rightarrow \Lambda$. Any FA leads to a CFG in exactly this way, and it is not hard to believe after studying our example that the language generated by the CFG is exactly that recognized by the FA. At each stage in the derivation of a string x, there is exactly one variable in the string, and if we think of it as the "state of the derivation," the derivation can be viewed as simulating the processing of x by the FA.

CFGs in which the productions are all of this distinctive form, or one very similar, are the ones involved in the next definition.

Definition 9.3. Let $G = (V, \Sigma, S, P)$ be a CFG. G is called a *regular* grammar if every production takes one of the three forms

$$B \rightarrow a$$

$$B \rightarrow aC$$

$$B \rightarrow \Lambda$$

where B and C are elements of V and $a \in \Sigma$.

Theorem 9.2. For any language $L \subseteq \Sigma^*$, L is regular if and only if $L = L(G)$ for some regular grammar G.

Proof. First suppose L is regular, and let $M = (Q, \Sigma, q_0, \delta, A)$ be an FA recognizing L. Define the CFG $G = (V, \Sigma, S, P)$ as follows:

$$V = Q$$

$$S = q_0$$

$$P = \{B \rightarrow aC \mid \delta(B, a) = C\} \cup \{B \rightarrow \Lambda \mid B \in A\}$$

(This is exactly what we did in our example.) Suppose $x = a_1 a_2 \ldots a_n$ is recognized by M. There is a sequence of transitions of the form

$$\rightarrow q_0 \xrightarrow{a_1} q_1 \xrightarrow{a_2} q_2 \xrightarrow{a_3} \cdots \xrightarrow{a_{n-1}} q_{n-1} \xrightarrow{a_n} q_n$$

where $q_n \in A$. But by definition of G, we have the derivation

$$S = q_0 \Rightarrow a_1 q_1 \Rightarrow a_1 a_2 q_2 \Rightarrow \cdots \Rightarrow a_1 a_2 \cdots a_{n-1} q_{n-1}$$
$$\Rightarrow a_1 a_2 \cdots a_n q_n \Rightarrow a_1 a_2 \cdots a_n \Lambda = x$$

Similarly, if x is generated by G, it is clear that $x \in L$.

In the converse direction, suppose $G = (V, \Sigma, S, P)$ is a regular grammar generating L. We can essentially reverse the construction above: that is, define states corresponding to all the variables and, for any production $B \rightarrow aC$, create a transition

$$B \xrightarrow{a} C$$

The only question is how to handle the other two types of productions. Let us add one additional state f, which will be the only accepting state; and every production

$$B \rightarrow \Lambda \quad \text{or} \quad B \rightarrow a$$

will correspond to a transition

$$B \xrightarrow{\Lambda} f \quad \text{or} \quad B \xrightarrow{a} f$$

respectively. Our machine $M = (Q, \Sigma, q_0, \delta, A)$ will be an NFA-Λ, defined as follows:

$Q = V \cup \{f\}$

$q_0 = S$

$A = \{f\}$

For any $q \in V$ and $a \in \Sigma$, the elements of $\delta(q, a)$ include all those states p for which there is a production $q \rightarrow ap$ in G, and, if the production $q \rightarrow a$ appears in G, the state f as well. For any $q \in V$, the set $\delta(q, \Lambda)$ is $\{f\}$ if the production $q \rightarrow \Lambda$ appears in G and $\emptyset$ otherwise. There are no transitions out of the state f.

If $x \in L = L(G)$, there is a derivation that begins

$$S \Rightarrow a_1 q_1 \Rightarrow a_1 a_2 q_2 \Rightarrow \cdots \Rightarrow a_1 a_2 \cdots a_{n-1} q_{n-1}$$

and the last step is either

$$a_1 a_2 \cdots a_{n-1} q_{n-1} \Rightarrow a_1 a_2 \cdots a_{n-1} a_n$$

or

$$a_1 a_2 \cdots a_{n-1} q_{n-1} \Rightarrow a_1 a_2 \cdots a_{n-1}$$

According to our definition of M, there will be the sequence of transitions

$$q_0 \xrightarrow{a_1} q_1 \xrightarrow{a_2} \cdots \xrightarrow{a_{n-1}} q_{n-1}$$

followed by either

$$q_{n-1} \xrightarrow{a_n} f$$

or

$$q_{n-1} \xrightarrow{\Lambda} f$$

In any case, it follows that x is accepted by M.

On the other hand, if $x = a_1 \ldots a_n$ is accepted by M, there is a sequence of transitions

$$q_0 \xrightarrow{a_1} q_1 \xrightarrow{a_2} \cdots \xrightarrow{a_{n-1}} q_{n-1}$$

followed either by

$$q_{n-1} \xrightarrow{a_n} q_n \xrightarrow{\Lambda} f$$

or by

$$q_{n-1} \xrightarrow{a_n} f$$

Each transition

$$q_{i-1} \xrightarrow{a_i} q_i$$

arises from a production $q_{i-1} \to a_i q_i$ in the grammar, and the last step corresponds to either the production $q_n \to \Lambda$ or the production $q_{n-1} \to a_n$. We conclude, therefore, that there is a derivation of x in G, and that $x \in L(G)$.

You can verify for yourself that the procedure described in the proof of the "only if" part of Theorem 9.2 can be applied to NFAs and NFA-Λs as well, and that in both cases, the resulting CFG generates the language recognized by the machine. If there are Λ-transitions, however, the CFG will contain productions of the form $B \to C$ and so will not be regular. This is just one illustration of a fact that is worth pointing out in any case: nonregular grammars can generate regular languages. Theorem 9.2 says, however, that if a regular language can be generated by a nonregular grammar, it is also possible to find a regular grammar that generates it.

Certain grammars that are less restrictive in form than regular grammars can be shown to generate regular languages. Some authors use the term "regular" to apply to grammars in which every production is of one of the forms

$$B \to xC$$
$$B \to x$$
$$B \to \Lambda$$

where B and C are elements of V and $x \in \Sigma^*$. Grammars of this type are also called *linear* grammars, and in Exercise 9.17 you are asked to show that these produce regular languages. It is also easy to show that another kind of linear grammar, in which all productions look like

$$B \to Cx$$
$$B \to x$$
$$B \to \Lambda$$

gives rise to regular languages. The exercises explore these grammars as well.

EXERCISES

9.1. In each case, say what language is generated by the context-free grammar with the indicated productions.

(a)
$$S \to aSa \mid bSb \mid \Lambda$$

(b)
$$S \to aSa \mid bSb \mid a \mid b$$

(c)

$$S \rightarrow aSa \mid bSb \mid A$$
$$A \rightarrow aBb \mid bBa$$
$$B \rightarrow aBa \mid bBb \mid a \mid b \mid \Lambda$$

(d)

$$S \rightarrow aS \mid aSbS \mid \Lambda$$

(e)

$$S \rightarrow aS \mid bS \mid a$$

(f)

$$S \rightarrow SS \mid bS \mid Sb \mid a$$

9.2. (a) Palindromes over $\{a, b\}$ are strings x of as and bs so that for any i with $1 \le i \le |x|/2$, the ith symbol from the left and the ith symbol from the right are the same. Find a CFG generating the set of strings x in which for every i with $1 \le i \le |x|/2$, the ith symbol from the left and the ith symbol from the right are different.

(b) Same as (a), but substitute $1 \le i \le |x|$ for $1 \le i \le |x|/2$.

9.3. Find a CFG corresponding to the "syntax diagram" in Fig. 9-3.

9.4. Let $L = \{x \in \{a, b\}^* \mid N_a(x) = N_b(x)\}$

(a) Show that if $x \in L$ and x begins and ends with the same symbol, $x = yz$ for some strings y and z in L with $|y|, |x| \ge 1$. (Suggestion: study the proofs in Example 9.5.)

(b) Use (a) to find a CFG generating L in which S is the only variable.

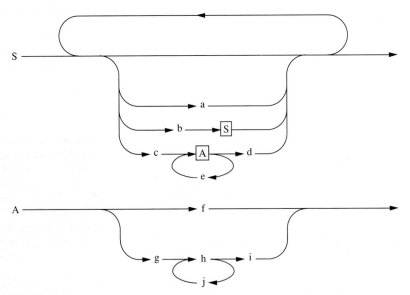

FIGURE 9-3

9.5. Let L be as in Exercise 9.4. Let $L_a = \{x \in \{a, b\}^* | N_a(x) = N_b(x) + 1\}$ and $L_b = \{x \in \{a, b\}^* | N_b(x) = N_a(x) + 1\}$.

(a) Show that if $x \in L_a$ and $x = by$ for some string y, then $y = wz$ for some strings $w, z \in L_a$.

(b) Using (a) and the corresponding result for L_b, find a CFG generating L that has exactly three variables S, A, and B, generating the strings in L, L_a, and L_b, respectively.

(c) Find a CFG generating L_a.

9.6. Find a CFG generating the language of all regular expressions over an alphabet Σ:

(a) If the definition of regular expression is interpreted strictly with regard to parentheses.

(b) If we interpret the definition so as to allow regular expressions that are not "fully parenthesized." Be careful to distinguish between Λ-productions and productions whose right side is the symbol Λ appearing in a regular expression; use λ in the second case.

9.7. Let G be the CFG whose productions are

$$S \rightarrow aS \mid Sb \mid a \mid b$$

Show using mathematical induction that no string in $L(G)$ contains the substring ba.

9.8. Let G be the CFG whose productions are

$$S \rightarrow aSb \mid ab \mid SS$$

Show using mathematical induction that no string in $L(G)$ begins with abb.

9.9. (a) Describe the language generated by the CFG with productions

$$S \rightarrow SS \mid (S) \mid \Lambda$$

(b) Show that the CFG with productions

$$S \rightarrow (S)S \mid \Lambda$$

generates the same language.

(c) Show that the CFG with productions

$$S \rightarrow S(S) \mid \Lambda$$

generates the same language.

9.10. Show using mathematical induction that if G_1 is the grammar having productions

$$A \rightarrow a \mid Aa \mid bAA \mid AAb \mid AbA$$

then every string in $L(G_1)$ has more as than bs.

9.11. This problem gives proposed alternative constructions for the CFGs G_U, G_C, and G^* in Theorem 9.1. In each case, either prove that the construction works or give an example of grammars for which it doesn't and say why it doesn't.

(a) (For G_U) $V_U = V_1 \cup V_2$; $\quad S_U = S_1$; $\quad P_U = P_1 \cup P_2 \cup \{S_1 \rightarrow S_2\}$

(b) (For G_C) $V_C = V_1 \cup V_2$; $\quad S_C = S_1$; $\quad P_C = P_1 \cup P_2 \cup \{S_1 \rightarrow S_1 S_2\}$

(c) (For G^*) $V = V_1$; $\quad S = S_1$; $\quad P = P_1 \cup \{S_1 \rightarrow S_1 S_1 \mid \Lambda\}$

9.12. Find CFGs for each of these languages.

(a) $\{a^i b^j c^k \mid i = j + k\}$

(b) $\{a^i b^j c^k \mid j = i + k\}$

(c) $\{a^i b^j c^k \mid i \neq j + k\}$
(d) $\{a^i b^j c^k \mid j \neq i + k\}$
(e) $\{a^i b^j c^k \mid j = i \quad \text{or} \quad j = k\}$
(f) $\{a^i b^j c^k \mid i = j \quad \text{or} \quad i = k\}$
(g) $\{a^i b^j c^k \mid i < j \quad \text{or} \quad i > k\}$
(h) $\{a^i b^j \mid i \leq 2j\}$
(i) $\{a^i b^j \mid i \leq j \leq 2i\}$

9.13. Give an inductive proof based on Theorem 9.1 that every regular language is context-free. (Suggestion: refer to Theorem 6.1.)

9.14. Describe the language generated by each of these regular grammars.
   (a) The grammar with productions

$$S \rightarrow aA \mid bC$$

$$A \rightarrow aS \mid bB$$

$$B \rightarrow aC \mid bA$$

$$C \rightarrow aB \mid bS \mid \Lambda$$

   (b) The grammar with productions

$$S \rightarrow bS \mid aA \mid \Lambda$$

$$A \rightarrow aA \mid bB$$

$$B \rightarrow bS \mid \Lambda$$

9.15. Let us say that a CFG $G = (V, \Sigma, S, P)$ is *left-regular* if every production takes one of the three forms

$$B \rightarrow a, \qquad B \rightarrow Ca, \qquad \text{or} \qquad B \rightarrow \Lambda$$

where $B, C \in V$ and $a \in \Sigma$. Show that a language $L \subseteq \Sigma^*$ is regular if and only if $L = L(G)$ for some left-regular CFG G. One approach is to mimic the proof of Theorem 9.2. Another, possibly easier, is to consider $REV(L)$.

9.16. Consider this statement: for any $L \subseteq \Sigma^*$, L is regular if and only if $L = L(G)$ for some CFG G in which every production takes one of the four forms $B \rightarrow a$, $B \rightarrow Ca$, $B \rightarrow aC$, or $B \rightarrow \Lambda$, where B and C are variables and $a \in \Sigma$. For each half of the statement (the "if" and the "only if") give either a proof or a counterexample.

9.17. Call a CFG *right-linear* if every production takes one of the forms $B \rightarrow xC$, $B \rightarrow x$, or $B \rightarrow \Lambda$, where B and C are variables and $x \in \Sigma^*$. *Left-linear* is defined similarly, but with $B \rightarrow Cx$ substituted for $B \rightarrow xC$. Show that if a CFG G is either right-linear or left-linear, $L(G)$ is regular.

9.18. Each of these CFGs, though not regular, generates a regular language. In each case, find a regular expression corresponding to the language, draw an NFA recognizing the language, and find a regular grammar generating the language.
   (a)

$$S \rightarrow AabB$$

$$A \rightarrow aA \mid bA \mid \Lambda$$

$$B \rightarrow Bab \mid Bb \mid ab \mid b$$

(*b*)

$$S \rightarrow AAS \mid ab \mid aab$$
$$A \rightarrow ab \mid ba \mid \Lambda$$

(*c*)

$$S \rightarrow SSS \mid a \mid ab$$

(*d*)

$$S \rightarrow AB$$
$$A \rightarrow aAa \mid bAb \mid a \mid b$$
$$B \rightarrow aB \mid bB \mid \Lambda$$

(*e*)

$$S \rightarrow AA \mid B$$
$$A \rightarrow AAA \mid Ab \mid bA \mid a$$
$$B \rightarrow bB \mid \Lambda$$

CHAPTER
10

DERIVATION TREES AND AMBIGUITY

10.1 DEFINITIONS AND EXAMPLES

Suppose we have a context-free language generated by a specific context-free grammar. When we examine a string x, we are interested in whether x is in the language, but if it is, we are also likely to be concerned with how it is derived. The derivation may provide information about the structure of the string or the way it is to be interpreted. Several of the examples we looked at in Chapter 9 illustrate this point. In English, one way you "understand" a sentence is to find a grammatical structure to which the sentence corresponds, which means a derivation of the sentence from the rules of English grammar. (To a native English speaker, this is usually an unconscious process, except perhaps in the case of very complicated syntax; someone whose native language is German is likely to be more aware of the process.) A Pascal compiler must *parse* each statement in the program; this means essentially that it must reconstruct the derivation of the statement in the BNF grammar, for this derivation is what determines what sort of statement it is. In our algebraic-expression example, we saw that how an expression is interpreted depends on the derivation one postulates for it.

Let us take a CFG $G = (V, \Sigma, S, P)$. There is a graphical way of describing derivations in G that exhibits clearly the essential structure of the derivation. This is to draw a *derivation tree*, or *parse tree*. At the root of the tree is the variable with which we begin the derivation (the start symbol of the grammar if we are speaking of a complete derivation, but we also want to include derivations from other variables); each time the right side α of a production $A \rightarrow \alpha$ is substituted for the variable A, A is represented as the root of a subtree, and its children are

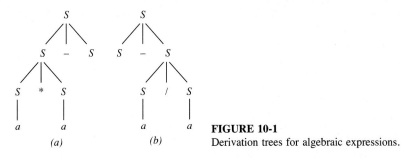

FIGURE 10-1
Derivation trees for algebraic expressions.

the symbols in α, in the same order, left-to-right, as they occur in the production. In the case of the production $A \rightarrow \Lambda$, the node labeled A has the single child Λ.

To illustrate: in Example 9.4, we used the productions

$$S \rightarrow S + S \mid S - S \mid S * S \mid S/S \mid (S) \mid a$$

The derivation

$$S \Rightarrow S - S \Rightarrow S * S - S \Rightarrow a * S - S \Rightarrow a * a - S \Rightarrow a * a - a$$

has the derivation tree shown in Fig. 10-1a. The derivation

$$S \Rightarrow S - S \Rightarrow S - S/S \Rightarrow \cdots \Rightarrow a - a/a$$

has the derivation tree shown in Fig. 10-1b.

As we have already noted, we sometimes consider a derivation from some variable other than the start symbol. It is also useful sometimes to consider trees representing "incomplete" derivations, as in Fig. 10-2. Thus, derivation trees always have variables at nonterminal, or interior, nodes, but may have them at leaf nodes as well. In a tree representing the complete derivation of a string in the language, each leaf node contains either a terminal symbol or Λ.

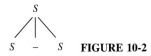

FIGURE 10-2

You have probably taken a computer science course in which you studied *expression trees*. These are normally described as *binary* trees in which terminal nodes correspond to identifiers or constants, and nonterminal nodes are operators. There is a close relationship between these and the derivation trees in Figure 10-1. The expression tree corresponding to the tree in Figure 10-1a would normally be drawn as in Figure 10-3. Figures 10-1a and 10-3 convey the same information, except that in the second case only the terminal symbols are drawn.

FIGURE 10-3
Expression tree corresponding to Fig. 10-1a.

A "derivation" means a sequence of steps in a particular order, each step being the replacement of a variable by the right side of a production. If the order is different, the derivation is different. For example,

$$S \Rightarrow S + S \Rightarrow a + S \Rightarrow a + a$$

is not the same derivation as

$$S \Rightarrow S + S \Rightarrow S + a \Rightarrow a + a$$

However, these are different only in a trivial way: at the point when our string contains $S + S$, we can obviously choose whether to replace the leftmost S first, as in the first derivation, or the rightmost S, as in the second. One way to say that these derivations are different only in a trivial way is to say that their derivation trees are identical. A derivation tree specifies completely which productions are used in the derivation, and for each production used the tree specifies where the right side of that production fits in the string being derived. If at some stage of the derivation there are several variables present in the current string, the derivation tree says nothing about the "temporal" order in which they are used. We would surely say that this order is irrelevant to any interpretation of the string's structure that might be made on the basis of the derivation; we think of two derivations that correspond to the same derivation tree as being "essentially" the same.

Another way to compare two derivations is to "normalize" them so that at each step, if there is a choice as to which variable to replace, the one chosen is the leftmost one in the current string. A derivation is a *leftmost* derivation if it has this property: at each step, the leftmost variable in the current string is replaced. If the two derivations being compared are both leftmost and are still different, it seems reasonable to say that they are not "essentially the same."

It may conceivably happen that a string of variables and terminals that is derivable in a grammar has *no* leftmost derivation: in a grammar containing productions

$$S \rightarrow AB \qquad A \rightarrow a \qquad B \rightarrow \Lambda$$

the string A can be derived from S, but there is no leftmost derivation of A. You can see, though, that if we don't "stop halfway" like this—i.e., if we are discussing a derivation of a string of terminals—we can always choose the derivation to be leftmost. Moreover, comparing two derivations in terms of their derivation trees is equivalent to comparing them by "normalizing" them so that they are both leftmost. In particular, if there are two distinct leftmost derivations of a string, the corresponding derivation trees are different. This is easy to see: consider the first step at which the derivations differ. This step must be $xA\beta \Rightarrow x\alpha_1\beta$ in the first derivation and $xA\beta \Rightarrow x\alpha_2\beta$ in the second, where x is a string of terminals, A is a variable, and $\alpha_1 \neq \alpha_2$. The two derivation trees both have a node labeled A, and the respective portions of the two trees to the left of this node are identical, since the leftmost derivations have been the same up to this point. However, the two nodes have different sets of children, so the trees cannot be the same.

Of course, it is also true that the leftmost derivations corresponding to different derivation trees are different. We conclude, therefore, that a string of terminals has more than one derivation tree if and only if it has more than one leftmost derivation. Notice that in this entire discussion, "leftmost" could just as easily be "rightmost." The important thing is not what order is followed, only that some clearly defined order be followed consistently, so that two derivations that are similarly constrained can be compared.

As we have already noticed, a string can certainly have two or more derivations in the same CFG that are not "essentially the same."

Definition 10.1. A CFG G is *ambiguous* if there is at least one string in $L(G)$ having two or more distinct derivation trees (or, equivalently, two or more distinct leftmost derivations).

Example 10.1. Let us return to the algebraic-expression CFG discussed in Example 9.4, with productions

$$S \rightarrow S + S \mid S - S \mid S * S \mid S/S \mid (S) \mid a$$

In that example, we considered two essentially different derivations of the string

$$a + (a * a)/a - a$$

—and in fact two distinct leftmost derivations of this string were presented. However, we don't need such a complicated string to illustrate the ambiguity of the grammar. The string $a - a + a$, or even $a + a + a$, will do just as well. In the second case, two distinct leftmost derivations are

$$S \Rightarrow S + S \Rightarrow a + S \Rightarrow a + S + S \Rightarrow a + a + S \Rightarrow a + a + a$$

and

$$S \Rightarrow S + S \Rightarrow S + S + S \Rightarrow a + S + S \Rightarrow a + a + S \Rightarrow a + a + a$$

The corresponding derivation trees are those in Figs. 10-4a and 10-4b, respectively.

In the case of a string like $a + (a * a)/a - a$, it is clear that two derivations beginning $S \Rightarrow S - S$ and $S \Rightarrow S/S$, respectively, correspond to quite different interpretations of the string: in one case the difference of two quantities, in the other the quotient of two quantities. In the case of $a + a + a$, the difference isn't quite that dramatic, since in either case the expression is viewed as the sum of two subexpressions, but the principle is the same. Different derivations correspond to different ways of grouping terms, or different orders in which the operations are viewed as occurring. In one case, the expression is interpreted as $a + (a + a)$, in the other $(a + a) + a$. Notice the role of parentheses here:

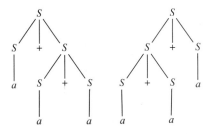

FIGURE 10-4
Two derivation trees for $a + a + a$.

informally, we might say they serve to remove the "ambiguity" in the interpretation of the expression. We will examine this property of parentheses more carefully a little later in this chapter, when we exhibit an unambiguous CFG equivalent to this one.

It is easy to see by looking at Example 10.1 that any CFG in which there is a production of the form $A \rightarrow A\alpha A$ (where α is any string) will be ambiguous. Unfortunately, there are more subtle ways in which ambiguity can occur, and to characterize the ambiguous grammars in a nontrivial way is not this simple. In fact, it turns out to be virtually impossible, as we shall see in Chapter 20.

Example 10.2. Ambiguity in the formal sense in which we have defined it is closely related to ambiguity as we often encounter it in everyday reading and conversation. Newspapers carry headlines like "WILDCAT STRIKES SPREAD," and Knuth, Larrabee, and Roberts [1989] mentions a story that actually appeared with the wonderful caption "DISABLED FLY TO SEE CARTER." In the first case, whether we read the headline as it is presumably intended or as a story of wild animals attacking campers' food supplies depends on whether we postulate a derivation such as

$$S \rightarrow \langle\text{modifier}\rangle \langle\text{noun}\rangle \langle\text{verb}\rangle$$

rather than one such as

$$S \rightarrow \langle\text{noun}\rangle \langle\text{verb}\rangle \langle\text{object}\rangle$$

Understanding a sentence means, among other things, picking the right derivation for it.

Example 10.3. A standard example of ambiguity in programming languages is the "dangling ELSE" phenomenon. Consider the BNF rules

$\langle\text{statement}\rangle ::=$ IF $\langle\text{expression}\rangle$ THEN $\langle\text{statement}\rangle \mid$
　　　　　　　IF $\langle\text{expression}\rangle$ THEN $\langle\text{statement}\rangle$ ELSE $\langle\text{statement}\rangle \mid$
　　　　　　　$\langle\text{otherstatement}\rangle$

which appear in a typical BNF grammar for Pascal, and the Pascal statement

　　　IF A1 THEN IF A2 THEN S1 ELSE S2

The ambiguity becomes clear when we encounter the ELSE; does it go with the first IF, as illustrated by the derivation tree in Fig. 10-5*a*, or the second, as illustrated in Fig. 10-5*b*? The answer is that it goes with the second. Typically, one reads in a Pascal book a rule such as "An ELSE belongs to the last preceding IF for which there is no ELSE already." The BNF grammar above does not say this; relative to this grammar, it is not a rule of *syntax*, but a rule of *semantics*. A Pascal compiler must be furnished with this information in order to process the statement correctly.

However, it is possible to find an equivalent grammar that incorporates this rule into its syntax. Suppose we use these BNF formulas instead:

　　　$\langle\text{statement}\rangle ::= \langle\text{st1}\rangle \mid \langle\text{st2}\rangle$
　　　　　　$\langle\text{st1}\rangle ::=$ IF $\langle\text{expression}\rangle$ THEN $\langle\text{st1}\rangle$ ELSE $\langle\text{st1}\rangle \mid \langle\text{otherstatement}\rangle$
　　　　　　$\langle\text{st2}\rangle ::=$ IF $\langle\text{expression}\rangle$ THEN $\langle\text{statement}\rangle \mid$
　　　　　　　　IF $\langle\text{expression}\rangle$ THEN $\langle\text{st1}\rangle$ ELSE $\langle\text{st2}\rangle$

These generate the same strings as the original rules and can be shown to be unambiguous. Although we shall not present a proof of either fact, it is not difficult to see the intuitive reason for the second. The variable $\langle\text{st1}\rangle$ represents an IF statement in which every IF

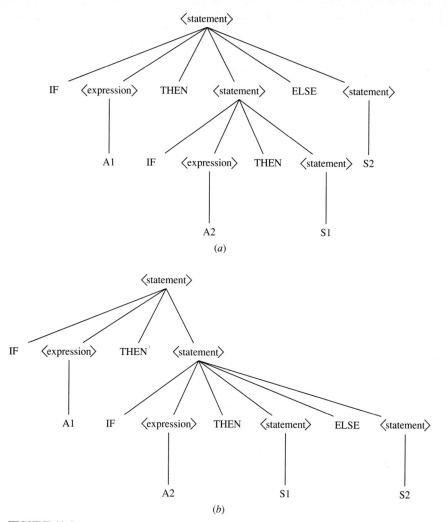

FIGURE 10-5
Two interpretations of a "dangling ELSE."

is matched by a corresponding ELSE, while any statement derived from ⟨st2⟩ contains at least one "unmatched" IF. The only variable appearing before ELSE in these formulas is ⟨st1⟩. Since the ELSE cannot match any of the IFs in the statement derived from ⟨st1⟩ (because they are already matched), the only choice for the matching IF is the one that appeared in the formula with the ELSE. It is the "last preceding IF for which there is no ELSE already."

It is interesting to compare both these sets of formulas with the corresponding BNF formulas in the official grammar for Modula-2, the "successor" to Pascal. These rules, in slightly less than the most general form, look something like this:

⟨statement⟩ ::= IF ⟨expression⟩ THEN ⟨statementsequence⟩ END |
　　　　　　IF ⟨expression⟩ THEN ⟨statementsequence⟩
　　　　　　ELSE ⟨statementsequence⟩ END | ⟨otherstatement⟩

Although they resemble the first version of the Pascal rules, one consequence of the change in syntax is that the "dangling ELSE" no longer occurs. The Modula-2 statement corresponding most closely to the tree in Fig. 10-5*a* is

IF A1 THEN IF A2 THEN S1 END ELSE S2 END

while Fig. 10-5*b* corresponds to

IF A1 THEN IF A2 THEN S1 ELSE S2 END END

Adding the explicit END after each statement sequence—even if it consists of only one statement—has eliminated the ambiguity as to how to match up ELSEs with IFs. If you indent both these statements as you are taught in programming classes, the difference between them is even more apparent.

Example 10.4. Regular grammars (see Section 9.4) can be ambiguous. Here is a simple example.

$$S \rightarrow aA \mid aB$$

$$A \rightarrow bA \mid \Lambda$$

$$B \rightarrow aB \mid b$$

The construction described in Theorem 9.1 produces the NFA-Λ in Fig. 10-6. The string *ab* has these two leftmost derivations:

$$S \Rightarrow aA \Rightarrow abA \Rightarrow ab$$

$$S \Rightarrow aB \Rightarrow ab$$

which, as you can see, correspond to two distinct paths in the NFA-Λ from the initial state to the accepting state. However, the regular grammar we obtain from an FA is clearly not ambiguous. For any state P and any input a, there is only one transition from P on a; therefore, for any variable P and any terminal a, there is only one production of the form $P \rightarrow aQ$. It follows that the derivation for a given string is completely determined—it must start with the start symbol, and the production to be used at each step is determined by the next symbol in the string.

We conclude that for regular grammars we already have an algorithm to remove ambiguity: construct the corresponding NFA-Λ, convert it into an FA, and find the regular grammar associated with the FA. You may verify that in this example the FA we get has six states, and the productions in the resulting grammar can be written

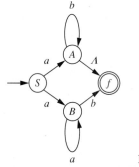

FIGURE 10-6

$$S \rightarrow aX \mid bE$$

$$X \rightarrow aB \mid bY$$

$$E \rightarrow aE \mid bE$$

$$B \rightarrow aB \mid bF$$

$$Y \rightarrow aE \mid bY \mid \Lambda$$

$$F \rightarrow aE \mid bE \mid \Lambda$$

One obvious way to simplify this grammar is to delete the productions involving E. Since both E-productions contain E on the right side, E is a 'useless' variable: it can never appear in the derivation of a string in the language. Although eliminating such variables isn't always quite this easy, an algorithm for doing it in general will be presented in the next chapter.

10.2 AN UNAMBIGUOUS CFG FOR ALGEBRAIC EXPRESSIONS

Normally, ambiguity is a property of the grammar, not of the language. There are exceptions to this generalization: it is possible to show that certain context-free languages are "inherently ambiguous," in the sense that they cannot be produced except by ambiguous CFGs. As a general rule, however, if a CFG is ambiguous, it is possible and often desirable to find an equivalent unambiguous CFG.

The rest of this chapter is devoted to solving this problem in a specific case: a slightly simplified version of the algebraic-expression grammar. One feature that this example will help to clarify is the role of parentheses in algebraic expressions.

It will simplify the discussion slightly to reduce the number of operators to two, $+$ and $*$. There is no real loss of generality in doing this, since if you like you can think of $+$ as standing for "any operation with the same precedence as $+$." This could be done by replacing $+$ and $-$ in the grammar by a new variable AO ("adding operator") and adding the productions $AO \rightarrow +|-$. Similarly for $*$. In any case, we shall consider the grammar G with productions

$$S \rightarrow S + S \mid S * S \mid (S) \mid a$$

We have seen that $S \rightarrow S + S$ by itself is enough to produce ambiguity, so it will be essential to eliminate this type of production. At the same time, we shall keep in mind our observations in Example 9.4 about the possibility of the grammar itself incorporating the rules of order and precedence: $*$ should have higher precedence than $+$, and $a + b + c$ should mean $(a + b) + c$, not $a + (b + c)$.

If we are not to have $S \rightarrow S + S$, we don't want to think of expressions that involve $+$ as being sums of other expressions. They are obviously sums of something—let's use "terms" to stand for the things that are added (combined using $+$'s) to create expressions. The corresponding variable in our grammar will be T. Expressions can also be products, but here it helps to remember precedence.

$a + b * c$ and $a * b + c$ are both sums: in other words, products are evaluated first and the results added. Rather than saying that *expressions* are products, then, it is more appropriate to say that *terms* can be products. Keep in mind that an expression can consist of a single term. Let's say that "factors" are the things that are multiplied (combined using $*$'s) to produce terms; they will be represented in our grammar by the variable F.

So far, we have a hierarchy of levels: expressions, the most general objects, are sums of one or more terms; terms are products of one or more factors. This hierarchy incorporates the fact that $*$ has precedence over $+$.

Where do parentheses come in? Expressions can consist of a pair of parentheses with something inside; so can terms; so can factors. If we include all these cases in our grammar, however, we are providing too many ways of deriving (a), for example, and the whole point of this discussion is to find a grammar with no ambiguity. Which is most appropriate? The crucial point is that you can't do anything with an object in parentheses until that object has been evaluated; in other words, evaluation of an expression in parentheses takes precedence over any operators outside the parentheses. In our hierarchy, factors are evaluated first; so the appropriate choice is to say that something that starts with "(" and ends with ")" is a factor. The things inside the parentheses can be arbitrary expressions.

We're almost ready to write down our grammar. Expressions are sums of one or more terms, terms are products of one or more factors, factors may be parenthetical expressions or simply identifiers. However, it's a little misleading to say that expressions are sums of terms, for this might suggest something like $S \rightarrow T + T \mid T$. Then, in order to get a sum of three terms, we would be forced to try $T \rightarrow T + T$ or something comparable, and we would have ambiguity again. The way out is easy enough: an expression is either a single term or the sum of a term and another expression. The only question is whether we want $S \rightarrow S + T$ or $S \rightarrow T + S$. This is the place to remember that $a + b + c = (a + b) + c$; the formula seems to suggest that $S \rightarrow S + T$ is more appropriate.

The grammar that we end up with after our discussion is $G1 = (V, \Sigma, S, P)$, where $V = \{S, T, F\}$ and P contains the productions

$$S \rightarrow S + T \mid T$$

$$T \rightarrow T * F \mid F$$

$$F \rightarrow (S) \mid a$$

Whether or not you were convinced by the preceding discussion, we are now faced with *proving* two things: first, that the new CFG $G1$ is indeed equivalent to the original one, and second, that it is unambiguous. Both proofs are slightly complicated, but both provide interesting and nontrivial examples of how mathematical induction is typically used with CFGs, and, as we noted earlier, the second involves some fundamental properties of parentheses that you may decide are not quite as obvious as you thought. To avoid confusion, we relabel the start symbol in $G1$.

Theorem 10.1. Let G be the CFG with productions

$$S \rightarrow S + S \mid S * S \mid (S) \mid a$$

Let $G1$ be the CFG with the productions

$$S1 \rightarrow S1 + T \mid T$$

$$T \rightarrow T * F \mid F$$

$$F \rightarrow (S1) \mid a$$

Then $L(G) = L(G1)$.

Proof.

   (1) **We show $L(G1) \subseteq L(G)$.** The proof is by induction on the length of a string in $L(G1)$. For the basis step, if $|x| = 1$ and $x \in L(G1)$, then clearly $x = a$, and so $x \in L(G)$.

   In the induction step, we assume that $K \geq 1$ and that for every y in $L(G1)$ with $|y| \leq K$, $y \in L(G)$. We wish to show that if $x \in L(G1)$ and $|x| = K + 1$, then $x \in L(G)$. We consider three cases, depending on how derivations of x in $G1$ begin.

(*a*) Suppose that x has a derivation in $G1$ that begins $S1 \Rightarrow S1 + T$. Then $x = y + z$, where $S1 \Rightarrow^*_{G1} y$ and $T \Rightarrow^*_{G1} z$. But since there is a production $S1 \rightarrow T$ in $G1$, we may say that $S1 \Rightarrow^*_{G1} z$ also. Therefore, since y and z are in $L(G1)$ and $|y| \leq K$ and $|z| \leq K$, the inductive hypothesis implies that y and z are both in $L(G)$. Since y and z are both derivable from S in G, and since there is a production $S \rightarrow S + S$ in G, we may conclude that $y + z = x$ is derivable from S in G, and thus $x \in L(G)$.

(*b*) Suppose x has a derivation in $G1$ beginning $S1 \Rightarrow T \Rightarrow T * F$. Then $x = y * z$, where $T \Rightarrow^*_{G1} y$ and $F \Rightarrow^*_{G1} z$. As before, it follows that $S1 \Rightarrow^*_{G1} y$ and $S1 \Rightarrow^*_{G1} z$. Again, the inductive hypothesis implies that y and z are in $L(G)$, and this time the fact that G contains the production $S \rightarrow S * S$ implies that $y * z = x \in L(G)$.

(*c*) The case when x has a derivation in $G1$ beginning $S1 \Rightarrow T \Rightarrow F \Rightarrow (S1)$ is handled similarly.

   Since $K + 1 \geq 2$, the cases (*a*), (*b*), and (*c*) account for all the strings in $L(G1)$; it follows that $L(G1) \subseteq L(G)$.

   (2) **We show $L(G) \subseteq L(G1)$.** Again, we use induction on $|x|$ and, just as in part (1), the basis step, $|x| = 1$, is straightforward. We assume that $K \geq 1$ and that for every y in $L(G)$ with $|y| \leq K$, $y \in L(G1)$; we wish to show that if $x \in L(G)$ and $|x| = K + 1$, then $x \in L(G1)$.

(*a*) Suppose x has a derivation in G beginning $S \Rightarrow (S)$. Then $x = (y)$, where $S \Rightarrow^*_G y$ and $|y| \leq K$. By the induction hypothesis, $y \in L(G1)$. Therefore, we may derive x in $G1$ by starting the derivation $S1 \Rightarrow T \Rightarrow F \Rightarrow (S1)$.

(*b*) Suppose x has a derivation in G beginning $S \Rightarrow S + S$. Starting at this point we must be a little more careful. Just as before, we can use the induction hypothesis to show that $x = y + z$, where y and z are both in $L(G1)$. However, this doesn't in itself imply that $x \in L(G1)$; we know that y is derivable from S, but what we need is for z to be derivable from T — in other words, we would like z to be a single term, the last of the terms whose sum is x. With this in mind, let $x = x_1 + x_2 + \cdots + x_n$, where each $x_i \in L(G1)$ and n is the largest integer for which we can find such strings $x_1, x_2, \cdots, x_n$. (We know $n \geq 2$, since we have already expressed x as $y + z$, where y and z are in $L(G1)$.)

For each x_i, the first step in any derivation of x_i is either $S1 \Rightarrow S1 + T$ or $S1 \Rightarrow T$, but the first case would imply that $x_i = x_i' + x_i''$, where $x_i', x_i'' \in L(G1)$, and this would contradict the fact that n is the largest integer j for which x can be decomposed into the sum of j elements of $L(G1)$. Therefore, each x_i is derivable from T in $G1$.

Let $y' = x_1 + \cdots + x_{n-1}$ and $z' = x_n$. The string y' is clearly derivable from $S1$, since $S1 \Rightarrow_{G1}^* T + T + \cdots + T$ $(n - 1$ terms). We have shown, then, that $x = y' + z'$, where $S1 \Rightarrow_{G1}^* y'$ and $T \Rightarrow_{G1}^* z'$. It obviously follows that $S1 \Rightarrow_{G1}^* x$, since we may start with the production $S1 \rightarrow S1 + T$. Therefore, $x \in L(G1)$.

(c) Finally, suppose every derivation of x in G begins $S \Rightarrow S * S$. The proof in this case is a little more delicate but we can use a modification of the idea in (b). We may write $x = y * z$, where $y, z \in L(G)$. Suppose $x = x_1 * x_2 * \cdots * x_n$, where each x_i is an element of $L(G)$ and n is the largest integer for which we can find such strings x_1, $\ldots, x_n$. (Note the slight difference between this and the corresponding decomposition of x in (b).) Then by the inductive hypothesis, each $x_i \in L(G1)$. Here we would like to show that each x_i is derivable from F in $G1$. Any derivation of x_i in $G1$ must begin either $S1 \Rightarrow S1 + T$, $S1 \Rightarrow T \Rightarrow T * F$, or $S1 \Rightarrow T \Rightarrow F$. Let us show that the first two cases are impossible.

In the first case, $x_i = x_i' + x_i''$, where $x_i', x_i'' \in L(G1)$. Therefore, by part (1), $x_i', x_i'' \in L(G)$. We have

$$x = x_1 * x_2 * \cdots * x_{i-1} * x_i' + x_i'' * x_{i+1} * \cdots * x_n$$

and $x_1, x_2, \ldots, x_{i-1}, x_i', x_i'', x_{i+1}, \ldots, x_n \in L(G)$. It is clear, then, that

$$w_1 = x_1 * x_2 * \cdots * x_{i-1} * x_i'$$

and

$$w_2 = x_i'' * x_{i+1} * \cdots * x_n$$

are both in $L(G)$; but this implies that $x = w_1 + w_2$, where $w_1, w_2 \in L(G)$, and thus that x has a derivation in G beginning $S \Rightarrow S + S$. We have assumed, however, that every derivation of x in G begins $S \Rightarrow S * S$.

In the second case, $x_i = x_i' * x_i''$, where $x_i', x_i'' \in L(G1)$. Again, part (1) implies that $x_i', x_i'' \in L(G)$. Then

$$x = x_1 * \cdots x_{i-1} * x_i' * x_i'' * x_{i+1} * \cdots * x_n$$

and since there are $n + 1$ factors, each in $L(G)$, we have contradicted our assumption that n such factors was the most possible.

Having ruled out the first two cases, we may conclude that for each i, x_i is derivable from F in $G1$. That's all we need: let $y' = x_1 * \ldots * x_{n-1}$ and $z' = x_n$. The string y' is clearly derivable from T, since $F * F * \ldots * F$ $(n - 1$ factors) is. We have $x = y' * z'$, where $T \Rightarrow_{G1}^* y'$ and $F \Rightarrow_{G1}^* z'$. It follows that $S1 \Rightarrow_{G1}^* x$, since we may start with the productions $S1 \Rightarrow T \Rightarrow T * F$. Therefore, $x \in L(G1)$.

The question of whether the grammar is ambiguous turns out to be closely related to the role of parentheses, and in order to prove that it is not ambiguous it will be helpful first to derive some basic results about parentheses, which are applicable in any situation where parentheses are used. Many of the observations we shall make about parentheses can be applied to other structures used as markers in the same way: {}, [], ⟨⟩, and even things like BEGIN END in programming languages.

As we have seen, one normally uses parentheses to remove ambiguity: if there is some doubt as to how $a + b + c$ should be interpreted, writing it as $(a + b) + c$ makes it clear. In a more complicated expression, parentheses are used to force one interpretation rather than another that would be the "default" interpretation: $((a + b) * c - (d + e))/f$ would be interpreted very differently if the parentheses were missing.

Inquiring into the role of parentheses in expressions like this one forces us to examine more carefully properties that are normally taken for granted. For example, in an algebraic expression, what does it mean for a subexpression to be "within parentheses"? If you're not careful, you might say it means that the subexpression lies between some left parenthesis and some right parenthesis. But consider the expression $(a) + b + (c)$. Since it starts with "(" and ends with ")," everything within it lies between "(" and ")," but we obviously do not say that b is within parentheses. "Within parentheses" means between some left parenthesis and the particular right parenthesis corresponding to it. So we are using strongly the fact that to every left (or right) parenthesis, there is one natural choice for the right (or left) parenthesis that corresponds to it. If this were not the case, then far from helping to remove ambiguity, the parentheses themselves would be an additional source of ambiguity. Our first job is to prove that this property we take for granted is indeed true. First we must define in some sort of formal way exactly what it means to say that one right parenthesis corresponds to another left parenthesis. For the moment, we won't need to worry about any symbols in the strings other than parentheses.

Definition 10.2. Suppose x is a string containing left and right parentheses and possibly other symbols as well. By taking into account the positions of the parentheses in x, we may view them as distinguishable objects; in other words, when we speak of a parenthesis in x, we mean a specific occurrence of the symbol "(" or ")". A *complete pairing* of x is a partition of the set of parentheses in x into (disjoint) subsets so that

1. Each subset in the partition contains exactly one "(" and one ")", with the "(" appearing somewhere before the ")"; and
2. For each subset S in the partition, the set of all parentheses in x *between* the two elements of S is the union of zero or more subsets in the partition.

The string x is said to be *completely paired* if there is a complete pairing of x. In a complete pairing P, the two parentheses in each subset in P are said to be *mates* with respect to P, or *mates in* P.

Lemma 10.1. If P and Q are two complete pairings of a string x, two parentheses that are mates in P are mates in Q. That is, there is no more than one way to pair a string completely.

Proof. Since symbols in x other than parentheses are irrelevant, we may simplify the discussion slightly by assuming that x contains only parentheses. The proof is by induction on the number of parentheses between the two in question. Let us formulate the statement to be proved this way: Any two parentheses in x that are mates in P and have exactly N parentheses between them are mates in Q.

For the basis step, suppose $(_0$ and $)_0$ are mates in P and $x = u(_0)_0v$. If $(_0$ and $)_0$ are not mates in Q, then denote by $)_1$ the mate of $(_0$ in Q. In this case $x = u(_0)_0w)_1y$, for some strings w and y of parentheses. By definition of "complete pairing," the set of parentheses in the string $)_0w$ is the union of subsets in the partition Q; but this is impossible, since the string begins with ")." Therefore, $(_0$ and $)_0$ are mates in Q.

For the induction step, suppose that $K \geq 0$ and that any two parentheses in x that are mates in P and have K or fewer parentheses between them are mates in Q. We wish to show that any two parentheses in x that are mates in P and have $K + 1$ parentheses between them are mates in Q. Let $(_0$ and $)_0$ be any such pair. Then $x = u(_0v)_0w$, where $|v| = K + 1$.

We know that the parentheses in v are partitioned into subsets in P. We now observe that they are also partitioned into subsets in Q. This follows from the inductive hypothesis: two parentheses in v that are mates in P have fewer than K parentheses between them and are therefore mates in Q.

It follows that the mate of $(_0$ in Q, say $)_1$, cannot be to the left of $)_0$, since the parentheses in v are already partitioned into pairs in Q. If $)_1$ were not the same as $)_0$, it would have to be to the right of $)_0$: $x = u(_0v)_0y)_1z$. In this case, the parentheses in $v)_0y$ would have to be partitioned into subsets in Q. But this is impossible. Since v is already partitioned this way, $)_0$, which is between $(_0$ and $)_1$, cannot have a mate in Q that is between $(_0$ and $)_1$. Therefore, $(_0$ and $)_0$ are mates in Q.

Lemma 10.1 tells us that if we know there *is* a complete pairing, it makes sense to talk of the "mate" of a parenthesis without specifying any particular complete pairing—there is only one. Once we know this, it is easy to say what "within parentheses" means: between some left parenthesis and its mate.

There is still one more step to be taken care of, before we are allowed to apply these facts about parentheses to strings generated by our CFG $G1$. In a string produced by $G1$, how do we know that there is a complete pairing in the first place? And even if we do know this, how can we be sure that the mate of some parenthesis $(_0$ is the right parenthesis we expect it to be—namely, the right parenthesis produced at the same time as $(_0$ by a single application of the production $F \rightarrow (S)$? Fortunately, the following lemma takes care of all our problems.

Lemma 10.2. In any derivation of a string x in $G1$, if we define a "pair" to be the set of two parentheses created by a single application of the production $F \rightarrow (S)$, the partition of the set of parentheses in x that is determined by these pairs is a complete pairing of x.

Proof. This is one of those results whose proof is almost easier than its statement. Condition 1 in the definition of "complete pairing" is obviously satisfied in this case. To see that condition 2 is also satisfied, take any two parentheses in x that constitute a pair, say $(_0$ and $)_0$. The step in the derivation where they appear looks like $\alpha F \beta \Rightarrow \alpha(_0S)_0\beta$. Any parentheses between these two in x must therefore be obtained during the subsequent derivation of a string from this S and are obviously obtained in "pairs"; therefore, condition 2 holds.

We now have the facts we need about parentheses and may proceed to apply them to our grammar.

Theorem 10.2. The CFG $G1$ with productions

$$S1 \rightarrow S1 + T \mid T$$

$$T \rightarrow T * F \mid F$$

$$F \rightarrow (S1) \mid a$$

is unambiguous.

Proof. We wish to show that every string x in $L(G1)$ has only one leftmost derivation from $S1$. The proof will be by mathematical induction on $|x|$, and it will actually be easier to prove something that is apparently slightly stronger: For any x derivable from $S1$, T, or F, x has only one leftmost derivation from that variable.

For the basis step, let $|x| = 1$, and suppose that x is derivable from $S1$, T, or F. It is obvious that $x = a$ and that in each case there's only one possible derivation: from F, $F \Rightarrow a$; from T, $T \Rightarrow F \Rightarrow a$; and from $S1$, $S1 \Rightarrow T \Rightarrow F \Rightarrow a$.

For the induction step, we assume that $K \geq 1$ and that for every y derivable from $S1$, T, or F with $|y| \leq K$, y has only one leftmost derivation from that variable. We wish to show that if $|x| = K + 1$ and x is derivable from $S1$, T, or F, there is only one leftmost derivation from that variable.

(1) Suppose the string x contains at least one $+$ that is not within parentheses. Let $x = x_1 +_0 x_2$, where $+_0$ is the last $+$ not within parentheses. Clearly x cannot be derived from T or F, since the only $+$'s in strings derivable from these variables are within parentheses. Therefore, any derivation of x must begin $S1 \Rightarrow S1 + T$. Moreover, this $+$ must be $+_0$; for if not, some other $+$ not within parentheses comes after it, and no $+$ not within parentheses is in any string derivable from T. Thus, any leftmost derivation of x has the form

$$
\begin{aligned}
S1 &\Rightarrow S1 + T \\
&\Rightarrow^* x_1 + T \\
&\Rightarrow^* x_1 + x_2
\end{aligned}
$$

where the last two steps represent leftmost derivations of x_1 from $S1$ and x_2 from T, respectively. However, since $|x_1| \leq K$ and $|x_2| \leq K$, the induction hypothesis tells us x_1 has only one leftmost derivation from $S1$ and x_2 has only one from T. Therefore, x has only one leftmost derivation from $S1$.

(2) Suppose x contains no $+$ outside parentheses, but x contains at least one $*$ outside parentheses. Let $x = x_1 *_0 x_2$, where $*_0$ is the last $*$ not within parentheses. x cannot be derived from F, and since x contains no $+$ not within parentheses, any derivation of x must begin $S1 \Rightarrow T \Rightarrow T * F$. Just as in (1), this $*$ must be $*_0$, and so any leftmost derivation of x has the form

$$
\begin{aligned}
S1 &\Rightarrow T \Rightarrow T * F \\
&\Rightarrow^* x_1 * F \\
&\Rightarrow^* x_1 * x_2
\end{aligned}
$$

where the last two steps represent leftmost derivations of x_1 and x_2 from T and F, respectively. By the inductive hypothesis, x_1 has only one leftmost derivation from T, and x_2 only one from F. It follows that x has only one leftmost derivation from $S1$.

(3) Finally, suppose x contains no + or * outside parentheses. Any derivation of x must begin $S1 \Rightarrow T \Rightarrow F \Rightarrow (S1)$. Therefore $x = (x_1)$, where $S1 \Rightarrow^* x_1$. By the inductive hypothesis x_1 has only one leftmost derivation from $S1$, and therefore x has only one from $S1$. The proof is complete.

EXERCISES

10.1. Refer to Example 9.4.

(a) Draw the derivation tree corresponding to each of the given derivations of $a + (a * a)/a - a$.

(b) Find the rightmost derivation corresponding to each of the trees in (a).

(c) Draw at least one more derivation tree for the same string.

(d) How many distinct derivation trees for this string are there?

(e) How many derivation trees are there for the string $a + a + a + a + a$?

(f) How many derivation trees are there for the string $(a + (a + a)) + (a + a)$?

10.2. Give an example of a CFG and a string of variables and terminals derivable from the start symbol for which there is no rightmost derivation.

10.3. Consider the Pascal statement

$$X:=1; \text{ IF } A > 2 \text{ THEN IF } A > 4 \text{ THEN } X:=2 \text{ ELSE } X:=3$$

(a) What is the resulting value of X if $A = 3$? If $A = 1$?

(b) Same questions as in (a), but this time assume that the statement is interpreted as in Fig. 10-5a.

10.4. Show that the CFG having productions

$$A \rightarrow a \mid Aa \mid bAA \mid AAb \mid AbA$$

is ambiguous. (Find a string for which there are at least two derivation trees.)

10.5. According to Exercise 9.9, the grammar with productions

$$S \rightarrow SS \mid (S) \mid \Lambda$$

and that with productions

$$S \rightarrow (S)S \mid \Lambda$$

generate the same language. The first is clearly ambiguous, because of the production $S \rightarrow SS$. Show that the second is unambiguous.

10.6. Show that the grammars in parts (a)–(c) of Exercise 9.1 are unambiguous.

10.7. Is the grammar obtained in Example 9.6 ambiguous? Give reasons.

10.8. In each case, show that the CFG is ambiguous and find an equivalent unambiguous CFG.

(a)

$$S \rightarrow SS \mid a \mid b$$

(b)

$$S \rightarrow ABA$$
$$A \rightarrow aA \mid \Lambda$$
$$B \rightarrow bB \mid \Lambda$$

(c)

$$S \rightarrow A \mid B$$
$$A \rightarrow aAb \mid ab$$
$$B \rightarrow abB \mid \Lambda$$

(d)

$$S \rightarrow aSb \mid aaSb \mid \Lambda$$

(e)

$$S \rightarrow aSb \mid abS \mid \Lambda$$

10.9. (a) Let x be a completely paired string of parentheses. Show that no prefix of x can have more right parentheses than left parentheses.

(b) Let x be a string of parentheses in which there are equal numbers of left and right parentheses and no prefix has more right than left. Show that x can be completely paired.

10.10. Consider the CFG G having productions

$$S \rightarrow AB$$
$$A \rightarrow aA \mid \Lambda$$
$$B \rightarrow ab \mid bB \mid \Lambda$$

Any derivation of a string in $L(G)$ must begin with the production $S \rightarrow AB$. Clearly, any string derivable from A has only one derivation from A; likewise for B. Therefore, G is unambiguous. True or false? Why? (Compare with the proof of Theorem 10.2.)

CHAPTER

11

SIMPLIFIED FORMS AND NORMAL FORMS

11.1 ELIMINATING Λ-PRODUCTIONS FROM A CFG

The previous chapter furnished us with examples in which, for certain languages, choosing one context-free grammar rather than another proves to be convenient. In the examples so far, the objective has been to remove the ambiguity from the grammar; but there are other reasons why it may be convenient to replace a given CFG by an equivalent one that is in some way simpler or more uniform. Questions about the grammar may be easier to answer if we can make certain simplifying assumptions about the form of the productions. In fact, there are several "normal forms" for CFGs, one of which we shall investigate in this chapter. In each case, for an arbitrary context-free grammar, it is possible to find an equivalent one that is in that normal form. Such results make it easier to answer questions, not only about a specific grammar or language but about context-free languages in general, since one can always assume that the CFG generating a language is in some appropriate normal form.

There are also several specific features that may make a CFG less convenient to work with. Two that we shall consider are "Λ-productions," of the form $A \rightarrow \Lambda$, and "unit productions," of the form $A \rightarrow B$, where A and B are variables. To illustrate, consider what might be said about a derivation in a grammar that contained neither type. Take an arbitrary step in the derivation, which takes us from some string α to some string β. If there are no Λ-productions, we know that β is at least as long as α; if there are no unit productions, the only way α and β

can be of equal lengths is for that step to have been the replacement of a variable by a single terminal. To say it another way, each step in the derivation either increases the length of the string or increases the number of terminal symbols. It follows that if $|x| = K$, a derivation of x can have no more than $2K - 1$ steps. This maximum number would be attained, for example, if the first $K - 1$ steps each increased the length by 1, to a total of K, and the last K steps each replaced a variable by a terminal. If we wished to determine whether a particular string of length K was in the language, a straightforward, if not necessarily efficient, way to proceed would be to examine all possible derivations of $2K - 1$ steps or fewer, and see if any of them produced the string. This is not to say that the question couldn't be answered without these assumptions or even that this is the best way to answer it in the presence of these assumptions, but at least it might suggest why it is sometimes convenient to eliminate Λ-productions and unit productions from a grammar. In any case, the first two results in this chapter say that, for all practical purposes, we can always eliminate both.

We begin with a qualification. We obviously *can't* eliminate all Λ-productions from a CFG if the string Λ is itself in the language L obtained from the CFG. The most we can hope for in that case is that $L - \{\Lambda\}$ can be generated by a CFG with no Λ-productions. In fact, this is possible. Before we prove it in general, let us consider an example that illustrates some of the potential complications. Let G be the grammar whose productions are

$$S \rightarrow ABCBCD$$

$$A \rightarrow CD$$

$$C \rightarrow a \mid \Lambda$$

$$B \rightarrow Cb$$

$$D \rightarrow bD \mid \Lambda$$

The first thing this example demonstrates was probably obvious already: you can't simply eliminate the Λ-productions without adding anything. In this case, if $D \rightarrow \Lambda$ is eliminated, nothing can be derived, since it is impossible to get rid of D from the current string. When Λ-productions are eliminated, we must add new productions that will allow us to derive every string whose derivation those Λ-productions made possible. This can mean adding a lot of productions, as we can see by considering $S \rightarrow ABCBCD$. Let us temporarily write this $S \rightarrow ABC_1BC_2D$. Since the right side contains three variables that begin Λ-productions, and since each of the three can also be used to derive something other than Λ, we may in a derivation replace none, any, or all of these three by Λ. Since in our modified grammar we will have no Λ-productions, the way to allow for all these options is to add to the grammar all possible productions that we obtain by deleting some subset of $\{C_1, C_2, D\}$ from ABC_1BC_2D. In other words, in addition to the original production, we will have

$$S \rightarrow ABBC_2D \mid ABC_1BD \mid ABC_1BC_2 \mid$$
$$ABBD \mid ABC_1B \mid ABBC_2 \mid$$
$$ABB$$

Notice that in some examples, this procedure would produce duplicate productions. For example, if we had $A \rightarrow CC$ and $C \rightarrow \Lambda$, we might write $A \rightarrow C_1C_2$, but $A \rightarrow C_1$ and $A \rightarrow C_2$ are really the same. Duplicate productions can obviously be discarded. The other type of extraneous production that might be obtained by the procedure is one of the form $A \rightarrow A$. These will clearly not contribute anything to the grammar and may be discarded as well.

The second point to observe is that if we followed literally the "adding" rule, we would be adding, among others, new Λ-productions. For example, applying the rule to $A \rightarrow CD$ would cause $A \rightarrow C \mid D \mid \Lambda$ to be added. We don't want $A \rightarrow \Lambda$ in the final grammar, but we must be a little careful how we get rid of it, if we are to be sure of keeping all the strings generated by the original grammar. One approach might be an iterative one:

1. Identify and record the variables that begin Λ-productions;
2. Delete the Λ-productions;
3. Identify all productions whose right sides contain variables recorded in step 1, and add all the necessary productions (possibly including Λ-productions), as discussed above; and
4. Repeat steps 1–3 until some sort of "equilibrium" is reached.

The iteration can be avoided, however, if we can determine at the outset which Λ-productions would eventually be added by this process, in addition to the ones present already. Another way to say this is: find out which variables are the "nullable" ones. If we knew this, we could apply the "adding" rule just once, to all productions whose right sides contained any of these nullable variables, and then simply discard any Λ-productions produced in this step.

These are the highlights of the algorithm, and at this point we proceed more systematically.

Definition 11.1. A *nullable* variable in a CFG $G = (V, \Sigma, S, P)$ is defined as follows:

1. If $A \in V$ and $A \rightarrow \Lambda$ is a production in P, then A is a nullable variable;
2. If $A \in V$, and for some $n \geq 1$, $A \rightarrow B_1B_2 \ldots B_n$ is a production in P, and B_1, B_2, $\ldots$, B_n are nullable variables, then A is a nullable variable;
3. Only those variables A in V for which there are productions as in rules 1 or 2 are nullable variables.

You can easily convince yourself that the nullable variables are precisely those variables A for which $A \Rightarrow^* \Lambda$. In addition, the definition suggests the following algorithm for finding all nullable variables: Start out with the set containing all variables that begin Λ-productions in the grammar; at each step add to the set all variables that begin productions whose right sides are made up entirely of variables already in the set; stop when this iterative step doesn't add anything to the set; the set obtained is the set of nullable variables. A more formal version is now given.

Algorithm FindNull (Finding the nullable variables in a CFG $G = (V, \Sigma, S, P)$).

$N_0 := \{A \in V | A \to \Lambda$ is a production$\}$;
$I := 0$;
REPEAT
$\quad I := I + 1$;
$\quad N_I := N_{I-1} \cup \{A | A \to \alpha$ is a production and α is a string of ele-
$\quad$ments of $N_{I-1}\}$
UNTIL $N_I = N_{I-1}$;
N_I is the set of nullable variables.

In our example above, the set N_0 contains C and D. N_1 contains A as well, because of the production $A \to CD$. Since no other productions have right sides containing only the variables A, C, and D, these three are the only nullable variables.

Algorithm 11.1 (Eliminating Λ-productions from a CFG $G=(V,\Sigma,S,P)$). To construct a CFG $G1 = (V, \Sigma, S, P1)$ equivalent to G but containing no Λ-productions.

1. Initialize $P1$ to be P.
2. Find all nullable variables using Algorithm FindNull.
3. For every production $A \to \alpha$ in P, add to $P1$ all productions that can be obtained from this one by deleting from α any subset of the occurrences in α of nullable variables.
4. Delete all Λ-productions from $P1$. Also delete any duplicates, as well as productions of the form $A \to A$.

Before proving that Algorithm 11.1 works correctly in every case, we finish showing what it gives us in the example above.

The productions in the original grammar were

$$S \to ABCBCD$$

$$A \to CD$$

$$C \to a \mid \Lambda$$

$$B \to Cb$$

$$D \to bD \mid \Lambda$$

We have already determined that the nullable variables are A, C, and D, and that seven productions are added as a result of two C's and a D appearing on the right side of the first production. It is easy to see that a total of eight additional productions are required and that the resulting grammar contains the productions

$$S \to ABCBCD \mid$$
$$ABBCD \mid ABCBD \mid ABCBC \mid BCBCD \mid$$

$$ABBD \mid ABCB \mid ABBC \mid BBCD \mid BCBD \mid BCBC \mid$$
$$ABB \mid BCB \mid BBC \mid BBD \mid$$
$$BB$$
$$A \rightarrow CD \mid C \mid D$$
$$C \rightarrow a$$
$$B \rightarrow Cb \mid b$$
$$D \rightarrow bD \mid b$$

Theorem 11.1. Let $G = (V, \Sigma, S, P)$. Let $G1 = (V, \Sigma, S, P1)$ be the CFG obtained by applying Algorithm 11.1 to G. Then $G1$ has no Λ-productions and $L(G1) = L(G) - \{\Lambda\}$.

Proof. That $G1$ has no Λ-productions is obvious. We show a statement that is slightly stronger than the stated equality: for any variable A in V, and any x other than Λ in Σ^*, $A \Rightarrow_G^* x$ if and only if $A \Rightarrow_{G1}^* x$.

(1) **We show: for any $n \geq 1$, if x can be derived from A in n steps in G, x can be derived from A in $G1$.** The proof is by induction on n. For the basis step, suppose x can be derived from A in one step in G. Then $A \rightarrow x$ is a production in G. Since $x \neq \Lambda$, this production is still in $G1$, and so x can be derived from A in $G1$.

For the induction step, we assume that $K \geq 1$ and that any string other than Λ derivable from A in K or fewer steps in G is derivable from A in $G1$. We wish to show that if $x \neq \Lambda$ and x is derivable from A in $K + 1$ steps in G, x is derivable from A in $G1$. Suppose the first step in a $(K + 1)$-step derivation of x in G is $A \rightarrow X_1 X_2 \ldots X_n$, where each X_i is either a variable or a terminal. Then $x = x_1 x_2 \ldots x_n$, where for each i, the string x_i is either equal to X_i or derivable from X_i in K or fewer steps. Any X_i for which the corresponding x_i is Λ is a nullable variable. If we delete these X_i's from the string $X_1 \ldots X_n$, there are still some left (since $x \neq \Lambda$), and the resulting production is an element of $P1$. Furthermore, the induction hypothesis tells us that for each i, if X_i is a variable remaining in the right side of this production, x_i is obtainable from X_i in $G1$. Therefore, x is obtainable from A in $G1$.

(2) **We show: for any $n \geq 1$, if x can be derived from A in n steps in $G1$, x can be derived from A in G.** Again, the proof is by induction on n. For the basis step, suppose x can be derived from A in one step in $G1$. Then $A \rightarrow x$ is a production in $G1$. This means that $A \rightarrow \alpha$ is a production in G, where x is obtained from α by deleting nullable variables, possibly none. Clearly it follows that x is obtainable from A in G, since a derivation can be obtained by starting with $A \Rightarrow \alpha$ and deriving Λ from each of the nullable variables in α.

Suppose that $K \geq 1$ and that every string other than Λ derivable from A in K or fewer steps in $G1$ is derivable from A in G; we wish to show the same result for a string x derivable from A in $K + 1$ steps in $G1$. Again, let the first step of a $(K + 1)$-step derivation of x in $G1$ be $A \rightarrow X_1 X_2 \ldots X_n$, where each X_i is either a variable or a terminal. We may write $x = x_1 x_2 \ldots x_n$, where for each i, x_i is either equal to X_i or derivable from X_i in $G1$ in K or fewer steps. By the induction hypothesis, each x_i is derivable from X_i in G. By definition of $G1$, there is a production $A \rightarrow \alpha$ in G so that $X_1 X_2 \ldots X_n$ can be obtained from α by deleting certain nullable variables. Clearly $X_1 \ldots X_n$ can be derived from A in G. Therefore we may derive x from A in G, by starting the derivation $A \Rightarrow^* X_1 \ldots X_n$ and then deriving each x_i from the corresponding X_i.

Example 11.1. Let $G = (V, \Sigma, S, P)$ be the CFG with $V = \{S, A, B\}$, $\Sigma = \{a, b, c\}$, and P containing the productions

$$S \rightarrow BAAB$$

$$A \rightarrow aAc \mid cAa \mid \Lambda$$

$$B \rightarrow AB \mid bB \mid \Lambda$$

All the variables are nullable. (Since S is not used on the right of any production, the fact that it is nullable isn't useful, except that we know $\Lambda \in L(G)$.) It is easy to check that the grammar $G1$ obtained by applying Algorithm 11.1 to G contains these productions:

$$S \rightarrow BAAB \mid$$
$$AAB \mid BAB \mid BAA \mid$$
$$AB \mid BB \mid BA \mid AA \mid$$
$$B \mid A$$

$$A \rightarrow aAc \mid cAa \mid ac \mid ca$$

$$B \rightarrow AB \mid A \mid bB \mid b$$

The first four lines of productions consist of the first production in G and those obtained from it by successively leaving out one, two, and three variables.

Clearly, the cost of eliminating Λ-productions from a grammar is that sometimes the number of productions is increased substantially (see Exercise 11.3). You might ask whether the algorithm introduces any other undesirable properties. One partial answer is that if the original grammar G is unambiguous, the new one $G1$ is also. The proof is not particularly difficult, but we shall not present it here.

11.2 ELIMINATING UNIT PRODUCTIONS FROM A CFG

The elimination of unit productions bears some resemblance to the elimination of Λ-productions. Again, we must be sure that in eliminating some productions we can still derive all the strings we could originally—in other words, we must typically add productions as well as delete them. If we have productions

$$A \rightarrow C$$

$$C \rightarrow B \mid \alpha$$

where A, B, and C are variables, when we eliminate $A \rightarrow C$ we must be sure that we are still able to get B and α from A, so we add $A \rightarrow B$ and $A \rightarrow \alpha$, even though the first is itself a unit production that must eventually be deleted. In Algorithm 11.1, we eliminated this iterative, or circular, aspect of the process by finding all the nullable variables at the outset. Here we may do something comparable: find at the outset all pairs of variables (A, B) so that B can be derived from A. For any such pair, the production $A \rightarrow B$ would eventually be added anyway, if we were to use an iterative algorithm. For every such pair, add the productions that are necessary to guarantee no strings will be lost when unit productions are deleted; finally, delete the unit productions.

Before, we had an algorithm to identify all nullable variables; here we need a systematic way to find all pairs of variables (A, B) for which $A \Rightarrow^* B$. At this point, however, a difficulty arises. If there are no Λ-productions in our grammar, a variable B can be derived from a variable A only by a sequence of unit productions and, as we shall see, such pairs can be identified without difficulty. But if there are Λ-productions, we can have derivations like $A \Rightarrow BC \Rightarrow B$, or more elaborate versions of the same thing, and the problem of identifying those pairs (A, B) for which $A \Rightarrow^* B$ will become complicated. As a result, we make the assumption that we have already applied Algorithm 11.1 if necessary, so that the grammar has no Λ-productions.

For any variable A, call a variable B other than A *A-derivable* if $A \Rightarrow^* B$. Clearly, since any such derivation consists entirely of unit productions,

1. If $A \to B$ is a production, B is A-derivable;
2. If C is A-derivable, $C \to B$ is a production, and $B \neq A$, then B is A-derivable;
3. Only variables obtained by rules 1 and 2 are A-derivable.

As this suggests, an algorithm for finding A-derivable variables is the following: Begin with a set containing all variables B for which $A \to B$ is a production; at each step, add to the set any variable B other than A such that $C \to B$ is a production for some variable C already in the set; when it is impossible to add any more variables to the set, it contains all A-derivable variables. Again, it may be useful to have a more formal version.

Algorithm Find-A-Derivable (Finding all A-derivable variables in a CFG $G = (V, \Sigma, S, P)$).

$AD_0 := \{B \in V | A \to B \text{ is a production}\};$
$I := 0;$
REPEAT
  $I := I + 1;$
  $AD_I := AD_{I-1} \cup \{B \in V | B \neq A \text{ and } C \to B \text{ is a production for some}$
    $C \in AD_{I-1}\}$
UNTIL $AD_I = AD_{I-1};$
AD_I is the set of A-derivable variables.

We note again that although one would normally say that a variable A itself is "A-derivable," our definition does not include it, simply because it would contribute nothing in the present discussion.

Algorithm 11.2 (Eliminating unit productions from $G = (V, \Sigma, S, P)$, assuming G has no Λ-productions). To construct $G1 = (V, \Sigma, S, P1)$ equivalent to G but having no unit productions.

1. Initialize $P1$ to be P.
2. For each variable A in V, find the set of A-derivable variables, variables B other than A for which $A \Rightarrow^* B$, using Algorithm Find-A-Derivable.

3. For every pair (A, B) such that B is A-derivable, and every non-unit production $B \rightarrow \alpha$ in P, add to $P1$ the production $A \rightarrow \alpha$.

4. Delete all unit productions from P_1.

Just as before, we must now verify that this construction does produce a grammar equivalent to the original.

Theorem 11.2. Let $G = (V, \Sigma, S, P)$ be a CFG without Λ-productions. Let $G1 = (V, \Sigma, S, P1)$ be the CFG obtained by applying Algorithm 11.2 to G. $G1$ contains no unit productions and $L(G1) = L(G)$.

Proof. It is clear from step 4 of the algorithm that $G1$ contains no unit productions. One half of the equality is almost obvious. Every production $A \rightarrow \alpha$ in $P1$ either is in P or can be "constructed" from productions in P by finding a variable B in G for which $A \Rightarrow_G^* B$ and a production $B \rightarrow \alpha$ in P. Therefore, no string can be derived in $G1$ that could not originally be derived in G—i.e., $L(G1) \subseteq L(G)$.

What remains is to show that $L(G) \subseteq L(G1)$. It will be a relatively straightforward induction proof once we formulate an appropriate statement to prove—that's the hardest part. Consider this statement: every string of variables and terminals that can be derived from S in G by a leftmost derivation with N steps, the last of which was not a unit production, can be derived from S in $G1$. Proving this statement for every $N \geq 1$ will be sufficient, since every string in $L(G)$ has a leftmost derivation whose last step is not a unit production. The basis step, $N = 1$, is clear, since any non-unit production in P is in $P1$. Suppose that $K \geq 1$ and that every string derivable from S in G by a leftmost derivation of K or fewer steps that doesn't end in a unit production is derivable from S in $G1$. We wish to show the same statement for $K + 1$. Take any string γ derivable from S in G by a leftmost derivation of $K + 1$ steps that doesn't end in a unit production. The last step in this derivation looks like

$$x B \alpha \Rightarrow x \beta \alpha$$

where $x \in \Sigma^*$, $B \in V$, $\alpha, \beta \in (V \cup \Sigma)^*$, $B \rightarrow \beta$ is a production in P, and $x \beta \alpha = \gamma$.

If there was a previous step in this derivation that was not a unit production, the string obtained by the *last* such step was $x A \alpha$, for some $A \in V$ for which $A \Rightarrow_G^* B$. This is where we are using the fact that the derivation is leftmost: all the unit productions between these two steps involve variables in the same position in the string. By definition of $P1$, $A \rightarrow \beta$ is a production in $P1$. The string $x A \alpha$ is derivable from S in $G1$, by the induction hypothesis, since its derivation in G has no more than K steps. Therefore,

$$S \Rightarrow_{G1}^* x A \alpha \Rightarrow_{G1} x$$

and $x \beta \alpha = \gamma$ is derivable from S in $G1$.

On the other hand, if all productions before this one in the leftmost derivation were unit productions, then $x = \alpha = \Lambda$ and $S \Rightarrow_G^* B$. But in this case $S \rightarrow \beta$ is a production in $P1$, so certainly $\beta = \gamma$ is derivable from S in $G1$.

It is worth remarking, again without proof, that if the original CFG is unambiguous, the new one obtained from Algorithm 11.2 is as well.

Example 11.2. Consider the unambiguous algebraic-expression grammar we derived in Section 10.3, with productions

$$S \rightarrow S + T \mid T$$

$$T \rightarrow T * F \mid F$$

$$F \rightarrow (S) \mid a$$

The S-derivable variables are T and F, and the only T-derivable variable is F. In step 3 of Algorithm 11.2, the productions $S \rightarrow T * F \mid (S) \mid a$ and $T \rightarrow (S) \mid a$ are added to $P1$. When unit productions have been deleted, we are left with

$$S \rightarrow S + T \mid T * F \mid (S) \mid a$$

$$T \rightarrow T * F \mid (S) \mid a$$

$$F \rightarrow (S) \mid a$$

11.3   ELIMINATING USELESS VARIABLES FROM A CFG

Another way to simplify a CFG is to eliminate any parts, variables or productions, that aren't contributing anything because they are never used in the derivation of a string in the language. Such excess baggage may have arisen as a byproduct of some previous modification of the grammar (see Example 10.4), or it may simply mean that the grammar has not been thought out carefully enough. Let's concentrate on variables. There are two obvious ways a variable may be "useless" in this sense: first, it may be "unreachable" (that is, it doesn't appear in any string derivable from S); second, it may be a "dead end" (no string of terminals can be derived from it). Notice the analogy to states in a nondeterministic finite automaton: any state in an NFA not reachable from the initial state and from which no final state can be reached can be eliminated, along with any transitions to or from it, without affecting the language recognized by the NFA. But the analogy with states in an NFA is not perfect, and there is a slightly less obvious way for a variable A to be useless. Even though A itself is neither unreachable nor a dead end, it may happen that every string derivable from S that contains A also contains at least one other variable that *is* a dead-end variable. Nevertheless, if we find algorithms to eliminate unreachable variables and dead-end variables, respectively, we shall see that combining them appropriately does in fact eliminate all useless variables.

Definition 11.2. Let $G = (V, \Sigma, S, P)$ be a CFG. A *live* variable in V is defined as follows:

1. If there is a production $A \rightarrow x$, for some $x \in \Sigma^*$, then A is live;
2. If there is a production $A \rightarrow \alpha$ and every variable in α is live, then A is live;
3. Only variables A satisfying rules 1 or 2 are live.

   A *reachable* variable is defined as follows:

4. If A appears in a string α for which there is a production $S \rightarrow \alpha$, then A is reachable,
5. If B is reachable and A appears in a string α for which there is a production $B \rightarrow \alpha$, then A is reachable,
6. Only variables A satisfying rules 4 or 5 are reachable.

A variable A is *useful* if it appears in a derivation of a string in $L(G)$—i.e., for some strings α and β in $(V \cup \Sigma)^*$ and some string $x \in \Sigma^*$, $S \Rightarrow^* \alpha A \beta \Rightarrow^* x$. Otherwise A is *useless*.

It is easy to check that reachable variables are precisely those variables that appear in strings derivable from S, and live variables are precisely those from which strings of terminals may be derived. Moreover, by this time, converting a recursive definition such as 1–3 or 4–6 of Definition 11.2 into an algorithm should seem like a relatively straightforward process, since this was what we did to obtain Algorithms FindNull and Find-A-Derivable.

Algorithm FindLive (Finding live variables in a CFG $G = (V, \Sigma, S, P)$).

> $L_0 :\ = \{A \in V \mid$ there is a production $A \to x$ for some $X \in \Sigma^*\}$;
> $I :\ = 0$;
> REPEAT
> $\quad I :\ = I + 1$;
> $\quad L_I :\ = L_{I-1} \cup \{A \in V \mid$ there is a production
> $A \to \alpha$ and every variable in α is in $L_{I-1}\}$
> UNTIL $L_I = L_{I-1}$;
> L_I is the set of live variables in G.

Algorithm FindReachable (Finding reachable variables in a CFG $G = (V, \Sigma, S, P)$).

> $R_0 :\ = \{S\}$;
> $I :\ = 0$;
> REPEAT
> $\quad I :\ = I + 1$;
> $\quad R_I :\ = R_{I-1} \cup \{A \in V \mid$ for some $B \in R_{I-1}$ and some α, $B \to \alpha$
> $\qquad\qquad$ is a production of P and A appears in $\alpha\}$
> UNTIL $R_I = R_{I-1}$;
> R_I is the set of reachable variables in G.

Algorithm 11.3 (Eliminating useless variables from a CFG $G = (V, \Sigma, S, P)$). To construct a CFG $G1 = (V1, \Sigma, S, P1)$ equivalent to G but having no useless variables.

1. Let L be the set of live variables in V, obtained by applying Algorithm FindLive to G, and let P' be the set of productions in P containing no variables other than elements of L. Let $G' = (L, \Sigma, S, P')$.
2. If $L = \varnothing$, then let $V1 = P1 = \varnothing$. Otherwise, let $V1$ be the set of reachable variables in L, obtained by applying Algorithm FindReachable to G', and let $P1$ be the set of productions in P' that contain no variables other than elements of $V1$. Let $G1 = (V1, \Sigma, S, P1)$.

It is easy to believe that in applying Algorithm 11.3 to a CFG we eliminate any variable that is not both reachable and live. What is less obvious, since there may be useless variables that *are* both reachable and live, is that we have eliminated these as well. But, in fact, we have.

Theorem 11.3. Let $G = (V, \Sigma, S, P)$ be a CFG, and let $G1 = (V1, \Sigma, S, P1)$ be the CFG obtained by applying Algorithm 11.3 to G. Then $G1$ is a CFG with no useless variables, and $L(G1) = L(G)$.

Proof. Let $G' = (L, \Sigma, S, P')$ be the intermediate CFG obtained by step 1 of the algorithm. Then $L(G) = L(G')$, since in obtaining G' from G the only productions left out are those containing variables of G from which no strings of terminals can be derived in G. Similarly, $L(G') = L(G1)$, since in constructing $G1$ from G' the only productions omitted are those containing variables that can never be obtained in any derivation in G' beginning with S.

To show that every variable in the new grammar is useful, let $A \in V1$. A is reachable in G'; i.e., there is a derivation $S \Rightarrow^* \alpha A \beta$ in G'. This means of course that not only A, but any variables in α and β as well, are reachable in G'—i.e., elements of $V1$—and so this is a legitimate derivation in $G1$, since any production in P' that involves only variables in $V1$ is still in $P1$.

On the other hand, since this is a derivation in G', all variables involved (in particular, A, as well as all variables in α and β) are elements of L, the set of variables in G'. This means that they are live variables in V. Thus, there is a derivation $\alpha A \beta \Rightarrow^* x$ in G, for some string $x \in \Sigma^*$. Obviously any variable involved in this derivation is also a live variable in V, so all the productions involved are elements of P'; thus, this is a legitimate derivation in G'. In fact, it's a derivation in $G1$ as well: $\alpha A \beta$ is derivable from S in G', so anything derivable from $\alpha A \beta$ in G' is also derivable from S in G'; since all variables involved are therefore in $V1$, all the productions involved must be in $P1$.

We now have

$$S \Rightarrow^*_{G_1} \alpha A \beta \Rightarrow^*_{G_1} x$$

which shows that A is a useful variable in $G1$.

Example 11.3. Consider the CFG with terminal set $\{a, b\}$ and productions

$$S \rightarrow AB \mid CD \mid ADF \mid CF \mid EA$$

$$A \rightarrow abA \mid ab$$

$$B \rightarrow bB \mid aD \mid BF \mid aF$$

$$C \rightarrow cB \mid EC \mid Ab$$

$$D \rightarrow bB \mid FFB$$

$$E \rightarrow bC \mid AB$$

$$F \rightarrow abbF \mid baF \mid bD \mid BB$$

$$G \rightarrow EbE \mid CE \mid ba$$

First, let us apply Algorithm FindLive to this CFG to find the live variables. $L_0 = \{A, G\}$; L_1 includes C as well, because of the production $C \rightarrow Ab$; L_2 includes E, because of the production $E \rightarrow bC$; finally, L_3 includes S, because of the production $S \rightarrow EA$. Since no other variables begin productions whose right sides contain only terminals and the variables A, G, C, E, and S, these five are the only live variables. Thus the intermediate grammar in Algorithm 11.3 contains the productions

$$S \rightarrow EA$$

$$A \rightarrow abA \mid ab$$

$$C \rightarrow EC \mid Ab$$

$$E \rightarrow bC$$

$$G \rightarrow EbE \mid CE \mid ba$$

We apply Algorithm FindReachable to this grammar, to find the reachable variables. You might wish to calculate R_0, R_1, and so on., but it's clear that all except G are reachable. The final grammar, equivalent to the original but with no useless variables, is the one with productions

$$S \rightarrow EA$$

$$A \rightarrow abA \mid ab$$

$$C \rightarrow EC \mid Ab$$

$$E \rightarrow bC$$

You may check that in Example 11.3 it would have worked just as well to apply Algorithms FindLive and FindReachable in the opposite order—i.e., let G' be obtained from G by eliminating all the unreachable variables in G, and let $G1$ be obtained from G' by eliminating all variables that are not live variables in G'. A legitimate question might be whether this always works. Perhaps surprisingly, the answer is no, although if you think about it, using our previous observations, you can see why. Suppose A is reachable and live (with a production $A \rightarrow a$, for example), but the only strings derivable from S that contain A also contain some non-live variable B. Since the second step would eliminate B, it would make it impossible to derive any string containing A. A itself, and in particular the production $A \rightarrow a$, would not be eliminated in the first step, since A is reachable; and this production would not be eliminated in the second step, since A is live. Even though A is useless, it would remain in $G1$.

The simplest example illustrating this is

$$S \rightarrow AB$$

$$A \rightarrow a$$

which is an extreme case: not only does it have useless variables, but the entire grammar is "useless," since it doesn't generate any strings. Nevertheless, if the two algorithms were applied in the wrong order, nothing would be eliminated in the first step and only the first production in the second step. You can check that Algorithm 11.3 does what it should: wipes out everything!

The following theorem summarizes the results of the first three sections of the chapter.

Theorem 11.4. Let G be a context-free grammar. There is a CFG $G1$ that has no Λ-productions, no unit productions, and no useless variables, so that $L(G1) = L(G)$.

Proof. The result is almost obvious from Theorems 11.1, 11.2, and 11.3. It remains only to observe that the algorithm to eliminate useless variables may remove productions but adds none; therefore, if we apply it to a CFG with no Λ-productions and no unit productions, the resulting CFG has none either.

11.4   CHOMSKY NORMAL FORM

In a sense, the first three sections of this chapter show how to simplify a CFG. However, the "simplified" grammar may have many more productions than the original, and it may be difficult because of the variety of types of productions to say much about the grammar. For this reason, it is often convenient to find an equivalent CFG in a "normal form," which not only eliminates certain specific types of productions, but places severe restrictions on the form of the remaining ones. We shall present one of these, the Chomsky normal form.

Definition 11.3. A CFG $G = (V, \Sigma, S, P)$ is in *Chomsky normal form* (CNF) if every production is of one of these two types:

$$A \to BC$$

$$A \to a$$

where $A, B, C \in V$, and $a \in \Sigma$.

Transforming a CFG $G = (V, \Sigma, S, P)$ into CNF may be done in three steps. The first is to apply Algorithms 11.1 and 11.2 to obtain a CFG $G1 = (V, \Sigma, S, P1)$ with no Λ-productions or unit productions so that $L(G1) = L(G) - \{\Lambda\}$. The second step is to obtain a grammar $G2 = (V2, \Sigma, S, P2)$ equivalent to $G1$ so that every production in $G2$ is either of the form

$$A \to B_1 B_2 \ldots B_k$$

where $k \geq 2$ and each B_i is a variable in $V2$, or of the form

$$A \to a$$

for some $a \in \Sigma$.

The idea behind the construction of $G2$ is very simple. Since $P1$ contains no Λ-productions or unit productions, every production in $P1$ that is not already of the form $A \to a$ looks like $A \to \alpha$, for some string α of length at least 2. For every terminal a appearing in such a string α, introduce a new variable X_a, introduce a new production $X_a \to a$, and replace a in all the productions where it appears, except those of the form $A \to a$, by the variable X_a.

For example, if there were two productions $A \to aAb$ and $B \to ab$, they would be replaced by $A \to X_a A X_b$ and $B \to X_a X_b$, and the productions $X_a \to a$ and $X_b \to b$ would be added. The sole use of the variable X_a is to derive the terminal symbol a, and thus it is reasonably clear that $G2$ is equivalent to $G1$.

The grammar $G2$ obtained this way now resembles a grammar in CNF, in the sense that the right side of every production is either a single terminal or a string of two or more variables. The last step is to replace each production whose right side has more than two variables by an equivalent set of productions, each one having exactly two variables on the right side. This process is best described by an example: the production

$$A \rightarrow BCDBCE$$

would be replaced by

$$A \rightarrow BY_1$$
$$Y_1 \rightarrow CY_2$$
$$Y_2 \rightarrow DY_3$$
$$Y_3 \rightarrow BY_4$$
$$Y_4 \rightarrow CE$$

The new variables Y_1, Y_2, Y_3, Y_4 are specific to this production and would be used nowhere else. This may conceivably be wasteful, in terms of the number of variables, but at least there is no doubt that the combined effect of this set of five productions is precisely equivalent to the original production, and adding these new variables and productions therefore does not change the language generated.

Let us denote by $G' = (V', \Sigma, S, P')$ the grammar obtained by this final step. G' is in CNF and is equivalent to $G1$, which, except possibly for Λ, is equivalent to G. If we are content to let these informal arguments take the place of a formal proof, we have obtained the following result.

Theorem 11.5. Let $G = (V, \Sigma, S, P)$ be a CFG. There is a CFG $G' = (V', \Sigma, S, P')$ in Chomsky normal form so that $L(G') = L(G) - \{\Lambda\}$.

Example 11.4. Let G be the grammar whose productions are

$$S \rightarrow AACD$$
$$A \rightarrow aAb \mid \Lambda$$
$$C \rightarrow aC \mid a$$
$$D \rightarrow aDa \mid bDb \mid \Lambda$$

Let us go through each step of the conversion to CNF.

(1) **Eliminating Λ-productions.** The nullable variables are A and D; Algorithm 11.1 produces the grammar with productions

$$S \rightarrow AACD \mid ACD \mid AAC \mid CD \mid AC \mid C$$
$$A \rightarrow aAb \mid ab$$
$$C \rightarrow aC \mid a$$
$$D \rightarrow aDa \mid bDb \mid aa \mid bb$$

(2) Eliminating unit productions. Here, we may simply add the productions

$$S \rightarrow aC \mid a$$

and delete $S \rightarrow C$.

(3) Restricting productions to either the form $A \rightarrow a$ or the form $A \rightarrow B_1B_2\ldots B_k$ (where $k \geq 2$ and each B_i is a variable). This step yields the productions

$$S \rightarrow AACD \mid ACD \mid AAC \mid CD \mid AC \mid X_aC \mid a$$

$$A \rightarrow X_aAX_b \mid X_aX_b$$

$$C \rightarrow X_aC \mid a$$

$$D \rightarrow X_aDX_a \mid X_bDX_b \mid X_aX_a \mid X_bX_b$$

$$X_a \rightarrow a$$

$$X_b \rightarrow b$$

(4) The final step to CNF. There are six productions whose right sides are too long. Applying our algorithm produces the grammar whose productions are

$S \rightarrow AT_1$	$T_1 \rightarrow AT_2 \quad T_2 \rightarrow CD$
$S \rightarrow AU_1$	$U_1 \rightarrow CD$
$S \rightarrow AV_1$	$V_1 \rightarrow AC$
$S \rightarrow CD \mid AC \mid X_aC \mid a$	
$A \rightarrow X_aW_1$	$W_1 \rightarrow AX_b$
$A \rightarrow X_aX_b$	
$C \rightarrow X_aC \mid a$	
$D \rightarrow X_aY_1$	$Y_1 \rightarrow DX_a$
$D \rightarrow X_bZ_1$	$Z_1 \rightarrow DX_b$
$D \rightarrow X_aX_b \mid X_bX_b$	
$X_a \rightarrow a$	
$X_b \rightarrow b$	

There is some room for simplification here, if it is important to reduce the number of variables as much as possible; in general, though, such simplifications are probably not worth the extra work.

EXERCISES

11.1. Show that the nullable variables defined by Definition 11.1 are precisely those variables A for which $A \Rightarrow^* \Lambda$.

11.2. In each case, given the context-free grammar G, find a CFG G' with no Λ-productions that generates the language $L(G) - \{\Lambda\}$.

(*a*) *G* has productions $S \rightarrow aA \mid \Lambda \quad A \rightarrow bA \mid \Lambda$

(*b*) *G* has productions

$$S \rightarrow AB \mid \Lambda$$
$$A \rightarrow aASb \mid a$$
$$B \rightarrow bS$$

(*c*) *G* has productions

$$S \rightarrow AB \mid ABC$$
$$A \rightarrow BA \mid BC \mid \Lambda \mid a$$
$$B \rightarrow AC \mid CB \mid \Lambda \mid b$$
$$C \rightarrow BC \mid AB \mid A \mid c$$

11.3. If a CFG has n non-Λ-productions, and no production has more than m variables on the right side, what is the maximum number of productions in the grammar obtained by eliminating the Λ-productions from the original?

11.4. Show that every regular grammar that does not generate Λ is equivalent to a regular grammar with no Λ-productions.

11.5. In each case, given the context-free grammar G, find a CFG G' with no Λ-productions and no unit productions that generates the language $L(G)$.

(*a*) *G* has productions

$$S \rightarrow ABA$$
$$A \rightarrow aA \mid \Lambda$$
$$B \rightarrow bB \mid \Lambda$$

(*b*) *G* has productions

$$S \rightarrow aSa \mid bSb \mid A$$
$$A \rightarrow aBb \mid bBa$$
$$B \rightarrow aB \mid bB \mid \Lambda$$

(*c*) *G* has productions

$$S \rightarrow A \mid B \mid C$$
$$A \rightarrow aAa \mid B$$
$$B \rightarrow bB \mid bb$$
$$C \rightarrow aCaa \mid D$$
$$D \rightarrow baD \mid abD \mid aa$$

11.6. In each case, given the context-free grammar G, find an equivalent CFG with no useless variables.

(a) G has productions

$$S \rightarrow ABC \mid BaB$$
$$A \rightarrow aA \mid BaC \mid aaa$$
$$B \rightarrow bBb \mid a$$
$$C \rightarrow CA \mid AC$$

(b) G has productions

$$S \rightarrow AB \mid AC$$
$$A \rightarrow aAb \mid bAa \mid a$$
$$B \rightarrow bbA \mid aaB \mid AB$$
$$C \rightarrow abCa \mid aDb$$
$$D \rightarrow bD \mid aC$$

11.7. In each case, given the context-free grammar G, find a CFG G' in Chomsky normal form that generates $L(G) - \{\Lambda\}$.
   (a) G has productions $S \rightarrow SS \mid (S) \mid \Lambda$
   (b) G has productions $S \rightarrow S(S) \mid \Lambda$
   (c) G is the CFG in Exercise 11.5a
   (d) G has productions

$$S \rightarrow AaA \mid CA \mid BaB$$
$$A \rightarrow aaBa \mid CDA \mid aa \mid DC$$
$$B \rightarrow bB \mid bAB \mid bb \mid aS$$
$$C \rightarrow Ca \mid bC \mid D$$
$$D \rightarrow bD \mid \Lambda$$

CHAPTER
12

PUSHDOWN AUTOMATA

12.1 INTRODUCTION BY WAY OF AN EXAMPLE

In studying regular languages, we started off with a notational scheme (regular expressions) for describing the way the languages were generated. The problem of recognizing such a language led to the formulation of an abstract machine, a finite automaton, corresponding exactly to this type of language. Context-free languages, like regular languages, take their name from a method of generating the languages. Here, the method is a context-free grammar. Since not every context-free language is regular, finite automata are not capable of recognizing arbitrary CFLs, and we would like an abstract machine, if there is one, that is just powerful enough to do this.

Finite automata are restricted in their memory to being able to distinguish among a finite number of states. Increasing the memory by increasing the number of states allows the machine to recognize regular languages of greater complexity, but no finite number of states will be enough to handle a nonregular language. On the other hand, the problem with an infinite number of states, unless this idea is qualified somehow, is that we are no longer able to describe in a finite way the specifications of the machine or how it should work. Instead, we consider augmenting the machine by adding a separate "memory." If the machine is to be able to recognize even a simple nonregular CFL, such as the set of palindromes over $\{a,b\}$, we know from the discussion in Section 4.4 that it will need to remember arbitrarily large amounts of information; this extra memory, therefore, will need to be potentially infinite, so one might say that in a sense the machine will have infinitely many "states"—there will be infinitely many distinct possibilities as to the contents of the memory. But viewing it this way is not especially helpful, since, as we shall see, at a particular instant the machine will not be able to distinguish among all these states; the step it takes next will be decided on the basis of a fixed number of bits of information. It will be appropriate to keep the idea of a finite set of states, which will include an initial state and some accepting states. The memory will be extra. In order to discover the appropriate way of organizing, or describing, this auxiliary memory, it will be helpful to look at an example.

Example 12.1 Consider the language

$$L = \{xcREV(x) | x \in \{a, b\}^*\}$$

Strings in L are palindromes of a particularly simple type: the c marks the middle of the string and thus simplifies the job of recognizing it.

In order to test a string for membership in L, a machine must remember each symbol occurring before the c until it encounters the matching symbol after the c. If when a pair of symbols is matched up they are discarded, then we see that each time a symbol after the c is encountered, the one it matches (if indeed it does match one) will be the one among the unmatched first symbols that came last—the one added to the memory most recently. This observation suggests that the memory can operate as a *stack*, which is simply a way of storing data values subject to the rule "last in, first out" (often abbreviated LIFO). If you think of a stack as a list, the LIFO rule means that items are always added ("pushed on the stack") and deleted ("popped off the stack") at the same end (the "top" of the stack), and at any time the top element is the only one accessible.

Our abstract machine will consist of a finite set of states, together with a potentially infinite stack that serves as the memory. As long as it hasn't yet read the c, it pushes each incoming symbol onto the stack. When it sees the c, it must remember that it has now finished the first half of the string: it can do this by changing states. Our set Q of states will have the three elements q_0, q_1, and q_2. The machine stays in q_0, the initial state, as long as it hasn't yet encountered c; in that state, each input symbol is added to the stack, regardless of what is currently on top. On the input c, the machine moves to state q_1, leaving the stack alone. In state q_1, each input is compared to the symbol currently on the top of the stack; if they agree, that symbol is popped off the stack and both are discarded—otherwise, the machine will crash and the string will not be accepted. Finally, if after the last input symbol has been read and matched, the stack is empty, the machine will move to q_2, the accepting state.

Each step in this process, each "move" of the machine, can be described as follows. An action will be taken depending on three things:

1. The current state;
2. The next input;
3. The symbol on top of the stack.

The action consists of

1. Changing states (or staying in the same state); and
2. Replacing the top stack symbol by a string of symbols in the stack alphabet.

Popping the top symbol off the stack is to be thought of as replacing it by Λ; pushing another symbol Y on the stack means replacing the top symbol X by YX, assuming that the left end corresponds to the top. In addition to these two basic actions, it is convenient to allow others as well: replacing X by Y (i.e., popping X and pushing Y), or even replacing X by some other longer string.

So far, this discussion suggests that we can describe moves, or transitions, by a "transition function" similar to the one that described moves of a finite automaton. There a move depended on two things, a state and an input, and consisted of one action, changing state, so an appropriate transition function was

$$\delta : Q \times \Sigma \to Q$$

Here, it looks as though we want

$$\delta : Q \times \Sigma \times \Gamma \to Q \times \Gamma^*$$

where Σ is the input alphabet, as usual, and Γ is the stack alphabet, possibly different from Σ. For a state q, an input a, and a stack symbol X, $\delta(q, a, X) = (p, \alpha)$ means we move to state p and replace X on the stack by the string α.

In order to make sense of this description, a few qualifications are necessary. First, how do we describe a move if the stack is empty ($\delta(q, a, ?)$)? We avoid this problem by saying that initially there is a special *start symbol* Z_0 on the stack, and the machine is not allowed to move when the stack is empty. Provided no symbol ever replaces Z_0 or gets placed "under" Z_0, whenever Z_0 is on top the stack is effectively empty—at least, as empty as when we started.

Second, remember that in our example we want to move to q_2 if the stack is empty when all the input has been read. How do we describe a move when the input is exhausted ($\delta(q, ?, X)$)? The solution we adopt here is a little different: we shall allow moves that use only Λ as input, just like Λ-transitions in an NFA-Λ. This suggests that we want

$$\delta : Q \times (\Sigma \cup \{\Lambda\}) \times \Gamma \to Q \times \Gamma^*$$

Of course, once we have moves of the form $\delta(q, \Lambda, X)$, we are not necessarily restricted to making them after all the input has been read. We might simply move without processing the next input symbol, which means that it's still there to be processed the next time.

Finally, we have said that there are situations when the machine will crash—i.e., when no move is specified. In the case of a finite automaton, when this happened we decided to make $\delta(q, a)$ a *subset* of Q, so that it could have the value $\varnothing$. And, of course, at the same time we allowed for the possibility that $\delta(q, a)$ might contain more than one element, so that the FA became nondeterministic. Here, we do the same thing, except that now, since $Q \times \Gamma^*$ is an infinite set, it is necessary to say explicitly that $\delta(q, a, X)$ and $\delta(q, \Lambda, X)$ will never be allowed to contain more than a finite number of elements. Although in this example it is not necessary to allow nondeterminism, in many cases it is. This leaves us with

$$\delta : Q \times (\Sigma \cup \{\Lambda\}) \times \Gamma \to \quad (\text{finite subsets of } Q \times \Gamma^*)$$

At last, we are ready to describe precisely how our simple-palindrome-recognizer will work. Q will be the set $\{q_0, q_1, q_2\}$; q_0 is the initial state, and the only accepting state is q_2; $\Sigma = \{a, b, c\}$; $\Gamma = \{a, b, Z_0\}$; and the transition function δ is given by the following transition table. Remember that when we specify a string to be placed on the stack, the top of the stack corresponds to the left end of the string. This convention may seem odd at first, since if we were to push the symbols on one at a time, we would have to do it right-to-left, or in reverse order. But the point is that when we get around to processing the symbols on the stack, the order in which we encounter them is the same as the order in which they occur in the string (see Table 12.1).

TABLE 12.1
Transition table for Example 12.1

Move number	State	Input	Stack symbol	Move(s)
1	q_0	a	Z_0	(q_0, aZ_0)
2	q_0	b	Z_0	(q_0, bZ_0)
3	q_0	a	a	(q_0, aa)
4	q_0	b	a	(q_0, ba)
5	q_0	a	b	(q_0, ab)
6	q_0	b	b	(q_0, bb)
7	q_0	c	Z_0	(q_1, Z_0)
8	q_0	c	a	(q_1, a)
9	q_0	c	b	(q_1, b)
10	q_1	a	a	(q_1, Λ)
11	q_1	b	b	(q_1, Λ)
12	q_1	Λ	Z_0	(q_2, Z_0)
(all other combinations)				none

Moves 1–6 push the next input onto the stack; 7–9 change state without affecting the stack; 10–11 match an input with a stack symbol and discard both; and the last move is to accept, provided there is nothing except Z_0 on the stack.

You can understand better how the machine works by tracing a few strings. To do that, let's keep track of the current state, all the unread input, and the entire contents of the stack, where the top corresponds to the left of the string. First, let's try a string in L, say $abcba$.

Move number	Resulting state	Unread input	Stack
(initially)	q_0	$abcba$	Z_0
1	q_0	$bcba$	aZ_0
4	q_0	cba	baZ_0
9	q_1	ba	baZ_0
11	q_1	a	aZ_0
10	q_1	—	Z_0
12	q_2	—	Z_0
(accept)			

Next, a string not in L, say acb.

Move number	Resulting state	Unread input	Stack
(initially)	q_0	acb	Z_0
1	q_0	cb	aZ_0
8	q_1	b	aZ_0
(crash)			

Another string not in L, say ab.

Move number	Resulting state	Unread input	Stack
(initially)	q_0	ab	Z_0
1	q_0	b	aZ_0
4	q_0	$-$	baZ_0
(crash)			

Finally, yet another string not in L: $acaa$.

Move number	Resulting state	Unread input	Stack
(initially)	q_0	$acaa$	Z_0
1	q_0	caa	aZ_0
8	q_1	aa	aZ_0
10	q_1	a	Z_0
12	q_2	a	Z_0

Notice the last move that occurs. There is no move $\delta(q_1, a, Z_0)$, but there is a move $\delta(q_1, \Lambda, Z_0)$, so the machine takes it. At this point, the machine is in an accepting state, but the input is not exhausted. We could say that the portion of the string input so far (i.e., aca) is accepted, but the entire string is not.

12.2 DEFINITIONS

The example in Section 12.1 should have prepared us for the following definition. Remember that what is being defined is in general nondeterministic.

Definition 12.1. A *pushdown automaton* (PDA) is a 7-tuple $M = (Q, \Sigma, \Gamma, q_0, Z_0, \delta, A)$, where

> Q is a finite set of states;
> Σ and Γ are finite alphabets (the input alphabet and the stack alphabet, respectively);
> $q_0 \in Q$ (the initial state);
> $Z_0 \in \Gamma$ (the initial stack symbol);
> $A \subseteq Q$ (the set of accepting states); and
> $\delta : Q \times (\Sigma \cup \{\Lambda\}) \times \Gamma \ \rightarrow \ $ (finite subsets of $Q \times \Gamma^*$).

δ is called the transition function of M.

In talking about the operation of a PDA, we will find it useful to keep track of the same three things we did when we traced the progress of the machine in our first example. We need to develop a little notation that will allow us to do this.

Let $M = (Q, \Sigma, \Gamma, q_0, Z_0, \delta, A)$ be a PDA. A *configuration* of M is specified by a state $q \in Q$, an input string $x \in \Sigma^*$, and a string of stack symbols $\alpha \in \Gamma^*$, and will be denoted by the triple (q, x, α). We interpret a configuration (q, x, α) to mean that q is the current state, x is the string of remaining unread input, and α is the current stack contents, where as usual, the top of the stack corresponds to the left end of the string α.

Suppose $(p, ay, X\beta)$ is a configuration of M, where $a \in \Sigma$, $y \in \Sigma^*$, $\beta \in \Gamma^*$, and $X \in \Gamma$, and suppose that $\delta(p, a, X)$ contains the pair (q, γ) for some $q \in Q$ and $\gamma \in \Gamma^*$. We write

$$(p, ay, X\beta) \vdash_M (q, y, \gamma\beta)$$

substituting $\vdash$ for $\vdash_M$, unless there is some possibility of confusion, and we say the configuration $(p, ay, X\beta)$ *derives* the configuration $(q, y, \gamma\beta)$ in one step, or one move. This simply means that if M is in state p and reads the first symbol a of the remaining input, one of the moves it is allowed to make is to move to state q and to replace the top stack symbol X by the string γ. Similarly, if $\delta(p, \Lambda, X)$ contains (q, γ), we write

$$(q, ay, X\beta) \vdash (q, ay, \gamma\beta)$$

Notice that no input has been read; this is a "Λ-transition." More generally, if $k \geq 0$ and (p, x, α) and (q, y, β) are configurations, we define

$$(p, x, \alpha) \vdash_M^k (q, y, \beta)$$

recursively, as follows.

$(p, x, \alpha) \vdash_M^0 (q, y, \beta)$ if $p = q$, and $\alpha = \beta$;

For $k \geq 1$, $(p, x, \alpha) \vdash_M^k (q, y, \beta)$ if there is a configuration (r, x, γ) so that $(p, x, \alpha) \quad \vdash_M^{k-1} (r, z, \gamma) \vdash_M (q, y, \beta)$

For two configurations (p, x, α) and (q, y, β),

$$(p, x, \alpha) \vdash_M^* (q, y, \beta)$$

will mean that $(p, x, \alpha) \vdash_M^k (q, y, \beta)$ for some $k \geq 0$; in other words, there is some sequence of (zero or more) moves that allows M to get from the first configuration to the second. Again, we usually write $\vdash^*$ instead of $\vdash_M^*$.

Using this new notation, we may define acceptance of a string by a PDA. Although so far we have been thinking of a string being accepted as a result of the PDA entering an accepting state, it is useful at this point to introduce another mode of acceptance. Using the notation we have developed, we can give precise definitions of both types.

Definition 12.2. If $M = (Q, \Sigma, \Gamma, q_0, Z_0, \delta, A)$ is a PDA and $x \in \Sigma^*$, x is *accepted by M by final state* if

$$(q_0, x, Z_0) \vdash^* (q, \Lambda, \alpha)$$

for some $\alpha \in \Gamma^*$ and some $q \in A$. x is *accepted by M by empty stack* if

$$(q_0, x, Z_0) \vdash^* (q, \Lambda, \Lambda)$$

for some $q \in Q$. The languages $L_f(M)$ and $L_e(M)$ are the sets of strings in Σ^* that M accepts by final state and by empty stack, respectively.

To say that M accepts x by final state means that there is a sequence of moves that takes M from the initial configuration (the initial state q_0, the entire string x yet to be read, and the start symbol Z_0 on the stack) to some configuration where the state is an accepting state and all the symbols of x have been read. The final contents of the stack are irrelevant in this case. If x is accepted by empty stack, on the other hand, the final state is irrelevant, but the stack is empty and the input has been completely read. In Example 12.1, M accepted the language L by final state. For the string in L that we considered, we could trace the processing by M as follows:

$$(q_0, abcba, Z_0) \vdash (q_0, bcba, aZ_0)$$
$$\vdash (q_0, cba, baZ_0)$$
$$\vdash (q_1, ba, baZ_0)$$
$$\vdash (q_1, a, aZ_0)$$
$$\vdash (q_1, \Lambda, Z_0)$$
$$\vdash (q_2, \Lambda, Z_0) \quad \text{(accept)}$$

It is worth emphasizing again that when we say a string x is accepted, by either method, we mean that *there is* a sequence of moves that causes the machine to go, in the process of reading the symbols of x, from the initial configuration to the appropriate final configuration. Since in general a PDA may be nondeterministic, there may be many other permissible sequences of moves that do not result in acceptance. Each time there is a choice of more than one move, you may view the PDA as making a guess as to which one to make. Viewed this way, acceptance means that if the PDA guesses right at each step, it can reach an accepting configuration. In our next example, we will see a little more clearly what it means to "guess right at each step."

If you have the impression at this point that PDAs are more complicated and harder to understand completely than finite automata or even NFA-Λs, it's not surprising: they are. On the one hand, a move depends on more factors than simply a state and an input, and on the other hand, describing the result of a move requires more than just specifying a state. We could, if we wished, draw a "finite-state diagram" for Example 12.1, modeling it after a transition diagram for an FA. Such a diagram is shown in Fig. 12-1. Each transition is labeled with an input (an alphabet symbol or Λ), a stack symbol X, a slash ("/"), and a string of stack symbols α; the interpretation is that the transition may occur on that particular input and involves replacing X on the stack by α.

There is no doubt that such a diagram contributes something towards understanding how the PDA operates, but it does not capture completely the PDA's behavior in the same way that a transition diagram for an FA does. The difference is not so much that more information is required to label each arrow, although that in itself makes the diagram harder to follow. The more important difference is that with an FA, all you need to know in order to trace the next move is the

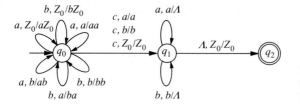

FIGURE 12-1

Transition diagram for the PDA in Example 12.1.

next input, and all you need to remember after making the move is the state you went to; in other words, if you are fed the input symbols one at a time, you can blithely follow the arrows, instantly forgetting everything else, and that's all there is to it. In Fig. 12-1, you can't even follow the arrows without keeping track of the stack contents as you go—not just the top symbol, but the entire stack. This brings us back to the essential difference between an FA and a PDA. A PDA must remember arbitrarily large amounts of information. The number of possible combinations of state and stack contents is infinite; thus, it is obviously not possible to draw a "finite-state diagram" in the same sense as for an FA (see Exercise 12.12).

Since we are comparing FAs and PDAs, this is an appropriate place to mention that there is a straightforward way of viewing any NFA-Λ, in particular any FA, as a particularly simple PDA. We may think of it as having a stack whose contents are never changed. It is easy to see that acceptance by the NFA-Λ is equivalent to acceptance by final state by the corresponding PDA. Once we have established that the languages that can be accepted by PDAs are precisely the context-free languages, we will have another easy proof that every regular language is a CFL.

12.3 MORE EXAMPLES

Example 12.2 In our first example, we made it easy for the PDA to recognize the palindromes in L, by giving them all a special middle symbol that served as an indicator to the PDA that it should switch from the "pushing-input-onto-stack" state to the "comparing-input-symbol-to-stack-symbol" state. Now we consider the language of all even-length palindromes over $\{a, b\}$, in which there is no such marker. Let

$$L = \{xREV(x) \mid x \in \{a, b\}^*\}$$

which, of course, is a context-free language. The general strategy for constructing a PDA to recognize this language will be the same as in the earlier case: remember the symbols we've seen so far, for as long as we have to until we can pair them with matching symbols in the second half. The obvious question is, how does the PDA know when it reaches the second half? The answer is that it doesn't; it guesses. Remember that it's permissible for a nondeterministic PDA to guess. There's no penalty for guessing wrong—the only question is, if it guesses right as to the midpoint of the string, will the symbols on either side of that midpoint match up correctly? To be sure of allowing the right guess, if there is one, we have the machine guess *at each step* that it has reached the middle. Of course, nearly all of these guesses will be wrong, but if none of the wrong guesses causes the machine

TABLE 12.2
Transition table for Example 12.3

Move number	State	Input	Stack symbol	Move(s)
1	q_0	a	Z_0	$(q_0, aZ_0), (q_1, Z_0),$
2	q_0	b	Z_0	$(q_0, bZ_0), (q_1, Z_0)$
3	q_0	a	a	$(q_0, aa), (q_1, a)$
4	q_0	b	a	$(q_0, ba), (q_1, a)$
5	q_0	a	b	$(q_0, ab), (q_1, b)$
6	q_0	b	b	$(q_0, bb), (q_1, b)$
7	q_0	Λ	Z_0	(q_1, Z_0)
8	q_0	Λ	a	(q_1, a)
9	q_0	Λ	b	(q_1, b)
10	q_1	a	a	(q_1, Λ)
11	q_1	b	b	(q_1, Λ)
12	q_1	Λ	Z_0	(q_2, Z_0)
	(all other combinations)			none

to accept a string it shouldn't, there's no harm done. If the string is actually in L, then one of the guesses—the one the machine makes when it actually *is* at the midpoint—will be correct, and the corresponding sequence of moves will lead to acceptance.

Let $Q = \{q_0, q_1, q_2\}$ and $\Gamma = \{a, b, Z_0\}$, as before. This PDA will also accept by final state, and again q_2 will be the only accepting state. The state q_0 represents "not having yet reached the midpoint of the string"; q_1 represents "having passed the midpoint, but not having reached the end"; and q_2 means accepting. In state q_0, guessing that we have not yet reached the middle means pushing the next input onto the stack and staying in q_0. Guessing that we have just reached the middle means treating the last symbol pushed onto the stack as the end of the first half, and moving to state q_1, without reading another input symbol, so as to be able to begin matching. An alternative would be to read the next symbol and to move to q_1 and make the first comparison on the same move, but this is less consistent with our decision to reserve q_1 as the state in which we make comparisons. Thus, the transition to q_1 will be a Λ-transition. Once we're in q_1, there's no more guessing—we're committed to the consequences of our earlier guess.

The transition table for our PDA is shown in Table 12.2.

Notice that this table is identical to Table 12.1 in Example 12.1, except for moves 7–9. In both cases, these three moves represented transitions from q_0 to q_1. The difference is that in Example 12.1 no guessing was required at this point; the signal to make the move was provided by the input c. Here, these moves are guesses, and they don't even take into account the next input symbol. If you compare move 1 and move 7, for example, you can see that there is genuine nondeterminism: in state q_0, with Z_0 the top stack symbol and a the next input symbol, the PDA can either read the a, push it onto the stack, and stay in q_0, or save the a to be read later and move to q_1. Although we shall return to this point later, it is worth pointing out here that a Λ-transition in itself does not represent nondeterminism. The PDA in Example 12.1 involved a move $\delta(q_1, \Lambda, Z_0)$, but since there were no moves $\delta(q_1, \sigma, Z_0)$ for any $\sigma \in \Sigma$, the Λ-transition was the only choice in this situation.

Let us trace the operation of the PDA for a string in L, say $baab$. The sequence of moves that leads to acceptance is

$$(q_0, baab, Z_0) \vdash (q_0, aab, bZ_0)$$
$$\vdash (q_0, ab, abZ_0)$$
$$\vdash (q_1, ab, abZ_0)$$
$$\vdash (q_1, b, bZ_0)$$
$$\vdash (q_1, \Lambda, Z_0)$$
$$\vdash (q_2, \Lambda, Z_0) \text{ (accept)}$$

Other possible sequences of moves are

(1)
$$(q_0, baab, Z_0) \vdash (q_1, baab, Z_0)$$
$$\vdash (q_2, baab, Z_0)$$

(2)
$$(q_0, baab, Z_0) \vdash (q_0, aab, bZ_0)$$
$$\vdash (q_1, aab, bZ_0) \text{ (crash)}$$

(3)
$$(q_0, baab, Z_0) \vdash (q_0, aab, bZ_0)$$
$$\vdash (q_0, ab, abZ_0)$$
$$\vdash (q_0, b, aabZ_0)$$
$$\vdash (q_1, b, aabZ_0) \text{ (crash)}$$

(4)
$$(q_0, baab, Z_0) \vdash (q_0, aab, bZ_0)$$
$$\vdash (q_0, ab, abZ_0)$$
$$\vdash (q_0, b, aabZ_0)$$
$$\vdash (q_0, \Lambda, baabZ_0)$$
$$\vdash (q_1, \Lambda, baabZ_0) \text{ (crash)}$$

These four sequences represent the four possible wrong guesses: that the midpoint was after zero, one, three, or four symbols, respectively. The last three lead to crashes, the first to an accepting state—but not to acceptance of the string we had in mind.

Example 12.3. In this example, we also try to recognize palindromes, but we make it even harder for our PDA by requiring it to recognize those of odd length as well as even.

$$L = \{x \in \{a, b\}^* \mid REV(x) = x\}$$

The idea here is that at each point before we have started the second half, we must allow for each of three possibilities:

1. That the next input is still in the first portion of the string, and should therefore be pushed onto the stack;
2. That the next input is the very middle of the (odd-length) string and should therefore be read but not saved, since it need not be compared to anything; and
3. That the next input is the first symbol in the second half of an even-length string.

With this in mind, we may construct the transition table (Table 12.3). Q, Γ, and A are as before. Again, notice the similarity between this table and those in Examples 12.1 and 12.2. The difference between this and the one in Example 12.2 is only that in the first six cases there is a second move that might be chosen.

TABLE 12.2
Transition table for Example 12.3

Move number	State	Input	Stack symbol	Move(s)
1	q_0	a	Z_0	$(q_0, aZ_0), (q_1, Z_0),$
2	q_0	b	Z_0	$(q_0, bZ_0), (q_1, Z_0)$
3	q_0	a	a	$(q_0, aa), (q_1, a)$
4	q_0	b	a	$(q_0, ba), (q_1, a)$
5	q_0	a	b	$(q_0, ab), (q_1, b)$
6	q_0	b	b	$(q_0, bb), (q_1, b)$
7	q_0	Λ	Z_0	(q_1, Z_0)
8	q_0	Λ	a	(q_1, a)
9	q_0	Λ	b	(q_1, b)
10	q_1	a	a	(q_1, Λ)
11	q_1	b	b	(q_1, Λ)
12	q_1	Λ	Z_0	(q_2, Z_0)
(all other combinations)				none

To take a typical case: line 5 says that if we're in state q_0, the next input is a, and the symbol on the top of the stack is b, we can either push the a, because we guess it's still in the first part of the string, or we can switch to q_1 and leave the stack alone, because we guess the input is the middle of the string and therefore doesn't need to be examined. Line 9 gives the third possible choice in this situation: do not read the input and go to state q_1 (because we guess the input is the start of the second half).

We shall trace two sequences of moves for the input string aba, and leave it to you to find all the others.

(1)
$$(q_0, aba, Z_0) \vdash (q_0, ba, aZ_0)$$
$$\vdash (q_1, a, aZ_0)$$
$$\vdash (q_1, \Lambda, Z_0)$$
$$\vdash (q_2, \Lambda, Z_0) \text{ (accept)}$$

(2)
$$(q_0, aba, Z_0) \vdash (q_0, ba, aZ_0)$$
$$\vdash (q_0, a, baZ_0)$$
$$\vdash (q_1, a, baZ_0) \text{ (crash)}$$

12.4   DETERMINISTIC PDAs

It is obvious that the PDA in Example 12.3 must be interpreted as a nondeterministic machine: the set $\delta(q_0, a, b)$, for example, contains two distinct moves. We also discussed the nondeterminism present in Example 12.2, although it takes a slightly less obvious form. There, no set $\delta(q, a, X)$ or $\delta(q, \Lambda, X)$ has more than one element, but at certain points the PDA still has a choice, since it can move by reading an input symbol or, for the same combination of state and stack symbol, leave the input symbol to be read later. In Example 12.1, even though there is a Λ-transition (namely, $\delta(q_1, \Lambda, Z_0)$), it seems appropriate to think of this PDA as deterministic, since there is no other move in state q_1 when the top stack symbol is Z_0.

These observations should make it easy to understand the next definition.

Definition 12.3. Let $M = (Q, \Sigma, \Gamma, q_0, Z_0, \delta, A)$ be a PDA. M is *deterministic* if there is no configuration for which M has a choice of more than one move; in other words, if

1. $\delta(q, a, X)$ has at most one element, for any $q \in Q$, $a \in \Sigma \cup \{\Lambda\}$, and $X \in \Gamma$; and
2. For any $q \in Q$ and $X \in \Gamma$, if $\delta(q, a, X) \neq \varnothing$ for some $a \in \Sigma$, then $\delta(q, \Lambda, X) = \varnothing$.

A language L is a *deterministic context-free language* (DCFL) if there is a deterministic PDA (DPDA) M for which $L = L_f(M)$.

The last sentence in Definition 12.3 deserves a comment. In Chapter 5, even though we had nondeterministic and deterministic finite automata, we did not define a "deterministic regular language." The reason, of course, was that for any NFA, or NFA-Λ, there is an FA that recognizes the same language. Thus, you might guess at this point that the corresponding result for PDAs is not true. In fact, it can be shown that the languages in Examples 12.2 and 12.3 are examples of CFLs that are not DCFLs. This is another indication that context-free languages are more complicated in a number of ways than regular languages.

Example 12.4. Consider the language L of all "balanced" strings of two types of parentheses, say "()" and "[]"—those strings that could be the strings of parentheses in a legal algebraic expression. (The word "parenthesis" here will be used for either type.) For example, [()[]] and ((([[]]))[] are such strings, and (] and ())(() are not. A CFG generating L contains the productions

$$S \rightarrow SS \mid (S) \mid [S] \mid \Lambda$$

Our discussion of "completely paired" strings of parentheses in Chapter 10 carries over without difficulty to this slightly more general case. There is only one way to pair up left and right parentheses in a balanced string: it is to pair two parentheses if they were both produced by the same application of one of the productions $S \rightarrow (S)$ or $S \rightarrow [S]$ in any derivation of the string.

Since each right parenthesis is matched with the *last* left parenthesis of the same type before it that does not already have a mate, it is clear that a stack will be the appropriate tool with which to recognize this language also.

We may construct a deterministic PDA to recognize L in a straightforward way. There will be two states: the initial state q_0, which is also the accepting state (note that Λ is one element of L), and another state q_1. In q_1, if there is at least one parenthesis on the stack, left parentheses of either type in the input are pushed onto the stack; a right parenthesis can be used to match a left parenthesis of the same type already on the stack, causing both to be discarded. Whenever all parentheses have been removed from the stack, indicating that the input string up to that point is balanced, the machine returns to q_0 by a Λ-transition, leaving the stack unchanged. At that point, if there is more input, the machine proceeds as if from the beginning.

Table 12.4 is a transition table for such a deterministic PDA. To avoid hopeless confusion, the parentheses with which we normally enclose a pair specifying a single move have been omitted.

TABLE 12.4
Transition table for Example 12.4

Move number	State	Input	Stack symbol	Move(s)
1	q_0	(	Z_0	$q_1, (Z_0$
2	q_0	[	Z_0	$q_1, [Z_0$
3	q_1	(	(	$q_1, (($
4	q_1	[	(	$q_1, [($
5	q_1	(	[	$q_1, ([$
6	q_1	[	[	$q_1, [[$
7	q_1	)	(	q_1, Λ
8	q_1	]	[	q_1, Λ
9	q_1	Λ	Z_0	q_0, Z_0
(all other combinations)				none

The input string ([])[], for example, results in the following sequence of moves. Again, to avoid confusion, the only parentheses shown are input symbols or stack symbols.

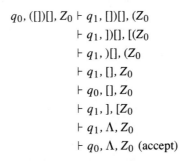

$$q_0, ([])[], Z_0 \vdash q_1, [])[], (Z_0$$
$$\vdash q_1,])[], [(Z_0$$
$$\vdash q_1,)[], (Z_0$$
$$\vdash q_1, [], Z_0$$
$$\vdash q_0, [], Z_0$$
$$\vdash q_1,], [Z_0$$
$$\vdash q_1, \Lambda, Z_0$$
$$\vdash q_0, \Lambda, Z_0 \text{ (accept)}$$

Before we leave this example, it seems appropriate to mention that you may very well have seen stacks used in a way similar to the way we're using them here, with a language closely related to the set of balanced strings of parentheses. If you have written or studied a computer program that reads in an algebraic expression and processes it (to "process" a string could mean to evaluate it, to convert it to postfix notation, to build an expression tree to store it, or simply to check it to see that it obeys the syntax rules), the program almost certainly involved at least one stack. If the program did not use recursion, the stack was explicit—storing values of subexpressions, perhaps, or parentheses and operators; if the algorithm was recursive, there was an implicit stack behind the scenes, since stacks are the data structures involved whenever recursive algorithms are implemented.

Example 12.5 For our last example, we consider

$$L = \{x \in \{a, b\}^* \mid N_a(x) > N_b(x)\}$$

The problem of comparing the number of as to the number of bs has a straightforward solution. A temporary excess of one symbol over the other is saved on the stack, and an input symbol of the opposite type is used to cancel out a symbol already on the stack. Thus, at any point where the stack contains only Z_0, equal numbers of both symbols have been read; an a on the stack indicates a surplus of as, and similarly for bs.

TABLE 12.5

Transition table for nondeterministic PDA recognizing
L

Move number	State	Input	Stack symbol	Move(s)
1	q_0	a	Z_0	(q_0, aZ_0)
2	q_0	b	Z_0	(q_0, bZ_0)
3	q_0	a	a	(q_0, aa)
4	q_0	b	b	(q_0, bb)
5	q_0	a	b	(q_0, Λ)
6	q_0	b	a	(q_0, Λ)
7	q_0	Λ	a	(q_1, a)
(all other combinations)				none

Table 12.5 represents a simple nondeterministic PDA with two states recognizing L. The PDA can quit (by taking a Λ-transition to the accepting state q_1) whenever it sees an a on the stack.

This approach must be modified slightly if we want our recognizer to be deterministic. In the machine we have, the current state doesn't play much of a role in the processing; the machine stays in q_0 until it decides to quit, which it does by checking that the stack has at least one a on it. This feature can be viewed as the cause of the nondeterminism, since from q_0 the PDA must be able either to quit or to continue reading (there are strings in L that are prefixes of longer strings in L). If we use the current state to indicate whether there is currently a surplus of as, we can avoid Λ-transitions altogether—and in particular avoid the nondeterminism introduced by the Λ-transition in our first PDA. Thus, our deterministic PDA will have the two states q_0 and q_1 as before, but this time it enters q_1 whenever it reads an a and the stack is empty. This move does not change the stack. If it pushed an a, to reflect the fact that there is now a surplus of as, there would be no way to discern at the point where that a was about to be popped off that the machine should leave q_1. The PDA leaves q_1 only by reading b when the stack is empty (i.e., by reading b when there is currently only one excess a), and that move also leaves the stack unchanged.

The deterministic PDA we have outlined has the transition table shown in (Table 12.6). Notice that there is no move specified from q_1 with stack symbol b or from q_0 with stack symbol a; neither of these combinations will ever occur.

TABLE 12.6

Transition table for deterministic PDA recognizing *L*

Move number	State	Input	Stack symbol	Move(s)
1.	q_0	a	Z_0	(q_1, Z_0)
2.	q_0	b	Z_0	(q_0, bZ_0)
3.	q_0	a	b	(q_0, Λ)
4.	q_0	b	b	(q_0, bb)
5.	q_1	a	Z_0	(q_1, aZ_0)
6.	q_1	b	Z_0	(q_0, Z_0)
7.	q_1	a	a	(q_1, aa)
8.	q_1	b	a	(q_1, Λ)
(all other combinations)				none

We illustrate the operation of this machine on the input string *abbabaa*.

$$(q_0, abbabaa, Z_0) \vdash (q_1, bbabaa, Z_0)$$
$$\vdash (q_0, babaa, Z_0)$$
$$\vdash (q_0, abaa, bZ_0)$$
$$\vdash (q_0, baa, Z_0)$$
$$\vdash (q_0, aa, bZ_0)$$
$$\vdash (q_0, a, Z_0)$$
$$\vdash (q_1, \Lambda, Z_0) \text{ (accept)}$$

12.5 THE TWO TYPES OF ACCEPTANCE ARE EQUIVALENT

We have defined two types of acceptance by a PDA: acceptance by final state and acceptance by empty stack. In all our examples, we have constructed PDA's that accepted by final state, although in practically all of them a PDA that accepted the language by empty stack would have looked virtually the same. (The exception is the DPDA in Example 12.4.) You may verify that in Examples 12.1–12.3, when a string is accepted, the stack ends up containing only the start symbol Z_0. In fact this was rather arbitrary; the move that got the PDA to the accepting state could just as easily have popped Z_0 off the stack. In general, of course, there is no reason to expect that a PDA that accepts a language by final state can be converted quite so simply into one that accepts the same language by empty stack. Nevertheless, the two types of acceptance turn out to be equivalent, in the sense that if a PDA accepts a language one way, another PDA can be found to accept the language the other way. This is the substance of the next two theorems.

Theorem 12.1. Let $M = (Q, \Sigma, \Gamma, q_0, Z_0, \delta, A)$ be a PDA, and let $L = L_f(M)$ (the language M accepts by final state). There is a PDA M_1 so that $L = L_e(M_1)$ (i.e., M_1 accepts L by empty stack).

Proof. We would like to construct M_1 so that when the two machines process the same input, M_1's stack will be empty precisely when M enters an accepting state. If we just make M_1 a replica of M but with some extra states that give it the ability to empty its stack automatically, without reading any more input, whenever M enters an accepting state, then we will have part of what we want: any time M enters an accepting state, the stack of M_1 will become empty. The difficulty is that M might crash with an empty stack—and if M_1 copied M exactly, its stack would be empty too, even though M was not in an accepting state. To avoid this, we let M_1 start by placing on its stack a special symbol U *under* the start symbol of M; this special symbol will keep M_1 from emptying its stack until it is really appropriate.

How does M_1 empty its stack automatically when M enters an accepting state? By including a Λ-transition from this state to a special "stack-emptying" state q_e, from which there are other Λ-transitions that just keep popping things off the stack until it's empty.

A precise definition of M_1 can be given as follows. What we choose to be the set of accepting states is arbitrary, since it will not be used; $\emptyset$ is the easiest choice. $M_1 = (Q_1, \Sigma, \Gamma_1, q_i, Z_0, \delta_1, A_1)$, where

$Q_1 = Q \cup \{q_e, q_i\}$ (where $q_e, q_i \notin Q$)
$\Gamma_1 = \Gamma \cup \{U\}$ (where $U \notin \Gamma$)
$A_1 = \varnothing$

The transition function δ_1 is defined as follows:

(1) $\delta_1(q_i, \Lambda, Z_0) = \{(q_0, Z_0 U)\}$
(2) For $q \in Q, a \in \Sigma$, and $X \in \Gamma, \delta_1(q, a, X) = \delta(q, a, X)$
(3) For $q \in Q - A$ and $X \in \Gamma, \delta_1(q, \Lambda, X) = \delta(q, \Lambda, X)$
(4) For $q \in A$ and $X \in \Gamma, \delta_1(q, \Lambda, X) = \delta(q, \Lambda, X) \cup \{(q_e, X)\}$
(5) For $X \in \Gamma_1, \delta_1(q_e, \Lambda, X) = \{(q_e, \Lambda)\}$

On the one hand, if $x \in L_f(M)$, then for some $q \in A$ and some $\gamma \in \Gamma^*$,

$$(q_i, x, Z_0) \vdash_{M_1} (q_0, x, Z_0 U) \text{ (by (1) above)}$$
$$\vdash^*_{M_1} (q, \Lambda, \gamma U) \text{ (by (2), (3), and (4) above)}$$
$$\vdash_{M_1} (q_e, \Lambda, \gamma U) \text{ (by (4) above)}$$
$$\vdash^*_{M_1} (q_e, \Lambda, \Lambda) \text{ (by (5) above)}$$

thus, $x \in L_e(M_1)$.
On the other hand, if $x \in L_e(M_1)$,

$$(q_i, x, Z_0) \vdash_{M_1} (q_0, x, Z_0 U) \vdash^*_{M_1} (p, \Lambda, \Lambda)$$

for some $p \in Q_1$. Since the only way U can be removed from the stack is by using (5), p must be q_e, and

$$(q_0, x, Z_0 U) \vdash^*_{M_1} (q_e, \Lambda, U)$$

Since the state q_e can be entered from another state only by (4), it must be the case that

$$(q_0, x, Z_0 U) \vdash^*_{M_1} (q, \Lambda, \alpha U)$$

for some $q \in A$ and some $\alpha \in \Gamma^*$. Since the only transitions that can be included in such a sequence of steps are transitions in M, it follows that

$$(q_0, x, Z_0) \vdash^*_M (q, \Lambda, \alpha)$$

so $x \in L_f(M)$.

Theorem 12.2. Let $M_1 = (Q_1, \Sigma, \Gamma_1, q_0, Z_0, \delta_1, \varnothing)$ be a PDA, and let $L = L_e(M_1)$. There is a PDA M so that $L = L_f(M)$.

Proof. This time we would like to construct M with an extra state q_f, which will be the accepting state, so that M enters q_f precisely when M_1's stack becomes empty. In constructing M so as to copy M_1, we will again place a special marker U at the bottom of the stack initially so that when M_1's stack empties, M will still be able to move to q_f by Λ-transitions.
Let $M = (Q, \Sigma, \Gamma, q_i, Z_0, \delta, \{q_f\})$ be defined as follows.

$Q = (Q_1 \cup \{q_i, q_f\}$ (where $q_i, q_f \notin Q_1$)
$\Gamma = \Gamma_1 \cup \{U\}$ (where $U \notin \Gamma_1$)

The transition function δ is defined as follows:

(1) $\delta(q_i, \Lambda, Z_0) = (q_0, Z_0 U)$
(2) For $q \in Q_1$, $a \in \Sigma$, and $X \in \Gamma_1$,
  $\delta(q, a, X) = \delta_1(q, a, X)$ and $\delta(q, \Lambda, X) = \delta_1(q, \Lambda, X)$
(3) For $q \in Q_1$, $\delta(q, \Lambda, U) = (q_f, U)$

Suppose first that $x \in L_e(M_1)$. Then

$$(q_0, x, Z_0) \vdash^*_{M_1} (q, \Lambda, \Lambda) \text{ for some } q \in Q_1$$

Therefore,

$$(q_i, x, Z_0) \vdash_M (q_0, x, Z_0 U) \vdash^*_M (q, \Lambda, U)$$

since all the transitions in M_1 are also transitions in M. It follows from (3) that

$$(q_i, x, Z_0) \vdash^*_M (q_f, \Lambda, U)$$

and thus, that $x \in L_f(M)$.
  On the other hand, if $x \in L_f(M)$, then

$$(q_i, x, Z_0) \vdash_M (q_0, x, Z_0 U) \vdash^*_M (q_f, \Lambda, \alpha)$$

for some $\alpha \in \Gamma^*$. Since the only transition to q_f is a Λ-transition from some $q \in Q_1$ with U on top of the stack, and since nothing is ever placed below U on the stack, we have $\alpha = U$ and

$$(q_0, x, Z_0 U) \vdash^*_M (q, \Lambda, U)$$

The only transitions that can appear in this sequence of moves are transitions in M_1; thus

$$(q_0, x, Z_0) \vdash^*_{M_1} (q, \Lambda, \Lambda)$$

Therefore, $x \in L_e(M_1)$.

You may verify for yourself that if the PDA M_1 in Theorem 12.2 happens to be deterministic, then so is the PDA M constructed in the proof of the theorem. The conclusion is that if L is accepted by empty stack by a DPDA, L is accepted by final state by another DPDA.

The corresponding modification of Theorem 12.1 is not true, and we can illustrate this by the language L in Example 12.4. There we gave a deterministic PDA accepting L by final state. Let's consider whether L could possibly be accepted by some other DPDA M_1 by empty stack. Λ is an element of L; therefore $(q_0, \Lambda, Z_0) \vdash^*_{M_1} (q, \Lambda, \Lambda)$ for some state q. Since M_1 is assumed to be deterministic, there is no choice in this sequence of moves: when starting in q_0, with Z_0 on the stack, M_1 is forced to empty the stack by a sequence of one or more Λ-transitions. But if that's true, the same sequence of moves must occur even if there's more input. For example, $(q_0, (), Z_0) \vdash^*_{M_1} (q, (), \Lambda)$. There is no way that any string other than Λ will be accepted, since M_1 will always start by immediately emptying its stack.

The problem here is that some strings in L, in particular Λ, are prefixes of longer strings in L. Whenever this happens, exactly the same sort of argument shows that L can't possibly be accepted by empty stack by a DPDA (see Exercise 12.8). However, if this prefix problem is "fixed up" by concatenating a new symbol onto the ends of all strings in L, making it impossible for any of the resulting strings to be prefixes of any others, the resulting language can be accepted by empty stack by a DPDA. See Exercise 12.9.

EXERCISES

12.1. For the PDA in Example 12.1, trace the sequence of moves made corresponding to each of the input strings $bbcbb$ and $baca$.

12.2. For the PDA in Example 12.2, trace every possible sequence of moves corresponding to the input string $aabbb$.

12.3. For the PDA in Example 12.3, two sequences of moves corresponding to the input string aba were shown. Trace each of the remaining sequences of moves corresponding to this string.

12.4. Give transition tables for PDAs that recognize each of the following languages.
   (a) The language of all odd-length palindromes over $\{a, b\}$.
   (b) The language of all non-palindromes over $\{a, b\}$.
   (c) The language $\{a^N x \mid N \geq 0, \ x \in \{a, b\}^* \text{ and } |x| \leq N\}$.

12.5. In both cases, a transition table is given for a PDA with initial state q_0 and accepting state q_2. In each case, describe the language that is accepted by final state.

Move number	State	Input	Stack symbol	Move(s)
1	q_0	a	Z_0	(q_1, aZ_0)
2	q_0	b	Z_0	(q_1, bZ_0)
3	q_1	a	a	$(q_1, a), (q_2, a)$
4	q_1	b	a	(q_1, a)
5	q_1	a	b	(q_1, b)
6	q_1	b	b	$(q_1, b), (q_2, b)$
	(all other combinations)			none

Move number	State	Input	Stack symbol	Move(s)
1	q_0	a	Z_0	(q_0, XZ_0)
2	q_0	b	Z_0	(q_0, XZ_0)
3	q_0	a	X	(q_0, XX)
4	q_0	b	X	(q_0, XX)
5	q_0	c	X	(q_1, X)
6	q_0	c	Z_0	(q_1, Z_0)
7	q_1	a	X	(q_1, Λ)
8	q_1	b	X	(q_1, Λ)
9	q_1	Λ	Z_0	(q_2, Z_0)
	(all other combinations)			none

12.6. In each case, describe a DPDA that accepts by final state the given language over $\{a, b\}$.

    (a) $\{x \mid N_a(x) = N_b(x)\}$

    (b) $\{a^N b^{2N} \mid N \geq 0\}$

    (c) $\{a^N b^{N+M} a^M \mid M, N \geq 0\}$

    (d) The language recognized by the PDA in Exercise 12.5(a)

12.7. Show that if the PDA M_1 in Theorem 12.2 is a DPDA, so is the PDA M that is obtained.

12.8. Show that if there are strings x and y in the language L so that x is a prefix of y and $x \neq y$, no DPDA can accept L by empty stack.

12.9. Show that if there is a DPDA accepting L by final state, and $ is not one of the symbols in the input alphabet, there is a DPDA that accepts the language $L\{\$\}$ by empty stack.

12.10. Suppose M_1 and M_2 are PDAs accepting L_1 and L_2, respectively, by final state. Describe a procedure for constructing a PDA accepting each of these languages by final state. (Note: in each case, nondeterminism will be necessary.)

    (a) $L_1 \cup L_2$

    (b) $L_1 L_2$

    (c) L_1^*

12.11. Give an example of a PDA and an input string x for which there are infinitely many possible sequences of moves corresponding to x.

12.12. Suppose a language L can be accepted (either by finite state or by empty stack) by a PDA in which, for some integer N, every string can be processed to completion without the stack's ever containing more than N items. What conclusion can be drawn about L? Give reasons for your answer.

CHAPTER
13

THE EQUIVALENCE
OF CFGs
AND PDAs

13.1 FOR ANY CFG THERE IS A PDA

This chapter contains two theorems. The second, in particular, is complicated, but the two are crucial because their purpose is to convince you that having an auxiliary memory in the form of a stack is exactly what is required for an abstract machine with finitely many states to be able to recognize an arbitrary context-free language.

There is some room for doubt at this point. Our first three examples of PDAs dealt with palindromes—obviously appropriate for recognition by a PDA, because of their symmetry, but for that reason too special to be completely typical CFLs. Only in the fourth example did we look at a language for which the CFG had a little more interesting structure, and you may feel that it also involved too much "symmetry" to be a representative example; in any case, the PDAs we constructed to recognize it had no obvious direct connection to CFGs for the language.

We are ready to confront an arbitrary CFL. In other words, we have a CFG generating the language, but that's all we know about it. Our first goal is to show that we can construct a PDA to recognize any such language. Obviously, the machine we end up with *will* be directly related to the grammar, and it will be possible at that point to get a better idea of why the two concepts are equivalent ways of describing languages. The second goal, which will complete the proof of this equivalence, will be to prove that the language recognized by any PDA can in fact be generated by a CFG.

The PDA we construct in the first part will have to test an arbitrary string and determine whether it can be derived from the grammar. It will do this by simulating a derivation, guessing which production to use whenever there is a choice, and comparing the terminal symbols as they are produced with those of the input string. Because of the guessing, we will be depending heavily on nondeterminism; if a derivation exists, and if the PDA guesses right at each step of its simulated derivation, the two will match and the input will be accepted.

The PDA will use the stack to keep track of the current string in the derivation it is simulating. It will start by pushing the start symbol S onto the stack. From that point on, the stack will contain the current string of the derivation, except for terminal symbols at the beginning that have already been popped and matched successfully with symbols in the input. To say it another way: at each step, the string of input symbols already read, followed by the contents of the stack (exclusive of Z_0), constitutes the current string in the derivation. The two types of moves the PDA can make are

1. To pop a terminal symbol from the stack, provided it matches the next input symbol. Both symbols are then discarded.
2. To pop a variable A from the stack and to replace it by the right side α of some production $A \rightarrow \alpha$. This is where the guessing takes place.

When a variable appears on top of the stack, it is the leftmost variable in the current string. Thus, the derivation being simulated is a leftmost one. If at some point there is nothing left of the current string on the stack, the attempted derivation must have been successful at producing the input string read so far, and the PDA can move to an accepting state.

We are now ready to give a more careful description of the PDA and to prove that the strings it recognizes are precisely those that can be generated by the grammar.

Theorem 13.1. Let $G = (V, \Sigma, S, P)$ be a CFG. There is a PDA M so that $L_f(M) = L(G)$.

Proof. We define $M = (Q, \Sigma, \Gamma, q_0, Z_0, \delta, A)$ as follows.

$Q = \{q_0, q_1, q_2\}$
$\Gamma = V \cup \Sigma \cup \{Z_0\}$, where $Z_0 \notin V \cup \Sigma$
$A = \{q_2\}$
(1) $\delta(q_0, \Lambda, Z_0) = \{(q_1, SZ_0)\}$
(2) For $A \in V$, $\delta(q_1, \Lambda, A) = \{(q_1, \alpha) | A \rightarrow \alpha$ is a production in $G\}$
(3) For each $a \in \Sigma$, $\delta(q_1, a, a) = \{(q_1, \Lambda)\}$
(4) $\delta(q_1, \Lambda, Z_0) = \{(q_2, Z_0)\}$

and (1)–(4) are the only moves M can make.

(*a*) **We show** $L(G) \subseteq L_f(M)$. We begin with the observation that for any strings y and z of terminal symbols and any string α of stack symbols,

(5) $(q_1, yz, y\alpha) \vdash^* (q_1, z, \alpha)$

(The moves are those in (3) above, as many as there are symbols in y.) With this in mind, let us consider this statement, which we shall prove using mathematical induction:

(6) If $x \in L(G)$ and the Nth step in a leftmost derivation of x is $yA\alpha \Rightarrow yy'\beta$, where $x = yy'z$ and β either is Λ or begins with a variable, then

$$(q_0, x, Z_0) = (q_0, yy'z, Z_0) \vdash^* (q_1, z, \beta Z_0)$$

In words, this says that if the current string in a leftmost derivation consists of a string of terminals, possibly followed by a string beginning with a variable, some sequence of moves will have read that initial sequence of terminals, matched it with terminals from the stack, and left the remaining portion of the current string on the stack.

It is easy to see that proving (6) will be sufficient: the last step in a leftmost derivation of x looks like

$$yA\alpha \Rightarrow yy' = x$$

(i.e., as in (6) but with $\beta = \Lambda$), and (6) will then tell us that

$$(q_0, x, Z_0) \vdash^* (q_1, \Lambda, Z_0)$$

It will follow from (4) that

$$(q_0, x, Z_0) \vdash^* (q_2, \Lambda, Z_0)$$

and thus that $x \in L_f(M)$.

In the basis step of the proof of (6), let $N = 1$. The first step in a derivation of x looks like $S \Rightarrow y'\beta$, so the string y in (6) is Λ. Since this is a production, we have

$$(q_0, x, Z_0) = (q_0, y'z, Z_0) \vdash (q_1, y'z, SZ_0) \vdash (q_1, y'z, y'\beta Z_0)$$

The first move here is from (1), the second from (2). It follows from (5) that

$$(q_0, x, Z_0) \vdash^* (q_1, z, \beta Z_0)$$

For the induction step, suppose that $K \geq 1$ and that (6) is true for every N with $N \leq K$. We wish to show that if the $(K + 1)$th step in a leftmost derivation of x is $yA\alpha \Rightarrow yy'\beta$, then $(q_0, x, Z_0) \vdash^* (q_1, z, \beta Z_0)$, where $x = yy'z$. Let us look at the Kth step in the leftmost derivation of x. It is of the form

$$wB\gamma \Rightarrow ww'\beta' = ww'A\alpha$$

where $ww' = y$; this means that $x = ww'(y'z)$, and the induction hypothesis implies that

$$(q_0, x, Z_0) \vdash^* (q_1, y'z, A\alpha Z_0)$$

If the production used in the $(K + 1)$th step is $A \to \alpha'$, so that $\alpha'\alpha = y'\beta$, then from (2) and (5),

$$(q_1, y'z, A\alpha Z_0) \vdash (q_1, y'z, \alpha'\alpha Z_0) = (q_1, y'z, y'\beta Z_0) \vdash^* (q_1, z, \beta Z_0)$$

This completes the proof of (6).

(b) **We show $L_f(M) \subseteq L(G)$.** Roughly speaking, this means we need to show the reverse of (6): that the configuration $(q_1, z, \beta Z_0)$ can occur only if some leftmost derivation in the grammar produces the string $y\beta$, where $x = yz$. To be precise, we prove

(7) If, starting with (q_0, x, Z_0), there is a sequence of N moves of M that results in the configuration $(q_1, z, \beta Z_0)$, then for some $y \in \Sigma^*$, $x = yz$ and $S \Rightarrow_G^* y\beta$.

Again, the proof is by induction on N. For the basis step, let $N = 1$. The only single move producing a configuration of this form is the move (1). Therefore, in this case, $z = x$ and $\beta = S$. The conclusion obviously follows from taking $y = \Lambda$.

For the induction step, suppose that $K \geq 1$ and that (7) is true for any N with $N \leq K$. Suppose some sequence of $K + 1$ moves produces the configuration $(q_1, z, \beta Z_0)$. We wish to show that $x = yz$ for some $y \in \Sigma^*$ and that $S \Rightarrow^* y\beta$. There are only two possibilities for the last move in this sequence of $K + 1$ moves: either the preceding configuration was $(q_1, az, a\beta Z_0)$ for some $a \in \Sigma$, or it was $(q_1, z, A\gamma Z_0)$ for some variable A for which there is a production $A \to \alpha$ with $\alpha\gamma = \beta$. These two possible moves correspond to (2) and (3), respectively.

In the first case, the induction hypothesis implies that for some $y' \in \Sigma^*$, $x = y'az$ and $S \Rightarrow^* y'a\beta$. If we let $y = y'a$, the conclusion follows immediately.

In the second case, the induction hypothesis implies that $x = yz$ for some $y \in \Sigma^*$ and $S \Rightarrow^* yA\gamma$. But then

$$S \Rightarrow^* yA\gamma \Rightarrow y\alpha\gamma = y\beta$$

This completes the induction.

Suppose $x \in L_f(M)$. Since M can enter q_2 only via a Λ-transition with Z_0 on top of the stack,

$$(q_0, x, Z_0) \vdash^* (q_1, \Lambda, Z_0) \vdash (q_2, \Lambda, Z_0)$$

Letting $y = x$ and $z = \beta = \Lambda$ in (7), we may conclude that $S \Rightarrow_G^* x$, and therefore $x \in L(G)$.

Example 13.1. Let us look again at the language L of balanced strings of parentheses, for which we constructed a PDA in Example 12.4 of the previous chapter. For the sake of simplicity, we assume that [and] are the only "parentheses" used. A CFG generating L contains the productions

$$S \to SS \mid [S] \mid \Lambda$$

The rules (1)–(4) in the proof of Theorem 13.1 give us the PDA $M = (\{q_0, q_1, q_2\}, \Sigma, \{S, Z_0\}, Z_0, \delta, \{q_2\})$, where the transition function δ is defined by this table.

Move number	State	Input	Stack symbol	Move(s)
1	q_0	Λ	Z_0	(q_1, SZ_0)
2	q_1	Λ	S	$(q_1, SS), (q_1, [S]), (q_1, \Lambda)$
3	q_1	[	[	(q_1, Λ)
4	q_1	]	]	(q_1, Λ)
5	q_1	Λ	Z_0	(q_2, Z_0)
	(all other combinations)			none

Let us choose a string in L and compare the moves made by M in accepting the string with a leftmost derivation of the string in the grammar. Let $x = [][[][]]$. The sequence of moves by which M accepts x is shown below. Each move in which a variable on the stack is replaced by a string corresponds to a step in a leftmost derivation of x, and that step is shown at the right. Observe that at each step, the stack contains (in addition to Z_0) the portion of the current string in the derivation that remains after an initial string of terminals is removed.

$(q_0, [][[][]], Z_0)$

$\vdash (q_1, [][[][]], SZ_0)$ S

$\vdash (q_1, [][[][]], SSZ_0)$ $\Rightarrow SS$

$\vdash (q_1, [][[][]], [S]SZ_0)$ $\Rightarrow [S]S$

$\vdash (q_1,][[][]], S]SZ_0)$

$\vdash (q_1,][[][]],]SZ_0)$ $\Rightarrow []S$

$\vdash (q_1, [[][]], SZ_0)$

$\vdash (q_1, [[][]], [S]Z_0)$ $\Rightarrow [][S]$

$\vdash (q_1, [][]], S]Z_0)$

$\vdash (q_1, [][]], SS]Z_0)$ $\Rightarrow [][SS]$

$\vdash (q_1, [][]], [S]S]Z_0)$ $\Rightarrow [][[S]S]$

$\vdash (q_1,][]], S]S]Z_0)$

$\vdash (q_1,][]],]S]Z_0)$ $\Rightarrow [][[]S]$

$\vdash (q_1, []], S]Z_0)$

$\vdash (q_1, []], [S]]Z_0)$ $\Rightarrow [][[[S]]$

$\vdash (q_1,]], S]]Z_0)$

$\vdash (q_1,]],]]Z_0)$ $\Rightarrow [][[][]]$

$\vdash (q_1,],]Z_0)$

$\vdash (q_1, \Lambda, Z_0)$

$\vdash (q_2, \Lambda, Z_0)$

13.2   FOR EVERY PDA THERE IS A CFG

In Theorem 13.1, we found a straightforward way of defining a PDA to simulate a leftmost derivation in a given CFG. If at some point in the derivation the current string looks like $x\alpha$, where x is a string of terminals, then at some point in the simulation, the input string read so far is x and the stack contains the string α. We accomplished this by simply taking as our new stack alphabet the set $\Sigma \cup \Gamma$ and by defining PDA moves so that variables are removed from the stack and replaced by the right sides of productions. The states are almost incidental: after the initial move, the PDA stays in the same state until it is ready to accept.

We wish to start with a PDA and produce a CFG that generates precisely the strings accepted by the PDA. The argument will be simplified somewhat if we assume that the PDA accepts the language by empty stack. By Theorem 12.1, we can make this assumption without loss of generality. It is not obvious what the variables in our grammar should be, and it seems as though the states of the PDA might introduce an extra degree of complexity, but we attempt to preserve the main feature of the earlier correspondence. The string read so far will be the initial portion of the current string in a leftmost derivation, and what remains on the stack will correspond to the remaining portion of the current string. In fact, we will define our CFG so that this remaining portion will consist entirely of variables, so as to highlight the correspondence between the stack contents and the remaining portion of the current string. In order to yield a string of terminals in the CFG, all the remaining variables must eventually be eliminated from the current string, and in order for the input string to be accepted by the PDA, all the symbols on the stack must eventually be popped off.

We might start by trying a very simple approach. Take the variables in the grammar to be all possible stack symbols in the PDA, renamed if necessary so that no input symbols are included; take the start symbol to be Z_0; ignore the states of the PDA completely; and for each PDA move that reads a (either Λ or an element of Σ) and replaces A on the stack by $B_1 B_2 \ldots B_m$, introduce the production

$$A \rightarrow aB_1B_2 \ldots B_m$$

This approach will give us the correspondence outlined above between the current stack contents and the string of variables remaining in the current string being derived. Moreover, it will allow the grammar to generate all strings accepted by the PDA. However, because we are ignoring the states of the PDA, we cannot be sure that these are the only strings derivable. To see an example, we need only look at Example 12.1. This PDA accepts the language $\{x \, cREV(x) \mid x \in \{a, b\}^*\}$ by final state, but to make it accept the same language by empty stack we can simply change move 12 to

$$\delta(q_1, \Lambda, Z_0) = \{(q_2, \Lambda)\}$$

instead of $\{(q_2, Z_0)\}$. We use A and B as stack symbols instead of a and b. The moves of the PDA include these:

$$\delta(q_0, a, Z_0) = \{(q_0, AZ_0)\}$$
$$\delta(q_0, c, A) = \{(q_1, A)\}$$
$$\delta(q_1, a, A) = \{(q_1, \Lambda)\}$$
$$\delta(q_1, \Lambda, Z_0) = \{(q_2, \Lambda)\}$$

Using the rule we have tentatively adopted, we obtain productions

$$Z_0 \rightarrow aAZ_0$$
$$A \rightarrow cA$$
$$A \rightarrow a$$
$$Z_0 \rightarrow \Lambda$$

The string aca has the leftmost derivation

$$Z_0 \Rightarrow aAZ_0 \Rightarrow acAZ_0 \Rightarrow acaZ_0 \Rightarrow aca$$

corresponding to the sequence of moves

$$(q_0, aca, Z_0) \vdash (q_0, ca, AZ_0) \vdash (q_1, a, AZ_0) \vdash (q_1, \Lambda, Z_0) \vdash (q_2, \Lambda, \Lambda)$$

But this grammar also allows the derivation

$$Z_0 \Rightarrow aAZ_0 \Rightarrow aaZ_0 \Rightarrow aa$$

which does not correspond to any sequence of moves of the PDA.

We must modify our grammar to eliminate this problem. A way to incorporate the states of the PDA is to take as the variables, instead of stack symbols A, things of the form

$$[p, A, q]$$

where p and q are states. For the variable $[p, A, q]$ to be replaced by a (either Λ or a terminal symbol), it must be the case that there is a PDA move, beginning in state p and ending in state q, that reads a and pops A from the stack. More generally, we may think of $[p, A, q]$ as representing any sequence of moves that takes the PDA from state p to state q and has the ultimate effect of removing A from the stack.

If the variable $[p, A, q]$ appears in the current string of a derivation, our "goal" is to replace it by Λ or a terminal symbol, and our corresponding goal, beginning in the PDA in state p with A on top of the stack, is to move to state q and pop A from the stack. Suppose now that instead there is a move from p to p_1 that reads a and replaces A on the stack by $B_1 B_2 \ldots B_m$. It is appropriate to introduce a into our current string at this point, since we want the initial string of terminals to correspond to the input read so far. But our new goal has become the following: to start in p_1 and make a sequence of moves—ending up in some state p_2, say—that result in B_1 being removed from the stack; then make some more moves that remove B_2 and in the process move from p_2 to some other state p_3; ...; to move from p_{m-1} to some p_m and remove B_{m-1}; and finally, to move from p_m to q and remove B_m. The actual moves need not do these steps directly, as described, but this is what we want their effect to be. Since we don't care what the states $p_2, \ldots, p_m$ are, it makes sense to allow any string of the form

$$a[p_1, B_1, p_2][p_2, B_2, p_3] \ldots [p_m, B_m, q]$$

to replace $[p, A, q]$ in the current string—in other words, to allow the productions

$$[p, A, q] \rightarrow a[p_1, B_1, p_2][p_2, B_2, p_3] \ldots [p_m, B_m, q]$$

for all possible sequences of states $p_2, \ldots, p_m$. Some such sequences will be dead ends, in the sense that there is no sequence of moves that follows this sequence of states and has this ultimate effect; but no harm is done by introducing these productions, since for any derivation that contains a dead end sequence, there will be at least one variable that can't be eliminated from the string. If we denote by S the start symbol of the grammar, the productions that we need to begin are those of the form

$$S \rightarrow [q_0, Z_0, q]$$

where q_0 is the initial state. Since in accepting a language by empty stack the final state is irrelevant, we include a production of this type for every possible state q.

This discussion should help you to understand the proof of Theorem 13.2, in which the grammar corresponding to a given PDA is defined more concisely, but essentially in the same way as above.

Theorem 13.2. Let $M = (Q, \Sigma, \Gamma, q_0, Z_0, \delta, A)$ be a PDA. There is a CFG G so that $L(G) = L_e(M)$.

Proof. We define $G = (V, \Sigma, S, P)$ as follows.

$V = \{S\} \cup \{[p, A, q] \mid A \in \Gamma, \ p, q \in Q\}$

P contains these productions, and only these:

(1) For every $q \in Q$, the production $S \rightarrow [q_0, Z_0, q]$ is in P;

(2) If $q, q_1 \in Q$, $a \in \Sigma \cup \{\Lambda\}$, $A \in \Gamma$, and $\delta(q, a, A)$ contains (q_1, Λ), then the production $[q, A, q_1] \rightarrow a$ is in P;

(3) If $m \geq 1$, $q, q_1 \in Q$, $a \in \Sigma \cup \{\Lambda\}$, $A \in \Gamma$, and $\delta(q, a, A)$ contains $(q_1, B_1 B_2 \ldots B_m)$, for some $B_1, B_2, \ldots, B_m \in \Gamma$, then for every choice of $q_2, \ldots, q_{m+1} \in Q$, the production

$$[q, A, q_{m+1}] \rightarrow a[q_1, B_1, q_2][q_2, B_2, q_3] \ldots [q_m, B_m, q_{m+1}]$$

is in P.

The main idea of the proof is to characterize the strings of terminals that can be derived from a variable $[q, A, q']$: specifically, to show that for any $q, q' \in Q, A \in \Gamma$, and $x \in \Sigma^*$,

(4) $[q, A, q'] \Rightarrow_G^* x$ if and only if $(q, x, A) \vdash_M^* (q', \Lambda, \Lambda)$

From this result, the theorem will follow. On the one hand, if $x \in L_e(M)$, then $(q_0, x, Z_0) \vdash_M^* (q, \Lambda, \Lambda)$ for some $q \in Q$; (4) then implies that $[q_0, Z_0, q] \Rightarrow_G^* x$; but then, from (1), $x \in L(G)$. On the other hand, if $x \in L(G)$, then $S \Rightarrow_G^* x$; but the first step of this derivation must be $S \Rightarrow [q_0, Z_0, q]$ for some $q \in Q$; thus $[q_0, Z_0, q] \Rightarrow_G^* x$. It follows from (4) that $x \in L_e(M)$.

Both parts of (4) are proved using mathematical induction. First, we show that for $N \geq 0$,

(5) If $[q, A, q'] \Rightarrow_G^N x$, then $(q, x, A) \vdash_M^* (q', \Lambda, \Lambda)$

In the basis step, suppose that $[q, A, q'] \Rightarrow_G^1 x$. By definition of the productions in G, this can happen only if x is Λ or an element of Σ and $\delta(q, x, A)$ contains (q', Λ). In this case, it is clearly true that $(q, x, A) \vdash (q', \Lambda, \Lambda)$.

In the induction step, suppose that $K \geq 1$ and that whenever $[q, A, q'] \Rightarrow_G^N x$ for some $N \leq K$, $(q, x, A) \vdash^* (q', \Lambda, \Lambda)$. Suppose that $[q, A, q'] \Rightarrow_G^{K+1} x$. We wish to show that $(q, x, A) \vdash_M^* (q', \Lambda, \Lambda)$. Since $K \geq 1$, the first step of this derivation is

$$[q, A, q'] \Rightarrow a[q_1, B_1, q_2][q_2, B_2, q_3] \ldots [q_m, B_m, q']$$

for some $m \geq 1$, some $a \in \Sigma \cup \{\Lambda\}$, some sequence $B_1, \ldots, B_m \in \Gamma$, and some sequence $q_1, \ldots, q_m \in Q$, so that $\delta(q, a, A)$ contains $(q_1, B_1 \ldots B_m)$. The remaining part of the derivation takes each of the variables $[q_i, B_i, q_{i+1}]$ to some string x_i, and the variable

$[q_m, B_m, q']$ to a string x_m. The strings $x_1, \ldots, x_m$ satisfy the formula $a x_1 \ldots x_m = x$, and each x_i is derived from its respective variable in K or fewer steps. The induction hypothesis, therefore, implies that for $1 \le i \le m - 1$,

$$(q_i, x_i, B_i) \vdash^* (q_{i+1}, \Lambda, \Lambda)$$

and that

$$(q_m, x_m, B_m) \vdash^* (q', \Lambda, \Lambda)$$

Suppose M is in the configuration $(q, x, A) = (q, a x_1 x_2 \ldots x_m, A)$. Since $\delta(q, a, A)$ contains $(q_1, B_1 \ldots B_m)$, M can go in one step to the configuration $(q_1, x_1 x_2 \ldots x_m, B_1 B_2 \ldots B_m)$; M can then go in a sequence of steps to $(q_2, x_2 \ldots x_m, B_2 \ldots B_m)$, then to $(q_3, x_3 \ldots x_m, B_3 \ldots B_m)$, and ultimately to (q', Λ, Λ). Thus, the result (5) follows.

To complete the proof of (4), we show that for $N \ge 0$,

(6) If $(q, x, A) \vdash^N_M (q', \Lambda, \Lambda)$, then $[q, A, q'] \Rightarrow^*_G x$

If $N = 1$, then $x \in \Sigma \cup \{\Lambda\}$ and $\delta(q, x, A)$ contains (q', Λ). In this case, we have from (2) that $[q, A, q'] \Rightarrow x$.

For the induction step, suppose that $K \ge 1$ and that for any $N \le K$, and any combination of $q, q' \in Q$, $x \in \Sigma^*$, and $A \in \Gamma$, if $(q, x, A) \vdash^N (q', \Lambda, \Lambda)$, then $[q, A, q'] \Rightarrow^*_G x$. Suppose now that $(q, x, A) \vdash^{K+1} (q', \Lambda, \Lambda)$. We wish to show that $[q, A, q'] \Rightarrow^*_G x$. We know that for some $a \in \Sigma \cup \{\Lambda\}$ and some $y \in \Sigma^*$, $x = ay$ and the first of the $K + 1$ moves is

$$(q, x, A) = (q, ay, A) \vdash (q_1, y, B_1 B_2 \ldots B_m)$$

Here $m \ge 1$, since $K \ge 1$, and the B_i's are elements of Γ. In other words, $\delta(q, a, A)$ contains $(q_1, B_1 \ldots B_m)$. Since the K subsequent moves result in the configuration (q', Λ, Λ), then for each i with $1 \le i \le m$ there must be intermediate points at which the stack contains precisely the string $B_i B_{i+1} \ldots B_m$. For each such i, let q_i be the state M is in the first time the stack contains $B_i \ldots B_m$, and let x_i be the portion of the input string that is consumed in going from q_i to q_{i+1} (or, if $i = m$, in going from q_m to the configuration (q', Λ, Λ)). Then it must be the case that

$$(q_i, x_i, B_i) \vdash^* (q_{i+1}, \Lambda, \Lambda)$$

for each i with $1 \le i \le m - 1$, and

$$(q_m, x_m, B_m) \vdash^* (q', \Lambda, \Lambda)$$

where each of the indicated sequences of moves has K or fewer. Therefore, by the inductive hypothesis,

$$[q_i, B_i, q_{i+1}] \Rightarrow^*_G x_i$$

for $1 \le i \le m - 1$ and

$$[q_m, B_m, q'] \Rightarrow^*_G x_m$$

From (3), we know that

$$[q, A, q'] \Rightarrow a[q_1, B_1, q_2][q_2, B_2, q_3] \ldots [q_m, B_m, q']$$

since $\delta(q, a, A)$ contains $(q_1, B_1 \ldots B_m)$, and thus $[q, A, q'] \Rightarrow^*_G a x_1 x_2 \ldots x_m = x$. This completes the induction and the proof of the theorem.

Example 13.2. We return to the language $L = \{xcREV(x) \mid x \in \{a, b\}^*\}$, which we used to introduce the construction in Theorem 13.2. We may construct a PDA M accepting L by empty stack that is almost the same as the PDA in Example 12.1. The only difference is that, since it accepts by empty stack, the state q_2 is not necessary, and the Λ-transition that formerly moved the PDA to state q_2 now pops Z_0 off the stack. To avoid confusion, we also use A and B as stack symbols instead of a and b. The transition table for M is shown.

Move number	State	Input	Stack symbol	Move(s)
1	q_0	a	Z_0	(q_0, AZ_0)
2	q_0	b	Z_0	(q_0, BZ_0)
3	q_0	a	A	(q_0, AA)
4	q_0	b	A	(q_0, BA)
5	q_0	a	B	(q_0, AB)
6	q_0	b	B	(q_0, BB)
7	q_0	c	Z_0	(q_1, Z_0)
8	q_0	c	A	(q_1, A)
9	q_0	c	B	(q_1, B)
10	q_1	a	A	(q_1, Λ)
11	q_1	b	B	(q_1, Λ)
12	q_1	Λ	Z_0	(q_1, Λ)
	(all other combinations)			none

The construction in Theorem 13.2 gives us the CFG $G = (V, \Sigma, S, P)$, where V contains S and all objects of the form $[p, X, q]$, where X is a stack symbol and p and q can each be either q_0 or q_1. P contains the following productions:

$$(0) \qquad S \to [q_0, Z_0, q]$$

$$(1) \quad [q_0, Z_0, q] \to a[q_0, A, p][p, Z_0, q]$$

$$(2) \quad [q_0, Z_0, q] \to b[q_0, B, p][p, Z_0, q]$$

$$(3) \quad [q_0, A, q] \to a[q_0, A, p][p, A, q]$$

$$(4) \quad [q_0, A, q] \to b[q_0, B, p][p, A, q]$$

$$(5) \quad [q_0, B, q] \to a[q_0, A, p][p, B, q]$$

$$(6) \quad [q_0, B, q] \to b[q_0, B, p][p, B, q]$$

$$(7) \quad [q_0, Z_0, q] \to c[q_1, Z_0, q]$$

$$(8) \quad [q_0, A, q] \to c[q_1, A, q]$$

$$(9) \quad [q_0, B, q] \to c[q_1, B, q]$$

$$(10) \quad [q_1, A, q_1] \to a$$

$$(11) \quad [q_1, B, q_1] \to b$$

$$(12) \quad [q_1, Z_0, q_1] \to \Lambda$$

(p and q can each be either q_0 or q_1; thus there are a total of 35 productions.)

Consider the string $bacab$. The PDA accepts it by the sequence of moves

$$(q_0, bacab, Z_0) \vdash (q_0, acab, BZ_0)$$
$$\vdash (q_0, cab, ABZ_0)$$
$$\vdash (q_1, ab, ABZ_0)$$
$$\vdash (q_1, b, BZ_0)$$
$$\vdash (q_1, \Lambda, Z_0)$$
$$\vdash (q_1, \Lambda, \Lambda)$$

The corresponding leftmost derivation is

$$S \Rightarrow [q_0, Z_0, q_1]$$
$$\Rightarrow b[q_0, B, q_1][q_1, Z_0, q_1]$$
$$\Rightarrow ba[q_0, A, q_1][q_1, B, q_1][q_1, Z_0, q_1]$$
$$\Rightarrow bac[q_1, A, q_1][q_1, B, q_1][q_1, Z_0, q_1]$$
$$\Rightarrow baca[q_1, B, q_1][q_1, Z_0, q_1]$$
$$\Rightarrow bacab[q_1, Z_0, q_1]$$
$$\Rightarrow bacab$$

From the sequence of PDA moves, it may look as though there are several choices of leftmost derivations. For example, we might start with the production $S \rightarrow [q_0, Z_0, q_0]$. Remember, though, that $[q_0, Z_0, q]$ represents a sequence of moves from q_0 to q that has the ultimate effect of removing Z_0 from the stack. Since the PDA ends up in state q_1, it is clear that q should be q_1. Similarly, it may seem as if the second step could have been

$$[q_0, Z_0, q_1] \Rightarrow b[q_0, B, q_0][q_0, Z_0, q_1]$$

However, we can see that the sequence of PDA moves that starts in q_0 and eliminates B from the stack ends with the PDA in state q_1, not q_0. In fact, since every move to state q_0 adds to the stack, the variable $[q_0, B, q_0]$ in this grammar is useless: no sequence of terminals can be derived from it.

EXERCISES

13.1. In each case below, you are given a CFG and a string x that it generates. For the PDA that is constructed from the grammar as in the proof of Theorem 13.1, trace a sequence of moves by which x is accepted, showing at each step the state, the unread input, and the stack contents. Show at the same time the corresponding leftmost derivation of x in the grammar. See Example 13.1 for a guide.

(a) The grammar has productions

$$S \rightarrow S + T \mid T$$
$$T \rightarrow T * F \mid F$$
$$F \rightarrow (S) \mid a$$

and $x = (a + a * a) * a$.

(b) The grammar has productions $S \rightarrow S + S \mid S * S \mid (S) \mid a$, and $x = (a * a + a)$.

(c) The grammar has productions $S \rightarrow (S)S \mid \Lambda$, and $x = ()(())$.

13.2. Let M be the PDA in Example 12.3, except that move number 12 is changed to (q_2, Λ), so that M does in fact accept by empty stack. Let $x = ababa$. Find a sequence of moves of M by which x is accepted, and give the corresponding leftmost derivation in the CFG obtained from M as in Theorem 13.2.

13.3. Under what circumstances, if any, is the PDA obtained in Theorem 13.1 deterministic? What kind of language would it accept in this case?

13.4. If the PDA in Theorem 13.2 is deterministic, what conclusion can be drawn about the grammar that is obtained? Can this conclusion ever hold without the PDA being deterministic?

13.5. Find the other useless variables in Example 13.2.

CHAPTER
14

PARSING

14.1 TOP-DOWN PARSING

Suppose we have a context-free language, generated by some context-free grammar that is preferably unambiguous. We have already seen that it is important to be able to find a derivation in that grammar of a given string. If the string is an algebraic expression, the derivation is what tells us how to interpret the expression; if the string is a statement in a programming language, the derivation tells us what type of statement it is, and, provided we know the *semantics* of the language, tells us how to execute the statement. The systematic study of taking a string and attempting to reconstruct a derivation is called *parsing*. The problem of finding efficient parsing algorithms has attracted a great deal of research. There is a large body of theory, and there are many specialized techniques that depend on specific properties of the grammar. In this chapter, we shall look briefly at two general approaches to the problem, which provide starting points for the development of efficient parsers.

On the face of it, it would seem that parsing a string is more difficult than just determining whether the string is in the language. In fact, though, an algorithm for recognizing a language can often, with only a little extra effort, be made to give us a parsing algorithm.

Example 14.1. Let's look at a language for which we have constructed a recognizer in the form of a PDA: the language L of balanced strings of parentheses. Again, we use []

as the parentheses. It will be convenient at this point, however, to modify the language slightly, by adding to the end of each string a special symbol that marks the end. Thus, let

$$L_1 = L\{\$\} = \{x\$ \mid x \in L\}$$

We constructed a deterministic PDA accepting L in Example 12.4, which can easily be modified to accept L_1; thus we have implicitly an algorithm for recognizing L_1. Instead, however, we begin with the general construction in the proof of Theorem 13.1, which takes an arbitrary CFG and produces a PDA recognizing the language it generates. The idea is that since the PDA we obtain is tied directly to a grammar, it will be more likely to suggest a parsing algorithm for an arbitrary CFL.

We have used the grammar having productions

$$S \;\rightarrow\; SS \mid [S] \mid \Lambda$$

to generate L, but it has the defect that it is ambiguous. Instead, we consider the grammar containing the productions

$$S \;\rightarrow\; [S]S \mid \Lambda$$

(see Exercise 10.5). L_1 is therefore generated by the CFG having productions

$$S \rightarrow T\$$$

$$T \rightarrow [T]T \mid \Lambda$$

The construction used to prove Theorem 13.1 produces the PDA with initial state q_0, accepting state q_2, and a third state q_1. The stack symbols are Z_0, S, T, [,], and \$, and the moves are given by the transition table, Table 14.1.

It is not quite correct to say that the machine represents an *algorithm* for recognizing L_1, since it is clearly nondeterministic. Ignoring this problem for the moment, let us see to what extent having a *recognizer* gives us a *parser*. We have seen that a correct series of guesses by the PDA parallels a leftmost derivation of the string in the grammar; the steps in the derivation correspond to those PDA moves in which a variable on top of the stack is replaced by the right side of a production. To obtain a parse of the string, all that is necessary is to keep a record of the moves of the PDA. We might accomplish this with a PDA that is enhanced by having an output capability; such a machine is sometimes

TABLE 14.1

A nondeterministic PDA for the language L_1

Move number	State	Input	Stack symbol	Move(s)
1	q_0	Λ	Z_0	(q_1, SZ_0)
2	q_1	Λ	S	$(q_1, T\$)$
3	q_1	Λ	T	$(q_1, [T]T), (q_1, \Lambda)$
4	q_1	[	[	(q_1, Λ)
5	q_1	]	]	(q_1, Λ)
6	q_1	\$	\$	(q_1, Λ)
7	q_1	Λ	Z_0	(q_2, Z_0)
	(all other combinations)			none

referred to as a *pushdown transducer*. We shall not describe these any more formally—the point is that for our present purposes it is enough to look at the "recognizer."

The other observation to make at this point is that to the extent that our PDA acts as a parser, it is a *top-down* parser: the first time a variable is replaced on the stack by the right side of a production, the root of the derivation tree and its children have been determined, and each subtree of the tree is constructed similarly from the top down. Since the derivation being simulated is leftmost, subtrees whose roots are on the same level will be constructed in such a way that the leftmost are constructed first.

We return to the problem of nondeterminism. One approach would be a "backtracking" algorithm that would simulate sequences of moves that might be made by the PDA. At any point where the PDA would crash or where it became clear that the current sequence of moves would not lead to acceptance, the algorithm would backtrack, at each step undoing the most recent move, until a point was found where there was a possible move that had not yet been tried. In terms of derivations, this approach simply amounts to numbering the productions beginning with each variable, trying sequences of productions, and backing up in the derivation whenever it becomes clear that the current string will never derive the desired string.

We illustrate this idea for the string []\$, assuming that of the two productions starting with T, the first to be tried is always $T \rightarrow [T]T$. At the left is shown the PDA moves, at the right the corresponding steps in the leftmost derivation. Each time the PDA crashes, the last dotted line above that point indicates how far we must backtrack. The number in parentheses in the preceding line is repeated at the point where the moves resume after that backtrack.

$$
\begin{aligned}
(q_0, []\$, Z_0) &\vdash (q_1, []\$, SZ_0) &&S \\
&\vdash (q_q, []\$, T\$Z_0) &&\Rightarrow T\$ \\
&\vdash (q_1, []\$, [T]T\$Z_0) &&\Rightarrow [T]T\$ \\
&\vdash (q_1,]\$, T]T\$Z_0)\ (1)
\end{aligned}
$$

$$
\begin{aligned}
&\vdash (q_1,]\$, [T]T]T\$Z_0) &&\Rightarrow [[T]T]T]\$ \\
&\text{(crash)}
\end{aligned}
$$

$$
\begin{aligned}
(1)\quad &\vdash (q_1,]\$,]T\$Z_0) &&\Rightarrow []T\$ \\
&\vdash (q_1, \$, T\$Z_0)\ (2)
\end{aligned}
$$

$$
\begin{aligned}
&\vdash (q_1, \$, [T]T\$Z_0) &&\Rightarrow [][T]T\$ \\
&\text{(crash)}
\end{aligned}
$$

$$
\begin{aligned}
(2)\quad &\vdash (q_1, \$, \$Z_0) &&\Rightarrow []\$ \\
&\vdash (q_1, \Lambda, Z_0) \\
&\vdash (q_2, \Lambda, Z_0) \\
&\text{(accept)}
\end{aligned}
$$

Things are not always quite as straightforward as in this example. It may not be possible to pursue a sequence of moves until the PDA either accepts or crashes—it may never do either, as we shall see shortly; in any case, it may be desirable to use some other empirical method to determine that it's necessary to backtrack. For example, if it can be determined that there are more terminal symbols in the current string than in the string being derived, or if there is some combination of terminal symbols in the current string that does not appear in the string being derived, then backtracking is appropriate.

It is likely that in a more complicated grammar, this backtracking approach will be unacceptably slow. Assuming that we are beginning with an unambiguous grammar, it seems likely that a given string can be accepted by at most one sequence of moves. Thus a better approach might be to confront the problem head-on: to consider whether there may be a way to decide, whenever the PDA has a choice of moves, which is the appropriate one. The only source of nondeterminism in our example is the choice of two different moves on input Λ when T is on the stack, corresponding to the two productions with left side T. The one that replaces T by $[T]T$ will cause [to become the top stack symbol, which is appropriate if the next input is [. Otherwise, if the next input is either] or \$, the only appropriate move is to pop T from the stack. It appears, then, that in this example we can eliminate the nondeterminism by "lookahead"—by using the next input symbol to determine the correct move. Moreover, if we are careful, our algorithm can still be embodied in a PDA, which will now be deterministic.

The only way a PDA can use the next input symbol in determining the next move is to consume it in making the move. Suppose, for example, that the next input is] and T is the top stack symbol. The correct move in the original PDA is to pop T, on the assumption that below T is], which will be popped on the following move as the] in the input is read. In our modified PDA with lookahead, the first move reads the [and pops the T. The PDA must then "remember," without using any more input, to pop the] that is under the T; this can be done by having the first move enter a special state, q_1, from which there is a Λ-transition that pops] from the stack.

Table 14.2 is a description of a deterministic PDA that is obtained from the original one by incorporating lookahead.

TABLE 14.2
Using lookahead to eliminate the nondeterminism from Table 14.1

Move number	State	Input	Stack symbol	Move(s)
1	q_0	Λ	Z_0	(q_1, SZ_0)
2	q_1	Λ	S	$(q_1, T\$)$
3	q_1	[	T	$(q_[, [T]T)$
4	$q_[$	Λ	[	(q_1, Λ)
5	q_1	]	T	$(q_], \Lambda)$
6	$q_]$	Λ	]	(q_1, Λ)
7	q_1	\$	T	$(q_\$, \Lambda)$
8	$q_\$$	Λ	\$	(q_1, Λ)
9	q_1	[	[	(q_1, Λ)
10	q_1	]	]	(q_1, Λ)
11	q_1	\$	\$	(q_1, Λ)
12	q_1	Λ	Z_0	(q_2, Z_0)
	(all other combinations)			none

The sequence of moves by which the PDA accepts the string []$, and the corresponding steps in the leftmost derivation of this string, are described below.

$$
\begin{aligned}
(q_0, []\$, Z_0) &\vdash (q_1, []\$, SZ_0) & & S \\
&\vdash (q_1, []\$, T\$Z_0) & & \Rightarrow T\$ \\
&\vdash (q_[,]\$, [T]T\$Z_0) & & \Rightarrow [T]T\$ \\
&\vdash (q_1,]\$, T]T\$Z_0) & & \\
&\vdash (q_], \$,]T\$Z_0) & & \Rightarrow []T\$ \\
&\vdash (q_1, \$, T\$Z_0) & & \\
&\vdash (q_\$, \Lambda, \$Z_0) & & \Rightarrow []\$ \\
&\vdash (q_1, \Lambda, Z_0) & & \\
&\vdash (q_2, \Lambda, Z_0) & & \\
&\quad\text{(accept)} & &
\end{aligned}
$$

You can see without much trouble that moves 9, 10, and 11, which were all moves in the original nondeterministic PDA, will never actually be used. We include them in the table, since in a more general example moves of this type may still be necessary. We shall not give a formal proof that this deterministic PDA accepts L, but you are invited to try it with a few longer input strings to convince yourself.

The PDA derived as in Theorem 13.1 does not always have the property that looking ahead to the next input is enough to determine what the next move should be. However, it may fail to have this property for relatively simple reasons, and it may be possible to correct the problem by a simple modification of the grammar. The next two examples illustrate this idea.

Example 14.2. Let's stay with the language L_1 in Example 14.1 but consider the other unambiguous grammar for L mentioned in Exercise 10.5, whose productions are

$$ S \rightarrow S[S] \mid \Lambda $$

The PDA for L_1 produced as in Theorem 13.1 has the transitions shown in Table 14.3.

TABLE 14.3
A second nondeterministic PDA for L_1

Move number	State	Input	Stack symbol	Move(s)
1	q_0	Λ	Z_0	(q_1, SZ_0)
2	q_1	Λ	S	$(q_1, T\$)$
3	q_1	Λ	T	$(q_1, T[T]), (q_1, \Lambda)$
4	q_1	[	[	(q_1, Λ)
5	q_1	]	]	(q_1, Λ)
6	q_1	$\$	$\$	(q_1, Λ)
7	q_1	Λ	Z_0	(q_2, Z_0)
	(all other combinations)			none

We can see the potential problem by trying a backtracking approach, where each time there is a choice we try first the move corresponding to $T \rightarrow T[T]$. In our first example, we waited to backtrack until the simulated PDA moves caused a crash. If we try this strategy here, T is replaced it by $T[T]$ whenever it appears on the stack; the new T is also replaced by $T[T]$; and we are in an infinite loop, which continues to add to the stack without reading any input.

If we were satisfied with a backtracking algorithm, the problem would not be too serious; we could just try the two choices in the opposite order or use some other criterion for deciding when to backtrack. However, when we attempt to use lookahead in order to remove the nondeterminism, the problem resurfaces in a different form. Consider the input string []\[][]\$. The leftmost derivation of this string is

$$S \Rightarrow T\$ \Rightarrow T[T]\$ \Rightarrow T[T][T]\$ \Rightarrow T[T][T][T]\$ \Rightarrow \ldots \Rightarrow [][][]\$$$

which means that the correct sequence of moves for this input begins

$$
\begin{aligned}
(q_0, [][][]\$, Z_0) &\vdash (q_1, [][][]\$, SZ_0) \\
&\vdash (q_1, [][][]\$, T\$Z_0) \\
&\vdash (q_1, [][][]\$, T[T]\$Z_0) \\
&\vdash (q_1, [][][]\$, T[T][T]\$Z_0) \\
&\vdash (q_1, [][][]\$, T[T][T][T]\$Z_0)
\end{aligned}
$$

In each of the last four configurations shown, the next input is [and T is the top stack symbol, but the correct sequences of moves beginning at each of these points are all different. Obviously looking ahead to the next input symbol is not enough to decide. In fact, even looking arbitrarily far ahead won't help. Since the remaining input is the same in all these configurations, there is no way to choose the next move on the basis of the input.

The problem arises because of the production $T \rightarrow T[T]$. Because the right side begins with T, the PDA must make a certain number of identical moves before it does anything else. The only way it can attempt to decide how many is to look ahead in the input and, as we have seen, even looking all the way to the end may not be sufficient. This phenomenon in a CFG is referred to as *left recursion*, and the problem can often be corrected by eliminating the left recursion from the grammar before we start. More generally, suppose that in a CFG the productions beginning with T are $T \rightarrow T\alpha$ and $T \rightarrow \beta$ (where β does not begin with T). Clearly the strings that can be obtained are those of the form $\beta\alpha^N$, where $N \geq 0$. If these two productions are replaced by

$$T \rightarrow \beta U$$

$$U \rightarrow \alpha U \mid \Lambda$$

the language is unchanged and the left recursion has been eliminated.

In our example, with $\alpha = [T]$ and $\beta = \Lambda$, we would replace

$$T \rightarrow T[T] \mid \Lambda$$

by

$$T \rightarrow U$$

$$U \rightarrow [T]U \mid \Lambda$$

and the resulting grammar for L_1 allows us to construct a deterministic PDA much as in Example 14.1. We shall not show it, because of the obvious similarity between this grammar and that in Example 14.1.

There are comparable, straightforward methods of eliminating left recursion in a CFG containing several productions of the form $T \to T\alpha$; see Exercise 14.5.

Example 14.3. Consider the CFG whose productions are

$$S \to T\$$$

$$T \to [T] \mid []T \mid [T]T \mid []$$

(The language generated is that of all balanced strings of parentheses other than Λ. The grammar is obtained by removing Λ-productions from the one in Example 14.1; the remark at the end of Section 11.1 implies that it is unambiguous.)

Although there is no left recursion, we can predict immediately that looking ahead one symbol in the input will not be enough to select the right move of the nondeterministic top-down PDA. The problem is that there are four T-productions whose right side begins with [; if T is the top stack symbol, knowing that the next input symbol is [is obviously not enough to decide which to use. An appropriate solution here is to "factor" the right sides, as follows:

$$T \to [U$$

$$U \to T] \mid]T \mid T]T \mid]$$

More factoring is necessary because of the U-productions. In the case of the U-productions whose right side begin with T, we may factor out $T]$; we obtain the productions

$$S \to T\$$$

$$T \to [U$$

$$U \to T]W \mid]W$$

$$W \to T \mid \Lambda$$

We simplify the grammar slightly by eliminating the variable T, to obtain

$$S \to [U\$$$

$$U \to [U]W \mid]W$$

$$W \to [U \mid \Lambda$$

Let us omit the transition table for the nondeterministic PDA based on this grammar, and go directly to the DPDA incorporating lookahead (see Table 14.4).

Finally, let us trace the moves of this machine on the input [][[]]\$:

$$
\begin{aligned}
(q_0, [][[]]\$, Z_0) &\vdash (q_1, [][[]]\$, SZ_0) &\quad S \\
&\vdash (q_1, [][[]]\$, [U\$Z_0) &\quad \Rightarrow [U\$ \\
&\vdash (q_1,][[]]\$, U\$Z_0) \\
&\vdash (q_1, [[]]\$,]W\$Z_0) &\quad \Rightarrow []W\$ \\
&\vdash (q_1, [[]]\$, W\$Z_0)
\end{aligned}
$$

$\vdash(q_[, []]\$, [U\$Z_0)$ $\Rightarrow [][U\$$

$\vdash(q_1, []]\$, U\$Z_0)$

$\vdash(q_[,]]\$, [U]W\$Z_0)$ $\Rightarrow [][[U]W\$$

$\vdash(q_1,]]\$, U]W\$Z_0)$

$\vdash(q_],]\$,]W]W\$Z_0)$ $\Rightarrow [][[]W]W\$$

$\vdash(q_1,]\$, W]W\$Z_0)$

$\vdash(q_], \$,]W\$Z_0)$ $\Rightarrow [][[]]W\$$

$\vdash(q_1, \$, W\$Z_0)$

$\vdash(q_\$, \Lambda, \$Z_0)$ $\Rightarrow [][[]]\$$

$\vdash(q_1, \Lambda, Z_0)$

$\vdash(q_2, \Lambda, Z_0)$

(accept)

In Examples 14.2 and 14.3, we were able by a combination of factoring and eliminating left recursion to transform the CFG into what is called an LL(1) grammar, meaning that the nondeterministic PDA produced from the grammar as in Theorem 13.1 can be turned into a deterministic top-down parser by "looking ahead" to the next input symbol. A grammar is LL(k) if looking ahead k symbols in the input is always enough to choose the next move of the PDA. Such a grammar allows the construction of a deterministic top-down parser.

14.2 RECURSIVE DESCENT

If a CFG is LL(1), there is a deterministic top-down parsing algorithm that decides what the next production in a leftmost derivation is, by looking at the next input symbol. A straightforward way to describe the algorithm is to specify a DPDA that embodies it. There are, however, other formulations of essentially the same

TABLE 14.4
A deterministic PDA for Example 14.3

Move number	State	Input	Stack symbol	Move(s)
1	q_0	Λ	Z_0	(q_1, SZ_0)
2	q_1	Λ	S	$(q_1, [U\$)$
3	q_1	[	U	$(q_[, [U]W)$
4	$q_[$	Λ	[	(q_1, Λ)
5	q_1	]	U	$(q_],]W)$
6	$q_]$	Λ	]	(q_1, Λ)
7	q_1	[	W	$(q_[, [U)$
8	q_1	]	W	$(q_], \Lambda)$
9	q_1	\$	W	$(q_\$, \Lambda)$
10	$q_\$$	Λ	\$	(q_1, Λ)
11	q_1	[	[	(q_1, Λ)
12	q_1	]	]	(q_1, Λ)
13	q_1	\$	\$	(q_1, Λ)
14	q_1	Λ	Z_0	(q_2, Z_0)
	(all other combinations)			none

algorithm. The method of *recursive descent* is one that is commonly used; the name refers to a collection of mutually recursive procedures corresponding to the variables in the grammar.

Example 14.4. To illustrate, we return to the CFG obtained in Example 14.3 by factoring; the productions are

$$S \rightarrow [U\$$$

$$U \rightarrow]W \mid [U]W$$

$$W \rightarrow [U \mid \Lambda$$

We shall give a Pascal version of a recursive-descent parser. ("Recognizer" is really a more accurate term, although it would be easy enough to add output statements to the program that would allow one to reconstruct the derivation of the string being recognized.) It involves procedures S, U, and W, that are mutually recursive in the same way that the productions in the grammar are. In cases where there is a choice of two actions (in the procedures U and W), the procedure examines the next input symbol in order to decide.

It is convenient to use a global variable for the "current symbol," and for that variable to have a value before a procedure is called. In the case of W, for example, the procedure is able then to look at the current symbol, and either consume it by reading another symbol (if its original value is "[") or terminate without consuming it. Each input symbol is echoed immediately when it is read. If at some point a symbol is discovered to violate the syntax of the grammar, it has already been output; at that point an error-handling procedure is called. An error flag, also a global variable, is set, and thereafter calls on the procedures have no effect.

There are two things to notice about the program. First, the structure mirrors the productions in the grammar almost exactly. During the execution of the program, with an input string in the language, the calls made on the procedures correspond exactly to the substitutions made for variables in a leftmost derivation of the string — or to the replacement of those variables on the stack during the processing of the string by the DPDA in Example 14.3.

Second, the program's correctness depends on the grammar's being LL(1), since each procedure is able to select the correct action on the basis of the current input symbol.

```
PROGRAM  Parser(Input,Output);
VAR
CurrentSymbol    : CHAR;
ErrorFlag        : BOOLEAN;
PROCEDURE  ReadAndEcho(VAR NextSymbol : CHAR);
BEGIN
    Read(NextSymbol);
    IF  NextSymbol <>  ' '  THEN
        Write(NextSymbol)
    ELSE
        Write('(END  OF  DATA)')
END;    (* ReadAndEcho *)

PROCEDURE  HandleError(CorrectSym : CHAR);
BEGIN
```

```
  WriteLn;
  IF  CorrectSym  <>  'E'  THEN
     WriteLn('    ERROR : EXPECTING ', CorrectSym)
  ELSE
     WriteLn('    ERROR : EXPECTING EITHER [ OR ]');
  ErrorFlag : TRUE
END;   (*  HandleError *)


PROCEDURE  U; Forward;   (*  necessary  in  Pascal   *)
PROCEDURE  W; Forward;   (*  because  of  the  mutual  recursion *)


PROCEDURE  S;
BEGIN
  IF  CurrentSymbol  =  '['  THEN
     BEGIN
        ReadAndEcho(CurrentSymbol);
        U;
        IF  NOT  ErrorFlag  THEN
           IF  CurrentSymbol  <>  '$'  THEN
              HandleError('$')
     END
  ELSE
     HandleError('[')
END;   (*  S  *)


PROCEDURE  U;
BEGIN
  IF  NOT  ErrorFlag  THEN
     IF  CurrentSymbol  =  ']'  THEN
        BEGIN
           ReadAndEcho(CurrentSymbol);
           W
        END
     ELSE IF  CurrentSymbol  =  '['  THEN
        BEGIN
           ReadAndEcho(CurrentSymbol);
           U;
           IF  CurrentSymbol  =  ']'  THEN
           ReadAndEcho(CurrentSymbol)
           ELSE
              HandleError(']');
           W
        END
     ELSE
        HandleError('E')
END;       (*  U  *)


PROCEDURE  W;
BEGIN
```

```
   IF NOT ErrorFlag THEN
     IF CurrentSymbol = '[' THEN
       BEGIN
         ReadAndEcho(CurrentSymbol);
         U
       END
   END;  (*  W  *)

BEGIN   (*  MAIN  *)
   ErrorFlag := FALSE;
   ReadAndEcho(CurrentSymbol);
   S;
   IF NOT ErrorFlag THEN
     BEGIN
       WriteLn;
       WriteLn('PARSING  COMPLETE.');
       WriteLn('THE  ABOVE  STRING  IS  IN  THE  LANGUAGE.');
     END
END.
```

Here is a sample of the output produced, for the input strings [][[][[]]]$, $,
[]], [][, and [[], respectively.

```
[][[][[]]]$
PARSING  COMPLETE.
THE  ABOVE  STRING  IS  IN  THE  LANGUAGE.
$
   ERROR : EXPECTING [
[]]
   ERROR : EXPECTING $
[][ (END  OF  DATA)
   ERROR : EXPECTING [ OR ]
[[] (END  OF  DATA)
   ERROR : EXPECTING ]
```

The program is less complete than it might be, in several respects. In the
case of a string not in the language, it reads and prints out only the symbols up
to the first illegal one—i.e., up to the point where the DPDA would crash. In
addition, it does not read past the symbol $; if the input string were []$], for
example, the program would merely report that []$ is in the language. Finally,
the error messages may seem slightly questionable. The four different messages
correspond to locations in the S- and U-procedures where terminal symbols are
expected. The second error, for example, is detected in the procedure S, after
the return from the call on U. The production is $S \rightarrow [U\$$, and the procedure
therefore "expects" to see $ at this point. Of course this doesn't mean that any
symbol other than $ would have triggered the error message: [would be valid
here, and would have resulted in a different sequence of procedure calls, so that
the program would not have made the same test at this point in S.

14.3 BOTTOM-UP PARSING

In the top-down approach to parsing, as implemented by a PDA, the derivation tree is constructed in a top-to-bottom manner by replacing a variable (i.e., the root of a subtree) on the stack by the right side of a production (the children of that node). The other moves of the PDA consist of removing from the stack terminals that match the incoming input symbols, in preparation for another move of the first type. This process corresponds to a leftmost derivation, since at each step the variables remaining on the stack are those in the current string of the derivation, and the one closest to the top is the one appearing farthest to the left in the string.

The opposite approach, in which the construction of the tree is from the bottom up, can also be formulated in terms of a PDA. Input symbols are "shifted" onto the stack, if necessary, until there is at the top of the stack a string of symbols comprising the right side of a production; at this point a sequence of moves begins that has the effect of "reducing" that string: replacing it on the stack by the variable on the left of the production. Thus, the string of children of a node is replaced on the stack by their parent. The last step of this process is to reduce a string to the start symbol S; the entire process simulates a derivation, in reverse order, of the input string. At each step, the current string in the derivation consists of the contents of the stack, followed by the string of unread input; since after each reduction the variable on top of the stack is the rightmost one in the current string, the derivation being simulated in reverse is a *rightmost* derivation. A parser that uses this approach is often referred to as a *shift-reduce* parser, after the two types of moves involved.

Let us use as an illustrative example a simplified version of the CFG G_1 in Section 10.2, with productions

$$(1)\ \ S_1 \to S_1 + T$$

$$(2)\ \ S_1 \to T$$

$$(3)\ \ T \to T * a$$

$$(4)\ \ T \to a$$

The reason for numbering the productions will be seen presently. Again, it will be helpful to add an endmarker to the strings, so we introduce the new start symbol S and the new production

$$(0)\ \ S \ \to\ S_1\$$$

to obtain a CFG we shall call G. Suppose we wish to parse the string $a + a * a\$$, which has the rightmost derivation

$$
\begin{aligned}
S &\Rightarrow S_1\$ \\
&\Rightarrow S_1 + T\$ \\
&\Rightarrow S_1 + T * a\$ \\
&\Rightarrow S_1 + a * a\$ \\
&\Rightarrow T + a * a\$ \\
&\Rightarrow a + a * a\$
\end{aligned}
$$

TABLE 14.5
A bottom-up parse of $a + a * a\$$ in the grammar G

Move	Production	Stack	Unread input
—		Z_0	$a + a * a\$$
shift		aZ_0	$+a * a\$$
reduce	$T \to a$	TZ_0	$+a * a\$$
reduce	$S_1 \to T$	$S_1 Z_0$	$+a * a\$$
shift		$+S_1 Z_0$	$a * a\$$
shift		$a + S_1 Z_0$	$*a\$$
reduce	$T \to a$	$T + S_1 Z_0$	$*a\$$
shift		$*T + S_1 Z_0$	$a\$$
shift		$a * T + S_1 Z_0$	$\$$
reduce	$T \to T * a$	$T + S_1 Z_0$	$\$$
reduce	$S_1 \to S_1 + T$	$S_1 Z_0$	$\$$
shift		$\$S_1 Z_0$	—
reduce	$S \to S_1\$$	SZ_0	—

The corresponding steps or groups of steps taken by a shift-reduce (bottom-up) parser are shown in Table 14.5. Remember that at each point, the reverse of the string on the stack (omitting Z_0), followed by the string of unread input, constitutes the current string in the derivation, and the reductions therefore occur in the opposite order from the corresponding steps in the derivation. For example, since the last step in the derivation is to replace T by a, the first reduction replaces a on the stack by T.

Let us first present a "nondeterministic bottom-up parser" for this grammar, comparable to the nondeterministic top-down parser produced by Theorem 13.1.

The "shift" moves allow the next input to be shifted onto the stack, regardless of the current stack symbol. A "reduce" sequence of moves can begin when the top stack symbol is the final symbol of the right side of some production $A \to \alpha$; if $|\alpha| > 1$, the moves in the sequence proceed on the assumption that the symbols below the top one are in fact the previous symbols of α; they remove these symbols, from back to front, and place A on the stack. Once such a sequence is started, a sequence of states unique to this sequence is what allows the PDA to remember how to complete the sequence. For example, suppose we wish to reduce the string $T * a$ to T. If we begin in some state q, with a on top of the stack, the first step will be to remove a and enter a state that we might call $q_{3,1}$. (Here is where the numbering of the productions is helpful; the notation is supposed to suggest that the PDA has completed one step of the reduction associated with production 3.) Starting in state $q_{3,1}$, the PDA expects to see $*$ on the stack. Assuming it does, it removes it and enters $q_{3,2}$. In $q_{3,2}$, the only possible move is to remove T from the stack, replace it by T, and return to q. Of course, all the moves of this sequence are Λ-transitions: they affect only the stack.

Aside from these special states used for reductions, we will be able to get by with two states, the state q and an accepting state q_1. The input alphabet Σ is $\{a, +, *, \$\}$, and the stack alphabet Γ is $\{a, +, *, \$, S, S_1, T, Z_0\}$. The transitions for the PDA are given in Table 14.6.

Notice that in the "shift" moves, there are a number of combinations of input and stack symbol that could be omitted; for example, in processing a string in the language, it will never be the case that + is the top stack symbol as well as the next input symbol. It does no harm to include these, however, since no string that contains these combinations will be reduced to S.

It can be shown without too much difficulty that this nondeterministic PDA does in fact recognize the language generated by the CFG. Moreover, for any CFG, a nondeterministic PDA can be constructed along the same lines that recognizes the corresponding language.

Just as in the top-down case, we would like a deterministic algorithm for bottom-up parsing. We can use backtracking, but it is likely to be inefficient. The example we have chosen will allow us to eliminate the nondeterminism from the PDA directly, much as we did in the top-down case, in a simple way. It is not the most widely applicable method of obtaining a deterministic bottom-up parser

TABLE 14.6
A nondeterministic bottom-up parser for G

State	Input	Stack symbol	Move(s)
	Shift moves (σ and X are arbitrary)		
q	σ	X	$(q, \sigma X)$
	Moves to reduce $S_1\$$ to S		
q	Λ	$\$$	$(q_{0,1}, \Lambda)$
$q_{0,1}$	Λ	S_1	(q, S)
	Moves to reduce $S_1 + T$ to S_1		
q	Λ	T	$(q_{1,1}, \Lambda)$
$q_{1,1}$	Λ	$+$	$(q_{1,2}, \Lambda)$
$q_{1,2}$	Λ	S_1	(q, S_1)
	Move to reduce T to S_1		
q	Λ	T	(q, S_1)
	Moves to reduce $T * a$ to T		
q	Λ	a	$(q_{3,1}, \Lambda)$
$q_{3,1}$	Λ	$*$	$(q_{3,2}, \Lambda)$
$q_{3,2}$	Λ	T	(q, T)
	Move to reduce a to T		
q	Λ	a	(q, T)
	Move to accept		
q	Λ	S	(q_1, Λ)
	(all other combinations)		none

without backtracking, but it is one of the simplest methods to describe, and it works well when it can be used.

In the PDA shown for our example, nondeterminism is present for two reasons. First, there may be a choice as to whether to shift an input symbol onto the stack or to attempt to reduce a string on top of the stack. For example, if T is the top stack symbol, it might be the T in the right side of $T \rightarrow T * a$, in which case a shift is correct, or it might be the T in one of the S_1-productions, in which case the correct move is to reduce. Second, if it is somehow determined that a reduction is the appropriate move, there may be some doubt as to which reduction it should be. (There are two productions whose right sides end with a, for example.) The second question is easily resolved in our example. To take the situation already mentioned: if a is on top of the stack, and if we pop it off and find $*$ below it, it is clear that we should attempt to reduce $T * a$ to T. Otherwise, we should reduce a to T. In either case, the correct reduction is the one that reduces the longest string possible.

Returning to the first question, we suppose the top stack symbol is T. Consider the possible values of the next input. If it is $+$, we should soon have the string $S_1 + T$, in reverse order, on top of the stack, and thus the correct move at this point is a reduction of either T or $S_1 + T$ to S_1. (Which one it is depends on what is below T in the stack.) If the next input is $*$, the eventual reduction will be that of $T * a$; since we already have T, we should shift. Finally, if it is $\$$, we should reduce either T or $S_1 + T$ to S_1 to allow the reduction of $S_1\$$. In any case, we can make the decision on the basis of the next input. What is true for this example is that there are certain combinations of top stack symbol and input symbol for which a reduction is always appropriate, and for all other combinations a shift is correct. The set of pairs for which a reduction is correct is an example of a *precedence relation*. (It is a relation from Γ to Σ, in the sense of Section 1.5.) There are a number of types of *precedence grammars*, for which precedence relations can be used to obtain a deterministic shift-reduce parser. Our example, in which the decision to reduce can be made by examining the top stack symbol and the next input symbol, and in which a reduction always reduces the longest possible string, is an example of a *weak precedence grammar*.

A deterministic PDA that acts as a shift-reduce parser for our grammar is shown in Table 14.7. In order to compare it to the nondeterministic PDA, it will be useful to make a few observations. The input and stack alphabets are the same as in the nondeterministic case. The stack symbols may be divided into three groups: those whose appearance on top of the stack requires a shift regardless of the next input (these are Z_0, S_1, $+$, and $*$); those that require a reduction or lead to acceptance (a, $\$$, and S); and those for which the correct choice can be made only by consulting the next input (T is the only one in this group). In the DPDA, shifts in which the top stack symbol is of the second type have been omitted, since they do not lead to acceptance of any string and their presence would introduce nondeterminism. Shifts in which the top stack symbol is of the first or third type are shown, labeled "shift moves." If the top stack symbol is of the second type, the moves that constitute the reduction are all Λ-transitions. But if the PDA reads a symbol and decides to reduce, the input symbol that has

TABLE 14.7

A deterministic bottom-up parser for *G*

Move Number	State	Input	Stack symbol	Move(s)
		Shift moves		
1	q	σ	X	$(q, \sigma X)$
	(σ is arbitrary; X is either Z_0, S_1, +, or *.)			
2	q	σ	T	$(q, \sigma T)$
	(σ is any input symbol other than + or $.)			
		Moves to reduce $S_1\$$ to S		
3	q	Λ	$\$$	$(q_\$, \Lambda)$
4	$q_\$$	Λ	S_1	(q, S)
		Moves to reduce either a or $T * a$ to T		
5	q	Λ	a	$(q_{a,1}, \Lambda)$
6	$q_{a,1}$	Λ	$*$	$(q_{a,2}, \Lambda)$
7	$q_{a,2}$	Λ	T	(q, T)
8	$q_{a,1}$	Λ	X	(q, TX)
	(X is any stack symbol other than *.)			
		Moves to reduce either $S_1 + T$ or T to S_1 and shift an input symbol		
9	q	σ	T	$(q_{T,\sigma}, \Lambda)$
10	$q_{T,\sigma}$	Λ	$+$	$(q'_{T,\sigma}, \Lambda)$
11	$q'_{T,\sigma}$	Λ	S_1	$(q, \sigma S_1)$
12	$q_{T,\sigma}$	Λ	X	$(q, \sigma S_1 X)$
	(σ is either + or $; X is any stack symbol other than +.)			
		Move to accept		
13	q	Λ	S	(q_1, Λ)
	(all other combinations)			none

been read will eventually be shifted onto the stack, once the reduction has been completed (the machine must remember the input symbol during the reduction); the eventual shift is shown, not under "shift moves," but farther down in the table, as part of the sequence of moves that effect the reduction.

We trace this PDA on the input string $a + a * a\$$:

$$
\begin{aligned}
(q, a + a * a\$, Z_0) \quad &\vdash (q, +a * a\$, aZ_0) \quad &&(\text{move } 1) \\
&\vdash (q_{a,1}, +a * a\$, Z_0) \quad &&(\text{move } 5) \\
&\vdash (q, +a * a\$, TZ_0) \quad &&(\text{move } 8) \\
&\vdash (q_{T,+}, a * a\$, Z_0) \quad &&(\text{move } 9) \\
&\vdash (q, a * a\$, +S_1 Z_0) \quad &&(\text{move } 12) \\
&\vdash (q, *a\$, a + S_1 Z_0) \quad &&(\text{move } 1) \\
&\vdash (q_{a,1}, *a\$, +S_1 Z_0) \quad &&(\text{move } 5)
\end{aligned}
$$

$$\vdash (q, *a\$, T + S_1 Z_0) \quad \text{(move 8)}$$
$$\vdash (q, a\$, *T + S_1, Z_0) \quad \text{(move 2)}$$
$$\vdash (q, \$, a * T + S_1 Z_0) \quad \text{(move 1)}$$
$$\vdash (q_{a,1}, \$, *T + S_1 Z_0) \quad \text{(move 5)}$$
$$\vdash (q_{a,2}, \$, T + S_1 Z_0) \quad \text{(move 6)}$$
$$\vdash (q, \$, T + S_1 Z_0) \quad \text{(move 7)}$$
$$\vdash (q_{T,\$}, \Lambda, +S_1 Z_0) \quad \text{(move 9)}$$
$$\vdash (q'_{T,\$}, \Lambda, S_1 Z_0) \quad \text{(move 10)}$$
$$\vdash (q, \Lambda, \$S_1 Z_0) \quad \text{(move 11)}$$
$$\vdash (q_\$, \Lambda, S_1 Z_0) \quad \text{(move 3)}$$
$$\vdash (q, \Lambda, S Z_0) \quad \text{(move 4)}$$
$$\vdash (q_1, \Lambda, Z_0) \quad \text{(move 13)}$$
(accept)

EXERCISES

14.1. In each case, the grammar with the given transitions satisfies the LL(1) condition. For each one, give a transition table for the deterministic PDA obtained as in Example 14.1.

    (a) $S \to S_1 \$$ $S_1 \to AS_1 \mid \Lambda$ $A \to aA \mid b$

    (b) $S \to S_1 \$$ $S_1 \to aA$ $A \to aA \mid bA \mid \Lambda$

    (c) $S \to S_1 \$$ $S_1 \to aAB \mid bBA$ $A \to bS_1 \mid a$ $B \to aS_1 \mid b$

14.2. In each case, the grammar with the given productions does not satisfy the LL(1) condition. Using the techniques discussed in Section 14.1 (eliminating left recursion and factoring), find an equivalent LL(1) grammar.

    (a) $S \to S_1 \$$ $S_1 \to aaS_1 b \mid ab \mid bb$

    (b)

$$S \to S_1 \$$$

$$S_1 \to aAb \mid aAA \mid aB \mid bbA$$

$$A \to aAb \mid ab$$

$$B \to bBa \mid ba$$

    (c) $S \to S_1 \$$ $S_1 \to S_1 A \mid \Lambda$ $A \to Aa \mid b$

    (d) $S \to S_1 \$$ $S_1 \to S_1 T \mid ab$ $T \to aTbb \mid ab$

14.3. Show that for the CFG in Exercise 14.2(d), if the last production were $T \to a$ instead of $T \to ab$, the grammar obtained by eliminating left recursion and factoring would not be LL(1). (Find a string that doesn't work; specify the point at which looking ahead one symbol in the input isn't enough to decide what move the PDA should make.)

14.4. Consider a modification of the unambiguous CFG discussed in Chapter 10 for the language L of all algebraic expressions involving the operators $+$ and $*$ and the identifier a:

$$S \rightarrow S_1\$$$

$$S_1 \rightarrow S_1 + T \mid T$$

$$T \rightarrow T * F \mid F$$

$$F \rightarrow (S_1) \mid a$$

(a) Write the CFG which is obtained from this one by eliminating left recursion, as discussed in Section 14.1.

(b) Give a transition table for a DPDA which acts as a top-down parser for L.

14.5. Section 14.1 gave a method for eliminating from a CFG the left recursion involving a variable T, assuming that the T-productions are $T \rightarrow T\alpha$ and $T \rightarrow \beta$ (where β does not begin with T). Suppose, more generally, that the T-productions are

$$T \rightarrow T\alpha_i \ (1 \leq i \leq m)$$

$$T \rightarrow \beta_i \ (1 \leq i \leq n)$$

where none of the strings β_i begins with T. Find a set of productions with which these can be replaced, so that the resulting grammar will be equivalent to the original and will have no left recursion involving T.

14.6. Let G be the CFG with productions

$$S \rightarrow S_1\$$$

$$S_1 \rightarrow [S_1 + S_1] \mid [S_1 * S_1] \mid a$$

($L(G)$ is the language of all "fully parenthesized" algebraic expressions involving the operators $+$ and $*$ and the identifier a.) Give a transition table for a deterministic bottom-up parser obtained from this grammar as in Section 14.3.

14.7. Let G have productions $S \rightarrow S_1\$, S_1 \rightarrow S_1[S_1] \mid S_1[] \mid [S_1] \mid []$, and let G_1 have productions $S \rightarrow S_1\$, S_1 \rightarrow [S_1]S_1 \mid [S_1] \mid []S_1 \mid []$.

(a) Give a transition table for a deterministic bottom-up parser obtained from G as in Section 14.3.

(b) Show that G_1 is not a weak precedence grammar (see Section 14.3).

14.8. In the nondeterministic bottom-up parser given for the grammar in Section 14.3, the implicit assumption in the transition table was that the start symbol S did not appear on the right side of any production. Why is there no loss of generality in making this assumption in general?

14.9. In the standard nondeterministic bottom-up parsing PDA for a grammar, obtained as in Section 14.3, consider a configuration in which the right side of a production is currently on top of the stack in reverse, and this string does not appear in the right side of any other production. Why is it always correct to reduce at this point?

14.10. (a) Say exactly what the precedence relation is for the grammar discussed in Section 14.3. In other words, for which pairs (X, σ), where $X \in \Gamma$ and $\sigma \in \Sigma$, is it correct to reduce when the top stack symbol is X and the next input symbol is σ?

(b) The larger grammar with productions

$$S \rightarrow S_1\$$$

$$S_1 \rightarrow S_1 + T \mid S_1 - T \mid T$$
$$T \rightarrow T * F \mid T/F \mid F$$
$$F \rightarrow (S_1) \mid a$$

is also a weak precedence grammar. Just as in part (a), say what the correct precedence relation is.

CHAPTER
15

CFLs AND
NON-CFLs

15.1 THE PUMPING LEMMA AND EXAMPLES

In Part II of this book, one feature of regular languages that made them relatively easy to study was the number of equivalent characterizations of regularity. In particular, Theorem 8.1 characterized regular languages as those for which a certain equivalence relation on Σ^*, defined in terms of the language, has only finitely many equivalence classes. That result provided a simple way of constructing a variety of nonregular languages.

So far, we have two characterizations of CFLs: one involving CFGs and the other involving PDAs. Neither makes it very obvious that there are languages that are not context-free. Of course, we decided in Chapter 9 that no CFG is likely to be able to capture all the subtlety of "normally spoken" English, but the difference between normally spoken English and something else may be more a matter of style or taste than of syntax. There are syntactically correct sentences that no one would ever say or write. It remains to be seen whether a *formal* language can be proved not to be a CFL. However, a second important method for showing languages nonregular was provided by the Pumping Lemma for regular languages (Theorem 8.2), and it turns out that there is also a Pumping Lemma for context-free languages, which is used in much the same way.

The Pumping Lemma for regular languages was proved by using the characterization of the languages in terms of finite automata; it depended on the fact that a sufficiently long string caused an FA to visit some state more than once. This allowed us to conclude that any sufficiently long string x could be written $x = uvw$, in such a way that all the strings of the form uv^iw were also accepted by the FA. In the case of CFLs, it is easier to derive the comparable result by looking at grammars, but the principle is similar. Suppose a derivation in a grammar G involves a variable A more than once, in this way:

$$S \Rightarrow^* vAz \Rightarrow^* vwAyz \Rightarrow^* vwxyz$$

where $v, w, x, y, z \in \Sigma^*$. In other words, $A \Rightarrow^* x$, but also $A \Rightarrow^* wAy$. We may write

$$A \Rightarrow^* wAy \Rightarrow^* w^2Ay^2 \Rightarrow^* w^3Ay^3 \Rightarrow^* \ldots$$

and we may conclude that all the strings vxz, $vwxyz$, vw^2xy^2z, $\ldots$ are in $L(G)$. If we can show that any sufficiently long string in $L(G)$ has a derivation in which this sort of phenomenon occurs, we will have a "pumping lemma"; and if we can in addition impose some restrictions on the strings v, w, x, y, and z, just as we were able to do on the strings u, v, and w in the simpler case, we will have an effective tool for proving certain languages non-context-free.

It will be convenient to discuss derivations in terms of derivation *trees*, and it will be even more convenient to be able to assume that they are *binary* trees— i.e., trees in which no node has more than two children. In order to do this, all we need is to transform the CFG into Chomsky Normal Form. The resulting grammar won't be able to produce Λ, but that won't matter, since we are only concerned about long strings.

Let us say that a *path* in a binary tree either is empty or consists of a node, one of its descendants (possibly itself), and all the nodes in between. We will say that the *length* of a path is the number of nodes it contains, and the *height* of a binary tree is the length of the longest path.

The way we get the sort of repeating we want is to force a variable to appear twice on the same path in a derivation tree; the way to do that is to make sure there is a sufficiently long path; and as Lemma 15.1 shows, that will follow if the length of the string, which is the same as the number of leaf nodes in any derivation tree for the string, is sufficiently large.

Lemma 15.1. For any $M \geq 1$, if the number of leaf nodes in a binary tree is greater than 2^{M-1}, there is a path whose length is greater than M.

Proof. An equivalent statement is that if the height of the tree is $\leq M$, the number of leaf nodes is $\leq 2^{M-1}$. We prove this by induction on M. The basis step, $M = 1$, is trivial since a tree with height ≤ 1 is either empty or a single node.

In the induction step, suppose that $K \geq 1$ and that any binary tree with height K or less has no more than 2^{K-1} leaf nodes. We wish to show that any binary tree with height $\leq K+1$ has no more than $2^{(K+1)-1} = 2^K$ leaf nodes. Assume that T is a binary tree with height $\leq K+1$. If T is empty or T consists of a single node, the result is clear. Otherwise, the left and right subtrees of T both have height $\leq K$. By the induction hypothesis, each has no more than 2^{K-1} leaf nodes. The number of leaf nodes in T is the sum of that in its left subtree and that in its right and is therefore no more than $2^{K-1} + 2^{K-1} = 2^K$.

Obtaining the result we want is now relatively straightforward.

Theorem 15.1. Let $G = (V, \Sigma, S, P)$ be a CFG in Chomsky Normal Form, with a total of n variables. If u is any string in $L(G)$ with $|u| \geq 2^{n+1}$, then u may be written as $u = vwxyz$, for some v, w, x, y, and z satisfying

$$|wy| > 0$$

$$|wxy| \leq 2^{n+1}$$

$$\text{for any } m \geq 0, \ vw^m x y^m z \in L(G)$$

Proof. Lemma 15.1 shows that any derivation tree for u must have height at least $n+2$. Let us consider a path of maximum possible length and look at the bottom portion, consisting of a leaf node and the $n + 1$ nodes above it, each of which corresponds to a variable. Since there are only n distinct variables in the grammar, this portion of the path contains some variable A twice. Let x be the portion of u derived from the A closest to the leaf; let $t = wxy$ be the portion of u derived from the other A. If v and z represent the beginning and ending portions of u, we have $u = vwxyz$. An illustration of what this might look like is given in Fig. 15-1.

The A closest to the root in this portion of the path can be considered the root of a binary derivation tree for wxy. Since we began with a path of maximum length, this tree has height $\leq n + 2$, so Lemma 15.1 implies that $|wxy| \leq 2^{n+1}$. The node containing this A has two children, both corresponding to variables. If we let B denote the one that is not an ancestor of the other A, then since x is derived from that other A, the string of terminals derived from B does not overlap x; therefore, either w or y is non-null, so $|wy| > 0$.

Finally, as we observed above, $A \Rightarrow^* x$ (the bottom A), and $A \Rightarrow^* wAy$ (the top A); therefore, $A \Rightarrow^* w^m x y^m$ for every $m \geq 0$. Since $S \Rightarrow^* vAz$, the third conclusion of the theorem follows.

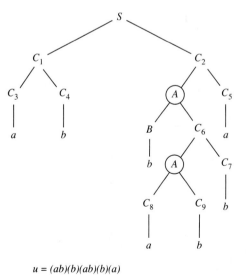

$u = (ab)(b)(ab)(b)(a)$
$\quad = v\,w\,x\,y\,z$

FIGURE 15-1

In this case, even more so than in Chapter 8, it is worth restating the result so as to emphasize the essential features.

Theorem 15.1a   **(The pumping lemma for CFLs).** Let L be a CFL. There is an integer N so that for any $u \in L$ with $|u| \geq N$, there are strings v, w, x, y, and z satisfying

$$|wy| > 0 \tag{15.1}$$

$$|wxy| \leq N \tag{15.2}$$

$$\text{For any } m \geq 0, vw^m xy^m z \in L \tag{15.3}$$

Proof. We may find a CFG in Chomsky Normal Form generating $L - \{\Lambda\}$. If n is the number of variables in this grammar and $N = 2^{n+1}$, the result is an immediate consequence of Theorem 15.1.

Just as in the case of the earlier pumping lemma, we must be careful to apply the theorem correctly when we use it to show a language is not context-free. First, since we start by assuming there is a CFG generating L and try to derive a contradiction, we don't know what the integer N in Theorem 15.1a is; thus, the u we choose is likely to be specified in terms of N. Second, once we have chosen u, the theorem does not tell us what the strings v, w, x, y, and z are, only that they exist; in order to complete the proof, we must show that *any* possible choice of these five strings satisfying the conditions (15.1)–(15.3) leads to a contradiction.

We are ready to demonstrate the existence of non-context-free languages, using Theorem 15.1a. What sort of language is a likely candidate? We know from Chapter 13 that all it takes to recognize a CFL is a finite-state machine with an auxiliary memory in the form of a stack. If we can find a language for which a single stack doesn't seem to provide enough memory or doesn't allow the machine to access the memory in the necessary way, the chances are we will be on the right track. We saw in Example 12.4 that a stack was sufficient to recognize strings of the form $(^n)^n$, for example, which could just as easily have been called $a^n b^n$. The a's are saved on the stack so that the number of a's can be compared with the number of b's that follow. What if we tried to recognize the strings $a^n b^n c^n$? It would be necessary somehow to save both the number of a's and the number of b's so that those numbers could be compared to the number of c's as well as to each other. It does not seem as though a single stack provides any way to do this, and this will be our first candidate for a non-context-free language. For the proof, however, we return to the pumping lemma. The argument about one stack not being sufficient may be appealing intuitively, and it might even be possible to develop it into a proof, but at this stage it is still at the level of "It doesn't seem as though it could work," and that is not a proof.

Example 15.1. Let $L = \{a^n b^n c^n \mid n \geq 1\}$. Using the pumping lemma (Theorem 15.1a), we show that L is not a CFL. The proof starts in exactly the same way as a proof using the pumping lemma for regular languages: Suppose L is a CFL, and let N be the integer in Theorem 15.1a. We choose a string u with $|u| \geq N$; one obvious choice is $u = a^N b^N c^N$. Suppose v, w, x, y, and z are any strings satisfying $u = vwxyz$ as well as (15.1)–(15.3) in the theorem. Since $|wxy| \leq N$, wxy can contain at most two of the three symbols a, b, and c, and since $|wy| > 0$, w and y together contain at least one. The string vw^2xy^2z contains additional occurrences of the symbols contained in w and y; therefore, it cannot contain equal numbers of all three symbols. But according to (15.3), $vw^2xy^2z \in L$. This is a contradiction, and our assumption that L was a CFL cannot have been correct.

Notice that to get the contradiction, we started with $u \in L$ and showed that vw^2xy^2z not only fails to be an element of L, but also fails to be an element of the larger language

$$L_1 = \{u \in \{a, b, c\}^* | \ u \text{ has equal numbers of } a\text{'s, } b\text{'s, and } c\text{'s}\}$$

Therefore, we have in fact proved L_1 to be non-context-free as well.

Example 15.2. Let $L = \{ss \mid s \in \{a, b\}^*\}$. This language is similar in one obvious respect to the language of even-length palindromes: in both cases, to recognize a string in the language, a machine needs to save the first half so as to compare it to the second. But for palindromes, the last-in-first-out principle is obviously the appropriate one. This time, when we encounter the first symbol in the second half (even assuming we are able to recognize it), the symbol we need to compare it to is the *first* in, not the last—in other words, it's at the bottom of the stack. Here again, though, arguing that the obvious approach to recognizing the language with a PDA doesn't work is not the same as proving that no approach works. Let's use the pumping lemma. Suppose that L is a CFL, and let N be the integer in Theorem 15.1a. We have our choice of u, subject to the condition $|u| \geq N$; let's try $u = a^N b^N a^N b^N$. Suppose $u = vwxyz$ and (15.1)–(15.3) in the theorem hold. As usual, we must derive a contradiction from these facts and nothing else—i.e., no other assumptions about v, w, x, y, and z.

As in the first example, condition (15.2) implies that wxy can overlap at most two of the four contiguous groups of symbols. We consider several cases.

(a) Suppose w or y contains at least one a from the first group of a's. Since $|wxy| \leq N$, neither w nor y can contain any symbols from the second half of u. Consider $m = 0$ in condition (15.3): $vw^0xy^0z = a^i b^j a^N b^N$, for some $i < N$ and some $j \leq N$. If this string were ss (i.e., if it were in L), what could s be? Unless $i = 0$, s must start with a (from the first s) and end with b (from the second), and this is obviously impossible. But if $i = 0$, the string is $b^N a^N b^N$, which is obviously not of the form ss. Since uw^0xy^0z cannot be in L, we have a contradiction in this case.

(b) Suppose wxy contains no a's from the first group, but w or y contains at least one b from the first group of b's. $vw^0xy^0z = a^N b^i a^j b^N$ for some $i < N$ and some $j \leq N$; again it is impossible for this string to be of the form ss.

The other two cases (wy contains no symbols from the first half of u but at least one a, and wy contains only b's from the second group) are handled the same way.

Just as in the first example, if we look carefully we can apply our proof to other languages besides this one. You can check, for example, that with only minor modifications our proof would also be sufficient to show that both the languages $\{a^n b^n a^n b^n | n \geq 0\}$ and $\{a^n b^m a^n b^m | n, m \geq 0\}$ are non-context-free. A similar proof shows also that $\{scs \mid s \in \{a, b\}^*\}$ is not context-free. The marker in the middle may appear to remove the need for nondeterminism, but the basic problem that makes a PDA incapable of recognizing this language is still there.

Examples of this type can be tricky. In the first place, it may not be obvious what string u to choose; in the second place, once u is chosen, it may not be obvious what cases need to be considered, or exactly where the contradiction is to come from in each case. In the example, $u = a^N b^N a^N b^N$ may not seem like the obvious choice, and it isn't the only one that will work, but you should at least convince yourself that there are some choices, such as $a^N a^N$ or $(ab)^N (ab)^N$, that would not work. Once we choose $a^N b^N a^N b^N$, we could consider different ways of breaking the problem into cases. An obvious way would be: (a) wy contains only a's from the first group; (b) wy contains a's from the first group and b's from the first; (c) wy contains only b's from the first group; $\ldots$; (g) wy contains only b's from the second group. It may not be necessary to consider cases at all, if you can come up with a convincing reason that works for *any* v, w, x, y, and z. If you divide the problem into cases, it is normally better, all other things being equal, to consider four than to consider seven. If you find yourself saying something like "Cases 1, 3, and 5 are handled exactly like cases 6, 8, and 10," perhaps you should try to reduce the number of cases. (Try to rephrase the proof above so that there are only two cases instead of four!) But in any case, the crucial thing to remember is that you must show convincingly that your choice of u leads to a contradiction, and you must do it by using only the facts about v, w, x, y, and z contained in (15.1)–(15.3).

Example 15.3. Let

$$L = \{x \in \{a, b, c\}^* \mid N_a(x) < N_b(x) \text{ and } N_a(x) < N_c(x)\}$$

where $N_a(x)$, $N_b(x)$, and $N_c(x)$ are the numbers of a's, b's, and c's, respectively, in x. The intuitive reason that no PDA can recognize L is similar to that in Example 15.1: the stack allows the machine to compare the number of a's to the number of b's or to compare the number of a's to the number of c's, but not both. Suppose L is a CFL, and let N be the integer in Theorem 15.1a. Let $u = a^N b^{N+1} c^{N+1}$. If $u = vwxyz$, where (15.1)–(15.3) hold, wxy can contain at most two distinct symbols. This time, two cases will suffice.

(a) Suppose w or y contains at least one a. wy cannot contain any c's, so $vw^2 xy^2 z$ cannot have fewer a's than c's. This is a contradiction, since (15.3) says $vw^2 xy^2 z \in L$.

(b) Suppose neither w nor y contains an a. wy contains either b or c. Therefore, $vw^0 xy^0 z$ contains either as many a's as b's, or as many a's as c's, which is also a contradiction of (15.3).

Note that $\{a^i b^j c^k \mid i < j \text{ and } i < k\}$ can be shown to be non-context-free by exactly the same argument.

Example 15.4. Let us consider the language Pascal: the set of strings that are syntactically correct Pascal programs. We have discussed in Chapter 9 the fact that most of the syntax of Pascal can be described by a BNF grammar, which is the same as a context-free grammar. At this point, however, we are in a better position to understand why a BNF grammar cannot encompass all the rules of the language, and why in fact it is not strictly correct to say that Pascal is a CFL. We do not assume, incidentally, that you are an expert in Pascal syntax; this discussion should make sense even if you have never programmed in Pascal, although unless you are willing to take on faith one or two assertions about what constitutes legal Pascal syntax, you may wish to consult a Pascal textbook.

One of the requirements in a Pascal program is that a variable identifier used in the main body of the program be declared previously in a variable declaration section.

Checking that this is the case is essentially the same as determining whether a certain string is of the form xcx, where x is the identifier and c is the string appearing between the declaration of x and its use. We observed in Example 15.2 that the language $\{xcx \mid x \in \{a, b\}^*\}$ is not a CFL; although in the previous discussion c was a single symbol, allowing it to be a longer string would not seem to remove the difficulty.

There are other examples as well of rules in Pascal, violations of which cannot be detected by a PDA. We noted that $\{a^n b^m a^n b^m\}$ is not a CFL. We can imagine a situation in which being able to recognize a string of this type is essentially what is required. Suppose that a procedure P is declared, having n formal parameters; another procedure Q is declared, having m parameters; subsequently, calls on P and Q are made, so that the numbers of parameters in the calls must agree with the numbers in the respective declarations.

Using the pumping lemma, we can construct a proof that Pascal is not a CFL, based on the first of these two ideas. Assume that Pascal is a CFL, and let N be the integer in Theorem 15.1a. We want a string u, with length at least N, that has both a declaration of a variable and a statement using the variable. If we keep everything else to an absolute minimum, we might let u be the string

$$\text{PROGRAM}\square\text{P;VAR}\square A^N B^N \text{:INTEGER;BEGIN}\square A^N B^N := 1\square\text{END.}$$

There are four embedded blanks in this string, which are indicated by $\square$, and all are necessary as separators. The portion beginning with VAR and extending to the next semicolon is the variable declaration section. "PROGRAM$\square$P" is the program header; the "BEGIN ... END" marks the body of the program. Everything but the variable declaration section and the statement in the program body is essential to a legal program. As for these two, the assignment statement is not legal unless a declaration similar to this one is also included, and the identifiers in the two places must be the same.

Theorem 15.1a says that $u = vwxyz$, where $|wy| > 0$, $|wxy| \leq N$, and (in particular) $vw^0 xy^0 z = vxz$ is also a legal Pascal program. We will use this to derive our contradiction.

First, notice that because $|A^N B^N| = 2N$, the string wxy can contain symbols from before the first $A^N B^N$, symbols after the second $A^N B^N$, or symbols between the two, but at most one of these possibilities can occur. In addition, wxy may contain symbols from $A^N B^N$ itself. Let's show, however, that each of these is impossible. If wxy contained any symbols from "PROGRAM$\square$P;VAR$\square$", then vxz would still have the complete assignment statement, which would be legal only if the "VAR$\square$" was there to identify the variable declaration section. Every program must have a program header, and it must be separated from the variable declaration section by a semicolon. Therefore, nothing at the beginning of the program can be eliminated. The program must end with "END."; if anything were missing from ":= 1$\square$" there would be an illegal statement. Thus, nothing can be eliminated from the end. Finally, the syntax for a variable declaration section with a single declaration is

"VAR <variable identifier>:<type identifier>;"

and the program body must start with "BEGIN$\square$". If you're willing to believe that "INTEGER" can't be shortened in any way so as to obtain a legal type identifier, it's clear that nothing can be omitted from the middle.

The only possibilities are for w and y to be completely within the first identifier, for them to be completely within the second identifier, or for w to be within the first and

y within the second. In either of the first two cases, deleting wy clearly leaves the two identifiers unequal. In the third case, the same is true since $|wxy| \leq N$. We may conclude that vxz cannot possibly be a legal Pascal program, and therefore that Pascal is not a CFL.

15.2 INTERSECTIONS AND COMPLEMENTS

Theorem 9.1 asserted that the set of context-free languages is closed under the operations of union, concatenation, and *. For regular languages, it was a straightforward process to add two more operations (intersection and complement) to the list. But another way in which context-free languages are more complex is that applying these two operations to CFLs does not always produce a CFL. Now that we have examples of non-CFLs, we can see this easily.

Theorem 15.2. There are CFLs L_1 and L_2 so that $L_1 \cap L_2$ is not a CFL; there is a CFL L so that L' is not a CFL.

Proof. We have already seen an example to illustrate the first statement: if we let

$$L_1 = \{a^i b^j c^k \mid i < j\}$$

and

$$L_2 = \{a^i b^j c^k \mid i < k\}$$

then $L_1 \cap L_2$ is the language that Example 15.3 shows to be non-context-free. (The proof given there was actually for a different language, but we observed that the same proof works for this one.) L_1 and L_2 are both CFLs, however. A CFG for L_1 has the productions

$$S \rightarrow ABC$$
$$A \rightarrow aAb \mid \Lambda$$
$$B \rightarrow bB \mid b$$
$$C \rightarrow cC \mid \Lambda$$

and one generating L_2 has the productions

$$S \rightarrow AC$$
$$A \rightarrow aAc \mid B$$
$$B \rightarrow bB \mid \Lambda$$
$$C \rightarrow cC \mid c$$

The proof that these two grammars do generate L_1 and L_2 is straightforward and we omit it.

The second statement follows from the first, since for any L_1 and L_2,

$$L_1 \cap L_2 = (L_1' \cup L_2')'$$

If complements of CFLs were always CFLs, then for any two CFLs L_1 and L_2, L_1' and L_2' would be CFLs, so would their union, and so would its complement. But we already know that for certain CFLs L_1 and L_2, $L_1 \cap L_2$ is not a CFL.

Example 15.5. The second part of the proof of Theorem 15.2 starts with the assumption that the complement of a CFL is always a CFL and derives a contradiction; the conclusion is that there exists a CFL whose complement is not one. That description makes it sound like a nonconstructive proof, but if we look more closely we can use it to come up with an example. If L_1 and L_2 are the languages defined in the first part of the proof above, $L_1 \cap L_2 = (L_1' \cup L_2')'$, and we know that this language is not a CFL. Therefore, either L_1 is a CFL whose complement is not a CFL, or L_2 is, or (since the union of two CFLs is a CFL) $L_1' \cup L_2'$ is. Let us determine which of these is true. There are two ways a string can fail to be in L_1. It can be a string not even in R, the regular language corresponding to the regular expression $a^*b^*c^*$, or it can be a string of the form $a^i b^j c^k$ for which $i \geq j$. In other words,

$$L_1' = R' \cup \{a^i b^j c^k \mid i \geq j\}$$

R' is regular, since R is, and so R' is context-free; $\{a^i b^j c^k \mid i \geq j\}$ is a CFL that has a CFG similar to the one shown in the theorem for L_1. Therefore, L_1' is a CFL. Similarly,

$$L_2' = R' \cup \{a^i b^j c^k \mid i \geq k\}$$

and L_2' is a CFL. It follows that $L_1' \cup L_2'$, which is equal to

$$R' \cup \{a^i b^j c^k \mid i \geq j \text{ or } i \geq k\}$$

is a CFL whose complement is not a CFL. In fact, the second part by itself would work also—see Exercise 15.8.

It might be interesting at this point to go back to Theorem 4.4, in which the intersection of two regular languages was shown to be regular, and to see what goes wrong when we try to use the same construction here to show that the intersection of two CFLs is a CFL. We started with FAs M_1 and M_2 recognizing the two languages, and we constructed a composite machine M whose states were pairs (p, q) of states in M_1 and states in M_2, respectively. M kept track of both machines at once—or, to say it a different way, it simulated running the two machines in parallel. A string was accepted by M if it was simultaneously accepted by M_1 and M_2.

If we have CFLs L_1 and L_2, and PDAs $M_1 = (Q_1, \Sigma, \Gamma_1, q_1, Z_1, \delta_1, A_1)$ and $M_2 = (Q_2, \Sigma, \Gamma_2, q_2, Z_2, \delta_2, A_2)$ accepting them, we can construct states of a new machine M in the same way: let $Q = Q_1 \times Q_2$. It also seems reasonable to construct the stack alphabet of M by letting $\Gamma = \Gamma_1 \times \Gamma_2$; if we see the pair on top of the stack, we will know the symbols on top of the stacks of M_1 and M_2. When we try to define the moves of M, however, things become complicated, even leaving aside the question of nondeterminism. If $\delta_1(p, a, X) = \{(p', X')\}$ and $\delta_2(q, a, Y) = \{(q', Y')\}$, where $X, X' \in \Gamma_1$ and $Y, Y' \in \Gamma_2$, it's obvious what to do:

$$\delta((p, q), a, (X, Y)) = \{((p', q'), (X', Y'))\}$$

But what if $\delta_1(p, a, X) = \{(p', X'X)\}$ and $\delta_2(q, a, Y) = \{(q', \Lambda)\}$? Or if $\delta_1(p, a, X) = \{(p', X)\}$ and $\delta_2(q, a, Y) = \{(q', YYY)\}$? There is no obvious way to have M keep track of both the states of M_1 and M_2 and the stacks of M_1 and M_2 and still operate like a PDA. Theorem 15.2 confirms that such an M is indeed impossible in general.

If we are careful, though, we can salvage something from this discussion. If M_1 is a PDA and M_2 is a PDA with *no* stack (in particular, a deterministic one — i.e., an FA), there is no obstacle to carrying out this construction. The stack on our new machine will simply be that on M_1. The result is the following theorem.

Theorem 15.3. If L_1 is a context-free language and L_2 is a regular language, then $L_1 \cap L_2$ is a context-free language.

Proof. As we indicated in the discussion earlier, the proof will be to construct a PDA recognizing $L_1 \cap L_2$ by final state. Let $M_1 = (Q_1, \Sigma, \Gamma_1, q_1, Z_1, \delta_1, A_1)$ be a PDA accepting L_1 by final state, and let $M_2 = (Q_2, \Sigma, q_2, \delta_2, A_2)$ be an FA recognizing L_2. We define a PDA $M = (Q, \Sigma, \Gamma, q_0, Z_0, \delta, A)$ as follows:

$Q = Q_1 \times Q_2 \qquad q_0 = (q_1, q_2)$
$\Gamma = \Gamma_1 \qquad Z_0 = Z_1$
$A = A_1 \times A_2$
(1) For $p \in Q_1, q \in Q_2, a \in \Sigma$, *and* $Z \in \Gamma$,

$$\delta((p, q), a, Z) = \{((p', q'), \alpha) \mid \delta_1(p, a, Z) \text{ contains } (p', \alpha) \text{ and } \delta_2(q, a) = q'\}$$

(2) For $p \in Q_1, q \in Q_2$, and $Z \in \Gamma$,

$$\delta((p, q), \Lambda, Z) = \{((p', q), \alpha) \mid (p', \alpha) \in \delta_1(p, \Lambda, Z)\}$$

You can see that (1) and (2) capture the idea of M keeping track of the states of M_1 and M_2. The contents of the stack at any time is exactly what it would be in the machine M_1.

Let us prove that if M_1 can by processing a string y get to a state p, with a string α on its stack, and M_2 can by processing y get to a state q, then M can by processing y get to the state (p, q), with α on the stack. More precisely, let us show that for any $n \geq 0$ and any $p \in Q_1, q \in Q_2, y, z \in \Sigma^*$, and $\alpha \in \Gamma^*$, if

$$(q_1, yz, Z_1) \vdash^n_{M_1} (p, z, \alpha) \qquad \text{and} \qquad \delta_2^*(q_2, y) = q$$

then

$$((q_1, q_2), yz, Z_1) \vdash^n_M ((p, q), z, \alpha)$$

This will imply that if

$$(q_1, x, Z_1) \vdash^*_{M_1} (p, \Lambda, \alpha) \text{ for some } p \in A_1 \text{ (i.e., } x \in L(M_1))$$

and

$$\delta_2^*(q_2, x) \in A_2 \quad \text{(i.e., } x \in L(M_2))$$

then

$$((q_1, q_2), x, Z_1) \vdash^*_M ((p, q), \Lambda, \alpha) \text{ for some } (p, q) \in A \text{ (i.e., } x \in L(M))$$

The proof is by induction on n, and, in spite of the intimidating notation, is easy. For the basis step, suppose

$$(q_1, yz, Z_1) \vdash^0_{M_1} (p, z, \alpha) \qquad \text{and} \qquad \delta_2^*(q_2, y) = q$$

Clearly $y = \Lambda$, $p = q_1$, $\alpha = Z_1$, and $q = q_2$. In this case, we obviously have

$$((q_1, q_2), yz, Z_1) \vdash_M^0 ((p, q), z, \alpha) = ((q_1, q_2), yz, Z_1)$$

Suppose that $K \geq 0$ and that the statement is true for $n = K$. Assume that

$$(q_1, yz, Z_1) \vdash_{M_1}^{K+1} (p, z, \alpha) \qquad \text{and} \qquad \delta_2^*(q_2, y) = q$$

We wish to show that

$$((q_1, q_2), yz, Z_1) \vdash_M^{K+1} ((p, q), z, \alpha)$$

Let us look at the last move in the sequence of $K + 1$ moves in M_1. If it is a Λ-transition, then

$$(q_1, yz, Z_1) \vdash_{M_1}^{K} (p', z, \beta) \vdash_{M_1} (p, z, \alpha)$$

for some $p' \in Q_1$ and some $\beta \in \Gamma_1^*$. In this case the inductive hypothesis implies that

$$((q_1, q_2), yz, Z_1) \vdash_M^{K} ((p', q), z, \beta)$$

and from (2) we have

$$((p', q), z, \beta) \vdash_{M_1} ((p, q), z, \alpha)$$

so the result follows. Otherwise, $y = y'a$ for some $a \in \Sigma$, and

$$(q_1, y'az, Z_1) \vdash_{M_1}^{K} (p', az, \beta) \vdash_{M_1} (p, z, \alpha)$$

Let $q' = \delta_2^*(q_2, y')$; the inductive hypothesis implies that

$$((q_1, q_2), y'az, Z_1) \vdash_{M_1}^{K} ((p', q'), az, \beta)$$

and from (1) we have

$$((p', q'), az, \beta) \vdash_M ((p, q), z, \alpha)$$

Again, the result follows.

The other half of the proof is to show that for any $n \geq 0$, and any p, q, y, z, and α, if

$$((q_1, q_2), yz, Z_1) \vdash_M^{n} ((p, q), z, \alpha)$$

then

$$(q_1, yz, Z_1) \vdash_{M_1}^{n} (p, z, \alpha) \qquad \text{and} \qquad \delta_2^*(q_2, y) = q$$

Again, the proof is by induction. The details are almost identical to those in the first half, and we omit them. This second statement implies that if $x \in L(M)$, then $x \in L(M_1) \cap L(M_2)$, and the theorem follows.

It is also worthwhile, in the light of Theorems 15.2 and 15.3, to re-examine the proof that the complement of a regular language is regular. If an FA $M = (Q, \Sigma, q_0, \delta, A)$ recognizes the language L, the FA $M' = (Q, \Sigma, q_0, \delta, Q - A)$ recognizes $\Sigma^* - L$. If a PDA $M = (Q, \Sigma, \Gamma, q_0, Z_0, \delta, A)$ recognizes the context-free language L by final state, we are free to apply the same construction and to consider the PDA $M' = (Q, \Sigma, \Gamma, q_0, Z_0, \delta, Q - A)$. Theorem 15.2 says that in general, M' does not recognize $\Sigma^* - L$. Why not?

Essentially, the problem is nondeterminism. In the PDA M, it may happen that for some $x \in \Sigma^*$, $(q_0, x, Z_0) \vdash^* (p, \Lambda, \alpha)$ for some $p \in A$, and $(q_0, x, Z_0) \vdash^*$ (q, Λ, β) for some other $q \notin A$. Thus, x is accepted by M as well as by M', since q is one of the accepting states in M'. Every NFA-Λ is equivalent to an FA, but the corresponding result about PDAs is not true. In fact, although we shall not present all the details, we are now in a position to see more clearly why there are CFLs that are not DCFLs.

We would expect that if M is a *deterministic* PDA recognizing L, then the PDA M' constructed as above, by making the nonaccepting states accepting and vice versa, would recognize $\Sigma^* - L$. Unfortunately, this is still not quite correct. One reason is that there might be input strings that cause M to enter an infinite sequence of Λ-transitions and are therefore never processed to completion. Any such string would be accepted neither by M nor by M'. However, it can be shown that difficulties of this sort can be resolved and that a DPDA can be constructed that recognizes $\Sigma^* - L$. Thus, the complement of a DCFL is a DCFL. It follows that any context-free language whose complement is not a CFL (see Theorem 15.2) cannot be a DCFL.

15.3 DECISION PROBLEMS FOR CFLs

At the end of Chapter 8, we considered a number of decision problems involving regular languages, beginning with the membership problem: given an FA M and a string x, does M accept x? We may formulate the same sorts of questions for context-free languages. For some of them, essentially the same algorithms work; for others, the inherent nondeterminism of PDAs requires us to find new algorithms; and for some, no algorithm is possible, although only later will we be in a position to prove this.

To the basic membership problem for CFLs, we can no longer simply answer "Run M with input x and see what happens." If we think of M as making a move once per second and choosing arbitrarily whenever it has a choice, there is at least one problem with this approach. A sequence of moves that ends with x being rejected does not necessarily mean that there isn't another sequence that would cause M to accept x. Only if the PDA is deterministic can we conclude that x is not in the language recognized by M, and as we remarked in the previous section, some context-free languages are not recognized by any deterministic PDA. If we have the specifications for the PDA, we could very likely formulate some backtracking algorithm, similar to those described in Chapter 14, that would be guaranteed to answer the question. But a completely different approach, suggested early in Chapter 11, is simpler to describe, even though it might be inefficient to carry out. It depends on the fact that a CFG with no Λ-productions and no unit productions can require no more than $2N - 1$ steps for the derivation of a string of length N.

Decision algorithm for membership problem. (**Given a PDA M and a string x, does M accept x?**) Use the construction in Theorem 13.2 to find a CFG G generating the language recognized by M. If $x = \Lambda$, use Algorithm FindNull in Section 11.1 to determine whether the start symbol of G is nullable. Otherwise, eliminate Λ-productions and unit productions from G using Algorithms 11.1 and 11.2. Examine all derivations with one step, all those with two steps, and so on., until either a derivation of x has been found or all derivations of length $2|x| - 1$ have been examined. If no derivation of x has been found, M does not accept x.

We note at this point that since the theorems in Chapter 13 let us go from a CFG to a PDA and vice versa, we can formulate any of these decision problems in terms of either a CFG or a PDA. We consider the decision problems corresponding to problems 2 and 3 in Chapter 8, but stated in terms of CFGs.

1. Given a CFG G, does it generate any strings? (Is $L(G) = \varnothing$?)
2. Given a CFG G, is $L(G)$ finite?

The pumping lemma for context-free languages, Theorem 15.1, provides us with a way of answering both questions. We transform G into Chomsky normal form. Let G' be the resulting grammar, n be the number of variables in G', and $N = 2^{n+1}$. If G' generates any strings, it must generate one of length less than N. Otherwise, apply the pumping lemma to a string u of minimal length ($\geq N$) generated by G'; then $u = vwxyz$ for some v, w, x, y, z with $|wy| > 0$ and $vxz \in L(G')$—but this contradicts the minimality of u. Similarly, if $L(G')$ is infinite, there must be a string $u \in L(G)$ with $N \leq |u| < 2N$; the proof is virtually identical to that of the corresponding result in Chapter 8. We therefore obtain these two decision algorithms:

Decision algorithms for problems 1 and 2. (**Given a CFG G, is $L(G) = \varnothing$? Is $L(G)$ finite?**) First, test whether Λ can be generated from G, using the algorithm for the membership problem. If it can, then $L(G) \neq \varnothing$. In any case, let G' be a CNF grammar generating $L(G) - \{\Lambda\}$, and let $N = 2^{n+1}$, where n is the number of variables in G'. For increasing values of I beginning with 1, examine all strings of length I. If for no $I < N$ is there a string of length I in $L(G')$, and $\Lambda \notin L(G)$, then $L(G') = L(G) = \varnothing$. If for no I with $N \leq I < 2N$ is there a string of length I in $L(G)$, then $L(G)$ is finite; if there is a string $x \in L(G)$ with $N \leq |x| < 2N$, then $L(G)$ is infinite.

These algorithms are easy to describe, not necessarily easy to carry out. Fortunately, for problems like the membership problem where it is important to be able to find practical solutions, there are more efficient algorithms (see the References). If we go any farther down the list of decision problems in Chapter 8, formulated for CFGs or PDAs instead of for regular expressions or FAs, we encounter problems for which there is no possible decision algorithm, even a horribly inefficient one. To take an example, given two context-free grammars, are there any strings generated by both? The algorithm we gave in Chapter 8 to solve the corresponding problem for FAs depended on the fact that the class of regular languages is closed under the operations of complement and intersection. We know that the class of CFLs is not; this in itself does not tell us that the problem is "unsolvable," but we shall see in Part IV that it is.

EXERCISES

15.1. Show in each case, using the pumping lemma, that the given language is not a CFL.

   (a) $L = \{a^i b^j c^k \mid i < j < k\}$
   (b) $L = \{x \in \{a, b\}^* \mid N_b(x) = N_a(x)^2\}$
   (c) $L = \{a^N b^{2N} a^N \mid N \geq 0\}$

15.2. Decide in each case whether the given language is a CFL. Prove your answer.

   (a) $L = \{a^n b^m a^m b^n \mid m, n \geq 0\}$
   (b) $L = \{xayb \mid x, y \in \{a, b\}^*$ and $|x| = |y|\}$
   (c) $L = \{xyx \mid x, y \in \{a, b\}^*, |x| \geq 1\}$
   (d) $L = \{x \in \{a, b\}^* \mid N_a(x) < N_b(x) < 2N_a(x)\}$

15.3. If L is a CFL, is it necessarily true that $REV(L)$ is a CFL? Either give a proof that it is in general, or give an example of a CFL for which it fails and a proof that it fails in that case.

15.4. State theorems that generalize Theorems 8.3 and 8.4 to CFLs. Then give examples of languages where

   (a) Theorem 15.1a can be used to show the language is not a CFL, but the generalization of Theorem 8.3 cannot.
   (b) The generalization of Theorem 8.3 can be used to show the language is not a CFL, but the generalization of Theorem 8.4 cannot.
   (c) The generalization of Theorem 8.4 can be used to show the language is not a CFL.

15.5. Give a proof not involving the pumping lemma that the language $L = \{x \in \{a, b, c\}^* \mid N_a(x) = N_b(x) = N_c(x)\}$ is not a CFL. Suggestion: use Example 15.1 and a theorem from this chapter.

15.6. (a) Show that the class of DCFLs is not closed under union. Example 15.5 may be helpful.

   (b) Show that the class of DCFLs is not closed under intersection.

15.7. (a) Show that if L is a CFL and F is finite, $L - F$ is a CFL.

   (b) Show that if L is not a CFL and F is finite, then $L - F$ is not a CFL.
   (c) Show that if L is not a CFL and F is finite, then $L \cup F$ is not a CFL.

15.8. In the preceding problem, suppose "finite" is replaced by "regular." In each case, determine whether the resulting statement is true or false, and prove your answer.

15.9. Show in each case that the given language is a CFL whose complement is not a CFL.

   (a) $\{a^i b^j c^k \mid i \geq j$ or $i \geq k\}$
   (b) $\{a^i b^j c^k \mid i \neq j$ or $i \neq k\}$

15.10. Give an example, including the transition table, of a DPDA M recognizing a language L for which the language recognized by the machine obtained from M by reversing the accepting and nonaccepting states is not L'.

PART
IV

TURING MACHINES, THEIR LANGUAGES, AND COMPUTATION

Someone trying to give a capsule description of computer science might begin by saying it is the study of algorithms to solve problems. Computer scientists are interested in designing algorithms, in developing ways of implementing them efficiently, and in analyzing and comparing them.

In the case of a typical problem that you encounter in a beginning programming course, such as sorting a mass of data values into increasing order, there is no doubt that the problem has a solution. The focus is on developing a solution in an organized, systematic way, and on recognizing the difference between an algorithm and a trial-and-error approach that may not provide complete solutions in every case or that may fail to terminate. The beginning student quickly learns some of the features that are necessary for something to be a genuine algorithm. As he progresses, he acquires tools that can assist in the solution of a variety of more and more complex problems.

It is an unfortunate fact that not all problems have solutions. This statement requires a little elaboration. There are problems for which no solution has yet been discovered; that in itself has a bright side, since these problems provide a challenge to researchers and an opportunity for fame and fortune to anyone who can meet the challenge. The more unfortunate fact is that there are problems— even interesting problems, solutions to which would be immensely useful—for which no general algorithmic solutions can possibly exist. In order to demonstrate this, we need a more precise way of formulating the notion of an algorithm, a precise model of computation in general. The abstract machines that we studied in Parts II and III can be viewed as embodiments of certain types of algorithms: those in which no more than a fixed amount of information can be "remembered," those in which information developed during the course of the algorithm can be retrieved only in accordance with a last-in-first-out rule, and so on. In this part, we begin by describing an abstract machine called a Turing machine that is generally accepted as a model for *any* effective computation, any algorithmic procedure.

There are a number of slightly different formulations of Turing machines, some of which we shall discuss and compare. Once we have the basic model, it will be possible to relate it to the more primitive machines we studied earlier. One way to do this is to consider the languages that can be recognized by these machines and to look for ways of generating such languages. By introducing grammars more general than regular or context-free grammars, we will be able to see a natural hierarchy into which these languages, and thus the corresponding machines, fit.

Our first example of an unsolvable problem is obtained by identifying a language that cannot be recognized by any Turing machine. The method by which this is done is interesting in itself and useful in other contexts; it uses a circular sort of argument known as a diagonal argument, and depends on encoding the specifications of a Turing machine as a string that can be processed by another Turing machine. As a result, the first type of unsolvable problem to be considered involves Turing machines themselves. However, once a single unsolvable problem is obtained, others can be derived from it. We examine one that is a general combinatorial problem, and several having to do with context-free languages.

After looking at problems that cannot be solved, it is appropriate to look more closely at those that can, and to try to characterize them independently of Turing machines. More generally, we characterize the functions that can be computed by Turing machines as those that can be built up, beginning with certain "initial" functions, by applications of three operations. Finally, we mention briefly a few other characterizations of "computability" and try to indicate why they are also equivalent to the Turing-machine characterization.

CHAPTER
16

TURING
MACHINES

16.1 MODELS OF COMPUTATION

With each of the two types of languages we have studied so far, there is associated a "model of computation": an abstract machine that is able to recognize precisely the languages of that type. The term "model of computation" is appropriate in the sense that each of these machines accepts a string of input symbols, makes certain "moves" in response to these inputs, and produces a rudimentary output, a yes-or-no answer. Of the two, the more sophisticated is a pushdown automaton. Such a machine can be in any of a finite number of "states," and it has a potentially infinite auxiliary memory organized as a stack. Any context-free language can be recognized by a machine of this type, but there is no *a priori* reason to think that such a machine is an appropriate model for computation in general. Indeed, we know that CFLs are the only languages that PDAs can recognize, and thus, since we have simple examples of languages that are not context-free, it is easy to describe "computations" no PDA can carry out. We now consider how we might generalize the notion of a PDA—and, ultimately, how we might enlarge our idea of a "computation."

One approach to the problem of generalizing the machine is to consider specific examples of non-context-free languages, and to see what extra features would be required in order to recognize them. This corresponds to what we did in Chapter 12, when we formulated the definition of a PDA. For example, let

$L_1 = \{a^n b^n c^n | \ n \geq 1\}$, as in Example 15.1. It is not hard to see that although one stack is not sufficient to recognize L_1, two stacks are. The machine could push a's onto the first stack until the first b is encountered, push bs onto the second until the input symbol c occurs, and then pop one element from each stack for every c that is read; if the input runs out just as the two stacks become empty, the string is accepted. For a second example, consider $L_2 = \{s s | \ s \in \{a, b\}^*\}$, as in Example 15.2. Here, the problem seems to be that in order to compare the second half of a string with the first, a "first in, first out" rule is more appropriate than the "last in, first out" rule by which a stack operates. In response to this example, one might postulate a *queue* as the appropriate way to organize the auxiliary memory of the machine.

These examples are suggestive. The first is obviously a generalization of PDAs, and the second, if defined properly, can be shown to be. In fact, these two seemingly different approaches turn out to produce machines with the same "computing power"; either would be a feasible way to proceed, and both have been introduced as "models of computation." Instead, however, we follow the approach taken by Alan Turing some 50 years ago. He formulated an abstract machine that is a model of computation in a somewhat more literal sense. He imagined a human "computer"—that is, a human with a pencil and paper solving some problem in an algorithmic way—and attempted to isolate the primitive steps into which the computation could be decomposed. He then defined a machine that is capable of the same kinds of primitive steps; in this way he was able to argue that any conceivable algorithm, or "effective procedure," could be carried out by his machine.

Turing decided that the primitive steps in a computation are examining an individual symbol on the paper, erasing a symbol or replacing it by another, and transferring one's attention from one part of the paper to another. He postulated further that a human computer can always be assumed to operate in such a way that his action at any point depends only on the symbol he is currently examining and on his "state of mind" at the time. His state of mind can change, as a result of the symbols he has seen or the computations he has made, but the crucial point is that there are only (according to Turing) a finite number of possible states of mind. In particular, the states of mind in themselves do not allow the computer to remember the entire sequence of moves he has made so far, just as an FA cannot recognize arbitrarily long strings of the form $0^N 1^N$.

There are a number of variations on the original Turing machine, some of which will be discussed in more detail in Chapter 17. The one we shall begin with is not exactly that proposed by Turing, but its basic features are similar. It has, in common with FAs and PDAs, a finite set of states, corresponding in Turing's terminology to the possible "states of mind" of the human computer. Instead of a sheet of paper, it has a linear "tape," which has a left end and is potentially infinite to the right, and which is divided into squares. Each square is capable of holding a single symbol, an element of some finite alphabet; if a square has no symbol in it, we say it contains the *blank* symbol. It will be helpful to distinguish between the *input* alphabet, which contains all the symbols that can be on the tape initially, and the *tape* alphabet, which may contain additional symbols to be used during the computation. The machine has a tape head that at any moment is centered on one of the squares of the tape. The basic actions the machine is capable of are reading the symbol in the current square, changing the symbol in the current square, moving the head one square to the right or left, and changing states. The decision to do one or more of the last three is made on the basis of the symbol that is read and the state the machine is in at that time. The tape serves as the input device (the input is simply the string, assumed to be finite, of nonblank symbols on the tape originally), the memory, and the output device (the output is the string of symbols left on the tape at the end of the computation). The most important feature is that the head can move in either direction on the tape and can erase or modify any symbol it encounters.

Does it seem as though an abstract machine of this type is sufficiently general that it can serve as a model for an arbitrary computation? When you sit down to compute something, you normally have a two-dimensional sheet of paper, not a one-dimensional tape, but it isn't hard to convince yourself that writing all the symbols on the same horizontal line, though it may be more awkward, does not really limit the type of computation. You might object that a human computer would not be restricted to moving just one square at a time—or, for that matter, to examining just one square at a time. In fact, Turing's original definition allowed the head to move any number of squares, up to some maximum value L. But as long as there is a limit to the number of squares the head can move in one step, and it certainly seems reasonable that there should be, making this limit one is really no less general: a jump of ten squares to the right would be accomplished in ten moves, and the machine could "remember" how far it had progressed in the sequence of moves by having a corresponding sequence of states set aside specifically for that ten-move sequence. Similarly, examining a block of contiguous squares, though it might be done by a human "at a glance," can be done by the machine one square at a time.

No doubt there are other ways in which the actions of such a machine differ from the actions of a human computer. Nevertheless, the nature of the model provides some basis for suspecting that it really is a general model for computation. To say that it is is simply to say that any "effective computation" whatsoever, any algorithmic procedure that can be carried out by a human being or a team of human beings or a computer, can be carried out by some Turing machine. This statement was first formulated by a logician named Alonzo Church, in the 1930s, and it has come to be known as *Church's thesis*, or the *Church–Turing thesis*. It is not a mathematically precise statement, since we don't have a precise definition of "effective computation" or "algorithmic procedure," so it is not something one can prove. But in the fifty years since the Turing machine's invention, a good bit of evidence has accumulated that has caused Church's thesis to be generally accepted. We shall examine some of the evidence later, after we have defined the machines more precisely and looked at some examples.

Before we proceed, however, notice in particular that we are no longer concentrating exclusively on language recognition when we speak of computation, although it will still make sense to consider the languages that can be "accepted" by Turing machines. Since we are not restricted to yes-or-no answers, we may attempt to compute any arbitrary function from strings of input symbols to strings of output symbols. As we shall see, it will be easy to include numerical functions in this discussion. If we find some functions that *cannot* be computed using Turing machines, and if we believe the Church–Turing thesis, we will be able to draw conclusions about computability in general.

16.2   DEFINITIONS; TMs AS LANGUAGE ACCEPTORS

Definition 16.1. A *Turing machine* (TM) is a 5-tuple $T = (Q, \Sigma, \Gamma, q_0, \delta)$, where

Q is a finite set of *states*, assumed not to contain h, the *halt* state (the same symbol will be used for the halt state of every TM);

Σ, the *input alphabet*, is a finite set of symbols;

Γ, the *tape alphabet*, is a finite set with $\Sigma \subseteq \Gamma$; Γ is assumed not to contain Δ, the *blank* symbol;

$q_0 \in Q$ (the *initial* state); and

δ is a partial function (i.e., possibly undefined at certain points) from $Q \times (\Gamma \cup \{\Delta\})$ to $(Q \cup \{h\}) \times (\Gamma \cup \{\Delta\}) \times \{R, L, S\}$.

We view the TM as having a *tape*, with a left end but infinite to the right, marked off into squares. Each square can hold a single symbol of $\Gamma \cup \{\Delta\}$, but at any point of a TM's operation all but a finite number of these squares will contain the symbol Δ, and initially the only nonblank symbols on the tape are elements of Σ. For convenience, we think of the squares being numbered, left-to-right, beginning with 0. The TM also has a *tape head*, which allows it to read from, and write to, one square of the tape. If $q \in Q$, $r \in Q \cup \{h\}$, $X, Y \in \Gamma \cup \{\Delta\}$, and $D \in \{R, L, S\}$, we interpret the formula

$$\delta(q, X) = (r, Y, D)$$

to mean that when the TM is in state q, and the symbol on the tape square being examined is X, the TM replaces X by Y on that square of the tape, changes to state r, and either moves the tape head one square left, moves it one square right, or leaves it stationary, depending on whether D is L, R, or S, respectively. If $r = h$, we say that the move causes the TM to *halt*. Notice that once it has halted, the TM cannot move further, since δ is not defined at any pair (h, X).

You will recall from Chapter 12 that for a pushdown automaton, the value of the transition function was a *set* of pairs, reflecting the fact that a PDA is an inherently nondeterministic machine. A Turing machine, at this point, is a deterministic machine. We do allow $\delta(q, X)$ to be undefined, but if it *is* defined, it is a single triple. In the next chapter we shall consider nondeterministic Turing machines, but it will turn out, just as in the case of FAs, that allowing nondeterminism does not increase the computing power of these machines.

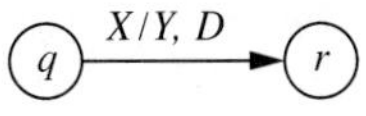

FIGURE 16-1
A single Turing machine move illustrated.

It is often helpful to illustrate the transition function of a TM by drawing a "transition diagram," much as we did for FAs. The move

$$\delta(q, X) = (r, Y, D)$$

(where D is R, L, or S) will be represented as in Fig. 16-1.

To describe the machine completely at any point, we must specify the state it is in, the contents of the tape, and the current head position. Accordingly, we will say that a *configuration* of the TM is a pair $(q, x\underline{a}y)$, where q is a state, $x, y \in (\Gamma \cup \{\Delta\})^*$, $a \in \Gamma \cup \{\Delta\}$, and the underlined symbol represents the current position of the head. This is interpreted to mean that x begins in square 0 on the tape, or that x is null and a is in square 0; that the string y appears immediately after a; and that all squares beyond y are blank. If w is a string of length > 1 and we write $(q, x\underline{w}y)$, we mean that the tape head is positioned at the first symbol of w. Normally, when we specify a configuration $(q, x\underline{a}y)$, y will either be the null string or have last symbol nonblank, although there would be no harm in thinking of $(q, x\underline{a}y)$ and $(q, x\underline{a}y\Delta)$, for example, as specifying the same configuration.

Just as in the case of pushdown automata, it is convenient to be able to trace a sequence of moves by examining the configurations at each step. We say

$$(q, x\underline{a}y) \vdash_T (r, z\underline{b}w)$$

if T passes from the configuration on the left to that on the right in one move, and

$$(q, x\underline{a}y) \vdash_T^* (r, z\underline{b}w)$$

if T passes from the first configuration to the second in zero or more moves. If there is no ambiguity, $\vdash_T$ and $\vdash_T^*$ are often shortened to $\vdash$ and $\vdash^*$, respectively. For example, if T is currently in the configuration $(q, aab\underline{a}\Delta a)$, and $\delta(q, a) = (r, \Delta, L)$, we would write

$$(q, aab\underline{a}\Delta a) \vdash (r, aa\underline{b}\Delta\Delta a)$$

Before long, we shall consider combining two or more TMs by "executing" them consecutively. This is reasonable. We may think of a TM as the embodiment of a specific algorithm, which is determined by the transition function of the TM. We often describe the solution to a problem in a way such as this: "First execute algorithm A; then execute algorithm B; . . . ," so it makes sense intuitively to imagine one TM picking up where another leaves off. For this reason, we do not assume that when a TM starts, its head is always scanning square 0 of the tape. However, there are conventions that we follow when we use one TM in isolation. The way we provide the *input* string x to a TM is to place x on the tape beginning in square 1, and to start the TM in the configuration $(q_0, \underline{\Delta}x)$. If this TM were to be used, and given input, as part of some larger computation, the important thing when it started would not be that it start in square 0, but only that it start with tape contents $y\underline{\Delta}x$, for some string y.

Now that we have defined the input to a TM, we can say how a TM *accepts* a string. An input string $x \in \Sigma^*$ is accepted by T if starting T with input x leads eventually to a halting configuration. In other words, x is accepted if for some strings y and z in $(\Gamma \cup \{\Delta\})^*$ and some $a \in \Gamma \cup \{\Delta\}$,

$$(q_0, \underline{\Delta}x) \vdash_T^* (h, y\underline{a}z)$$

In this situation we say *T halts on input x*. The *language accepted by T* is the set of input strings that are accepted by T.

Notice that there are several ways that an input string can fail to be accepted by a TM. First, it can lead to some nonhalting configuration from which the TM cannot move (i.e., to some combination of nonhalting state and current tape symbol for which the transition function is undefined). Second, it is conceivable that at some point in processing the string, the head is at square 0 and the next move calls for moving the head left, off the end of the tape. In either of these cases, we shall say that the TM *crashes*, which of course is not the same as saying that it halts. Third, an input string might cause the TM to begin a never-ending sequence of moves (an infinite loop). To put it another way, we might say that a string can fail to be accepted by being explicitly *rejected*, as a result of the machine's crashing, or it can fail to be accepted because the machine is unable to make up its mind as to whether to accept. The difference between these outcomes is that in the second case there *is* no outcome. Someone waiting for the answer is left in suspense; the machine continues to make moves, but the observer can never be sure that it is not about to halt. This difference cannot be defined away, as it turns out. The potential indecisiveness of the TM, because of the possibility of infinite loops, will have significant implications in the theory of computation, and we shall be discussing it in more detail later. For now, however, we shall look at examples in which the problem doesn't arise—languages that are accepted in such a way that every input string is either accepted or explicitly rejected.

Example 16.1. Let's not be too ambitious with our first example; consider $L = \{x \in \{a, b\}^* |\ x$ contains the substring $aba\}$. Of course, we can easily draw an FA recognizing L, as in Fig. 16-2a. It is not surprising that constructing a TM is also easy, and that we can do it so that the two transition diagrams look much alike. The TM is illustrated in Fig. 16-2b.

There are five states in our TM, and the input and tape alphabets are both $\{a, b\}$. A few observations about the machine are in order. First, since the language is regular, the TM is able to process input strings essentially the way an FA is forced to: without changing any tape symbols, and moving the head to the right at each step. We would expect that to recognize a nonregular language, this type of processing will not be sufficient. Second, notice that as soon as the TM discovers aba on the tape it halts, and thereby accepts the entire input string, even though it may not have read to the end. This is in contrast to an FA or a PDA; in either of these cases, "accept" means to accept the string of input symbols read so far. Of course, some TMs must read all the input, even if the languages they accept are regular. For $L_1 = \{x \in \{a, b\}^* |\ x$ ends with $aba\}$, for example, an FA and a TM are shown in Fig. 16-3. Since all moves in the TM are to the right, the TM cannot halt without reading the blank to the right of the last input symbol.

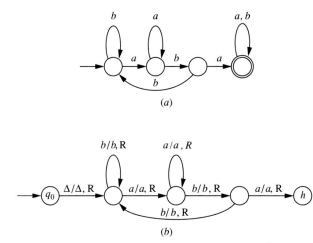

FIGURE 16-2
An FA and a TM to accept $\{a, b\}^*\{aba\}\{a, b\}^*$.

Example 16.2. Example 16.1 does not really exhibit very much of the power of Turing machines; it's really just a dressed-up FA. Let us consider the nonregular language L of palindromes over $\{a, b\}$ and construct a TM to accept it. You can get a hint as to how to proceed by imagining how you might check a long string by hand to see if it was a palindrome. One way would be to position your two forefingers at the two ends; as your eyes jump repeatedly back and forth comparing the two end symbols, your fingers, which are the markers that tell your eyes how far to go, gradually move toward the center. This is very close to the way our TM will do it. The markers at each end will be blank squares. Moving the markers toward the center corresponds to erasing (i.e., changing to blanks) symbols that have already been tested. The head moves repeatedly back and forth, comparing the symbol at one end of the remaining nonblank string to the symbol at the

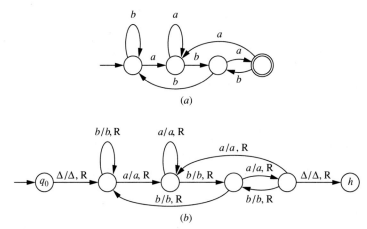

FIGURE 16-3
An FA and a TM to accept $\{a, b\}^*\{aba\}$.

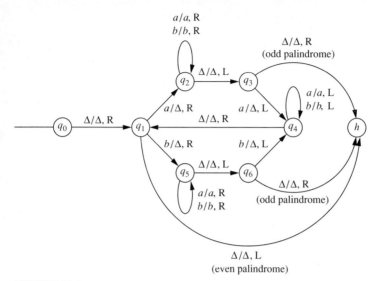

FIGURE 16-4
A TM to accept palindromes over $\{a, b\}$.

other. The transition diagram is shown in Fig. 16-4. Again the tape alphabet is the same as the input alphabet $\{a, b\}$.

We trace the moves made by the machine for three different input strings: a non-palindrome, an even-length palindrome, and an odd-length palindrome.

$(q_0, \underline{\Delta}abaa)$	$\vdash (q_1, \Delta\underline{a}baa)$	$\vdash (q_2, \Delta\Delta\underline{b}aa)$	$\vdash^* (q_2, \Delta\Delta baa\underline{\Delta})$
	$\vdash (q_3, \Delta\Delta b\underline{a}a)$	$\vdash (q_4, \Delta\Delta b\underline{a})$	$\vdash^* (q_4, \Delta\underline{\Delta}ba)$
	$\vdash (q_1, \Delta\Delta\underline{b}a)$	$\vdash (q_5, \Delta\Delta\Delta\underline{a})$	$\vdash (q_5, \Delta\Delta\Delta a\underline{\Delta})$
	$\vdash (q_6, \Delta\Delta\Delta\underline{a})$	(crash)	
$(q_0, \underline{\Delta}aa)$	$\vdash (q_1, \Delta\underline{a}a)$	$\vdash (q_2, \Delta\Delta\underline{a})$	$\vdash (q_2, \Delta\Delta a\underline{\Delta})$
	$\vdash (q_3, \Delta\Delta\underline{a})$	$\vdash (q_4, \Delta\underline{\Delta})$	$\vdash (q_1, \Delta\Delta\underline{\Delta})$
	$\vdash (h, \Delta\Delta\Delta\underline{\Delta})$	(accept)	
$(q_0, \underline{\Delta}aba)$	$\vdash (q_1, \Delta\underline{a}ba)$	$\vdash (q_2, \Delta\Delta\underline{b}a)$	$\vdash^* (q_2, \Delta\Delta ba\underline{\Delta})$
	$\vdash (q_3, \Delta\Delta b\underline{a})$	$\vdash (q_4, \Delta\Delta\underline{b})$	$\vdash (q_4, \Delta\underline{\Delta}b)$
	$\vdash (q_1, \Delta\Delta\underline{b})$	$\vdash (q_5, \Delta\Delta\Delta\underline{\Delta})$	$\vdash (q_6, \Delta\Delta\underline{\Delta})$
	$\vdash (h, \Delta\Delta\Delta\underline{\Delta})$	(accept)	

Example 16.3. For our third example illustrating a TM as a language recognizer, we try recognizing a language we know to be non-context-free. Let $L = \{ss \mid s \in \{a, b\}^*\}$ (see Example 15.2). The idea behind the TM will be to divide the processing into two parts: first, finding the middle of the string, and making it easy for the TM to distinguish the symbols in the second half from those in the first half; second, comparing the two halves. We accomplish the first task by working our way in from both ends simultaneously, gradually changing symbols closer and closer to the middle to their upper-case versions. This means that although the input alphabet is $\{a, b\}$, our tape alphabet will include A and B as well. Eventually we end up in the middle—assuming, of course, that the string is of even length—and then we may change the symbols in the first half back to their original

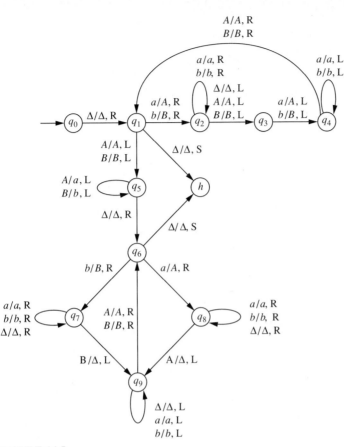

FIGURE 16-5
A Turing machine to accept $\{ss \mid s \in \{a, b\}^*\}$.

form. Now we can start at the beginning of the string again and, for each lower-case symbol in the first half, compare it to the corresponding upper-case symbol in the second. We keep track of our progress by changing lower-case symbols to upper-case and erasing the matching upper-case symbols. There are two ways a string can be rejected. If its length is odd, the TM will discover this in the first part of the processing; if it has even length but a symbol in the first half doesn't match the corresponding symbol in the second half, the TM will crash during the second phase. The TM suggested by this discussion is shown in Fig. 16-5.

On a machine such as this one, you can certainly increase your confidence that it correctly recognizes the desired language by tracing it on a variety of input strings. Again, let us consider three strings: one of odd length, which should be rejected during the first phase of the processing; one of even length that is not of the desired form; and a string in the language.

$(q_0, \underline{\Delta}aba)$ $\vdash (q_1, \Delta\underline{a}ba)$ $\vdash (q_2, \Delta A\underline{b}a)$ $\vdash^* (q_2, \Delta Aba\underline{\Delta})$
$\vdash (q_3, \Delta Ab\underline{a})$ $\vdash (q_4, \Delta A\underline{b}A)$ $\vdash (q_4, \Delta \underline{A}bA)$
$\vdash (q_1, \Delta A\underline{b}A)$ $\vdash (q_2, \Delta AB\underline{A})$ $\vdash (q_3, \Delta A\underline{B}A)$ (crash)

$(q_0, \underline{\Delta}abaa)$ $\vdash (q_1, \Delta\underline{a}baa)$ $\vdash (q_2, \Delta A\underline{b}aa)$ $\vdash^* (q_2, \Delta Abaa\underline{\Delta})$

$\vdash (q_3, \Delta Ab\underline{a}\underline{a})$ $\vdash (q_4, \Delta Ab\underline{a}A)$ $\vdash^* (q_4, \Delta\underline{A}baA)$

$\vdash (q_1, \Delta A\underline{b}aA)$ $\vdash (q_2, \Delta AB\underline{a}A)$ $\vdash (q_2, \Delta ABa\underline{A})$

$\vdash (q_3, \Delta AB\underline{a}A)$ $\vdash (q_4, \Delta A\underline{B}AA)$ $\vdash (q_1, \Delta AB\underline{A}A)$

$\vdash (q_5, \Delta A\underline{B}AA)$ $\vdash (q_5, \Delta\underline{A}bAA)$ $\vdash (q_5, \underline{\Delta}abAA)$

(first phase completed)

$\vdash (q_6, \Delta\underline{a}bAA)$ $\vdash (q_8, \Delta A\underline{b}AA)$ $\vdash (q_8, \Delta Ab\underline{A}A)$

$\vdash (q_9, \Delta A\underline{b}\Delta A)$ $\vdash (q_9, \Delta A\underline{b}\Delta A)$ $\vdash (q_6, \Delta A\underline{b}\Delta A)$

$\vdash (q_7, \Delta AB\underline{\Delta}A)$ $\vdash (q_7, \Delta AB\Delta\underline{A})$ (crash)

$(q_0, \underline{\Delta}abab)$ $\vdash^* \dots$

(same moves as in previous case, down to the third-from-last)

$\vdash (q_6, \Delta A\underline{b}\Delta B)$ $\vdash (q_7, \Delta AB\underline{\Delta}B)$ $\vdash (q_7, \Delta AB\Delta\underline{B})$

$\vdash (q_9, \Delta AB\underline{\Delta})$ $\vdash (q_9, \Delta A\underline{B})$ $\vdash (q_6, \Delta AB\underline{\Delta})$

$\vdash (h, \Delta AB\underline{\Delta})$ (accept)

16.3   COMBINING TURING MACHINES

Just as a complicated algorithm is formulated by decomposing it into subalgorithms, a complicated Turing machine can often be described by specifying smaller TMs that are combined to form it. At this point, we must say a little more precisely how this is done. Suppose $T_1 = (Q_1, \Sigma_1, \Gamma_1, q_1, \delta_1)$ and $T_2 = (Q_2, \Sigma_2, \Gamma_2, q_2, \delta_2)$. We assume that $\Gamma_1 \subseteq \Sigma_2$; we may also assume, by renaming states if necessary, that $Q_1 \cap Q_2 = \varnothing$. We form the composite machine $T = (Q, \Sigma_1, \Gamma_2, q_0, \delta)$ by letting T start in the initial state of T_1 and identifying the halt state of T_1 with the initial state q_2 of T_2. More precisely,

$$Q = Q_1 \cup Q_2 \quad \text{and} \quad q_0 = q_1$$

For any $q \in Q_1$ and $X \in \Gamma_1 \cup \{\Delta\}$, if

$$\delta_1(q, X) = (r, Y, D)$$

then

$$\delta(q, X) = \begin{cases} (r, Y, D) & \text{if } r \neq h \\ (q_2, Y, D) & \text{if } r = h \end{cases}$$

For any $q \in Q_2$ and $X \in \Gamma_2 \cup \{\Delta\}$,

$$\delta(q, X) = \delta_2(q, X)$$

T acts like T_1, up to the point where T_1 would halt or crash; if T_1 halts, T begins to act like T_2, as if it were starting in the initial state of T_2, with its head scanning the square of the tape at which T_1 stopped.

We might write this composite machine T_1T_2. If we were trying to illustrate it in a larger context, in a manner similar to a transition diagram but without explicitly showing the states, we might also write

$$T_1 \to T_2$$

We can also make the composition conditional, depending on the current tape symbol when T_1 halts. Thus for some $a \in \Gamma_1 \cup \{\Delta\}$, we might write

$$T_1 \overset{a}{\to} T_2$$

to stand for the composite machine $T_1 T' T_2$, where T' is described by the diagram in Fig. 16-6.

$\longrightarrow \bigcirc \overset{a/a,\,\mathrm{S}}{\longrightarrow} (h)$ **FIGURE 16-6**

This composite TM's action can be described informally as follows: execute the TM T_1; if and when T_1 halts, either begin to execute T_2 (if the current tape symbol is a) or crash (if the current symbol is not a).

In order to be able to describe TMs with smaller TM components and still avoid developing a new notation in which every primitive operation is formulated as a separate TM, it will occasionally be useful to use a "mixed" notation, in which some but not all of the states of a TM are shown. For example, the diagram in Fig. 16-7a, which is an abbreviated version of the one in Fig. 16-7b, has an obvious meaning: If the current tape symbol is a, execute the TM T; if it is b, halt; and if it is anything else, crash; in the first case, repeat the execution of T until T halts scanning some symbol other than a; if at that point the tape symbol is b, halt, otherwise crash.

In the case of a simple composition of two TMs, we have given a precise description of the composite machine—its states and its individual transitions. We stop short of doing this in sufficient generality to take care of all more complicated combinations, such as the one above, but it is usually clear in specific examples what is involved.

There is, however, one possible source of confusion relating to the notation we are adopting. Consider a TM of the form $T = T_1 \overset{a}{\to} T_2$. If T_1 halts scanning some symbol not explicitly specified (i.e., any symbol other than a), T crashes. However, when T_2 halts, T halts—even though *no* tape symbols are explicitly specified. This might seem slightly inconsistent. We could avoid the problem by saying that if T_1 halts scanning a symbol other than a, T *halts*, but then $T_1 \overset{a}{\to} T_2$ would not be equivalent to the composition $T_1 T' T_2$ described above, and this

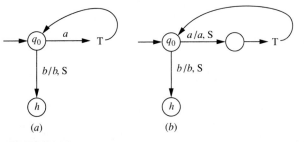

(a)   (b)

FIGURE 16-7

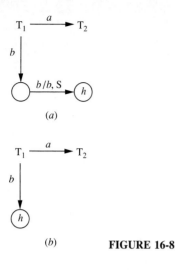

(a)

(b)   **FIGURE 16-8**

seems undesirable also. In our notation, if at the end of one sub-TM's operation at least one way is specified for the composite TM to continue, then any option that allows the composite TM to halt at that point must be shown explicitly, as in Fig. 16-8a and 16-8b. (The second is a shortened form of the first.)

We have previously said that a single TM is usually thought of as starting at square 0 of the tape, at least if it is to process an input string. However, some TMs that wouldn't make much sense in isolation if this convention were observed (for example, the TM that executes the algorithm "move the tape head one square left") can still be useful in combination with others. It is appropriate to consider the opposite question as well: can a TM that works by itself be depended upon to do its job without crashing when it is used as part of a larger TM? Yes—provided that when it begins, the tape has been properly prepared. For example, as we have already observed, a TM expecting to find an input string needs to begin in a configuration of the form $(q_0, y\underline{\Delta}z)$, where z is a string, possibly null, of nonblank symbols. The symbols of y are irrelevant. The reason is that if the TM avoids crashing when started with the configuration $(q_0, \underline{\Delta}z)$, the head will never attempt to move to the left of the blank; therefore, starting with $(q_0, y\underline{\Delta}z)$, the TM will never see any of the symbols of y.

Notice that at this point we have begun to pay more attention to the *output* of a TM, the string of symbols left on the tape when the TM halts, than we did in our first three examples. There we were not concerned at all with the final configuration of the machine, except for the question of whether it was a halting configuration. In the case of a TM that is used as an intermediate component of a larger machine, however, it is likely that its sole purpose is to change in some specific way the tape contents and/or head position, so as to create a beginning configuration appropriate for the component that follows.

There are a number of standard tape operations that will obviously be useful in many settings, and that are therefore candidates for TM building blocks. Some of them, such as moving the head a specified number of positions in one direction or the other, writing a specific symbol in the current square, and searching to the right for a specified symbol, are straightforward and don't need to be spelled out. We consider a few slightly more involved operations.

Example 16.4 (Copying a string). Let us construct a TM that creates a copy of the input string, to the right of the input but with a blank separating the original from the copy. We must be careful to specify the final position of the head as well; let's say that if the initial configuration is $(q_0, \underline{\Delta}x)$ (where x is a string of nonblank symbols), the final configuration should be $(h, \underline{\Delta}x\Delta x)$. The TM will examine the first symbol, copy it in the right place, examine the second, copy it, and so on. It will keep track of its progress by changing the symbols in the input string to uppercase. We shall assume for simplicity that the input alphabet is $\{a, b\}$, but all that is needed in a more general situation is a new "uppercase" symbol in the tape alphabet for each symbol in the input alphabet, from which the original symbol can be reconstructed. Finally, when the string has been copied, the uppercase letters will be changed back to lowercase. The resulting TM is shown in Fig. 16-9.

Example 16.5 (Deleting a symbol). It may sometimes be necessary to delete a symbol from a string—i.e., to change the tape contents from $y\underline{a}z$ to $y\underline{z}$, where $y \in (\Sigma \cup \{\Delta\})^*$, $z \in \Sigma^*$, and $a \in \Sigma \cup \{\Delta\}$. (Remember: $y\underline{z}$ means that the head is centered on the first symbol of z.) Again, we assume that the input alphabet and the tape alphabet are both $\{a, b\}$. The TM starts by replacing the symbol in the current square by a blank, so that the square can be located easily later. Then it moves to the right end of the string and makes a single pass from right to left through the string, moving symbols one square to the left as it goes. The diagram appears in Fig. 16-10. The states labeled q_Δ, q_a, and q_b are what allow the machine to remember the symbol from the previous square (the square to the right), which it will write in the current square. In state q_a, for example, the symbol to be written is a, and the current symbol, which the a replaces, determines whether the TM should stay in state q_a and move left, change to state q_b and move left, or halt.

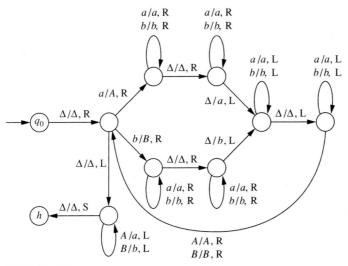

FIGURE 16-9
A Turing machine to copy strings.

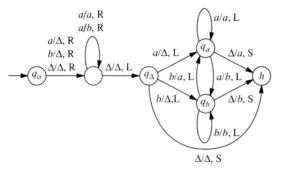

FIGURE 16-10
A Turing machine to delete a symbol.

Notice that *inserting* a symbol a, or changing the tape contents from $y\underline{z}$ to $ya\underline{z}$, would be done virtually the same way, except that the single pass would go from left to right, and the move that starts it off would be writing a instead of Δ. You are asked to complete this machine in Exercise 16.8.

Another observation is in order at this point, and it applies not only to this example but to many other situations as well. We have formulated the "Delete" TM so that it transforms $ya\underline{z}$ to $y\underline{z}$. What if it is called when the the tape contents are not $ya\underline{z}$, but $ya\underline{z}\Delta w$, where w is some arbitrary string of tape symbols and blanks? It might seem as though the TM should finish with $y\underline{z}\Delta w$ on the tape, so that every nonblank symbol to the right of a is moved over. Of course, the machine we designed doesn't do this, and in fact it could not reasonably be expected to. Unless we know something about the computations that have gone on before, or unless we have previously managed to mark the rightmost nonblank symbol so that the TM can recognize it, there is no way of finding it. The instructions "Move the head to the square containing the rightmost nonblank symbol" are not ordinarily something that a TM can execute. In general, a TM is designed according to specifications, which say that if it starts in a particular sort of configuration, it should halt in some other specified configuration. The specifications may say nothing about the result if the TM starts in some different configuration; the TM may meet its specifications and yet behave unpredictably, perhaps even crash, in these abnormal situations.

16.4   COMPUTING A FUNCTION WITH A TM

In the sense that the purpose of a computer program is to produce a specified output string for every legal input string, it can be thought of as "computing" a function from one set of strings to another. Let us define how a TM computes a similar function.

Definition 16.2. Let $T = (Q, \Sigma, \Gamma, q_0, \delta)$ be a TM. Let $S \subseteq \Sigma^*$ and $f : S \to \Gamma^*$. T computes f if for each $x \in S$,

$$(q_0, \underline{\Delta}x) \vdash_T^* (h, \underline{\Delta}f(x))$$

and for each x in Σ^* that is not in S, T fails to halt on input x. More generally, a TM can compute a function of several variables. If $k \geq 0$, $S \subseteq (\Sigma^*)^k = \Sigma^* \times \Sigma^* \times \ldots \times \Sigma^*$ (k factors), and $f : S \to \Gamma^*$, then T computes f if for each k-tuple $(x_1, x_2, \ldots, x_k) \in S$,

$$(q_0, \underline{\Delta} x_1 \Delta x_2 \ldots \Delta x_k) \vdash_T^* (h, \underline{\Delta} f(x_1, x_2, \ldots, x_k))$$

and for any other input that is a k-tuple of strings, T fails to halt.

One feature of the definition is worth noting. It is not quite correct to say that a TM computes only one function. For example, if T computes $f : (\Sigma^*)^2 \to \Gamma^*$, then T also computes $f_1 : \Sigma^* \to \Gamma^*$ defined by $f_1(x) = f(x, \Lambda)$. For that matter, since we view functions defined by the same rule on the same domain as different if they have different codomains, it is not correct to say that for some domain S, at most one function on S is computed by a given TM. However, it is true according to our definition that for any specified k and any set $C \subseteq \Gamma^*$, a TM computes at most one function of k variables having codomain C.

Notice that our definition does not allow a TM to compute $f : \Sigma_1^* \to \Sigma_2^*$ unless $\Sigma_1 \subseteq \Sigma_2$. This is not a significant limitation, however, since we can define $f' : \Sigma_1^* \to (\Sigma_1 \cup \Sigma_2)^*$ by the formula $f'(x) = f(x)$. Our definition can accommodate the function f', and the only difference between the two functions is that their codomains are different. For this reason it is sometimes convenient to be a little less precise and speak of a TM computing $f : \Sigma_1^* \to \Sigma_2^*$ even when $\Sigma_1 \not\subseteq \Sigma_2$.

Numerical functions of numerical arguments can be described in this context, once we choose a way of representing the numbers by strings. We shall restrict ourselves to nonnegative integers, and we shall use the "unary" representation, in which the integer n is represented by the string $1^n = 11 \ldots 1$.

Definition 16.3. Let $T = (Q, \{1\}, \Gamma, q_0, \delta)$ be a TM. Denote by $\mathcal{N}$ the set of natural numbers. If $S \subseteq \mathcal{N}$, T computes $f : S \to \mathcal{N}$ if for every $n \in S$,

$$(q_0, \underline{\Delta} 1^n) \vdash_T^* (h, \underline{\Delta} 1^{f(n)})$$

and for every n not in S, T fails to halt on input 1^n. If $k \geq 0$ and $S \subseteq \mathcal{N}^k$, T computes $f : S \to \mathcal{N}$ if for every $(n_1, n_2, \ldots, n_k) \in S$,

$$(q_0, \underline{\Delta} 1^{n_1} \Delta 1^{n_2} \ldots \Delta 1^{n_k}) \vdash_T^* (h, \underline{\Delta} 1^{f(n_1, \ldots, n_k)})$$

and T fails to halt if the input is a k-tuple not in S.

Later we shall discuss some systematic ways of constructing TMs to compute functions; for now, here are two examples. More examples are to be found in the exercises.

Example 16.6   (Concatenation/addition). We may consider the concatenation function $Concat : \Sigma^* \times \Sigma^* \to \Sigma^*$. A TM computing this function is obtained very simply from the *Delete* TM of Example 16.5 and is shown in Fig. 16-11 for the alphabet $\{a, b\}$. Since nonnegative integers are represented by strings of 1's, and concatenating two such strings corresponds to adding the numbers they represent, a simplified version of this TM computes the addition function from $\mathcal{N} \times \mathcal{N} \to \mathcal{N}$.

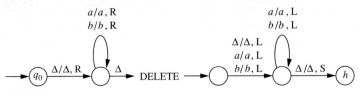

FIGURE 16-11
A Turing machine for concatenating strings.

Example 16.7 (The characteristic function of a set). Let L be a language in Σ^*. The *characteristic function* of L is the function $\chi_L : \Sigma^* \to \{0, 1\}$ defined by

$$\chi_L(x) = \begin{cases} 1 & \text{if } x \in L \\ 0 & \text{otherwise} \end{cases}$$

Computing the function χ_L is therefore very similar to something we have already done, in special cases, in Section 16.2: building a TM that accepts L. The difference is that any string that previously caused the machine to halt will now cause our TM to halt in the configuration $(h, \underline{\Delta}1)$, and any other string will cause our TM to halt in the configuration $(h, \underline{\Delta}0)$. If we take L to be the language of palindromes in $\{a, b\}^*$, as in Example 16.2, the new TM is illustrated in Fig. 16-12. Compare this to the TM shown in Fig. 16-4.

As we observed in Section 16.2, a TM *accepting* a language L "recognizes" L only in a weak sense: it halts if the input string is in L and not otherwise, but it may fail to halt by looping forever. A TM computing the function χ_L is better. It is guaranteed to decide explicitly, for each $x \in \{a, b\}^*$, whether $x \in L$, and it does so in such a way that an observer watching the computation is assured of getting the answer in a finite amount of

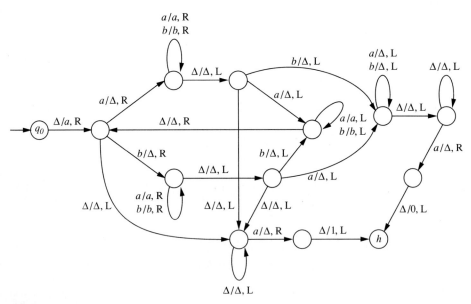

FIGURE 16-12
Computing χ_L for the set of palindromes.

time. It might seem, of course, as though this is what TMs should always do. Why would anyone want a TM of the first type, which may provide an answer only if the answer is yes? The answer is that a machine of this type might be the best possible! We shall return to this question in Chapter 18.

EXERCISES

16.1. Trace the TM in Fig. 16-5 on the input string $a\,a\,b\,a$. Keep track of the state, tape contents, and head position, as in Example 16.3.

16.2. Table 16-1 is a transition table for a TM.
  (a) What is the final tape configuration if the input is ab?
  (b) What is the final tape configuration if the input is $ba\,a$?
  (c) Describe in general what the TM does, given an arbitrary input in $\{a, b\}^*$.

16.3. Draw transition diagrams for TMs accepting the following languages.
  (a) $\{a^i b^j \,|\, i < j\}$
  (b) $\{x \in \{a, b\}^* \,|\, N_a(x) = N_b(x)\}$
  (c) $\{a^{3i} b^i \,|\, i \geq 0\}$
  (d) $\{a^n b^n c^n \,|\, n \geq 0\}$
  (e) The language of balanced strings of parentheses
  (f) The language of all nonpalindromes over $\{a, b\}$

16.4. In Example 16.3, a TM is given that accepts the language $\{ss \,|\, s \in \{a, b\}^*\}$. Draw a TM that accepts this language and has no tape symbols other than a and b.

16.5. Show that any language that can be accepted by a TM can be accepted by a TM that does not crash on any input.

16.6. Suppose L is accepted by the TM T. What can be said about L in each of the following cases?
  (a) T moves its tape head right on each move.
  (b) T never changes any symbol on its tape.

16.7. Suppose T is a TM. We would like to construct a new TM U that operates as follows. First T is executed; if and when T halts, another TM is executed, which halts if and only if the number of nonblank symbols left on the tape by T is even.
  (a) Why may it not be possible to express U in the form TT_1 for any TM T_1?
  (b) Describe a modification T' of T, and a TM T_1, so that U can be constructed by the formula $U = T'T_1$.

TABLE 16.1

q	σ	$\delta(q, \sigma)$	q	σ	$\delta(q, \sigma)$
q_0	Δ	$(q_1, \Delta, \mathrm{R})$	q_4	b	(q_4, b, R)
q_1	a	(q_1, a, R)	q_4	Δ	(q_7, a, L)
q_1	b	(q_1, b, R)	q_5	Δ	(q_6, b, R)
q_1	Δ	$(q_2, \Delta, \mathrm{L})$	q_6	a	(q_6, a, R)
q_2	a	$(q_3, \Delta, \mathrm{R})$	q_6	b	(q_6, b, R)
q_2	b	$(q_5, \Delta, \mathrm{R})$	q_6	Δ	(q_7, b, L)
q_2	Δ	(h, Δ, R)	q_7	a	(q_7, a, L)
q_3	Δ	(q_4, a, R)	q_7	b	(q_7, b, L)
q_4	a	(q_4, a, R)	q_7	Δ	$(q_2, \Delta, \mathrm{L})$

16.8. Draw the *Insert*(σ) TM, which changes the tape contents from $y\underline{z}$ to $y\underline{\sigma}z$. Here $y \in (\Sigma \cup \{\Delta\})^*$, $\sigma \in \Sigma \cup \{\Delta\}$, and $z \in \Sigma^*$. You may assume that $\Sigma = \{a, b\}$.

16.9. In each case, draw a TM that computes the indicated function. (In the first six parts, the function is from $\mathcal{N}$ to $\mathcal{N}$. In the last two parts, let $\Sigma = \{a, b\}$.)
  (a) $f(x) = x + 2$
  (b) $f(x) = 2x$
  (c) $f(x) = x^2$
  (d) $f(x) = x \bmod 2$
  (e) $f(x) = x \operatorname{div} 2$
  (f) $f(x)$ = the smallest integer greater than or equal to $\log_2(x + 1)$ (i.e., $f(0) = 0$, $f(1) = 1$, $f(2) = f(3) = 2$, $f(4) = f(5) = f(6) = f(7) = 3$, etc.)
  (g) $f : \Sigma^* \times \Sigma^* \to \{0, 1\}$ defined by $f(x, y) = 1$ if $x = y$, $f(x, y) = 0$ otherwise
  (h) $f : \Sigma^* \to \Sigma^*$ defined by $f(x) = REV(x)$

16.10. The TM shown in Fig. 16-13 computes a function f from $\{a, b\}^*$ to $\{a, b\}^*$. For any string $x \in \{a, b\}^*$, describe the string $f(x)$.

16.11. Draw a TM that takes as input a string of 0s and 1s, interprets it as the binary representation of a nonnegative integer, and leaves as output the unary representation of that integer (i.e., a string of that many 1's).

16.12. In Fig. 16-14 is a TM that accepts the language $\{scs | s \in \{a, b\}^*\}$. Modify it so as to obtain a TM that computes the characteristic function of the same language.

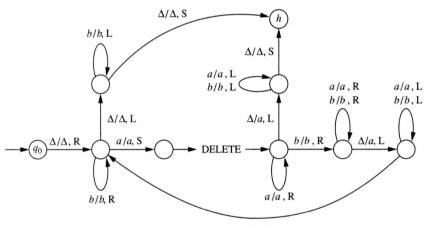

FIGURE 16-13

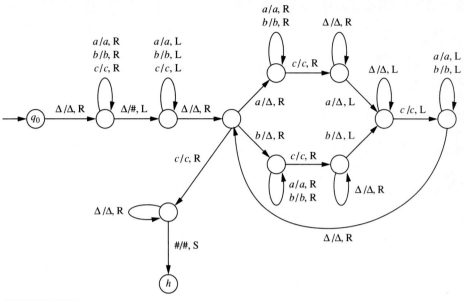

FIGURE 16-14

CHAPTER
17

VARIATIONS OF TURING MACHINES

17.1 TMS WITH DOUBLY-INFINITE TAPES

We have in Chapter 16 described a specific abstract machine that is the primary model of computation we will be using for the remainder of the book. Although there are obvious analogies between the operation of such a machine and the actions of a human "computer," it is certainly not the only possible way to formulate a general model of computation, and it may not even be the most natural. In this chapter, we consider possible variations on, and generalizations of, the basic Turing machine. One reason for studying these is simply that they are viable alternatives to our basic model and have been investigated for their own sake. Another reason is that they are representative of a number of possible modifications of the TM that might seem to have the potential for increasing its computing power, yet can be shown not to increase it. Thus, they constitute a sort of evidence of the generality of the Turing machine, evidence to support the Church–Turing thesis; by considering them, and by seeing in each case that an ordinary TM can do everything they can, one can perhaps appreciate better the TM's flexibility and power.

When we compare two classes of abstract machines as to their "computing power," it is important to pin down precisely the criteria that we are using. At this point, we are not discussing speed, efficiency, or convenience; we are concerned

298

only with whether the two types of machines are able to solve the same problems and get the same answers. Of course, even if we know that two machines have the same power in this sense, we may find that one is more convenient to use; in fact, the most important reason for introducing some of the generalizations of Turing machines is that they *are* more convenient, or easier to understand, in specific applications. Any machine in the extended family of Turing machines gives an "answer," first by halting or failing to halt, and second by producing a particular output. Thus, if we wish to show that of machines in this family, those of type B are at least as powerful as those of type A, we will need to show that for any machine T_A of type A, there is a machine T_B of type B that halts on exactly the same input strings as T_A and, when it halts on a particular input, produces the same output as T_A.

First, we mention briefly a few minor variations on the basic model, each of them slightly more restrictive, which are often used. One possibility is to require that in each move the tape head move either to the right or to the left. In this version, the values of the transition function δ are elements of $Q \times (\Gamma \cup \{\Delta\}) \times \{L,R\}$ instead of $Q \times (\Gamma \cup \{\Delta\}) \times \{L,R,S\}$. A second possibility is to say that a move can include writing a tape symbol or moving the tape head but not both. In this case δ would take values in $Q \times (\Gamma \cup \{\Delta\} \cup \{L,R\})$ (where L and R are assumed not to be elements of Γ). It is not difficult to see that neither restriction changes the power of the machine; you are referred to Exercises 17.1 and 17.2 for the details.

The first generalization we shall discuss in detail is one in which the tape is infinite in both directions and, as before, initially blank in all but a finite number of squares. We think of the squares as being numbered left to right, but now the numbers include all negative integers as well as all nonnegative. A configuration can still be described by a pair $(q, x\underline{a}y)$, except that there is no assumption about which square x begins in. All squares preceding x and following y are blank; the tape head is scanning the square containing a; x either is null or has a nonblank leftmost symbol; and y either is null or has a nonblank rightmost symbol. As before, we assume that if the TM receives an input string x, it begins in configuration $(q_0, \Delta x)$. If the TM is viewed as producing output, the output consists of the symbols left on the tape, extending from the leftmost nonblank through the rightmost, when the machine halts.

It may not be obvious how this type of machine compares to the basic model, except that in some sense these have more "room to work." A potentially more important difference is that a TM with a doubly infinite tape cannot crash by attempting to move the head to the left. We now prove that neither of these differences is really significant. The first theorem says, not surprisingly, that machines of this new type are at least as powerful as ordinary TMs. The second theorem states the converse.

Theorem 17.1a. Let $T_1 = (Q_1, \Sigma, \Gamma_1, q_1, \delta_1)$ be an ordinary TM. There is a TM $T_2 = (Q_2, \Sigma, \Gamma_2, q_2, \delta_2)$ with a doubly infinite tape satisfying these properties:

1. $\Gamma_1 \subseteq \Gamma_2$;

2. For any $x \in \Sigma^*$, T_2 halts on input x if and only if T_1 halts on input x; and
3. For any $x \in \Sigma^*$, if $(q_1, \underline{\Delta} x) \vdash_{T_1}^* (h_1, y\underline{a}z)$, then $(q_2, \underline{\Delta} x) \vdash_{T_2}^* (h_2, y'\underline{a}z)$, where

$y = \Delta^k y'$ for some $k \geq 0$. In other words, if T_1 halts on input x, then T_2 halts on input x with the same output as T_1.

Proof. Let

$$\Gamma_2 = \Gamma_1 \cup \Gamma_1' \cup \{\#\} \cup \{\Delta'\}$$

where $\# \notin \Gamma_1$, and $\Gamma_1' \cup \{\Delta'\}$ contains for every symbol $\sigma \in \Gamma_1 \cup \{\Delta\}$ a corresponding symbol σ'. $\#$ will be placed immediately by T_2 in square -1, where it will serve the same purpose in T_2 as the end of the tape in T_1. A symbol in $\Gamma_1' \cup \{\Delta'\}$ will be used only at the end of T_2's operation, to mark temporarily the position in which T_2 is to halt, while T_2 erases the extraneous symbol $\#$. Returning to this position on the tape, T_2 will be able to restore the original symbol in $\Gamma_1 \cup \{\Delta\}$ before halting.

The set Q_2 will contain all the elements of Q_1 in addition to the new states $q_2, q_i,$ $q_h, q_l,$ and q_r. Two moves of T_2 are

$$\delta_2(q_2, \Delta) = (q_i, \Delta, L)$$

$$\delta_2(q_i, \Delta) = (q_1, \#, R)$$

These allow T_2 to place the symbol $\#$ in square -1 and enter essentially the starting configuration of T_1. The moves of T_2 also include all the nonhalting moves of T_1; thus, up to the point where T_1 either halts or tries to move off the tape, T_2's moves will copy those of T_1 exactly. From a state in Q_1, there is no move defined for the tape symbol $\#$. Thus, if T_1 crashes trying to execute the move $\delta(p, X) = (q, Y, L)$, where $q \neq h$, T_2 will crash one move later because its head will be reading the symbol $\#$.

Moves of T_1 that attempt to halt must be handled differently. For each move $\delta_1(p, X) = (h, Y, D)$, we let T_2 make the move $\delta_2(p, X) = (q_h, Y, D)$. $\delta_2(q_h, \#)$ is not defined, so if T_1 actually crashed in trying to halt, T_2 will also crash. Any tape symbol other than $\#$ must be to the right of $\#$; what T_2 must do in this case is to erase the symbol $\#$, return to the current tape position, and halt. It does this by the moves

$$\delta_2(q_h, X) = (q_l, X', L) \qquad \text{(for every } X \in \Gamma_1 \cup \{\Delta\})$$

$$\delta_2(q_l, X) = (q_l, X, L) \qquad \text{(for every } X \in \Gamma_1 \cup \{\Delta\})$$

$$\delta_2(q_l, \#) = (q_r, \Delta, R)$$

$$\delta_2(q_r, X) = (q_r, X, R) \qquad \text{(for every } X \in \Gamma_1 \cup \{\Delta\})$$

$$\delta_2(q_r, X') = (h, X, S) \qquad \text{(for every } X' \in \Gamma_1' \cup \{\Delta'\})$$

It should be clear that T_2 has the desired properties.

Theorem 17.1b. Let $T_1 = (Q_1, \Sigma, \Gamma_1, q_1, \delta_1)$ be a TM with a doubly-infinite tape. There is an ordinary TM $T_2 = (Q_2, \Sigma, \Gamma_2, q_2, \delta_2)$ satisfying these properties:

1. $\Gamma_1 \subseteq \Gamma_2$;
2. for any $x \in \Sigma^*$, T_2 halts on input x if and only if T_1 does; and

3. for any $x \in \Sigma^*$, if $(q_1, \underline{\Delta}x) \vdash_{T_1}^* (h, y\underline{a}z)$, then $(q_2, \underline{\Delta}x) \vdash_{T_2}^* (h, y\underline{a}z)$.

Proof. This time our problem is more complicated: to simulate T_1, a TM having a doubly-infinite tape, using T_2, whose tape has a left end. The basic idea of the simulation will be to treat the tape in T_2 as if it is a "folded" tape, containing the positive side of T_1's tape as well as the portion of the negative side that has been used. Roughly speaking, at any point where T_1 has moved its head k squares and no further beyond square 0, either to the left or to the right, T_2's tape will show the first k negative squares as "folded over," in the sense that the portion of the tape from 1 to k will contain two "tracks"—the first representing the squares from 1 to k, the second those from -1 to $-k$. Square 0 will also contain an extra symbol representing the fold, so that any time T_1's head crosses from one side of the tape to the other, T_2's head can change from one track to the other.

The following diagram shows what we imagine the two tapes to look like at some point. If T_1 is currently scanning square -2, T_2 will be scanning square 2, paying attention to the lower part only.

	-4	-3	-2	-1	0	1	2	3	4	
...		Δ	a	b	a	a	b	a	a	Δ

(↓ above square -2)

0	1	2	3	4	...
a	b	a	a	Δ	
f	a	b	a		

(↑ below square 2)

At this point, we must consider two technical problems: first, how to store two symbols on a single square of T_2's tape, and second, how to let T_2 remember whether it is supposed to be looking at the first symbol (upper track) or second symbol (lower track) in the current square. The first problem can be resolved by letting T_2 have a larger alphabet, containing not only symbols of Γ_1 but *pairs* of symbols of Γ_1, as well as pairs of the form $(\sigma, \mathbf{f})$, where $\sigma \in \Gamma_1$ and $\mathbf{f}$ represents the fold. (In fact, for reasons we shall mention shortly, it will be convenient to enlarge the alphabet even more.) To take care of the second problem, we can allow T_2 to remember both the state of T_1 it is supposed to be in in its simulation of T_1, and which of the two symbols on its tape it is supposed to be examining, by giving it states of the form $(q, \mathbf{r})$ and $(q, \mathbf{l})$, where $q \in Q_1$. $\mathbf{r}$ means it's supposed to be on the right half of T_1's tape and should therefore look at the first symbol in the current square, the one in the upper track; $\mathbf{l}$ refers to the left half.

The first part of T_2's operation will be to place the "fold" marker $\mathbf{f}$ in square 0 and move to state $(q_1, \mathbf{r})$, at which point it is simulating T_1's initial configuration and ready to begin simulating the actual moves of T_1. During this simulation phase, whenever T_1 would move the tape head, T_2 does also, except that if it is currently in one of the states $(q, \mathbf{l})$, it moves in the opposite direction, and whenever it encounters the fold marker it may change tracks. Each time T_2 moves farther from square 0 than it has gone up to that point, it will be able to detect this from the fact that the symbol it sees is a single symbol, not a pair. At this point it will extend the folded portion by converting the single symbol to the appropriate pair before continuing.

After this discussion, it is relatively straightforward to describe more precisely the moves T_2 makes in simulating T_1, up to the point where T_1 halts. Recall that Γ_2 includes

$\Gamma_1 \cup (\Gamma_1 \times \Gamma_1) \cup (\Gamma_1 \times \{\mathbf{f}\})$ as a subset, and that Q_2 includes, in addition to the initial state q_2, the subset $Q_1 \times \{\mathbf{l}, \mathbf{r}\}$.

T_2 starts with the move

$$\delta_2(q_2, \Delta) = ((q_1, \mathbf{r}), (\Delta, \mathbf{f}), S)$$

which has the effect of placing a marker at the fold in the tape and starting off preparing to examine the symbols in the upper track of the tape. It begins to simulate T_1. For each move

$$\delta_1(p, X) = (q, Y, D)$$

made by T_1, where $p \in Q_1$, $q \in Q_1 \cup \{R\}$, $X, Y \in \Gamma_1 \cup \{\Delta\}$, and $D \in \{L, R, S\}$, we need the following moves of T_2. To simplify the notation, let $-D$ denote the direction opposite to D: $-R = L$, $-L = R$, $-S = S$.

(1) For every $Z \in \Gamma_1 \cup \{\Delta\}$,

$$\delta_2((p, \mathbf{r}), (X, Z)) = ((q, \mathbf{r}), (Y, Z), D)$$
$$\delta_2((p, \mathbf{l}), (Z, X)) = ((q, \mathbf{l}), (Z, Y), -D)$$

(2) $\delta_2((p, \mathbf{r}), (X, \mathbf{f})) = \delta((p, \mathbf{l}), (X, \mathbf{f}) = \begin{cases} ((q, \mathbf{l}), (Y, \mathbf{f}), R) & \text{if } D = L \\ ((q, \mathbf{r}), (Y, \mathbf{f}), D) & \text{if } D = R \text{ or } S \end{cases}$

The moves in the first group represent moves of T_1 that occur in any square other than 0. Those in the second represent moves of T_1 from square 0 and may involve shifting T_2's head from one track to the other.

In addition, for each move

$$\delta_1(p, X) = (q, Y, D)$$

T_2 has the moves

(3)

$$\delta_2((p, \mathbf{r}), X) = ((q, \mathbf{r}), (Y, \Delta), D) \qquad \text{and (if } X = \Delta)$$

$$\delta_2((p, \mathbf{l}), \Delta) = ((q, \mathbf{l}), (\Delta, Y), -D)$$

These moves extend the two tracks by one square, as a result of T_1's moving farther away from square 0. In the second case, a nonblank symbol should not be encountered, since the symbol on T_1's tape is in a square to the left of 0 that T_1 is visiting for the first time.

We shall not give a formal proof that these moves allow T_2 to simulate faithfully the moves of T_1 up to the point where it halts, but you should trace a few examples if you're not convinced. (See Exercise 17.3).

If and when T_1 does halt, T_2 moves instead to some state that still allows it to remember which track of the tape it is supposed to be looking at. Before it can halt, it must fix up its tape so that it really is a duplicate of T_1's, with the obvious exception that the nonblank symbols will begin in square 0 or somewhere to the right. For example, if its tape contains

a	b	$\underline{a}$	a	Δ	b	a	a
$\mathbf{f}$	Δ	b	a	a			

it must transform it to

a	a	b	Δ	a	b	$\underline{a}$	a	Δ	b	a	a

where in each case the underlined symbol represents the head position.

It is not hard to outline a series of basic steps T_2 might take to do this, in which each step consists of operations similar to those we have seen before. Starting in the configuration shown above, for example, it might first change the a in the current head position to a', so as to be able to relocate this symbol later. This will mean adding to the alphabet sets like

$$(\Gamma_1 \times (\Gamma_1' \cup \{\Delta'\})) \cup ((\Gamma_1' \cup \{\Delta'\}) \times (\Gamma \cup \{\mathbf{f}\}))$$

It might then change every Δ (or Δ') in the folded portion of the tape to the new symbol Δ_1 (or Δ_1'), for reasons that will be apparent shortly. This requires more additions to the alphabet. At this point, it begins a sequence of iterations, in each of which the folded portion is reduced as the symbols are shifted by one square. The first of these iterations applied to the folded configuration above would yield

Δ_1	a	b	a'	a	Δ_1	b	a	a
$\mathbf{f}$	b	a	a					

This can be thought of as deleting the b at the beginning of the second track, and inserting it at the beginning of the first; thus, we could adapt the TMs discussed in Example 16.5. The "insert" operation is where we use the fact that Δ has been replaced by Δ_1—the insertion is completed when all the symbols up to the first actual Δ have been shifted to the right.

When the second track has been completely eliminated, the $\mathbf{f}$ and any leading occurrences of Δ_1 are deleted; all remaining occurrences of Δ_1 are changed back to Δ; the final position of the head is located, and the symbol there changed back to its original form; and T_2 can finally halt.

17.2 TMs WITH MORE THAN ONE TAPE

Another obvious way in which we might try to strengthen the basic Turing machine is to provide it with more than one tape. We saw early in Chapter 16 that two stacks would allow a pushdown automaton to recognize languages that it could not handle with only one; perhaps adding extra tapes will enhance the TM in a corresponding way.

By an *n-tape Turing machine* ($n \geq 1$), we mean a machine similar to a TM and specifiable as before by a 5-tuple $T = (Q, \Sigma, \Gamma, q_0, \delta)$, but with n separate one-sided tapes, each with its own independent tape head. This TM makes a move on the basis of the state it's in and the n-tuple of tape symbols currently being examined on the tapes. Since the tape heads can move independently, we describe the transition function as a partial function

$$\delta \ : \ Q \times (\Gamma \cup \{\Delta\})^n \rightarrow (Q \cup \{h\}) \times (\Gamma \cup \{\Delta\})^n \times \{R,L,S\}^n$$

We can generalize the notion of configuration in a straightforward way: a configuration is specified by an $(n + 1)$-tuple of the form

$$(q, x_1\underline{a_1}y_1, \ldots, x_n\underline{a_n}y_n)$$

with the same restrictions as before on the strings x_i and y_i.

The initial configuration with input x is

$$(q_0, \underline{\Delta}x, \underline{\Delta}, \ldots, \underline{\Delta})$$

In other words, the first tape is the one used for input. We shall say that the output of an n-tape TM is also the final contents of tape 1. There are alternative notions of output that would take into account the contents of the other tapes as well, but our choice is to view tapes 2 through n as auxiliary working space and to disregard their contents when the TM halts. In particular, such a TM computes a function f if, whenever it begins with an input string x in (or representing an element in) the domain of f, it halts in some configuration $(h, \underline{\Delta}f(x), \ldots)$, where the contents of tapes 2 through n are arbitrary, and otherwise it fails to halt.

It is obvious that for any $n \geq 2$, n-tape TMs are at least as powerful as ordinary 1-tape TMs: to simulate an ordinary TM exactly, a TM with n tapes simply acts as if tape 1 were its only one and leaves the others blank. We now show the converse.

Theorem 17.2. Let $n \geq 2$ and let $T_1 = (Q_1, \Sigma, \Gamma_1, q_1, \delta_1)$ be an n-tape TM. There is a 1-tape TM $T_2 = (Q_2, \Sigma, \Gamma_2, q_2, \delta_2)$ satisfying these properties:

1. $\Gamma_1 \subseteq \Gamma_2$
2. for any $x \in \Sigma^*$, T_2 halts on input x if and only if T_1 halts on input x; and
3. for any $x \in \Sigma^*$, if $(q_1, \underline{\Delta}x, \underline{\Delta}, \ldots, \underline{\Delta}) \vdash_{T_1}^* (h, y\underline{az}, y_2\underline{a_2}z_2, \ldots, y_n\underline{a_n}z_n)$ for some $a, a_2, \ldots, a_n \in \Gamma_1 \cup \{\Delta\}$ and some $y, y_2, \ldots, y_n, z, z_2, \ldots, z_n \in (\Gamma_1 \cup \{\Delta\})^*$, then $(q_2, \underline{\Delta}) \vdash_{T_2}^* (h, y\underline{az})$.

Proof. We give the proof for $n = 2$, but it will be obvious that the argument extends easily to the general case.

First, a single tape can be made to look like two tapes exactly as in the proof of Theorem 17.1*b*, by using alphabet symbols that are actually pairs of symbols—thereby creating, in effect, two tracks on the tape. In the proof of Theorem 17.1*b*, a symbol a on one of the tracks was changed to a' in order to identify the head position. Here, there is a head on each tape and the two move independently; thus we must include pairs of the form (a', b') as well as (a', b), (a, b'), and (a, b). In other words, if we denote by Γ the set $\Gamma_1 \cup \{\Delta\}$, the alphabet Γ_2 must include the subset

$$(\Gamma \times \Gamma) \cup (\Gamma \times \Gamma') \cup (\Gamma' \times \Gamma) \cup (\Gamma' \times \Gamma'),$$

as well as Γ_1 itself. We also add an extra symbol #, and the first moves of T_1 are to insert this symbol in square 0, shifting the blank and the input string over. This makes it easy to locate square 0 any time we wish. The second step in T_2 is to change the blank that is now in square 1 to the pair (Δ', Δ'), signifying that the "head" on each track starts at this location. T_2 is ready to begin simulating the moves of T_1.

T_1 makes moves of the form

$$\delta(p, a_1, a_2) = (q, b_1, b_2, D_1, D_2) \tag{17.1}$$

where a_1 and a_2 are the symbols in the current squares of the respective tapes. If T_2 is to simulate the next move of T_1, its first problem is to determine which move that is. Since it has only one tape head, this will require locating the primed symbols on the two tracks of its tape. Once this has been done, T_2 must make the appropriate changes to the two tracks, including the creation of new primed symbols to reflect the changes in the positions of the tape heads of T_1.

It is obviously possible for T_2 to "remember" the current state p of T_1. With this in mind, we can describe more precisely the steps T_2 might follow in simulating a single move of T_1:

1. Move the head left to the symbol #; move it right until a pair of the form (a_1', y) is found, and remember a_1;

2. Locate the "head" on the second track the same way, by starting from the # in square 0 and finding the pair of the form (z, a_2');

3. If the move of T_1 that has now been determined is that in (17.1), remember the state q; change the pair (z, a_2') to (z, b_2), and move the tape head in direction D_2;

4. If the current square contains #, crash, since T_1 would have crashed by trying to move the tape head off tape 2; if not, and if the new square doesn't contain a pair of symbols (because $D_2 = R$ and T_2 has not previously examined positions this far to the right), convert the symbol c there to the pair (c, Δ'); if the new square does contain a pair, say (c, d), convert it to (c, d');

5. Locate the pair (a_1', y) again, as in step 1; change it to (b_1, y) and move the head in direction D_1; and

6. As in step 4, either crash, or change the single symbol c to the pair (c', Δ), or change the pair (c, d) to (c', d).

It is clear that as long as the halt state has not been reached, iterating these six steps allows T_2 to simulate the moves of T_1 correctly. If and when the state q in (17.1) is h, T_2 must carry out these additional steps in order to finish up:

7. Convert each pair (c, d) on the tape to the single symbol c;

8. Delete the #, so that the remaining symbols begin in square 0; and

9. Move the head to the primed symbol, change it to the corresponding unprimed symbol, and halt with the head in that position.

Corollary 17.1. Any language that is accepted by a k-tape TM can be accepted by an ordinary TM, and any function that is computed by a k-tape TM can be computed by an ordinary TM.

Proof. The proof is immediate from Theorem 17.2.

17.3   NONDETERMINISTIC TMS

With both the simpler models of computation that we have considered, FAs and PDAs, we have considered the effect of adding the element of nondeterminism.

In the case of FAs, it often simplified the discussion, since for many regular languages it is easier to find an NFA-Λ than it is to find an FA, but it did not actually change the class of languages we were able to recognize. In the case of PDAs, it did: there are CFLs that cannot be recognized by any DPDA. With Turing machines, perhaps surprisingly, we find once again that nondeterminism fails to add any genuine computing power; any language that can be accepted by a nondeterministic TM can be accepted by an ordinary one. The argument that shows this is the most complex so far in this chapter, even though we will take advantage of the result we have just established, by allowing our ordinary TM to have three separate tapes. Nevertheless, the proof depends ultimately on the same sorts of routine manipulations that we have seen so far, and it is a good illustration of the fact that by combining *enough* of these simple, routine manipulations, we can produce Turing machines that are able to perform very complex operations.

A *nondeterministic Turing machine* $T = (Q, \Sigma, \Gamma, q_0, \delta)$ is defined exactly the same way as an ordinary TM, except in one respect. The transition function δ is still defined on the set $Q \times (\Gamma \cup \{\Delta\})$, but its values, instead of being elements of $(Q \cup \{h\}) \times (\Gamma \cup \{\Delta\}) \times \{R,L,S\}$, are now subsets of this set. We do not need to say that δ is a *partial* function, as we did before; instead of saying that $\delta(q, a)$ is undefined, we will say that $\delta(q, a) = \varnothing$—either way, the TM cannot move in state q if the current tape symbol is a. In this new setting, we can refer to a configuration of a TM in the same way; to say

$$(p, x\underline{a}y) \vdash (q, w\underline{b}z)$$

means that beginning in the first configuration, there is a move that will produce the second. Similarly,

$$(p, x\underline{a}y) \vdash^* (q, w\underline{b}z)$$

means that there is at least one sequence of zero or more moves that takes the TM from the first configuration to the second. With this definition, we may still say that a string $x \in \Sigma^*$ is accepted if for some $a \in \Gamma \cup \{\Delta\}$ and some $y, z \in (\Gamma \cup \{\Delta\})^*$,

$$(q_0, \underline{\Delta}x) \vdash^* (h, y\underline{a}z)$$

It is less obvious what an appropriate definition of *output* would be in the nondeterministic case; it is conceivable that the final tape contents could be any one of an infinite number of possibilities, depending on which sequence of moves is chosen. TMs of this type will be useful (see Exercises 17.7 and 17.8, for example), but primarily as components of larger TMs. When we compare nondeterministic TMs to ordinary ones, we will be concerned with them only as language acceptors. Since every TM can be interpreted as a nondeterministic TM, it is obvious that any language that can be accepted by a TM can be accepted by a nondeterministic TM. The converse is less obvious, and we will prove it.

Theorem 17.3. Let $T_1 = (Q_1, \Sigma, \Gamma_1, q_1, \delta_1)$ be a nondeterministic TM accepting the language $L \subseteq \Sigma^*$. There is an ordinary (deterministic) TM $T_2 = (Q_2, \Sigma, \Gamma_2, q_2, \delta_2)$ accepting L.

Proof. The TM T_2 we are looking for will have the property that for any $x \in \Sigma^*$, T_2 halts on input x if and only if there is *some* sequence of moves T_1 might make on input x that will cause it to halt. This suggests a strategy for constructing T_2 that will be foolproof if we can actually implement it—have T_2 try if necessary every conceivable sequence of moves T_1 could make, one sequence at a time, and halt if and only if it finds a sequence that would cause T_1 to halt. We must be a little careful: if one sequence of moves leads T_1 into an infinite loop, we don't want T_2 to get bogged down in the same infinite loop, for it would never get around to trying other sequences of moves that might actually halt. To avoid this problem, we shall have T_2 try every *finite* sequence of moves T_1 can make. We must see to it that when T_2 carries out a sequence of moves that would cause T_1 to crash, T_2 is able to recover, abandon that sequence, and go on to try the next sequence. If T_2 ever finds a sequence that causes T_1 to halt, it can halt; otherwise it continues to try unsuccessful sequences of moves forever.

Here is a more precise description of how T_2 will work: it will try all possible single moves, then all possible sequences of two moves, then all possible sequences of three, and so on. This approach may seem inefficient, in the sense that every sequence of $n + 1$ moves that is tried will involve repeating some sequence of n moves that was previously tried. In the extreme case that for some n, T_1 cannot execute any sequence of n moves without crashing, T_2 will essentially go into an infinite loop. It will attempt to try longer and longer sequences of moves, but the effect will be that it ends up repeating the same sequences of moves, in the same order, over and over. Aside from the question of efficiency, however, there is no doubt that the approach will produce the correct result if it can be carried out. If $x \in L$, then for some n there is a sequence of n moves T_1 could take on input x that would cause it to halt, and eventually T_2 will get around to trying that particular sequence of n moves. If $x \notin L$, every finite sequence of moves either causes T_1 to crash or ends in a nonhalting state, and in this case T_2 will continue to move without halting.

There is another way of describing the simulation we are trying to carry out, a way that may make it seem more natural. The possible sequences of moves T_1 can make may be represented by a *computation tree*. Nodes in the tree represent configurations of T_1; the root is the initial configuration, and the children of any node N correspond to the configurations to which T_1 might move in one step from the configuration N. T_2's job is simply to perform a *breadth-first search* of this tree: to examine the paths in the tree in order of length, to see if any of them lead to a halting configuration.

Let's suppose for the sake of simplicity that the maximum size of any set $\delta(q, a, X)$ is 3; i.e., T_1 sometimes has a choice of three moves, but it never has more than three choices. What we come up with in this case will generalize easily. In any configuration from which there is at least one move, we can label the possible moves using the digits 0, 1, and 2; the order is arbitrary. If there are only one or two moves from a certain configuration, we will still assign all three digits to moves; thus, distinct digits may represent the same move. In this simple case, the computation tree is shown in Fig. 17–1.

It will be convenient to construct T_2 so that it has three tapes. The first is used only to save the original input, and its contents are never changed. The second will be used to keep track somehow of the sequence of moves of T_1 that T_2 is currently attempting to execute. The third will be the "working tape," corresponding to T_1's tape, where T_2 will actually carry out the steps specified in the current sequence of moves; every time T_2 begins trying a new sequence, the third tape will be erased and the input from the first recopied onto the third.

Let's continue to assume that T_1 has no more than three choices at any time; what we come up with in this case will generalize easily. Using the digits 0, 1, and 2 to label

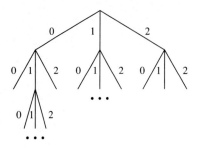

FIGURE 17-1
The computation tree for a nondeterministic TM.

the possible moves at any point, as described above, provides T_2 with a way to keep track on the second tape of the sequences of moves it has tried and to generate the sequence that is to be tried next. A string of digits represents a sequence of moves of T_1. The string 120, for example, represents the following sequence: first, move number 1 (actually the second move, since the first is move 0) from the initial configuration; second, move 2 of the three possible moves starting from the configuration that results from the first move; finally, move 0 from the configuration resulting from the first two moves. Notice again that at each step we assume that if there are any choices at all, there are three, which may not all be distinct. The only disadvantage of doing this is that there may be several strings representing the same sequence of moves; thus, the process will be less efficient. Even so, of course, there may be strings of digits that do not correspond to sequences of that many moves, because the first few moves of the sequence cause T_1 to halt or crash. T_2 abandons a string as soon as it is no longer possible to carry out the specified moves. We will say that the string that follows string 00 is 01; the one that follows 01 is 02; the one that follows 02 is 10; and so on. You should now be able to see that given a string representing a sequence of moves, T_2 can generate the *next* string by interpreting the first one as a base-3 representation and adding 1—unless the given string is 22...2, in which case the next string is the string of 0's with one more symbol.

Figure 17-2 shows a one-tape TM that executes precisely this transformation on an input string of 0's, 1's, and 2's. To make this TM into one of the components of T_2, which

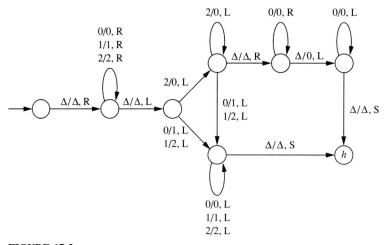

FIGURE 17-2
The one-tape version of *NextSequence*.

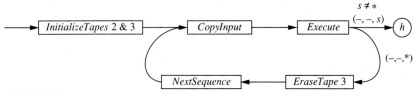

FIGURE 17-3
Simulating a nondeterministic TM by a 3-tape TM.

we might call *NextSequence*, we merely change it into a three-tape TM that acts on the second tape only, irrespective of the contents of the first and third. Moreover, it is easy to see the modifications that would be necessary in the general case where 3 is replaced by n; the only requirement is that if $n > 10$, we agree on n symbols to represent the values $0, 1, \ldots, n - 1$ in an n-ary representation.

It is now easy to describe the general structure of T_2. We may think of it as composed of five sub-TMs called *InitializeTapes2&3*, *CopyInput*, *Execute*, *EraseTape3*, and *NextSequence*. These are combined as in Fig. 17-3.

InitializeTapes2&3 writes the symbol 0 in square 1 of tape 2, to represent the sequence of moves to be tried first, and places the symbol # in square 0 of tape 3. This marker will allow T_2 to detect, and recover from, an attempt by T_1 to move its head off the tape. *CopyInput* copies the original input string x from tape 1 onto tape 3, so that tape 3 ends up with the contents $\#\Delta x$. *Execute* is the TM that actually simulates the action of T_1 on this input, by executing the sequence of moves currently specified on tape 2. We shall discuss this component in a little more detail shortly, but its crucial feature is that it finishes with a symbol s in the current square of tape 3, and $s = *$ if and only if the sequence of moves would not cause T_1 to halt (i.e., if and only if either T_1 would crash at some point along the way, or the sequence would conclude with T_1 in a nonhalting state). In this case T_2 continues with the *EraseTape3* sub-TM, and otherwise (if T_1 would halt) it halts. *EraseTape3* restores tape 3 to the configuration $\#\Delta$. (There is one slight subtlety here that we have run into before. If we have no information about the computation that has produced a particular configuration of a TM, and no information about the final head position relative to the nonblank symbols left on the tape, then 'erasing the tape' is not possible. No matter how far to the right we go, we have no way of knowing whether we have found all the nonblank symbols. In our situation, however, we do have more information: tape 2, which tells us in particular how many moves there were in the sequence we just finished executing. The nonblank symbols on tape 3 can extend no more than one square past the nonblank portion of tape 2.) We have already discussed the TM *NextSequence*.

The problem of constructing T_2 has therefore been reduced to that of constructing the component *Execute*, which must simulate the sequence of moves of T_1 specified by the string of digits on tape 2. To describe *Execute* in complete detail would be very tedious. Instead, we consider what a typical small portion of the transition diagram for T_1 might look like (Fig. 17-4a), and we show the corresponding portion of the diagram of *Execute* (Fig. 17-4b). The states of *Execute* include all those of T_1, and others as well. We have continued to make the simplifying assumption that the maximum number of choices at any point in T_1 is 3. We simplify things still further by assuming that $\Gamma_1 = \{a\}$, so that a and Δ are the only symbols on T_1's tape. Finally, since tape 1 is ignored by *Execute*, we have presented the portion of *Execute* in Fig. 17-4b as a two-tape machine.

Suppose that Fig. 17-4a shows all possible transitions from state p. Thus, if the current tape symbol is a, there are two moves, one of which halts, and if the

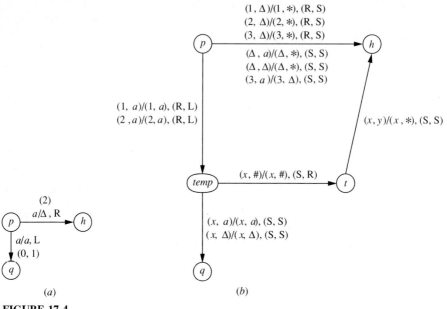

FIGURE 17-4
A typical small portion of *Execute*.

current symbol is Δ, T_1 crashes. The nonhalting move with tape symbol a may also cause a crash, since it attempts to move the head left. Since there is at least one move given the state-symbol combination (p, a), our scheme calls for us to specify moves 0, 1, and 2 (not all distinct). We have arbitrarily designated the nonhalting move as both move 0 and move 1, and the halting move as move 2. *Execute* should *not* crash; thus, we need to specify eight possible moves from state p, since there are four possible symbols on tape 2 and two on tape 3. (Note: # is an additional symbol on tape 3, but it will be evident shortly why it is not necessary to consider that possibility in state p.)

In five of the eight moves, *Execute* will halt with the tape head on tape 3 reading $*$. One way this can happen is for the symbol on tape 2 to be a digit and that on tape 3 to be blank. There are three such moves, and they all represent a crash of T_1 during the specified sequence of moves. The other way, accounting for the other two moves of the five, is for the tape symbol on tape 2 to be blank. This signifies that the current sequence of moves has been completed, and, since $p \neq h$, T_1 has not halted.

One of the eight is also a halt, but with the tape head on tape 3 reading something other than $*$; Δ was chosen arbitrarily. This is the halting move shown in Fig. 17-4a. Since T_1's move involves moving the tape head right, there is no chance of T_1 crashing on that move, so it really does halt.

The remaining two cases correspond to the two nonhalting moves in Figure 17.4b. These occur when the symbol on tape 2 is either 0 or 1 and that on tape 3 is a. The reason these two moves do not go directly to state q in *Execute* is that T_1's move involved moving the head left; thus *Execute* must test to see if the moves cause a crash. It does this by moving the head on tape 3 left and entering a "temporary" state created specifically for this purpose. From the temporary state, any symbol on tape 3 other than # indicates that T_1 made the move safely, and in this case *Execute* goes to state q, as T_1 would have in the first place. The symbol # on tape 3, however, indicates a crash. *Execute* moves the head to the first square to the right of #, writes the symbol ∗, and halts. In Fig. 17-4*b*, the symbol *x* in the moves from *temp* and *t*, and the symbol *y* in the move from *t*, stand for any arbitrary symbol.

Although this small example does not illustrate every conceivable situation that might occur (see Exercise 17.11), it should now be obvious that the complete transition diagram for T_1 can eventually be transformed into a corresponding diagram for *Execute*, and therefore that it is indeed possible for T_2 to simulate every finite sequence of moves of T_1.

17.4 UNIVERSAL TURING MACHINES

We have discussed the TM as a general model of computation, and you should by this time be comfortable with the idea of a TM as a rudimentary computer— rudimentary, that is, in its relative inefficiency and cumbersome operations, but able ultimately to carry out computations as complex as those of any other computer. Up to this point, one apparent difference between a TM and a "computer," as you usually think of one, is that a single TM can execute a single algorithm only, whereas a computer can execute an essentially unlimited variety of algorithms, depending on the "program" currently in its memory. This may seem like a substantial difference. But in fact, the original electronic computers were limited in the same way: The program was inherent in the way the computer was wired, and as a result, changing the program was a tedious and awkward job. What happened subsequently was not so much that the computer changed in any radical way, as that people began to conceive of a different way of using it, which involved viewing the program as part of the data to be loaded into its memory. Turing had the same idea. In addition to special-purpose machines, he described a "universal computing machine" that works as follows. It is a TM T_U whose input consists of two parts: a string specifying some other (special-purpose) TM T_1, and a second string *x* that is interpreted as input to T_1. T_U then simulates the processing of *x* by T_1. Thus, the essential concept of the stored-program computer dates back at least to Turing's 1936 paper. In this section, we shall describe such a "universal Turing machine" T_U. It seems appropriate to class this with "generalizations of TMs," although, to repeat, what is more general is not the type of machine, but only the use that is being made of it. (The fact that there is such a universal TM, however, is in itself another indication of the power of the Turing machine concept. You should convince yourself, for example, that there is no such thing as a "universal pushdown automaton.") The universal TM we construct will be useful at several points in our subsequent discussions; in addition, the encoding scheme on which it depends will play an important part in the next chapter.

The first step in constructing T_U is to formulate a notational system in which we can encode an arbitrary TM T_1 as a string $e(T_1)$ over some fixed alphabet, and encode an arbitrary input string *z* as a string $e(z)$ over the same fixed alphabet. There are many ways we might do this, and it doesn't matter which method we use. It will not even matter that in our encoding scheme, several different strings represent essentially the same TM. The only crucial thing is that given a string encoding a TM, we must be able to reconstruct the TM. We shall use an alphabet of only the two symbols x and y, even though the TM T_1 we are encoding may have many more symbols in its alphabet. The string of x's and y's that encodes a TM will be constructed by assigning positive integers to each state, each tape symbol, and each of the three "directions" S, L, and R.

At this point, a slight technical problem arises. We want a string of x's and y's to be the encoding of at most one TM; in other words, we want the encoding function e to be one-to-one. Consider two TMs T_1 and T_2 that are identical except that the tape symbols of T_1 are a and b, and those of T_2 are a and c. If we really want to call these two TMs different, then in order to guarantee that their encodings are different, we must make sure that the integers assigned to b and c are different. To accommodate *any* TM and still ensure that the encoding is one-to-one, we must somehow fix it so that no symbol in any TM's alphabet receives the same number as any other symbol in any other TM's alphabet; similarly with states. The easiest way to handle this problem is to fix once and for all the set of symbols that can be used by TMs, and the set of states that can be used by TMs, and to number the elements of these two sets at the outset. This is the reason for the following

Convention. We assume from this point on that there are two fixed infinite sets $\mathcal{Q} = \{q_1, q_2, \ldots\}$ and $\mathcal{S} = \{a_1, a_2, \ldots\}$ so that for any TM $T = (Q, \Sigma, \Gamma, q_0, \delta)$, we have $Q \subseteq \mathcal{Q}$ and $\Gamma \subseteq \mathcal{S}$.

It should be clear that this assumption about states is no restriction at all, since the names that are chosen for the states of a TM are irrelevant. And as long as $\mathcal{S}$ contains all the symbols we would ever want in our input alphabets, the other assumption is equally harmless.

Definition 17.1   (The encoding function e). The first step in defining our encoding is to associate to each tape symbol, including Δ, to each state, including h, and to each of the three "directions," a string of x's. Accordingly, let

$$s(\Delta) = x$$

$$s(a_i) = x^{i+1} \qquad \text{(for each } a_i \in \mathcal{S})$$

$$s(h) = x$$

$$s(q_i) = x^{i+1} \qquad \text{(for each } q_i \in \mathcal{Q})$$

$$s(S) = x$$

$$s(L) = xx$$

$$s(R) = xxx$$

Each move m of a TM, described by the formula

$$\delta(p, a) = (q, b, D)$$

is encoded by the string

$$e(m) = s(p)y\,s(a)y\,s(q)y\,s(b)y\,s(D)y$$

and for any TM T, T is encoded by the string

$$e(T) = s(q)ye(m_1)ye(m_2)y \ldots e(m_k)y$$

where q is the initial state of T and $m_1, m_2, \ldots, m_k$ are the distinct moves of T, arranged in some arbitrary order. Finally, any string $z = z_1 z_2 \ldots z_k$, where each $z_i \in \mathcal{S}$, is encoded by

$$e(z) = yys(z_1)ys(z_2)y \ldots s(z_k)y$$

The yy at the beginning of the string $e(z)$ is there so that in a composite string of the form $e(T)e(z)$, there will be no doubt as to where $e(T)$ stops. Notice that one consequence of this is that the encoding $s(a)$ of a single symbol $a \in \mathcal{S}$ is different from the encoding $e(a)$ of the one-character string a.

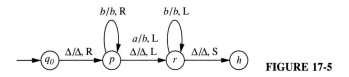

FIGURE 17-5

Example 17.1. Consider the TM illustrated in Fig. 17-5, which transforms an input string of a's and b's by changing the leftmost a, if there is one, to b. Let us assume for simplicity that the tape symbols a and b are assigned the numbers 1 and 2 (so that $s(a) = xx$ and $s(b) = xxx$) and that the states q_0, p, and r are given the numbers 1, 2, and 3, respectively. If we take the six moves in the order they appear, left-to-right, the first move $\delta(q_0, \Delta) = (p, \Delta, R)$ is encoded by the string

$$x^2 y x^1 y x^3 y x^1 y x^3 y = xxyxyxxxyxyxxxy$$

and the entire TM by the string

$$xxyxxyxyxxxyxyxxxyyxxxxyxxxxyxxxxyxxxxyxxxxyyxxxxyxxxyxxxxyxxxyxxyy$$

$$xxxyxyxxxxyxyxxxyyxxxxyxxxxyxxxxyxxxxyxxxyxxyyxxxxyxyxyxyxyxyy$$

Remember that the first part of the string, in this case xxy, is to identify the initial state of the TM.

The entire input to the universal TM T_U will consist of a string of the form $e(T)e(z)$, where T is some TM and z is interpreted as input to T. In Example 17.1, if the input string to T were baa, the portion of T_U's input tape after the string $e(T)$ would contain the string $yyxxxyxxyxxy$.

Although we know from Section 17.2 that it is not really necessary, it will be convenient to let T_U be a three-tape TM. The first tape is the input tape, containing the string $e(T)e(z)$. This tape will also be the output tape: if T halts, T_U will halt, and the final contents of T_U's first tape will be the encoded form of the final tape of T. The second tape will be the working tape during the simulation of T, and the third tape will contain the encoded form of the state that T is currently in. Initially, T_U moves the string $e(z)$ representing T's input, all except the initial yy, from the end of tape 1 to tape 2, beginning in square 3. Since T begins with square 0 blank, xy is written in squares 1 and 2 of tape 2. Square 0 of tape 2 remains

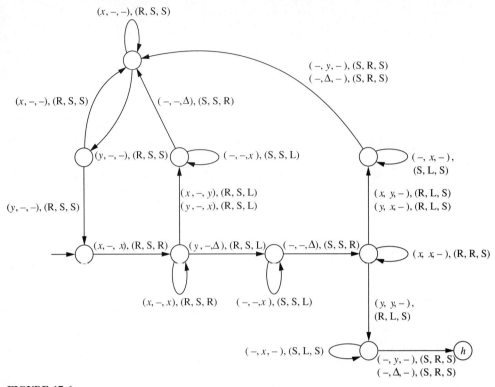

FIGURE 17-6
Finding the right move on tape 1.

blank. T_U leaves the tape head in square 1 on tape 2. T_U copies the encoded form of T's initial state from the beginning of tape 1 onto tape 3, beginning in square 1, and deletes it from tape 1.

After these initial steps, T_U is ready to begin simulating the action of T on the input string represented by the contents of tape 2. Before any moves of T have been simulated, T_U's three tape heads are all in square 1. The appropriate move at any point is determined by the current symbol on T's tape, which is encoded by the string on tape 2 of T_U, beginning with the current head position and extending up to the next y, and by the current state of T, encoded by the string on tape 3 of T_U. Thus, in order to make the move, T_U must first search tape 1, the specifications of T, for the 5-tuple whose first two parts match this state-input combination. This search is perhaps the most complicated part of the entire process. A TM that does this is shown in Fig. 17-6. Since the search operation never changes any tape symbols, the labeling in the figure is simplified somewhat: what would normally be written

$$(a, b, c)/(a, b, c), (D_1, D_2, D_3)$$

is written

$$(a, b, c), (D_1, D_2, D_3)$$

instead.

Once the appropriate 5-tuple is found, the last three parts are used to carry out the actual simulation of the move. To illustrate, suppose that before the search, T_U's three tapes look like this:

$\Delta \underline{x} x y x y x x x y x y x x x y y x x x y x x y x x x x y x x x y x x y y x x y \ldots$

$\Delta x y x x y \underline{x} x y x x x y \Delta \ldots$

$\Delta \underline{x} x x \Delta \ldots$

The corresponding tape of T would be

$\Delta a \underline{a} b \Delta \ldots$

assuming that the symbols numbered 1 and 2 are a and b, respectively, and T would be in state 2. After the search of tape 1, the tapes look like this:

$\Delta x x y x y x x x y x y x x x y y x x x y x x y \underline{x} x x x y x x x y x x y y x x y \ldots$

$\Delta x y x x y \underline{x} x y x x x y \Delta \ldots$

$\Delta \underline{x} x x \Delta \ldots$

The 5-tuple on tape 1 specifies that T's current symbol should be changed to b, the head should be moved left, and the state should be changed to state 4. These operations can be carried out by T_U in a fairly straightforward way, and we do not include the details (see Exercise 17.13). The final result is

$\Delta \underline{x} x y x y x x x y x y x x x y y x x x y x x y x x x x y x x x y x x y y x x y \ldots$

$\Delta x y \underline{x} x y x x x y x x x y \Delta \ldots$

$\Delta \underline{x} x x x \Delta \ldots$

and T_U is now ready for the next move.

There are several ways in which the sequence of moves might come to an end. First, T might crash by being unable to move. In this case, the search operation pictured in Fig. 17-6 also crashes, since after the last 5-tuple on tape 1 has been tried unsuccessfully, the second of the y's at the end takes the machine back to the initial state, but there is no move from that state with y on tape 1. Second, T might crash by attempting to move off the tape. We can easily arrange things so that in this case T_U crashes also. Finally, T may halt. T_U detects this when it processes a 5-tuple on tape 1 whose third part is x. In this case, after T_U has changed tape 2 appropriately, it erases tape 1, copies tape 2 onto tape 1, and halts.

EXERCISES

17.1. In Section 17.1, we mentioned a variation of TMs in which the transition function δ takes values in $Q \times (\Gamma \cup \{\Delta\}) \times \{L, R\}$, so that the tape head must move left or right on each move. It is not difficult to show that any ordinary TM can be simulated by one of these. Explain how the move $\delta(p, a) = (q, b, S)$ could be simulated by such a restricted TM.

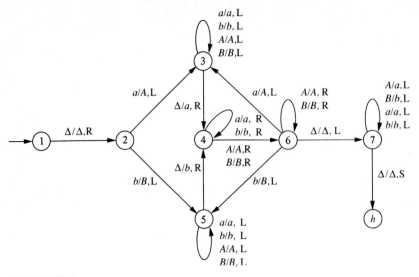

FIGURE 17-7

17.2. An ordinary TM can also be simulated by one in which δ takes values in $Q \times (\Gamma \cup \{\Delta\} \cup \{L,R\})$, so that writing a symbol and moving the tape head are not both allowed on the same move. Explain how the move $\delta(p, a) = (q, b, R)$ of an ordinary TM could be simulated by one of these restricted TMs.

17.3. In Fig. 17-7 is a transition diagram for a TM M with a doubly-infinite tape. First, trace the moves it makes on the input string abb. Then trace the moves that the ordinary TM of Theorem 17.1b makes in simulating M on the same input, up to the point where M halts.

17.4. Draw a transition diagram for a TM that would have the effect of 'shifting' over by one the symbols in a folded configuration as discussed in the proof of Theorem 17.1b, assuming that the tape head is initially in square 0. For example,

Δ	a	b	a	b	b
f	b	a			

would be transformed to

b	Δ	a	b	a	b	b
f	a					

17.5. Construct a TM with a doubly-infinite tape that does the following: if it begins with the tape blank except for a single a somewhere on it, it halts with the head scanning the square with the a.

17.6. Draw the portion of the transition diagram for the one-tape TM M_2 embodying the six steps shown in the proof of Theorem 17.2 corresponding to the move $\delta_1(p, a_1, a_2) = (q, b_1, b_2, R, L)$ of M_1.

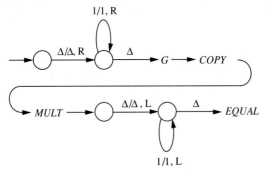

1/1, R

Δ/Δ, R   Δ

G → COPY

Δ/Δ, L   Δ

MULT →   EQUAL

1/1, L   **FIGURE 17-8**

17.7. Draw a transition diagram for a three-tape TM that works as follows: starting in the configuration $(q_0, \underline{\Delta}x, \underline{\Delta}y, \underline{\Delta})$, where x and y are strings of 0's and 1's of the same length, it halts in the configuration $(h, \underline{\Delta}x, \underline{\Delta}y, \underline{\Delta}z)$, where z is the string obtained by interpreting x and y as binary representations and adding them.

17.8. What is the effect of the nondeterministic TM whose transition table is shown here?

q	σ	$\delta(q, \sigma)$
q_0	Δ	$\{(q_1, \Delta, R)\}$
q_1	Δ	$\{(q_1, 1, R), (q_2, \Delta, L)\}$
q_2	1	$\{(q_2, 1, L)\}$
q_2	Δ	$\{(h, \Delta, S)\}$

17.9. Call the nondeterministic TM in the previous exercise G. Let *MULT* be a TM that computes the product of two numbers (i.e., transforms the tape $\underline{\Delta}1^m\Delta1^n$ to the tape $\underline{\Delta}1^{mn}$). Let *COPY* be the TM in Example 16.4, which transforms $\underline{\Delta}x$ to $\underline{\Delta}x\Delta x$ for an arbitrary string x of 1's. Finally, let *EQUAL* be a TM that works as follows: starting with the tape $\underline{\Delta}x\Delta y$, *EQUAL* halts if and only if $x = y$. Consider the nondeterministic TM shown in Fig. 17-8. It is nondeterministic because the component G is. What language does it accept?

17.10. Using the idea in the previous exercise, construct a nondeterministic TM that accepts the language of all strings 1^n for which n is a nonprime integer greater than 1.

17.11. Fig. 17-4b shows the portion of the Execute TM corresponding to the portion of M_1 shown in Fig. 17-4a. Consider the portion of M_1 shown in Fig. 17-9. Assume again that the maximum number of choices at any point in M_1 is 3, and that the moves shown are the only ones from state r. Draw the corresponding portion of Execute.

a/a, L

r → h

Δ/Δ, R

s

FIGURE 17-9

17.12. Assuming the same encoding method discussed in Section 17.4, draw the TM that is encoded by the string

$$xxyxxyxyxxxyxyxxxyyxxxyxxyxxxyxxyxxxyyxxxyxxxyxxxyxxxyxxxyy$$

$$xxxyxyxxxxyxyxxyyxxxxyxxyxxxxyxxyxxxyyxxxxyxxxyxxxxxy$$

$$xxxyxxxyyxxxxxyxyxxxxxxxyxxyxxyyxxxxxxyxyxxxxxxxyxxxyxxyy$$

$$xxxxxxxyxxyxxxxxxxyxxyxxyyxxxxxxxyxxyxxxxxxxyxxxyxxyy$$

$$xxxxxxxyxyxyxyxyy$$

17.13. Draw the portion of the universal TM M that is responsible for changing the tape symbol and moving the tape head after the search operation has identified the correct 5-tuple on tape 1. For example, the configuration

$$\Delta xxyxyxyxxxyxyxyxxxyyxxxyxxy\underline{x}xxxyxxxyxxyyxxy \ldots$$

$$\Delta xyxxy\underline{x}xyxxxy\Delta \ldots$$

$$\Delta \underline{x}xxx\Delta \ldots$$

would be transformed to

$$\Delta \underline{x}xyxyxyxxxyxyxyxxxyyxxxyxxyxxxxyxxxyxxyyxxy \ldots$$

$$\Delta xy\underline{x}xyxxxyxxxy\Delta \ldots$$

$$\Delta \underline{x}xxx\Delta \ldots$$

17.14. Show that if there is a TM T computing the function $f : \mathcal{N} \to \mathcal{N}$, then there is another one, T', whose tape alphabet is $\{1, 0\}$. Suggestion: suppose T has tape alphabet $\Gamma = \{a_1, \ldots, a_n\}$, one of whose symbols is 1; encode Δ and each a_i as a string of 0's and 1's, of some fixed length K; have T' begin by replacing nonblank symbols of the input string by their encoded versions; then show how T' can simulate T, but using blocks of tape K squares long instead of single squares. T' will obviously require many more states than T.

CHAPTER
18

RECURSIVELY ENUMERABLE LANGUAGES

18.1 RECURSIVELY ENUMERABLE AND RECURSIVE

In earlier sections of this book, we began with methods of generating certain types of languages and developed abstract machines specifically to recognize these languages. In Part IV, we have started with the machines (TMs) because we view them as general models of computation. Nevertheless, as we have seen in Chapter 16 a TM can be a language recognizer, and it is therefore appropriate to discuss the languages that can be recognized in this way.

At this point, we make an official distinction between the two methods mentioned in Chapter 16 in which a TM can "recognize" a language.

Definition 18.1. Let $L \subseteq \Sigma^*$ be a language. A TM T with input alphabet Σ *accepts L* if $L = \{x \in \Sigma^* | T$ halts with input $x\}$. T *recognizes L* if T computes the characteristic function $\chi_L : \Sigma^* \to \{0, 1\}$. In other words, T recognizes L if T halts for any input x in Σ^*, with final tape contents $\underline{\Delta}1$ if $x \in L$ and $\underline{\Delta}0$ otherwise. (Some authors say that in this situation T *decides L*.)

A language L is *recursively enumerable* if there is a TM that accepts L. L is *recursive* if there is a TM that recognizes L.

Every recursive language is recursively enumerable: if T is a TM recognizing L, T can easily be modified so that it accepts L instead. In the converse direction, suppose T is a TM accepting L. If for every input string x, T's processing terminates, by either halting or crashing, then for any input string an observer can find out in a finite amount of time whether the string is in L. It is not hard to believe that in this case T can be modified so that it recognizes L. In fact, we may state a slightly more general result, which will be useful in the next chapter.

Theorem 18.1. Suppose T is a nondeterministic TM accepting L, and for every input string x, every possible sequence of moves either halts or crashes. Then L is recursive.

Proof. In the proof of Theorem 17.3, we constructed a deterministic three-tape TM T' that simulates if necessary every possible finite sequence of moves of a given nondeterministic TM T. T' is able to detect, and recover from, crashes of T. It continues trying longer and longer sequences of moves, as long as it has not found one that halts.

We wish to construct a deterministic TM T_1 that recognizes L. It will be a modification of T' and in particular will retain the three tapes. The first change we make is easy: if and when T_1 finds a sequence of moves of T that halts, then instead of merely halting, it will halt with tape 1 having the configuration $\underline{\Delta}1$. The other change that is required is more substantial. T_1 must be able to determine at some point that it will never be able to find a sequence of moves of T that halts, and it must then halt with $\underline{\Delta}0$ on tape 1. The question is how it can determine this.

Recall that T' keeps track of the sequence of moves it should try next by keeping a string of digits on tape 2. The ith digit specifies the choice T should make at the ith step. Obviously, if there is some number N so that every possible string of N digits represents a sequence of moves that crashes, the input is not accepted, since any longer sequence of digits must start out with a sequence of length N. The crucial observation in constructing T_1 is that if x is not accepted, then since there can be no infinite sequence of moves, there must be such an integer N. (If this seems obvious, fine; if not, see Exercise 18.16.) With this observation, it is easy to describe in general how T_1 works. Although a detailed description would be messy, it would be fairly straightforward. Each time T_1 simulates a sequence of moves of T that crashes, T_1 copies in the blank portion of tape 1 the sequence of digits currently on tape 2. If each digit in the sequence is the maximum possible (for example, if T has three choices at some point and never any more than three, this would mean each digit in the string was a 2), and if the sequence has length n, T_1 searches the strings on tape 1 to see whether all possible sequences of length n appear. If not, it continues simulating the next sequence of moves, just like T'. But if so, it concludes that the input is not accepted, and it erases tape 1 and halts with tape 1 containing $\underline{\Delta}0$.

If L is accepted by a TM, what might yet prevent L from being recursive is the possibility that L loops forever on some input strings and that no TM accepting L can avoid infinite loops. We shall return to this problem later in the chapter. At this point, it is probably not even obvious that there are any nonrecursive languages, much less that there are recursively enumerable languages that are not recursive.

It will be helpful to establish some conditions that are sufficient for a language to be recursively enumerable and some that are sufficient for a language to be recursive. Several of these results depend on a way of constructing a TM that can simulate two other TMs simultaneously.

Theorem 18.2. If L_1 and L_2 are recursively enumerable subsets of Σ^*, $L_1 \cup L_2$ and $L_1 \cap L_2$ are recursively enumerable.

Proof. Suppose $T_1 = (Q_1, \Sigma, \Gamma_1, q_1, \delta_1)$ and $T_2 = (Q_2, \Sigma, \Gamma_2, q_2, \delta_2)$ are TMs accepting L_1 and L_2, respectively. We wish to construct TMs accepting $L_1 \cup L_2$ and $L_1 \cap L_2$. The idea is very similar to that in Chapter 4, where we constructed FAs recognizing $L_1 \cup L_2$ and $L_1 \cap L_2$, given FAs recognizing L_1 and L_2: we include in our set of states the pairs in $Q_1 \times Q_2$. This technique did not work with PDAs, for reasons having to do with the stack, and of course the corresponding statement about CFLs is false (see Theorem 15.2). The reason it will work with TMs is that, according to 16.2, it is sufficient to find a two-tape TM that does what we want. Let's describe the solution for $L_1 \cup L_2$.

We want our machine $T = (Q, \Sigma, \Gamma, q_0, \delta)$ to accept a string x if and only if x is accepted by T_1 or T_2 or both. T starts by copying the input x onto the second tape and inserting the marker # at the beginning of each tape. It proceeds to simulate T_1 on the first tape and at the same time T_2 on the second, using the marker to recover from a crash of either T_1 or T_2. The simulation is accomplished by allowing every possible move

$$\delta((p_1, p_2), (a_1, a_2)) = ((q_1, q_2), (a_1', a_2'), (D_1, D_2))$$

where, for both values of i, $\delta_i(p_i, a_i) = (q_i, a_i', D_i)$. This simulation continues up to the point where one or both of T_1 and T_2 would halt or crash. As in previous arguments of this type, T does not detect a crash caused by moving off the tape until one move later, when the current symbol is #. If and when either one halts, T halts. If T_1 or T_2 crashes, T ignores that tape from that point on and continues to simulate the other machine on the other tape until it halts or crashes. If both machines eventually crash, T can simply crash. Finally, if one crashes and the other loops forever, or if they both loop forever, T will loop forever. It should now be clear that T accepts the language $L_1 \cup L_2$.

A TM to accept $L_1 \cap L_2$ is constructed the same way, except that it can crash as soon as either T_1 or T_2 crashes, and it can halt only after both T_1 and T_2 have halted.

We leave as an exercise the fact that the class of recursive languages is also closed under the operations of union and intersection (Exercise 18.1). For recursive languages, however, we may add another set operation to the list, as the next result indicates.

Theorem 18.3. If $L \subset \Sigma^*$ is recursive, so is L'.

Proof. If T is a TM recognizing L, we may modify T to form a TM T', which leaves output $\underline{\Delta}1$ any time T leaves output $\underline{\Delta}0$ and vice versa. Then T' recognizes L'.

The fact that the corresponding statement about recursively enumerable languages cannot be proved as easily as Theorem 18.3 (you should make sure you understand why not), does not in itself mean that the statement is false. But the next result suggests that it is at least less likely to be true.

Theorem 18.4. If $L \subseteq \Sigma^*$ is a recursively enumerable language for which L' is also recursively enumerable, L is recursive.

Proof. Let T_1 and T_2 be TMs accepting L and L', respectively. We construct a two-tape TM T to recognize L, using the same idea as in the proof of Theorem 18.2. We proceed as if we wanted T to accept $L \cup L'$, and as if we didn't realize that $L_1 \cup L_2 = \Sigma^*$. However, since $L \cup L' = \Sigma^*$ and $L \cap L' = \varnothing$, for any input string $x \in \Sigma^*$, one and only one of T_1 and T_2 will halt on input x. This means that we can complete the proof by letting T be the following modification of the TM in Theorem 18.2: if T_1, being simulated on tape 1, halts, let T halt with tape 1 containing $\underline{\Delta}1$, and if T_2, on tape 2, halts, let T halt with tape 1 containing $\underline{\Delta}0$.

There is one slight obstacle to our doing this. In both cases, T is required at some point to erase tape 1 and to leave blank every square but square 1. You remember from the proof of Theorem 17.3 that in general, "erasing the tape" is not a feasible operation for a TM. To get around this difficulty, we first have T insert a marker in square 0 of tape 1, so as to be able to find the beginning of the tape. Then, in the simulation of T_1 on tape 1, every time T_1 writes Δ, T writes a different symbol, say Δ'. As soon as T_1 or T_2 halts, T finds the beginning of tape 1 and erases all symbols from square 1 up to the first occurrence of Δ, which marks the furthest extent of T_1's moves on the tape. T may then return to the beginning of the tape and leave it containing the appropriate symbol.

18.2   ENUMERATING A LANGUAGE

To "enumerate" a set of items means either to count the elements or to list them. We consider an alternative characterization of recursively enumerable languages. Roughly speaking, a language L is recursively enumerable if and only if there is an algorithm for listing all the strings in L and no others. As usual, the appropriate way to formulate the idea of an algorithm is to use a Turing machine. It is convenient to use a TM with at least two tapes, one on which the strings in L are listed and the others for auxiliary working space.

Definition 18.2. Let T be a k-tape TM, where $k \geq 2$. T is said to enumerate a language $L \subseteq \Sigma^*$ if, beginning with all the tapes empty, T operates so as to satisfy these conditions:

1. On each move, the head on tape 1 either remains stationary or moves right;
2. At each step, tape 1 contains either

$$\Delta x_1 \# x_2 \# \ldots \# x_n \underline{\#} \qquad \text{or} \qquad \Delta x_1 \# x_2 \# \ldots \# x_n \# \underline{y}$$

where $n \geq 0$, each $x_i \in L$, and $y \in \Sigma^*$; and
3. For every $x \in L$, eventually one of the strings x_i on tape 1 is x.

If L is finite, T may halt when it has printed all the elements of L on tape 1, or it may continue to make moves without printing any other strings on tape 1. If L is infinite, T continues to move forever.

Theorem 18.5. If there is a TM T enumerating L, then L is recursively enumerable.

Proof. The idea of the proof is to use a TM T_1 with one more tape than T, tape 1 serving as the input tape and the others corresponding to the tapes of T. T_1 simulates T, except that every time $\#$ is written on tape 2, the simulation of T pauses while T_1 compares its input string to the string listed just before the $\#$. If the two strings match, T_1 halts. It is clear that the strings accepted by T_1 are precisely those generated on tape 2, which by assumption are the elements of L. In order to carry out the construction of T_1, we may use intact the transitions of T, treating the tapes other than tape 1 as the tapes of T and ignoring tape 1, with this change: every transition that involves writing # on tape 2 is replaced by a sequence of transitions in which the tapes other than 1 and 2 are ignored, the input string is compared to the string just before the # on tape 2, and if they don't match, T_1 is returned to the configuration that would have resulted from the original transition.

We wish to prove the converse of Theorem 18.5; if there is a TM T accepting L, we wish to construct a TM T_1 enumerating L. Again, the idea is simple. T_1 has one output tape and other auxiliary tapes. On its auxiliary tapes, it will generate all possible strings, one at a time; on each string it will simulate T, and if T halts during the simulation, T_1 will list the string on its output tape. Unfortunately, there is a problem with this approach. If L is recursive, the strategy works and hardly requires any further elaboration, but if L is not recursive, there will be at least one string for which T_1 will never finish the simulation of T. As a result of this complication, the proof requires T_1 to be more sophisticated.

Theorem 18.6. If $L \subseteq \Sigma^*$ is recursively enumerable, there is a TM enumerating L.

Proof. Let T be a TM accepting L. We shall construct a three-tape TM T_1 enumerating L. Tape 1 will be the output tape. On tape 2, T_1 will generate strings in Σ^*, and on tape 3, T_1 will simulate the action of T on each string generated. To avoid the difficulty mentioned earlier when L is not recursive, we use a technique similar to that of Theorem 17.3: rather than attempting to complete the processing of a string, T_1 will simulate longer and longer finite sequences of moves of T. Accordingly, tape 2 will save not only the strings that have been generated so far, but the number of moves of T that have been carried out on each one.

If we impose an ordering on the alphabet Σ, the obvious order in which to generate elements of Σ^* is "lexicographic," or alphabetic, order. To illustrate: if $\Sigma = \{a, b\}$ and the ordering on Σ is the usual one, the elements of Σ^* would be generated in the order

$$\Lambda, a, b, aa, ab, ba, bb, aaa, aab, \ldots, bbb, aaaa, aaab, \ldots$$

One simple way to organize the simulation of sequences of moves of T on these strings is as follows. On the first pass, T_1 will generate Λ and simulate one move on that input. On the second pass, T_1 will simulate two moves on input Λ, then generate a and simulate one move on it. On the third pass, T_1 will simulate three moves on Λ and two on a, then generate b and simulate one move on it. After the ith complete pass, the contents of tape 2 might be something like this:

$$\Delta\Delta \overbrace{11 \ldots 1}^{i} \Delta\ a\ \Delta \overbrace{11 \ldots 1}^{i-1} \Delta\ b\ \Delta \overbrace{11 \ldots 1}^{i-2} \ldots \Delta\ x\ \Delta 1$$

where x is the ith element of Σ^* with respect to lexicographic order. During the next pass, T_1 processes each of the i strings already on tape 2 by adding an extra 1 after it, copying the string onto tape 3, simulating T on that input string for the specified number of steps, and erasing tape 3. If the simulation halts, T_1 copies that string onto tape 1 and follows it by #. The last step in this pass is to generate at the end of tape 2 the next element of Σ^* (the one that comes after x), place a single 1 after it, and simulate one move of T on that input.

We have not shown explicitly the bookkeeping devices that T_1 might use in carrying out these steps, but to do so would not be difficult. The process could be made more efficient by marking a string at the point when the current sequence of moves on that input causes T to crash, so that that string need not be tested again. In any case, it is clear that every string accepted by T will eventually be listed on tape 1, and that no other string will.

18.3   NOT ALL LANGUAGES ARE RECURSIVELY ENUMERABLE

In this section, we consider the question of whether every language is recursively enumerable. In previous sections of this book, we were able to produce nonregular languages and non-context-free languages fairly easily, by exploiting certain features of finite automata and context-free grammars. These features forced regular and context-free languages to satisfy certain "regularity conditions" (the conditions described in the two pumping lemmas, Theorems 8.2a and 15.1a) that are obviously not satisfied by all languages. This approach will not work here, however. There is no "pumping lemma for recursively enumerable languages." According to the Church–Turing thesis, any conceivable algorithm can be implemented by some Turing machine, and it is difficult to imagine any regularity condition comparable to those in the pumping lemmas that would be forced on a language simply by virtue of its being recognizable using some algorithmic procedure. Demonstrating that a particular language is not recursively enumerable will require a more subtle analysis.

In this section, before we attempt to exhibit a specific such language, we give a nonconstructive argument to show that there must be one. The essence of the argument is very simple, perhaps even anticlimactic. There are, in a sense to be made precise, many more languages than there are Turing machines to accept them; therefore, there must be languages to which no TM corresponds! We will, eventually, be able to find a specific language that is not recursively enumerable. Nevertheless, there is another reason for giving the nonconstructive proof, apart from its simplicity. It will introduce us to a remarkable type of "diagonal" argument, which we will be able to use again when we actually look for an example.

Much of the remainder of this section could have been included in Part I, Mathematical Notation and Techniques. It was saved until now, partly because Chapter 1 was long enough already, and partly because the material wasn't needed until now.

If we are to compare the "number" of Turing machines with the "number" of languages, we must obviously have a general criterion for comparing the sizes of two infinite sets. The criterion commonly used for finite sets can be misleading here. One can reasonably say that a set of three elements is bigger than a set of two elements because the set of three contains a subset with two and an additional element as well. In particular, $\{1, 2, 3\}$ is bigger than $\{1, 2\}$. If we could apply the same argument to infinite sets, we could conclude that the set $\mathcal{N}$ of natural numbers is bigger than the set $2\mathcal{N}$ of nonnegative even integers, since $\mathcal{N}$ contains all the elements of $2\mathcal{N}$ and odd integers as well. But this doesn't work: suppose we relabeled all the even integers, so that 0 is still called 0, but 2 is called 1, 4 is called 2, and so on. We haven't changed the "size," but now the set $2\mathcal{N}$ looks just as big as $\mathcal{N}$.

A better approach is to use the idea of a bijection, or "one-to-one correspondence": two finite sets are the same size if and only if there is a bijection from one to the other. We say that a set of two elements is smaller than a set of three because, although there is a bijection from the first set to a *subset* of the second, there is *no* bijection from the first to the second. This approach is better because it works with infinite sets too. It tells us that $\mathcal{N}$ and $2\mathcal{N}$ are the same size, since our "relabeling" of $2n$ so that it is called n is simply the bijection $f : 2\mathcal{N} \rightarrow \mathcal{N}$ defined by $f(m) = m/2$.

Surprisingly, this criterion leads to many different sizes of infinite sets—different "orders of infinity" (see Exercise 18.11). For our purposes, however, it is enough to distinguish two kinds of infinite sets: those that are the same size as $\mathcal{N}$, and those that are bigger, which account for all the rest.

Definition 18.3. A set S is *countably infinite* if there is a bijection from $\mathcal{N}$ to S, and *countable* if it is either finite or countably infinite. A set S is *uncountably infinite,* or simply *uncountable,* if it is not countable.

Saying that there is a bijection from $\mathcal{N}$ to S is the same as saying that the elements of S can be "listed" as $f(0), f(1), \ldots$, so that every element appears exactly once in the list. Countably infinite sets are the smallest infinite sets, because any infinite set has a countably infinite subset. This can be seen informally as follows. Choose any element in S and call it $f(0)$. In general, for any $n \geq 0$, assume that distinct elements $f(0), f(1), \ldots, f(n)$ of S have been chosen. Since S is infinite, there is an element of S that is not one of these; choose any such element and call it $f(n + 1)$. The function f constructed this way is a bijection from $\mathcal{N}$ to a subset of S, and so this subset is countably infinite. It is correct, therefore, to think of any uncountably infinite set as *bigger* than any countably infinite set.

One other fact about countably infinite sets will be useful: any infinite subset of a countably infinite set is countably infinite. This is almost obvious, but see Exercise 18.7.

An immediate example of a countably infinite set is $\mathcal{N}$ itself. We have seen that $2\mathcal{N}$ is also, and it is not difficult to find many more examples, including some that seem at first to be much bigger, such as the set of rational numbers. A large class of examples is provided by the following.

Theorem 18.7. Suppose $S_0, S_1, \ldots$ are countable sets. The set $\cup_{n=0}^{\infty} S_n$ is countable.

Proof. Again, we settle for an informal proof. We describe, without actually providing a formula, a way of listing in order the elements of the union. Consider the two-dimensional "array" whose n^{th} row contains the elements of S_n; notice that since S_n may be finite, these rows may be of unequal length. Now consider the path shown in Fig. 18-1. It is clear that this path will eventually hit each element of $\cup_{n=0}^{\infty} S_n$ at least once. It will hit an element more than once if that element belongs to S_n for more than one n. The function f defined by

$$f(i) = \text{the } i^{\text{th}} \text{ distinct element of } \bigcup_{n=0}^{\infty} S_n \text{ to be hit by the path}$$

is a bijection—either from $\{0, 1, \ldots, m\}$ to $\cup_{n=0}^{\infty} S_n$ or from $\mathcal{N}$ to this union, depending on whether the union is finite or infinite. Therefore, the union is a countable set.

Example 18.1. Let $S = \mathcal{N} \times \mathcal{N}$, the set of all ordered pairs of natural numbers. It follows easily from Theorem 18.7 that S is countable, since

$$\mathcal{N} \times \mathcal{N} = \bigcup_{m=0}^{\infty} (\{m\} \times \mathcal{N})$$

and there is an obvious bijection from $\mathcal{N}$ to each of the sets $\{m\} \times \mathcal{N}$. However, we can be more explicit about the bijection f from $\mathcal{N}$ to $\mathcal{N} \times \mathcal{N}$ illustrated in Fig. 18-1 and described in the proof of Theorem 18.7. Let's give the formula for $f^{-1}(m, n)$—in other words, the formula that "counts" the pairs in $\mathcal{N} \times \mathcal{N}$.

We refer again to the path shown in Fig. 18-1. Let $j \geq 0$; as the path loops through the array the jth time, it hits all the pairs (m, n) for which $m + n = j$, and there are $j + 1$ such pairs. Furthermore, for a specific pair (m, n) with $m + n = j$, there are m other pairs (p, q) with $p + q = j$ that get hit by the path before this one. Therefore, the total number of pairs that precede (m, n) in the enumeration corresponding to f is

$$1 + 2 + \ldots + (m + n - 1) + (m + n) + m = (m + n)(m + n + 1)/2 + m$$

(see Exercise 2.1). This is just another way of saying that

$$f^{-1}(m, n) = (m + n)(m + n + 1)/2 + m$$

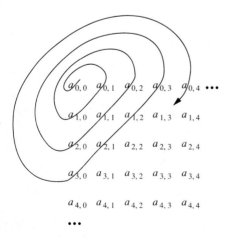

$a_{0,0}$ $a_{0,1}$ $a_{0,2}$ $a_{0,3}$ $a_{0,4}$ $\cdots$

$a_{1,0}$ $a_{1,1}$ $a_{1,2}$ $a_{1,3}$ $a_{1,4}$

$a_{2,0}$ $a_{2,1}$ $a_{2,2}$ $a_{2,3}$ $a_{2,4}$

$a_{3,0}$ $a_{3,1}$ $a_{3,2}$ $a_{3,3}$ $a_{3,4}$

$a_{4,0}$ $a_{4,1}$ $a_{4,2}$ $a_{4,3}$ $a_{4,4}$

$\cdots$

FIGURE 18-1
Listing the elements of $\cup_{n=0}^{\infty} S_n$.

The function f is often referred to as a *pairing* function and is useful in a number of counting arguments.

Corollary 18.1. If Σ is a finite alphabet, the set Σ^* is countable.

Proof. We may write Σ^* as the union

$$\bigcup_{n=0}^{\infty} S_n$$

where for each n, S_n is the set of all strings over Σ of length n. S_n is finite and therefore countable, and the corollary follows from Theorem 18.7.

We are now ready to produce sets that are uncountable. The most well known is the set of real numbers, and you are encouraged to consult any book on set theory for the classic diagonal proof due to Cantor. We begin instead with a set that will be more directly useful to us, although the argument here is also due to Cantor and is very similar—see Exercise 18.12.

Theorem 18.8. If S is a countably infinite set, then 2^S, the set of all subsets of S, is uncountably infinite. In particular, the set of all languages over a nonempty alphabet Σ is uncountable.

Proof. It is sufficient to show that $2^{\mathcal{N}}$ is uncountable, for if there is a bijection from $\mathcal{N}$ to S, there is also one from $2^{\mathcal{N}}$ to 2^S, and therefore, if $2^{\mathcal{N}}$ is uncountable, 2^S must be—see Exercise 18.8. The proof is by contradiction. Suppose $2^{\mathcal{N}}$ is countably infinite. The subsets of $\mathcal{N}$ can be listed $A_0, A_1, \ldots$, so that every subset is A_i for some i. Let

$$A = \{i \,|\, i \geq 0 \quad \text{and} \quad i \notin A_i\}$$

A is a subset of $\mathcal{N}$, and so $A = A_I$ for some I. Consider the statement $I \in A_I$. On the one hand, if it is true, then I does not satisfy the membership condition for the set A, and thus $I \notin A = A_I$. But on the other hand, if $I \notin A_I$, then I *does* satisfy the condition for membership in A, and thus $I \in A = A_I$. You may wish to stop at this point and read the last four or five sentences again.

To summarize: starting with the assumption that $2^{\mathcal{N}}$ is countably infinite, we have found a set $A \subseteq \mathcal{N}$ so that

1. If $I \in A$, then $I \notin A$;
2. If $I \notin A$, then $I \in A$.

We have a contradiction, since we must have $I \in A$ or $I \notin A$, but statements 1 and 2 say we can have neither. Therefore, $2^{\mathcal{N}}$ is not countably infinite.

The *diagonal* nature of the above argument has to do with the definition of the set A and can be described in geometric terms. Consider an infinite two-dimensional array as shown below, with rows indexed by I and columns by J, whose $(I, J)^{\text{th}}$ entry is the truth value of the statement $I \notin A_J$.

$$\begin{array}{ccccc}
 & 0 & 1 & 2 & 3 & \cdots \\
0 & \underline{0 \notin A_0} & 0 \notin A_1 & 0 \notin A_2 & 0 \notin A_3 & \cdots \\
1 & 1 \notin A_0 & \underline{1 \notin A_1} & 1 \notin A_2 & 1 \notin A_3 & \\
2 & 2 \notin A_0 & 2 \notin A_1 & \underline{2 \notin A_2} & 2 \notin A_3 & \\
3 & 3 \notin A_0 & 3 \notin A_1 & 3 \notin A_2 & \underline{3 \notin A_3} & \\
 & \cdots & & & &
\end{array}$$

The diagonal entries of this matrix are underlined in the diagram. A is the set of elements I for which the diagonal entry $I \notin A_I$ of the matrix is true. As we mentioned earlier, this type of argument can be applied in a number of settings. We will see it again in the next section and several times thereafter.

We have the ingredients we need for the main result of this section. Let us consider languages over a finite alphabet, say $\{x, y\}$.

Theorem 18.9. Not all languages over $\{x, y\}$ are recursively enumerable.

Proof. The result will follow from Theorem 18.8 and the fact, which we now prove, that the set $\mathcal{RE}$ of recursively enumerable languages over $\{x, y\}$ is countable.

We assume x and y are both elements of the fixed alphabet $\mathcal{S}$ introduced in Section 17.4; every recursively enumerable language $L \subseteq \{x, y\}^*$ can be accepted by some TM $t(L)$, all of whose states are in the set $\mathcal{Q}$ and all of whose tape symbols are in $\mathcal{S}$. Let Θ be the set of all such TMs. The encoding e discussed in Section 17.4 is a one-to-one function from Θ to $\{x, y\}^*$. We have

$$t : \mathcal{RE} \to \Theta$$

$$e : \Theta \to \{x, y\}^*$$

and therefore

$$e \circ t : \mathcal{RE} \to \{x, y\}^*$$

The function t is also one-to-one, since a TM accepts only one language, and thus $e \circ t$ is one-to-one. We obtain a bijection from $\mathcal{RE}$ to a subset of $\{x, y\}^*$. According to Corollary 18.1, the set $\{x, y\}^*$ is countable. It follows that every subset is, and therefore that $\mathcal{RE}$ is.

One might question whether the result in Theorem 18.9 is necessarily significant in the theory of computation. The result was established by showing that there are not enough Turing machines to recognize all possible languages, because there are not enough strings available to specify Turing machines. Specifying a TM to accept a language is one way of specifying the language, but it is not the only way. We could carry the argument slightly farther and observe that there aren't enough strings to specify all possible languages in *any* way. Since there are uncountably many languages, there must be some that are so complex, or so bizarre, that they can never even be described precisely, much less accepted by a TM. This might even be viewed as reassuring, in the following sense: perhaps it is still true that any language we would ever be interested in—any language whose existence we were aware of, because we were at least able to describe it in some way—*could* be accepted by some TM. At this point in our discussion, such a possibility is conceivable. In the next section, however, we will see that things do not turn out this way.

18.4   EXAMPLES

As advertised, we are about to produce an example of a non-recursively-enumerable language. Theorem 18.9 tells us that there are plenty of them (uncountably many, in fact—see Exercise 18.9), but on the face of it, actually producing one doesn't seem so easy. According to the Church–Turing thesis, this involves describing a language, the strings of which cannot be recognized by any conceivable algorithmic procedure. A subtle approach is called for, and "subtle"' is an excellent description of the diagonal argument from the preceding section. There we began with a matrix whose rows corresponded to integers I and whose columns corresponded to sets A_J. The $(I, J)^{\text{th}}$ entry was formed by using the set inclusion operation to relate I to J.

Here we can use an argument that parallels the earlier one closely but is even more ingenious. To visualize it in the same geometric way, think of the set of all Turing machines as being enumerated $T_0, T_1, \ldots$, and consider for each I the encoded string $e(T_I) \in \{x, y\}^*$, where e is the encoding function discussed in Section 17.5. Then repeat the previous diagonal argument, with these changes: instead of I, use $e(T_I)$; instead of A_J, use T_J; and replace "$I \notin A_J$" by "$e(T_I)$ is not accepted by T_J." You might wish to stop at this point and see if you can finish the construction by yourself, and produce a language that cannot be accepted by any TM. Our official definition is slightly different, in part because it does not use the countability of the set of TMs explicitly, but primarily because it is convenient in some of the later applications to consider a larger language.

Definition 18.4. Let *NonSelfAccepting* be the following subset of $\{x, y\}^*$:

$$NonSelfAccepting = NSA_1 \cup NSA_2$$

where

$$NSA_1 = \{w \in \{x, y\}^* | w = e(T) \quad \text{and} \quad T \text{ does not accept } w\}$$

$$NSA_2 = \{w \in \{x, y\}^* | w \text{ is not } e(T) \text{ for any TM } T\}$$

Let *SelfAccepting* be the complement of *NonSelfAccepting* in $\{x, y\}^*$, so that

$$SelfAccepting = \{w \in \{x, y\}^* | w = e(T) \quad \text{and} \quad T \text{ accepts } w\}$$

Theorem 18.10. *NonSelfAccepting* is not recursively enumerable.

Proof. First, notice that the way the definition is stated uses the fact that the encoding function e is one-to-one: if w is of the form $e(T)$, there is only one such T. As you would expect from the earlier diagonal argument, the proof is by contradiction. Suppose there is a TM T_0 accepting *NonSelfAccepting*; i.e., T_0 accepts an input string w if and only if $w \in$ *NonSelfAccepting*. Let $w_0 = e(T_0)$. We may ask the question: does T_0 accept w_0? On the one hand, if T_0 accepts w_0, then $w_0 \in$ *NonSelfAccepting*, since T_0 accepts *NonSelfAccepting*. Since $w_0 \in$ *NonSelfAccepting* and $w_0 = e(T_0)$, $w_0 \in NSA_1$. But by definition, a string $w = e(T)$ can be in NSA_1 only if T does not accept w. Thus, if T_0 accepts w_0, T_0 does not accept w_0. On the other hand, if T_0 does not accept w_0, w_0 satisfies the membership condition for NSA_1, and thus T_0 accepts w_0 since T_0 accepts *NonSelfAccepting*. Since we must have either $w_0 \in$ *NonSelfAccepting* or $w_0 \notin$ *NonSelfAccepting*, we have a contradiction; therefore, the TM T_0 accepting *NonSelfAccepting* cannot exist.

Even after you understand this proof thoroughly—which may require re-reading it—your reaction might be, So what? The language *NonSelfAccepting* seems somewhat contrived, to say the least, and since we know from Section 18.2 that there must be many languages that cannot be accepted by TMs, it may not strike you as especially significant that this strange-sounding language happens to be one of them. However, Theorem 18.10, and Theorem 18.11, whose proof uses Theorem 18.10, will turn out to have a number of important consequences. We will use it to show that certain problems, including some very reasonable-sounding ones, are "unsolvable." These matters will be investigated further in Chapter 20; for now, at least we have one example of a language that is not recursively enumerable, and we can use it to produce other examples that illustrate the relationship between recursive enumerability and recursiveness.

Theorem 18.11. *SelfAccepting* is recursively enumerable but not recursive. In other words, *SelfAccepting* can be *accepted* by a TM, but any such TM will loop forever on at least one input string.

Proof. The proof of the second statement is easy: if *SelfAccepting* were recursive, its complement *NonSelfAccepting* would be recursive and therefore recursively enumerable, contradicting Theorem 18.10. Thus, it is sufficient to construct a TM T_{SA} accepting *Self-Accepting*.

Recall that $SelfAccepting = \{w | w = e(T)$ and T accepts $w\}$. T_{SA} begins by determining whether the input string w is of the form $e(T)$ for some T. If it is not, T_{SA} crashes; if $w = e(T)$, T_{SA} simulates the processing of w by T and halts if and only if T would halt on w. We already have a TM to carry out the second part—it is the universal TM T_U introduced in Section 17.4, operating on the string $we(w) = e(T)e(w)$. Thus, T_{SA} is constructed in the form $T_1 T_U$. If the input string w is $e(T)$ for some T, T_1 halts leaving the string $we(w)$ on the tape for T_U, and otherwise T_1 crashes. The problem is therefore reduced to constructing T_1.

In order for a string w to be $e(T)$ for some T, it must consist of a string $x^k y$ followed by strings that encode TM moves—in other words, it must correspond to the regular expression

$$x^+ y (x^+ y x^+ y x^+ y x^+ y)^+$$

Second, there can be at most one move specified for each state-symbol combination; i.e., there cannot be two "5-tuples" with identical first two parts. Third, the fifth part of each 5-tuple must be x, xx, or xxx, so that it represents a valid direction. Finally, no 5-tuple is allowed to have first part x, since a TM is not allowed to move from the halt state.

Any string that satisfies these conditions is $e(T)$ for some T, even if the TM T crashes immediately or fails for other reasons to do anything 'meaningful."

All but the second of these conditions are easily tested. To test for the second, T_1 can execute a loop, during the ith iteration of which T_1 searches for 5-tuples after the ith that have the same first two parts as the ith. The details are slightly complicated but substantially the same as the "search" portion of the universal TM shown in Fig. 17-6, and we shall not spell them out.

If any of the four conditions for w to be of the form $e(T)$ is not met, T_1 simply crashes. If it tests successfully for all four, then T_1 must restore the input $w = e(T)$ to its original form and add to the end of it the string $e(w)$. Since w is itself a string of x's and y's, generating the string $e(w)$ is straightforward: $e(w)$ begins with yy; if the two symbols x and y are a_i and a_j, respectively, in the alphabet $\mathcal{S}$, each x in w will be encoded by x^{i+1} and each y by x^{j+1}, each such string being followed by y. For example, $xxyxy$ would become $yyx^{i+1}yx^{i+1}yx^{j+1}yx^{i+1}yx^{j+1}y$. When T_1 has left the string $we(w)$ on the tape, it halts with its head on square 0.

EXERCISES

18.1. Show that if L_1 and L_2 are both recursive languages in Σ^*, then $L_1 \cup L_2$ and $L_1 \cap L_2$ are also recursive.

18.2. In the proof of Theorem 18.1, if L_1 and L_2 are recursively enumerable subsets of Σ^* and T_1 and T_2 are TMs accepting L_1 and L_2, respectively, a new TM with two tapes is constructed that simulates both T_1 and T_2 simultaneously. Consider instead the idea of simulating the two machines sequentially, which can easily be done using only one tape, as follows. First, the tape Δx is transformed to $\Delta x \# \Delta x$. T_1 is then simulated, using the second copy of x as input and using the marker $\#$ to represent the end of the tape. If and when T_1 stops, either by halting or by crashing, the tape is erased except for the original input, and T_2 is simulated.

    (a) Could such a TM be used in Theorem 18.1 to show that the union of two recursively enumerable languages is recursively enumerable? Why?

    (b) Could such a TM be used to show that the intersection of two recursively enumerable languages is recursively enumerable? Why?

18.3. Suppose L is recursively enumerable but not recursive. Show that for any TM T accepting L, there must be infinitely many input strings x for which T loops forever.

18.4. Is the following statement true or false? If $L_1, L_2, \ldots$ are recursively enumerable subsets of Σ^*, then $\cup_{i=1}^{\infty} L_i$ is recursively enumerable.

18.5. Suppose that the languages $L_1, L_2, \ldots, L_N$ form a partition of Σ^* (i.e., their union is Σ^* and the intersection of any two is empty), and that each L_i is recursively enumerable. Show that each L_i is recursive.

18.6. Sketch a proof that if L_1 and L_2 are recursively enumerable subsets of Σ^*, then both $L_1 L_2$ and L_1^* are recursively enumerable, by constructing nondeterministic TMs to accept these languages.

18.7. Show that any subset of a countable set is countable.

18.8. Show that if there is a bijection from the set S to the set T, and S is uncountable, then T is uncountable.

18.9. Show that if the set S is uncountable and the subset T of S is countable, then the set $S - T$ is uncountable.

18.10. Let $\mathcal{N}$ denote the set of nonnegative integers and $\mathcal{Q}$ the set of all rational numbers, or fractions, negative as well as nonnegative. Show that the set $\mathcal{Q}$ is countable by describing explicitly a bijection from $\mathcal{N}$ to $\mathcal{Q}$. A formula is not necessary, but specify the bijection precisely.

18.11. Extend Theorem 18.8 to show that if S is *any* set (not necessarily countable), the set 2^S is bigger than S; i.e., there is a bijection from S to a subset of 2^S, but there is not a bijection from S to 2^S. This result is one way of showing that there are an infinite number of "orders of infinity."

18.12. Let S be the set of all infinite sequences $a_0, a_1, \ldots$, where each a_i is either 0 or 1.

    (a) Describe a bijection from S to the set $2^{\mathcal{N}}$. It follows from Theorem 18.8, then, that this set is uncountable.

    (b) Show directly, using a diagonal argument, that S is uncountable. Begin by supposing that there is an enumeration $s_0, s_1, \ldots$ of the elements of S, and find an $s \in S$ that is not in the list. Convince yourself, using your solution to part (a), that this proof is essentially the same as the proof given to Theorem 18.8.

18.13. In each case, determine whether the given set is countable or uncountable. Prove your answer.

    (a) The set of all finite subsets of $\mathcal{N}$

    (b) The set of all finite partitions of $\mathcal{N}$ (Hint: for any $A \subseteq \mathcal{N}$, the partition consisting of the two subsets A and A' is a finite partition of $\mathcal{N}$)

    (c) The set of all functions from $\mathcal{N}$ to $\{0, 1\}$ (see Exercise 18.12)

    (d) The set of all functions from $\mathcal{N}$ to $\mathcal{N}$

    (e) The set of all functions from $\{0, 1\}$ to $\mathcal{N}$

    (f) The set of all periodic functions from $\mathcal{N}$ to $\mathcal{N}$ (A function $f : \mathcal{N} \to \mathcal{N}$ is periodic if, for some integer $P_f > 0$, $f(x) = f(x + P_f)$ for every x; such a function is completely determined, once its values on the set $\{0, 1, \ldots, P_f - 1\}$ are specified.)

    (g) The set of all eventually constant functions from $\mathcal{N}$ to $\mathcal{N}$ (A function $f : \mathcal{N} \to \mathcal{N}$ is eventually constant if there are numbers C_f and N_f so that $f(x) = C_f$ for every $x \geq N_f$.)

18.14. We know $2^{\mathcal{N}}$ is uncountable. Give an example of a subset $S \subseteq 2^{\mathcal{N}}$ so that both S and $2^{\mathcal{N}} - S$ are uncountable.

18.15. Show that there exists a language L so that neither L nor L' is recursively enumerable. Can you give an example of such a language?

18.16. The proof of Theorem 18.1 involved a result sometimes known as the "infinity lemma," which may be formulated in terms of trees. Think of a configuration of a nondeterministic TM as a node in a tree. The root is the initial configuration with some input string x, and in general the children of any node N correspond to the configurations that could be reached from configuration N in one move. Since a nondeterministic TM has only a finite number of possible moves from any configuration, any node in the corresponding tree has only finitely many children. Saying that every sequence of moves leads to a halt or a crash is equivalent to saying that there is no infinite path in the tree from the root. The infinity lemma says that under these circumstances, the tree has a longest path; i.e., there is a number K so that the TM must halt or crash within K moves, no matter what choices it makes.

Complete the following proof of the infinity lemma. Suppose there is no longest path—i.e., for any integer n, there is a path from the root with more than n nodes. This means that the root node must have infinitely many descendants. But since the root node has only finitely many children, at least one of its children must also have infinitely many descendants.

18.17. This exercise has to do with actual computers. While it involves recursively enumerable languages only indirectly, it should be obvious after you have studied it why it is included in this chapter. The assumption is made throughout that the computer we are referring to uses some fixed operating system, under which all our programs run. A "program" can be thought of as a function from strings to strings: it takes one string as input and produces another as output. On the other hand, a program written in any particular programming language can be thought of as a string itself. By definition, a program P spreads a *virus* on input x if running P with input x causes the operating system to be altered. It is safe on input x if this doesn't happen, and it is safe if it is safe on every input string. A *virus tester* is a program IsSafe that when given the input Px, where P is a program and x is a string, produces the output "YES" if P is safe on the input x and "NO" otherwise. (We assume that in a string of the form Px, there is no ambiguity as to where the program P stops.) Prove that if there actually is the possibility of a virus—i.e., there is a program and an input that would cause the operating system to be altered—then there can be no virus tester that is both safe and correct. (Suppose there is such a virus tester IsSafe. Then it is possible to write a program D—for "diagonal"—that operates as follows when given a program P as input. It evaluates IsSafe(PP); if this is "NO", it prints "XXX", and otherwise it alters the operating system. Consider what D does on input D.)

CHAPTER
19

MORE
GENERAL
GRAMMARS

19.1 UNRESTRICTED GRAMMARS

The two general ways we have discussed for describing languages are specifying a procedure for generating all strings in the language, and specifying an algorithm, embodied in an abstract machine, for determining whether a given string is in the language or not. Regular languages are those that can be recognized by finite automata and those that can be generated by regular grammars or regular expressions. Context-free languages can be recognized by pushdown automata and generated by context-free grammars. Recursively enumerable languages have been defined as those that can be accepted by Turing machines, and we shall see in this chapter that they are precisely the languages that can be generated by certain "grammars" more general than context-free grammars. In addition, there is a type of grammar falling between a CFG and the most general type, and a corresponding class of machines slightly less general than TMs but more general than PDAs. These will be discussed briefly, starting in Section 19.3.

The "context-freeness" of a CFG lies in the fact that at any point in a derivation any variable A in the current string can be replaced by the right side of any A-production, regardless of the context. Another way to view this is to say that the left sides of productions are always single variables: as long as a variable on the left side of a production is present, that production can be applied. It is the context-freeness that allows us to prove the pumping lemma, since any sufficiently long derivation in a CFG is bound to contain a variable A that is "self-embedded"—i.e., for which $S \Rightarrow^* vAz \Rightarrow^* vwAyz$. Thus, it is the context-freeness that produces the "regularity" conditions described by the pumping lemma. We may remove this restriction by allowing the left side of a production to be more than a single variable. For example, if we wanted to specify that a variable A can be replaced by the string γ only when A is preceded by α and followed by β, we could use the production

$$\alpha A \beta \rightarrow \alpha \gamma \beta$$

Grammars in which all productions are of this type, with the additional requirement that $\gamma \neq \Lambda$, have been studied and will be mentioned later. It would seem that even without this extra restriction, such grammars are less than completely general, since their productions still involve replacing a single variable by a string and leaving everything else alone. An even more general sort of production might have the form

$$\alpha A \beta \rightarrow \gamma$$

Since α and β can both contain variables, it is more appropriate to think of such a production as simply a substitution of one string for another, with the idea of strings replacing variables retained only in the sense that the left side of a production must contain at least one variable. In fact, it turns out that every production of this second type can be replaced by a set of productions of the first type. Nevertheless, it is usually more convenient to allow the second type in defining our new grammars.

Definition 19.1. An *unrestricted grammar*, or *phrase-structure* grammar, is a 4-tuple $G = (V, \Sigma, S, P)$, where

V and Σ are finite sets, of *variables* and *terminals*, respectively, with $V \cap \Sigma = \varnothing$;
$S \in V$ (the *start* symbol);
P is a finite set of *productions* of the form $\alpha \rightarrow \beta$ where $\alpha \in (V \cup \Sigma)^+$, α contains at least one variable, and $\beta \in (V \cup \Sigma)^*$.

Much of the notation developed for context-free grammars can be carried over intact. In particular,

$$\alpha \Rightarrow_G^* \beta$$

means that β can be derived from α in zero or more steps, and

$$L(G) = \{x \in \Sigma^* | S \Rightarrow_G^* x\}$$

To illustrate the generality of these grammars, we consider two examples, which were our first two examples of non-context-free languages in Chapter 15.

Example 19.1. Let $L = \{a^n b^n c^n | n > 0\}$. Our grammar will involve variables A, B, and C, as well as two others to be explained shortly. First, we will have productions that produce strings with equal numbers of A's, B's, C's. Second, we will have productions that allow strings of A's, B's, and C's to transform themselves so that all the A's come first and all the C's last. Finally, we will have productions that change the variables to the corresponding terminals—but only if they are in the desired order.

The first two types of productions are easy to come up with. The context-free productions

$$S \rightarrow ABCS \mid ABC$$

generate all strings of the form α^N, where $\alpha = ABC$. Next, saying that the symbols A, B, and C are in the correct order is the same as saying that the string contains none of the substrings BA, CA, or CB. It is therefore appropriate to include productions that change these illegal strings to legal ones:

$$BA \rightarrow AB$$
$$CA \rightarrow AC$$
$$CB \rightarrow BC$$

Simply adding the productions $A \rightarrow a$, and so on, would not be correct, since they might be used too soon, before the variables line themselves up properly. Instead we say that C can be replaced by c *if* it is preceded by c or b:

$$cC \rightarrow cc$$
$$bC \rightarrow bc$$

B can be replaced by b if it is preceded by b or a:

$$bB \rightarrow bb$$
$$aB \rightarrow ab$$

and, tentatively, A can be replaced by a if it is preceded by a:

$$aA \rightarrow aa$$

Ignoring the obvious problem for a moment, we see that with only these productions, the illegal combinations ba, ca, and cb can never occur. But now for the problem: where does the first a come from? It is still not correct to have $A \rightarrow a$, even with our restrictions on b's and c's, because this would allow a substring in which all the variables were in the correct order to change itself into a string of terminals, even though the entire string still had illegal combinations. Somehow, we need the leftmost A to become an a to start things off. We solve the problem by using an extra variable F to stand for "the left end of the string". Then we can use the same argument as above and say that A can be replaced by a only when it is preceded by a or F:

$$FA \rightarrow a$$

We get F at the left end initially by the production

$$S \rightarrow FS_1$$

so that the two context-free productions above will involve S_1 instead of S. The final grammar G has $V = \{S, F, S_1, A, B, C\}$, $\Sigma = \{a, b, c\}$, and productions

$$S \rightarrow FS_1 \qquad S_1 \rightarrow ABCS_1 \mid ABC$$
$$BA \rightarrow AB \qquad CA \rightarrow AC \qquad CB \rightarrow BC$$
$$FA \rightarrow a \qquad aA \rightarrow aa \qquad aB \rightarrow ab$$
$$bB \rightarrow bb \qquad bC \rightarrow bc \qquad cC \rightarrow cc$$

The string *aabbcc*, for example, can be derived as follows. At each point, the underlined substring is the one that is replaced in the subsequent step.

$$S \Rightarrow F\underline{S_1} \qquad \Rightarrow FABC\underline{S_1} \quad \Rightarrow FABCABC\underline{S_1}$$

$$\Rightarrow FAB\underline{C}ABC \Rightarrow FA\underline{BA}CBC \Rightarrow FAAB\underline{C}BC$$

$$\Rightarrow \underline{FA}ABBCC \Rightarrow \underline{a}ABBCC \quad \Rightarrow a\underline{a}BBCC$$

$$\Rightarrow aa\underline{b}BCC \quad \Rightarrow aab\underline{b}CC \quad \Rightarrow aabb\underline{c}C$$

$$\Rightarrow aabbcc$$

It is easy to see that any string in L can be derived from this grammar, but it may not be quite so obvious that no other strings can. Notice first, however, that if $S \Rightarrow^* \alpha$, α cannot have a terminal symbol appearing after a variable; thus $\alpha \in \Sigma^* V^*$. Second, any subsequent production leaves the string of terminals intact and either rearranges the variables or adds one more terminal. Suppose $u \in L(G)$ and u has an illegal combination of terminals, say ba. Then $u = vbaw$, and there is a derivation of u of the form $S \Rightarrow^* vb\beta$ for some $\beta \in V^*$. But this is impossible, since no matter what β is, it is impossible to produce a as the next terminal.

If you study the derivation given in the first example, you may be reminded of the moves of a Turing machine. Transformations of the string resemble the way a TM transforms its tape, and the movement of A's to the left and C's to the right, as well as the "propagation" of terminal symbols to the right in the last phase of the derivation, are reminiscent of the motion of a TM's tape head. This is not mere coincidence, as we shall see presently: a grammar this general has the potential for carrying out the same sorts of "computations" as a TM. For the moment, we use this idea of symbols migrating through the string again in our next example.

Example 19.2. Let $L = \{ss \mid s \in \{a, b\}^*\}$. Consider first how we might construct a nondeterministic TM to generate strings of this type. One way would be to generate an arbitrary sequence of symbols representing the first half, then make a copy immediately following. Instead, we build the two halves simultaneously, one symbol at a time. Suppose we use a marker M to denote the middle of the string, and suppose that at some point we have the string sMs. To produce a longer string of the same type, we may insert an extra symbol at the beginning, then move just past the M to insert the same symbol. Equivalently, we may insert two identical symbols at the beginning, and let the second migrate to the right until it passes the M. This is the approach we take in constructing our grammar G. It will be helpful to use a second marker variable F to designate the front of the string. The first production in any derivation will be

$$S \rightarrow FM$$

Each time a new symbol σ is added, the migrating duplicate symbol will be the variable that is the uppercase version of σ. Thus, we have the productions

$$F \rightarrow FaA$$

$$F \rightarrow FbB$$

to produce the symbols, and the productions

$$Aa \rightarrow aA$$

$$Ab \rightarrow bA$$

$$Ba \rightarrow aB$$

$$Bb \rightarrow bB$$

to allow A or B to move to the right past any terminals. Eventually, this migrating variable hits M, at which point it passes M and immediately changes to the appropriate terminal, using one of the productions

$$AM \rightarrow Ma$$

$$BM \rightarrow Mb$$

To complete a derivation, we need the productions

$$F \rightarrow \Lambda$$

$$M \rightarrow \Lambda$$

The string *abbabb* has the following derivation. Again, the underlined portion of each string is the left side of the production to be used next.

$$S \Rightarrow \underline{F}M \qquad \Rightarrow Fb\underline{BM} \qquad \Rightarrow \underline{F}bMb$$

$$\Rightarrow Fb\underline{Bb}Mb \qquad \Rightarrow Fbb\underline{BM}b \qquad \Rightarrow \underline{F}bbMbb$$

$$\Rightarrow Fa\underline{Ab}bMbb \Rightarrow Fab\underline{Ab}Mbb \Rightarrow Fabb\underline{AM}bb$$

$$\Rightarrow \underline{F}abbMabb \Rightarrow abb\underline{M}abb \quad \Rightarrow abbabb$$

It is reasonably clear that any string in L can be generated by our grammar. We argue informally that no other strings are generated, as follows. First, it is clear that every string in $L(G)$ has even length, since the only productions that increase the ultimate length of the string increase it by 2. Second, when M is finally eliminated in the derivation, all the terminal symbols in the final string are present, and half come before M. Those preceding M are the terminals in the productions $F \rightarrow FaA$ and $F \rightarrow FbB$, since the only other productions that create terminals create them to the right of M. The farther to the left a terminal in the first half is, the later it appeared in the derivation, since the relative order of terminals in the first half never changes. But consider the A's and B's created by these same two productions. For any two, the one that appeared first reaches M first, since the two can never be transposed. Therefore, of two terminals in the second half, the one to the left came from the variable appearing later, so the second half matches the first.

19.2 GRAMMARS AND TURING MACHINES

The first two examples in this chapter make it clear that unrestricted grammars are more general than context-free grammars. In this section, we show first that any language generated by such a grammar can be accepted by some TM; this is straightforward. Next, we show that these grammars are really as general as TMs: the languages they generate account for all of the recursively enumerable languages.

Theorem 19.1. If $G = (V, \Sigma, S, P)$ is an unrestricted grammar, there is a TM $M = (Q, \Sigma, \Gamma, q_0, \delta)$ accepting $L(G)$.

Proof. According to Theorem 17.3, it is sufficient to find a nondeterministic TM M. The idea behind the construction of M is fairly simple. It will move its head to the right of the input string, nondeterministically choose a derivation in G to simulate on its tape, then compare the derived string to the input string. If the input string is in $L(G)$, some choice of moves will cause M to simulate the derivation of that string, and M will discover that the two strings are equal and halt. Otherwise, no matter what moves M makes, it will either generate a string that doesn't match the input or fail to complete a derivation at all, and in neither case will it halt. M may be described as this composite machine:

$$MovePastInput \to Simulate \to Equal$$

MovePastInput simply moves the tape head to the first blank square following the input string. *Equal* starts with the tape looking like $\underline{\Delta}x\Delta y$, where x is the input string and y is the string produced by the simulated derivation. It halts if and only if $x = y$. Both *MovePastInput* and *Equal* are easy to construct, and the problem is reduced to constructing the *Simulate* TM.

Simulate will include in its tape alphabet all the symbols of $\Sigma \cup V$ and possibly others. It begins by moving one square to the right and writing the start symbol S. Beginning at this point it enters a loop, which it may terminate after any number of iterations. A single iteration corresponds to a particular production of G, selected nondeterministically, and consists of selecting if possible from the string on the tape an occurrence of the first symbol in the left side of that production, attempting to find beginning at that point the entire left side of the production, replacing it by the right side, and returning the head to the beginning of the string. When *Simulate* chooses to exit the loop, it makes one more pass through the string until it encounters Δ, searches the string right-to-left for variables, and if it finds none returns the tape head to square 0 and halts. Nondeterminism is present in three places: choosing a production to use in a single iteration of the loop, selecting on the tape an occurrence of the beginning symbol in the left side of that production, and deciding when to exit the loop. If an incorrect choice is made at any of these points, the machine may crash. It should be clear, however, that for any string x in $L(G)$, *Simulate* can choose a sequence of moves that will result in x ending up on the tape, beginning in the square following that in which *Simulate* starts. Conversely, a string is left on the tape by *Simulate* only if the string can be derived in G.

Example 19.3. Consider the grammar with productions

$$S \to aBS \mid \Lambda$$

$$aB \to Ba$$

$$Ba \to aB$$

$$B \to b$$

It is easy to convince yourself that this grammar generates the languages of strings x with $N_a(x) = N_b(x)$. Figure 19-1 shows the *Simulate* TM discussed in the proof of Theorem 19.1. Note that in this example, the only productions in which the left and right sides are of unequal length are the S-productions, and S appears only at the right end of the string. In a more general example, applying a production like $S \to aBS$ could be

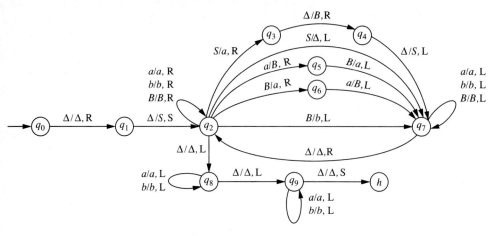

FIGURE 19-1
The *Simulate* TM for Example 19.3.

accomplished by using an Insert TM (see Example 16.5) twice, and $S \rightarrow \Lambda$ would require a deletion. You should trace the moves of *Simulate* as it simulates the derivation of a string in the language, say $abba$.

Theorem 19.2. If $L \subseteq \Sigma^*$ is a recursively enumerable language, there is an unrestricted grammar G generating L.

Proof. Let $M = (Q, \Sigma, \Gamma, q_0, \delta)$ be a TM accepting L. We have seen that derivations in a general grammar can resemble sequences of Turing machine moves. We shall exploit that feature, since the grammar we construct will do no less than simulate the moves of M. More specifically, the productions of G will be of three types:

1. Productions that generate two copies of an arbitrary element of Σ^*, along with other symbols that act as markers to keep the two copies separate;
2. Productions that simulate the moves of M, using as input one of the two copies of the string, while leaving the other copy unchanged; and
3. Productions that erase everything but the unmodified copy of the string, *provided* that the simulated moves of M applied to the other copy lead to a halt.

The two copies of the original string $a_1 a_2 \ldots a_k$ will take the form

$$(a_1 a_1)(a_2 a_2) \ldots (a_k a_k)$$

The symbols "(" and ")" are used here as variables. The first terminal symbol of each pair will stay the same, while the second is liable to be changed during the simulation.

When M begins, there is a blank in square 0 of the tape. In addition, M may use some of the blank portion of the tape to the right of the input string. Thus, we actually need to begin with a string of the form

$$(\Delta\Delta)(a_1 a_1) \ldots (a_k a_k)(\Delta\Delta) \ldots (\Delta\Delta)$$

The symbol Δ is also acting as a variable in G. If M accepts x by making a sequence of moves using n blank squares to the right of the input string, a derivation of x in G will begin by placing at least n copies of $(\Delta\Delta)$ at the end of the string.

It is now obvious how M's tape is represented during the simulation. In order to represent the complete TM configuration, we need a way of indicating both the state and the head position. We can do both by adding to our set of variables the states of M, and letting a state appear in the string just before the symbol-pair corresponding to the current head position. Thus, the string with which the simulation begins is

$$q_0(\Delta\Delta)(a_1 a_1)\ldots(a_k a_k)(\Delta\Delta)\ldots(\Delta\Delta)$$

If at some point during the processing M is in the configuration $(q, b_0 \ldots \underline{b_i} b_{i+1} \ldots b_m)$, the corresponding string in the derivation will be

$$(\Delta b_0)(a_1 b_1)\ldots(a_{i-1} b_{i-1})q(a_i b_i)\ldots(a_k b_k)(\Delta b_{k+1})\ldots(\Delta b_m)(\Delta\Delta)\ldots(\Delta\Delta)$$

(This assumes that m is greater than k, the length of the original input string; otherwise the string will be slightly different.)

The productions that generate the starting string are these:

$$S \rightarrow S(\Delta\Delta) \mid T$$

$$T \rightarrow T(\sigma\sigma) \mid q_0(\Delta\Delta)$$

where there is a production $T \rightarrow T(\sigma\sigma)$ for every symbol $\sigma \in \Sigma$. Corresponding to each move

$$\delta(p, a) = (q, b, \text{R})$$

where $a, b \in \Sigma \cup \{\Delta\}$, we have productions

$$p(\sigma a) \rightarrow (\sigma b)q$$

one for each $\sigma \in \Sigma \cup \{\Delta\}$. Note that the symbol σ stays unchanged and the state variable has moved to the right of the symbol-pair. For each move

$$\delta(p, a) = (q, b, \text{S})$$

we have all the productions

$$p(\sigma a) \rightarrow q(\sigma b)$$

$(\sigma \in \Sigma \cup \{\Delta\})$, and for each move

$$\delta(p, a) = (q, b, \text{L})$$

we have the productions

$$(\sigma_1 \sigma_2)p(\sigma_3 a) \rightarrow q(\sigma_1 \sigma_2)(\sigma_3 b)$$

one for every possible combination of $\sigma_1, \sigma_2, \sigma_3 \in \Sigma \cup \{\Delta\}$.

If the sequence of moves of M leads to the halt state (and only in this case), the derivation produces a string with the symbol h in it. At this point, we need productions that allow us to erase from any string containing h all the variables (elements of Q, Δ, "(", ")", and h), as well as all the terminal symbols in the second position of each pair, so as to leave only the terminal symbols of the input string accepted by M. Productions that accomplish this are

$$h(\sigma_1\sigma_2) \rightarrow h(\sigma_1\sigma_2)h \quad (\sigma_1, \sigma_2 \in \Sigma \cup \{\Delta\})$$

$$(\sigma_1\sigma_2)h \rightarrow h(\sigma_1\sigma_2)h \quad (\sigma_1, \sigma_2 \in \Sigma \cup \{\Delta\})$$

$$h(\sigma_1\sigma_2) \rightarrow \sigma_1 \quad (\sigma_1 \in \Sigma, \sigma_2 \in \Sigma \cup \{\Delta\})$$

$$h(\Delta\sigma) \rightarrow \Lambda \quad (\sigma \in \Sigma \cup \{\Delta\})$$

The productions in the first two lines simply propagate copies of h throughout the string, and those in the last two do the necessary erasing.

We shall not give a rigorous proof that this grammar generates precisely the strings accepted by M, but it is not difficult to convince yourself that this is the case. In the example that follows, a sample derivation is included.

Example 19.4. This example refers to Example 16.2 and the TM pictured in Fig. 16-4, which accepts the language of palindromes over $\{a, b\}$. We shall not list all the productions in the grammar obtained as in Theorem 19.2, since there are 251 of them. Many are unnecessary, since they involve combinations $(\sigma_1\sigma_2)$ that never occur. Instead, we show a derivation of the string aba in this grammar. The corresponding sequence of moves of the TM from which the grammar is derived is shown to the right. Since the TM moves its head to the blank square to the right of the input string and no farther, the derivation begins by producing a string with one copy of $(\Delta\Delta)$ on the right. At each step in the derivation, the underlined portion shows the left side of the production to be used in the next step.

$$
\begin{aligned}
\underline{S} &\Rightarrow \underline{S}(\Delta\Delta) \\
&\Rightarrow \underline{T}(\Delta\Delta) \\
&\Rightarrow \underline{T}(aa)(\Delta\Delta) \\
&\Rightarrow \underline{T}(bb)(aa)(\Delta\Delta) \\
&\Rightarrow \underline{T}(aa)(bb)(aa)(\Delta\Delta) \\
&\Rightarrow \underline{q_0}(\Delta\Delta)(aa)(bb)(aa)(\Delta\Delta) && (q_0, \underline{\Delta}aba) \\
&\Rightarrow (\Delta\Delta)\underline{q_1(aa)}(bb)(aa)(\Delta\Delta) && \vdash (q_1, \Delta\underline{a}ba) \\
&\Rightarrow (\Delta\Delta)(a\Delta)\underline{q_2(bb)}(aa)(\Delta\Delta) && \vdash (q_2, \Delta\Delta\underline{b}a) \\
&\Rightarrow (\Delta\Delta)(a\Delta)(bb)\underline{q_2(aa)}(\Delta\Delta) && \vdash (q_2, \Delta\Delta b\underline{a}) \\
&\Rightarrow (\Delta\Delta)(a\Delta)(bb)(aa)\underline{q_2(\Delta\Delta)} && \vdash (q_2, \Delta\Delta ba\underline{\Delta}) \\
&\Rightarrow (\Delta\Delta)(a\Delta)(bb)\underline{q_3(aa)}(\Delta\Delta) && \vdash (q_3, \Delta\Delta b\underline{a}) \\
&\Rightarrow (\Delta\Delta)\underline{(a\Delta)q_4(bb)}(a\Delta)(\Delta\Delta) && \vdash (q_4, \Delta\Delta\underline{b}) \\
&\Rightarrow (\Delta\Delta)\underline{q_4(a\Delta)}(bb)(a\Delta)(\Delta\Delta) && \vdash (q_4, \Delta\underline{\Delta}b) \\
&\Rightarrow (\Delta\Delta)(a\Delta)\underline{q_1(bb)}(a\Delta)(\Delta\Delta) && \vdash (q_1, \Delta\Delta\underline{b}) \\
&\Rightarrow (\Delta\Delta)(a\Delta)(b\Delta)\underline{q_5(a\Delta)}(\Delta\Delta) && \vdash (q_5, \Delta\Delta\Delta\underline{\Delta}) \\
&\Rightarrow (\Delta\Delta)(a\Delta)\underline{q_6(b\Delta)}(a\Delta)(\Delta\Delta) && \vdash (q_6, \Delta\Delta\underline{\Delta}) \\
&\Rightarrow (\Delta\Delta)(a\Delta)(b\Delta)\underline{h(a\Delta)}(\Delta\Delta) && \vdash (h, \Delta\Delta\Delta\underline{\Delta}) \\
&\Rightarrow (\Delta\Delta)(a\Delta)\underline{(b\Delta)h}(a\Delta)h(\Delta\Delta) \\
&\Rightarrow (\Delta\Delta)(a\Delta)\underline{h(b\Delta)}h(a\Delta)h(\Delta\Delta) \\
&\Rightarrow (\Delta\Delta)\underline{h(a\Delta)}h(b\Delta)h(a\Delta)h(\Delta\Delta) \\
&\Rightarrow \underline{h(\Delta\Delta)}h(a\Delta)h(b\Delta)h(a\Delta)h(\Delta\Delta)
\end{aligned}
$$

$\Rightarrow h(a\Delta)h(b\Delta)h(a\Delta)h(\Delta\Delta)$

$\Rightarrow a\underline{h(b\Delta)}h(a\Delta)h(\Delta\Delta)$

$\Rightarrow ab\underline{h(a\Delta)}h(\Delta\Delta)$

$\Rightarrow aba\underline{h(\Delta\Delta)}$

$\Rightarrow aba$

19.3   CONTEXT-SENSITIVE GRAMMARS

Most of the languages we have seen so far can be characterized in terms of grammars. Context-free languages are those generated by grammars in which the left side of every production is a single variable, and regular languages are those generated by context-free grammars in which there are additional restrictions on the right sides of productions. There are various other restrictions that might be imposed upon unrestricted grammars. One that has been widely studied produces a class of languages that lies strictly between the class of context-free languages and the class of all recursively enumerable languages.

Definition 19.2. A *context-sensitive grammar* (CSG) is a phrase-structure grammar in which every production has the form $\alpha \rightarrow \beta$, where $|\beta| \geq |\alpha|$. A context-sensitive language (CSL) is a language that is generated by some CSG.

Two notes on the terminology may be in order. First, the phrase "context-sensitive" sounds as though in particular it should mean "non-context-free," but of course it follows from Definition 19.2 that any context-free grammar having no Λ-productions is context-sensitive. We have run into similarly awkward phrases before: a nondeterministic TM, for example, may in fact be deterministic. It is more precise to say that a context-sensitive grammar *need* not be context-free. Second, it is easier to understand how the phrase "context-sensitive" arose if we use a different characterization of these languages. It can be shown that a language is context-sensitive if and only if it can be generated by a grammar $G = (V, \Sigma, S, P)$ in which every production has the form $\alpha A \beta \rightarrow \alpha X \beta$, where $\alpha, \beta \in (V \cup \Sigma)^*, A \in V$, and $X \in (V \cup \Sigma)^+ = (V \cup \Sigma)^* - \{\Lambda\}$.

Example 19.5. Consider the language of Example 19.1: $L = \{a^n b^n c^n | n > 0\}$. Although the grammar given in Example 19.1 is not a CSG, L is a CSL. Instead of using a separate variable F to indicate the front of the string, simply distinguish between the first A in the string and the remaining A's. You may check that the context-sensitive grammar with these productions generates L.

$$S \rightarrow \mathcal{A}BCS_1 \mid \mathcal{A}BC$$

$$S_1 \rightarrow ABCS_1 \mid ABC$$

$$BA \rightarrow AB \qquad CA \rightarrow AC \qquad CB \rightarrow BC$$

$$\mathcal{A} \rightarrow a \qquad aA \rightarrow aa \qquad aB \rightarrow ab$$

$$bB \rightarrow bb \qquad bC \rightarrow bc \qquad cC \rightarrow cc$$

Most languages you can think of are context-sensitive—in particular, programming languages: the non-context-free aspects of Pascal mentioned in Section 15.1, such as variables having to be declared before being used, can be accommodated by CSGs. However, the next result together with Theorem 18.11 shows that not all unrestricted grammars can be replaced by context-sensitive grammars.

Theorem 19.3. Every context-sensitive language is recursive.

Proof. Let L be generated by the CSG G. In the proof of Theorem 19.1, we began with an arbitrary grammar and constructed a nondeterministic TM to accept it. Our goal now is to use the extra assumption on G, that the right side of any production is at least as long as the left, to modify this TM in such a way that it cannot loop forever on an input string, no matter what choice of moves it makes. Theorem 18.1 will then imply that the language it accepts is recursive.

Our TM in Theorem 19.1 had the form

$$MovePastInput \rightarrow Simulate \rightarrow Equal$$

The possibility of an infinite loop occurs within *Simulate*: the machine could choose to repeat forever the loop, during one iteration of which it replaces the left side of some production by the right side. We can now avoid this as follows. *Simulate* begins by creating the tape configuration

$$\Delta x \# S \Delta \dots \underline{\Delta \Delta S}$$

where the current tape position is at the first S and the underlined portion of the tape is precisely the length of the input string x. *Simulate* then begins a loop. Each iteration now consists of these two steps:

1. In the string following $\#$, attempting to replace some occurrence of the left side of a production in G by the right side (nondeterministically, as before), but without moving the second S shown above any farther to the right, and crashing if the resulting string is longer than the allotted space—i.e., longer than x;
2. If the first step is successfully completed, searching the tape to the right of the resulting string (the resulting string being the portion to the right of $\#$ and up to the next Δ) for another occurrence of it, and crashing if it finds it, otherwise copying the resulting string to the right of the last nonblank symbol on the tape, separated from it by Δ.

The idea is that we are keeping on the tape the entire history of the derivation: after k iterations, the tape will have the form

$$\Delta x \# \alpha_k \Delta \dots \Delta S \Delta \alpha_1 \Delta \alpha_2 \Delta \dots \Delta \alpha_k$$

where for each $i \leq k$, α_i is the string obtained after the first i steps of the derivation. Clearly, the loop cannot be iterated forever: if it is repeated too many times, either the string α_k will exceed x in length or α_k will duplicate some previous α_j, and in either case *Simulate* crashes. *Simulate* exits the loop nondeterministically, as before, and either crashes, if the most recent α_k still contains nonterminals, or halts. *Equal* compares the input string x to the string immediately following $\#$.

It remains to check that this TM still accepts L. If $x \in L$, there is a derivation of x of the form

$$S \Rightarrow \alpha_1 \Rightarrow \alpha_2 \Rightarrow \dots \Rightarrow \alpha_k = x$$

where $|\alpha_i| \leq |x|$ for each i and $\alpha_i \neq \alpha_j$ for $i \neq j$. The inequality is true since the length of the string cannot decrease at any step of the derivation. Therefore, if the machine chooses the moves that simulate this derivation, it can successfully finish the derivation without crashing: α_i will never be too long and will never duplicate any previous α_j. On the other hand, if $x \notin L$, no sequence of moves will produce an α_k equal to x, and thus *Equal* will eventually crash.

Finally, the class of recursive languages is strictly larger than the class of context-sensitive languages. A trivial example of a recursive, non-context-sensitive language is any recursive language containing Λ, but as the next result indicates, there are nontrivial examples as well.

Theorem 19.4. There is a recursive language L such that $L - \{\Lambda\}$ is not context-sensitive.

Proof. Once again, we rely on a diagonal argument, very similar to that in Theorem 18.8. Let us consider the alphabet $\{a, b\}$. We may fix an infinite set $\mathcal{A} = \{A_1, A_2, \ldots\}$ so that any context-sensitive language over $\{a, b\}$ is generated by a CSG in which the start variable is A_1 and all variables are elements of $\mathcal{A}$.

The remainder of the proof depends on finding an explicit way to enumerate all such CSGs: $G_1, G_2, \ldots$. One way is described as follows. First, list all CSGs for which every production $\alpha \rightarrow \beta$ has $|\alpha|, |\beta| \leq 1$ and for which only the variable A_1 is involved; there are only finitely many. Then list those not already listed for which every production $\alpha \rightarrow \beta$ has $|\alpha|, |\beta| \leq 2$ and for which only the variables A_1 and A_2 are involved; and so on. It is clear that any CSG with the properties above will eventually be listed by this process.

Let $x_1, x_2, \ldots$ be the non-null elements of $\{a, b\}^*$ listed in lexicographic order, and let L be the language of all strings x_i for which $x_i \notin L(G_i)$. We claim L is recursive and not context-sensitive.

Each $L(G_i)$ is recursive, according to Theorem 19.3. Therefore, given $x \in \{a, b\}^*$, we can determine whether $x \in L$ by finding the i for which $x = x_i$ and then testing x for membership in $L(G_i)$. On the other hand, if L were context-sensitive L would be $L(G_i)$ for some i. In this case, take the corresponding x_i and ask whether x_i is an element of L. If it is, then by definition of L, $x_i \notin L(G_i) = L$. If it is not, then $x_i \notin L(G_i)$, and therefore by definition of L, $x_i \in L$. This contradiction proves that L is not context-sensitive.

19.4 LINEAR-BOUNDED AUTOMATA AND THE CHOMSKY HIERARCHY

Having described a type of language more general than CFLs and less general than recursively enumerable languages, we may ask whether there is a corresponding abstract recognizing device, something between a PDA and a TM. It turns out that we can obtain the machine we want by making a slight addition to the rules of a nondeterministic Turing machine, comparable to the way we modified the rules of unrestricted grammars to obtain CSGs. We can anticipate the sort of extra restriction that is appropriate by looking carefully at the TM constructed in Theorem 19.1 to accept a language L. The TM simulates a derivation of a string in the space to the right of the input string, and the tape head never needs to move farther right than the square to the right of the current string of the derivation. If the grammar used in the construction is context-sensitive, the strings in a derivation are never longer than the string of terminals being derived, and thus there is a fixed point on the tape, depending only on the length of the input string, beyond which the tape head never needs to move in order to decide whether to accept the input. In the definition below, the extra restriction is sharpened somewhat.

Definition 19.3. A *linear-bounded automaton* (LBA) is a 5-tuple $M = (Q, \Sigma, \Gamma, q_0, \delta)$ that is the same as a nondeterministic Turing machine except in the following respect: there are two extra tape symbols $\langle$ and $\rangle$, assumed not to be elements of Γ; M begins in the configuration $(q_0, \langle x \rangle)$, where x is the input string, and M is not permitted to replace the symbols $\langle$ or $\rangle$, or to move its head left from the square with $\langle$ or right from the square with $\rangle$.

Theorem 19.5. If $L \subseteq \Sigma^*$ is a CSL, L is accepted by an LBA.

Proof. Suppose $G = (V, \Sigma, S, P)$ is a CSG generating L. As we noted earlier, in proving Theorem 19.1, we used in the simulated derivation a portion of the tape no longer than the input string, but it was to the right of the input. That option is not available to us, but a satisfactory alternative is to convert the portion of the tape between $\langle$ and $\rangle$ into two tracks, so that the second provides the necessary space. Thus, let the tape alphabet of our machine M contain pairs (a, b), where $a, b \in \Sigma \cup V \cup \{\Delta\}$, in addition to elements of Σ. There may be other symbols needed as well.

The first action of M is to convert the tape configuration

$$\langle x_1 x_2 \ldots x_n \rangle$$

to

$$\langle (x_1, \Delta)(x_2, \Delta) \ldots (x_n, \Delta) \rangle$$

This step corresponds to the *MovePastInput* component of the TM in Theorem 19.1. M places S in the second track of square 1 and starts a loop exactly as before, except that the machine will crash if the string produced in the second track during any iteration has length $> n$. As before, M may exit the loop at any time; after exiting, it crashes if there are still nonterminals in the second track of the tape or if the second track does not match the input in the first track. Since G is context-sensitive, a string appearing in the derivation of a string $x \in L$ cannot be longer than x, and therefore, if the LBA begins with input x it can execute a sequence of moves that cause it to halt. If $x \notin L$, M will either crash or loop forever.

As you might guess from the proof of Theorem 19.5, the significant feature of the LBA is not that the tape head doesn't move past the input string at all, but that the tape head is restricted to a portion of the tape bounded by some linear function of the input length (this explains the origin of the phrase "linear-bounded"). As long as this is the case, an argument using multiple tracks can be used to find an equivalent machine satisfying the stricter condition in Definition 19.3.

The converse of Theorem 19.5 does not hold, since an LBA might accept Λ and Λ cannot be produced by any CSG. But the obvious modification of the statement is true.

Theorem 19.6. If $L \subseteq \Sigma^*$ is accepted by the LBA $M = (Q, \Sigma, \Gamma, q_0, \delta)$, there is a CSG generating $L - \{\Lambda\}$.

Proof. The proof is very similar to that of Theorem 19.2. The grammar is constructed so as to generate two copies of a string, simulate the action of M on one, and eliminate from the string everything except the other, if and when the simulated moves of M lead to a halt. We begin with objects of the form $(\sigma\sigma)$, as before. However, instead of viewing this as two terminal symbols enclosed between two variables, we view it as a single variable—so that when $(\sigma_1\sigma_2)$ is ultimately replaced by the terminal σ_1, the context-sensitive condition will still be satisfied. In the simulation, we must pay attention to the tape markers $\langle$ and $\rangle$. Thus, we may also have single variables such as $(\sigma_1\langle\sigma_2), (\sigma_1\sigma_2\rangle)$, and $(\sigma_1\langle\sigma_2\rangle)$, corresponding to points during the simulation when σ_2 is the leftmost, rightmost, and only symbol between the markers, respectively. In each case, σ_1 represents the terminal symbol originally in that position and is not modified during the simulation. In addition to these variables, we will have even more complicated ones of the form $q(\sigma_1\sigma_2), q(\sigma_1\langle\sigma_2)$, and so on, where $q \in Q \cup \{h\}$. The reason for incorporating the state q *into* the variable, rather than simply calling q a variable itself, as we did before, is again so that we can eventually eliminate the states from the string without violating the context-sensitivity. A variable of this sort appearing in a derivation signifies that at that stage of the simulation the LBA is in state q and σ_2 is the current tape symbol. Finally, since M's tape head can move to the tape squares containing the symbols $\langle$ and $\rangle$, we will also have variables of the form $q(\sigma_1\langle\sigma_2)^L, q(\sigma_1\sigma_2\rangle)^R, q(\sigma_1\langle\sigma_2\rangle)^L$, and $q(\sigma_1\langle\sigma_2\rangle)^R$. The first one, for example, signifies that M is in state q, its tape head is on the square containing $\langle$, and the next square contains σ_2 now but originally contained σ_1. The grammar need not produce $(\Delta\Delta)$, since initially there are no Δ's between the tape markers of M.

The first step in a derivation is to produce a string of the form

$$q_0(\sigma_1\langle\sigma_1)^L(\sigma_2\sigma_2)\ldots(\sigma_{n-1}\sigma_{n-1})(\sigma_n\sigma_n\rangle)$$

or

$$q_0(\sigma_1\langle\sigma_1\rangle)^L$$

These can be generated using the productions

$$S \to q_0(\sigma\langle\sigma\rangle)^L \mid T(\sigma\sigma\rangle)$$

$$T \to T(\sigma\sigma) \mid q_0(\sigma\langle\sigma)^L$$

for every choice of $\sigma \in \Sigma$.

Because of the endmarkers, and because the states have been incorporated into the variables, there are more combinations to consider when describing the productions used in the LBA simulation. We give those corresponding to LBA moves in which the tape head moves right, and leave the other two cases as exercises. The example following the proof gives a derivation illustrating several of these cases. Corresponding to the move

$$\delta(p, a) = (q, b, R)$$

we have these productions:

$$p(\sigma_1 a)(\sigma_2\sigma_3) \to (\sigma_1 b)q(\sigma_2\sigma_3)$$

$$p(\sigma_1\langle a)(\sigma_2\sigma_3) \to (\sigma_1\langle b)q(\sigma_2\sigma_3)$$

$$p(\sigma_1\langle a\rangle(\sigma_2\sigma_3)) \to (\sigma_1\langle b\rangle q(\sigma_2\sigma_3))$$

$$p(\sigma_1 a\rangle) \to q(\sigma_1 b\rangle)^R$$

$$p(\sigma_1\langle a\rangle) \to q(\sigma_1\langle b\rangle)^R$$

for every combination of $\sigma_1, \sigma_2 \in \Sigma$ and $\sigma_3 \in \Gamma \cup \{\Delta\}$. Notice that in the first three cases both sides of the production consist of two variables, and in the last two cases both sides consist of one variable. Corresponding to the move

$$\delta(p, \langle) = (q, \langle, R)$$

we have the productions

$$p(\sigma_1\langle\sigma_2)^L \to q(\sigma_1\langle\sigma_2)$$

$$p(\sigma_1\langle\sigma_2\rangle)^L \to q(\sigma_1\langle\sigma_2\rangle)$$

for each $\sigma_1 \in \Sigma$ and $\sigma_2 \in \Gamma \cup \{\Delta\}$.

If and when a variable of the form $h(\sigma_1\sigma_2)$ (or $h(\sigma_1\langle\sigma_2)$, etc.) shows up in a derivation, we need a way to eliminate everything but the symbols representing the original input. Again, the idea is first to let the h's propagate through the string. The necessary productions are

$$h(\sigma_1\sigma_2)(\sigma_3\sigma_4) \to h(\sigma_1\sigma_2)h(\sigma_3\sigma_4)$$

$$h(\sigma_1\langle\sigma_2)(\sigma_3\sigma_4) \to h(\sigma_1\langle\sigma_2)h(\sigma_3\sigma_4)$$

$$h(\sigma_1\sigma_2)(\sigma_3\sigma_4\rangle) \to h(\sigma_1\sigma_2)h(\sigma_3\sigma_4\rangle)$$

$$h(\sigma_1\langle\sigma_2)(\sigma_3\sigma_4\rangle) \to h(\sigma_1\langle\sigma_2)h(\sigma_3\sigma_4\rangle)$$

$$(\sigma_1\sigma_2)h(\sigma_3\sigma_4) \to h(\sigma_1\sigma_2)h(\sigma_3\sigma_4)$$

$$(\sigma_1\langle\sigma_2)h(\sigma_3\sigma_4) \to h(\sigma_1\langle\sigma_2)h(\sigma_3\sigma_4)$$

$$(\sigma_1\sigma_2)h(\sigma_3\sigma_4\rangle) \to h(\sigma_1\sigma_2)h(\sigma_3\sigma_4\rangle)$$

$$(\sigma_1\langle\sigma_2)h(\sigma_3\sigma_4\rangle) \to h(\sigma_1\langle\sigma_2)h(\sigma_3\sigma_4\rangle)$$

Here $\sigma_1, \sigma_3 \in \Sigma$ and $\sigma_2, \sigma_4 \in \Gamma \cup \{\Delta\}$. Finally, the productions

$$h(\sigma_1\sigma_2) \to \sigma_1$$

$$h(\sigma_1\langle\sigma_2) \to \sigma_1$$

$$h(\sigma_1\sigma_2\rangle) \to \sigma_1$$

$$h(\sigma_1\langle\sigma_2\rangle) \to \sigma_1$$

replace variables by terminals.

It is clear from the way we have defined variables that the grammar with these productions is context-sensitive. It is easy to convince yourself that it generates precisely the non-null strings accepted by M, but we do not attempt to give a rigorous proof.

Example 19.6. Again, we use the language L of palindromes over $\{a, b\}$ to illustrate. An LBA accepting L is essentially the same as the TM in Example 16.2, and it is shown in Fig. 19-2.

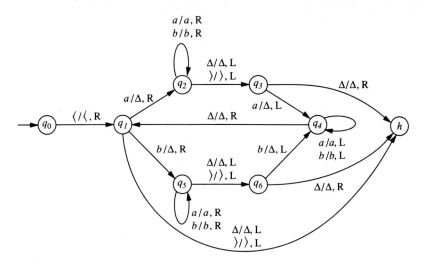

FIGURE 19-2
An LBA accepting the language of palindromes.

A derivation of aa in the grammar is shown, with the underlined portions indicating the left sides of productions to be used next, and the corresponding LBA moves appear to the right.

$$\underline{S} \Rightarrow \underline{T(aa\rangle)}$$

$$\Rightarrow \underline{q_0(a\langle a\rangle^L(aa\rangle)} \qquad (q_0, \langle aa\rangle)$$

$$\Rightarrow \underline{q_1(a\langle a\rangle(aa\rangle)} \qquad \vdash (q_1, \langle \underline{a}a\rangle)$$

$$\Rightarrow \underline{(a\langle\Delta\rangle q_2(aa\rangle)} \qquad \vdash (q_2, \langle\Delta\underline{a}\rangle)$$

$$\Rightarrow \underline{(a\langle\Delta\rangle q_2(aa\rangle)^R} \qquad \vdash (q_2, \langle\Delta a\rangle)$$

$$\Rightarrow \underline{(a\langle\Delta\rangle q_3(aa\rangle)} \qquad \vdash (q_3, \langle\Delta\underline{a}\rangle)$$

$$\Rightarrow \underline{q_4(a\langle\Delta\rangle(a\Delta\rangle)} \qquad \vdash (q_4, \langle\Delta\underline{\Delta}\rangle)$$

$$\Rightarrow \underline{(a\langle\Delta\rangle q_1(a\Delta\rangle)} \qquad \vdash (q_1, \langle\Delta\underline{\Delta}\rangle)$$

$$\Rightarrow \underline{h(a\langle\Delta\rangle(a\Delta\rangle)} \qquad \vdash (h, \langle\underline{\Delta\Delta}\rangle)$$

$$\Rightarrow \underline{h(a\langle\Delta\rangle h(a\Delta\rangle)}$$

$$\Rightarrow \underline{ah(a\Delta\rangle)}$$

$$\Rightarrow aa$$

Context-sensitive languages and recursively enumerable languages, along with the corresponding grammars and abstract machines, constitute the last two levels of the *Chomsky hierarchy*, which we summarize in Table 19.1. Chomsky designated the four types of languages as type 0, type 1, type 2, and type 3, from most general to most restrictive.

TABLE 19.1
The Chomsky hierarchy

Type	Languages (grammars)	Form of productions in grammar	Accepting device
3	Regular	$A \rightarrow aB,\ A \rightarrow a,\ A \rightarrow \Lambda$ $(A, B \in V,\ a \in \Sigma)$	Finite automaton
2	Context-free	$A \rightarrow \alpha$ $(A \in V,\ \alpha \in (V \cup \Sigma)^*)$	Pushdown automaton
1	Context-sensitive	$\alpha \rightarrow \beta$ $(\alpha, \beta \in (V \cup \Sigma)^*,\ |\beta| \geq |\alpha|,$ α contains a variable)	Linear-bounded automaton
0	Recursively enumerable (unrestricted or phrase-structure)	$\alpha \rightarrow \beta$ $(\alpha, \beta \in (V \cup \Sigma)^*,\ \alpha$ contains a variable)	Turing machine

The phrase "type 0 grammar" was actually applied to a grammar in which all productions are of the form $\alpha \rightarrow \beta$, where α is a string of one or more variables, but it is easy to see that any unrestricted grammar is equivalent to one of this type (Exercise 19.13).

We have seen that for each i between 1 and 3, the set of type i languages is a proper subset of the set of type $(i - 1)$ languages—except that a type 2 language is type 1 only if it doesn't contain Λ. The table leaves out two classes of languages we have considered for which there is no known characterization in terms of grammars: recursive languages, which fall strictly between context-sensitive and recursively enumerable languages; and deterministic context-free languages, which are between regular and context-free. And finally, of course, there are the languages that go off the chart: languages like *NonSelfAccepting*, which are so complex that no conceivable algorithmic procedure can be specified to recognize whether a given string is an element.

EXERCISES

19.1. In each case, describe the language generated by the unrestricted grammar with the given productions. a, b, and c are terminals; all other symbols are variables.

(a)

$$S \rightarrow LaR \qquad L \rightarrow LD$$

$$Da \rightarrow aaD \qquad DR \rightarrow R$$

$$L \rightarrow \Lambda \qquad R \rightarrow \Lambda$$

(b)

$$S \rightarrow ABCS \mid ABC$$

$$AB \rightarrow BA \qquad AC \rightarrow CA \qquad BC \rightarrow CB$$

$$BA \rightarrow AB \qquad CA \rightarrow AC \qquad CB \rightarrow BC$$

$$A \rightarrow a \qquad B \rightarrow b \qquad C \rightarrow c$$

(c)

$$S \rightarrow LA * R \qquad A \rightarrow a$$

$$L \rightarrow LI \qquad IA \rightarrow AI \qquad I* \rightarrow A * IJ \qquad IR \rightarrow A * R$$

$$JA \rightarrow AJ \qquad J* \rightarrow *J \qquad JR \rightarrow AR$$

$$LA \rightarrow EA \qquad EA \rightarrow AE \qquad E* \rightarrow E \qquad ER \rightarrow \Lambda$$

19.2. Consider the unrestricted grammar with the following productions.

$$S \rightarrow TD_1D_2 \qquad T \rightarrow ABCT \mid \Lambda$$

$$AB \rightarrow BA \qquad CD_1 \rightarrow D_1C \qquad A \rightarrow a$$

$$BA \rightarrow AB \qquad CD_2 \rightarrow D_2a \qquad D_1 \rightarrow \Lambda$$

$$CA \rightarrow AC \qquad BD_1 \rightarrow D_1b \qquad D_2 \rightarrow \Lambda$$

$$CB \rightarrow BC$$

(a) Describe the language generated by this grammar.
(b) Find a single production that could be substituted for $BD_1 \rightarrow D_1b$ so that the resulting language would be

$$\{xa^N \mid N \geq 0, \quad |x| = 2N, \quad \text{and} \quad N_a(x) = N_b(x) = N\}$$

19.3. Find unrestricted grammars to generate each of the following languages.
(a) $\{a^N b^N a^N b^N \mid N \geq 0\}$
(b) $\{a^N x b^N \mid x \in \{a, b\}^*, |x| = N\}$
(c) $\{sss \mid s \in \{a, b\}^*\}$
(d) $\{s\text{REV}(s)s \mid s \in \{a, b\}^*\}$
(e) $\{x \in \{a, b, c\}^* \mid N_a(x) < N_b(x), N_a(x) < N_c(x)\}$
(f) $\{x \in \{a, b, c\}^* \mid N_a(x) < N_b(x) < 2N_c(x)\}$
(g) $\{a^N \mid N = j(j + 1)/2 \text{ for some } j \geq 1\}$ (Suggestion: use the formula in Exercise 2.1. If a string has j groups of a's, the ith group containing i a's, then you can create $j + 1$ such groups by adding an a to each of the j groups and adding a single extra a at the beginning.)

19.4. In Example 19.3, trace the moves of *Simulate* as it simulates the derivation of the string $abba$. Show the state and tape contents at each step.

19.5. Suppose a nondeterministic TM is constructed as in the proof of Theorem 19.1 to accept $L(G)$, where G is the grammar in Exercise 19.1(a). Draw the *Simulate* component of the TM.

19.6. In the grammar in Example 19.4, give a derivation for the string $abba$.

19.7. Find a CSG generating $L - \{\Lambda\}$, where L is the language in Example 19.2.

19.8. Find CSG's equivalent to each of the grammars in Exercise 19.1.

19.9. Adapt the proofs of the appropriate theorems in Chapter 18 to show that the class of context-sensitive languages is closed under the operations of union and intersection.

19.10. Show that if there is a nondeterministic TM accepting L so that for any input string x, the TM never moves its tape head farther right than square $2|x|$, then $L - \{\Lambda\}$ is a CSL. (In fact, the same result is true if $2|x|$ is replaced by $K|x|$, where K is any positive integer.)

19.11. Show that if G is an unrestricted grammar generating L, and there is a constant K so that for any $x \in L$, any string appearing in a derivation of x has length $\leq K|x|$, then L is recursive.

19.12. In the proof of Theorem 19.6, the CSG productions corresponding to an LBA move of the form $\delta(p, a) = (q, b, R)$ are given. Give the productions corresponding to the move $\delta(p, a) = (q, b, L)$ and those corresponding to the move $\delta(p, a) = (q, b, S)$.

19.13. Show that any unrestricted grammar is equivalent to one in which the left side of every production is a string of one or more variables.

19.14. Theorem 9.1 asserts that if L_1 and L_2 are context-free languages, then L_1L_2 and L_1^* are also. The proof in both cases uses a simple construction to obtain a CFG generating the new language, given CFGs generating L_1 and L_2.

(a) Give an example to show that the construction used for L_1L_2 does not work to show that the concatenation of two recursively enumerable languages is recursively enumerable.

(b) Give an example to show that the construction used for L_1^* does not work to show that the $*$ of a recursively enumerable language is recursively enumerable.

Note: both results are nevertheless true in the more general case; see Exercise 18.6.

CHAPTER
20

UNSOLVABLE DECISION PROBLEMS

20.1 THE HALTING PROBLEM

For the languages and abstract machines studied in Parts II and III of this book, we have considered certain *decision problems*, and in many cases we have presented decision algorithms to solve them. An example of particular interest is the membership problem: Given a language L of a certain type and a string x, is x an element of L? We can solve this problem for regular languages, no matter whether L is specified by a regular expression, an FA, or a regular grammar (see Section 8.3). In the case of context-free languages, we can solve the problem if we are given either a CFG or a PDA specifying L (see Section 15.3). Although we have not discussed this problem directly for context-sensitive languages, the proof of Theorem 19.3 suggests an algorithm to solve the following: Given a CSG G and a string x, is x generated by G? The algorithm reduces essentially to trying all possible derivations if necessary; this approach is feasible at least theoretically because the length of the string cannot decrease at any step of a derivation.

A decision problem poses a general question, which can be thought of as a set of specific questions, one for each instance of the problem. In the case of the membership problem for regular languages, for example, the general question is Given a regular language L and a string x, is $x \in L$? An instance of the problem consists of a particular language L and a string x. According to the Church–Turing thesis, an appropriate way to formulate precisely the idea of a decision algorithm is to use a Turing machine. For example, a solution to the problem Given a finite automaton M and a string x, is $x \in L(M)$? might be a TM that begins with an input string encoding a specific instance of the problem and returns the answer 1 if $x \in L(M)$, 0 otherwise. In other words, the TM recognizes the language of all strings encoding instances of the problem for which the answer is yes. Saying that this decision problem is solvable is the same as saying that this language is recursive.

From Chapter 18, we have an example of a nonrecursive language:

$SelfAccepting = \{w \in \{x, y\}^* | w = e(T)$ for some TM T, and T accepts $w\}$

Therefore, using the discussion above, it makes sense to say that the problem

Given a Turing machine T, does T accept its own encoding $e(T)$?

is an *unsolvable* decision problem. In general, to say that a decision problem is unsolvable means that there is no general algorithm capable of solving every instance of the problem—or more precisely, that there is no TM recognizing the language of all strings that encode instances of the problem for which the answer is yes.

It is important to realize that a problem may be unsolvable even though we are able to answer the question in many specific instances. There are obviously TMs T for which we can decide easily whether T accepts $e(T)$. What makes the problem unsolvable is that there is no single algorithm guaranteed to provide an answer in every case.

Although the question of whether a Turing machine accepts its own encoding may not seem especially important, this first example of an unsolvable problem is significant for at least two reasons. First, it demonstrates that such problems exist: just because one can pose a reasonable-sounding problem, it does not follow automatically that there is an algorithm to solve it. Second, if one cannot even answer the question of whether a given TM T accepts the particular string $e(T)$, obviously one cannot expect to solve in general the membership problem for recursively enumerable languages. This is the most well-known unsolvable decision problem; because of the way a TM accepts a string, the problem is known as the *halting* problem.

Halting Problem. Given a Turing machine T and a string w, does T halt on input w?

The instance of the problem determined by a particular T and a particular w can be encoded by the string $e(T)e(w)$. The fact that the halting problem is unsolvable means that the language

$$Halting = \{e(T)e(w) | T \text{ halts on input } w\}$$

is not recursive. Although this should be obvious intuitively from the discussion above, let us give a more careful proof, since it is typical of many unsolvability proofs.

Theorem 20.1. The halting problem is unsolvable; i.e., the language *Halting* is not recursive.

Proof. We argue by contradiction that if *Halting* were recursive, then *SelfAccepting* would have to be. Suppose T_H is a TM recognizing *Halting*. Let

$$T_S = T_1 T_H$$

where T_1 is a TM with input alphabet $\{x, y\}$ that transforms a tape of the form $\underline{\Delta}w$ to the tape $\underline{\Delta}we(w)$. We have seen in the proof of Theorem 18.11 how to construct such a TM.

On the one hand, if $w \in$ *SelfAccepting*, then $w = e(T)$ for some T, where T accepts w. In this case T_S halts on input w with output 1, since the string $we(w) = e(T)e(w)$ is in *Halting* and T_H recognizes *Halting*.

On the other hand, if T_S halts with output 1 on the input string w, then $we(w) \in$ *Halting*. This means that for some TM T and some w' such that T accepts w', $we(w) = e(T)e(w')$. But since $e(w)$ and $e(w')$ both begin with yy, $e(w)$ and $e(w')$ must be the same. This implies that $w = w' = e(T)$ and thus that $w \in$ *SelfAccepting*.

We have shown that T_S recognizes the language *SelfAccepting*. This contradiction allows us to conclude that *Halting* is not recursive.

To understand the significance of the halting problem's unsolvability, it is helpful to translate it into informal terms, with the aid of the Church–Turing thesis. If any algorithmic procedure can be embodied in some TM, Theorem 20.1 might be restated like this: there is no general method for determining whether a given algorithmic procedure will terminate when applied to a given set of inputs. In another form that might hit closer to home, there is no general method for determining whether a computer program will enter an infinite loop when executed with a given set of data. In particular, there is no such thing as a "loop-finding" program that examines other computer programs and data sets in order to determine whether they will loop forever on those data values. That is no doubt enough to make the point. Theorem 20.1 is a profound result, because it points out a fundamental, inherent limit on what can be accomplished by computation. The halting problem is a problem that one might well wish to solve, for very practical reasons—but wish as one might, a general solution is impossible. You should review the steps that we took to arrive at Theorem 20.1, beginning with Theorem 18.10. The result may well be an increased respect for the diagonal argument!

We began our discussion of the halting problem with what sounded like a simpler problem, in which the TM T was arbitrary but we asked the question only for the specific string $e(T)$. The "simpler" problem was also unsolvable. We might turn this around, and ask the question for some fixed TM T_0 and an arbitrary string w. In other words, can we find an algorithm that is specific to T_0, but able to answer the question Given w, does T_0 accept w? Again, it is obvious that for *some* T_0's this is possible, but there is at least one for which it is not. Let T_0 be the universal TM T_U of Section 17.4. T_U takes as input a string of the form $e(T)e(w)$ and simulates the processing of w by T, halting if and only if T halts on input w. If it were possible to decide, for any string z, whether T_U halted on input z, then by considering arbitrary z's of the form $e(T)e(w)$, it would be possible to decide for a given T and a given w whether T halted on input w—i.e., it would be possible to solve the halting problem. Therefore, this "simplification" of the halting problem is also unsolvable for this T_0. In the next section, we consider other special cases of the halting problem.

Finally, since we have other characterizations of recursively enumerable languages that do not involve TMs, it is appropriate to consider another way of formulating the membership problem for recursively enumerable languages:

Given an unrestricted grammar G and a string x, can x be generated by G?

It should not be surprising that this problem is also unsolvable. If we had an algorithm to solve it, the following would constitute an algorithm for solving the halting problem. Given a TM T and a string w, construct the grammar G generating the language accepted by T (see the proof of Theorem 19.2). Apply the algorithm to determine whether w can be generated by G. G generates w if and only if T halts on w.

We summarize the last two results in the following

Corollary 20.1.

(a) There is at least one TM T_0 so that the problem Given w, does T_0 accept w? is unsolvable.

(b) The problem Given an unrestricted grammar G and a string x, can x be generated by G? is unsolvable.

20.2 OTHER UNSOLVABLE PROBLEMS RELATING TO TM's

In this section, we consider other decision problems relating to TMs, and we find that almost without exception they are also unsolvable. In our first example, we give a proof that the associated language is not recursive, but thereafter we rely on more informal arguments. In all cases, however, the basic method is similar and is essentially a proof by contradiction. To show that a problem P is unsolvable, we show that another problem P' that we already know is unsolvable can be reduced to P. In other words, we show that if we had an algorithm for solving P in every instance, we could obtain an algorithm for solving P' in every instance. It is easy to get confused in such arguments; one point to keep in mind is that a contradiction is obtained only if the assumption that we can solve P allows us to show that any *arbitrary* instance of P' can be solved. Thus, the approach is as follows: to show P is unsolvable, using the fact that P' is unsolvable,

1. Start with an arbitrary instance of P' (not P!); and
2. Construct an instance of P, the answer to which would allow us to answer the instance of P'.

Our next example of an unsolvable problem illustrates this procedure.

Theorem 20.2. The problem **Accepts(Λ):** Given a TM T, does T halt on input Λ? is unsolvable.

Proof. We show that if this problem could be solved, so could the halting problem. Accordingly, assume that Accepts(Λ) is solvable and consider an arbitrary instance of the halting problem: an arbitrary TM T' and an arbitrary string w. Let $T = Write(w)T'$, where $Write(w)$ is a TM that, starting with an empty tape, halts with tape contents $\underline{\Delta}w$. Clearly T halts on input Λ if and only if T' halts on input w. By applying the algorithm to determine whether T halts on Λ, we have determined whether T' halts on w.

Let's adapt this intuitive argument to show that

$$L_\Lambda = \{e(T) | T \text{ halts on input } \Lambda\}$$

is not recursive, by showing that if it were, *Halting* would be too. Specifically, we show that if we have a TM T_Λ recognizing L_Λ, we can construct a TM T_H to recognize *Halting*. In order for a TM to recognize *Halting*, it must leave output 1 if its input string z is of the form $e(T')e(w)$, where T' halts on input w, and leave output 0 otherwise. We construct T_H so that it first examines the input string z to determine whether it is of the form $e(T')e(w)$ (see the proof of Theorem 18.11). If z is not of this form, T_H halts with output 0. The next part of T_H's operation uses as above the fact that $T = Write(w)T'$ halts on input Λ if and only if T' halts on input w. If $z = e(T')e(w)$, T_H creates the tape configuration $\underline{\Delta}e(T) = \underline{\Delta}e(Write(w)T')$ and executes T_Λ. Therefore, if T' accepts w (i.e., $z = e(T')e(w) \in Halting$), then T accepts Λ, and T_H halts with output 1 as a result of executing T_Λ on the string $e(T)$; if T' does not accept w (i.e., $z \notin Halting$), T_H halts with output 0, since in this case $e(T) \notin L_\Lambda$. We have obtained the desired contradiction, that T_H recognizes *Halting*.

We have glossed over the problem of how T_H creates the string $e(Write(w)T')$ on the tape. But $e(Write(w))$ can be constructed from the string $e(w)$ in a straightforward way, and except for two slight complications, $e(Write(w)T')$ is obtained from $e(Write(w))$ and $e(T')$ by removing the symbols up through the first y from $e(T')$ and concatenating. The two complications are that the states of $Write(w)$ need to be renamed so that they are separate from those of T', and the halting moves in $Write(w)$ must be replaced by moves to the initial state of T'. Both these operations can obviously be performed by T_H; thus the proof is complete.

We give four more examples of unsolvable problems involving TMs. This is not by any means an exhaustive list, and several others may be found in the exercises.

Theorem 20.3. The following problems are all unsolvable.

AcceptsNothing. Given a TM T, is the language accepted by T empty?

AcceptsEverything. Given a TM T with input alphabet Σ, is the language accepted by T all of Σ^*?

Equivalence. Given two TMs T_1 and T_2, do they accept the same language?

WritesSymbol. Given a TM T and a symbol a in its tape alphabet, does T ever write a on its tape when started with an empty tape?

Proof. We show that AcceptsNothing is unsolvable by showing that Accepts(Λ), which we know is unsolvable, can be reduced to it. Consider an arbitrary TM T', an instance of Accepts(Λ). Construct a TM T as follows: $T = EraseTapeT'$, where *EraseTape* is a TM that transforms the initial tape $\underline{\Delta}x$ to $\underline{\Delta}$. T accepts at least one string if and only if

T' accepts Λ. If we had an algorithm for determining whether the language accepted by T was empty, we could use it to determine whether T' accepted Λ.

The proof that AcceptsEverything is unsolvable is identical, since the TM T constructed above accepts the entire set Σ^* if and only if T' accepts Λ.

Next, we show AcceptsEverything can be reduced to Equivalence, thereby showing that Equivalence is unsolvable. Take any T, an instance of AcceptsEverything. Construct an instance of Equivalence by letting T_1 be T and T_2 a TM that immediately halts on every input. T_1 and T_2 accept the same language if and only if T accepts everything.

Finally, we show that Accepts(Λ) can be reduced to WritesSymbol. Consider any TM T', an instance of Accepts(Λ). Construct an instance of WritesSymbol as follows. Let T be a TM with the same input and tape alphabets as T' except for one extra tape symbol a. T has exactly the same transitions as T' except that any halting move

$$\delta(p, \sigma) = (h, \tau, D)$$

of T' becomes

$$\delta(p, \sigma) = (h, a, D)$$

instead. T' halts on input Λ if and only if T writes the symbol a, starting with input Λ. If we could determine whether T wrote a, we could decide whether T' accepted Λ.

For the sake of variety, we present an example of a problem involving TMs that is actually solvable. At first, after seeing the last part of Theorem 20.3, you may be surprised that a superficially similar problem is solvable; see Exercise 20.7.

Theorem 20.4. The problem **WritesNonblank:** Given a TM T, does it ever write a nonblank symbol on its tape, starting with an empty tape? is solvable.

Proof. Suppose T has n states. Within n moves, T either will have crashed or will have entered some state q for the second time. If no nonblank symbol has been written by that time, in the first case it is obvious that none will be; in the second case, the sequence of moves beginning from q the second time will repeat exactly the moves from q the first time, since the tape will look the same, and T will be in an infinite loop, during which no nonblank symbol will ever be written. A decision algorithm for WritesNonblank is therefore to execute T for n moves: T writes a nonblank symbol if and only if it has done so by that time.

Theorem 20.4 tells us we cannot quite say that all decision problems regarding TMs are unsolvable. Yet in a way, we may view this example as the exception that proves the rule. It can be shown (see the book by Hopcroft and Ullman for details) that any decision problem involving the *language accepted* by a TM, as opposed to a problem involving the operation of the TM itself, is either trivial, in a sense that can be made precise, or unsolvable.

We close this section by pointing out that the decision problems for TMs in Theorems 20.2 and 20.3 all have counterparts involving grammars. See Exercise 20.6.

20.3 POST'S CORRESPONDENCE PROBLEM

In this section, we show that a combinatorial problem known as Post's Correspondence Problem (PCP) is unsolvable. The proof is long and somewhat complicated, but the result will allow us in the next section to exhibit a number of unsolvable decision problems relating to context-free grammars.

An instance of the problem, first stated by Emil Post, is called a *correspondence system*. It consists of a sequence of pairs $(\alpha_1, \beta_1), (\alpha_2, \beta_2), \ldots, (\alpha_n, \beta_n)$, each α_i and each β_i a string over the alphabet Σ. A *solution* to the problem instance consists of a sequence of one or more integers $i_1, i_2, \ldots, i_k$, each i_j satisfying $1 \leq i_j \leq n$ and the i_j's not necessarily distinct, so that

$$\alpha_{i_1}\alpha_{i_2} \ldots \alpha_{i_k} = \beta_{i_1}\beta_{i_2} \ldots \beta_{i_k}$$

It may be helpful in visualizing the problem to think of a sequence of n distinct groups of *dominoes*, one from the ith group having the string α_i on the top half and β_i on the bottom half (see Fig. 20-1a), and to imagine that there are an unlimited number of identical dominoes in each group. To solve this instance of the problem means to line up k dominoes, some of which may be duplicates, in a horizontal row, each one positioned vertically, so that the string formed by their top halves matches the string formed by their bottom halves (see Fig. 20-1b).

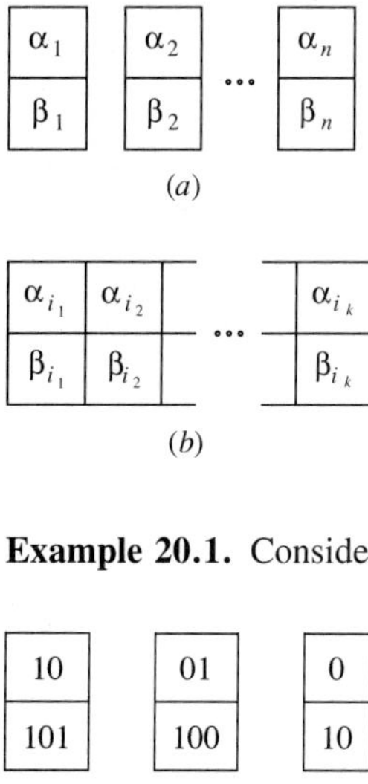

(a)

(b)

FIGURE 20-1

Example 20.1. Consider the correspondence system described by this picture:

10	01	0	100	1
101	100	10	0	010

Clearly, in any solution, domino 1 must be used first, since it is the only one in which the two strings begin with the same symbol. One solution is the following:

10	1	01	0	100	100	0	100
101	010	100	10	0	0	10	0

In fact, there is also a solution beginning

10	100
101	0

Can you find one?

If you spent much time on Example 20.1, you may be prepared to believe that there is no general algorithm to determine whether a given problem instance has a solution. The proof we shall give, however, is to show that a slightly different problem is unsolvable and to demonstrate from that the unsolvability of the original problem. An instance of the *Modified* Post's Correspondence Problem (MPCP) is exactly the same as an instance of PCP, but now solutions are required to begin with domino 1. In other words, a solution consists of a sequence of zero or more integers $i_2, i_3, \ldots, i_k$ so that

$$\alpha_1 \alpha_{i_2} \ldots \alpha_{i_k} = \beta_1 \beta_{i_2} \ldots \beta_{i_k}$$

We shall prove that because the halting problem is unsolvable, MPCP is unsolvable. Let us first show that that is sufficient to prove PCP unsolvable.

Theorem 20.5. MPCP can be reduced to PCP. In other words, if MPCP is unsolvable, so is PCP.

Proof. We begin with an arbitrary instance I of MPCP, represented by the pairs (α_1, β_1), $\ldots$, (α_n, β_n), and construct an instance J of PCP that would have a solution if and only if I did. In other words, we want a J so that there is a sequence of pairs solving J if and only if there is a sequence of pairs solving I and beginning with pair 1. The trick is to construct the pairs of J to correspond, generally speaking, to pairs in I, so that a solution to J would correspond to *some* selection of pairs in I for which the two concatenations match—but at the same time to make J have only one pair that could possibly begin a solution: the one corresponding to pair 1 in I.

Here is the way we do it. Let Σ be the alphabet for the instance I, and let # and $ be two symbols not in Σ. For each pair

$$(\alpha_i, \beta_i) = (a_1 a_2 \ldots a_r, b_1 b_2 \ldots b_s)$$

of I $(1 \le i \le n)$, define the pair

$$(\alpha_i', \beta_i') = (a_1 \# a_2 \# \ldots a_r \#, \# b_1 \# b_2 \ldots \# b_s)$$

in J. In addition, introduce two additional pairs as follows:

$$(\alpha_0', \beta_0') = (\# \alpha_1', \beta_1')$$

$$(\alpha_{n+1}', \beta_{n+1}') = (\$, \# \$)$$

The instance J of PCP now consists of the pairs (α_i', β_i') for $0 \le i \le n+1$. It is easy to check that if $i_2, \ldots, i_k$ is any solution for the instance I of MPCP, then $0, i_2, \ldots, i_k, n+1$ is a solution to the instance J of PCP. In other words, if

$$\alpha_1 \alpha_{i_2} \ldots \alpha_{i_k} = \beta_1 \beta_{i_2} \ldots \beta_{i_k}$$

then

$$\alpha'_0 \alpha'_{i_2} \dots \alpha'_{i_k} \alpha'_{n+1} = \beta'_0 \beta'_{i_2} \dots \beta'_{i_k} \beta'_{n+1}$$

On the other hand, suppose $i_1, \dots, i_k$ is a solution to J, so that

$$\alpha'_{i_1} \dots \alpha'_{i_k} = \beta'_{i_1} \dots \beta'_{i_k}$$

Clearly, $i_1 = 0$ and $i_k = n + 1$ (since the strings of the first pair must begin with the same symbol and those of the last pair must end with the same symbol). It is conceivable that some of the other i_j's are also $n + 1$, but if i_m is the last i_j to equal $n + 1$, then $0, i_2, \dots, i_m$ is also a solution to J, and it is now easy to check that $i_2, \dots, i_{m-1}$ is a solution to I.

If we had an algorithm for determining whether J had a solution, we could by using this construction determine whether I had a solution. Therefore, if PCP is solvable, so is MPCP.

We are ready to show that MPCP is unsolvable. As we have done several times already, we use the fact that the halting problem for TMs is unsolvable.

Theorem 20.6. MPCP is unsolvable (and therefore, by Theorem 20.5, PCP is unsolvable).

Proof. Let $T = (Q, \Sigma, \Gamma, q_0, \delta)$ be an arbitrary TM and let $w \in \Sigma^*$. It will be slightly more convenient to be able to assume that T never crashes. Since there is an algorithm to convert any TM into an equivalent one that will enter an infinite loop whenever the original one would have crashed, we may make this assumption without loss of generality. We show that an algorithm to solve MPCP would provide us with a way of determining whether T halted on input w. Thus, we wish to construct an instance $(\alpha_1, \beta_1), \dots, (\alpha_n, \beta_n)$ of MPCP (a *modified correspondence system*) that will have a solution if and only if T accepts w.

Some terminology and notation will be helpful. For an instance $(\alpha_1, \beta_1), \dots, (\alpha_n, \beta_n)$ of MPCP, we will say that a *partial solution* is a sequence $i_2, \dots, i_j$ so that $\alpha = \alpha_1 \alpha_{i_2} \dots \alpha_{i_j}$ is a prefix of $\beta = \beta_1 \beta_{i_2} \dots \beta_{i_j}$. Or, to be a little less precise, we might simply say that the string α obtained this way is a partial solution, or that the two strings α and β represent a partial solution. Secondly, we introduce temporarily a new notation for representing TM configurations. Let x and y be elements of $(\Gamma \cup \{\Delta\})^*$ with y not ending in Δ, and let $q \in Q$. The string xqy will represent the configuration we normally denote by (q, xy) (or by $(q, x\Delta)$, if $y = \Lambda$)—i.e., the symbols in x are those preceding the tape head, which is centered on the first symbol of y if $y \neq \Lambda$ and on Δ otherwise.

In order to simplify the notation, let's assume that $w \neq \Lambda$; this assumption will play no essential part in the proof. We also assume that $\#$ is a symbol not in Γ.

We want to specify pairs (α_i, β_i) in our modified correspondence system so that for any sequence

$$q_0 \Delta w, x_1 q_1 y_1, \dots, x_j q_j y_j$$

of successive configurations of T (note: $q_0 \Delta w$ is the initial configuration), a partial solution can be obtained that looks like

$$\alpha = \# q_0 \Delta w \# x_1 q_1 y_1 \# x_2 q_2 y_2 \# \dots \# x_j q_j y_j$$

Moreover, we want any partial solution to be an initial portion of one like this—or at least, to start deviating from this form only after an occurrence of a halting configuration xhy in the string. Next, if we have a partial solution

$$\alpha = \#q_0\Delta w\#x_1q_1y_1\#\ldots\#x_jhy_j$$

which will imply in particular, given our earlier remarks, that T accepts w, we want additional pairs (α_i, β_i) that will allow α to "catch up with" β, so that there will actually be a solution. Finally, we want to guarantee that *only* in that case do we have a solution. If we can specify the modified correspondence system in a way that accomplishes these things, it will follow fairly easily that the system has a solution if and only if T accepts w.

Before we say exactly what the pairs (α_i, β_i) are, let's outline the general strategy. We choose the pair (α_1, β_1), with which a solution must start, as follows:

$$\alpha_1 = \#$$

$$\beta_1 = \#q_0\Delta w\#$$

The portion of β_1 between the #'s represents the initial configuration of T. Suppose, for example, that $\delta(q_0, \Delta) = (q_1, a, \mathrm{R})$. Corresponding to that move of T, we will have a pair

$$(q_0\Delta, aq_1)$$

and we will make sure this is the only possible choice for the next pair $(\alpha_{i_2}, \beta_{i_2})$ in a partial solution. Using this pair next produces the partial solution

$$\alpha = \alpha_1\alpha_{i_2} = \#q_0\Delta$$

$$\beta = \beta_1\beta_{i_2} = \#q_0\Delta w\#aq_1$$

At this point, the only correct way to add to α is to add the symbols of w. Moreover, given the string we are aiming for, it is appropriate to add the same symbols to β. Therefore, we include in our modified correspondence system pairs (σ, σ), for every $\sigma \in \Gamma \cup \{\Delta\}$, as well as the pair $(\#, \#)$. Using these, we can obtain the partial solution

$$\alpha = \#q_0\Delta w\#$$

$$\beta = \#q_0\Delta w\#aq_1w\#$$

Note that α has caught up to the *original* string β, but the new β has a second portion representing the configuration of T after the first move. The process of extending the partial solution continues in the same way. At each step, as long as the halt state h has not appeared, the string β in the partial solution is one step ahead of α. Thus, the next portion to be added to α is determined, but the pairs (α_i, β_i) will be such that every time α_i's are used to complete the required configuration of T in the string α, the corresponding β_i's, which are added to β, will specify the configuration of T one move later. In this way, we guarantee that any partial solution is of the desired form. Roughly speaking, it remains only to include pairs (α_i, β_i) that allow α to catch up to β once the configuration includes the halt state h.

This discussion should make it easier to understand the choice of pairs (α_i, β_i) that form the instance of MPCP. They may be grouped into several types, as follows. (The order is not significant, and therefore no indices are specified except for the first pair.)

$$(\alpha_1, \beta_1) = (\#, \#q_0\Delta w\#)$$

Pairs of Type 1 (a is any element of $\Gamma \cup \{\Delta\}$)

$$(a, a)$$

$$(\#, \#)$$

Pairs of Type 2 $(q \in Q, p \in Q \cup \{h\}$, and $a, b, c \in \Gamma \cup \{\Delta\})$

(qa, pb) (if $\delta(q, a) = (p, b, \mathrm{S})$)

(qa, bp) (if $\delta(q, a) = (p, b, \mathrm{R})$)

(cqa, pcb) (if $\delta(q, a) = (p, b, \mathrm{L})$)

$(q\#, pa\#)$ (if $\delta(q, \Delta) = (p, a, \mathrm{S})$)

$(q\#, ap\#)$ (if $\delta(q, \Delta) = (p, a, \mathrm{R})$)

$(cq\#, pca\#)$ (if $\delta(q, \Delta) = (p, a, \mathrm{L})$)

Pairs of Type 3 $(a, b \in \Gamma \cup \{\Delta\})$

$$(ha, h)$$

$$(ah, h)$$

$$(ahb, h)$$

Pairs of Type 4

$$(h\#\#, \#)$$

The proof of the theorem now follows the intuitive argument above. First, we make the following

Claim: If we have any partial solution

$$\alpha = \gamma\#$$
$$\beta = \gamma\#z\#$$

to the modified correspondence system, where z represents a nonhalting configuration of T, we may extend it to a partial solution

$$\alpha' = \gamma\#z\#$$
$$\beta' = \gamma\#z\#z'\#$$

where z' represents the configuration of T one move later. Moreover, the string β' shown is the only one that can correspond to this α' in a partial solution.
We establish the claim in the case when

$$\alpha = \gamma\#$$
$$\beta = \gamma\#a_1 \ldots a_k q a_{k+1} \ldots a_{k+m}\#$$

and $m > 0$ and $\delta(q, a_{k+1}) = (p, b, \mathrm{R})$. The other cases are similar. The pairs that allow us to extend the partial solution are these: first, the pairs (a_1, a_1), $\ldots$, (a_k, a_k) of type 1; then, the pair (qa_{k+1}, bp) of type 2; next, any remaining pairs (a_{k+2}, a_{k+2}), $\ldots$, (a_m, a_m); and finally, the pair $(\#, \#)$. The partial solution produced is

$$\alpha' = \gamma\#a_1 \ldots a_k q a_{k+1} \ldots a_m\#$$
$$\beta' = \gamma\#a_1 \ldots a_k q a_{k+1} \ldots a_m\#a_1 \ldots a_k b p a_{k+2} \ldots a_m\#$$

Indeed, the substring of β' between the last two #'s is the TM configuration resulting from the move indicated. Furthermore, it is easy to see that at no point in this process is there any choice as to which pair to use; thus, the claim is established in this case.

Suppose, on the one hand, that T halts on input w; i.e., there is a sequence of consecutive configurations of T, beginning with $(q_0, \underline{\Delta}w)$ and ending with a halting configuration. If these configurations are represented by the strings $z_0, \ldots, z_j$, it follows easily from the claim above that there is a partial solution

$$\alpha = \#z_0\# \ldots \#z_{j-1}\#$$

$$\beta = \#z_0\# \ldots \#z_{j-1}\#z_j\#$$

to the modified correspondence system. (The proof uses mathematical induction on the number of successive configurations, and the inductive step is supplied by the claim.) The string z_j representing the halting configuration is of the form

$$uhv$$

where the strings u and/or v may be null. If at least one is non-null, we may extend the partial solution, using one pair of type 3 and others of type 1, to obtain

$$\alpha' = \alpha z_j\#$$

$$\beta' = \alpha z_j\#z_j'\#$$

where z_j' still contains h but has at least one fewer symbol than z_j. In a similar way, we can continue to extend the partial solution, so that the strings between consecutive #'s decrease in length by either one or two symbols at each step, until we have a partial solution of the form

$$\alpha''\#$$

$$\alpha''\#h\#$$

Applying the pair of type 4 now yields a solution.

Conversely, suppose T loops forever on input w. The last statement of the claim above implies that for any partial solution of the modified correspondence system of the form

$$\alpha = \#z_0\#z_1\# \ldots \#z_k\#$$

$$\beta = \#z_0\#z_1\# \ldots \#z_k\#z_{k+1}\#$$

where no z_i contains #, the strings z_i represent consecutive configurations of T. Again, the proof uses mathematical induction, this time on the number of #'s in the partial solution, and again the inductive step is furnished by the earlier claim. Therefore, h never appears in any partial solution—in particular, the pair of type 4 is never used. This implies that there can be no solution to the system, since α_1 and β_1 have different numbers of #'s and the pair of type 4 is the only other one with this property. It follows that the modified correspondence system has a solution if and only if T halts on input w, and the proof is complete.

The only modification of the proof that is necessary in the case $w = \Lambda$ is that the initial pair is $(\#, \#q_0\#)$ instead of $(\#, \#q_0\Delta w\#)$.

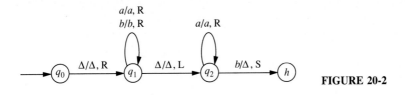

FIGURE 20-2

Example 20.2. Let T be the TM pictured in Fig. 20-2, which accepts all strings in $\{a, b\}^*$ that end with b. Let's examine the modified correspondence system constructed as in the proof of Theorem 20.6, both for a string w accepted by T and for one that is not. The only difference is in the initial pair.

The pairs of type 2 are these:

$$(q_0\Delta, \Delta q_1) \qquad (q_1 a, a q_1) \qquad (q_2 a, a q_2)$$

$$(q_0\#, \Delta q_1\#) \qquad (q_1 b, b q_1) \qquad (q_2 b, h\Delta)$$

$$(a q_1\#, q_2 a\Delta\#) \qquad (a q_1\Delta, q_2 a\Delta)$$

$$(b q_1\#, q_2 b\Delta\#) \qquad (b q_1\Delta, q_2 b\Delta)$$

$$(\Delta q_1\#, q_2\Delta\Delta\#) \qquad (\Delta q_1\Delta, q_2\Delta\Delta)$$

For the input string Λ, pair 1 is $(\#, \#q_0\#)$. The following partial solution is the longest possible, and the only one (except for smaller portions of it) ending in $\#$.

#	$q_0\#$	$\Delta q_1\#$
$\#q_0\#$	$\Delta q_1\#$	$q_2\Delta\Delta\#$

Clearly no solution exists.

For the input string b, which is accepted by T, pair 1 is $(\#, \#q_0\Delta b\#)$, and the solution follows.

#	$q_0\Delta$	b	#	Δ	$q_1 b$	#	Δ	$b q_1\#$	Δ	$q_2 b$	Δ	#
$\#q_0\Delta b\#$	Δq_1	b	#	Δ	$b q_1$	#	Δ	$q_2 b\Delta\#$	Δ	$h\Delta$	Δ	#

$\Delta h\Delta$	Δ	#	$h\Delta$	#	$h\#\#$
h	Δ	#	h	#	#

20.4 APPLICATIONS TO CONTEXT-FREE LANGUAGES

In Chapter 15, we were able to solve some of the basic decision problems involving context-free languages, including the membership problem for CFLs, the problem of whether a given CFG generates any strings of terminals, and the problem of whether a given CFG generates an infinite language. As we remarked at the time, however, many of the problems that are solvable for regular languages turn out to be unsolvable in the case of CFLs, and Theorem 20.6 provides us with a way of demonstrating this. We give three examples of unsolvable problems involving CFLs, and others may be found in the Exercises.

Theorem 20.7. The problem **CFGEmptyIntersection:** Given two CFGs G_1 and G_2, is $L(G_1) \cap L(G_2) = \varnothing$? is unsolvable.

Proof. We use the fact that PCP is unsolvable to show that this problem is also unsolvable. Suppose that $(\alpha_1, \beta_1), \ldots, (\alpha_n, \beta_n)$ is an arbitrary instance of PCP, where α_i and β_i are strings over the alphabet Σ. We show how to construct two CFGs G_1 and G_2 so that there is a string in $L(G_1) \cap L(G_2)$ if and only if there is a solution to the correspondence system. If there were an algorithm to solve CFGEmptyIntersection, there would be one to solve PCP.

Let $A = \{a_1, a_2, \ldots, a_n\}$, where none of the symbols a_i is in Σ. Let $G_1 = (\{S_1\}, \Sigma \cup A, S_1, P_1)$ and $G_2 = (\{S_2\}, \Sigma \cup A, S_2, P_2)$, where P_1 contains the $2n$ productions

$$S_1 \rightarrow \alpha_i S_1 a_i \mid \alpha_i a_i \qquad (1 \leq i \leq n)$$

and P_2 contains the productions

$$S_2 \rightarrow \beta_i S_2 a_i \mid \beta_i a_i \qquad (1 \leq i \leq n)$$

Then $L(G_1)$ is the language of all strings of the form

$$\alpha_{i_1} \alpha_{i_2} \ldots \alpha_{i_k} a_{i_k} a_{i_{k-1}} \ldots a_{i_1} \qquad (k \geq 1)$$

and $L(G_2)$ can be expressed similarly. Although it may be possible for a string of α_i's to match another unrelated string of β_i's, the symbols a_i act as a control. If $x \in L(G_1) \cap L(G_2)$, on the one hand

$$x = \alpha_{i_1} \alpha_{i_2} \ldots \alpha_{i_k} a_{i_k} a_{i_{k-1}} \ldots a_{i_1}$$

and on the other hand

$$x = \beta_{j_1} \beta_{j_2} \ldots \beta_{j_m} a_{j_m} a_{j_{m-1}} \ldots a_{j_1}$$

Since the last parts match, it must be true that $k = m$, $i_p = j_p$ for $1 \leq p \leq k$, and the correspondence system has a solution. Conversely, if there is such a solution $i_1, \ldots, i_k$, clearly the string x constructed as above is in both $L(G_1)$ and $L(G_2)$.

Theorem 20.8. The problem **CFGGeneratesAll:** Given a CFG G over the alphabet Σ, is $L(G) = \Sigma^*$? is unsolvable.

Proof. Again, we begin with an arbitrary correspondence system $(\alpha_1, \beta_1), \ldots, (\alpha_n, \beta_n)$ over some alphabet Σ. This time, we wish to construct a CFG G so that $L(G) \neq \Sigma^*$ if and only if the correspondence system has a solution.

Let G_1 and G_2 be the CFGs constructed as in the proof of Theorem 20.7, so that $L(G_1) \cap L(G_2) \neq \varnothing$ if and only if there is a solution to the correspondence system. But $L(G_1) \cap L(G_2) \neq \varnothing$ if and only if $(L(G_1) \cap L(G_2))' \neq \Sigma^*$, so if we can construct G to generate the language

$$(L(G_1) \cap L(G_2))' = L(G_1)' \cup L(G_2)'$$

we will have what we need.

We have an algorithm for finding a CFG to generate the union of two other CFGs (Theorem 9.1). Therefore, if we had a method for constructing a CFG G_1' to generate the language $L(G_1)'$, the same method would work for $L(G_2)'$, and G could be constructed to generate their union.

The construction of G_1' is slightly circuitous. First, construct a deterministic PDA M to recognize $L(G_1)$. (Although we do not include all the details, the principle is a simple one. The machine works by initially reading and pushing onto its stack all input symbols that are elements of Σ. If and when one of the a_i's is read for the first time, M crashes unless it is able to pop from its stack the symbols of the corresponding α_i in reverse. Thereafter, the only legal inputs are a_i's, and M continues matching them with the reverse of the strings on the stack. If this continues successfully until M finally pops from the stack the first α_i put there, so that the stack has only the initial stack symbol, M moves to an accepting state.) Next, interchange the accepting and nonaccepting states of M to obtain another PDA M'. Although we pointed out in Chapter 15 that this procedure may not always produce a PDA accepting the complement of the original language, it is easy to see that in this case it does. Finally, apply the method of Theorem 13.2 to construct a CFG G_1' to generate the language accepted by M', which is $L(G_1)'$.

We now have a method for constructing G so that $L(G) \neq \Sigma^*$ if and only if the given correspondence system has a solution, and the proof is complete.

Note that since we do have an algorithm for determining whether a given CFL is empty, one side-effect of the last two results is to confirm emphatically what we saw in Chapter 15: the intersection of two CFL's is not always a CFL, nor is the complement of a CFL always a CFL.

Theorem 20.9. The problem **IsAmbiguous:** Given a CFG, is it ambiguous? is unsolvable.

Proof. Given an arbitrary instance I of PCP, consisting of the pairs $(\alpha_1, \beta_1), \ldots, (\alpha_n, \beta_n)$, we construct a CFG G so that G is ambiguous if and only if I has a solution. Once again, we construct G_1 and G_2 exactly as in the proof of Theorem 20.7. G is the standard grammar generating the language $L(G_1) \cup L(G_2)$: the variables of G are S, S_1, and S_2, and the productions those of G_1 and G_2, along with the two extra productions

$$S \;\rightarrow\; S_1 \mid S_2$$

If the correspondence system has a solution $i_1, \ldots, i_k$, then

$$\alpha_{i_1} \ldots \alpha_{i_k} = \beta_{i_1} \ldots \beta_{i_k}$$

thus, the string

$$\alpha_{i_1} \ldots \alpha_{i_k} a_{i_k} \ldots a_{i_1}$$

which is in $L(G_1) \cap L(G_2)$, has two leftmost derivations in G, beginning with the productions $S \rightarrow S_1$ and $S \rightarrow S_2$, respectively. On the other hand, since each G_i is clearly unambiguous, the only way G can be ambiguous is for some string in $L(G)$ to be derivable from both S_1 and S_2. But this string is then in $L(G_1) \cap L(G_2)$, and so the correspondence system has a solution.

EXERCISES

20.1. In Section 20.1, a TM T_0 was given for which the decision problem Given a string w, does T_0 accept w? is unsolvable. Show that any T_0 accepting a nonrecursive language would also have this property.

20.2. Show that the following decision problems are all unsolvable. For a TM T, $L(T)$ denotes the language accepted by T.

(*a*) Given a TM T and a nonhalting state q, does T ever enter state q, starting with an empty tape?

(*b*) Given a TM T, does it accept more than one string?

(*c*) Given two TMs T_1 and T_2, is $L(T_1) \subseteq L(T_2)$?

(*d*) Given two TMs T_1 and T_2, is $L(T_1) \cap L(T_2) = \varnothing$?

20.3. (*a*) Show that the problem Given a TM T, is the language T accepts regular? is unsolvable. Suggestion: show that an algorithm to solve this problem would lead to an algorithm to solve the problem Accepts(Λ), as follows. Given a TM T_1, construct a TM T so that if T_1 halts on Λ, T accepts some nonregular language, say *Halting*, and if T_1 doesn't halt on Λ, T accepts the language $\varnothing$. Thus, if it were possible to decide whether T accepted a regular language, it would be possible to decide whether T_1 accepted Λ.

(*b*) Suggest some other problems that can be shown to be unsolvable in the same way as in (a). (Substitute other properties for "regular.")

(*c*) Show that the problem Given a TM T, is the language it accepts the complement of a recursively enumerable language? is unsolvable.

20.4. The proof of Theorem 20.2 shows that the language $L_\Lambda = \{e(T) \mid T \text{ halts on input } \Lambda\}$ is not recursive. Show that it is recursively enumerable.

20.5. One part of Theorem 20.3 says that the problem *AcceptsNothing* is unsolvable. Show explicitly that the language $L_\varnothing = \{e(T) \mid T \text{ accepts } \varnothing\}$ is not recursive.

20.6. For Theorem 20.2 and each part of Theorem 20.3, state a corresponding unsolvable problem having to do with unrestricted grammars.

20.7. Here is a "proof" that the problem Given a TM T, does T ever write a nonblank symbol, starting with an empty tape? is unsolvable.

> Given a TM T, construct a TM T_1 as follows: T_1 has the same tape alphabet as T, except that it has an additional symbol #. The states of T_1 are the same as those of T. The transitions of T_1 are the same, except that for any transition of T in which a nonblank symbol is written, the corresponding transition of T_1 writes # and halts. Then T writes a nonblank symbol, starting with an empty tape, if and only if T_1 writes the symbol #, starting with an empty tape. Since the problem: Given T_1, does it ever write the symbol #, starting with an empty tape? is unsolvable (see Theorem 20.3), then the problem: given T, does it ever print a nonblank symbol, starting with an empty tape? is unsolvable.

The result being "proved" here is false, according to Theorem 20.4, so this "proof" cannot possibly be correct. Explain as precisely as you can what is wrong with it.

20.8. Refer to the correspondence system in Example 20.2, in the case where the input string is a. Find the longest possible partial solution.

20.9. In each case below, either give a solution to the correspondence system or show that none exists.

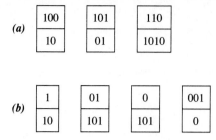

20.10. Show that the problem **CSLIsEmpty**: Given a linear-bounded automaton, is the language it accepts empty? is unsolvable. Suggestion: use the fact that Post's correspondence problem is unsolvable, by starting with an arbitrary correspondence system and constructing an LBA that accepts precisely the strings α representing solutions to the correspondence system.

20.11 Show that each of these decision problems for CFGs is unsolvable.

(a) Given two CFGs G_1 and G_2, is $L(G_1) = L(G_2)$?

(b) Given two CFGs G_1 and G_2, is $L(G_1) \subseteq L(G_2)$?

CHAPTER
21

COMPUTABILITY: PRIMITIVE RECURSIVE FUNCTIONS

21.1 COMPUTABLE FUNCTIONS

Up to this point in our study of Turing machines, the emphasis has been on the associated languages: those that can be accepted, the recursively enumerable, and those that can be recognized, the recursive. Another way to say this is that we have emphasized computations that can have only two results. In the case of a TM that is viewed as accepting a language, the two possible results are that the TM halts and that it doesn't. If the TM recognizes a language, it computes a function whose only two values are 0 and 1.

We are ready to consider other functions in more detail, and to try to determine what it means for a function to be *computable*. To start with, we will be considering only *numerical* functions: specifically, functions of zero or more nonnegative integer variables, whose values are nonnegative integers. We will see later that this is not unduly restrictive, since more general functions, from strings to strings for example, can be discussed by finding some suitable method of encoding both the arguments and the function values as numbers.

A word about terminology is in order at this point. If f is a function of k variables, up to this point our approach has been to specify the domain D of f, some subset of $\mathcal{N}^k$, and not to write $f(x)$ unless $x \in D$. However, we want to consider a TM computing f, and we are used to thinking of a TM with input alphabet Σ as processing an input string that can be any arbitrary element of Σ^*. This suggests, perhaps, a slight shift in the way we view our function. Rather

370

than thinking of f as a function from D to $\mathcal{N}$, we could describe f as a *partial* function from $\mathcal{N}^k$ to $\mathcal{N}$ that might be undefined at points not in D. If it happened that f was in fact defined at each point in $\mathcal{N}^k$, we would say explicitly that f was a *total* function. This is simply a shift in emphasis, largely as a matter of convenience. It allows us, for example, to add two functions whose domains are different—the result is also viewed as a partial function from $\mathcal{N}^k$ to $\mathcal{N}$, which is defined at every point where both the original functions are defined. From now on, we adopt this terminology. In particular, the word *function* is now understood to mean *partial* function. The main effect of this change will be to simplify the statements in definitions and theorems.

A partial function $f : \mathcal{N}^k \to \mathcal{N}$ is *computable* if there is a TM T that computes f (see Definition 16.3). In other words, for any input representing a point X in $\mathcal{N}^k$ at which f is defined, T halts with an output string representing $f(X)$, and for any other input $X \in \mathcal{N}^k$, T fails to halt.

We have encountered *uncomputable* (nonnumerical) functions defined on Σ^*. If $L \subseteq \Sigma^*$, saying that L is not recursive is the same as saying that the characteristic function $\chi_L : \Sigma^* \to \{0, 1\}$ is not computable. Although these examples do not provide us immediately with an uncomputable numerical function, we shall produce one shortly. In any case, an argument like that of Theorem 18.9 can be used to show that not all numerical functions of one variable can be computed: the set of Turing machines is countable, the set of functions from $\mathcal{N}$ to $\mathcal{N}$ is uncountable, and a single TM can compute at most one such function.

Beginning in the next section, we discuss an important class of functions, which will represent a first step toward an alternative characterization of computable functions. The discussion will involve various ways of creating new functions from given ones, and at this point it is necessary to enlarge slightly upon the definition of one such method, that of composition, given in Chapter 1. First a word about notation: in Definition 21.1, and frequently in what follows, it will be convenient to use some sort of notation that distinguishes integers from m-tuples of integers. We will generally use lower-case letters to represent integers, upper-case to represent vectors, or m-tuples.

Definition 21.1. Suppose f is a (partial) function from $\mathcal{N}^k$ to $\mathcal{N}$, and for each i with $1 \leq i \leq k$, g_i is a (partial) function from $\mathcal{N}^m$ to $\mathcal{N}$. The (partial) function $h = f(g_1, g_2, \ldots, g_k)$ from $\mathcal{N}^m$ to $\mathcal{N}$ defined by the formula

$$h(X) = f(g_1(X), g_2(X), \ldots, g_k(X)) \qquad \text{(for } X \in \mathcal{N}^m)$$

is said to be obtained from f and $g_1, g_2, \ldots, g_k$ by composition.

Notice that in the phrase "obtained from f and $g_1, g_2, \ldots, g_k$ by composition," the order of the functions is significant. In particular, the phrase describes only one function.

In this definition, in order for $h(X)$ to be defined, it is necessary and sufficient that each $g_i(X)$ be defined and that f be defined at the point $(g_1(X), \ldots, g_k(X))$. If all the functions $f, g_1, \ldots, g_k$ are total, h is total. Notice also that the function h could be written simply as $f \circ g$ if we took g to be the function from $\mathcal{N}^m$ to $\mathcal{N}^k$ defined by $g(X) = (g_1(X), \ldots, g_k(X))$; however, we have chosen to limit ourselves in these discussions to integer-valued, as opposed to vector-valued, functions.

For a familiar example, let $ADD : \mathcal{N} \times \mathcal{N} \rightarrow \mathcal{N}$ be the usual addition function ($ADD(x, y) = x + y$), and let f and g be partial functions from $\mathcal{N}^k$ to $\mathcal{N}$. The partial function h from $\mathcal{N}^k$ to $\mathcal{N}$ obtained from ADD, f, and g by composition is the sum of f and g:

$$h(X) = ADD(f(X), g(X)) = f(X) + g(X)$$

Theorem 21.1. If $f : \mathcal{N}^k \rightarrow \mathcal{N}$ and $g_1, g_2, \ldots, g_k : \mathcal{N}^m \rightarrow \mathcal{N}$ are computable functions and $h : \mathcal{N}^m \rightarrow \mathcal{N}$ is obtained from f and $g_1, \ldots, g_k$ by composition, then h is computable.

Proof. Let T_f and $T_1, T_2, \ldots, T_k$ be TM's computing f and $g_1, \ldots, g_k$, respectively. We will use them to construct a TM T_h to compute h. T_h begins with tape contents

$$\underline{\Delta}1^{x_1}\Delta1^{x_2} \ldots \Delta1^{x_m}$$

To simplify notation, let us denote by X the k-tuple $(x_1, \ldots, x_k)$ and by 1^X the string $1^{x_1}\Delta1^{x_2} \ldots \Delta1^{x_k}$. T_h must use this input k times, once for each of the T_i's. In order to do this, it makes an additional copy of the input each time before processing it. During the first iteration, T_h creates the tape

$$\Delta1^X\underline{\Delta}1^X$$

and executes T_1 to produce

$$\Delta1^X\underline{\Delta}1^{g_1(X)}$$

During the second iteration, it makes another copy of the input, to obtain

$$\Delta1^X\Delta1^{g_1(X)}\underline{\Delta}1^X$$

then executes T_2. After k iterations, the tape looks like

$$\Delta1^X\Delta1^{g_1(X)}\Delta1^{g_2(X)} \ldots \underline{\Delta}1^{g_k(X)}$$

T_h deletes the original input, so that the tape contains the input required for T_f:

$$\underline{\Delta}1^{g_1(X)}\Delta1^{g_2(X)} \ldots \Delta1^{g_k(X)}$$

The last step is to execute T_f, which produces the desired output.

For any choice of X at which the composition is undefined, T_h fails to halt: during the execution of T_i if $g_i(X)$ is undefined, and during the execution of T_f if each $g_i(X)$ is defined but $f(g_1(X), \ldots, g_k(X))$ is undefined. Therefore, the TM T_h we have defined computes h.

Notice also that in the simple case when $k = 1$, so that h reduces to the ordinary composition $f \circ g$, the original input is used only once, so that T_h can be constructed more simply by letting

$$T_h = T_g T_f$$

Before we start to look in more detail at the computable functions, let's see one example of a function that is not.

Example 21.1. Define a function $f : \mathcal{N} \to \mathcal{N}$ as follows. For each $n \geq 0$, $f(n)$ is the largest possible number of 1's that can be left on the tape by any TM having n states and tape alphabet $\{0, 1\}$, given that the TM starts with input 1^n and eventually halts. (You must first convince yourself that this is a meaningful definition. If we restrict our TM to have tape alphabet $\{0, 1\}$ and n states, there is no harm in assuming that the states are $q_1, \ldots, q_n$, and thus there are only a finite number of such machines. Some may crash or loop forever on the input 1^n, but of the remaining ones there is one that halts with at least as many 1's on its tape as any of the others; this number of 1's is what we are calling $f(n)$.) Let's agree in addition that $f(0) = 0$. Let us show that there is no TM that can compute the function f.

Suppose there were such a machine. It is possible to find another one T_f with tape alphabet $\{0, 1\}$ (see Exercise 17.14). Let $T = T_f T_1$, where T_1 is a TM that prints 1 in the first blank square to the right of its initial head position and halts with the tape head in its original position. Clearly, T computes the function g defined by $g(n) = f(n) + 1$. But this is impossible. On the one hand, if T has m states, then by definition of the function f, if T starts with input 1^m it can have no more than $f(m)$ 1's on its tape when it halts. On the other hand, $g(m) = f(m) + 1$, and since T computes g, when T starts with input 1^m it must halt with output $1^{f(m)+1}$. This contradiction shows that f is not computable.

The function f is known as the *busy-beaver* function, since its value for a given integer n is a measure of how busy a TM with n states that starts with input 1^n can be before it halts. It might be worthwhile to compare this proof of uncomputability to the proof of "unacceptability" in Theorem 18.10. There, we used a diagonal argument to show that no TM could accept the language *NonSelfAccepting*. Do you see anything "diagonal-like" in this example?

21.2 PRIMITIVE RECURSIVE FUNCTIONS

We have introduced the idea of a computable function, and although we have not examined many examples explicitly, we can certainly say with confidence that most if not all of our familiar functions are computable. However, the countability argument mentioned in the last section makes it clear that there are many uncomputable functions, and Example 21.1 contained one that can be defined reasonably simply. The question is, which functions are computable?

At first there is something almost paradoxical about the idea of *defining* a function that cannot be *computed*. When we define a function, we specify in some unambiguous way what its value is at each point in its domain. We certainly did this in Example 21.1. Yet, having described the number $f(n)$ perfectly precisely, we have no idea how to evaluate $f(1234)$. (The simple-minded approach of examining all 1234-state TMs with tape alphabet $\{0, 1\}$ is hopeless—not because of the large number of such machines, but because of a more serious problem: we have no general way of determining which ones halt on input 1^n.) By contrast, when we define a function g using a formula like

$$g(n) = |2^{n+5} - (3n + 1)^8|$$

the definition immediately suggests a sequence of steps we could take that would give us the value of $g(1234)$.

It is not just the fact that f is defined in words rather than by an algebraic formula that makes f uncomputable. Consider the function h defined as follows:

$h(n)$ is the largest number of 1's that can be left on the tape of a 2-state TM with tape alphabet $\{0, 1\}$, if it starts with input 1^n and eventually halts; you should be able to convince yourself that h is computable. Rather, f is uncomputable because the definition in words cannot be replaced by some more constructive definition. Our goal is to come up with a precise formulation of "constructive," so that any function defined in a way that meets this criterion will be computable, and any computable function can be defined in such a way. (Of course, we will still have the problem of deciding, given some definition in words, whether there is a better, more "constructive" definition. We won't be able to do much with that question, since the notion of "definable in words" is too nebulous.)

The function g defined above is obtained from a number of simpler functions by repeated applications of the composition operation. If we can show that the simpler functions are computable, it follows from Theorem 21.1 that g is. In order to be able to apply this type of reasoning more systematically, we need a class of "initial" functions, known to be computable, that we can start with. However, if we are to have any hope of producing all computable functions and still keeping to a manageable size our class of initial functions, we will need other methods of generating new functions in addition to composition (see Exercise 21.6). In Chapter 2, we considered functions that were defined recursively, and in fact we noticed by looking at functions like the factorial function that one of the important features of a recursive definition is its algorithmic quality: a recursive definition of a function f specifies how to obtain $f(n + 1)$, provided earlier values of f have already been computed. We will pin down a little more precisely the type of recursive definition we want to allow, and we will then be able to define a class of functions that contains many, though not all, of the computable functions.

Definition 21.2   (Initial functions). The functions that are included in the set of *initial functions* are the following:

1. *Constant* functions: for each $k \geq 0$, and each $a \geq 0$, the constant function $C_a^k :$ $\mathcal{N}^k \to \mathcal{N}$ is defined by the formula

$$C_a^k(X) = a \qquad \text{for every } X \in \mathcal{N}^k$$

   In the case $k = 0$, we may identify the function C_a^k with the number a.

2. The *successor* function $s : \mathcal{N} \to \mathcal{N}$ is defined by the formula

$$s(x) = x + 1$$

3. *Projection* functions: for each $k \geq 1$, and each i with $1 \leq i \leq k$, the projection function $p_i^k : \mathcal{N}^k \to \mathcal{N}$ is defined by the formula

$$p_i^k(x_1, x_2, \ldots, x_i, \ldots, x_k) = x_i$$

It is clear that each of the initial functions is a total function.

In Chapter 2, the simplest way we considered of defining a function f from $\mathcal{N}$ to $\mathcal{N}$ recursively was to say first what $f(0)$ is, then for any $k \geq 0$ to say what $f(k + 1)$ is in terms of $f(k)$. The prototypical example is the factorial function: here $f(0) = 1$ and $f(k + 1) = (k + 1) * f(k)$. The recursive step in the definition gives an expression for $f(k + 1)$ involving both k and $f(k)$. In generalizing this, it would be reasonable to allow, instead of the expression $(k + 1) * f(k)$, any expression of the form $h(k, f(k))$, where h is a function of two variables. (In this example, $h(x, y) = (x + 1)*y$.) We must adapt this for functions f of more than one variable. The easiest way is simply to restrict the recursion to one coordinate, say the last. In other words, we shall start by saying what $f(x_1, \ldots, x_n, 0)$ is, for any choice of $(x_1, \ldots, x_n)$ (this means specifying a constant if $n = 0$, and in the general case it means specifying a function of n variables), and in the recursive step we shall say what $f(x_1, \ldots, x_n, k + 1)$ is in terms of $f(x_1, \ldots, x_n, k)$. As usual, let X stand for $(x_1, \ldots, x_n)$. In the most general case, $f(X, k + 1)$ may depend on X and k directly, in addition to $f(X, k)$, just as $f(k + 1)$ depended on k as well as on $f(k)$ in the one-variable case. Thus, a reasonable way to formulate the recursive step is to say that

$$f(X, k + 1) = h(X, k, f(X, k))$$

for some function h of $n + 2$ variables.

Definition 21.3 (**The primitive recursion operation**). Suppose $n \geq 0$, and g and h are functions of n and $n + 2$ variables, respectively. The function $f : \mathcal{N}^{n+1} \to \mathcal{N}$ defined by the formulas

$$f(X, 0) = g(X)$$

$$f(X, k + 1) = h(X, k, f(X, k))$$

for every $X \in \mathcal{N}^n$ and every $k \geq 0$, is said to be obtained from g and h by the operation of *primitive recursion*.

To return again to the factorial example: g is the number, or the function of 0 variables, $C_1^0 = 1$, and we have seen above what $h(x, y)$ is. We shall see a number of other examples after the next definition.

Here again, if the functions g and h are total functions, f is total. If either g or h is not total, the situation is slightly more complicated. Let's see exactly what can be said in this case. Consider a fixed $X \in \mathcal{N}^n$. If $g(X)$ is undefined, then $f(X, 0)$ is undefined, $f(X, 1) = h(X, 0, f(X, 0))$ is undefined, $\ldots$, and in general, $f(X, k)$ is undefined for every k. For exactly the same reason, if $f(X, k)$ is undefined for *some* value of k, say $k = k_0$, then $f(X, k)$ is undefined for every $k \geq k_0$. This is the same as saying that if $f(X, k_1)$ is defined, then $f(X, k)$ is defined for every $k \leq k_1$. These observations will play a role in the next result, which is the analogue of Theorem 21.1 for the primitive recursion operation.

Theorem 21.2. If $g : \mathcal{N}^n \to \mathcal{N}$ and $h : \mathcal{N}^{n+2} \to \mathcal{N}$ are computable partial functions, the function f obtained from g and h by primitive recursion is also computable.

Proof. Let T_g and T_h be TMs computing g and h, respectively; we wish to construct a TM T_f to compute f.

The initial tape of T_f looks like

$$\underline{\Delta}1^{x_1}\Delta 1^{x_2}\Delta \ldots \Delta 1^{x_n}\Delta 1^{x_{n+1}}$$

which we abbreviate $\underline{\Delta}1^X\Delta1^{x_{n+1}}$. As usual, X denotes $(x_1, \ldots, x_n)$. In order to describe as simply as possible the action of T_f on this input, we assume that $f(X, x_{n+1})$ is defined. We shall take care of the case when it is not in a moment. T_f works as follows. First, it determines whether x_{n+1} is 0. If it is, T_f returns the tape head to square 0, executes T_g, and halts. Otherwise, the tape contents are $\Delta1^X\Delta1^{k+1}$ for some k. In this case, T_f will compute $f(X, 0)$, use it to compute $f(X, 1)$, use that to compute $f(X, 2), \ldots$, and ultimately use $f(X, k)$ to compute $f(X, k + 1)$. It prepares to do this by creating the tape

$$\#1^X\Delta1^k\Delta1^X\Delta1^{k-1}\Delta1^X\Delta\ldots\Delta1^2\Delta1^X\Delta1^1\Delta1^X\Delta1^0\underline{\Delta}1^X$$

(Of course $1^0 = \Lambda$; it is written this way for clarity's sake.) T_f starts the calculation by executing T_g and moving the tape head, to obtain

$$\#1^X\Delta1^k\Delta1^X\Delta\ldots\Delta1^1\underline{\Delta}1^X\Delta1^0\Delta1^{f(X,0)}$$

Here we are using the fact that $f(X, 0) = g(X)$. At this point T_f begins a loop, during each iteration of which it executes T_h and moves the tape head. After the first iteration, since $f(X, 1) = h(X, 0, f(X, 0))$, the tape looks like

$$\#1^X\Delta1^k\Delta1^X\Delta\ldots\underline{\Delta}1^X\Delta1^1\Delta1^{f(X,1)}$$

and T_f is ready to execute T_h again to compute $f(X, 2)$. A second iteration yields

$$\#1^X\Delta1^k\Delta1^X\Delta\ldots\underline{\Delta}1^X\Delta1^2\Delta1^{f(X,2)}$$

Continued iterations of this loop finally produce

$$\underline{\#}1^X\Delta1^k\Delta1^{f(X,k)}$$

at which point changing $\#$ to Δ and executing T_h once more produces the desired result.

We know from the remarks preceding the theorem that if $f(X, k + 1)$ is defined, each of the steps in the computation we have described can be carried out successfully. If $f(X, k + 1)$ is undefined, either the execution of T_g on the input 1^X will fail to halt, or, for some i with $0 \le i \le k$, the execution of T_h on the input $1^X\Delta1^i\Delta1^{f(X,i)}$ will fail to halt. Thus, we may conclude that T_f halts on the input $1^X\Delta1^{k+1}$ if and only if $f(X, k + 1)$ is defined.

Definition 21.4 **(Primitive recursive functions).** The set $\mathscr{PR}$ of *primitive recursive* functions is defined as follows:

1. All initial functions are elements of $\mathscr{PR}$.
2. For any $k \ge 0$ and $m \ge 0$, if $f : \mathscr{N}^k \to \mathscr{N}$ and $g_1, \ldots, g_k : \mathscr{N}^m \to \mathscr{N}$ are elements of $\mathscr{PR}$, then the function $f(g_1, \ldots, g_k)$ obtained from f and $g_1, \ldots, g_k$ by composition is an element of $\mathscr{PR}$.
3. For any $n \ge 0$, any function $g : \mathscr{N}^n \to \mathscr{N}$ in $\mathscr{PR}$, and any function $h : \mathscr{N}^{n+2} \to \mathscr{N}$ in $\mathscr{PR}$, the function $f : \mathscr{N}^{n+1} \to \mathscr{N}$ obtained from g and h by the operation of primitive recursion is an element of $\mathscr{PR}$.
4. No function is in $\mathscr{PR}$ unless it can be obtained by statements 1, 2, or 3.

As usual in the case of a definition like Definition 21.4, there are other ways we might describe the set $\mathscr{PR}$ (see the discussion in Section 2.3 and Exercise 2.27). One is to say that $\mathscr{PR}$ is the smallest set of functions that contains the initial functions and is closed under the operations of composition and primitive recursion. (In other words, $\mathcal{PR}$ is the smallest set S such that S contains the initial functions and S contains any function obtained from elements of S by composition or primitive recursion.) Another way that describes more explicitly the properties of a specific primitive recursive function, and often lends itself more easily to precise proofs, is to introduce the idea of a *primitive recursive derivation*. A function f has a primitive recursive derivation if there is a finite sequence of functions $f_0, f_1, \ldots, f_j$ so that $f_j = f$ and each function f_i in the sequence is an initial function, can be obtained from earlier functions in the sequence using composition, or can be obtained from earlier functions in the sequence using primitive recursion. The primitive recursive functions are precisely those having primitive recursive derivations.

Example 21.2. Let $ADD(x, y) = x + y$, so that $ADD : \mathcal{N}^2 \rightarrow \mathcal{N}$. Let's try to find a primitive recursive derivation for this function. Since it is not an initial function and there is no obvious way to obtain it by composition, we try to obtain it by primitive recursion, and hope that, assuming we are successful, the functions from which it is obtained are even simpler. If it is to be obtained from g and h using primitive recursion, g must be a function of one variable and h a function of three variables. The equations are

$$ADD(x, 0) = g(x)$$

$$ADD(x, k + 1) = h(x, k, ADD(x, k))$$

and we must find g and h that satisfy them. The first is easy. Obviously $ADD(x, 0) = x$, and x is the formula for the initial function p_1^1. The question is, how do we obtain $x + k + 1$ (i.e., $ADD(x, k + 1)$) from the three quantities x, k, and $x + k$? In this case, it's very easy: we don't use x and k directly at all, and we simply take the successor of $x + k$. In other words, we want $h(x, k, ADD(x, k))$ to be $ADD\,(x, k) + 1$, or $s(ADD(x, k))$. This means that for any x_1, x_2, and x_3, $h(x_1, x_2, x_3)$ should be $s(x_3)$, which is the same as $s(p_3^3(x_1, x_2, x_3))$. Therefore, a derivation for ADD could be obtained this way:

$f_0 = p_1^1$ (an initial function)

$f_1 = s$ (an initial function)

$f_2 = p_3^3$ (an initial function)

$f_3 = s(p_3^3)$ (obtained from f_1 and f_2 by composition)

$f_4 = ADD$ (obtained from f_0 and f_3 by primitive recursion)

There is considerable flexibility in the order here; we could have taken the sequence

$$s, p_1^1, p_3^3, s(p_3^3), ADD$$

the sequence

$$p_3^3, s, s(p_3^3), p_1^1, ADD$$

or any of a number of others. The only requirements are that both s and p_3^3 come before $s(p_3^3)$ and that ADD be the last one.

We go through one more example in detail.

Example 21.3. Let $MULT(x, y) = x * y$. Again, we attempt to obtain the function using primitive recursion. We have

$$MULT(x, 0) = 0$$

$$\begin{aligned} MULT(x, k + 1) &= x * (k + 1) \\ &= x * k + x \\ &= ADD(x * k, x) \\ &= ADD(x, x * k) \\ &= ADD(x, MULT(x, k)) \end{aligned}$$

Remember that we are attempting to write this in the form $h(x, k, MULT(x, k))$. Since x can be obtained from $(x, k, MULT(x, k))$ by using the projection p_1^3 and $MULT(x, k)$ can be obtained by using p_3^3, it is appropriate to write

$$MULT(x, k + 1) = ADD(p_1^3(x, k, MULT(x, k)), p_3^3(x, k, MULT(x, k)))$$

These formulas now say that $MULT$ is obtained from the two functions C_0^1, the zero function of one variable, and $ADD(p_1^3, p_3^3)$, a function of three variables, by primitive recursion. With this, we can write a complete primitive recursive derivation of $MULT$ without too much trouble. Since it will involve the function ADD, we begin our sequence with the derivation in the previous example. Any function in the list that is not explicitly stated to be derived from earlier functions is an initial function.

$$f_0 = p_1^1$$

$$f_1 = s$$

$$f_2 = p_3^3$$

$$f_3 = s(p_3^3) \qquad \text{(from } f_1 \text{ and } f_2 \text{ using composition)}$$

$$f_4 = ADD \qquad \text{(from } f_0 \text{ and } f_3 \text{ using primitive recursion)}$$

$$f_5 = C_0^1$$

$$f_6 = p_1^3$$

$$f_7 = ADD(p_1^3, p_3^3) \qquad \text{(from } f_4, f_6, \text{ and } f_2 \text{ using composition)}$$

$$f_8 = MULT \qquad \text{(from } f_5 \text{ and } f_7 \text{ using primitive recursion)}$$

You can probably imagine after this example that it will not often be worthwhile to construct a complete primitive recursive derivation of a function—usually it will suffice to show how the function can be obtained, either by composition or by primitive recursion, from simpler functions. Nevertheless, you should study these examples until you are comfortable with the idea, since it is a way of giving a complete, self-contained proof that a function is primitive recursive. In the Exercises you are asked to use this method to show that several other functions are primitive recursive.

Before we continue with more examples of primitive recursive functions, let us derive two properties of primitive recursive functions in general. Since we know that every primitive recursive function has a primitive recursive derivation, a reasonable method of showing that primitive recursive functions have some property P is to use mathematical induction on the number of steps in the derivation. But as we saw in Section 2.3, we will be able to complete such an inductive proof easily if we can show these statements:

1. Initial functions satisfy property P.
2. If f can be obtained, either by composition or by primitive recursion, from functions satisfying property P, then f also satisfies property P.

In other words, we simply need to show that the set of functions satisfying property P contains the initial functions and is closed under these two operations.

Theorem 21.3. Every primitive recursive function is a total function.

Proof. This is obvious from the remarks above: we have already observed that initial functions are total, the composition of total functions is total, and any function obtained from total functions by primitive recursion is total.

Theorem 21.4. Every primitive recursive function is computable.

Proof. It is almost obvious that the initial functions are all computable, and we omit the detailed proof of that statement. The result follows immediately from Theorems 21.1 and 21.2.

21.3   MORE EXAMPLES

In this section, we give several more examples of primitive recursive functions and make a few observations that in many cases simplify the proofs of primitive recursiveness.

Example 21.4. Let $f(x, y) = x^y$. In order to guarantee that f is total, let's agree that $0^0 = 1$. f can be obtained by primitive recursion as follows:

$$f(x, 0) = 1 = C_1^1(x)$$

$$\begin{aligned} f(x, k + 1) &= x^{k+1} \\ &= MULT(x, x^k) \\ &= MULT(x, f(x, k)) \\ &= MULT(p_1^3(x, k, f(x, k)), p_3^3(x, k, f(x, k))) \end{aligned}$$

$MULT(p_1^3, p_3^3)$ is primitive recursive, since it is obtained by composition from functions we already know to be primitive recursive; and C_1^1 is an initial function. Therefore, since f is obtained from these two by primitive recursion, f is primitive recursive.

At this point, let us compare Examples 21.3 and 21.4. In both cases, in the process of obtaining f from two other functions by primitive recursion, we obtained the formula

$$f(x, k + 1) = h_1(x, f(x, k))$$

for some function h_1 of two variables. In Example 21.3, h_1 was *ADD*; in Example 21.4, h_1 was *MULT*. What we needed in both cases, in order to obtain the exact form required by Definition 21.3, was $h(x, k, f(x, k))$, for some function h of three variables. This situation is common enough that it is worthwhile to prove the result we need once and for all, so that we don't have to clutter up the derivation with p_3^3 and p_1^3 every time the situation comes up. At the same time, we note several other equally simple results that often facilitate arguments of this type.

Theorem 21.5. Let f be a primitive recursive function of n variables. Then

1. For any $k \geq 1$, any function g of $n + k$ variables obtained from f by introducing "dummy" variables (e.g., if $n = 2$ and $k = 1$, $g(x_1, x_2, x_3) = f(x_1, x_3)$) is primitive recursive.
2. Any function g of n variables obtained from f by *permuting* variables (e.g., if $n = 2$, $g(x_1, x_2) = f(x_2, x_1)$) is primitive recursive.
3. For any k with $1 \leq k \leq n$, any function g of $n - k$ variables obtained from f by *substituting constants* for k of the variables of f (e.g., if $n = 2$ and $k = 1$, $g(x) = f(5, x)$) is primitive recursive.
4. For any k with $1 \leq k \leq n$, any function g of $n - k$ variables obtained from f by *repeating a variable* k times (e.g., if $n = 3$ and $k = 1$, $g(x_1, x_2) = f(x_1, x_2, x_1)$) is primitive recursive.

Proof. These are all variants of the same general situation:

$$g(x_1, x_2, \ldots, x_r) = f(z_1, z_2, \ldots, z_n)$$

where for each i, z_i is either $p_j^r(x_1, \ldots, x_r)$ for some j, or $C_a^r(x_1, \ldots, x_r)$ for some a. For example, the function g shown in part 1 could be written

$$g(x_1, x_2, x_3) = f(p_1^3(x_1, x_2, x_3), p_3^3(x_1, x_2, x_3))$$

In part 3 we could write

$$g(x) = f(C_5^1(x), p_1^1(x))$$

In all four cases, the result is true because all the functions p_j^r and C_a^r are primitive recursive, and g is obtained from f and some of these functions by composition.

These four cases can be combined in every which way. If

$$g(x_1, x_2, x_3) = f(x_1, x_1, x_2, x_2, 3, x_1, 7)$$

and f is primitive recursive, then g is, by exactly the same argument. Having made these observations, we shall often give shortened proofs of primitive recursiveness and leave it to you to convince yourself that Theorem 21.5 can be used to fill in the details.

Theorem 21.5 is useful not only in derivations by primitive recursion; it can be used directly. Here are some examples of functions f that are easily seen to be primitive recursive, using Theorem 21.5 and Examples 21.2, 21.3, and 21.4.

$$f(x_1, y_1, z_1) = ADD(x_1, y_1)$$
$$f(x) = x + 2$$

Similarly, we can define the predicates *GT* (greater than), *LE* (less than or equal), *GE*, and *NE* (not equal). These are all primitive recursive. For example,

$$\chi_{LT}(x, y) = Sg(y \dot{-} x)$$

where *Sg* is the function defined in Example 21.9, since $x < y$ if and only if $y \dot{-} x > 0$, and this condition holds if and only if $Sg(y \dot{-} x) = 1$.

$$\chi_{EQ}(x, y) = 1 \dot{-} (Sg(x \dot{-} y) + Sg(y \dot{-} x))$$

(If $x < y$ or $x > y$, one of the terms $x \dot{-} y$ and $y \dot{-} x$ is nonzero, and therefore the expression in parentheses is nonzero, causing the final result to be 0. If $x = y$, the parenthesized expression is 0, since $x \dot{-} y = y \dot{-} x = 0$; thus the final result is 1.) In both these cases, since the characteristic function has been obtained by composition from functions already known to be primitive recursive, it is also primitive recursive.

Although it would be straightforward to take care of the other relational predicates in the same way, let us return to them after the next result, when it will be even easier.

Predicates take the values true and false, and therefore we may apply the logical operators $\wedge$ (AND), $\vee$ (OR), and $\neg$ (NOT) to them. $(P_1 \wedge P_2)(X)$ is true if and only if $P_1(X)$ and $P_2(X)$ are true, and so on. Not surprisingly, these operations preserve the primitive recursive property.

Theorem 21.6. If P_1 and P_2 are primitive recursive n-place predicates, then so are the predicates $P_1 \wedge P_2$, $P_1 \vee P_2$, and $\neg P_1$.

Proof. The result follows from these three equations, which are easily verified.

$$\chi_{P_1 \wedge P_2} = \chi_{P_1} * \chi_{P_2}$$

$$\chi_{P_1 \vee P_2} = \chi_{P_1} + \chi_{P_2} \dot{-} \chi_{P_1 \wedge P_2}$$

$$\chi_{\neg P_1} = 1 \dot{-} \chi_{P_1}$$

Example 21.10 (continued). We have shown that the two relational predicates *LT* and *EQ* are primitive recursive. To take care of the other four, we observe that

$$LE = LT \vee EQ$$

$$GT = \neg LE$$

$$GE = \neg LT$$

$$NE = \neg EQ$$

so by Theorem 21.6, all are primitive recursive.

If P is an n-place predicate, and $f_1, \ldots, f_n : \mathcal{N}^k \to \mathcal{N}$, we may form the k-place predicate $Q = P(f_1, \ldots, f_n)$. It is clear that $\chi_Q = \chi_P(f_1, \ldots, f_n)$, and therefore, if P is a primitive recursive predicate and the functions $f_1, \ldots, f_n$ are all primitive recursive, Q is primitive recursive. As a simple example, consider the predicate

$$f < g$$

where $f, g : \mathcal{N}^k \to \mathcal{N}$. Since the predicate LT is primitive recursive, this one is if the two functions f and g are. Combining this general fact with Theorem 21.6, we see that arbitrarily complicated predicates constructed using relational and logical operators, such as

$$(f_1 = (3f_2)^2 \wedge (f_3 < f_4 + f_5)) \vee \neg(P \vee Q)$$

are primitive recursive as long as the basic constituents (in this case, the functions $f_1, \ldots, f_5$ and the predicates P and Q) are.

We return to the idea with which we began this section, that of defining a function by cases. The next result says that if all the individual functions and all the predicates specifying the individual cases are primitive recursive, the function being defined is also.

Theorem 21.7. Suppose $f_1, \ldots, f_k : \mathcal{N}^n \to \mathcal{N}$ are primitive recursive functions, $P_1, \ldots, P_k$ are primitive recursive n-place predicates, and for every $X \in \mathcal{N}^n$, exactly one of $P_1(X), \ldots, P_k(X)$ is true. The function $f : \mathcal{N}^n \to \mathcal{N}$ defined by

$$f(X) = \begin{cases} f_1(X) & \text{if } P_1(X) \text{ is true} \\ f_2(X) & \text{if } P_2(X) \text{ is true} \\ \cdots \\ f_k(X) & \text{if } P_k(X) \text{ is true} \end{cases}$$

is primitive recursive.

Proof. The last of the three assumptions is what guarantees that the definition of f is unambiguous. It implies that for every X, exactly one of the values $\chi_{P_i(X)}$ is 1 and the others are all 0. Therefore,

$$f = f_1\chi_{P_1} + f_2\chi_{P_2} + \ldots + f_k\chi_{P_k}$$

and the result follows from the primitive recursiveness of all the functions appearing on the right side of this equation.

Example 21.11. We know that ADD, SUB, and $MULT$ are primitive recursive. The fourth member of the quartet, DIV, is a little harder, but we are now in a position to take care of it as well as the related function MOD. There is an obvious question as to how to define them, since division by 0 is not usually defined. It is customary to say, in order to make both functions total, that $DIV(x, 0) = 0$ and $MOD(x, 0) = x$ for any x. Otherwise, $DIV(x, y)$ is the integer quotient when x is divided by y, and $MOD(x, y)$ is the remainder. For $y > 0$ these relationships are summarized by the two formulas

$$x = y * DIV(x, y) + MOD(x, y)$$

$$0 \le MOD(x, y) < y$$

We shall show that MOD is primitive recursive and use that result to show that DIV is also. We begin by letting

$$R(x, y) = MOD(y, x)$$

since in the derivation we use the first parameter of MOD for the recursion. According to Theorem 21.5, if we can show that R is primitive recursive, it will follow that MOD is as well. These formulas can easily be verified:

$$R(x, 0) = MOD(0, x) = 0$$

$$R(x, k + 1) = MOD(k + 1, x) = \begin{cases} R(x, k) + 1 & \text{if } x \neq 0 \quad \text{and} \quad R(x, k) + 1 < x \\ 0 & \text{if } x \neq 0 \quad \text{and} \quad R(x, k) + 1 = x \\ k + 1 & \text{if } x = 0 \end{cases}$$

For example,

$$R(5, 6 + 1) = MOD(7, 5) = MOD(6, 5) + 1$$

since $5 \neq 0$ and $MOD(6, 5) + 1 = 1 + 1 < 5$, and

$$R(5, 9 + 1) = MOD(10, 5) = 0$$

since $5 \neq 0$ and $MOD(9, 5) + 1 = 4 + 1 = 5$. The function h defined by

$$h(x_1, x_2, x_3) = \begin{cases} x_3 + 1 & \text{if } x_1 \neq 0 \quad \text{and} \quad x_3 + 1 < x_1 \\ 0 & \text{if } x_1 \neq 0 \quad \text{and} \quad x_3 + 1 = x_1 \\ x_2 + 1 & \text{if } x_1 = 0 \end{cases}$$

is not a total function, since it is undefined if $x_1 \neq 0$ and $x_3 + 1 > x_1$. But this isn't a serious problem. If we change the definition to

$$h(x_1, x_2, x_3) = \begin{cases} x_3 + 1 & \text{if } x_1 \neq 0 \quad \text{and} \quad x_3 + 1 < x_1 \\ 0 & \text{if } x_1 \neq 0 \quad \text{and} \quad x_3 + 1 \geq x_1 \\ x_2 + 1 & \text{if } x_1 = 0 \end{cases}$$

it works just as well: R is still obtained by primitive recursion from the two functions C_0^1 and h. It is clear from Theorem 21.7 that h is primitive recursive, and thus so is R. *DIV* is handled in a similar way. Let

$$Q(x, y) = DIV(y, x)$$

We have

$$Q(x, 0) = 0$$

$$Q(x, k + 1) = DIV(k + 1, x) = \begin{cases} Q(x, k) & \text{if } x \neq 0 \quad \text{and} \quad MOD(k, x) + 1 < x \\ Q(x, k) + 1 & \text{if } x \neq 0 \quad \text{and} \quad MOD(k, x) + 1 = x \\ 0 & \text{if } x = 0 \end{cases}$$

Thus, Q is obtained by primitive recursion from C_0^1 and the primitive recursive function h_1 defined by

$$h_1(x_1, x_2, x_3) = \begin{cases} x_3 & \text{if } x_1 \neq 0 \quad \text{and} \quad MOD(x_2, x_1) + 1 < x_1 \\ x_3 + 1 & \text{if } x_1 \neq 0 \quad \text{and} \quad MOD(x_2, x_1) + 1 = x_1 \\ 0 & \text{if } x_1 = 0 \end{cases}$$

Notice that for any (x_1, x_2, x_3), it *is* the case that exactly one of the predicates used in the definition of h_1 is true.

21.5 SOME BOUNDED OPERATIONS

In this section, we discuss certain related operations on functions and predicates that preserve the property of primitive recursiveness. One of these operations, however, will suggest in a natural way another operation that does not preserve this property but does preserve the property of computability. This new operation, which along with composition and primitive recursion will allow us to generate all the computable functions, will be discussed in the next chapter.

Let's begin by considering two simple and well-known functions:

$$f(x) = \sum_{i=0}^{x} i$$

$$x! = \prod_{i=1}^{x} i$$

The notation in the second case is precisely analogous to the summation notation in the first. In general,

$$\prod_{i=j}^{k} p_i$$

denotes the product $p_j * p_{j+1} * \ldots * p_k$ if $k \geq j$ and 1 if $k < j$. (A comment may be in order here concerning the convention with regard to the "empty" sum $\sum_{i=j}^{k} p_i$ where $k < j$, and the corresponding empty product $\prod_{i=j}^{k} p_i$. The natural value in the first case is 0, since the empty sum added to any other sum produces that other sum. The natural value in the second case is 1, for similar reasons.)

$f(x)$ can be written more simply as $DIV(x*(x+1), 2)$, and we have already shown the factorial function to be primitive recursive, but it will be useful to show that more general functions defined by the same method are primitive recursive. The added generality will come by allowing the terms being added or multiplied to be more general than i and in fact to involve other variables—so that the function being defined is a function of more than one variable.

Theorem 21.8. Let $n \geq 0$, and suppose $g : \mathcal{N}^{n+1} \to \mathcal{N}$ is primitive recursive. The two functions f_1 and f_2 from $\mathcal{N}^{n+1}$ to $\mathcal{N}$ obtained by *bounded sums* and *bounded products* from g as follows:

$$f_1(X, k) = \sum_{i=0}^{k} g(X, i)$$

$$f_2(X, k) = \prod_{i=0}^{k} g(X, i)$$

for any $X \in \mathcal{N}^n$ and $k \geq 0$, are both primitive recursive.

Proof. We give the proof for f_1, and that for f_2 is almost identical. We have

$$f_1(X, 0) = g(X, 0)$$

$$f_1(X, k+1) = f_1(X, k) + g(X, k+1)$$

Therefore, f_1 is obtained by primitive recursion from the two primitive recursive functions g_1 and h, where

$$g_1(X) = g(X, 0)$$

$$h(X, y, z) = z + g(X, y + 1)$$

It follows that f_1 is primitive recursive.

There is a slight discrepancy between the definition of the bounded product in Theorem 21.8 and the definition of $x!$ above: in one case the product begins with the $i = 0$ term, in the other case with $i = 1$. It is not difficult to generalize the theorem slightly so as to allow the sum or product to begin with the $i = i_0$ term, for any fixed i_0 (see Exercise 21.17). There are other ways to generalize it as well, but we will have no direct use for them. We shall see a better example of how bounded sums and products are used very shortly.

Although bounded sums and products are usually described as "bounded operations," the term is more properly applied to the other operations we are going to consider, since it will be clear that there is an "unbounded" counterpart. Again, we start with an example. Consider the one-place predicate *PerfectSquare*: *PerfectSquare*(x) is true if and only if x is a perfect square. In other words,

$$\textit{PerfectSquare}(x) = (\text{there exists } y \text{ with } y^2 = x)$$

If *Sq* is the two-place predicate defined by

$$\textit{Sq}(x, y) = (y^2 = x)$$

it would make sense to say that *PerfectSquare* is obtained from *Sq* by applying the *existential quantifier*, "there exists," to the second variable of *Sq* (see Section 1.3). The predicate *Sq* is clearly computable—in fact, it is primitive recursive. Does it follow that its "existential quantification" is computable? In this example, it obviously is: in order to determine whether there exists y with $x = y^2$, it is unnecessary to consider any values of y greater than x; thus there is an algorithm that can carry out the test. In a more general situation, however, the result is not true. Unless there is a *bound* to the values of y that need to be tested, it is possible that the answer can't be determined.

We can see this last statement by considering a situation familiar from Chapter 20. Given an alphabet Σ, we may impose an ordering on it, which gives rise to the standard lexicographic order on Σ^*; for $x \geq 0$, denote by s_x the xth string with respect to that ordering. Let T_U be the universal Turing machine of Section 17.4, and let H be the two-place predicate defined by

$$H(x, y) = (T_U \text{ halts after exactly } y \text{ moves on input } s_x)$$

H is clearly computable. However, the one-place predicate

$$\textit{Halts}(x) = (\text{there exists } y \text{ so that } T_U \text{ halts after } y \text{ moves on input } s_x)$$

is not, since to compute it would mean solving the Halting problem.

Let's return to the first example, and, to make things slightly clearer, assume $x \geq 2$. In this case, we may reduce even more the number of y's that need to be tested. We can say, for example, that

$$PerfectSquare(x) = (\text{there exists } y \leq DIV(x, 2) \text{ such that } y^2 = x)$$

We may think of this as $P(x, DIV(x, 2))$, where

$$P(x, k) = (\text{there exists } y \leq k \text{ such that } y^2 = x)$$

(Without any assumptions on x, we would need a larger bound on the set of y's to be tested; for example, we could write $PerfectSquare(x) = P(x, x)$.) We have applied the existential quantifier to the second variable of Sq, but only over the range specified by k. It seems clear that the predicate obtained this way from any computable predicate will still be computable; in fact this operation also preserves primitive recursiveness. The situation is similar if we use the *universal quantifier*, "for every," instead.

Definition 21.6. Let P be an $(n + 1)$-place predicate. The *bounded existential quantification* of P is the $(n + 1)$-place predicate E_P defined by

$$E_P(X, k) = (\text{there exists } y \text{ with } 0 \leq y \leq k \text{ such that } P(X, y))$$

The *bounded universal quantification* of P is the $(n + 1)$-place predicate A_P defined by

$$A_P(X, k) = (\text{for every } y \text{ with } 0 \leq y \leq k, P(X, y))$$

Theorem 21.9. If P is a primitive recursive $(n + 1)$-place predicate, the two bounded quantifications E_P and A_P are also primitive recursive.

Proof. $A_P(X, k)$ is true if and only if all the terms $P(X, i)$ are true for $0 \leq i \leq k$, and thus $\chi_{A_P}(X, k) = 1$ if and only if all the terms $\chi_P(X, i)$ are 1. Therefore,

$$\chi_{A_P}(X, k) = \prod_{i=0}^{k} \chi_P(X, i)$$

and the primitive recursiveness of A_P follows immediately from Theorem 21.8. Saying that there is an i with $0 \leq i \leq k$ for which $P(X, i)$ is true is the same as saying it is not the case that $P(X, i)$ is false for all i satisfying $0 \leq i \leq k$. In other words,

$$E_P(X, k) = \neg A_{(\neg P)}(X, k)$$

It follows that E_P is also primitive recursive.

We introduce the last type of bounded operation with another example. This time, consider the function *RoundUp*, which returns the first multiple of 10 greater than or equal to its argument. In other words,

$$RoundUp(x) = \min\{y \mid y \geq x \quad \text{and} \quad MOD(y, 10) = 0\}$$

If the two-place predicate T is defined by

$$T(x, y) = (y \geq x \quad \text{and} \quad MOD(y, 10) = 0)$$

RoundUp is obtained from T by applying to the second parameter an operation we might call *minimalization*. It is clear that T is primitive recursive, hence computable. Again, we may ask whether applying this operation to a computable predicate yields a computable function, and again it is clear that in this example the answer is yes: for any x, there is a multiple of 10 at least as large as x and no larger than $x + 9$, so there is an algorithm to find the minimal such multiple greater than or equal to x. Just as in the case of the quantification operators, it is necessary in general to restrict the minimalization to a bounded set of values if we wish to guarantee that the resulting function will be as well-behaved as the original predicate. The unbounded version of the operation will be discussed in the next chapter. Even in the bounded case, though, if we want the resulting function to be total, we must introduce an appropriate default value in case there is no number satisfying the predicate in the specified range.

Definition 21.7. If P is an $(n + 1)$-place predicate, the *bounded minimalization* of P is the function $m_P : \mathcal{N}^{n+1} \to \mathcal{N}$ defined by

$$m_P(X, k) = \begin{cases} \min\{y \mid 0 \le y \le k \quad \text{and} \quad P(X, y)\} & \text{if this set is not empty} \\ k + 1 & \text{otherwise} \end{cases}$$

The symbol μ is often used for the minimalization operator, and we will sometimes write

$$\overset{k}{\mu} y [P(X, y)] = m_P(X, k)$$

An important special case is that in which P is the predicate defined by $P(X) = (f(X) = 0)$ for some function f. In this case m_P is written m_f and referred to as the bounded minimalization of the function f.

Theorem 21.10. If P is a primitive recursive $(n + 1)$-place predicate, its bounded minimalization m_P is a primitive recursive function.

Proof. For any $X \in \mathcal{N}^n$, $m_P(X, 0)$ is 0 if $P(X, 0)$ is true and 1 otherwise. For $m_P(X, k + 1)$, there are three possibilities. If there exists $y \le k$ for which $P(X, y)$ is true, then $m_P(X, k + 1) = m_P(X, k)$. If there is no such y but $P(X, k + 1)$ is true, then $m_P(X, k + 1) = k + 1$. Finally, if neither of these conditions holds, $m_P(X, k + 1) = k + 2$. This means that m_P can be obtained by primitive recursion from the functions g and h, where

$$g(X) = \begin{cases} 0 & \text{if } P(X, 0) \text{ is true} \\ 1 & \text{otherwise} \end{cases}$$

$$h(X, y, z) = \begin{cases} z & \text{if } E_P(X, y) \text{ is true} \\ y + 1 & \text{if } \neg E_P(X, y) \wedge P(X, y + 1) \text{ is true} \\ y + 2 & \text{if } \neg E_P(X, y) \wedge \neg P(X, y + 1) \text{ is true} \end{cases}$$

Since P and E_P are primitive recursive predicates, g and h are primitive recursive, and therefore m_P is primitive recursive.

Example 21.12. For $x, y \ge 0$, let $LCM(x, y)$ be the least common multiple of x and y—the smallest integer that is both a multiple of x and a multiple of y. $LCM(x, y) = 0$ if either x or y is 0. We may obtain the function LCM by applying minimalization to the predicate CM, defined by

$$CM(x, y, z) = (z \text{ is a multiple of } x \text{ and } z \text{ is a multiple of } y)$$

Since $x * y$ is a multiple of x and a multiple of y, we may use bounded minimalization:

$$LCM(x, y) = m_{CM}(x, y, x * y)$$

Therefore, in order to show that LCM is primitive recursive, it is sufficient according to Theorem 21.10 to show that CM is primitive recursive. But this follows from the formula

$$CM(x, y, z) = (MOD(z, x) = 0 \wedge MOD(z, y) = 0))$$

Example 21.13. Let $d(n)$ be the nth digit of the infinite decimal expansion of $\sqrt{2} = 1.414213\ldots$. That is, $d(0) = 1$, $d(1) = 4$, and so forth. Let us show that the function d is primitive recursive.

One difficulty in this problem is resisting the temptation to start the solution with an equation like $x^2 = 2$, which has no integer solution. We begin with the observation that the last digit in the decimal representation of an integer N is $MOD(N, 10)$. Therefore, we will have accomplished our goal if we can show that the function f is primitive recursive, where $f(0) = 1$, $f(1) = 14$, $f(2) = 141$, and so on.

$f(i)$ is the integer part of (i.e., the greatest integer less than or equal to) the real number $10^i \sqrt{2}$. Another way to say this is that $f(i)$ is the largest integer whose square is less than or equal to $(10^i * \sqrt{2})^2 = 2 * 10^{2i}$. But this means that $f(i) + 1$ is the smallest integer whose square is *greater* than $2 * 10^{2i}$. Therefore, if we apply the minimalization operator to the primitive recursive predicate P defined by

$$P(x, y) = (y^2 > 2 * 10^{2*x})$$

$f(x)$ is obtained by subtracting 1 from the result. The only remaining problem is to show how a *bounded* minimalization can be used in this last step. We can do this by specifying a value of y for which y^2 is certain to be greater than $2 * 10^{2*x}$. Clearly, $y = 2 * 10^x$ is such a value, since $(2 * 10^x)^2 = 4 * 10^{2x} > 2 * 10^{2x}$. Therefore,

$$f(x) = m_P(x, 2 * 10^x) \dot{-} 1$$

Our last example will be very useful in the next chapter.

Example 21.14. Let $PrNo(n)$ be the nth prime number, so that $PrNo(0) = 2$, $PrNo(1) = 3$, $PrNo(2) = 5$, and so on. We show that the function $PrNo$ is primitive recursive.

First, we observe that the one-place predicate $PRIME$ defined by $PRIME(n) = (n$ is a prime) is primitive recursive, since

$$PRIME(n) = (n \geq 2) \wedge \neg(\text{ there exists } y \leq n \dot{-} 1 \text{ so that } y \geq 2 \wedge MOD(n, y) = 0)$$

$PrNo(k + 1)$ is the smallest prime greater than $PrNo(k)$. Therefore, if we can just place a bound on the set of integers greater than $PrNo(k)$ that may have to be tested in order to find a prime, we can use the bounded minimalization operator to obtain $PrNo$ by primitive recursion. But for any positive integer m, there is a prime greater than m and no larger than $m! + 1$. (If this were not the case, every prime factor p of $m! + 1$ would be $\leq m$. This is impossible; in fact, *no* prime factor of $m! + 1$ can be $\leq m$, since any prime $\leq m$ is a divisor of $m!$ and therefore not a divisor of $m! + 1$.) Let

$$P(x, y) = (y > x \wedge PRIME(y))$$

Then

$$PrNo(0) = 2$$

$$PrNo(k + 1) = m_P(PrNo(k), PrNo(k)! + 1)$$

From this we may conclude that $PrNo$ is obtained by primitive recursion from the two primitive recursive functions C_2^0 and h, where

$$h(x, y) = m_P(y, y! + 1)$$

Therefore, $PrNo$ is primitive recursive.

EXERCISES

21.1. Let $f : \mathcal{N} \to \mathcal{N}$ be the busy-beaver function discussed in Example 21.1. Show that f is eventually larger than any computable function—i.e., for any computable total function $g : \mathcal{N} \to \mathcal{N}$, there is an integer K so that $f(n) > g(n)$ for every $n \geq K$.

21.2. Let $f : \mathcal{N} \to \mathcal{N}$ be the function defined as follows: $f(n)$ is the maximum number of moves an n-state TM having tape alphabet $\{0, 1\}$ can make, assuming that it starts with input 1^n and always halts. Show that f is not computable.

21.3. Define $f : \mathcal{N} \to \mathcal{N}$ by: $f(n)$ is the maximum number of 1's that an n-state TM with no more than n tape symbols can leave on the tape, assuming that it starts with input 1^n and always halts. Show that f is not computable.

21.4. Show that the total function $f : \mathcal{N} \to \mathcal{N}$ is not computable if and only if the problem Given natural numbers n and C, is $f(n) > C$? is unsolvable.

21.5. Suppose that instead of including all constant functions in the set of initial functions, C_0^0 were the only constant function included. Describe what the set $\mathcal{PR}$ obtained by Definition 21.5 would be.

21.6. Suppose that in Definition 21.5, only the operation of composition were allowed (and not primitive recursion). What functions could be obtained?

21.7. What function is obtained from g and h by primitive recursion, where $g(x) = x$ and $h(x, y, z) = z + 2$?

21.8. Find two functions g and h so that the function f defined by $f(x) = x^2$ is obtained from g and h by primitive recursion.

21.9. Give complete primitive recursive derivations for each of the following functions.
   (a) $f : \mathcal{N}^2 \to \mathcal{N}$ defined by $f(x, y) = 2x + 3y$
   (b) $f : \mathcal{N} \to \mathcal{N}$ defined by $f(n) = n!$
   (c) $f : \mathcal{N} \to \mathcal{N}$ defined by $f(n) = 2^n$
   (d) $f : \mathcal{N} \to \mathcal{N}$ defined by $f(n) = n^2 \dot{-} 1$

21.10. Show that for any $n \geq 1$, the function $ADD_n : \mathcal{N}^n \to \mathcal{N}$ defined by

$$ADD_n(x_1, \ldots, x_n) = x_1 + \ldots + x_n$$

is primitive recursive.

21.11. Here is a primitive recursive derivation.

$$f_0 = C_1^0 \qquad \text{(an initial function)}$$

$$f_1 = C_0^2 \qquad \text{(an initial function)}$$

f_2 (obtained from f_0 and f_1 by primitive recursion)

$f_3 = p_2^2$ (an initial function)

f_4 (obtained from f_2 and f_3 by composition)

$f_5 = C_0^0$ (an initial function)

f_6 (obtained from f_5 and f_4 by primitive recursion)

$f_7 = p_1^1$ (an initial function)

$f_8 = p_3^3$ (an initial function)

$f_9 = s$ (an initial function)

f_{10} (obtained from f_9 and f_8 by composition)

f_{11} (obtained from f_7 and f_{10} by primitive recursion)

$f_{12} = p_1^2$ (an initial function)

f_{13} (obtained from f_6 and f_{12} by composition)

f_{14} (obtained from f_{11}, f_{13}, and f_3 by composition)

f_{15} (obtained from f_5 and f_{14} by primitive recursion)

Give simple formulas for f_2, f_6, f_{14}, and f_{15}.

21.12. Show that if $f : \mathcal{N} \to \mathcal{N}$ is primitive recursive, $A \subseteq \mathcal{N}$ is a finite set, and g is a total function agreeing with f at every point not in A, then g is primitive recursive.

21.13. Show that if $f : \mathcal{N} \to \mathcal{N}$ is a total function that is *eventually periodic* (i.e., for some integer N_0 and some $p > 0$, $f(x + p) = f(x)$ for every $x \geq N_0$), then f is primitive recursive.

21.14. Show that each of the following functions is primitive recursive.
(a) $f : \mathcal{N}^2 \to \mathcal{N}$ defined by $f(x, y) = max\{x, y\}$
(b) $f : \mathcal{N}^2 \to \mathcal{N}$ defined by $f(x, y) = min\{x, y\}$
(c) $f : \mathcal{N} \to \mathcal{N}$ defined by $f(x) = \lfloor \sqrt{x} \rfloor$ (the largest natural number less than or equal to $\sqrt{x}$)
(d) $f : \mathcal{N} \to \mathcal{N}$ defined by $f(x) = \lfloor \log_2(x + 1) \rfloor$

21.15. (a) Show that the function $f : \mathcal{N}^2 \to \mathcal{N}$ defined by: $f(x, y) =$ (the number of integer divisors of x less than or equal to y) is primitive recursive. Use this to show that the one-place predicate *PRIME* (see Example 21.14) is primitive recursive.
(b) Show that the function $f : \mathcal{N}^3 \to \mathcal{N}$ defined by: $f(x, y, z) =$ (the number of integers less than or equal to z that are divisors of both x and y) is primitive recursive. Use this to show that the two-place predicate P defined by $P(x, y) = (x$ and y are relatively prime) is primitive recursive.

21.16. Show that the function f defined by: $f(x) =$ (the leftmost digit in the decimal representation of 2^x) is primitive recursive.

21.17. Show that if $g : \mathcal{N}^{n+1} \to \mathcal{N}$ is primitive recursive, and $l, m : \mathcal{N} \to \mathcal{N}$ are both primitive recursive, then the functions f_1 and f_2 from $\mathcal{N}^{n+1}$ to $\mathcal{N}$ defined by

$$f_1(X, k) = \prod_{i = l(k)}^{m(k)} g(X, i)$$

$$f_2(X, k) = \sum_{i = l(k)}^{m(k)} g(X, i)$$

are primitive recursive.

21.18. Suppose P is a primitive recursive $(k + 1)$-place predicate, and f and g are primitive recursive functions of one variable. Show that the predicates $A_{f,g}P$ and $E_{f,g}P$ defined by

$$A_{f,g}P(X, k) = (\text{for every } i \text{ with } f(k) \le i \le g(k), P(X, i))$$

$$E_{f,g}P(X, k) = (\text{there exists } i \text{ with } f(k) \le i \le g(k) \text{ with } P(X, i))$$

are both primitive recursive.

21.19. Show that if $g : \mathcal{N}^2 \to \mathcal{N}$ is primitive recursive, then $f : \mathcal{N} \to \mathcal{N}$ defined by

$$f(x) = \sum_{i=0}^{x} g(x, i)$$

is primitive recursive.

21.20. In addition to the bounded minimalization of a predicate, we might define the bounded maximalization of a predicate P to be the function m^P defined by

$$m^P(X, k) = \begin{cases} \max\{y \le k | P(X, y) \text{ is true}\} & \text{if this set is not empty} \\ 0 & \text{otherwise} \end{cases}$$

(a) Show m^P is primitive recursive by finding two primitive recursive functions from which it can be obtained by primitive recursion.

(b) Show m^P is primitive recursive by using bounded minimalization.

CHAPTER
22

COMPUTABILITY: μ-RECURSIVE FUNCTIONS

22.1 A COMPUTABLE TOTAL FUNCTION THAT IS NOT PRIMITIVE RECURSIVE

The results in the last three sections of Chapter 21 should have convinced you that the set of primitive recursive functions is a large one and contains many of the standard functions that can be described by algebraic formulas. In fact, it is not an exaggeration to say that any total function from $\mathcal{N}$ to $\mathcal{N}$ that you will ever have occasion to compute in "real life" (that is, outside of courses on computation theory) is primitive recursive. Since primitive recursive functions are total, a non-primitive-recursive computable function can be obtained in a trivial way by leaving the function undefined somewhere. However, we begin this chapter by showing that there are computable total functions that are not primitive recursive. This result will set the stage for the introduction of another operation, in addition to composition and primitive recursion. The new operation preserves the property of computability but *not* that of primitive recursiveness. It will turn out that this third operation is what allows us to make precise our intuitive notion of "constructive definition" (see Section 21.2): the computable functions are essentially those that can be obtained from the initial functions by repeated applications of the three operations.

Theorem 22.1. There is a computable total function from $\mathcal{N}$ to $\mathcal{N}$ that is not primitive recursive.

Proof. Our proof will be an informal one. In showing that the function we construct is computable, we will not attempt to present a specific TM to compute it, but we will

394

describe in general terms an algorithm for computing it. The proof therefore depends on the Church–Turing thesis.

We begin by fixing a finite alphabet Σ containing all the symbols we might need to describe functions. Any primitive recursive function is specified by a primitive recursive derivation (see Section 21.2), which can in turn be specified by a finite string of symbols over Σ. A given function can have many different derivations, but that will not matter. The proof hinges on this statement: There is an algorithmic procedure for determining, given some string in Σ^*, whether it represents a primitive recursive derivation of a function of one variable. This is certainly plausible intuitively, even though spelling out the algorithm in detail would be very messy. If you are willing to accept the statement, however, the rest of the proof is straightforward—at least to the extent that any proof involving a diagonal argument can be called straightforward.

The strings in Σ^* may be ordered lexicographically. We now define the function $f : \mathcal{N} \to \mathcal{N}$ as follows. For each i, examine the strings in order, discarding those that do not represent primitive recursive derivations of functions of one variable, until the ith string is found that does represent such a derivation; let the function being derived be f_i, and let

$$f(i) = f_i(i) + 1$$

This clearly defines a total function. On the one hand, f is computable, since we have described an algorithm for finding the derivation of f_i and the derivation constitutes an algorithm for computing $f(i)$. On the other hand, f cannot be primitive recursive. Every primitive recursive function of one variable is f_i for some i, but f cannot be one of the f_i's, since for any i, $f(i) \neq f_i(i)$.

As you can imagine, the function constructed in the proof of Theorem 22.1 is not especially useful in itself. There are total, computable functions defined in more conventional ways that can be shown not to be primitive recursive. One of the most well known is a function introduced by Ackermann. It is interesting for several reasons, but one of its features is that although it is defined "recursively," in such a way that it is easily seen to be computable, it grows so rapidly that it cannot be primitive recursive. The details of the argument get to be involved, but a very readable discussion can be found in the book by Hennie.

22.2 UNBOUNDED MINIMALIZATION AND μ-RECURSIVE FUNCTIONS

Since not all computable functions are primitive recursive, we are interested in other ways of generating new functions, in addition to composition and primitive recursion. The last two types of "bounded operations" introduced in Section 21.5 can be generalized in an obvious way, by removing the boundedness requirement. As we have seen, however, the "unbounded existential quantification" operation does not preserve computability, and it is easy to check that the corresponding universal quantification doesn't either (see Exercise 22.1). Let's look more closely at the minimalization operation.

For a predicate P, we defined $\overset{k}{\mu}y[P(X, y)]$ to be the smallest y in the range $0 \leq y \leq k$ for which $P(X, y)$ is true. Since we wanted this to be a total function, we specified the default value $k + 1$ if there is no such y. In the unbounded case, if P is an $(n + 1)$-place predicate the minimalization will be a function of n variables, since there is no need for a parameter specifying the bound.

Definition 22.1. If P is an $(n + 1)$-place predicate, the *unbounded minimalization* of P is the partial function $M_P : \mathcal{N}^n \to \mathcal{N}$ defined by

$$M_P(X) = \min\{y \mid P(X, y) \text{ is true}\}$$

At any point X for which there is no y with $P(X, y)$ true, $M_P(X)$ is undefined.

The notation $\mu y[P(X, y)]$ is also used for $M_P(X)$. In the special case when $P(X, y) = (f(X, y) = 0)$, we write $M_P = M_f$ and refer to this function as the unbounded minimalization of f.

We choose not to specify a default value for M_P at a point X for which there is no y satisfying $P(X, y)$. The intuitive reason is that we want M_P to be computable wherever it is defined. If for some X, $P(X, y)$ is never true, and if the only way we have of determining this is by testing values of y in order, the testing process will never terminate. This is acceptable if $M_P(X)$ is undefined, but if $M_P(X)$ were given some default value, we would have to have some way of determining eventually that $M_P(X)$ took that value. Thus, an obvious difference between the unbounded minimalization operation and the others we have studied is that it may produce a partial function, even when applied to total functions.

The fact that we want M_P to be a computable function for any computable P has another consequence as well. Again, suppose that the only algorithm available for computing $M_P(X)$ is that of evaluating $P(X, y)$ for each y, and suppose that for a particular y_0, $P(X, y_0)$ is undefined. There might be a value $y_1 > y_0$ for which $P(X, y_1)$ is true, but if we get stuck in an infinite loop trying to evaluate $P(X, y_0)$, we will never get around to considering $P(X, y_1)$. We can avoid this problem by stipulating that unbounded minimalization be applied only to total predicates or total functions.

We are ready to define the class of functions that we shall show ultimately to be the same as the class of computable functions. Notice that in the following definition, the unbounded minimalization operator is applied only to predicates defined by some numerical function being zero.

Definition 22.2. The set $\mathcal{M}$ of μ-*recursive*, or simply *recursive*, partial functions is defined as follows.

1. All initial functions are elements of $\mathcal{M}$.
2. For any $k \geq 0$ and $m \geq 0$, if $f : \mathcal{N}^k \to \mathcal{N}$ and $g_1, \ldots, g_k : \mathcal{N}^m \to \mathcal{N}$ are elements of $\mathcal{M}$, the function $f(g_1, \ldots, g_k)$ obtained from f and $g_1, \ldots, g_k$ by composition is an element of $\mathcal{M}$.
3. For any $n \geq 0$, any function $g : \mathcal{N}^n \to \mathcal{N}$ that is in $\mathcal{M}$, and any function $h : \mathcal{N}^{n+2} \to \mathcal{N}$ that is in $\mathcal{M}$, the function $f : \mathcal{N}^{n+1} \to \mathcal{N}$ obtained from g and h by the operation of primitive recursion is an element of $\mathcal{M}$.
4. For any $n \geq 0$ and any total function $f : \mathcal{N}^{n+1} \to \mathcal{N}$ in $\mathcal{M}$, the function $M_f : \mathcal{N}^n \to \mathcal{N}$ defined by

$$M_f(X) = \mu y[f(X, y) = 0]$$

is an element of $\mathcal{M}$.

5. No function is in $\mathcal{M}$ unless it can be obtained by statements 1, 2, 3, or 4.

Just as in the case of primitive recursive functions, we may describe the μ-recursive functions as those obtainable by a finite sequence of steps, each step being the application of one of the specified operations to initial functions and/or functions obtained by previous steps in the sequence. Any such sequence yields only primitive recursive functions until such time as unbounded minimalization is used. At that point, the functions may cease to be primitive recursive or even total. Notice that if f is obtained by composition or primitive recursion, f may be total even though not all of the functions from which it is obtained are. Thus, it is conceivable that in the sequence of steps used to derive a μ-recursive function, unbounded minimalization could be used more than once, even if its first use produces a nontotal function. However, it will actually be shown later in this chapter that any μ-recursive function can be obtained by a sequence of steps containing only one use of unbounded minimalization.

Theorem 22.2. All μ-recursive functions are computable.

Proof. According to Theorems 21.1 and 21.2, it is sufficient to show that if $f : \mathcal{N}^{n+1} \rightarrow \mathcal{N}$ is a total computable function, its unbounded minimalization M_f is also computable. If T_f is a TM computing f, we have mentioned already the intuitive idea behind the construction of a TM T to compute M_f: for any input value X, T simply computes $f(X, 0), f(X, 1), \ldots$, until it discovers an i for which $f(X, i) = 0$, and halts with i as its output. If there is no such i, the computation will continue forever, but that is acceptable since $M_f(X)$ is undefined in that case. The details of constructing such a T are straightforward.

Much of the rest of this chapter is devoted to deriving the converse of Theorem 22.2.

22.3 GÖDEL NUMBERING

In the English language, we often formulate statements *about* the English language, and we don't consider it especially remarkable. (As the previous sentence indicates, we may also make statements about statements about the English language, etc.) We did something roughly comparable in the last section of Chapter 17, but in a formal language. We constructed strings of x's and y's that in a sense described languages of strings of x's and y's—in the sense that they specified Turing machines "describing" languages. Again, it seemed fairly innocuous; all we were doing was encoding certain strings of symbols by other strings of symbols. However, the technique proved very helpful, since it led to profound results about the limits of computation. The diagonal argument of Theorem 18.10, with its characteristic "circularity" (Turing machines accepting or not accepting their own encodings), was made possible by this trick.

The logician Kurt Gödel used a similar idea in the 1930s, around the time of the initial papers by Turing, Church, Post, *et al*, developing an encoding scheme to assign numbers to statements and formulas in an axiomatic system. As a result, he was able to describe logical relations between objects in the system by numerical formulas expressing relations between numbers. His ingenious use of these techniques led him to revolutionary and far-reaching results concerning the unprovability of statements in logical systems.

We will not be discussing Gödel's results directly, but the idea of "Gödel numbering" is a very general one, which will be useful to us in several ways. The first step is simply to encode sequences of several numbers as single numbers. One application will be to show that a more general type of "recursive definition" than we have considered so far gives rise to a primitive recursive function. A little later we extend our "arithmetization" to objects such as Turing machines. This will allow us to represent an arbitrary sequence of calculations involving numbers by a sequence of numbers, and it will be the principal ingredient in the proof that all computable functions are μ-recursive.

There are a number of Gödel-numbering schemes, but most of them depend on a familiar result about numbers: every positive integer can be factored into prime factors, and this factorization is unique except for differences in the order of the factors.

Definition 22.3. For any finite sequence $x_0, x_1, \ldots, x_n$ of natural numbers, the *Gödel number* of the sequence is the number

$$GN(x_0, \ldots, x_n) = 2^{x_0} 3^{x_1} 5^{x_2} \ldots (PrNo(n))^{x_n}$$

where $PrNo(n)$ is the nth prime—see Example 21.14.

For any sequence $x_0, \ldots, x_n$, $GN(x_0, \ldots, x_n) \geq 1$, and every integer ≥ 1 is the Gödel number of some sequence. It is not quite true that every integer is the Gödel number of only one sequence: for example,

$$GN(0, 1, 2) = GN(0, 1, 2, 0, 0) = 2^0 3^1 5^2$$

But in general, if

$$2^{x_0} 3^{x_1} \ldots (PrNo(m))^{x_m} = 2^{y_0} 3^{y_1} \ldots (PrNo(m))^{y_m} \ldots (PrNo(m + k))^{y_{m+k}}$$

then, since a number can have only one prime factorization,

$$x_0 = y_0, \quad x_1 = y_1, \quad \ldots, \quad x_m = y_m, \qquad \text{and} \qquad y_{m+1} = \ldots = y_{m+k} = 0$$

Therefore, two sequences having the same Gödel number are identical except that they may end with a different number of 0's. In particular, given $n \geq 1$, any positive integer is the Gödel number of at most one sequence of n integers.

For any fixed n, we may consider the function f from $\mathcal{N}^{n+1} \to \mathcal{N}$ defined by

$$f(x_0, \ldots, x_n) = GN(x_0, \ldots, x_n)$$

We shall be imprecise and use the name *GN* for any of these functions; it will generally be clear from the context which one is intended. All of them are primitive recursive.

Definition 22.3 says how to encode a sequence of integers. If we are given a positive integer g and we wish to *decode* g to find a sequence $x_0, \ldots, x_n$ for which $GN(x_0, \ldots, x_n) = g$, we may calculate the x_i's by factoring g into primes. For each i, x_i is the number of times $PrNo(i)$ appears as a factor. For example, the number 59895 has the factorization

$$59895 = 3^2 5^1 11^3 = 2^0 3^2 5^1 7^0 11^3$$

and is therefore the Gödel number of the sequence 0,2,1,0,3 (or, as we noticed above, of the sequence 0,2,1,0,3,0, . . . ,0). The prime number 31 is the Gödel number of the sequence 0,0,0,0,0,0,0,0,0,0,1, since $31 = PrNo(10)$. This type of calculation will be used frequently enough that we introduce a function specifically for this purpose.

Example 22.1. The function *Exponent*: $\mathcal{N}^2 \to \mathcal{N}$ is defined as follows:

$$Exponent(i, x) = \begin{cases} 0 & \text{if } x = 0 \\ \text{the number of times } PrNo(i) \text{ appears as a factor of } x & \text{if } x > 0 \end{cases}$$

For example, *Exponent*(4, 59895) = 3, as we saw above: The fourth prime, 11, appears three times as a factor of 59895. (Remember, 2 is the *zero*th prime.)

Exponent is primitive recursive. For $x > 0$, *Exponent*$(i, x) + 1$ is the smallest y for which $(PrNo(i))^y$ does not divide x evenly; this can be expressed as a bounded minimalization, since clearly $(PrNo(i))^x$ does not divide x evenly, and thus for $x > 0$,

$$Exponent(i, x) = \overset{x}{\mu}y[MOD(x, (PrNo(i))^y) > 0] \overset{\cdot}{-} 1$$

Let's demonstrate one way in which Gödel numbers are useful: allowing us to show that certain functions defined "recursively" are in fact primitive recursive.

Example 22.2. The Fibonacci numbers (see Exercise 2.13) are defined as follows.

$$FIB(0) = 0$$

$$FIB(1) = 1$$

$$FIB(n + 1) = FIB(n) + FIB(n - 1) \text{ for } n \geq 1$$

We shall show $FIB : \mathcal{N} \to \mathcal{N}$ is primitive recursive. The reason we would have trouble using the definition directly is that $FIB(n + 1)$ is defined not only in terms of n and $FIB(n)$, but also in terms of $FIB(n - 1)$. Intuitively, what we would like is a function f for which

1. Knowing $f(n)$ would allow us to calculate $FIB(n)$;
2. $f(n + 1)$ depends only on n and $f(n)$.

If we relaxed temporarily the requirement that $f(n)$ be a number, we might consider the *pair* $f(n) = (FIB(n - 1), FIB(n))$, where $f(0)$ is defined arbitrarily to be the pair $(0, FIB(0))$. This choice of f seems to satisfy statements 1 and 2: we can obviously get $FIB(n)$ from the pair $(FIB(n - 1), FIB(n))$, and the pair $(FIB(n), FIB(n + 1))$ depends only upon the previous pair $(FIB(n-1), FIB(n))$, since $FIB(n+1) = FIB(n-1) + FIB(n)$. How to avoid functions whose values are pairs? Just use the Gödel numbers of the pairs instead. Thus let

$$f(n) = \begin{cases} GN(0, FIB(0)) = 2^0 3^{FIB(0)} & \text{if } n = 0 \\ GN(FIB(n-1), FIB(n)) = 2^{FIB(n-1)} 3^{FIB(n)} & \text{if } n > 0 \end{cases}$$

If we can show f is primitive recursive, it will follow from the formula

$$FIB(n) = Exponent(1, f(n))$$

that FIB is as well. We have

$$f(0) = 1$$
$$f(k+1) = GN(FIB(k), FIB(k+1))$$
$$= GN(FIB(k), FIB(k-1) + FIB(k))$$
$$= GN(Exponent(1, f(k)), Exponent(0, f(k)) + Exponent(1, f(k)))$$

Since the function $h : \mathcal{N}^2 \to \mathcal{N}$ defined by

$$h(x, y) = GN(Exponent(1, y), Exponent(0, y) + Exponent(1, y))$$

is primitive recursive, and f is obtained from C_1^0 and h by primitive recursion, then f is primitive recursive.

In the definition of FIB the value of the function for $k+1$ is defined in terms of the previous two values. It should be clear that if 2 is replaced by r, for any fixed r, the same argument can be used to show that a function defined this way is primitive recursive. But we may carry this idea even further. It is possible to define a function $f : \mathcal{N}^{n+1} \to \mathcal{N}$ recursively so that $f(X, k+1)$ depends on *all* the values $f(X, 0), f(X, 1), \ldots, f(X, k)$. This type of recursion is known as *course-of-values* recursion. It bears the same relation to ordinary primitive recursion that the strong principle of mathematical induction does to the ordinary principle (see Section 2.2). This time, in order even to formulate the concept precisely, Gödel numbering is useful. Instead of saying that $f(X, k+1)$ depends directly on $f(X, 0)$, $\ldots, f(X, k)$ (which might seem to require some function with differing numbers of variables!) we accomplish the same thing indirectly by saying that $f(X, k+1)$ depends on the single value $GN(f(X, 0), \ldots, f(X, k))$. These two versions are intuitively equivalent, since from the number $GN(f(X, 0), \ldots, f(X, k))$ each of the values $f(X, i)$ can be derived.

Theorem 22.3. Suppose $g : \mathcal{N}^n \to \mathcal{N}$ and $h : \mathcal{N}^{n+2} \to \mathcal{N}$ are primitive recursive functions, and $f : \mathcal{N}^{n+1} \to \mathcal{N}$ is obtained from g and h by course-of-values recursion; i.e.,

$$f(X, 0) = g(X)$$
$$f(X, k+1) = h(X, k, GN(f(X, 0), \ldots, f(X, k)))$$

Then f is primitive recursive.

Proof. First, we define $f_1 : \mathcal{N}^{n+1} \to \mathcal{N}$ by the formula

$$f_1(X, k) = GN(f(X, 0), \ldots, f(X, k))$$

f can be obtained from f_1 by the formula

$$f(X, k) = Exponent(k, f_1(X, k))$$

Thus, it is sufficient to show that f_1 is primitive recursive. The details are very much the same as in Example 22.1 and are left to the Exercises.

There are still more general ways of defining functions recursively that give rise to primitive recursive functions, but we shall not discuss them here. In the Exercises, you are asked to consider one or two applications of Theorem 22.3.

We are ready to apply our Gödel numbering techniques to Turing machines. A function f computed by a TM is computed by a sequence of steps—the individual moves executed by the TM. If we can represent these steps as operations on numbers, we will have a way of building the function f from more rudimentary functions, and we will eventually be able to show that f is μ-recursive. A move of a TM takes it from one configuration to another; in order to describe the move numerically, all we need is a way of representing a TM configuration by a number.

We begin by assigning a number to each state. The halt state h will be assigned the number 0, and if Q is the state set we let the elements of Q be q_1, $q_2, \ldots, q_s$, where q_1 is always assumed to be the initial state.

Next, the tape head position can be described by specifying the number of the tape square it is scanning. Finally, we assign to the blank symbol Δ the number 0 (we will often write 0 instead of Δ), and we assume that the nonblank tape symbols are $1, 2, \ldots, t$. This allows us to define the *tape number* of the TM at any point to be the Gödel number of the sequence $a_0, \ldots, a_m$ of symbols currently on the tape. Notice that since we are identifying Δ with 0, the tape number will be the same no matter how many trailing blanks we include in this sequence. The tape number of a blank tape is 1.

Since the configuration of the TM is determined by the state, the tape head position, and the current contents of the tape, we define the *configuration number* to be the number

$$GN(q, P, tn)$$

where q is the number of the current state, P is the current head position, and tn is the current tape number. Of course, from the configuration number we can reconstruct all the details of the configuration; we shall be more explicit about this in the next section.

22.4 ALL COMPUTABLE FUNCTIONS ARE μ-RECURSIVE

Theorem 22.4. Every computable function $f : \mathcal{N}^n \to \mathcal{N}$ is μ-recursive.

Before beginning the official proof, which will be divided into a number of separate pieces, we give a sketch of the argument. Suppose T is a TM computing the function $f : \mathcal{N}^n \to \mathcal{N}$. Gödel numbering allows us to view the processing performed by T as a sequence of transformations performed on the configuration numbers of T. For any $X \in \mathcal{N}^n$ where f is defined, the ultimate effect is that the number representing the initial configuration of T with input X is transformed to the number representing the final (halting) configuration of T, in which the tape contents represent the value $f(X)$. Let's give a name to this transformation. Let $f_T : \mathcal{N} \to \mathcal{N}$ be the function that takes the initial configuration number to the final configuration number. (We ignore for the moment the problem of how to define $f_T(m)$ if m is not the Gödel number of an initial configuration representing an input value for which f is defined.) In order to relate the function f_T to the function f, we need two other functions, $InitConfig^{(n)} : \mathcal{N}^n \to \mathcal{N}$ and $Result_T : \mathcal{N} \to \mathcal{N}$, which are defined as follows.

For $X \in \mathcal{N}^n$, $InitConfig^{(n)}(X)$ is the number of the initial configuration of a Turing machine with input X. Notice that it doesn't matter what TM we use, since we have agreed that the initial state of any TM will be labeled q_1.

For an integer m that is a configuration number for T, $Result_T(m)$ is the number of the tape square containing the last nonblank symbol in that configuration, or 0 if the tape is blank. For any other integer m, $Result_T(m)$ is 0. The configurations we are interested in, of course, are those that result from T's computing $f(X)$—in other words, those in which the tape contents are $\Delta 1^{f(X)}$. If m is the configuration number of such a configuration, $Result_T(m)$ is simply $f(X)$.

What we can now say is that

$$f(X) = Result_T(f_T(InitConfig^{(n)}(X)))$$

This formula says simply that starting with an n-tuple X, $f(X)$ can be obtained in three stages. First, use $InitConfig^{(n)}$ to find the number of the initial configuration corresponding to that input. Second, use f_T to carry out the transformation of the configuration number corresponding to the moves carried out by T. Finally, use $Result_T$ to obtain $f(X)$ from the number of the final halting configuration. The proof of Theorem 22.4 begins by showing that the two functions $Result_T$ and $InitConfig^{(n)}$ are primitive recursive. The function f_T is more involved, but the remainder of the proof will consist of defining it precisely and showing that it is μ-recursive.

$Result_T$ is one example, and there will be a number of others, of a function whose value at a point m is defined one way if m is a configuration number for T and differently otherwise. The first step, therefore, is to examine the one-place predicate $IsConfig_T$ defined by

$$IsConfig_T(n) = (n \text{ is a configuration number for } T)$$

Lemma 22.1. $IsConfig_T$ is a primitive recursive predicate.

Proof. Let s_T be the number of nonhalting states of T and ts_T the number of nonblank tape symbols. m is a configuration number for T if and only if

$$m = 2^q 3^p 5^{tn}$$

where $q \leq s_T$, p is arbitrary, and tn is the Gödel number of a sequence of natural numbers, each one between 0 and ts_T. The conditions on q and tn can be stated as follows.

1. $q \leq s_T$
2. $tn \geq 1$
3. For every i, $Exponent(i, tn) \leq ts_T$

The extra condition on m, that it be of the form $2^q 3^p 5^{tn}$, is the same as saying

4. For every $i > 2$, $Exponent(i, m) = 0$

which in turn is equivalent to

4'. For every i, $i \leq 2$ or $Exponent(i, m) = 0$

In condition 3, "for every i" is really the same as "for every $i \leq tn$," since it is clear that $Exponent(i, tn) = 0$ for every $i > tn$. It follows that if we let P_1 be the predicate defined by

$$P_1(x, i) = (Exponent(i, x) \leq ts_T)$$

statement 3 can be restated as

3'. For every $i \leq tn$, $P_1(tn, i)$

or more concisely,

3''. $A_{P_1}(tn, tn)$

Using the same reasoning, we can replace "for every i" in statement 4' by "for every $i \leq m$." Therefore, if we let

$$P_2(x, i) = (i \leq 2 \ \bigvee \ Exponent(i, m) = 0)$$

then statement 4' is the same as

4''. $A_{P_2}(m, m)$

We know that $q = Exponent(0, m)$ and $tn = Exponent(2, m)$. Collecting the statements 1, 2, 3'', and 4'', and making these two substitutions, we obtain the formula

$$IsConfig_T(m) = (Exponent(0, m) \leq s_T)$$
$$\bigwedge \ (Exponent(2, m) \geq 1)$$
$$\bigwedge \ A_{P_1}(Exponent(2, m), Exponent(2, m))$$
$$\bigwedge \ A_{P_2}(m, m)$$

from which it follows that $IsConfig_T$ is primitive recursive.

Lemma 22.2. $InitConfig^{(n)} : \mathcal{N}^n \rightarrow \mathcal{N}$ is primitive recursive.

Proof. $InitConfig^{(n)}(x_1, \ldots, x_n)$ may be written as

$$GN(1, 0, t^{(n)}(x_1, \ldots, x_n))$$

where $t^{(n)}(x_1, \ldots, x_n)$ is the tape number of the tape containing $\Delta 1^{x_1} \Delta \ldots \Delta 1^{x_n}$. It is therefore sufficient to show that the function $t^{(n)}$ is primitive recursive. The proof is by mathematical induction on n. The basis step, $n = 0$, is clear, since $t^{(n)}$ is constant in that case. Suppose that for some $k \geq 0$, $t^{(k)}$ is primitive recursive.

$t^{(k+1)}(x_1, \ldots, x_k, x_{k+1}) = t^{(k+1)}(X, x_{k+1})$ is the tape number for the tape containing

$$\Delta 1^{x_1} \Delta \ldots \Delta 1^{x_k} \Delta 1^{x_{k+1}}$$

Counting the symbols in the string $\Delta 1^{x_1} \Delta \ldots \Delta 1^{x_k}$, we find that the string $1^{x_{k+1}}$ begins in tape square

$$k + \sum_{i=1}^{k} x_i + 1$$

and extends through tape square

$$k + \sum_{i=1}^{k} x_i + x_{k+1}$$

This means that the additional factors in the tape number resulting from the 1's in this last block are

$$PrNo(k + \sum_{i=1}^{k} x_i + 1)$$

$$PrNo(k + \sum_{i=1}^{k} x_i + 2)$$

$$\ldots$$

$$PrNo(k + \sum_{i=1}^{k} x_i + x_{k+1})$$

In other words, we may write

$$tn^{(k+1)}(X, x_{k+1}) = tn^{(k)}(X) * \prod_{i=1}^{x_{k+1}} PrNo(k + \sum_{i=1}^{k} x_i + i)$$

The first factor, viewed as a function of X, is primitive recursive according to the induction hypothesis, and so by Theorem 21.5 it is still primitive recursive when viewed as a function of $k + 1$ variables. The second is of the form

$$\prod_{i=1}^{x_{k+1}} g(X, i)$$

for a primitive recursive function g, and is therefore primitive recursive because of Theorem 21.8. The result follows, since the set of primitive recursive functions is closed under multiplication.

Lemma 22.3. *Result$_T$: $\mathcal{N} \to \mathcal{N}$ is primitive recursive.*

Proof. For any n that is the number of a configuration, *Result$_T(n)$* is the number of the tape square containing the last nonblank symbol in this configuration. Since the tape number for the configuration is $Exponent(2, n)$, and since the prime factors of the tape number correspond to the squares with nonblank symbols, we may write

$$Result_T(n) = \begin{cases} HighestPrime(Exponent(2, n)) & \text{if } IsConfig(n) \\ 0 & \text{otherwise} \end{cases}$$

where for any k, $HighestPrime(k)$ is the number of the largest prime factor of k. (For example, $HighestPrime(2^3 5^5 19^2) = 7$, since $19 = PrNo(7)$. $HighestPrime(0) = 0$.) The function $HighestPrime$ is primitive recursive, since

$$HighestPrime(k) = Max\{y \le k | Exponent(y, k) > 0\}$$

(see Exercise 21.20), so it follows that $Result_T$ is also.

We are almost ready to examine the processing done by T itself, and the resulting function f_T taking an initial configuration number to the corresponding final configuration number. We make the simplifying assumption that T never crashes by attempting to move its head left from square 0. This involves no loss of generality, since any T is equivalent to one with this property. It will be helpful next to introduce explicitly the functions that produce the current state, tape head position, tape number, and tape symbol from the configuration number. The respective formulas are

$$State(m) = Exponent(0, m)$$
$$Posn(m) = Exponent(1, m)$$
$$TapeNum(m) = Exponent(2, m)$$
$$Symbol(m) = Exponent(PrNo(Posn(m)), TapeNum(m))$$

for any m that is a configuration number for T, and 0 otherwise. It is clear, since $IsConfig_T$ is a primitive recursive predicate, that all four functions are primitive recursive.

The main ingredient in the description of f_T will be another function

$$Move_T : \mathcal{N} \to \mathcal{N}$$

Roughly speaking, $Move_T$ calculates the effect on the configuration number of a single move of T. More precisely, if m is the number for a configuration of T in which T can move, $Move_T(m)$ is the configuration number of T after the move, and if m is the number of a halting configuration or any other configuration in which T cannot move, $Move_T(m) = m$. If m is not a configuration number, $Move_T(m) = 0$.

Lemma 22.4. $Move_T : \mathcal{N} \to \mathcal{N}$ is primitive recursive.

Proof. We may write

$$Move_T(m) = \begin{cases} GN(NewState(m), NewPosn(m), NewTapeNum(m)) \\ \quad \text{if } m \text{ is a configuration number} \\ 0 \text{ otherwise} \end{cases}$$

The three functions *NewState*, *NewPosn*, and *NewTapeNum* all have the value 0 at any point m that is not a configuration number. For a configuration number m, *NewState*(m) is the resulting state if T can move from configuration m, and *State*(m) otherwise; the other two functions are defined similarly. Thus, in order to show that *Move*$_T$ is primitive recursive, it is sufficient to show that these three "New" functions are. In the argument it will help to have one more function, *NewSymbol*, defined analogously.

So far, our description of *NewState*(m) has involved three cases. One case corresponds to the primitive recursive predicate $\neg$*IsConfig*$_T$. The other two cases may be divided into subcases, corresponding to the various possible combinations of *State*(m) and *Symbol*(m). Since these two functions are primitive recursive, so are the predicates defining the subcases. In each subcase, the value of *NewState*(m) is either m or the value specified by the transition table for T. Therefore, since *NewState* is defined by cases, and the predicates and functions involved in the definition are all primitive recursive, it must be also. The argument to show that *NewSymbol* is primitive recursive is exactly the same.

The proof for *NewPosn* is almost the same. This function may also be defined by cases—the same cases involved in the definition of *NewState*. In each case, *NewPosn*(m) is either 0, if m is not a configuration number; *Posn*(m), if T cannot move from configuration m, or if the move does not change the head position; *Posn*$(m) + 1$, if the move shifts the head to the right; or *Posn*$(m) - 1$, if the move shifts the head to the left. Therefore, *NewPosn* is primitive recursive.

The definition of *NewTapeNum* can also be made using the same cases, but the formula in a given subcase is slightly more involved. Suppose that *Posn*$(m) = i$, *Symbol*$(m) = j$, and *NewSymbol*$(m) = j'$. The difference between *TapeNum*(m) and *NewTapeNum*(m) is that the first number involves the factor $PrNo(i)^j$ and the second has $PrNo(i)^{j'}$ instead; the exponents differ by $j - j' = $ *NewSymbol*$(m) - $ *Symbol*(m). Thus, in this subcase *NewTapeNum*(m) can be expressed as

$$TapeNum(m) * PrNo(Posn(m))^{NewSymbol}(m) \dot{-} Symbol(m)$$

if *NewSymbol*$(m) \geq$ *Symbol*(m), and

$$DIV(TapeNum(m), PrNo(Posn(m))^{Symbol(m) \dot{-} NewSymbol(m)}$$

otherwise. Since both formulas define primitive recursive functions, the function *NewTapeNum* is primitive recursive.

Now that we are able to describe the effect of one move of T on the configuration number, we generalize to a sequence of k moves. Consider the function *Trace*$_T : \mathcal{N}^2 \to \mathcal{N}$ defined as follows:

$$Trace_T(m, 0) = \begin{cases} m & \text{if } IsConfig_T(m) \\ 0 & \text{otherwise} \end{cases}$$

$$Trace_T(m, k + 1) = \begin{cases} Move_T(Trace(m, k)) & \text{if } IsConfig_T(m) \\ 0 & \text{otherwise} \end{cases}$$

It is clear from Lemma 22.4 that *Trace*$_T$ can be obtained by primitive recursion from two primitive recursive functions and is therefore primitive recursive itself. Assuming m is a configuration number, we may describe *Trace*$_T(m, k)$ as the number of the configuration after k moves, if T starts in configuration m—or, if T is unable to make as many as k moves from configuration m, as the number of the last configuration T reaches starting from configuration m.

We need just one more auxiliary function before we can complete the proof of Theorem 22.4. Let $Halting_T : \mathcal{N} \to \mathcal{N}$ be defined by

$$Halting_T(m) = \begin{cases} 0 & \text{if } IsConfig_T(m) \wedge Exponent(0, m) = 0 \\ 1 & \text{otherwise} \end{cases}$$

$Halting_T(m)$ is 0 if and only if m is the number of a halting configuration for T, and $Halting_T$ is clearly primitive recursive.

Proof of Theorem 22.4. Let T be a TM computing f as discussed above. For any m and k, $Halting_T(Trace_T(m, k))$ is 0 if and only if m is a configuration number for T and, beginning in configuration m, T halts within k moves. Let $MovesToHalt : \mathcal{N} \to \mathcal{N}$ be defined by

$$MovesToHalt(m) = \mu k[Halting_T(Trace_T(m, k)) = 0]$$

and define $f_T : \mathcal{N} \to \mathcal{N}$ by

$$f_T(m) = Trace_T(m, MovesToHalt(m))$$

We may describe the functions $MovesToHalt$ and f_T as follows. If m is a configuration number for T and T eventually halts when starting from configuration m, $MovesToHalt(m)$ is the number of moves from that point before T halts, and $f_T(m)$ is the number of the halting configuration that is eventually reached. For any other m, both functions are undefined. Since $MovesToHalt$ is obtained from a primitive recursive (total) function by unbounded minimalization, $MovesToHalt$ is μ-recursive, and since f_T is obtained by composition from μ-recursive functions, f_T is also μ-recursive.

We claim that

$$f = Result_T(f_T(InitConfig^{(n)}))$$

—i.e., that for any X, $f(X)$ is defined if and only if $Result_T(f_T(InitConfig^{(n)}(X)))$ is, and that if these numbers are defined, they are equal. To see this, suppose $f(X)$ is defined. In this case, if T begins in the configuration $InitConfig^{(n)}(X)$, it eventually halts. Therefore, $f_T(InitConfig^{(n)}(X))$ is the configuration number of the halting configuration $(h, \Delta 1^{f(X)})$, and when $Result_T$ is applied to this configuration number it produces $f(X)$. On the other hand, if $f(X)$ is undefined, T fails to halt with input X, and this means that $f_T(InitConfig^{(n)}(X))$ is undefined. The proof is complete.

22.5   NONNUMERIC FUNCTIONS

Using Gödel numbering again, we may extend the ideas of primitive recursiveness and μ-recursiveness to functions involving strings. For simplicity, we restrict ourselves in this section to functions of one variable, although everything we do can be generalized in a natural way to functions of several variables (see Exercise 22.11). The idea is that if f takes the string x to a string $f(x)$, we may consider the related numerical function ρ_f that takes the Gödel number of x to the Gödel number of $f(x)$. Once we have defined things precisely, it will be possible to extend Theorem 22.4 to this more general case as well.

Suppose Σ_1 and Σ_2 are finite alphabets and

$$f : \Sigma_1^* \to \Sigma_2^*$$

is a (partial) function. We would like to define $\rho_f : \mathcal{N} \to \mathcal{N}$ as follows: if $n \in \mathcal{N}$ is the Gödel number of a string $x \in \Sigma_1^*$, $\rho_f(n)$ is the Gödel number of the string $f(x)$. Notice that in order for this to make sense, two different strings in Σ_1^* cannot have the same Gödel number, so we must make sure that our numbering scheme has this property.

Definition 22.4. Let Σ be a finite alphabet. We assign Gödel numbers to the elements of Σ^* as follows. Let the elements of Σ be denoted

$$a_1, a_2, \ldots, a_s$$

For any string $x = a_{i_0} a_{i_1} \ldots a_{i_m} \in \Sigma^*$, we define

$$gn(x) = GN(i_0, i_1, \ldots, i_m) = 2^{i_0} \ldots (PrNo(m))^{i_m}$$

$gn(\Lambda)$ is defined to be 1.

The Gödel number of a string depends on the way we order the elements of Σ, which is arbitrary. The function $gn : \Sigma^* \to \mathcal{N}$ is indeed one-to-one. If $gn(x) = gn(y)$, then $|x| = |y|$, since otherwise one Gödel number would have a prime factor the other didn't (none of the exponents in the formula for $gn(x)$ or $gn(y)$ can be 0); thus, $x = y$, since each prime must appear to the same power in both numbers. One more thing to notice about Gödel numbers of strings is that not every positive integer is one. One reason is that a number like $3 = 2^0 3^1$ or $10 = 2^1 3^0 5^1$ cannot be a Gödel number, and another is that no Gödel number can have a prime appearing to a power higher than the number of symbols in Σ.

Since $gn : \Sigma^* \to \mathcal{N}$ is not a bijection, it is not correct to speak of gn^{-1}. But since gn is one-to-one, we may define $gn' : \mathcal{N} \to \Sigma^*$ as follows:

$$gn'(n) = \begin{cases} x & \text{if } n = gn(x) \\ \Lambda & \text{if } n \text{ is not } gn(x) \text{ for any } x \end{cases}$$

The value Λ is arbitrary here; any "default" value would work. We may conclude that gn' is a "left inverse" of gn: for any $x \in \Sigma^*$,

$$gn'(gn(x)) = x$$

We now have the ingredients we need. If $f : \Sigma_1^* \to \Sigma_2^*$, we may let $g_1 : \Sigma_1^* \to \mathcal{N}$ and $g_2 : \Sigma_2^* \to \mathcal{N}$ be the Gödel numbering functions, and g_1' and g_2' their respective left inverses as described above. We may define $\rho_f : \mathcal{N} \to \mathcal{N}$ by the formula

$$\rho_f(n) = g_2(f(g_1'(n)))$$

To understand this formula better, "trace" it in Fig. 22-1. The formula says that beginning at the lower left of the diagram, ρ_f is obtained by following the arrows up, over, and down.

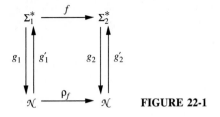

FIGURE 22-1

If x is any string in Σ_1^*, we have

$$\rho_f(g_1(x)) = g_2(f(g_1'(g_1(x))))$$
$$= g_2(f(x))$$

This formula says that in Fig. 22-1, both ways of getting from the upper left to the lower right produce the same result. The point is that the numerical function ρ_f "mirrors" the action of the string function f: whenever f takes a string x to a string y, ρ_f takes the Gödel number of x to the Gödel number of y.

With these tools, it is possible to say what it means for a function from strings to strings to be primitive recursive or μ-recursive.

Definition 22.5. Let $f : \Sigma_1^* \to \Sigma_2^*$, and let $\rho_f : \mathcal{N} \to \mathcal{N}$ be defined as above. The function f is said to be primitive recursive if and only if ρ_f is. Similarly, f is μ-recursive if and only if ρ_f is.

You can easily verify that only total functions $f : \Sigma_1^* \to \Sigma_2^*$ can be primitive recursive. Just as in the case of numerical functions, there are total μ-recursive functions that are not primitive recursive. The fundamental result of this section is just what you would expect from Theorems 22.2 and 22.4.

Theorem 22.6. Let $f : \Sigma_1^* \to \Sigma_2^*$. Then f is computable if and only if f is μ-recursive.

Proof. Suppose on the one hand that f is computable, and let T_f be a TM computing f. (Recall the remarks in Section 16.4: if $\Sigma_1 \not\subseteq \Sigma_2$, then when we speak of a TM computing f, we are really referring to a function with codomain $(\Sigma_1 \cup \Sigma_2)^*$.) We wish to show that the function $\rho_f : \mathcal{N} \to \mathcal{N}$ is μ-recursive, and according to Theorem 22.4, it is sufficient to show that ρ_f is computable. We omit the details, but it is easy to see from the definition of ρ_f that a TM T can be constructed by combining three TM's: one that takes the initial tape $\Delta 1^n$ and halts with tape $\Delta g_1'(n)$; the TM T_f, which halts with tape $\Delta f(g_1'(n))$; and a third that calculates the Gödel number of this string to yield the result, $g_2(f(g_1'(n))) = \rho_f(n)$.

On the other hand, suppose f is μ-recursive. By definition, ρ_f is μ-recursive. According to Theorem 22.2, ρ_f is computable; let T be a TM computing ρ_f. From the formula for ρ_f it follows that

$$g_2'(\rho_f(n)) = g_2'(g_2(f(g_1'(n))))$$
$$= f(g_1'(n))$$

Let x be any string in Σ_1^*. Applying this formula when $n = g_1(x)$, we obtain

$$f(x) = f(g_1'(g_1(x))) = g_2'(\rho_f(g_1(x)))$$

(You should refer to Fig. 22-1 for the correct interpretation of this formula.) Just as before, we may use T and two other TM's to construct a TM T_f to compute f. Therefore, f is computable.

We have now established the equivalence of two seemingly different approaches to the idea of computability. The theory of recursive functions is a large and well-developed subject with many aspects, and our discussion barely scratches the surface. For a comprehensive survey, consult the book by Rogers. Before we leave the subject of computability, however, it is appropriate to mention at least briefly a few other approaches.

Just as unrestricted grammars provide a way of generating languages, these grammars can be used to formulate a definition of computable functions. If $G = (V, \Sigma, S, P)$ is a grammar, and f is a partial function from Σ^* to Σ^*, G is said to compute f if there are variables A, B, C, and D in V so that for any x and y in Σ^*,

$$f(x) = y \text{ if and only if } AxB \Rightarrow_G^* CyD$$

It can be shown, by arguments not unlike those in Theorems 19.1 and 19.2, that the functions computable by grammars are precisely those that can be computed by Turing machines.

You have written programs in various high-level programming languages that, although you may not have thought of them in this way, compute certain functions from strings to strings. It is natural to consider the set of functions that can be computed by such programs—say those in Pascal. If we specify an "ideal" implementation of Pascal on an "ideal" computer, so that there is an unlimited amount of memory, no limit to the size of integers, and so on, then "Pascal-computable" and "Turing-computable" are the same.

Although high-level languages such as Pascal have many features that make it much easier to write programs to compute functions, these features make absolutely no difference as far as which functions can be computed. For simplicity, let's restrict ourselves to the numerical functions we have discussed in the last two chapters. We might consider a drastically pared-down programming language, which has variables whose values are natural numbers; statements of the form

$$X \leftarrow X + 1$$

and

$$X \leftarrow X \dot{-} 1$$

which cause variables to be incremented and decremented; "conditional go-to" statements of the form

$$\text{IF } X \neq 0 \text{ GO TO } L$$

where L is an integer label in the program; statements of the form

$$\text{READ}(X)$$

and

$$\text{WRITE}(X)$$

and nothing else. Even with a language like this, it turns out, it is possible to compute all computable functions. One approach to proving this would be to write a program in this language to simulate an arbitrary given Turing machine. This would involve some sort of "arithmetization" of the TM similar to Gödel numbering: one integer variable would represent the state, another the head position, a third the tape contents, and so on. Another approach would be via Theorem 22.4 — to show the class of functions that can be computed using this language contains the initial functions and is closed under the operations of composition, primitive recursion, and unbounded minimalization, and thus contains all μ-recursive functions.

Finally, this language, or even a less restricted programming language, can compute only the Turing-computable functions. Again, there are at least two ways to prove this. It might be shown directly, by simulating on a TM each feature of the language, and in this way building a TM to "execute" a program in the language, but it can also be shown with the help of Theorem 22.2. Just as a TM configuration can be described by specifying a state, a tape head position, and a string, a program "configuration" can be described by specifying a statement (the next statement to be executed) and the current values of all variables. These parameters can be assigned Gödel numbers, "configuration numbers" can be defined, and each step in the execution of the program can be viewed as a transformation of the Gödel number, very much as in the proof of Theorem 22.4. As a result, any function computed by a program in the language can be shown to be μ-recursive. You are referred to the text by Davis and Weyuker for a much more complete discussion.

There are many other formalisms that have been introduced to describe computable functions, and many other abstract machines that can be shown to be equivalent to Turing machines. Up to this point, every attempt to formulate precisely the idea of "effective computability" has produced the same set of functions: those that can be computed by Turing machines. As a result, we may feel justified at this point in accepting with even more confidence the Church–Turing thesis, that "effectively computable" does indeed mean "Turing-computable."

EXERCISES

22.1. Give an example to illustrate the fact that the unbounded universal quantification of a computable predicate need not be computable.

22.2. Show that the unbounded minimalization of any predicate can be written in the form $\mu y[f(X, y) = 0]$, for some function f.

22.3. Is the problem Given a Turing machine T computing some partial function f, is f a total function? solvable? Explain.

22.4. Suppose we copied the proof of Theorem 22.1 but using recursive derivations instead, as follows. Consider the strings in Σ^* in lexicographic order; for each i, find the ith string representing a "μ-recursive derivation" of a function of one variable, and let the function be called f_i; define f by the formula $f(i) = f_i(i) + 1$. Then (apparently) we have exhibited an algorithm for computing f, but f cannot be μ-recursive. Explain the seeming contradiction.

22.5. Complete the proof of Theorem 22.3.

22.6. Below are two recursive definitions of functions f, given some other function g assumed to be defined and primitive recursive. Show in each case that the function f is primitive recursive.

(a) $f(0) = 1$; for $x > 0$, $f(x) = g(x, f(DIV(x, 2)))$

(b) $f(0) = f(1) = 1$; for $x > 1$, $f(x) = g(x, f(\lfloor \sqrt{x} \rfloor))$ (See Exercise 21.14.)

22.7. Suppose $f : \mathcal{N} \to \mathcal{N}$ is a μ-recursive total function that is a bijection from $\mathcal{N}$ to $\mathcal{N}$. Show that its inverse f^{-1} is also μ-recursive.

22.8. In Section 22.5, we discussed the function $gn: \Sigma^* \to N$. Show that the predicate *Isgn* defined by

$$Isgn(x) = (x = gn(s) \text{ for some string } s \in \Sigma^*)$$

is primitive recursive.

22.9. In each case below, show that the function from $\{a, b\}^*$ to $\{a, b\}^*$ is primitive recursive.

(a) f is defined by $f(x) = xa$

(b) f is defined by $f(x) = ax$

(c) f is defined by $f(x) = REV(x)$

22.10. (a) Give reasonable definitions of primitive recursiveness and recursiveness for a function $f : \Sigma^* \to \mathcal{N}$, where Σ is a finite alphabet.

(b) Using your definition, show that $f : \{a, b\}^* \to \mathcal{N}$ defined by $f(x) = |x|$ is primitive recursive.

22.11. (a) Give definitions of primitive recursiveness and μ-recursiveness for a function $f : (\Sigma^*)^n \to \Sigma^*$ of n string variables.

(b) Using your definition, show that the concatenation function from $(\Sigma^*)^2$ to Σ^* is primitive recursive.

PART
V

INTRODUCTION
TO COMPUTATIONAL
COMPLEXITY

In discussing a decision problem like the ones in Sections 8.3 and 15.3, we have emphasized the question of whether there exists an algorithm to solve it. Unfortunately, this is not the same as the question of whether there is a *usable* algorithm, which lets us find the answer for a reasonable-sized instance of the problem using reasonable amounts of space and time. The area of computation theory that deals with this issue is known as the theory of *computational complexity*. The purpose of this part is to provide a brief, noncomprehensive introduction to it.

The key word in our definition of a usable algorithm is "reasonable." We shall be concerned primarily with what constitutes a reasonable amount of time, and, in Chapter 23, we shall try to pin that down. We will use a Turing machine as our model of computation and formulate a criterion that allows us to distinguish between *tractable* and *intractable* problems. There is fairly general agreement as to what the criterion should be: *polynomial-time* solvability on a Turing machine—even though problems that must according to this criterion be considered intractable in general can often be solved in many concrete instances, and even though some practical instances of "tractable" problems may require unacceptably large computation times with current algorithms and current hardware.

We shall see that there are decision problems that are genuinely intractable according to the criterion in Chapter 23 or just about any other criterion. Perhaps even more interesting are problems that are suspected to be intractable but have never been proven to be. Into this category fall a great many "real-world" problems that have been studied exhaustively but have resisted all attempts to find efficient solutions. If we generalize the polynomial-time criterion mentioned above by allowing our TMs to be nondeterministic, we may define a class of problems, referred to as $\mathcal{NP}$, that includes many of these. In Chapter 24, we study a subclass of $\mathcal{NP}$, consisting of problems that can be shown to be particularly difficult: if any one of these *NP-complete* problems could be shown to be tractable, it would follow that every problem in $\mathcal{NP}$ is also, and in particular that many important problems must have more efficient solutions than have so far been found. Although most people are doubtful that this is the case, the question remains one of the outstanding open problems in theoretical computer science.

CHAPTER 23

TRACTABLE
AND INTRACTABLE
PROBLEMS

23.1 GROWTH RATES OF FUNCTIONS

In order to talk about a problem being tractable or intractable with regard to the run time required for a solution, we must have a reasonable way to compare the run time of one algorithm to that of another. We begin with some preliminary definitions and notation having to do with the "growth rates" of quantities such as run time.

Definition 23.1. If $f, g : \mathcal{N} \to \mathcal{N}$ are partial functions that are undefined on at most a finite set of natural numbers, we write

$$f(n) = \mathcal{O}(g(n))$$

or

$$f = \mathcal{O}(g)$$

if there are constants C and N_0 so that for every $n \geq N_0$, $f(n)$ and $g(n)$ are defined and $f(n) \leq C g(n)$. In this case, we say f is *of the order of g,* or f is "big oh" of g.

The statement $f(n) = \mathcal{O}(g(n))$ describes a relationship between two functions. It is not an equation. In particular, it makes no sense to write $\mathcal{O}(g(n)) = f(n)$. It might be less misleading to write $f\mathcal{O}g$, as in Section 1.5, when f is related to g in this way, but the notation in Definition 23.1 is well established.

It will be useful to state explicitly what it means for f *not* to be of the order of g, which we write $f \neq \mathcal{O}(g)$. Let us make the assumption that f and g are both defined for all sufficiently large n, since this will be the case in most of our applications. In this case, $f \neq \mathbb{O}(g)$ means that for any constants C and N_0, there is an $n \geq N_0$ with $f(n) > C g(n)$. Another way to say this is that for any C, $f(n) > C g(n)$ for infinitely many values of n. If $g(n)$ is nonzero, at least for sufficiently large n, $f \neq O(g)$ means simply that the ratio $f(n)/g(n)$ is unbounded.

There are at least two things to notice about Definition 23.1. First, it ignores multiplicative constants: if $f(n) = \mathbb{O}(g(n))$, then for any constant D, $Df(n) = \mathbb{O}(g(n))$. Second, it ignores "small" values of n, since the inequality is assumed to hold only for sufficiently large n. For both these reasons, it makes sense to interpret the statement $f = \mathbb{O}(g)$ as a statement about the *growth rates* of f and g. If $f = \mathbb{O}(g)$, $f(n)$ may be greater than $g(n)$ for many or even all values of n, and it may exceed it by a large factor, but in the long run f is no larger than a function proportional to g. The "growth rate" terminology is particularly appropriate when the functions f and g are both nondecreasing, or at least eventually nondecreasing (i.e., their values *grow* as n increases), and many of the functions we are interested in will have this property. If $f = \mathbb{O}(g)$ and $g = \mathbb{O}(f)$, we say f and g have the same growth rate. This means that f and g are roughly proportional in the sense that for sufficiently large n, either $f(n)$ and $g(n)$ are both 0 or their ratio varies only between two fixed positive values. If $f = \mathbb{O}(g)$ and $g \neq \mathbb{O}(f)$, we say the growth rate of g is greater than that of f.

We should be a little careful here: talking about one growth rate being equal to, or greater than, another, makes it sound as though the growth rate is a numerical quantity to which we can apply the usual relational operators. While this is not exactly the case, there is no harm in adopting this approach. The properties such as transitivity that are suggested by the phrase "less than or equal" hold for the corresponding relation defined by $\mathbb{O}$, and the same is true for the various other relations of this sort. The next theorem makes this official. In each case, the indicated relation is on the set of partial functions from $\mathcal{N}$ to $\mathcal{N}$ that are defined for all sufficiently large n.

Theorem 23.1.

(a) The relation R_1 defined by

$$f R_1 g \quad \text{if and only if} \quad f = \mathbb{O}(g)$$

interpreted informally to mean the growth rate of f is no larger than that of g, is reflexive and transitive.

(b) The relation R_2 defined by

$$f R_2 g \quad \text{if and only if} \quad (f = \mathbb{O}(g) \text{ and } g \neq \mathbb{O}(f))$$

interpreted to mean the growth rate of f is less than that of g, is transitive and asymmetric (i.e., if $f R_2 g$, then $\neg g R_2 f$).

(c) The relation R_3 defined by

$$f R_3 g \quad \text{if and only if} \quad (f = \mathbb{O}(g) \text{ and } g = \mathbb{O}(f))$$

(f and g have the same growth rate) is an equivalence relation.

Proof. We check the second statement in (a) and leave the remaining ones as exercises. Suppose $f = \mathbb{O}(g)$ and $g = \mathbb{O}(h)$; i.e., for some constants C_1 and N_1, $f(n) \leq C_1 g(n)$ for all $n \geq N_1$, and for some other constants C_2 and N_2, $g(n) \leq C_2 h(n)$ for all $n \geq N_2$. Let N_0 be the larger of N_1 and N_2. For $n \geq N_0$, the inequalities involving f and g both hold. Thus, for $n \geq N_0$,

$$f(n) \leq C_1 g(n) \leq C_1 C_2 h(n)$$

We may conclude that $f = \mathbb{O}(h)$ by using the constants $C_1 C_2$ and N_0 in Definition 23.1.

Two special cases will be common enough to justify special terminology. First, a *polynomial* function with *integer coefficients* is a function p that either is identically 0 or may be written in the form

$$p(n) = a_k n^k + a_{k-1} n^{k-1} + \cdots + a_1 n + a_0$$

where each coefficient a_i is an integer and $a_k > 0$. In the latter case, k is the *degree* of the polynomial. Since we want such a function to take natural numbers to natural numbers, we may simply regard $p(n)$ as undefined if it is negative; it is easy to check that since the leading coefficient a_k is positive, $p(n) > 0$ for all sufficiently large n (see the proof of Theorem 23.2). An *exponential* function is a function q of the form

$$q(n) = a^n$$

for some fixed $a > 1$. We could allow the base a to be nonintegral by defining the value of the function at n to be the greatest integer not exceeding a^n.

Accordingly, we say that f has *polynomial growth rate* if there is a polynomial p so that $f = \mathbb{O}(p)$ and $p = \mathbb{O}(f)$, and g has *exponential growth rate* if there is an exponential function q with $g = \mathbb{O}(q)$ and $q = \mathbb{O}(g)$. Less formally, we might say f has at most polynomial growth rate if $f = \mathbb{O}(p)$ for some polynomial p, and g has at least exponential growth rate if $q = \mathbb{O}(g)$ for some exponential function q. Every function could be said to have at *least* polynomial growth rate, since by our definition 0 is a polynomial; although there are functions whose growth rate is greater than exponential—see Exercise 23.4— you don't often hear the phrase "at most exponential growth rate," since to grow exponentially is to get very large very fast. In fact, sometimes "exponential" is taken to mean "exponential or larger."

We shall establish results that to some extent clarify the ideas of polynomial and exponential growth rates and their relationship to each other, but it is instructive to see an example first.

Example 23.1. Let $p_1(n) = n^2$, $p_2(n) = n^2 + 3n + 7$, and $q(n) = 2^n$. Table 23-1 shows the values of these three functions for some selected values of n. Certain trends are apparent here, even though we have considered only a few values of n. In the first place, although $p_2(n)$ is several times larger than $p_1(n)$ for small values of n, it quickly settles down, and by the time we reach $n = 1000$ their difference is relatively negligible. This is easy to understand intuitively. $p_2(n)$ consists of a "higher-order" term n^2 and certain lower-order terms. Higher-order means higher growth rate (see the second statement in Theorem 23.2).

TABLE 23.1
Selected values of polynomial and exponential functions

n	$p_1(n) = n^2$	$p_2(n) = n^2 + 3n + 7$	$q(n) = 2^n$
1	1	11	2
2	4	17	4
3	9	25	8
5	25	47	32
10	100	137	1024
20	400	467	1048576
50	2500	2657	$1.13 * 10^{15}$
100	10000	10307	$1.27 * 10^{30}$
1000	1000000	1003007	$1.07 * 10^{301}$

Eventually, this higher-order term predominates, and it is the only determining factor in the growth rate of the function.

An even more striking trend is the explosive growth of the exponential function. Again, the first few values of n are inconclusive—only by $n = 5$ has q surpassed p_1. But by $n = 10$ the function q has an imposing lead, and thereafter it is no contest. Whereas the values of p_1 and p_2 for $n = 1000$ are still of manageable size (a million dollars doesn't buy that much these days, and it's not unusual to have flown a million miles), that of q is almost unimaginably big, bigger by a couple of hundred orders of magnitude than the number of atomic particles in the universe.

Of course a tabulation like this would look different for higher-degree polynomials and for exponential functions with a different base. At $n = 1000$, for example, $(1.01)^n$ is still only about 20959. But the "exponential growth" is still there—it just takes a little longer for its effects to become apparent. $(1.01)^{10000}$ is greater than 10^{43}, while $(10000)^2$ is just a hundred million. The next two theorems help to confirm that the two features we noticed in our example will persist in general.

Theorem 23.2. Let p be the polynomial

$$p(n) = a_k n^k + a_{k-1} n^{k-1} + \cdots + a_1 n + a_0$$

where $a_k > 0$. The growth rate of $p(n)$ is the same as that of n^k. Furthermore, the growth rate of n^j is greater than that of n^k if $j > k$.

Proof. We show first that $p(n) = \mathbb{O}(n^k)$. We may write

$$\frac{p(n)}{n^k} = a_k + \frac{a_{k-1}}{n} + \cdots + \frac{a_1}{n^{k-1}} + \frac{a_0}{n^k}$$

and we may choose N_0 so that for any $n \geq N_0$, each of the k terms

$$\left|\frac{a_{k-1}}{n}\right|, \; \left|\frac{a_{k-2}}{n^2}\right|, \ldots, \left|\frac{a_1}{n^{k-1}}\right|, \; \left|\frac{a_0}{n^k}\right|$$

is less than $1/k$. It follows in the first place that for $n \geq N_0$, $p(n)$ is defined (i.e., nonnegative), since even if all the coefficients $a_{k-1}, \ldots, a_0$ were negative, the quantity

$$\frac{a_{k-1}}{n} + \ldots + \frac{a_1}{n^{k-1}} + \frac{a_0}{n^k}$$

would still be less than 1 in absolute value, so that

$$\frac{p(n)}{n^k} > a_k - 1 \geq 0$$

In the second place, for $n \geq N_0$,

$$\frac{p(n)}{n^k} \leq a_k + 1$$

thus, the inequality in Definition 23.1 is satisfied with $C = a_k + 1$.

The proof that $n^k = \mathbb{O}(p(n))$ is similar. Choosing N_0 even slightly larger if necessary, so that each of the terms $|a_{k-1}/n|, \ldots, |a_0/n^k|$ is $\leq 1/(2k)$ for all $n \geq N_0$, we have

$$\frac{p(n)}{n^k} \geq a_k - \frac{1}{2}$$

which can be rewritten

$$n^k \leq \left(\frac{1}{a_k - 1/2} \right) * p(n)$$

For the last statement in the theorem, suppose $j > k$. It is obvious that $n^k = \mathbb{O}(n^j)$, since $n^k \leq n^j$ for every $n \geq 0$. Since the ratio $n^j/n^k = n^{j-k}$ is unbounded, $n^j \neq \mathbb{O}(n^k)$. Thus, the growth rate of n^j is greater than that of n^k.

Theorem 23.3. Any exponential function has a growth rate greater than that of any polynomial.

Proof. Let

$$q(n) = a^n$$

for some $a > 1$, and let

$$p(n) = a_k n^k + \cdots + a_1 n + a_0$$

We wish to show that $p = \mathbb{O}(q)$ and $q \neq \mathbb{O}(p)$. If we use Theorem 23.1(a), it will suffice to show that $n^k = \mathbb{O}(a^n)$ and $a^n \neq \mathbb{O}(n^k)$.

Our proof will use a simple fact from calculus: that the ratio $\log n/n$ approaches 0 as n becomes increasingly large, where "log" means the natural logarithm to the base e. For a proof that does not depend on calculus, see Exercise 23.6.

You may verify easily that

$$n^k = (z(n))^n$$

where $z(n)$ is the real number

$$z(n) = e^{k(\log n/n)}$$

Since the exponent in this expression approaches 0 as n gets large, and since $e^0 = 1 < a$, we may choose N_0 so that $z(n) \leq a$ for all $n \geq N_0$. It follows that for $n \geq N_0$,

$$n^k = z(n)^n \leq a^n$$

thus, $n^k = \mathcal{O}(a^n)$.

To show that $a^n \neq \mathcal{O}(n^k)$, we must show that the ratio a^n/n^k is unbounded. We may write

$$\frac{a^n}{n^k} = n\,\frac{a^n}{n^{k+1}}$$

The argument in the first part shows that

$$n^{k+1} \leq a^n$$

for large n. But this is the same as

$$\frac{a^n}{n^{k+1}} \geq 1$$

Thus, multiplying the left side by n produces an unbounded quantity.

23.2 THE TIME COMPLEXITY OF A TURING MACHINE

In examining the time and space requirements of an algorithm, it is appropriate to take into account the size of the specific instance of the problem to which the algorithm is applied. If we use a Turing machine to implement the algorithm, a good measure of the size of the problem instance is the length of the input string. Thus, to study execution time we consider how the number of moves made by the TM depends on the input length. It is most common to look at the *worst*-case execution time, for at least two reasons: a conservative approach is the safest, and the worst-case estimate is usually the easiest to obtain. In order for this approach to make sense, however, it is necessary to start with a TM that does not loop forever on any input.

Definition 23.2   (The time complexity of a TM). Let $T = (Q, \Sigma, \Gamma, q_0, \delta)$ be a TM that halts or crashes on every input string. The *time complexity* of T is the function τ_T, where for $n \geq 0$, $\tau_T(n)$ is the maximum number of moves T can make if it begins with an input string $x \in \Sigma^*$ satisfying $|x| = n$.

Example 23.2. We consider the TM T of Example 16.3, which accepts the language $\{ss \mid s \in \{a, b\}^*\}$. This TM is pictured in Fig. 23-1. The formula for $\tau_T(n)$ will depend on whether n is even or odd. We derive the formula in the first case and leave the second as an exercise.

The first phase of the processing of a non-null even-length string is to convert the second half of the string to upper-case. This can be divided into two subphases: subphase 1, corresponding to the large loop at the top of Fig. 23-1, ends with *all* the symbols changed to upper-case and the tape head reading the last symbol of the first half; subphase 2 ends when the first half has been converted back to its original form, the tape head is at the beginning of the string, and T is in state q_6. Subphase 1 consists of a single move followed by a sequence of passes. We illustrate for the string $aabaab$. The first pass begins in the configuration

$$(q_1, \Delta \underline{a}abaab)$$

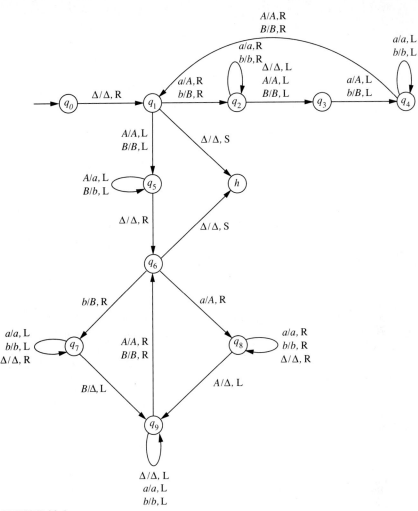

FIGURE 23-1

The a is changed to A, the head is moved to the rightmost lower-case symbol, and that symbol is changed to upper-case, yielding

$$(q_4, \Delta Aaba\underline{a}B)$$

Finally, the head is moved back to the leftmost lower-case symbol, resulting in the configuration

$$(q_1, \Delta A\underline{a}baaB)$$

If the input has length $2k$, $2k$ moves to the right and one to the left are required to find the rightmost symbol, then $2k - 1$ moves to the left and one to the right to find the leftmost lower-case symbol. Thus, the first pass contains $4k + 1$ moves. Each subsequent pass requires four fewer moves, since there are two fewer lower-case symbols, and so subphase 1 contains a total of

$$1 + (4k + 1) + (4(k - 1) + 1) + \cdots + (4(0) + 1)$$

$$= 1 + 4 \sum_{i=0}^{k} i + (k + 1)$$

$$= 1 + 4k(k + 1)/2 + (k + 1)$$

$$= 2k^2 + 3k + 2$$

moves. (The second equality uses Exercise 2.1.) In the case of our sample string, subphase 2 would transform the configuration

$$(q_5, \Delta A A \underline{B} A A B)$$

to

$$(q_6, \Delta \underline{a} a b A A B)$$

It is easy to see that in general this uses $k + 1$ moves if the original input has length $2k$; thus in the first phase of the processing there are

$$2k^2 + 4k + 3$$

moves.

So far, the processing time is independent of the input, as long as its length is even. In the second phase, the way to avoid a crash, and thus the way to obtain the maximum number of moves, is to consider an input string of the form ss, where $|s| = k$. This phase also consists of a sequence of passes, and we use the same string as before to illustrate. The first complete pass begins in configuration

$$(q_6, \Delta \underline{a} a b A A B)$$

It changes a to A, finds the leftmost upper-case symbol, and, assuming it is A, replaces it by Δ, yielding

$$(q_9, \Delta A a \underline{b} \Delta A B)$$

T completes the pass by leaving the head at the leftmost lower-case symbol, so that the configuration is

$$(q_6, \Delta A \underline{a} b \Delta A B)$$

It is easy to see that in general this pass involves k moves to the right, k moves back to the left, and one more to the right. The effect of each pass is to compare one symbol in the first half to the corresponding symbol in the second, and therefore k passes are required, each one having the same number of moves. If we include the last move to the halt state, we obtain

$$k(2k + 1) + 1$$

moves in the second phase. Our final total for a non-null input string of length $2k$ is

$$4k^2 + 5k + 4$$

This formula does not apply when $k = 0$, but at this point we can obviously conclude, since the number of moves for odd-length input is even smaller, that

$$\tau_T(n) = \mathbb{O}(n^2)$$

Before we leave this example, a comment is in order. It can be shown, although the proof is messy, that the TM we constructed to solve this problem is essentially the best possible, in the sense that the time complexity of any other TM that is a solution has growth rate at least that of n^2. However, a "machine-independent" description of the algorithm we used (find the middle of the string; compare the symbols in the first half with those in the second) suggests intuitively that the algorithm should require time that is only *linear* in the length of the string, rather than quadratic. In particular, you could without any difficulty write a Pascal program to solve the problem in linear time. This should not come as a surprise. Although a TM is a general model of computation, we know this does not mean it is always an efficient way of carrying out the computation. It turns out that using a TM as a yardstick is still an adequate way of distinguishing between those problems that can be solved in a reasonable amount of time and those that cannot; we shall return briefly to this question in the next section. It is not difficult to see, incidentally, that in this example we can improve on the quadratic run time by using a multitape TM—see Exercise 23.8.

23.3 TRACTABLE DECISION PROBLEMS: THE CLASS $\mathcal{P}$

We have noticed previously that a language can be identified with a decision problem. The decision problem associated with the language in Example 23.2, for example, is Given $x \in \{a, b\}^*$, is x of the form ss for some string s? Recognizing the language is equivalent to solving the corresponding problem. Conversely, once a method of encoding instances of a decision problem is established, the problem may be identified with the language of all the strings representing "yes-instances" (i.e., strings that are encodings of instances for which the answer is yes).

The TM in Example 23.2 accepts the language $L = \{ss \mid s \in \{a, b\}^*\}$ in quadratic time—that is, it accepts the language, and its time complexity function has growth rate equal to that of n^2. A weaker statement is that the language L can be accepted in *polynomial* time. The class of all languages with this property has been the object of much study.

Definition 23.3 (The class $\mathcal{P}$). The class $\mathcal{P}$ is the set of all languages L that can be accepted in polynomial time—i.e., for which there exists a TM T accepting L and a natural number k so that $\tau_T(n) = \mathbb{O}(n^k)$.

We are interested particularly in decision problems corresponding to languages in $\mathcal{P}$. However, we must be a little careful here. If we choose an extremely inefficient way of encoding instances of a problem, it may happen that the idea of polynomial time based on the length of the encoded strings doesn't mean much. When we speak of a decision problem "corresponding to a language in $\mathcal{P}$," we mean one for which some "reasonable" encoding produces a language in $\mathcal{P}$.

The reason $\mathcal{P}$ is significant is that the decision problems corresponding to languages in $\mathcal{P}$ have come to be regarded as the problems that are *tractable*—for which we can realistically expect to find answers to all reasonable-sized instances of the problem. One can question this characterization on a number of grounds.

It could reasonably be objected that if two TMs solving some problem had time complexities $(1.000001)^n$ and n^{1000}, respectively, a typical instance would have a greater chance of being solved on the first than on the second, Theorem 23.3 notwithstanding. While this is true, it is also true that in real life, "polynomial" is more likely to mean n^2 or n^3 or n^4 than n^{1000}, and "exponential" to mean 2^n than $(1.000001)^n$. For that matter, there are functions whose growth rates are greater than any polynomial, yet smaller than any exponential function (see Exercise 23.5); but again, the empirical evidence is that a problem of genuine interest that cannot be solved in polynomial time is likely to require at least exponential time and is therefore likely to be "intractable" in the most general case.

Since we have already seen an example of a problem that can be solved in linear time on a modern computer but in no better than quadratic time on a Turing machine, one might raise the question of whether defining the class $\mathscr{P}$ in terms of TMs is appropriate. The answer, which we state without proof, is that it doesn't make any difference which model of computation is used. The idea of "polynomial-time computability" seems to be independent of the particular computing device: roughly speaking, if a problem can be solved in polynomial time on some computer, its language is in $\mathscr{P}$.

Even if we accept the idea that the tractable decision problems are those corresponding to the languages in $\mathscr{P}$, one other qualification is in order. Saying that a problem is intractable doesn't mean that every instance of the problem takes a long time to solve, or even necessarily that every large instance does. It means that for any polynomial p, there is a natural number n, and an instance I of size n, so that answering the question for I will inevitably take more time than $p(n)$. For an intractable problem, it may still happen that there is an algorithm providing an answer for most instances, or at least most instances of interest, in an acceptably short time.

We consider briefly the intractable problems: those that no Turing machine, and therefore no computer, can solve in polynomial time. Are there any? We begin by recalling the results in Chapter 20, which should keep us from ever being too optimistic. There are decision problems that are unsolvable: no algorithm—no polynomial-time algorithm, no exponential-time algorithm—can ever solve them in general. Even aside from this, however, there are problems that are solvable in principle but *arbitrarily* complicated in practice. Theorem 23.4 uses a variation of the diagonal argument of Theorem 18.10 to show that for any computable function $f : \mathcal{N} \to \mathcal{N}$, no matter how large its growth rate, there is a decision problem that is solvable, but not by any TM having time complexity less than or equal to f.

Theorem 23.4. Let $f : \mathcal{N} \to \mathcal{N}$ be any computable (total) function. There is a recursive language $L \subseteq \{x, y\}^*$ for which no TM T satisfying $\tau_T \leq f$ can accept L. (Thus, although the membership problem for L is solvable, no TM T with $\tau_T \leq f$ can solve it.)

Proof. We use the encoding function e from Section 17.4, which encodes any TM as a string of x's and y's. Let

$$L = \{w \in \{x, y\}^* | w = e(T) \text{ for some TM } T$$

$$\text{that crashes on input } w \text{ in } f(|w|) \text{ or fewer moves}\}$$

First, we argue informally that L is recursive. Given a string w, its membership in L can be tested by following these steps:

1. Determine whether w is of the form $e(T)$ for some TM T;
2. Assuming w is of this form, compute the number $f(|w|)$, using a TM that computes f; and
3. If $w = e(T)$, simulate T on the input w for $f(|w|)$ moves, unless T halts or crashes within that time.

Suppose for the sake of contradiction that L is accepted by some TM T_1, and that $\tau_{T_1}(n) \le f(n)$ for every n. Consider the string $w = e(T_1)$. Within $f(|w|)$ moves, T_1 either halts or crashes on input w. If it crashes, w satisfies the defining condition for membership in L; therefore, T_1 must halt on input w since T_1 accepts L. On the other hand, if T_1 halts on input w, $w \notin L$ by definition of L; but since T_1 accepts L, T_1 cannot accept w. We now have the desired contradiction.

Theorem 23.4 can be strengthened considerably. It is possible to show that if f and g are functions for which the ratio

$$\frac{g(n)}{f(n) \log f(n)}$$

is unbounded, and g satisfies certain other requirements that are more stringent than mere computability but still fairly general, there are decision problems that can be solved by a TM with time complexity $\le g$, but not by any TM with time complexity $\le f$. In this way, the existence of a hierarchy of decision problems can be demonstrated. In addition, there are similar results for *space* complexity, which has to do with the number of squares of tape a TM needs for a computation as a function of the input length. See the book by Hopcroft and Ullman for a more complete discussion.

Of course, the decision problems described in the proof of Theorem 23.4 have an artificial feel to them. We already knew that not all problems were solvable; it is not especially alarming that there are other problems that can't be solved efficiently, if they are problems we have no interest in solving anyway. However, the situation at this point is somewhat similar to that in Chapter 20. Once it is known that there *are* problems that are inherently difficult in this sense, it is possible to exhibit problems of more general interest that fall into this category. We mention just one example. There are certain logical systems that are *undecidable*—i.e., for which there is no algorithm that can determine the truth or falsity of all statements in the system. Gödel showed, for example, that the logical system of arithmetic on the nonnegative integers has this property. On the other hand, it is easy to describe a logical system that is decidable but has the following remarkable property: for any positive integer k, the problem of deciding the truth value of a statement of length n cannot be solved by any TM with time complexity less than that of

$$2^{2^{2^{.^{.^{.^{2^n}}}}}}$$

with k successive exponentiations! The exponentiations in this formula are performed from the top down; for example,

$$2^{2^{2^3}} = 2^{2^8} = 2^{256}$$

This is a statement about growth rates; it might be hoped that solutions could still be obtained for all instances of reasonable size. No such luck: it has been shown that in order to find a solution for all statements of length less than about 700 in this system, a computing device with as many components as there are elementary particles in the universe would still require more time than the age of the universe. It is clear from results like these that whether such a problem is theoretically solvable or not, in practical terms a solution is out of the question.

23.4 NONDETERMINISM AND THE CLASS $\mathcal{NP}$

Many problems that are known to have polynomial-time solutions are still the objects of intensive study. If you have studied sorting algorithms, for example, you already know that the difference between an algorithm with run time $\mathcal{O}(n^2)$ and another with run time $\mathcal{O}(n \log n)$ can be dramatic, and enough to justify considerable research and effort. At the opposite extreme, it might well be worthwhile to study a problem that has been proven intractable—not to find a general solution, but perhaps to find an approximate solution, or a way to solve the problem in special cases. There is a third group of problems that is in some ways the most interesting of all and contains a wide variety of problems with important practical applications. For these problems, no one has been able to find either a polynomial-time solution or a proof that none exists. In this section, we shall define a class of such problems, and in the next chapter, we shall look at some examples in more detail. Before proceeding with the definition, it may be helpful to look at an example.

Example 23.3. We consider a decision problem from logic called the *satisfiability* problem. It involves logical expressions containing Boolean variables x_i and the logical connectives $\wedge$, $\vee$, and $\neg$ (AND, OR, and NOT, respectively). The problem is to determine whether a given expression can be *satisfied*—made to have the value true—by some choice of truth values for its variables. We shall formulate the problem in an apparently more restricted setting, although the first theorem in the next chapter shows that there is really no loss of generality.

Let us use the notation $\overline{x}_i$ to denote the expression $\neg x_i$. A logical expression is said to be in *conjunctive normal form* (CNF), if it is the *conjunction* of several subexpressions (that is, formed by joining the subexpressions by $\wedge$'s), each of which is a disjunction (formed with $\vee$'s) of x_i's and $\overline{x}_i$'s. For example,

$$(x_1 \vee x_3 \vee x_4) \wedge (\overline{x}_1 \vee x_3) \wedge (\overline{x}_1 \vee x_4 \vee \overline{x}_2) \wedge \overline{x}_3 \wedge (x_2 \vee \overline{x}_4)$$

is a CNF expression with five *conjuncts*. You can verify easily that this expression is satisfied by the assignment

$$x_2 = x_4 = \text{ true,} \qquad x_1 = x_3 = \text{ false}$$

The satisfiability problem is this: Given an expression in conjunctive normal form, is there a truth assignment that satisfies it?

The satisfiability problem is a *combinatorial* problem. It asks whether there is a particular combination of values for the x_i's for which some desired condition holds. As such, it has a solution that is trivial conceptually: try all combinations, if necessary, and see! We may think of this solution as consisting of two phases: generating possible combinations, and testing each one that is generated. If you did actually verify for yourself the correctness of the solution given above for our instance of the problem, you should already be convinced that testing a given combination is simple and relatively efficient. What makes this trivial solution not very interesting is that there are too many combinations for it to be generally feasible to test each one. If there are k distinct variables in the expression, the number of ways of assigning truth values to them is 2^k; thus, the worst-case run time grows exponentially with k.

We have encountered an abstract "machine" that can in a sense execute this brute-force algorithm quickly. A nondeterministic Turing machine can *guess* a choice of truth values for the variables, then test the guess to see if it works. If the expression can be satisfied, and *if* the TM guesses correctly and chooses a sequence of moves corresponding to a truth assignment that satisfies the expression, the moves can be carried out in short order; if the expression cannot be satisfied, any choice of moves leads to the correct answer. Of course, in observing that a nondeterministic TM doesn't need much time to find the answer, we have not removed the difficulty of the problem: there is no physical realization of a nondeterministic TM, and no obvious way of transforming such a "machine" into a deterministic algorithm without increasing the execution time substantially. Nevertheless, since the solution to many other combinatorial problems can be described in essentially this way, the concept of nondeterminism provides us with an appropriate way to define the class of decision problems, or languages, that we wish to consider. We shall return to the satisfiability problem shortly.

Definition 23.4 (The nondeterministic time complexity of a TM). Let $T = (Q, \Sigma, \Gamma, q_0, \delta)$ be a nondeterministic TM having the property that for each $x \in \Sigma^*$, every possible sequence of moves on input x leads to either a halt or a crash.

First, for $x \in \Sigma^*$, we let τ_x be the length of the longest sequence of moves on input x (see Exercise 18.16). The (nondeterministic) time complexity of T is the function τ_T defined by

$$\tau_T(n) = \max \{\tau_x \mid |x| = n\}$$

In other words, for any input string x, T must halt or crash on input x within $\tau_T(|x|)$ moves, and τ_T is the smallest function having this property.

Notice that if T happens to be deterministic, the two definitions of time complexity given in Definitions 23.2 and 23.4 agree.

Definition 23.5 (The class $\mathcal{NP}$). The class $\mathcal{NP}$ is the set of all languages L that can be accepted in nondeterministic polynomial time—i.e., for which there exist a nondeterministic Turing machine T accepting L and a natural number k so that $\tau_T(n) = \mathcal{O}(n^k)$.

Since every TM may be viewed as a nondeterministic TM, it is obvious from Definitions 23.3 and 23.5 that $\mathcal{P} \subseteq \mathcal{NP}$.

If we keep in mind our previous remarks about "reasonable" encodings of instances of a decision problem, we may now refer to decision problems as being in $\mathcal{P}$ or in $\mathcal{NP}$. Before we discuss what can be said about the *actual* time required to solve a problem in $\mathcal{NP}$, we return to our satisfiability example.

Example 23.3   (continued). We show that the satisfiability problem is in $\mathcal{NP}$ by constructing a nondeterministic TM to solve it. The first step is to specify precisely what the instances of the problem will look like and to come up with a reasonable way of encoding them for input to our TM. The assumptions we make about the CNF expressions are that each conjunct (i.e., each of the subexpressions joined by $\wedge$'s) will contain at least one variable, and for some $v \geq 1$, the distinct variables appearing in the expression will be precisely the variables $x_1, x_2, \ldots, x_v$. One variable might appear more than once in a single conjunct, and the conjuncts themselves may be duplicated. Since v, the number of distinct variables, is arbitrary, it is necessary to distinguish the variables by encoding their subscripts. We use a unary encoding for this: x_i will be represented by the string $x1^i$, and its negation $\overline{x}_i$ by the string $\overline{x}1^i$. Beyond that, an example will be sufficient to indicate our encoding scheme. The expression

$$(x_1 \vee \overline{x}_2) \wedge (x_2 \vee x_3 \vee \overline{x}_1) \wedge (\overline{x}_4 \vee x_2)$$

will be represented by the string

$$\wedge x1\overline{x}11 \wedge x11x111\overline{x}1 \wedge \overline{x}1111x11$$

We define *Satisfiable* to be the language over the alphabet $\Sigma = \{\wedge, x, \overline{x}, 1\}$ that contains the encodings of all expressions in CNF that satisfy the conditions described above and can be satisfied.

Let's use the term *literal* to refer to one of the occurrences of a variable x_i or $\overline{x}_i$ in our expression. If k denotes the number of literals in the expression, k is at least v and may be arbitrarily large. We denote by c the number of conjuncts in the expression, and by n the length of the string encoding the expression.

Is the encoding we have chosen a reasonable one? One answer is that

$$n \leq k(v + 1) + c$$
$$\leq k^2 + 2k$$

The first inequality uses the fact that the variables are $x_1, \ldots, x_v$. Each string $x1^i$ or $\overline{x}1^i$ has length $\leq v + 1$, and there is one $\wedge$ for each of the c conjuncts. The second inequality is true since v and c are both $\leq k$. It follows from these inequalities that if a quantity is bounded by a polynomial in n, it must also be bounded by a polynomial in k. Since k seems like a reasonable measure of the "size" of the problem instance, we conclude that our encoding is reasonable. Thus, if we can find a nondeterministic TM that has polynomial time complexity and accepts the language *Satisfiable*, it will be fair to say that the satisfiability problem is in $\mathcal{NP}$.

We now outline the steps that our nondeterministic TM T will take in order to accept *Satisfiable*. Once we have done this, we will be able to find the time complexity of T.

First, T must determine whether the input string does in fact represent a valid CNF expression in which each conjunct is non-null. For this to be true, it is sufficient that the string begin with $\wedge$, that every $\wedge$ be followed immediately by x or $\overline{x}$, and that every x

or $\overline{x}$ be followed immediately by 1. T can obviously test this condition in a single pass through the input, during which it moves its head only to the right.

Testing whether the distinct variables present are $x_1, \ldots, x_v$ for some v is more complicated but can be done as follows. T makes a sequence of passes through the input, during which it will need to mark certain literals; it can do this by changing x to y or $\overline{x}$ to $\overline{y}$. On each pass, T marks the first literal not already marked, marks each subsequent literal involving the same variable, and adds a 1 to the portion of the tape following the input, separated from the input by a single Δ. When there are no more unmarked literals, the string following the input contains v 1's, where v is the number of distinct variables in the expression. T then makes one more pass through the input, to determine whether there is a string of more than v consecutive 1's. If there is, the input is invalid and T crashes. Otherwise, the input is valid, and T restores the tape to its original form.

T begins another sequence of passes in an attempt to satisfy the expression. A single pass begins by T's examining the first conjunct that has not yet been satisfied. T may then try to satisfy the conjunct by choosing within it a literal that does not yet have a truth value; the marking scheme for keeping track of this is described in step 2 below. If it chooses such a literal, it makes it true, by assigning to the corresponding variable the value true if the literal is an x, false if it is an $\overline{x}$. This is the only point in T's operation where there is any nondeterminism. Each time T sees a literal in this conjunct that has no truth value, it can select it or pass it by. If it chooses to pass by all the literals in this conjunct, it crashes. Assuming that T does in fact select a literal, the remainder of the pass consists of the following steps.

1. T marks that literal by changing the x to y or the $\overline{x}$ to $\overline{y}$.
2. It examines each subsequent conjunct not yet satisfied for occurrences of the variable corresponding to that literal. Each time T finds a literal involving that variable, it marks it by changing x to z or $\overline{x}$ to $\overline{z}$. If the original assignment to that variable results in this literal's now having the value true, T marks the conjunct that is now satisfied by changing the $\wedge$ to # and proceeds to the next conjunct. Thereafter, no conjunct marked with # needs to be considered again.
3. After T has marked all the conjuncts that have been satisfied as a result of the assignment to this variable, it returns to the literal marked with y, changes the y to z, and marks that conjunct, which is now satisfied, with #. T is now ready for the next pass.

The sequence of passes terminates in one of two ways. Either all conjuncts are marked with #, in which case the expression has been satisfied, or all the literals in the first unsatisfied conjunct have been marked with z. In the first case, T halts; in the second, it crashes. It should be clear that if the expression is satisfiable, and only in this case, T can choose a sequence of moves that will cause it to halt.

It remains to find the nondeterministic time complexity of T. Recall that v, c, and n denote the number of distinct variables, the number of conjuncts, and the length of the input string, respectively.

The actions of T consist of two phases: testing that the input is valid, and, provided it is, attempting to satisfy the CNF expression. But in both phases, except for a few steps that obviously take time proportional to n, all the actions of T consist merely of repetitions of the following operation: beginning with some string of one or more consecutive 1's in the input, delimited at both ends by some symbol other than 1, and locating some or all of the other occurrences of strings of 1's that have the same length and are similarly delimited. The last operation in the first phase is slightly different, since there T searches for a *longer* string of 1's, but the time required is virtually the same. The operation is performed no more than $v + 1$ times in the first phase and no more than c times in the second.

A single operation of this type consists of several pattern-matching operations involving the same pattern. Since the only places in the string that can begin occurrences of the pattern are places that look like $x1$ or $\overline{x}1$, no tape square needs to be compared to a square in the pattern more than once during the entire operation. Of course, a one-tape Turing machine must continue moving its head back and forth between the pattern and the suspected occurrence of the pattern; thus, a single such comparison may take as many as $2n$ moves. But the conclusion is that the time required for one operation of this type is no more than $2n^2$.

Since v and c are both $\leq n$, it follows that the time complexity of T is $\mathbb{O}(n^3)$, and therefore in particular it is polynomial. This completes our example; the result we have obtained is summarized in Theorem 23.5.

Theorem 23.5. The satisfiability problem is in $\mathcal{NP}$.

23.5 $\mathcal{NP}$-COMPLETENESS

The only difference between the definition of $\mathcal{P}$ and that of $\mathcal{NP}$ is that the second contains the extra word "nondeterministic," but this difference seems to be significant indeed. With Example 23.3 in mind, we might try to summarize the difference intuitively by saying that a problem is in $\mathcal{P}$ if it can be *solved* in polynomial time, while a problem is in $\mathcal{NP}$ if a guess at a solution can be *tested* in polynomial time to see if it is in fact a solution. Another analogy that is often advanced to explain nondeterminism uses the idea of *parallel* computation. If a nondeterministic TM can make several possible choices of moves, one can imagine several "parallel processors" carrying out the possible computations simultaneously. While this analogy is suggestive, it does not suggest how an arbitrary computation that is possible in nondeterministic polynomial time can be performed in deterministic polynomial time. It is not possible to build an arbitrarily large army of parallel processors, and attempting to carry out all the computations sequentially—essentially what happens when we use a deterministic TM to simulate a nondeterministic one, as in the proof of Theorem 17.3—can lead to exponential time complexity or worse.

In any case, there does not *seem* to be any reason to believe that every problem in $\mathcal{NP}$ is in $\mathcal{P}$. To say it another way: there *seems* every reason to believe that at least some of the problems in $\mathcal{NP}$ are indeed intractable. However, nobody knows for sure. The question of whether $\mathcal{P} = \mathcal{NP}$ has become notorious and is one of the outstanding open questions in theoretical computer science. On the one hand, many important and practical problems are in $\mathcal{NP}$, and a great deal of labor has been expended in unsuccessful attempts to find polynomial-time solutions. On the other hand, although many problems are known to be intractable, no one has been able to produce any that are in $\mathcal{NP}$.

Some progress has been made in this area of research. In 1971, a paper by Cook introduced the idea of an "NP-complete" problem and proved that the satisfiability problem of Example 23.3 had this property. We shall give a precise definition later, but roughly speaking, to be NP-complete means to be as hard as any problem in $\mathcal{NP}$. If a polynomial-time solution were ever to be found for a problem known to be NP-complete, it would follow that *every* problem in $\mathcal{NP}$ had such a solution—i.e., that $\mathcal{P} = \mathcal{NP}$. In the twenty years following Cook's paper, a great many other well-known problems have been shown to be NP-complete. Moreover, the weight of opinion supports the view that $\mathcal{P} \neq \mathcal{NP}$. As a result, if a problem is known to be in $\mathcal{NP}$, and there is no obvious polynomial-time algorithm, it is now less likely that an enterprising researcher will launch a direct assault on the problem, or that he will try to give a direct proof of intractability. Instead, he is more likely to try to determine whether the problem is NP-complete. If it is, deciding whether it is tractable will be as difficult as deciding whether $\mathcal{P} = \mathcal{NP}$.

In Chapter 20, once certain problems were known to be unsolvable, a typical proof that a problem P was unsolvable was to show that some other unsolvable problem could be reduced to P. Here there is an analogous procedure, depending on the idea of a *polynomial-time reduction*.

Definition 23.6. Let Σ_1 and Σ_2 be finite alphabets, and L_1 and L_2 languages in Σ_1^* and Σ_2^*, respectively. L_1 is said to be *polynomial-time reducible* to L_2 if there is a total function $f : \Sigma_1^* \to \Sigma_2^*$ for which

$$x \in L_1 \text{ if and only if } f(x) \in L_2$$

and f can be computed in polynomial time—i.e., there is a TM computing f that has polynomial time complexity. We shall use the notation

$$L_1 <_p L_2$$

to mean that L_1 is polynomial-time reducible to L_2.

The statement $L_1 <_p L_2$ should be interpreted to mean that the difficulty of recognizing L_1 is no greater, or not much greater, than that of recognizing L_2. If the languages are those corresponding to decision problems, the statement says the first problem is not much harder than the second. This interpretation is reasonable: the first part of the statement $L_1 <_p L_2$ says that in order to test a string x for membership in L_1, it is sufficient to test $f(x)$ for membership in L_2; and the second part asserts that computing $f(x)$ isn't too difficult. The next theorem gives two properties of the relation $<_p$, both of which are consistent with this interpretation.

Theorem 23.6. Let $L_1 \subseteq \Sigma_1^*$, $L_2 \subseteq \Sigma_2^*$, and $L_3 \subseteq \Sigma_3^*$.

(a) If $L_1 <_p L_2$ and $L_2 <_p L_3$, then $L_1 <_p L_3$.
(b) If $L_2 \in \mathcal{P}$ and $L_1 <_p L_2$, then $L_1 \in \mathcal{P}$.

Proof.

(a) Suppose $f : \Sigma_1^* \to \Sigma_2^*$; $g : \Sigma_2^* \to \Sigma_3^*$; for $x \in \Sigma_1^*$, $x \in L_1$ if and only if $f(x) \in L_2$; and for $y \in \Sigma_2^*$, $y \in L_2$ if and only if $g(y) \in L_3$. Then $g \circ f : \Sigma_1^* \to \Sigma_3^*$, and for $x \in \Sigma_1^*$, $x \in L_1$ if and only if $g \circ f(x) \in L_3$. It remains to show that $g \circ f$ is polynomial-time computable. Let T_f and T_g be TMs computing f and g, and assume

$$\tau_{T_f}(n) = \mathcal{O}(n^j) \qquad \text{and} \qquad \tau_{T_g}(n) = \mathcal{O}(n^k)$$

It follows, in fact, that there are positive constants C, D, E, and F so that for *every* n,

$$\tau_{T_f}(n) \leq Cn^j + D$$

and

$$\tau_{T_g}(n) \leq En^k + F$$

We may combine the TMs T_f and T_g to obtain a TM T computing $g \circ f$. Consider the number τ_x of moves made by T_f in computing $f(x)$. If $\tau_x \leq |x|$, then T_f cannot change the rightmost symbol in the input string x or write any symbols to the right of it, and thus $|f(x)| = |x|$. Otherwise, we can say that $|f(x)| \leq \tau_x$, since to create an output string of length $|f(x)|$ will then require at least $|f(x)|$ moves. In either case, we have

$$|f(x)| \leq \tau_x + |x| \leq \tau_{T_f}(|x|) + |x|$$

We may conclude that for any $x \in \Sigma_1^*$,

$$\begin{aligned}
\tau_T(|x|) &\leq \tau_{T_f}(|x|) + \tau_{T_g}(|f(x)|) \\
&\leq C|x|^j + D + E|f(x)|^k + F \\
&\leq C|x|^j + D + E(\tau_{T_f}(|x|) + |x|)^k + F \\
&\leq C|x|^j + D + E(C|x|^j + D + |x|)^k + F
\end{aligned}$$

Since the last expression is a polynomial in $|x|$ (of degree jk if j and k are both nonzero, otherwise of degree j or degree k), the TM T has polynomial time complexity.

(b) Let T_2 be a TM with polynomial time complexity accepting L_2; let $f : \Sigma_1^* \to \Sigma_2^*$ be such that $x \in L_1$ if and only if $f(x) \in L_2$; and assume that the TM T_f computing f also has polynomial time complexity. Let T be the composite TM $T_f T_2$. It is clear that the strings in L_1 are precisely the input strings in Σ_1^* for which T halts, and the argument in (a) shows that T also has polynomial time complexity. It follows that $L_1 \in \mathcal{P}$.

Definition 23.7. A language $L \in \Sigma^*$ is *NP-hard* if for every language $L' \in \mathcal{NP}$, $L' <_p L$. If L is an NP-hard language that is itself in $\mathcal{NP}$, L is said to be *NP-complete*.

Theorem 23.7.

(a) If L is NP-hard and $L <_p L_1$, then L_1 is NP-hard.
(b) Let L be any NP-complete language. $L \in \mathcal{P}$ if and only if $\mathcal{P} = \mathcal{NP}$.

Proof. Both parts follow immediately from the previous theorem.

By using our intuitive idea of "reasonable" encodings of decision problems, we may extend Definition 23.7 so as to talk about NP-hard, or NP-complete, decision problems. A problem P is NP-hard, for example, if there is a reasonable encoding of instances of P so that the language obtained by encoding all "yes-instances" is NP-hard. Similarly, we may use the $<_p$ notation to compare two decision problems: $P_1 <_p P_2$ if this relation holds for the corresponding languages, given reasonable encodings of instances of P_1 and P_2. In this way, we can also extend part (a) of Theorem 23.7 so that it applies to decision problems. At this point, of course, it is not obvious that there are any NP-complete problems, much less that there are any of practical interest. In the next chapter, we shall look at several examples, beginning with the satisfiability problem.

EXERCISES

23.1. (a) Suppose $f, g, h : \mathcal{N} \to \mathcal{N}$, and $f = \mathbb{O}(h)$ and $g = \mathbb{O}(h)$. Show that $f + g = \mathbb{O}(h)$.

(b) Show that if $f, g : \mathcal{N} \to \mathcal{N}$, then $f(n) + g(n) = \mathbb{O}(\max(f(n), g(n)))$.

23.2. Let $f_1(n) = 2n^2; f_2(n) = n^2 + 3n^{3/2}; f_3(n) = n^3 / \log n;$ and

$$
f_4(n) = \begin{cases} 2n^2 & \text{if } n \text{ is even} \\ n^2 \log n & \text{if } n \text{ is odd} \end{cases}
$$

For each of the twelve combinations of i and j, determine whether $f_i = \mathbb{O}(f_j)$. Give reasons.

23.3. Suppose $f : \mathcal{N} \to \mathcal{N}$ is a total function, and $f = \mathbb{O}(p)$ for some polynomial p. Show that there is a polynomial q so that $f(n) \le q(n)$ for every n.

23.4. (a) Show that each of the functions $n!$, n^n, and 2^{2^n} has a growth rate greater than that of any exponential function.

(b) Of these three functions, which has the largest growth rate and which the smallest?

23.5. (a) Show that each of the functions $2^{\sqrt{n}}$ and $n^{\log n}$ has a growth rate greater than that of any polynomial and less than that of any exponential function.

(b) Which of these two functions has the larger growth rate?

23.6. Give a proof of Theorem 23.3 that does not use calculus. Suggestion: write $n = N_0 + m$,

$$
n^k = N_0^k \left(\frac{N_0 + 1}{N_0} \right)^k \cdots \left(\frac{N_0 + m}{N_0 + m - 1} \right)^k
$$

and choose N_0 sufficiently large.

23.7. In Example 23.2, find a formula for $\tau_T(n)$ when n is odd.

23.8. Show that it is possible to construct a two-tape TM accepting the language of Example 23.2 that has *linear* time complexity rather than quadratic.

23.9. Find the time complexity function for each of these TMs:

(a) The TM shown in Fig. 16-4.

(b) The *Copy* TM shown in Fig. 16-9.

(c) The *Delete* TM shown in Fig. 16-10.

23.10. Draw a TM computing the function f defined by $f(n) = n^2$ (see Exercise 16.9), and find its time complexity.

23.11. Show that any polynomial function $p : \mathcal{N} \to \mathcal{N}$ is computable in polynomial time.

23.12. Show that for any solvable decision problem, there is a way to encode instances of the problem so that there is a TM solving the problem and having polynomial complexity.

23.13. Prove the following generalization of Theorem 23.4. For any computable function $f : \mathcal{N} \rightarrow \mathcal{N}$, there is a recursive language $L \subseteq \{x, y\}^*$ so that for any TM T accepting L, $\tau_T(n) > f(n)$ for infinitely many values of n. (Hint: for any TM T, there are TMs T' that have the same time complexity and accept the same language as T but for which $e(T')$ is arbitrarily large.)

23.14. Let $\Sigma = \{a, b\}$, let L_1 be the language of palindromes over Σ, and let $L_2 = \{yy | y \in \Sigma^*\}$.
   (a) Show that $L_1 <_p L_2$.
   (b) Is there any language in Σ^* (other than $\emptyset$ and Σ^*) to which L_1 is *not* polynomial-time reducible? Why? What generalization does this suggest?

23.15. (a) Let L_1 and L_2 be languages over alphabets Σ_1 and Σ_2, respectively. Show that if $L_1 <_p L_2$, then $L_1' <_p L_2'$.
   (b) Show that if there is an NP-complete language L whose complement is in $\mathcal{NP}$, then the complement of any language in $\mathcal{NP}$ is also in $\mathcal{NP}$.

23.16. Let L, L_1, and L_2 be languages over Σ with $L_1 \neq \Sigma^*$ and $L = L_1 \cap L_2$. Show that if L is NP-complete, $L_1 \in \mathcal{NP}$, and $L_2 \in \mathcal{P}$, then L_1 is NP-complete.

CHAPTER
24

SOME
NP-COMPLETE
PROBLEMS

24.1 NP-COMPLETENESS OF THE SATISFIABILITY PROBLEM

We described in the last section of the preceding chapter what it means for a problem to be NP-complete. It is now time to demonstrate that such problems exist. An appropriate problem to take as our first example is the one that was first proved to be NP-complete: the satisfiability problem discussed in Example 23.3. The proof was provided in 1971 by Stephen Cook, and our Theorem 24.1 is often called Cook's theorem. The details of the proof are complicated, but once we have one NP-complete problem, producing others will be considerably easier.

First, a word about notation: often in what follows, something like

$$\bigwedge_{i=1}^{n} A_i$$

is used to denote the conjunction

$$A_1 \wedge A_2 \wedge \cdots \wedge A_n$$

The same shorthand can be used with disjunctions, and other variants of this notation can be interpreted similarly. As in Example 23.3, if a is a Boolean variable, $\bar{a}$ stands for $\neg a$.

In one section of the proof of Theorem 24.1, the following basic result about Boolean formulas is useful.

Lemma 24.1. Let F be any Boolean formula involving the variables $a_1, a_2, \ldots, a_t$. Then F is equivalent to a formula in conjunctive normal form—i.e., of the form

$$\bigwedge_{i=1}^{k} \bigvee_{j=1}^{l_i} b_{i,j}$$

where each $b_{i,j}$ is either an a_r or an $\overline{a}_r$.

Proof. It will be easiest to show first that any such F is equivalent to a formula in *disjunctive normal form*, that is, of the form

$$\bigvee_{i=1}^{k} \bigwedge_{j=1}^{l_i} b_{i,j}$$

To see this, we introduce a little notation. For an assignment θ of truth values to the variables, and for any j between 1 and t, we let

$$\alpha_{\theta,j} = \begin{cases} a_j & \text{if assignment } \theta \text{ makes } a_j \text{ true} \\ \overline{a}_j & \text{otherwise} \end{cases}$$

It is clear from this definition that for each θ, the conjunction $\bigwedge_{j=1}^{t} \alpha_{\theta,j}$ is satisfied by assignment θ and by no others. Therefore, if we let S be the set of assignments satisfying F, the assignments that satisfy one of the disjuncts of the formula

$$F_1 = \bigvee_{\theta \in S} \bigwedge_{j=1}^{t} \alpha_{\theta,j}$$

are precisely those that satisfy F. Since F and F_1 are satisfied by exactly the same assignments, they must be equivalent.

To finish the proof we apply our preliminary result to $\neg F$. If $\neg F$ is equivalent to

$$\bigvee_{i} \bigwedge_{j} b_{i,j}$$

then it follows from De Morgan's law that F is equivalent to

$$\bigwedge_{i} \bigvee_{j} \neg b_{i,j}$$

Theorem 24.1 (Cook's Theorem). The satisfiability problem is NP-complete.

Proof. In Example 23.3, we saw that the language *Satisfiable* is in $\mathcal{NP}$. What we must now show is that it is NP-hard. In other words, if $L \subseteq \Sigma_1^*$ is in $\mathcal{NP}$, and $\Sigma = \{\wedge, x, \overline{x}, 1\}$, we must find a polynomial-time computable function $f : \Sigma_1^* \to \Sigma^*$ so that for any $x \in \Sigma_1^*$, $x \in L$ if and only if $f(x) \in$ *Satisfiable*.

Recall that strings in *Satisfiable* are encodings over Σ of conjunctive-normal-form expressions that involve Boolean variables $x_1, x_2, \ldots, x_v$, for some $v \geq 1$. The construction of f will be easier to understand if we proceed indirectly, by constructing a function g from Σ_1^* to *CNF*, the set of all CNF expressions (with arbitrarily many variables, whose names are arbitrary) so that $x \in \Sigma_1^*$ is in L if and only if $g(x)$ is satisfiable. The remainder of the construction then consists simply of specifying a way of relabeling variables so as to encode the CNF expressions as discussed in Example 23.3. Finding g is the hard part; showing that the corresponding function f is polynomially computable will be comparatively simple.

At this point, all we know about L is that it is in $\mathcal{NP}$. Somehow we must use this fact to find our function $g : L \to CNF$. Saying that L is in $\mathcal{NP}$ means that there exist a nondeterministic TM $T = (Q, \Sigma_1, \Gamma, q_0, \delta)$ accepting L and a polynomial p so that for any $x \in \Sigma_1^*$, T must halt or crash within $p(|x|)$ moves on input x. We may assume without loss of generality that for any n, $p(n) \geq n$. We may also assume that T never crashes by attempting to move the head left from square 0, since modifying T if necessary to obtain a new TM with this property will obviously not destroy the polynomial time complexity. It will be convenient to extend slightly the idea of "consecutive" configurations of T. If C and C' are configurations of T, we will say that C and C' are consecutive if C' can be obtained from C by a single move of T, or if C is a configuration from which T cannot move and $C' = C$. Using this convention, we may say that the strings in L are precisely those strings x for which there exist consecutive configurations $C_0, C_1, \ldots, C_{p(|x|)}$ of T, C_0 being the initial configuration corresponding to input x and $C_{p(|x|)}$ being a halting configuration. Thus, our goal is to find, for any $x \in \Sigma_1^*$, a CNF expression $g(x)$ that can be satisfied if and only if there is such a sequence of consecutive configurations of T.

In order to do this, we introduce three groups of Boolean variables. We associate with variables in the three groups statements about the current state, tape contents, and current head position of T, respectively, after a certain number of moves. A CNF formula constructed from these variables will therefore correspond to, and have the same logical structure as, a statement about configurations of T. In particular, we will be able, for any $x \in \Sigma_1^*$, to come up with a CNF formula $g(x)$ so that the statement identified with it says, roughly speaking: T begins with input x and processes it in a way that is consistent with all the rules of TMs in general, is consistent with the specific rules in its transition table, and leads to acceptance of x in a sequence of $p(|x|)$ moves. An assignment of truth values to our Boolean variables will correspond to specifying the state, the tape head position, and the contents of each tape square of T at each step, and we will be able to see that such an assignment satisfies the formula $g(x)$ precisely when the corresponding set of choices for states, tape symbols, and so on, constitutes a computation of T that results in x being accepted.

To simplify things, we begin by enumerating all states and tape symbols of T. Let

$$Q = \{q_0, q_1, \ldots, q_{r-1}\}$$

$$q_r = h$$

$$\sigma_0 = \Delta$$

$$\Sigma_1 = \{\sigma_1, \ldots, \sigma_s\}$$

$$\Gamma = \{\sigma_1, \ldots, \sigma_s, \ldots, \sigma_{s'}\}$$

Let us fix a string $x = \sigma_{i_1}\sigma_{i_2}\ldots\sigma_{i_n} \in \Sigma_1^*$, and let $N = p(|x|) = p(n)$. Because the time complexity of T is bounded by p, the statement we want to end up with involves only the first $N + 1$ configurations of T, and thus involves only the tape squares 0, 1, $\ldots, N$ (since in N moves T can never move its head past square N). With this in mind, we can now present the three classes of "atoms" we will use to construct our CNF formula $g(x)$. After each one, we give the statement with which it is associated, which describes one individual feature of a configuration of T. The phrase "at time i" is used to mean after i moves of T.

$Q_{i,j}$ $(0 \leq i \leq N, 0 \leq j \leq r)$: at time i, T is in state q_j

$H_{i,j}$ $(0 \leq i \leq N, 0 \leq j \leq N)$: at time i, the tape head is centered on square j

$S_{i,j,k}$ $(0 \leq i \leq N, 0 \leq j \leq N, 1 \leq k \leq s')$: at time i, the symbol in square j is σ_k

Our CNF formula $g(x)$ will be the conjunction of seven clauses:

$$g(x) = g_1(x) \wedge g_2(x) \wedge \cdots \wedge g_7(x)$$

In order to explain how it is constructed, it will be helpful to start with the statement we want to be associated with each clause.

1. $g_1(x)$ will be the CNF formula associated with the statement that the configuration of T at time 0 is the initial configuration corresponding to input x. This means that T is in state q_0, its tape head is in square 0, the symbol in square 0 is Δ, the symbols in squares 1 through n are those of x, and the remaining squares, up through square N, are blank. $g_1(x)$ is therefore the formula

$$Q_{0,0} \wedge H_{0,0} \wedge S_{0,0,0} \wedge \bigwedge_{j=1}^{n} S_{0,j,i_j} \wedge \bigwedge_{j=n+1}^{N} S_{0,j,0}$$

$g_1(x)$ will in fact be the only portion of $g(x)$ that depends directly on x.

2. $g_2(x)$ will correspond to the statement that after N steps T will be in the halt state. Thus $g_2(x)$ will consist of the single atom

$$Q_{N,r}$$

3. The statement corresponding to $g_3(x)$ is the primary one that involves the specifications (i.e., the transition function) of T, and it is the most complicated. It says that whenever T is in a configuration from which it can move, the state and current symbol one step later are those resulting from one of the legal moves of T. Suppose we denote by CM ("can move") the set of pairs (j, k) for which $\delta(q_j, \sigma_k) \neq \emptyset$. We want our statement to say: For every i between 0 and $N - 1$, for every tape square l between 0 and N, and for every pair $(j, k) \in CM$, if at time i the tape head is at square l and the current state-symbol combination is (j, k), there is one of the moves in $\delta(q_j, \sigma_k)$ so that at time $i + 1$, the state, the symbol at square l, and the new head position are precisely those specified by that move. If there were only one move in the set $\delta(q_j, \sigma_k)$, say $\delta(q_j, \sigma_k) = \{(q_{j'}, \sigma_{k'}, D)\}$, the appropriate formula for that choice of i, j, k, and l could be written

$$(Q_{i,j} \wedge H_{i,l} \wedge S_{i,l,k}) \rightarrow (Q_{i+1,j'} \wedge H_{i+1,l'} \wedge S_{i+1,l,k'})$$

where

$$l' = \begin{cases} l + 1 & \text{if } D = R \\ l & \text{if } D = S \\ l - 1 & \text{if } D = L \end{cases}$$

Since $\delta(q_j, \sigma_k)$ may in general have several elements, we will need

$$(Q_{i,j} \wedge H_{i,l} \wedge S_{i,l,k}) \rightarrow \bigvee_m (Q_{i+1,j_m} \wedge H_{i+1,l_m} \wedge S_{i+1,l,k_m})$$

where m ranges over all moves in $\delta(q_j, \sigma_k)$ and, for a given m, (j_m, k_m, l_m) is the corresponding triple (j', k', l') for that move. Thus, the complete formula we want (except that it is not in conjunctive normal form) looks like

$$\bigwedge_{i,j,k,l} ((Q_{i,j} \wedge H_{i,l} \wedge S_{i,l,k}) \rightarrow \bigvee_m (Q_{i+1,j_m} \wedge H_{i+1,l_m} \wedge S_{i+1,l,k_m}))$$

where i ranges from 0 to $N-1$, l ranges from 0 to N, and (j,k) varies over all pairs in CM. To obtain $g_3(x)$, we apply Lemma 24.1 to each of the conjuncts of this formula. The result is of the form

$$\bigwedge_{i,j,k,l} F_{i,j,k,l}$$

where $F_{i,j,k,l}$ is in conjunctive normal form, and the number of literals in $F_{i,j,k,l}$ is bounded independent of n.

4. Next, we formulate a statement saying that for any i, if T cannot move at time i, then at time $i+1$ the configuration is unchanged. Following the notation in the preceding part, we let CM' be the set of pairs (j, k) for which $\delta(q_j, \sigma_k)$ is empty. In particular, CM' includes every pair (r, k), since $q_r = h$. An appropriate formula is

$$\bigwedge_{i,j,k,l} (Q_{i,j} \wedge H_{i,l} \wedge S_{i,l,k} \rightarrow ((Q_{i+1,j} \leftrightarrow Q_{i,j}) \wedge (H_{i+1,l} \leftrightarrow H_{i,l}) \wedge (S_{i+1,j,k} \leftrightarrow S_{i,j,k})))$$

where i and l have the same ranges as in part 3, and this time $(j, k) \in CM'$. Here again, we may apply the lemma to each conjunct to obtain $g_4(x)$, which is of the form

$$\bigwedge_{i,j,k,l} G_{i,j,k,l}$$

Just as in part 3, each $G_{i,j,k,l}$ is in conjunctive normal form and is bounded in length independently of n.

It might seem as though taking our formula to be $g_1(x) \wedge g_2(x) \wedge g_3(x) \wedge g_4(x)$ would be sufficient. The corresponding statement says, roughly: T begins with input x, and after processing it for N moves, according to the transitions specified by its transition table, it ends in the halt state. However, things are not quite this simple. Although the requirement that the formula we have so far be satisfied places a number of constraints on the truth values of the atoms $Q_{i,j}$, and so on, it does not place enough. There are still truth assignments we could make that would satisfy the formula but would not correspond to an actual computation of T—that would in fact violate basic rules of TMs. For example, an assignment could specify that $Q_{0,0}$ and $Q_{0,1}$ were both true, or that $S_{1,2,3}$ and $S_{1,2,4}$ were both true, or that $S_{1,2,k}$ was false for every k. Fortunately, these problems can be corrected fairly easily.

5. $g_5(x)$ is the formula corresponding to the statement that T is in exactly one state at each step. "Exactly one" means at least one and never as many as two. The formula corresponding to "at least one" is

$$\bigwedge_{i=0}^{N} (Q_{i,0} \vee Q_{i,1} \vee \cdots \vee Q_{i,r})$$

and the one corresponding to "never two," by De Morgan's law, is

$$\bigwedge_{i,j_1,j_2} (\overline{Q}_{i,j_1} \vee \overline{Q}_{i,j_2})$$

where the conjunction is from $i = 0$ to $i = N$ and over every pair (j_1, j_2) with $j_1 \neq j_2$. $g_5(x)$ is the conjunction of these two.

6. $g_6(x)$ represents the statement that at each step, there is exactly one symbol in each square of the tape. Following the model in the preceding part, we may write $g_6(x)$ as the conjunction of the two formulas

$$\bigwedge_{i,j}(S_{i,j,0} \vee S_{i,j,1} \vee \cdots \vee S_{i,j,s'})$$

and

$$\bigwedge_{i,j,k_1,k_2} (\overline{S}_{i,j,k_1} \vee \overline{S}_{i,j,k_2})$$

Here i and j range from 0 to N, and (k_1, k_2) ranges over all pairs with $k_1 \neq k_2$.

7. Finally, we need our statement to guarantee that the *only* changes in the tape are those resulting from legal moves of T. In other words, for each i and each j, if the tape head at time i is not at square j, the symbol in that square is unchanged at time $i + 1$. We can write the corresponding formula as

$$\bigwedge_{i,j,k} (\overline{Q}_{i,j} \rightarrow (S_{i,j,k} \leftrightarrow S_{i+1,j,k}))$$

Here i goes from 0 to $N - 1$, j from 0 to N, and k from 0 to s'. Although it would be simple enough to transform this directly into conjunctive normal form, to obtain $g_7(x)$ we will settle for applying Lemma 24.1 to each conjunct.

The formula $g(x)$ that we have constructed has exactly the same structure as the statement (complicated, to be sure) that says there is a sequence of consecutive configurations of T, beginning with input x and ending in the halt state. On the one hand, if T accepts x, this statement is true—it is made true by a particular way of specifying the state, the tape head position, and the contents of each tape square at each time from 0 to N. Therefore, the corresponding formula $g(x)$ is satisfied by the corresponding truth assignments to the atoms in our three classes. Conversely, if $g(x)$ is satisfiable, there is a way of specifying the state, and so on, at each step so that the statement corresponding to $g(x)$ is true. But built into the statement are clauses that guarantee that these assignments of states and symbols are consistent with the operation of the TM T and therefore constitute a computation of T by which x is accepted. It follows, therefore, that a string x is an element of L if and only if $g(x)$ is satisfiable.

The rest of the proof consists of showing that the function $f : \Sigma_1^* \rightarrow \Sigma^*$ can be computed by a TM in polynomial time. $f(x)$ is calculated by computing $g(x)$ and then relabeling the variables. Let's consider what is involved in constructing a TM T_g to write the formula $g(x)$. We will have T_g write it in the same form as that in which we want the output to end up, except for the variable names. For example, the expression

$$(\overline{S}_{i,j,2} \vee \overline{S}_{i,j,3}) \wedge (\overline{S}_{i,j,2} \vee \overline{S}_{i,j,4})$$

which might appear in the second portion of $g_6(x)$, could be written on the tape as

$$\overline{S}1^i, 1^j, 11\overline{S}1^i, 1^j, 111 \wedge \overline{S}1^i, 1^j, 11\overline{S}1^i, 1^j, 1111$$

T_g uses a number of ingredients in the process of constructing $g(x)$. Among them are the input string x, the integers $n = |x|$ and $N = p(n)$, the integers r, s, and s', and the transition table for the TM T, which consists of a set of 5-tuples (u, v, u', v', D) representing moves $(q_{u'}, \sigma_{v'}, D)$ in the set $\delta(q_u, \sigma_v)$. The first job for T_g is to enter all this information at the beginning of its tape, in a "reference" section that will not be disturbed, except for temporary bookkeeping markers, until T_g has finished writing $g(x)$ and is ready to erase everything else. Following this reference section of the tape will also be enough room for all active integer variables i, j, k, and so on, used in the formula $g(x)$. The computation of $p(n)$ can be done in polynomial time; thus T_g can create this reference area in polynomial time.

It would be very tedious to go in detail through each step of the process by which T_g writes the formula $g(x)$, and we shall not attempt to do this. Looking briefly at a few typical portions should be enough to convince you that everything that needs to be done can be done in polynomial time. We may summarize the argument as follows. The total number of literals in the formula $g(x)$ is bounded by a polynomial function of $|x|$, and the time required for computing and writing each one is no worse than polynomial; therefore T_g has polynomial time complexity. We won't worry about doing things in the most efficient way—being sloppy will simply make the polynomials a little bigger. Let's look again at the second of the two portions of $g_6(x)$, which is typical of the ones that we were able to write directly in conjunctive normal form. It may help to rewrite it in the form

$$\bigwedge_{i=0}^{N} \bigwedge_{j=0}^{N} \bigwedge_{k_1=0}^{s'} \bigwedge_{k_2 \neq k_1} (\overline{S}_{i,j,k_1} \vee \overline{S}_{i,j,k_2})$$

Since s' is constant, the number of literals in this formula is $\mathcal{O}(N^2) = \mathcal{O}(p(|x|)^2)$. Suppose for example that for some specific values of i, j, k_1, and k_2, T_g has just written the conjunct $\overline{S}_{i,j,k_1} \vee \overline{S}_{i,j,k_2}$. Let's go briefly through the steps it must take to write the next literal on the tape. It begins by incrementing k_2, if possible, until another value not equal to k_1 is found. (If this is not possible, it increments k_1 if possible and sets k_2 to 0; if k_1 is already s', it increments j if possible; etc.) Assuming that T_g is able to find a new 4-tuple (i, j, k_1, k_2) in the appropriate range, it then writes $\overline{S}$, followed by the strings representing i, j, and k_1. How long does all this take? In order to test whether k_2 can be incremented, k_2 must be compared with s'. The number of moves required depends on the sizes of k_2 and s', as well as as the distance between them on the tape. k_2 and s' are bounded independently of $|x|$, and the two portions of the tape being compared are no farther apart than the length of the reference section plus the length of the portion of $g(x)$ already written. If all these quantities are bounded by polynomials in $|x|$, the resulting number of moves is also. A similar argument applies if further comparisons (k_1 to s', j to N, etc.) are necessary. Once the new values of i, j, k_1, k_2 are set, then writing the literal involves copying the strings 1^i, 1^j, and 1^{k_1}. In each case, since the three integers are bounded by polynomials, and the total distance that the head must travel in order to write each new symbol is likewise bounded, the total time for writing $\overline{S}_{i,j,k_1}$ is at worst polynomial.

In the case of a clause like $g_3(x)$, things may be a little less obvious. The formula looks like

$$\bigwedge_{i=0}^{N-1} \bigwedge_{l=0}^{N} \bigwedge_{j=0}^{N} \bigwedge_{(j,k)\in CM} F_{i,j,k,l}$$

where the fourth conjunction is over the indicated values of k. Each $F_{i,j,k,l}$ is itself in conjunctive normal form and involves certain variables that depend on $\delta(q_j, \sigma_k)$, as well as $Q_{i,j}$, $H_{i,l}$, and $S_{i,l,k}$. The important point is that there is a fixed number, independent of n, that bounds the number of literals in $F_{i,j,k,l}$, and therefore the number of literals in $g_3(x)$ is also no more than a polynomial function of n. Once T_g has finished writing one of these literals, it uses rules in its program (i.e., its transition table) to determine which type of literal to write next and how to compute the correct subscripts; and the number of steps required to write it is no worse than polynomial, for the same reasons that we saw in the case of g_6.

To obtain $f(x)$ from $g(x)$, the only job remaining is to relabel the variables so that they are $x_1, \ldots, x_v$ for some v. This is straightforward. At each step, the first of the literals that haven't yet been relabeled is found, it is given the next available number, and all other occurrences of it are located and relabeled. We leave it to you to check that a TM can accomplish this job in time that is bounded by a polynomial function of $|g(x)|$ and thus by a polynomial function of $|x|$. The proof is now complete.

24.2   OTHER NP-COMPLETE PROBLEMS

We have one example of an NP-complete problem, and we wish to find more. According to Theorem 23.7(a), the way to proceed is to follow the model in Chapter 20. To show that a problem is unsolvable, show that some other problem known to be unsolvable can be reduced to it; to show that a problem is NP-hard, show that some other problem known to be NP-hard can be polynomially reduced to it.

The next example is just a special case of the satisfiability problem, but it is sometimes more useful in showing other problems NP-complete. It is called the 3-satisfiability problem, and it asks, Given an expression in conjunctive normal form in which every conjunct is the disjunction of exactly three literals, is there a satisfying truth assignment? On the one hand, there is an obvious sense in which this problem is at least as easy as the general satisfiability problem. However, as Theorem 24.2 shows, the general problem can be reduced to this one. We denote by *3-SAT* the language obtained by encoding instances of the problem, using the encoding discussed in Example 23.3.

Theorem 24.2. *Satisfiable* $<_p$ *3-SAT*. The 3-satisfiability problem is NP-complete.

Proof. *Satisfiable* and *3-SAT* are both languages in $\Sigma^* = \{x, \overline{x}, \Lambda, 1\}^*$. Proving the first statement requires that we find a polynomial-time-computable function $f : \Sigma^* \to \Sigma^*$ so that for any x, $x \in$ *Satisfiable* if and only if $f(x) \in$ *3-SAT*.

Let $C \subseteq \Sigma^*$ be the set of strings in Σ^* representing expressions in conjunctive normal form, and let *3-C* be the subset of C corresponding to those expressions in which each conjunct contains exactly three literals. Since a TM can easily determine in polynomial time whether an element of Σ^* is in C, it is sufficient to find a function

$$f_1 : C \to 3\text{-}C$$

so that for any $x \in C$, x represents a satisfiable expression if and only if $f_1(x)$ does. (To simplify things, we will ignore the encoding and write elements of C and 3-C in the ordinary CNF notation.)

Let

$$x = \bigwedge_{i=1}^{n} A_i$$

where each A_i is a disjunction of literals. By definition,

$$f_1(x) = \bigwedge_{i=1}^{n} B_i$$

where $B_i = A_i$ if A_i contains exactly three literals, and otherwise B_i is constructed from A_i as follows. In each case where an atom α or β or α_j is introduced, it is assumed not to occur in the expression x, and it is unique to the particular B_i in which it appears.

1. If $A_i = a$, then $B_i = (a \vee \alpha \vee \beta) \wedge (a \vee \overline{\alpha} \vee \beta) \wedge (a \vee \alpha \vee \overline{\beta}) \wedge (a \vee \overline{\alpha} \vee \overline{\beta})$
2. If $A_i = a \vee b$, then $B_i = (a \vee b \vee \alpha) \wedge (a \vee b \vee \overline{\alpha})$
3. If $A_i = a_1 \vee a_2 \vee \cdots \vee a_k$, where $k > 3$, then

$$B_i = (a_1 \vee a_2 \vee \alpha_1) \wedge (a_3 \vee \overline{\alpha}_1 \vee \alpha_2) \wedge (a_4 \vee \overline{\alpha}_2 \vee \alpha_3) \wedge \cdots$$

$$\wedge (a_{k-3} \vee \overline{\alpha}_{k-5} \vee \alpha_{k-4}) \wedge (a_{k-2} \vee \overline{\alpha}_{k-4} \vee \alpha_{k-3}) \wedge (a_{k-1} \vee a_k \vee \overline{\alpha}_{k-3})$$

In cases 1 and 2, it is easy to verify that for every possible assignment to α and β, A_i and B_i, both viewed as expressions involving a and b, are equivalent. It follows that whenever an A_i belonging to either of these cases is replaced by B_i, the resulting expression is satisfiable if and only if the original was.

Suppose a single $A_i = a_1 \vee a_2 \vee \cdots \vee a_k$ (where $k > 3$) is replaced by B_i. If a truth assignment θ satisfies the original expression, it must make one of the a_j's true. Let us show that with the same assignment θ, we can make the new expression true by specifying values for the α_j's. We consider three cases.

1. If θ makes a_1 or a_2 true, then specifying all α_j's false satisfies the new expression, since every conjunct after the first involves an $\overline{\alpha}_j$.
2. If θ makes a_{k-1} or a_k true, then specifying all α_j's true satisfies the new expression, since every conjunct except the last involves an α_j.
3. For any m with $2 < m < k - 1$, the conjuncts before the one containing a_m all contain an α_j for some j with $1 \leq j \leq m - 2$; and the conjuncts after this one all contain an $\overline{\alpha}_j$ for some j with $m - 1 \leq j \leq k - 3$. Therefore, if θ makes a_m true, then specifying α_j true for $1 \leq j \leq m - 2$ and the remaining α_j's false satisfies the new expression.

It follows that if θ is a truth assignment satisfying x, the expression $f_1(x)$ that has all the A_i's replaced by B_i's can also be satisfied by the assignment θ together with some choice of truth values for the additional variables.

On the other hand, if θ does not satisfy the expression x, θ fails to satisfy some A_i and therefore makes all the a_j's in A_i false. It is easy to see that with the assignment θ, no truth assignment to the additional variables can cause the corresponding B_i to be true. (For the first conjunct of B_i to be true, α_1 must be true; for the second to be true, α_2 must be true; $\ldots$; for the next-to-last to be true, α_{k-3} must be true; at this point, the last conjunct is forced to be false.) Therefore, if the original expression x is unsatisfiable, $f_1(x)$ is also unsatisfiable.

We now have the function f we want. To show the first statement of the theorem, it remains to check that f is computable in polynomial time. But this follows almost immediately from the fact that the length of $f(x)$ is no worse than proportional to that of x. The second part of the theorem follows from the first, Theorem 24.1, and the fact that *3-SAT* is a subset of *Satisfiable*.

A number of important NP-complete combinatorial problems can be formulated in terms of *graphs*. We begin with some basic terminology and then give two related examples of such problems.

Definition 24.1. An (undirected) *graph* is a pair $G = (V, E)$, where V is a finite nonempty set of *vertices* and E is a finite set of *edges*, or unordered pairs of vertices. ("Unordered" means that the pair (v_1, v_2) is considered to be the same as the pair (v_2, v_1).) The edge (v_1, v_2) is said to join the vertices v_1 and v_2, or to have end points v_1 and v_2, and in this case v_1 and v_2 are *adjacent*. A *subgraph* of G is a graph whose vertex set and edge set are subsets of the respective sets of G. A *complete* graph is one in which any two vertices are joined by an edge. A *vertex cover* for G is à set C of vertices so that any edge of G has an endpoint in C.

A schematic diagram of a graph G with seven vertices and ten edges is shown in Fig. 24-1. G has a complete subgraph with four vertices (3, 5, 6, and 7), and obviously, therefore, several complete subgraphs with fewer than four vertices. $\{1, 3, 5, 7\}$ is a vertex cover for G, and it is easy to see that there can be no vertex cover with fewer than four vertices.

The *complete subgraph problem* is this: Given a graph G and an integer k, does G have a complete subgraph with k vertices? The *vertex cover problem* is Given G and k, is there a vertex cover for G with k vertices?

Theorem 24.3. The complete subgraph problem is NP-complete.

Proof. It is easy to see that this problem is in $\mathcal{NP}$. A nondeterministic TM can take a string encoding an instance of the problem (i.e., a graph and an integer k), nondeterministically select k of the vertices, and then examine the edges to see whether any two of the k vertices are adjacent. A reasonable encoding of the problem uses the alphabet $\Sigma_1 = \{1, /\}$ and involves the unary representations of the vertices and vertex-pairs, with $/$'s used as separators. With respect to this encoding, the nondeterministic TM can complete the solution in polynomial time.

We show that the complete subgraph problem is NP-hard by showing that the satisfiability problem is polynomial-time reducible to it. Following the proof of Theorem 24.2, we proceed by constructing for each conjunctive-normal-form expression x, an instance $f_1(x)$ of the complete subgraph problem consisting of a graph G_x and an integer

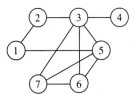

FIGURE 24-1

k_x, so that for any x, x is satisfiable if and only if G_x has a complete subgraph with k_x vertices. Once we have such an f_1, it will be straightforward to check that the corresponding function $f : \Sigma^* \to \Sigma_1^*$ is polynomially computable.

Let x be the expression

$$x = \bigwedge_{i=1}^{c} \bigvee_{j=1}^{d_i} a_{i,j}$$

where each $a_{i,j}$ is a literal. We want the vertices of G_x to correspond precisely to the occurrences of the terms $a_{i,j}$ in x; thus let

$$V_x = \{(i, j) | 1 \leq i \leq c \text{ and } 1 \leq j \leq d_i\}$$

The edges of G_x will now be specified in such a way that the vertex (i, j) is adjacent to (l, m) if and only if the corresponding literals are in different conjuncts of x and there is a truth assignment to x that makes them both true. The way to do this is to let

$$E_x = \{((i, j), (l, m)) | i \neq l \text{ and } a_{i,j} \neq \neg a_{l,m}\}$$

Finally, we take the integer k_x to be c, the number of conjuncts in the expression x.

If x is satisfiable, then there is a truth assignment θ so that for each i there is a literal a_{i,j_i} that is given the value true by θ. But then the vertices

$$(1, j_1), (2, j_2), \dots, (k, j_k)$$

determine a complete subgraph of G_x, since we have specified the edges of G_x so that any two of these vertices are adjacent.

On the other hand, suppose there is a complete subgraph of G_x with k vertices. Since none of the corresponding literals is the negation of another, there is a truth assignment that makes them all true; and since these literals must be in distinct conjuncts, this assignment results in at least one literal in each conjunct being true—i.e., x is satisfiable.

Checking that this construction leads to a function $f : \Sigma^* \to \Sigma_1^*$ that is computable in polynomial time is now straightforward, and we omit the details.

Theorem 24.4. The vertex cover problem is NP-complete.

Proof. As in the case of the complete subgraph problem, an instance of the problem consists of a graph and an integer k. Just as in the previous case, a nondeterministic TM can quickly select k vertices and determine whether they form a vertex cover. Thus, the problem is in $\mathcal{NP}$. To see that it is NP-hard, we show that an instance $I = (G, k)$ of the complete subgraph problem can be transformed to an instance $f_1(I) = (G_1, k_1)$ of the vertex cover problem in such a way that G has a complete subgraph with k vertices if and only if G_1 has a vertex cover with k_1 vertices.

If $G = (V, E)$, let G_1 be the *complement* of G:

$$G_1 = (V, E_1)$$

where

$$E_1 = \{(i, j) | i, j \in V \text{ and } (i, j) \notin E\}$$

Let $k_1 = |V| - k$. On the one hand, if vertices $v_1, v_2, \dots, v_k$ determine a complete subgraph of G, then since no edge in G_1 joins two of the v_i's, every edge in G_1 must have as an endpoint an element of $V - \{v_1, \dots, v_k\}$; and thus, this set is a vertex cover for G_1 with k_1 vertices. Conversely, suppose $U = \{u_1, \ldots, u_{|V|-k}\}$ is a vertex cover for G_1. Every edge of G_1 has an end point in U, so two vertices in $V - U$ cannot be joined by an edge in G_1. But any two vertices are joined either by an edge in G or by one in its complement, and therefore any two vertices in $V - U$ are joined by an edge in G. In other words, $V - U$ determines a complete subgraph of G with k vertices.

Since the transformation from G to G_1 can clearly be carried out in polynomial time, the proof is complete.

We finish up by showing that a combinatorial problem known as the *three-dimensional matching problem* is NP-complete. An instance of the problem consists of three disjoint sets A, B, and C, each with N elements, and a set M of triples in $A \times B \times C$. The problem is to determine whether M has a subset M' containing N triples that account for every element of $A \cup B \cup C$. Such an M' is called a matching. The two-dimensional counterpart of the problem, involving only the sets A and B, is called the *marriage* problem and can be understood by thinking of A as prospective husbands and B as prospective wives. M is obtained as a result of each person, male and female, listing all persons of the opposite sex that he or she would find acceptable as a mate. In other words, M is a set of male-female pairs. Finding a matching means finding a way to marry everyone off so that no one has more than one spouse and everyone has an acceptable mate. To visualize the three-dimensional version in the same way, imagine sets of men, women, and children, and create M by having each person list all man-woman-child triples including him- or herself that he or she would find satisfactory. Is there a way to form N man-woman-child families so that everyone is included and everyone is satisfied?

We shall use the NP-completeness of *3-SAT* to show that this problem is NP-complete. The proof will be easier to understand, however, if we do this indirectly, by introducing another related problem called the three-dimensional *relaxed* matching problem, or *3DRM* for short. An instance of this problem consists of disjoint sets A, B, and C, with $|A| \geq |B| = |C| = N$, and a subset $M \subseteq A \times B \times C$. The problem is to determine whether there is a subset M' of M containing N elements so that every element of $B \cup C$ appears exactly once in a triple in M' and every element of A appears at most once. (If $|A| > N$, some elements of A will be left out.) Such an M' is called a *relaxed matching*.

Theorem 24.5. *3DRM* is NP-complete.

Proof. As in the last few examples, we ignore specific encodings and work directly with problem instances. We also omit the proof, which is straightforward, that *3DRM* is in $\mathcal{NP}$, and proceed directly to the proof that the 3-satisfiability problem is polynomial-time reducible to *3DRM*. Given an instance I of the 3-satisfiability problem (i.e., a conjunctive normal form expression x in which every conjunct contains three literals), we must associate to I an instance $f(I) = (A, B, C, M)$ of *3DRM*, in such a way that I is satisfiable if and only if there is a relaxed matching M' for the instance $f(I)$.

Suppose

$$x = \bigwedge_{j=1}^{N} C_j$$

and that the distinct variables involved in x are $u_1, u_2, \ldots, u_m$. We begin by specifying the sets A, B, and C.

$$A = \{u_{i,j}, \overline{u}_{i,j} | 1 \le i \le m, 1 \le j \le n\}$$
$$B = \{b_{i,j} | 1 \le i \le m, 1 \le j \le n\} \cup \{\beta_1, \ldots, \beta_n\}$$
$$C = \{c_{i,j} | 1 \le i \le m, 1 \le j \le n\} \cup \{\gamma_1, \ldots, \gamma_n\}$$

Thus $|A| = 2mn$, and $|B| = |C| = mn + n$.

M is the union of the following sets of triples.

1. $T_i = \{(u_{i,j}, b_{i,j}, c_{i,j}) | 1 \le j \le n\}$ (for each i with $1 \le i \le m$)
2. $\overline{T}_i = \{(\overline{u}_{i,j}, b_{i,j+1}, c_{i,j}) | 1 \le j \le n - 1\} \cup \{(\overline{u}_{i,n}, b_{i,1}, c_{i,n})\}$ (for each i with $1 \le i \le m$)
3. $S = \{(u_{i,j}, \beta_j, \gamma_j) | 1 \le i \le m, \ 1 \le j \le n,$ and the literal u_i appears in $C_j\}$
4. $\overline{S} = \{(\overline{u}_{i,j}, \beta_j, \gamma_j) | 1 \le i \le m, \ 1 \le j \le n,$ and the literal $\overline{u}_i$ appears in $C_j\}$

Notice that for each i, the triples in T_i contain (collectively) exactly one occurrence of each $u_{i,j}$, each $b_{i,j}$, and each $c_{i,j}$, and those in $\overline{T}_i$ contain exactly one occurrence of each $\overline{u}_{i,j}$, each $b_{i,j}$, and each $c_{i,j}$. Moreover, the triples in T_i and those in $T_{i'}$ do not contain any symbols in common if $i \ne i'$, and similarly for $\overline{T}_i$ and $\overline{T}_{i'}$.

Suppose there is a truth assignment θ satisfying x. We show how to construct a relaxed matching M'. For each conjunct C_j of x, choose the triple containing β_j and γ_j to be added to M' by selecting a literal in C_j that is true under θ, say one involving the variable u_i. If the literal is u_i, let the triple be $(u_{i,j}, \beta_j, \gamma_j)$, and if it is $\overline{u}_i$ let the triple be $(\overline{u}_{i,j}, \beta_j, \gamma_j)$. In the first case, also add to M' all pairs in $\overline{T}_i$, in the second all pairs in T_i. (Note: in either case, the pairs may have been added already, since the same variable u_i may be selected for several different C_j's. But it will never happen that the literal u_i is selected in one conjunct and $\overline{u}_i$, for the same i, in another.) It is easy to check that no element of $A \cup B \cup C$ appears more than once in these triples. After these steps are completed, there may still be values of i for which neither T_i nor $\overline{T}_i$ has been added. In this case, it doesn't matter which we pick; let us arbitrarily choose T_i for every such i. The resulting set M' is a relaxed matching.

Conversely, suppose that M' is a relaxed matching. First we claim that for any i, $(u_{i,j}, \beta_j, \gamma_j)$ and $(\overline{u}_{i,j'}, \beta_{j'}, \gamma_{j'})$ cannot both be in M' if $j \ne j'$. Assume for the moment that this claim is true. We may use M' to specify a truth assignment θ as follows: for each i, θ makes u_i false if $(\overline{u}_{i,j}, \beta_j, \gamma_j) \in M'$ for some j, and otherwise θ makes u_i true. For each j, β_j is one of the elements of B, so M' has to contain either $(u_{i,j}, \beta_j, \gamma_j)$ or $(\overline{u}_{i,j}, \beta_j, \gamma_j)$ for some i. In the first case, u_i appears in C_j, and in the second case, $\overline{u}_i$ appears in C_j; thus θ makes one of the literals in C_j true in either case. Since this is true for any j, θ must satisfy x.

Now to take care of the claim. Suppose $(u_{i,j}, \beta_j, \gamma_j), (\overline{u}_{i,j'}, \beta_{j'}, \gamma_{j'}) \in M'$. Assume for simplicity that $j < j'$. Since $(u_{i,j}, \beta_j, \gamma_j) \in M'$, M' cannot contain $(u_{i,j}, b_{i,j}, c_{i,j})$. $c_{i,j}$ must appear in some triple of M', and the only other possibility is that $(\overline{u}_{i,j}, b_{i,j+1}, c_{i,j}) \in M'$. This means that M' cannot contain $(u_{i,j+1}, b_{i,j+1}, c_{i,j+1})$, and the same reasoning shows that $(\overline{u}_{i,j+1}, b_{i,j+2}, c_{i,j+1}) \in M'$. Eventually, using the same argument, we obtain $(\overline{u}_{i,j'}, b_{i,j'+1}, c_{i,j'}) \in M'$ (or, if $j' = n$, $(\overline{u}_{i,j'}, b_{i,1}, c_{i,j'}) \in M'$). However, this is inconsistent with the assumption that $(\overline{u}_{i,j'}, \beta_{j'}, \gamma_{j'}) \in M'$. This completes the proof of the claim, and we have shown that x is satisfiable if and only if there is a relaxed matching.

It is easy to see that the function taking a string in *3-SAT* to the appropriate string encoding the instance M can be computed in polynomial time, since M contains $2mn + 3n$ triples and each one can be constructed in polynomial time. The proof is therefore complete.

Theorem 24.6. The three-dimensional matching problem is NP-complete.

Proof. According to Theorem 24.5, it is sufficient to show that the problem is in $\mathcal{NP}$ and that *3DRM* is polynomial-time reducible to it. The first statement is straightforward, and we omit the details. Suppose $I = (A, B, C, M)$ is an instance of *3DRM*; let $|B| (= |C|) = N$, and let $|A| = N + k$. We show how to construct an instance $f(I) = (A_1, B_1, C_1, M_1)$ of the matching problem so that there is a relaxed matching for I if and only if there is a matching for $f(I)$. Let

$$A_1 = A$$
$$B_1 = B \cup \{b_1, \ldots, b_k\}$$
$$C_1 = C \cup \{c_1, \ldots, c_k\}$$

where the b_i's and c_i's are not in $A \cup B \cup C$. Let

$$M_1 = M \cup \{(a, b_i, c_j) | a \in A, \ 1 \le i \le k, \ \text{and} \ 1 \le j \le k\}$$

Suppose there is a relaxed matching M' for I. The triples of M' include N of the elements of A; let $a_1, \ldots, a_k$ be the elements that are not included. Let

$$M_1' = M' \cup \{(a_i, b_i, c_i) | 1 \le i \le k\}$$

It is obvious that M_1' is a matching for M_1.

On the other hand, suppose M_1' is a matching for M_1. Every element of $B \cup C$ appears in exactly one of the triples in M_1', and it is one of the triples that don't include the b_i's or c_i's. Therefore, the subset M' of all triples not involving b_i's or c_i's constitutes a relaxed matching for I.

The mapping from I to $f(I)$ is easily computable in polynomial time, and the proof is complete.

EXERCISES

24.1. In each case, find an equivalent expression that is in conjunctive normal form.
  (a) $(a \wedge b) \vee (c \wedge d)$
  (b) $a \to (b \wedge (c \to (d \vee e)))$
  (c) $\bigvee_{i=1}^{n}(a_i \wedge b_i)$

24.2. Suppose x is a Boolean formula involving n distinct variables. What is the maximum number of literals that might be required in a conjunctive-normal-form formula equivalent to x?

24.3. In the proof of Theorem 24.1, given a nondeterministic TM T with input alphabet Σ_1, we constructed a function $g : \Sigma_1^* \to CNF$ so that for any $x \in \Sigma_1^*$, x is accepted by T if and only if $g(x)$ is satisfiable. The idea is that the formula $g(x)$ "says" x is accepted by T, in the sense that $g(x)$ is constructed from a number of atoms, each of which is associated with a statement about some detail of T's configuration after a certain number of steps. Consider the following much simpler function $g_1 : \Sigma_1^* \rightarrow CNF$. For any $x \in \Sigma_1^*$, $g_1(x)$ is a single atom, labeled a_x. For each x, we associate the atom a_x with the statement "T accepts x." There is an obvious similarity between the statements $g(x)$ and $g_1(x)$: both depend on x, and both are associated with statements that say x is accepted by T. Explain what the essential difference is. Why isn't it possible to construct a trivial, one- or two-line proof of Cook's theorem using the function g_1? And, assuming you are convinced that any such proof has a fatal defect, why doesn't the proof given for the theorem suffer from the same defect?

24.4. Determine in each case whether the indicated expression is satisfiable.

(a) $(a \vee b) \wedge (a \vee \bar{b}) \wedge (\bar{a} \vee \bar{b})$

(b) $(a \vee b \vee c) \wedge (a \vee \bar{b}) \wedge (\bar{a} \vee c) \wedge (\bar{b} \vee \bar{c}) \wedge (b \vee \bar{c})$

24.5. Find an unsatisfiable conjunctive-normal-form expression involving three variables, in which each conjunct has exactly three literals and contains all three variables, so that the number of conjuncts is as small as possible.

24.6. (a) Show that the 2-satisfiability problem is in $\mathscr{P}$.

(b) Show that if $k \geq 4$, the k-satisfiability problem is NP-complete.

24.7. (a) In the proof of Theorem 24.3, could the 3-satisfiability problem have been used instead of the satisfiability problem?

(b) In the proof of Theorem 24.5, could *Satisfiable* have been used instead of *3-SAT*?

24.8. Determine whether there is a matching for the following instance of the three-dimensional matching problem: $A = \{1, 2, 3, 4, 5\}$; $B = \{a, b, c, d, e\}$; $C = \{r, s, t, u, v\}$; $M = \{(1, a, t), (4, c, s), (2, a, u), (1, d, s), (4, e, v), (3, b, u), (5, b, r), (3, d, s), (2, e, t), (5, c, t)\}$. If there is, find one.

24.9. (a) Show that the four-dimensional matching problem is NP-complete.

(b) Show that the marriage problem (the two-dimensional matching problem) is in $\mathscr{P}$.

REFERENCES

GENERAL REFERENCES

There are a number of textbooks covering the topics in this book—and, in some cases, many other topics as well. Two of the most prominent are Hopcroft and Ullman (1979) and Lewis and Papadimitriou (1981). These are both excellent and authoritative texts, and I have occasionally borrowed from both in terms of notation and organization. Other texts that cover much of this material and will be useful complements to this book are Davis and Weyuker (1983), Révész (1983), McNaughton (1982), Harrison (1978), Salomaa (1973), and Minsky (1967). Three more recent books, all of which are very readable, are Cohen (1986), Wood (1987), and Sudkamp (1988). In general, all these books assume more mathematical maturity on the part of the reader than I have assumed (Cohen is an exception, for he uses very little mathematical notation at all), and some of them, in addition to being more comprehensive, are written much more concisely.

PART II

The idea of a finite automaton appears in McCulloch and Pitts (1943) as a way of modeling neural nets. Properties of FAs are developed more extensively in Mealy (1955) and Moore (1956). Kleene (1956) introduces regular expressions and proves the equivalence of regular expressions and FAs; the proof given in this book is closer to that in McNaughton and Yamada (1960). NFAs are discussed in Rabin and Scott (1959), and their equivalence to FAs is proved. Theorems 7.1 and 8.1, having to do with the equivalence classes of the relation I_L, are due to Nerode (1958), and a related characterization of regular languages can be found in Myhill (1957). The algorithm in Sections 7.2 and 7.3 for minimizing the number of states in an FA appears in Huffman (1954) and in Moore (1956), and the presentation here follows that in Hopcroft and Ullman. The Pumping Lemma, Theorem 8.2a, is proved in Bar-Hillel, Perles, and Shamir (1961).

PART III

Context-free grammars were introduced in Chomsky (1956). In Chomsky (1959), many of the properties of CFGs are discussed, and Chomsky normal form is introduced. Chomsky and Miller (1958) includes the equivalence of regular grammars and finite automata. Backus (1959) and Naur (1960) introduce BNF notation as a way of describing the syntax of programming languages, and in Ginsburg and Rice (1962) this is shown to be equivalent to CFGs. Ambiguity in CFGs is studied in Floyd (1962), Cantor (1962), and Chomsky and Schützenberger (1963). The material in Chapter 10 on parentheses is adapted from McNaughton (1982). The pumping lemma for context-free languages is proved in Bar-Hillel, Perles, and Shamir (1961), and more general versions can be found in Ogden (1968), and Wise (1976).

Pushdown automata are described in Oettinger (1961), and the equivalence between PDAs and CFGs is shown in Chomsky (1962), Evey (1963), and Schützenberger (1963). Deterministic PDAs are discussed in Schützenberger (1963), and properties of deterministic CFLs are derived in Ginsburg and Greibach (1966). Ginsburg (1966) is a useful compendium of much of the theory of CFLs as of the time it was written, and Harrison (1978) is a comprehensive study of languages from the point of view of grammars.

LL(1) grammars are introduced in Lewis and Stearns (1968) and LL(k) grammars in Rosenkrantz and Stearns (1970). Knuth (1965) characterizes the grammars (the so-called LR(k) grammars) corresponding to DCFLs. For a comprehensive study of general parsing techniques, see Aho and Ullman (1972), and for an up-to-date treatise on parsing, see Sippu and Soisalon-Soininen (1987). Much of our Chapter 14 follows the discussion in Lewis and Papadimitriou (1981).

In addition to the easy-to-describe algorithm presented in Chapter 15 for solving the membership problem for context-free languages, there are more efficient and practical algorithms. One simple one due independently to Cocke, Younger, and Kasami is discussed in Hopcroft and Ullman (1979).

PART IV

Turing machines were introduced in Turing (1936), where they were referred to as "computing machines." In the same year, Post (1936) introduced a similar type of abstract machine. Turing's paper, which included the idea of a universal Turing machine, gave a proof that the halting problem is unsolvable. Church (1936) contains the first explicit statement of the Church–Turing thesis, as well as proofs of the existence of unsolvable problems. All three of these papers are reprinted in Davis (1965). There are a number of books containing excellent introductions to Turing machines, including Hennie (1977), Minsky (1967), and Lewis and Papadimitriou (1981).

The "Infinity Lemma" (Exercise 18.16) is due originally to König and is discussed in Knuth (1968). Exercise 18.17 is taken from Dowling (1989).

Chomsky (1956) and (1959) contain the definition of the Chomsky hierarchy and the proof of Theorems 19.1 and 19.2. Proofs of Theorems 19.5 and 19.6 may be found in Kuroda (1964).

Post's correspondence problem was stated and proved to be unsolvable in Post (1946). The unsolvable problems in Section 20.4 relating to context-free languages appeared in Bar-Hillel, Perles, and Shamir (1961), Cantor (1962), Floyd (1962), and Chomsky and Schützenberger (1963).

Gödel (1931) was one of the first, and one of the most significant, of a number of papers in the 1930s that might be described in part as demonstrating the limits of mathematical reasoning and computation. One aspect of Gödel's work that is very generally applicable is the "arithmetization" of formal or computational systems, as discussed in Section 22.3. Many of the properties of primitive recursive and μ-recursive functions were discussed in Kleene (1936), and that paper proved the equivalence of μ-recursiveness and Turing computability. These papers of Gödel and Kleene are both reprinted in Davis (1965), the former in an English translation. General references on primitive recursive functions and recursive function theory are Péter (1967), Hermes (1965), and Rogers (1967). Kleene (1952) contains an extensive treatment of the Church–Turing thesis, computability, and recursive functions, and Davis (1958) is another advanced reference on these topics.

PART V

Rabin (1963) and Hartmanis and Stearns (1965) are two early papers dealing with the subject of computational complexity. The class $\mathcal{P}$ was introduced in Cobham (1964), and, at the opposite extreme, certain solvable problems were proven to be intractable in Meyer and Stockmeyer (1973). Cook (1971) introduced the concept of NP-completeness and contained the proof of Theorem 24.1, that the satisfiability problem is NP-complete. Karp (1972) exhibited a number of NP-complete problems and helped to establish the idea as a fundamental one in complexity theory. Since 1971, a large number of problems have been shown to be NP-complete, and Garey and Johnson (1978) gives, in addition to a readable general discussion, a catalogue of the problems known to be NP-complete at that time. Hopcroft and Ullman (1979) and Machtey and Young (1978) are general references on computational complexity, while Stockmeyer and Chandra (1979), Cook (1983), and Karp (1986) are introductory survey articles in the area. The proofs given for Theorems 24.5 and 24.6 are essentially those in Wood (1987).

BIBLIOGRAPHY

Aho, A. V., and J. D. Ullman: *The Theory of Parsing, Translation and Compiling, Vol. I: Parsing*, Prentice Hall, Englewood Cliffs, New Jersey, 1972.

Backus, J. W.: "The Syntax and Semantics of the Proposed International Algebraic Language of the Zürich ACM-GAMM Conference," *Proceedings of the International Conference on Information Processing*, UNESCO, 1959, 125–132.

Bar-Hillel, Y., M. Perles, and E. Shamir: "On Formal Properties of Simple Phrase Structure Grammars," *Zeitschrift für Phonetik Sprachwissenschaft und Kommunikations-forschung*, 14 (1961), 143–172.

Boas, R. P.: "Can We Make Mathematics Intelligible?" *American Mathematical Monthly,* 88 (1981), 727–731.

Cantor, D. C.: "On the Ambiguity Problem of Backus Systems," *Journal of the ACM*, 9 (1962), 477–479.

Chomsky, N.: "Three Models for the Description of Language," *IRE Transactions on Information Theory*, 2 (1956), 113–124.

Chomsky, N.: "On Certain Formal Properties of Grammars," *Information and Control*, 2 (1959), 137–167.

Chomsky, N.: "Context-free Grammars and Pushdown Storage," *Quarterly Progress Report*, No. 65, MIT Research Laboratory of Electronics, Cambridge, Mass., 1962, 187–194.

Chomsky, N., and G. A. Miller: "Finite-state Languages," *Information and Control*, 1 (1958), 91–112.

Chomsky, N., and M. P. Schützenberger: "The Algebraic Theory of Context Free Languages," *Computer Programming and Formal Systems*, North Holland, Amsterdam, 1963, 118–161.

Church, A.: "An Unsolvable Problem of Elementary Number Theory," *American Journal of Mathematics*, 58 (1936), 345–363.

Cobham, A.: "The Intrinsic Computational Difficulty of Functions," *Proceedings of the 1964 Congress For Logic, Mathematics, and Philosophy of Science,* North Holland, New York, 1964, 24–30.

Cohen, D. I. A.: *Introduction to Computer Theory*, Wiley, New York, 1986.

Cook, S. A. "The Complexity of Theorem Proving Procedures," *Proceedings of the Third Annual ACM Symposium on the Theory of Computing*, Association for Computing Machinery, New York, 1971, 151–158.

Cook, S. A.: "An Overview of Computational Complexity," *Communications of the ACM*, 26 (1983) 400–408.

Davis, M. D.: *Computability and Unsolvability*, McGraw-Hill, New York, 1958.

Davis, M. D.: *The Undecidable*, Raven Press, Hewlett, NY, 1965.

Davis, M. D., and E. J. Weyuker: *Computability, Complexity and Languages: Fundamentals of Theoretical Computer Science*, Academic Press, New York, 1983.

Dowling, W. F.: "There Are No Safe Virus Tests," American Mathematical Monthly, 96 (1989), 835–836.

Evey, J.: "Application of Pushdown Store Machines," *Proceedings, 1963 Fall Joint Computer Conference*, AFIPS Press, Montvale, New Jersey, 1963, 215–227.

Floyd, R. W.: "On Ambiguity in Phrase Structure Languages," *Communications of the ACM*, 5 (1962), 526–534.

Garey, M. R., and D. S. Johnson: *Computers and Intractability: A Guide to the Theory of NP-Completeness*, Freeman, New York, 1979.

Ginsburg, S.: *The Mathematical Theory of Context-free Languages*, McGraw-Hill, New York, 1966.

Ginsburg, S., and S. A. Greibach: "Deterministic Context-free Languages," *Information and Control*, 9 (1966), 563–582.

Ginsburg, S., and H. G. Rice: "Two Families of Languages Related to ALGOL," *Journal of the ACM*, 9 (1962), 350–371.

Gödel, K.: "Über Formal Unentscheidbare Sätze der Principia Mathematica und Verwandter Systeme, I," *Monatshefte für Mathematik and Physik*, 38 (1931), 173–198.

Harrison, M. A.: *Introduction to Formal Language Theory*, Addison-Wesley, Reading, Mass., 1978.

Hartmanis, J., and R. E. Stearns: "On the Computational Complexity of Algorithms," *Transactions of the American Mathematical Society*, 117 (1965), 285–306.

Hennie, F. C.: *Introduction to Computability*, Addison-Wesley, Reading, Mass., 1977.

Hermes, H.: *Enumerability, Decidability, Computability*, Academic Press, New York, 1965.

Hopcroft, J. E., and J. D. Ullman: *Introduction to Automata Theory, Languages, and Computation*, 2d ed., Addison-Wesley, Reading, Mass., 1979.

Huffman, D. A.: "The Synthesis of Sequential Switching Circuits," *Journal of the Franklin Institute*, 257 (1954), 161–190, 275–303.

Karp, R. M.: "Reducibility Among Combinatorial Problems," in *Complexity of Computer Computations*, Plenum Press, New York, 1972, 85–104.

Karp, R. M.: "Combinatorics, Complexity, and Randomness," *Communications of the ACM*, 29 (1986), 98–109.

Kleene, S. C.: "General Recursive Functions of Natural Numbers," *Mathematische Annalen*, 112 (1936), 727–742.

Kleene, S. C.: *Introduction to Metamathematics*, Van Nostrand, New York, 1952.

Kleene, S. C.: "Representation of Events in Nerve Nets and Finite Automata," in Shannon, C. E., and J. McCarthy (eds.), *Automata Studies*, Princeton University Press, Princeton, New Jersey (1956), 3–42.

Knuth, D. E.: "On the Translation of Languages from Left to Right," *Information and Control*, 8 (1965), 607–639.

Knuth, D. E.: *The Art of Computer Programming*, Vol. I: *Fundamental Algorithms*, Addison-Wesley, Reading, Mass., 1968.

Knuth, D. E., T. Larrabee, and P. M. Roberts: *Mathematical Writing*, MAA Notes #14, Mathematical Association of America, 1989.

Kuroda, S. Y.: "Classes of Languages and Linear-Bounded Automata," *Information and Control*, 7 (1964), 207–223.

Lewis, H. R., and C. Papadimitriou: *Elements of the Theory of Computation*, Prentice Hall, Englewood Cliffs, New Jersey, 1981.

Lewis, P. M., II, and R. E. Stearns: "Syntax-directed Transduction," *Journal of the ACM*, 15 (1968), 465–488.

Machtey, M., and P. R. Young: *An Introduction to the General Theory of Algorithms*, Elsevier North-Holland, New York, 1978.

McCulloch, W. S., and W. Pitts: "A Logical Calculus of the Ideas Immanent in Nervous Activity," *Bulletin of Mathematical Biophysics*, 5 (1943), 115–133.

McNaughton, R.: *Elementary Computability, Formal Languages, and Automata*, Prentice Hall, Englewood Cliffs, New Jersey, 1982.

McNaughton, R., and H. Yamada: "Regular Expressions and State Graphs for Automata," *IEEE Transactions on Electronic Computers*, 9 (1960), 39–47.

Mealy, G. H.: "A Method for Synthesizing Sequential Circuits," *Bell System Technical Journal*, 34 (1955), 1045–1079.

Meyer, A. R., and L. J. Stockmeyer: "The Equivalence Problem for Regular Expressions with Squaring Requires Exponential Space," *Proceedings of the Thirteenth Annual IEEE Symposium on Switching and Automata Theory*, 1973, 125–129.

Minsky, M. L.: *Computation: Finite and Infinite Machines*, Prentice Hall, Englewood Cliffs, New Jersey, 1967.

Moore, E. F.: "Gedanken Experiments on Sequential Machines," in Shannon, C. E., and J. McCarthy (eds.), *Automata Studies*, Princeton University Press, Princeton, New Jersey, 1956, 129–153.

Myhill, J.: "Finite Automata and the Representation of Events," *WADD TR-57-624*, Wright Patterson AFB, Ohio, 1957, 112-137.

Naur, P. (ed.): "Report on the Algorithmic Language ALGOL 60," *Communications of the ACM*, 3 (1960), 299-314, revised in *Communications of the ACM*, 6 (1963), 1–17.

Nerode, A.: "Linear Automaton Transformations," *Proceedings of the AMS*, 9 (1958), 541–544.

Oettinger, A. G.: "Automatic Syntactic Analysis and the Pushdown Store," *Proceedings of the Symposia in Applied Mathematics*, 12, American Mathematical Society, Providence, Rhode Island, 1961, 104–109.

Ogden, W.: "A Helpful Result for Proving Inherent Ambiguity," *Mathematical Systems Theory*, 2 (1968), 191–194.

Péter, R.: *Recursive Functions*, Academic Press, New York, 1967.

Post, E. L.: "Finite Combinatory Processes–Formulation I," *Journal of Symbolic Logic*, 1 (1936), 103–105.

Post, E. L.: "A Variant of a Recursively Unsolvable Problem," *Bulletin of the American Mathematical Society*, 52 (1946), 246–268.

Rabin, M. O., and D. Scott: "Finite Automata and their Decision Problems," *IBM Journal of Research and Development*, 3 (1959), 115–125.

Rabin, M. O.: "Real-Time Computation," *Israel Journal of Mathematics*, 1 (1963), 203–211.

Révész, G. E.: *Introduction to Formal Language Theory*, McGraw-Hill, New York, 1983.

Rogers, H., Jr.: *Theory of Recursive Functions and Effective Computability*, McGraw-Hill, New York, 1967.

Rosenkrantz, D. J., and R. E. Stearns: "Properties of Deterministic Top-down Grammars," *Information and Control*, 17 (1970), 226–256.

Salomaa, A.: *Formal Languages*, Academic Press, New York, 1973.

Schützenberger, M. P.: "On Context-free Languages and Pushdown Automata," *Information and Control*, 6 (1963), 246-264.

Sippu, S., and E. Soisalon-Soininen: *Parsing Theory*, Springer-Verlag, New York, 1987.

Stockmeyer, L. J., and A. K. Chandra: "Intrinsically Difficult Problems," *Scientific American*, 240 (1979), 140–159.

Sudkamp, T. A.: *Languages and Machines: An Introduction to the Theory of Computer Science*, Addison-Wesley, Reading, Mass., 1988.

Turing, A. M.: "On Computable Numbers with an Application to the Entscheidungsproblem," *Proceedings of the London Mathematical Society*, 2, No. 42, 1936, 230–265.

Wise, D. S.: "A Strong Pumping Lemma for Context-free Languages," *Theoretical Computer Science*, 3 (1976), 359–370.

Wood, D.: *Theory of Computation*, Wiley, New York, 1987.

INDEX

A

Abstract machine, 27, 69, 278
Acceptance
    by an FA, 69, 74
    by an NFA, 90
    by an NFA-Λ, 94
    by a PDA
        by empty stack, 218, 229-230
        equivalence of two types, 227
        by final state, 218
    by a TM
        of a language, 284, 319
        of a string, 284
Accepting states
    in an FA, 69, 70
    in a PDA, 217
Ackermann, W., 395
Addition function, 10, 377, 391
    primitive recursive derivation for, 377
A-derivable variables, 202
    algorithm to find, 202
Adjacent vertices, 444
Algebraic expressions
    a CFG for, 165
    as an example of a nonregular language, 142
    fully parenthesized, 47
    an unambiguous CFG for, 188
Algorithm, (xv), 278, 280
    usable, 413
Alphabet, 24
Ambiguity
    in context-free grammars, 183-184, 367
    in programming languages, 184
    in regular grammars, 186

Ambiguous, 166, 183
AND, 12, 383, 426
Arbitrarily complicated problems, 424
Arithmetic progression, 146, 154
Associative laws, 5
Atoms, 437
Axioms, 17

B

Backtracking, 246
Backus, J., 164
Backus-Naur Form, 164
Balanced strings of parentheses. *See* Parentheses
Basis step, 37
Biconditional, 13
Big-oh notation, 415
Bijection, 8, 325
Binary tree, 264
    height of, 264
    path in, 264
Blank symbol, 280
BNF. *See* Backus-Naur Form
Boas, R., 70
Bottom-up parsing, 255
Bound variable, 14
Bounded existential quantification, 388
Bounded maximalization, 393
Bounded minimalization, 389
Bounded operations, 387
Bounded sums and products, 386
Bounded universal quantification, 388
Breadth-first search, 307
Busy-beaver function, 373

C

Cantor, G., 327
Cartesian product, 6, 10
Cases
definition by, 384
proof by, 20
CFG. *See* Context-free grammar
CFL. *See* Context-free language
Characteristic function
of a language, 294
of a predicate, 382
Chomsky, N., (xvii) 349
Chomsky hierarchy, 349
Chomsky Normal Form, 208
converting a CFG to, 208
Church, A., 281, 398
Church's thesis. *See* Church-Turing thesis
Church-Turing thesis, 281, 324, 353, 355, 411
Closed under an operation, 54
Closure, 54
CNF. *See* Chomsky Normal Form or Conjunctive
normal form
Codomain, 7
Combinatorial problem, 427
Combining Turing machines, 288
Commutative laws, 5
Complement
of a CFL, 271, 367
of a DCFL, 274
of a graph, 445
of a recursive language, 321
of a recursively enumerable language,
321
of a regular language, 80
of a set, 4
Complete graph, 444
Complete pairing, 191
Complete subgraph problem, 444
NP-completeness of, 444
Completely paired, 191
Composite TM, 289
Composition, 9, 371
of computable functions, 372
Computability, 278, 282, 370
in terms of grammars, 410
Computable functions, 371, 373-374, 394
μ-recursiveness of, 401-407
Computation, 150, 279, 355
Computation tree, 307
Computational complexity, 413
Computer as an FA, 152
Computer virus, 333
Computing a function with a TM, 292-293
Computing power, 298

Concatenation
of CFLs, 168
of languages, 26
of recursively enumerable languages, 331,
352
of regular languages, 62
of strings, 26
Concatenation function, a TM to compute, 293
Conditional statement, 12
alternative formulations of, 13
Configuration
of a PDA, 217-218
of a TM, 283
Configuration number, 401
Congruence mod n, 22
Conjunct, 427
Conjunction, 426
Conjunctive normal form, 426, 436
Consecutive configurations of a TM, 437
Constant functions, 374
Constructive definition, 48, 374
Constructive proof, 18
Context (in a CFG), 163–164
Context-free grammar, (xvii), 157, 160, 334
corresponding to a given PDA, 236–240
language generated by, 160
Context-free languages, 160
complement of, 270
concatenation and * of, 168
deterministic, 224
complement of, 274
intersection of, 270
intersection with regular languages, 272
union of, 168
Context-sensitive grammar, 343
Context-sensitive language, 343
corresponding to a given LBA, 347
recursiveness of, 344
Contradiction, proof by, 20
Contrapositive, 19
Converse, 13
Copying a string, 291
Cook, S., 430
Cook's Theorem, 436
Correspondence system, 359
Countable, 325
Countable union of countable sets, 325
Countably infinite, 325
Counterexample, 18
Course-of-values induction. *See* Strong principle
of mathematical induction
Course-of-values recursion, 400
Crash, 284
CSG. *See* context-sensitive grammar
CSL. *See* context-sensitive language

D

Dangling ELSE, 184
Davis, M., 411
DCFL. *See* Deterministic context-free language
Decidable system, 425
Decision algorithms, 149–150, 274-275, 353
Decision problems, 147, 274–275, 353
   involving context-free languages, 275
   involving regular languages, 148
   involving TMs, 354–358
   unsolvable. *See* Unsolvable problems
Degree of a polynomial, 417
Deleting a tape symbol, 291
DeMorgan laws, 5
Derivation in a CFG, 160, 180, 182
   simulation by a PDA, 233, 255
Derivation tree, 180
Deterministic context-free language, 224, 274, 350
   complement of, 274
Deterministic PDA, 224
Diagonal argument, 327–328, 329, 333, 345, 373, 395, 397, 424
Difference of two sets, 5
Direct proof, 17
Disjoint sets, 4
Disjunction, 426
Disjunctive normal form, 436
Disproving a statement, 18
Distinguishable with respect to a language, 77
Distinguishing one string from another, 76
Distributive laws, 5
Domain, 7
Dominoes, 359
Doubly infinite tape, 299
DPDA. *See* Deterministic PDA
Dummy variables in a function, 380

E

Edges of a graph, 444
Effective computation, 280
Effectively computable, 411
Empty language, 59
   algorithm to determine whether a given CFG generates, 275
   algorithm to determine whether a given FA accepts, 149
Empty set, 4
Empty stack, acceptance by *See* Acceptance
Empty sum and product, 386
Encoding TMs as strings, 311-312
English, grammar rules for, 162
Enumerating a language, 322

Equivalence class, 23
   of the relation I_L, 122
Equivalence relation, 22
Erasing a symbol, 285
Erasing the tape of a TM, 309, 322
Eventually constant, 333
Eventually periodic, 154
Existential quantification
   bounded, 388
   unbounded, 395
Existential quantifier, 387
Exponential function, 417
Exponential growth rate, 417
Expression tree, 181
Extended transition function
   for FA, 73
   for NFA, 89
   for NFA-Λ
      nonrecursive definition, 93
      recursive definition, 94

F

FA. *See* Finite automaton
Factorial function, 44, 374
Factoring in a CFG, 250
Factors in an algebraic expression, 188
Fibonacci numbers, 52, 399
Final state, acceptance by. *See* acceptance
Finer (of partitions), 126
Finite automaton, (xvii), 56, 70
   language accepted by, 74
   string accepted by, 74
Finite language, 62
   algorithm to determine whether a given FA accepts, 150
   algorithm to determine whether a given CFG generates, 275
Finite-state machine. *See* Finite automaton
First in, first out, 280
Five-tuple, 70
Folded tape, 301
Free variable, 14
Fully parenthesized, 47
Function, 7
   of several variables, 10

G

Generating languages, 27
Gödel, K., 398, 425
Gödel number, 398
   of a pair, 400
   of a string, 408

Gödel numbering, 398
  of a TM, 401
Grammar, 159, 334
  context-free. *See* Context-free grammar
  context-sensitive. *see* Context-sensitive grammar
  regular. *See* Regular grammar
  unrestricted. *See* Unrestricted grammar
Grammar rules, 160
Graph, 444
Growth rate, 416
Guessing in a PDA, 219, 220–221

H

Halt on input x, 284
Halt state in a Turing machine, 282
Halting configuration, 284
Halting problem, 354
Height of a derivation tree, 265
Hennie, F., 395
Hierarchy of decision problems, 425
Higher-order term, 417
Hopcroft, J., 358

I

If and only if, 12
Indirect proof, 19
Indistinguishability relation on Σ^*, 79, 122
Induction hypothesis, 37
Induction step, 37
Inductive definition. *See* Recursive definitions
Infinite loop, 284
Infinity lemma, 332
Inherently ambiguous CFL, 187
Initial function, 374
Initial stack symbol, 215
Initial state
  in an FA, 70
  in a PDA, 217
  in a TM, 282
Injection, 8
Input alphabet of a Turing machine, 282
Input string to a TM, 283
Input symbols to FA, 69, 70
Inserting a tape symbol, 292
Instance of a decision problem, 147, 353
Intersection, 4
  of a CFL and a regular language, 272
  of CFLs, 270, 367
  of recursively enumerable languages, 321
  of regular languages, 80
Intractable problem, 413

Inverse function, 10
Isomorphic, 136
Isomorphism from one FA to another, 136

K

Kleene's theorem
  part 1, 108
  part 2, 114
Λ-closed, 104
Λ-closure, 94
  algorithm to calculate, 94
Λ-productions, 196
  eliminating from a CFG, 199
Λ-transition
  in an NFA, 91
    eliminating, 96-98
  in a PDA, 218

L

Language, 25
  accepted by a PDA, 219
  accepted by a TM, 284
  context-free. *See* Context-free language
  describing a, 27
  finite, 62
  generating a, 27
  recognition, 27
  recognized by an FA, 74
  recognizer, (xvii)
  recursive. *See* Recursive language
  recursively enumerable. *See* Recursively enumerable languages
  regular. *See* Regular languages
Largest prime factor, 405
Last in, first out, 214
LBA. *See* Linear-bounded automaton
Least common multiple, 389
Left recursion in a CFG, 249
  algorithm to eliminate, 249–250
Left-linear CFG, 178
Leftmost derivation, 182
Left-regular CFG, 178
Length of a string, 25
Lexical analysis, 152
Lexicographic order, 323
LIFO. *See* Last in, first out
Linear grammar, 175
Linear-bounded automaton, 346
  corresponding to a given CSG, 346
Literal in a logical expression, 428
Live variables in a CFG, 204
  algorithm to find, 205

LL(k) grammar, 251
Logical operations, 12
Logical reasoning, general principle of, 17
Logical statements, 11
Logically equivalent, 11
Logically implies, 11
Lookahead, 247
Loop-finding program, 355
Loops in paths in an FA, 143

M

Marking pairs of states, 128
  a more efficient algorithm for, 131
Marriage problem, 446
Mate of a parenthesis, 191
Mathematical induction. *See* Principle of mathematical induction
Maximal PD set, 121
McCulloch, W., (xvii)
Membership problem, 353
  for CFLs, an algorithm to solve, 274
  for CSLs, 353
  for recursively enumerable languages, 354
  for regular languages, an algorithm to solve, 148
Memory required to recognize a language, 66
Merging states in an FA, 127
Migrating symbols, 337
Minimal counterexample, 44
Minimalization operation, 389
Minimum-state FA
  algorithm to construct, 129
  for a given language, 124
  obtained from a given FA, 126
Model of computation, (xvi), 279-281
Modified correspondence system, 361
Modified Post's correspondence problem, 360
Modula-2, 185
Monus operation. *See* Proper subtraction
MPCP. *See* Modified Post's correspondence problem
Multiplication function, primitive recursive derivation for, 378
Multi-tape TM, 303–305
μ-recursive partial functions, 396
  computability of, 397
  non-numeric, 409
Myhill-Nerode Theorem, 141

N

Natural languages, 161

Natural numbers, 8
Negating a quantified statement, 16
Next-state function. *See* Transition function
NFA. *See* Nondetermistic finite automaton
NFA-Λ. *See* Nondeterministic finite automaton
Non-context-free languages, 266–270
Non-context-sensitive language, 345
Nondeterminism
  eliminating from an NFA, 98–99
  in an FA, 88
  in a PDA, 215, 219, 274
Nondeterministic finite automaton, 88
  language recognized by, 90
  string accepted by, 90
  transition function for, 88
Nondeterministic finite automaton with Λ-transitions, 93
  to accept $L_1 \cup L_2$, L_1L_2, and L^*, 109–112
  corresponding to a given regular grammar, 173–175
  language accepted by, 94
  string accepted by, 94
  transition function for, 93
Nondeterministic polynomial time, 427
Nondeterministic time complexity, 427
Nondeterministic TM, 306
  equivalent to a given unrestricted grammar, 339
  for solving combinatorial decision problems, 427
Nonnumeric functions, 407–409
Nonpalindromes, 160–161
Non-primitive-recursive function, 394
Non-recursively-enumerable language, 328
  example of, 329
Nonregular languages, 142
NonSelfAccepting, 329–330
Nonterminal symbols, 160
Normal forms for CFGs, 196
NOT, 12
$\mathcal{NP}$, 427
NP-complete problem, 430–432
  examples of, 436, 442, 444, 445, 446, 448
NP-hard problem, 432
n-place predicate, 382
Null input, 91
Null string, 25
Nullable variables in a CFG, 198
  algorithm to find, 199
Numerical function, 293, 370

O

One-to-one, 8

One-to-one correspondence, 325
Only if, 13
Onto, 8
OR, 12
Order of, of the, 415
Ordered n-tuple, 6
Ordered pair, 6
Orders of infinity, 325
Output of a TM, 290

P

$\mathcal{P}$, 423
$\mathcal{P} = \mathcal{NP}$ problem, 430-431
Pairing function, 327
Pairs of states (p, q) with $p \not\equiv q$. *See* Marking pairs of states
Pairwise distinguishable set of strings, 121
Palindromes, 46
    alternate definition of, 50
    nonregularity of, 78–79
    PDAs to recognize, 220–223
    recognizing the language of, 67
    TM to accept, 285–286
Parallel computation, 430
Parentheses
    in algebraic expressions, 190–193
    balanced strings of, 138, 224–225, 235–236, 244–251
Parse tree, 180
Parser
    deterministic bottom-up, 259
    deterministic top-down, 247, 251
    nondeterministic bottom-up, 256–257
    nondeterministic top-down, 246
Parsing, 244
Partial function, 7, 371
Partial solution to a modified correspondence system, 361
Partition, 23
Pascal, 25
    context-sensitiveness of, 343–344
    non-context-freeness of, 268
    nonregularity of, 151
    real constant in, 62
    syntax of, 164
Pascal-computable, 410
Path going through a state, 115
Path in a binary tree, 264
PCP. *See* Post's correspondence problem
PD set. *See* Pairwise distinguishable set of strings
PDA. *See* Pushdown automaton

Peano axioms, 44
Periodic functions, 333
Permuting the variables of a function, 380
Phrase-structure grammar. *See* Unrestricted grammar
Pigeonhole principle, 53
Pitts, W., (xvii)
Polynomial function, 417
Polynomial growth rate, 417
Polynomial time, 423
Polynomial-time reducible, 431
Polynomial-time solvability, 413
Post, E., 359
Post's correspondence problem, 359
Power set, 6
Precedence
    in algebraic expressions, 166
    in regular expressions, 59
Precedence grammar, 258
Precedence relation, 258
Predecessor function, 381
Predicate, 382
Prefix property, 54
Prime, 15
Prime, the nth, 390
Primitive recursion, 375
    applied to computable functions, 375
Primitive recursive derivation, 377
Primitive recursive functions, 376
    closure under addition and multiplication, 381
    computability of, 379
    nonnumeric, 409
Principle of mathematical induction, 36
Production
    in a context-free grammar, 160
    in an unrestricted grammar, 334–335
Programming languages, 25, 151, 343-344, 410-411
Programs, verifying the correctness of, 43
Projection function, 374
Proofs, 17
    by cases, 20
    by contradiction, 20
    direct, 17
    indirect, 19
    by induction. *See* Principle of mathematical induction
Propagation of symbols, 337
Proper subtraction, 381
Pumping lemma for CFLs, 266
Pumping lemma for regular languages, 144
    application to decision problems, 149
    weaker forms, 146

Pushdown automaton, 217
  acceptance
    by empty stack, 218
    by final state, 218
  configuration of, 217
  corresponding to a given CFG, 232-235
  definition, 217
  deterministic, 224
  equivalence of two types of acceptance,
    227
  generalizations of, 280
  guessing by, 220
  simulating a CFG derivation, 233
  transition diagram for, 220
Pushdown transducer, 246

Q

Quantifier, 14
Queue, 280

R

Range, 8
Reachable states in an FA, 81, 84
  algorithm to calculate, 126
Reachable variables in a CFG, 204
  algorithm to find, 205
Reasonable encoding, 423
Recognizing languages, 27
Recursive algorithms, runtime analysis of, 52
Recursive definitions, 45
  of functions, 374
Recursive descent parsing, 252
Recursive language, 319
  complement of, 321
Recursive partial function. *See* μ-recursive
  partial function
Recursively enumerable languages, 319
  complement of, 321
  concatenation and * of, 331, 352
  nonrecursive, 330
  unions and intersections of, 321
Reduce, 255
Reflexive, 22
Regular expression, 57
  corresponding to a given FA, 114–119
  formal definition, 58
  the language corresponding to, 58
  simplifying, 60, 61
Regular grammar, 173
  corresponding to a given FA, 173

Regular languages, 58, 171
  union, concatenation, and * of, 62
  union, intersection, difference, and comple-
    ment of, 80
Regularity conditions, 324
Relation
  from one set to another, 22
  on a set, 22
Relational predicates, 382
Relaxed matching, 446
Repeating a variable, 380
Reverse of a string, 46
Right invariant, 123
Right-linear CFG, 178
Rightmost derivation, 183
Rightmost nonblank symbol, 292
Rogers, H., 410

S

Satisfiability problem, 426
Scope of quantifier, 14
SelfAccepting, 329–330
Self-embedded variable, 264, 334
Semantics, 165
Sets, 3
  complement of, 4
  equality of, 4
Shift, 255
Shift-reduce parser, 255
Simulating a nondetermistic TM, 307–311
Size of an infinite set, 324
Space complexity, 425
Specifying languages, 27, 328-329
Stack, 214
Stack alphabet, 217
Stack-emptying state, 227
Start symbol in a CFG, 160
State diagram. *See* Transition diagram
States, 69
States of mind, 280
Stored-program computer, 311
String, 25
  accepted by FA, 74
  length of, 25
Strong principle of mathematical induction,
  41
Subgraph, 444
Subset, 4
Subset construction, 98
Substituting constants for variables, 380
Substring, 26
Successor function, 374

Surjection, 8
Symmetric, 22
Syntax diagram, 164

T

Tape alphabet, 282 Tape head, 282
Tape number, 401
Tape square, 282
Tape symbol, 282
Tape of a Turing machine, 282
Terminal, 160
Terms in an algebraic expression, 187
Testing in polynomial time, 427, 430
Three-dimensional matching problem, 446
    NP-completeness of, 448
Three-dimensional relaxed matching problem,
    446
    NP-completeness of, 448
Three-satisfiability problem, 442
    NP-completeness of, 442
Time complexity of a TM, 420
TM. *See* Turing machine
Tokens, 151
Top-down parsing, 246
Total function, 8, 371
Tracks on TM tape, 301
Tractable problem, 413, 423
Transition diagram
    for an FA, 71
        as an algorithm for recognizing a language,
        68-69
    for a PDA, 219–220
    for a TM, 283
Transition function
    for an FA, 70
    for an NFA, 88
    for an NFA-Λ, 93
    for a PDA, 217
    for a TM, 282
Transition table, 71
Transitive, 22
Truth set, 11
Truth table, 30
Truth values, 11
Turing, A., xv, 280
Turing machine, xv, 282
    accepting a language, 319
    accepting a string, 284
    configuration of, 283
    corresponding to an unrestricted grammar,
        339

language accepted by, 284
multitape, 303
nondeterministic, 306
    simulation by a deterministic TM, 309
output of, 290
recognizing a language, 319
rejecting a string, 284
with two-symbol alphabet, 318
universal, 311
variations of, 299, 303, 306
Turing-computable, 410, 411
Type i language, 350

U

Ullman, J., 358
Unambiguous, 166
Unary representation, 293
Unbounded existential quantification, 395
Unbounded minimalization, 396
Uncomputable function, 373
Uncountable, 325
Uncountably infinite set, 325
    existence of, 327
Undecidable system, 425
Union, 4
    of CFLs, 168
    of countable sets, 325
    of recursively enumerable languages, 321
    of regular languages, 62, 80
Uniqueness of minimimum-state FA, 134–137
Unit productions in a CFG, 196
    elimination of, 202
Universal quantifier, 388
Universal set, 4
Universal TM, 311, 355
    input to, 313
Universe, 11
Unrestricted grammar, 335
    corresponding to a given TM, 340
Unsolvable problems, 150, 357
    involving CFLs, 366
    involving TMs, 357
Useful variable, 205
Useless variable, 187, 205
    elimination of, 205

V

Vacuously true, 20
Variables
    in a context-free grammar, 159
    in logical statements, 11, 14
    in an unrestricted grammar, 334–335

Vertex cover, 444
Vertex cover problem, 444
  NP-completeness of, 445
Vertices of a graph, 444
Virus tester, 333

W

Weak precedence grammar, 258
Well-ordering principle, 44
Weyuker, E., 411
Within parentheses, 191